WORLD
CATHOLICISM
IN
TRANSITION

WORLD CATHOLICISM IN TRANSITION

Edited by

Thomas M. Gannon, S.J.

MACMILLAN PUBLISHING COMPANY

NEW YORK

Collier Macmillan Publishers

LONDON

Macmillan Publishing Company
866 Third Avenue, New York, NY 10022

Collier Macmillan Canada, Inc.

Library of Congress Catalog Card Number: 88-1644

Printed in the United States of America

printing number
1   2   3   4   5   6   7   8   9   10

Library of Congress Cataloging-in-Publication Data
World Catholicism in transition / edited by Thomas M. Gannon.
    p. cm.
    Bibliography: p.
    Includes index.
    ISBN 0-02-911280-X
    1. Catholic Church—History—1965- I. Gannon, Thomas M.
BX1390.W67 1988
282'.09'04—dc19

Contents

Part Four   The Third Church   263

List of Contributors

MADELEINE ADRIANCE is director of the Liberal Arts Program at Mount Ida College (Newton, Massachusetts) and lecturer in sociology at the University of Massachusetts/Boston. She received her Ph.D. in sociology from Boston University in 1984 after completing field research in Brazil. She is the author of *Opting for the Poor: Brazilian Catholicism in Transition*, and of articles in *Sociological Analysis, Social Compass*, and *Cross Currents*.

JEAN AUCAGNE, S.J., worked in Lebanon from 1946 to 1948 and in Egypt from 1954 to 1956; since 1959 he has resided in Lebanon. In addition to numerous journalistic activities, he has been professor of linguistics at the University of Saint Joseph in Beirut since 1977.

JOHN J. CARROLL, S.J., went to the Philippines in 1946. After completing his Ph.D. in sociology and Southeast Asian Studies at Cornell University, he returned to the Philippines, engaging in research and training social action workers. Between 1973 and 1981 he taught sociology and was dean of the faculty of social sciences at the Gregorian University in Rome. Currently he is director of the Institute on Church and Social Issues at the Ateneo de Manila University.

JOHN A. COLEMAN, S.J., is professor of religion and society at the Graduate Theological Union, Berkeley, California. He serves as sociology of religion editor for the international Catholic journal *Concilium* and is editor-in-chief for the Isaac Hecker series in American culture and religion at the Paulist Press. Among his many books are *An American Strategic Theology* and, with Gregory Baum, *Christians and Party Politics*.

MARGARET E. CRAHAN is Henry R. Luce professor of religion, power, and the political process at Occidental College, Los Angeles. In addition to field work throughout Central and South America, Spain, and Switzerland, she has published widely on Spanish colonial administration, church–state relations, religion and politics, twentieth-century Cuba, and the African cultural heritage in the Caribbean. Her most recent books include *Africa and the Caribbean, Human Rights and Basic Needs in the Americas*, and the forthcoming *Power and Piety: The Political Dimensions of Religion in Latin America* and *Cuba: Social Transformations, 1963–1958*.

KAREL DOBBELAERE is professor of sociology and the sociology of religion at the Catholic University of Leuven (Belgium) and professor of sociological research at the University of Antwerp. Currently he is president of the International Conference for the Sociology of Religion and has been a visiting fellow at All Souls College (Oxford), the Nanzan Institute for Religion and Culture (Japan), and a visiting professor at Kent State University (Ohio).

WALTER FERNANDES, S.J., is director of the Indian Social Institute in New Delhi, where he has worked since 1977. Born in Mangalore (India), he pursued graduate studies in the sociology of religion at the Sorbonne, taking his Ph.D. from the Institut Catholique de Paris. He has written on tribal and the forest-dweller economy, people's participation in development, inequality, trade unions and industrial relations in India, caste and conversion, and the Catholic church in India.

PAUL F. FURLONG is lecturer in politics at the University of Hull (England). He holds degrees from the Gregorian University in Rome, from Oxford, and from the University of Reading (England). He has published mainly in the field of Italian politics and on political theory; his main research interests include the Christian Democrat party, its role and strategy in government, its relations with the Vatican, and in general the impact of social and economic change on the Italian political system.

KAREL GABRIEL is professor of sociology at the Catholic School of Social Work in Osnabrück/Vechta in West Germany. He earned his Ph.D. at the University of Bielefeld, after studying theology and sociology at the Universities of Tübingen and Frankfurt. With F. X. Kaufmann he edited *Zur Soziologie des Katholizismus* and has published articles in the sociology of religion, the sociology of organizations, and social work.

THOMAS M. GANNON, S.J., was director of the Woodstock Theological Center at Georgetown University from 1983 to 1986 and for the previous ten years chaired the department of sociology at Loyola University of Chicago, He received his Ph.D. in sociology from the University of Chicago and holds advanced degrees in philosophy and theology. He has served as president of both the Religious Research Association and the Association for the Sociology of Religion, and has been visiting professor at universities in England, Germany, Austria, Japan, and India. His most recent book is *The Catholic Challenge to the American Economy.*

ADRIAN HASTINGS has been professor of theology at the University of Leeds since 1985. He worked in Uganda from 1958 to 1966 after which he was based in Tanzania and Zambia, working for four years with the Association of Catholic Bishops of Eastern and Central Africa on post-Vatican II reorientation. In 1971–1972 he undertook a study on marriage in Africa for the Anglican Archbishops and from 1982 to 1985 he was professor of religious studies at the University of Zimbabwe. He has also taught at the University of London's School of Oriental and African Studies and at the University of Aberdeen. His numerous books include *Church and Mission in Modern Africa, A Concise Guide to the Second Vatican Council, A History of African Christianity, 1950–1975,* and *A History of English Christianity, 1920–1985.*

PETER HEBBLETHWAITE has been Vatican affairs writer for *The National Catholic Reporter* since 1979. His first professional task was to report the final session of the Second Vatican Council for the British Jesuit magazine *The Month,* which he edited from 1967 to 1974. Since parting amicably with the Jesuits in 1974, he has published *The Runaway Church, Christian-Marxist Dialogue, Beyond: The Year of Three Popes,* and *John XXIII, Shepherd of the Modern World,* which received a Christopher Award in 1986. He has since published *Synod Extraordinary and the Vatican,* and is currently engaged on a major biography of Pope Paul VI.

MEINRAD P. HEBGA, S.J., was born in Cameroon and pursued studies in philosophy and theology at the Gregorian University in Rome. He holds doctorates in philosophy and psychology from the University of Rennes and the Sorbonne. He is currently professor of philosophy at the University of Yaoundé (Cameroon) and has taught at Harvard Divinity School, the Gregorian University, and the Institut Catholique de l'Afrique de l'Ouest (Abidjan). He has written numerous articles on Christianity and the church in West Africa.

MICHAEL P. HORNSBY-SMITH is senior lecturer in sociology, University of Surrey (England). He has been researching change in English Catholicism since the mid-1970s and is author of *Catholic Education: The Unobtrusive Partners, Roman Catholic Opinion,* and *Roman Catholics in England: Studies in Social Structure Since the Second World War,* as well as many research articles in *Sociology, Sociological Review, Review of Religious Research,* and the *Journal for the Scientific Study of Religion.*

FRANZ-XAVER KAUFMANN is professor of sociology and social policy and director of the Institute for Population Research and Social Policy at the University of Bielefeld in West Germany. He has published widely in the sociology of religion; his current research is focused on the theory of the welfare state, the family, and social policy.

HENRI MADELIN, S.J., is director of the Centre Sèvres in Paris (an institute that combines the Jesuit faculties of philosophy and theology) and lectures at the Institut d'Etudes Politiques de Paris. An economist with a Ph.D. in political science, he is author of a study of the relationship between oil and politics in the western Mediterranean. He has also written on the confrontation between Christians and Marxists in France and the political behavior of Christians.

DAVID MARTIN has chaired the department of sociology at the London School of Economics and has been professor of sociology there since 1971. He has written eight books (mostly in the sociology of religion) and is currently studying the growth of conservative Protestantism in Latin America, as well as the relation of religion and politics. From 1975 to 1983 he was president of the International Conference of the Sociology of Religion and is currently Elizabeth Scurlock University Professor of Human Values at Southern Methodist University in Dallas.

HANS MOL is professor of religious studies at McMaster University in Ontario. He is author of many books dealing with religion and identity, including *The Faith of Australians, Faith and Fragility, The Fixed and the Fickle,* and *Identity and the Sacred.* He was lecturer in sociology at the University of Canterbury in New Zealand from 1961 to 1963 and fellow in sociology at the Institute of Advanced Studies of the Australian National University from 1963 to 1970.

JUAN CARLOS NAVARRO chairs the department of sociology in the School of Social Sciences at the Universidad Católica Andrés Bello, Caracas. He is also a researcher at the Instituto Internacional de Estudios Avanzados, doing work on the Venezuelan political system and on internal conflicts in the Venezuelan Catholic church.

AURELIO ORENSANZ, born in Larues, Spain, has lived in New York City since 1979. He pursued graduate studies in sociology at the London School of Economics and the New School for Social Research in New York City, and is now lecturer in sociology at the Graduate School of Management and Urban Professions, New School for Social Research. His long-term research interests center on Hispanic communities in the United States. He has written on popular culture in Franco's Spain, presentations of art in society, and the organization of Spanish tourism.

MÁIRE NIC GHIOLLA PHÁDRAIG is lecturer in sociology at University College, Dublin. She has written on religious practice and secularization in Ireland and on social and cultural factors in family planning, and is currently involved in studying the relationship between family and work in Dublin.

BARBARA STRASSBERG was born in Cracow, Poland, and has lived in Chicago since 1984. Before coming to the United States she taught at the Institute of Sociology of Jagiellonian University (Cracow) where she received her Ph.D. She has also been an honorary fellow of the University of Chicago Divinity School. Her research interests focus on the relation of religion to national identity. She is the author of *The Church in the Process of Assimilation of Polish Americans.*

JAN SWYNGEDOUW is professor of religious studies at Nanzan University in Nagoya, Japan, where he is also permanent fellow of the Nanzan Institute for Religion and Culture and editor of the *Japanese Journal of Religious Studies.* Born in Belgium, he was ordained a Roman Catholic priest in the Immaculate Heart of Mary Mission Society and has worked in Japan since 1961. He completed the doctoral course in religious studies at Tokyo University. He has published several books (in Japanese) on Japanese religiosity and has been a frequent contributor to various scholarly journals.

MIKLÓS TOMKA is professor of sociology at the University of Budapest. From 1978 to 1986 he was vice-president of the research committee for the sociology of religion of the International Sociological Association. He has published several books and numerous articles on the sociology of religion, mass communications, and time-budget research. His current research interests include religious socialization, religion and the life-cycle, and the relationship between religion and the social system.

Preface

Roman Catholicism today is going through one of its most important periods of change and transition. In its relation to nation-states and secular culture and in dealings with non-Christians and other Christian groups, its boundaries have been appreciably modified, providing it with new normative reference points and differing conceptions of task. Correspondingly, notions of office, status, and authority have undergone notable changes: where formal status earlier legitimated the exercise of authority, it now increasingly depends on the qualities of the person who occupies the office as well as on the style with which directives and admonitions are tendered. One-way vertical communication—from top to bottom—is rapidly being juxtaposed by both bottom-to-top and lateral patterns (e.g., the International Synod of Bishops, regional and national bishops' conferences). These changes are not merely institutional but extend to the level of lived experience: Catholics behave and think today in ways that would have seemed extraordinary in the 1950s. Theologians can dispute the official interpretation of a point of doctrine, Catholics can refuse to obey a directive of the pope, priests can abandon their ministry—and they can do these things while continuing to retain membership in the church and the respect of the social community to which they belong.

Of all the factors contributing to these changes, surely one of the most significant has been the growing recognition of Catholicism as a world church.[1] Although in its central goals and corporate tradition the church has always been a religious organization positioned at the transnational level as a symbolic and cultural leader, the time has ended when Catholicism as a whole can be equated with its Greco-Roman Mediterranean or European expressions. Over the last twenty years a multicultural Catholicism has emerged in which regional churches are expected to interact, mutually criticizing and enriching one another to the benefit of the universal church.

It is widely accepted that the Second Vatican Council was a key event in this emergence of a world church. One need only compare it with previous councils to recognize that the church at Vatican II exhibited greater geographic and ethnic inclusiveness than ever before in its history. Even though the Asian and African bishops played a relatively minor part compared with their European colleagues, they represented an indigenous hierarchy (rather than missionary bishops of European or North American origin) gathering as a world episcopate with the pope and under his leadership to function as the final teaching and decision-making body of the church.[2] In its formal teaching the council also revealed a new perspective. It admitted vernacular languages into the church's liturgy, established the International Synod of Bishops, called for the "internationalization" of the Roman Curia, conferred new status to regional and national bishops' conferences, endorsed the principles of missionary accommodation to indigenous cultures and of religious liberty, and for the first time in the church's doctrinal history rendered a truly positive evaluation of the great non-Christian world religions. Since the council this trend has been carried forward by the virtual abolition of the Latin liturgy, the global travels of Paul VI and John Paul II, and the increasing vitality of the church in the Third World.

The statistical growth of Catholicism in the Third World probably best illustrates the novelty of the present situation. As of the mid-1980s, the total membership of the church stood at approximately 840 million persons who were distributed in the major regions of the world in roughly these proportions: 277 million in Western and Central Europe, 352 million in the countries of Latin America; 64 million in North America, 70 million in Africa, 71 million in Asia, and 6 million in Oceania (including Australia and New Zealand). The professional personnel of the church amounted to 1.4 million, including nearly 406,000 priests (diocesan and religious), 926,000 sisters, 66,000 brothers, and about 4,000 bishops (residential and titular).[3] Until 1960, the church's main constituency was found in areas typically designated as the Western world. Today, Latin America contains more Catholics than Europe and North America taken together, and more Catholics live in the southern hemisphere than in the northern. By the year 2000, it is estimated that approximately 70 percent of all Catholics (and 60 percent of all Christians) will live in the south.[4]

We are, therefore, witnessing an epochal shift that is dramatically altering the predominance of the Western church. Catholicism has become a world church with an evident presence in all six continents. Regional and national hierarchies are acquiring a new sense of their own distinctive identity. They no longer simply learn from Europe but now feel a responsibility to shape the future of the church in their own parts of the world and to contribute insights based on their own experience. This experience is shaped both by the originality of different cultures and by the relative social position of Catholicism: in 30 of the 263 countries of the world all Christians together form less than 1 percent of the population; in 86 countries they comprise 50 percent or less; in 147 countries they are in the majority.

These developments raise imposing challenges. Only once before, as Karl Rahner has observed, has Christianity been forced to undergo an abrupt cultural shift: the first-century transition from a Jewish to a Gentile Christianity.[5] While this change introduced a radically new period in church history, the end result was a monocultural Catholicism that began to unravel only with the demise of European colonialism. The current transition is far more complex than that of the first century: it involves not just two but many cultures. How, for example, can the church adjust itself to the secular society and new scientific technological culture of the West, which has replaced the classical culture that provided the intellectual framework of European Catholicism, and at the same time implant itself in the more traditional cultures of Asia and Africa? Can a church that simultaneously responds to the corrosive acid of secularization and the urgent demand for inculturation—that is, the process of a deep, sympathetic adaptation to local cultures—retain sufficient internal coherence and solidarity to remain a single social body? How can the church adopt new symbols, language, structures, and behavior on a massive scale without losing continuity with its own origins and tradition?[6]

It is by no means easy to formulate answers to these questions without a deeper understanding of the changing situation of Roman Catholicism across the world. Although there has been some theological discussion of the emergence of a world church since the end of the Second Vatican Council, there is little available—certainly in the social science literature on religion—that takes seriously Catholicism's various historical and cultural contexts and its differing relationships with the political sector. Nor has much attention been paid to the interesting convergences and divergences in Catholicism worldwide. This volume seeks to stimulate that broader perspective by bringing together a series of original and critical reflections on the development and condition of contemporary Catholicism in a variety of situations, no two of which are exactly alike.

The chapters in this book have been organized into four parts. The first focuses on some of the major challenges and strategic issues facing world Catholicism. David Martin, in a unifying introductory essay, probes the church's embodiment and activity in various ecological niches and demonstrates that Catholicism's center–periphery patterns have been neither static through time nor uniform from one segment of the periphery to another. Peter Hebblethwaite (Chapter 2) analyzes the post-Vatican II developments with regard to the papacy and the reality of local churches. The essays in Parts II and III examine specific contexts in Catholicism's European heartland and in the English-speaking world. A key issue here is the process of secularization and its impact on the shape and influence of Catholicism. Part IV considers what Walbert Buhlmann has called the "Third Church"—the church of the new nations of Latin America, Africa, and Asia now entering as a force into both world history and the history of the church.[7] Central themes running through these last chapters include the church's relationship to revolution and the problems of religious "inculturation"—a term that made its first appearance in official Catholic literature in the public message issued by the International Synod of Bishops in 1977.

The book is intended for two audiences. On the one hand, it is aimed at professional students and scholars of religion and addresses a number of issues pertinent to the relationship between Christianity and culture that fall at the intersection of social science and theology. On the other hand, the general reader will find interest in the work as an account of the changing face of Roman Catholicism and its worldwide diversity. Obviously the full range of this diversity cannot be treated in a single volume. We hope, however, that the case studies included in the following chapters will offer sufficient variety to be typical of situations elsewhere. The objective was not to provide an encyclopedia of world Catholicism but an introduction to the comparative sociology of Catholicism.

Three convictions underlie this objective. First, the church, as a transnational actor, comes into play vis-à-vis different cultures and political arrangements under certain conditions; each set of conditions calls forth specialized problem-solving initiatives both by the center and by local/regional churches. Second, the church's actions have different consequences for diverse historical and cultural situations because the parameters that constrain problem-solving efforts differ. They also carry direct consequences for domestic political developments, intergroup conflict or alliance, and cultural and symbolic meanings. In short, the transnational capacities of the church are mediated through different systems of religious control according to different historical filters and national contexts.[8] Third, despite its multiple inculturation, Catholicism is more than a federation of particular churches. Local churches, Paul VI warned, could easily fall prey to local separatist forces.[9] What is essential is that the church retain its capacity, so astonishing to the ancient world, of bringing Jews and Gentiles, Greeks and barbarians, into a single people. In the early church, the feeling of worldwide fellowship was cultivated by adherence to a single rule of faith, concelebration of the liturgy, eucharistic communion, letters of peace, mutual hospitality, and charitable assistance.[10] But how is this common culture to be maintained today? As the various essays collected in this volume demonstrate, the problems accompanying Catholicism's transition to a world church cannot be adequately handled without a comprehensive pastoral strategy, which will undoubtedly involve formation of new structures and new methodologies. The emergence of a world church sets the main agenda for Catholicism in the decades to come.

This book was begun at the Woodstock Theological Center at Georgetown University; editorial work was completed in England at St. Edmund's College, Cambridge. Both places provided a congenial atmosphere, encouragement, and support. Special thanks are due to Jacqueline Sheldon and Alison Roberts for their translations of chapters originally written in French and Spanish, and to Anne Waites and her team of typists who prepared the manuscript for publication.

THOMAS M. GANNON, S.J.

NOTES

1. The first to enunciate this thesis was Karl Rahner, speaking at Weston School of Theology in Cambridge, Massachusetts, in 1979. See "Towards a Fundamental Theological Interpretation of Vatican II," *Theological Studies* 40 (1979):716–27. See also Walbert Buhlmann, *The Church of the Future: A Model for the Year 2001* (Maryknoll, N.Y.: Orbis, 1986) and Avery Dulles, S.J., "The Emerging World Church: A Theological Reflection," Address to the Catholic Theological Society of America, Washington, D.C., June 13, 1984. Several of Dulles's formulations are included in this preface, as are those of Ivan Vallier, "The Roman Catholic Church as a Transnational Actor," in R. O. Keohane and J. S. Nye (eds.), *Transnational Relations in World Politics* (Cambridge, Mass.: MIT Press, 1972).
2. Rahner, *Theological Investigations*, p. 718.
3. These figures are taken from *The Statistical Yearbook of the Church* (Rome: Office of the Secretary of State, 1984).
4. For statistics to support this estimate, see Buhlmann, *Church of the Future*, pp. 117–30.
5. Rahner, *Theological Investigations*, p. 721.
6. What these questions imply theologically for the church is discussed by Dulles, "The Emerging World Church." See also Ary A. Roest Crollius, "What Is So New About Inculturation," *Gregorianum* 59 (1978):721–38, and William Reiser, "Inculturation and Doctrinal Development," *Heythrop Journal* 22 (1981):135–48.
7. Walbert Buhlmann, *The Coming of the Third Church* (Maryknoll, N.Y.: Orbis, 1977).
8. See Vallier, "The Roman Catholic Church as Transnational Actor."
9. Paul VI, *Evangelii nuntiandi*, n. 62; an English translation is available in A. Flannery (ed.), *Vatican Council II: More Postconciliar Documents* (Northport, N.Y.: Costello, 1982), pp. 741–42.
10. For a discussion of these and similar practices, see L. Hertling, *Communio: Church and Papacy in Early Christianity* (Chicago: Loyola University Press, 1972).

PART
ONE

The Emerging World Church

1

Catholicism in Transition

David Martin

The Roman Catholic church, comprising at the present time over 800 million people, is both universal and local in character. The fundamental character of Catholicism as a social organism is to achieve expansion in this or that ecological niche. According to the nature of the niche in which it finds itself Catholicism encounters different challenges and chances, different constraints and opportunities. At the same time, Catholicism also responds to certain social processes that are widespead without necessarily all moving in the same direction. Secularization, for example, is such a widespread process, usually associated with the breakup and fragmentation of organic societies. But some societies are shifting toward a new form of organic unity, which may be religious in character as in the case of Islam, or ideological as in the case of Marxism. In the course of this chapter we must first consider the varieties of ecological niche and then briefly consider the broader tendencies.[1]

Western Europe

The first niche to be considered is the one in which Catholicism was originally cradled: Europe. In Europe the outward forms of Catholicism constitute a passable holy ghost of the Roman Empire, the spirit of a political body long since dead. Indeed, given that the Lutheran churches, and even more so the Anglican church, continue to some extent in the same spirit and retain so many of the original Catholic forms, there is still a sense in which the whole of Catholic Europe is present, albeit in fractured form in the northern third of the continent. True, the northern provinces threw off the colonial tutelage of Rome, though not necessarily Latinity, but they also retained a great deal. Even where much was lost much was later revived, and that process of

3

loss and recovery recurred almost as often within those churches retaining the Roman obedience as among the conservative national churches emerging at the Reformation. In the eighteenth century the continuity of Catholicism, Roman and non-Roman, was partly interrupted, by defalcation from the faith among the upper clergy, for example, in France, and by a nationalization of the churches usually by absolute monarchies, which extended from England to Russia, Spain to Austria, France to Portugal—and indeed to Latin America. In the light of historical realities the Brazilian church was less Catholic following the changes wrought by the Marquis de Pombal than even the Anglican church during Sir Robert Walpole's time.

Naturally such reflections as these in part point to neglected historical realities and in part imply estimates as to what is or is not of the *esse* of "Roman Catholicism." These estimates hover over a great deal of what follows so they might as well be indicated at the very beginning. The church is *more or less* Roman, and in the Spain of Charles III, the Austria of Joseph II, the Brazil of Pedro I and II, and the Sweden of Charles XII it has been less so in several different ways. The same reflection applies to the Chinese church during the Cultural Revolution.

The norms of Catholicity that lie behind what we write, and control what we consider to be the scope of our topic, need particularly to be noted because in the present period we are witnessing a departure from a distinctive variant or version of Catholicism. This was created at Trent in the sixteenth century and then more specifically devised to counter the problems of the period from 1860–1950. Catholicism was organized as a social ghetto and an ecclesiastical fortress, dug into the Roman rock or base, and the whole of Catholicism was organized and directed by the almost absolute authority incarcerated—sometimes literally—in that base. Influences flowed into and out of the base through channels that were steeply vertical. Organizations like Catholic Action were devised as part of the outer defense system of the Roman base.[2]

Many have seen this exclusive focus and this vertical nature of authority as of the *esse* of *Roman* Catholicism. It is part of the object of this volume to chart the changing core of what is to be regarded as "essential." It is also part of its object to extend Vaticanology toward a view of Catholicism as a system, assimilating impulses from a worldwide net and then redistributing those impulses once again to a worldwide net. It is important, for example, to look at the way the European "center" has redistributed resources, especially the resources of the priesthood, toward Latin America, and how Latin American Catholicism in turn has influenced the center. It may well be that powerful signals will soon be fed into Rome from the African church.

These reflections arise because we are dealing with the center: the so-called traditional center of the earth in the Mediterranean (literally, Middle Land). Yet curiously enough the demographic heartlands of relatively "orthodox" Catholicism are not to be found on the Mediterranean littoral. Much of southern Europe from southern Portugal to Bosnia is weakly Christianized and exhibits a religion that is diffuse and/or superstitious.[3]

Even if we balk at the normative implications involved in speaking of "orthodoxy," the strength of Catholicism in terms of practice is more often located in the central rather than in the southernmost parts of Europe. There is a richly Catholic center in the Alpine area of Switzerland, Austria, Bavaria, and parts of northern

Italy. It extends northwest along much of the southern Rhineland up to Cologne and into the southern part of the Netherlands. It then extends further into Flanders with isolated bastions in Brittany and southern Ireland (Eire). It extends southwest through the Massif Central and parts of the Pyrenees to the Basque country, and thence to most of northern Spain, Galicia, and northern Portugal, with powerful tentacles in parts of Aragon and Catalonia. It extends northeast into Slovakia, Poland, Lithuania, and parts of Latvia. The southeastern extension has suffered historical truncation by the combined effects of the Eastern Schism, based on the Eastern and Byzantine empire, and of the Ottoman empire, which took over from Byzantium. It extends from the Veneto to Slovenia and Croatia, and reaches down the Yugoslav (Dalmatian) littoral as far as Dubrovnik.[4]

In the interstices of belief exist major areas of secularity, in the Paris basin, in parts of Emilio-Tuscany, and in Czech Lands. Of course, almost the whole of post-Protestant Europe is deeply secularized, with the capitals of secularity being found in the major metropolitan centers of London, Birmingham, Amsterdam, Hamburg, Berlin, Copenhagen, Oslo, Stockholm, and Helsinki.

Within Catholicism various declines can be discerned that parallel those once largely confined to Protestant cultures. Historically, secularity has attended the appearance of large-scale mobile concentrations of populations, the creation of heavy industry, and also of certain kinds of primary industry—for example, the coalfields of Décazeville and Asturias. In today's perspective we can see that as social conditions in general approximate those of northern Protestant countries so Catholic practice moves closer to Protestant practice. In France weekly practice has dramatically decreased over the past decade until the church in France is not so very different from the Church of England. In parts of urban, lowland Switzerland, Catholic practice, considered in terms both of mass attendance and of moral behavior, has begun to approximate that of Protestants.

It is important in these matters to focus not only on mass attendance but also on identification with "Catholicity" and with the church, and with Catholic moral norms. In Ireland (Eire), for example, Catholicism is strong with regard to mass attendance, identification with the church, and Catholic moral norms. In 1986 only 35 percent of Irish citizens voted in favor of legalizing divorce. Ireland comes closest of all countries to exemplifying and embodying Catholicism in terms of official Catholic social doctrine.[5] In Poland, moral perceptions and behavior are less strongly Catholic than is identification with the church and attendance at mass. In France residual Catholicism may remain at the level of some sense of identity but it rarely extends to mass attendance or to the enthusiastic embrace of official Catholic moral theology. In Flanders and the southern Netherlands Catholic identification remains strong, but we also see a formerly very high level of practice lowered considerably, and loyalty to Catholic moral norms greatly eroded.

It is worth noting some interesting evidence on the beliefs, practices, and values of Catholic Europe as provided by the European Values Survey.[6] This evidence is compatible with the detailed evidence on France provided by Henri Madelin in Chapter 3. In general, it may be said that the majority of practicing Catholics accept basic Catholic doctrines. At the same time the baptized Catholic population taken as a whole and descending from older to younger generations is decreasingly inclined to believe in a *personal* God and in an "after life." Most Catholics accept the standards embodied in the Ten Commandments, more especially the specifically moral ones concerning honesty, truthfulness, marital faithfulness, respect for parents, and respect for life. But there is a decreasing acceptance, age group by age group, of ecclesiastical pronouncements on such matters as divorce and abortion. This decreasing acceptance is clearly visible even among Catholics who attend mass weekly. Of those Catholics who attend mass weekly 75 percent approve of abortion where the mother's health is endangered, and 55 percent approve of abortion where the fetus is likely to be born handicapped. The majority of Catholics, practicing or nonpracticing, long ago rejected the prohibition of contraceptives. This decline in moral orthodoxy exists everywhere in Western Europe and echoes data obtained in North America and Eastern Europe. Of course, the decline varies greatly country by country. The Irish (South and North) are most clearly attached to official ecclesiastic rulings, which are indeed built into the polity in Eire, whereas the French are least attached. The shift in moral attitudes and disregard for ecclesiastical authority are paralleled by a decrease in regular mass attendance. This again is least visible in Ireland and most visible in France.

The difference in all these matters between Ireland and France is not surprising since in the one control of socialization is fully maintained by the church, whereas in the other such control has been largely conceded to other agencies, following a century of struggle with the state. Declines in weekly practice have also been notable in the historic Catholic heartlands of Spain and Italy. It is important to notice that as women's lifestyles begin to approximate those of men so does their religious practice approach the level of males. There is no "intrinsic" female religiosity or, at any rate, there is no specific propensity to religious practice. It is also worth noting in general that while practice and moral orthodoxy and obedience to ecclesiastical authority have declined, respect for the church remains high. The image of the church in Catholic Europe is fairly positive.

The traditional relationships between regular practice and political conservatism still hold, in spite of changes in the attitudes of priests. It seems that the laity, though exalted by progressive theologians, remain politically inclined to conservatism. Another connection, which continues to be visible, is the antagonistic symbiosis between Catholicism and radicalism. Catholic countries over the last two centuries have bred both more conservatism *and* more radicalism. Communism as a version of radical politics has been important largely in the Latin countries, above all in France and in Italy. And radical anarchism too has had its greatest influence in Latin countries, above all in Spain.

How has the decomposition of regular religious practice affected politics? I would note a tendency, present since the 1960s, for the church to move away from the kind of explicit support of Christian Democracy offered after World War II. This tendency was rooted in several changes. The left had relaxed its traditional anticlericalism. The right for its part appeared caught up in a profane economic dynamism. In any case, the restabilization of Western Europe in which Catholic leaders like Konrad Adenauer were so prominent had been sufficiently accomplished. Ecclesiastical interventions became more specific, as, for example, the unsuccessful attempt to prevent the legalization of divorce in Italy. On the other hand, a partial move back to support for Christian Democracy has been evident since 1980, particularly in Italy.

Here I would quote from Suzanne Berger, whose focus is on France but who also draws attention to a wider European context.

> In France where the dimensions of religious change have been the most striking, weekly mass attendance dropped from about one-third of all Catholics in the 1950s to about 15 per cent at the end of the seventies. The numbers of those taking confession, communion, and confirmation fell. Ordinations declined from over 600 a year to about 150 between the mid-sixties and mid-seventies. Surveys of the faithful find growing pockets of doubt and resistance to central tenets of doctrine. The subcultural institutions which sheltered the Catholic community from the onslaught of secular culture and from the Republic are in ruin. Catholic Action associations, among the largest mass movements of the post-war period, have become sects with small audiences beyond the immediate participants.
>
> These phenomena appear in all of Catholic Western Europe, more advanced in France, the Netherlands, and Germany than in Spain, Italy, or Portugal; but everywhere the trends seem to move in the same directions. There are, to be sure, countertendencies: an upsurge of charismatic religious practice, some revival of monastic recruitment, continued mass support for private, i.e., Catholic schools, the success of new styles of Catholic politics, particularly in the Italian *Communione e liberazione* movement. The dominant fact, however, is the collapse of old patterns of religious practice and of long-established religious institutions.[7]

Berger shows, as does Henri Madelin, that there is continued support for conservatism among the faithfully practicing minority, and she emphasizes yet again how the historic church–state confrontation forced politics to turn around the axis of Catholic believers against anticlericals. She shows that in certain areas, such as the west of France, where practice has dropped, the voting behavior of the population now approximates the national average, which means that voting for the left has increased.

But the core of what she has to say is of wider significance. It concerns the emergence of Catholic militants somewhat disengaged from traditional practice, and the transfer of active commitments following the collapse of associations like Catholic Action. While Madelin mentions tendencies toward a religiosity based on self-construction and toward a skepticism vis-à-vis *all* central authorities, Berger's focus is on the political redirection of religious commitments. Perhaps a comparison may be suggested here between what happened in terms of religiously motivated politics when Jews left the ghetto and what has happened recently as Catholics have left the ghetto. Certainly the tendencies observable in France at an advanced stage invite comparisons as far afield as contemporary Chile and Brazil. "Christians for Socialism" and other groups flourish inside the church when it takes a radical stand and move outside when it does not.

Berger is concerned with a Catholic population that has shifted to the left, bringing new electors to the Socialist Party and even to the Communist Party, and also contributing to single-issue movements concerned with regional cultural integrity, the nuclear threat, and ecology. Catholics in Catholic trade unions such as the Confédération Française Démocratique du Travail (CFDT) have continued to express their new militancy within the framework of the union. However, some of those Catholics brought up in movements like Catholic Action have tended to leave the institutions of the Catholic subculture and to engage in militant politics. At a time when party political adherence overall is in decline these passionate sometime members of associations for cultural defense enter the explicitly political realm.

This, however, is not a simple transfer of loyalties. The converts bring with them a distinctive concern about community, race, feminism, the Third World, and a commitment to worker self-management and decentralization. The impact of these concerns has been sufficiently great to stir up adherents of the older left so that they actually prodded Mittérand toward the nationalization of the Catholic schools. Clearly this kind of semidetached religiosity, seeking a focus for a faith friendly to religion though not to ecclesiastical authority, is an important phenomenon in contemporary Catholicism, among both priests and laity. It invites comparison with the religiosity that animates the cells emerging among the East European intelligentsia and that is found among the base communities of South America. It also invites comparison with certain elements within communism itself. Many neo-Marxists seem concerned with precisely those issues that might animate those once involved in the Catholic subculture, for example, the preservation of local skills, languages, and traditions against cosmopolitan capitalism and against a pervasive technicist mentality. (Indeed, as Catholic authority is becoming desacralized so also is Marxist authority.)

The school issue is, of course, a residue from older conflicts, and has cropped up again recently in Latin America as well as Europe. It derives from two rival claims: the claim of the Catholic church to provide a "formation" for its children, and the claim of the state to provide comprehensive socialization for all those who constitute the sacred vessel of "the nation." The recent conflict in France has received most publicity, but it has arisen also in Spain, Italy, and Malta. Moreover, it was Allende's proposals to take over Catholic education in Chile that crucially increased ecclesiastical alarm over the direction of his policies. The issue of who educates the next generation is central in Nicaragua today. All communist governments insist on "thought control" as basic to their aims, as indeed has the Catholic church in the whole Counter Reformation period. However, the claim that the Catholic church now advances is presumably based on a right to educate the children of the faithful according to the general assumptions of a pluralist society. (Indeed, Madelin emphasizes the breakup of "totalities" in contemporary France and the pluralism that pervades both church and society.) The church has now evolved a long way from the position which claimed that Catholics could not tolerate the propagation of error.

Madelin characterizes the controversy over the schools as one in which the majority of French people were not only aggressively in favor of an education informed or at least toned by religion but also concerned to save a private system from the bureaucratic rigidities of public education. Vast demonstrations occurred in spite of the fact that only a minority is involved in Catholic education. This is precisely the controversy over Christian schools in general in Australia, Britain, and the United States. It touches on the specific character and values of Christian education and the right of parents to choose the atmosphere in which children may be brought up. In other words, the "rights of conscience" are slowly changing sides, and the ejection of the church from the state, which is partial in Western countries and total in communist ones, has offered the church the role of defender of subcultural values (and by extension of minorities of every kind).

Eastern Europe

The situation of Catholicism in Eastern Europe presents quite specific problems, as well as broader long-term ones almost coextensive with the onset of urbanization and industrialization. The map of practice is very varied. Poland and Lithuania are countries where the majority attends weekly mass. For Poles and for Lithuanians (excluding Russians intruded into Lithuania), Catholic practice and national identity are almost coextensive.[8] The same can almost be said of the subnationalities of Croatia and Slovakia. The resentment of Croatians against Belgrade and of Slovakians against Prague are additional spurs to piety. The areas of lowest practice are undoubtedly Czech Lands and Moravia, and this weakness has a long history. Czech liberalism and the effects of modernization had bitten deep into Catholic practice long before the communist takeover.

The intermediate case is Hungary.[9] Hungary is only partly Catholic since eastern Hungary managed to retain its Calvinism under Turkish rule and thereafter. But insofar as Hungary has been by tradition 75 percent Catholic, certain changes there are common to a lesser or greater degree in most Catholic cultures of Eastern Europe. From being the established state religion Catholicism became first a harassed church deeply opposed to the state, and then a church more or less coexisting with the state. In the new situation following 1948 the church lost its lands, its schools, its welfare bodies, and its hospitals. It also faced the dissolution of its religious orders and was deprived of every kind of chaplaincy. This was all part of a massive process of state-managed social differentiation removing the web of interconnection, at all levels from parish to government, and forcibly restricting the church to a sphere of private religiosity. Naturally all this, together with steady pressure and antireligious propaganda, enormously reduced the capacity of the church to reproduce itself, so that the younger generations and those occupying roles in the new echelons of power and education have become increasingly nonreligious.

However, the decline of religious practice was not only related to the effects of antireligious socialization and the patent disadvantages of admitting a religious adherence. The state also set about massive programs of social, educational, and geographical mobility, which tore up the roots of local and family tradition. Women in particular were moved into the sphere of work, disrupting the capacity of religion to reproduce itself through "the distaff side." The result was a decline in those professing a faith from 50 percent in 1972 to 40 percent in 1981. There was a parallel erosion of attendance at Sunday mass to some 15 percent of Catholics and a diminution even of the rites of passage. Religious practice tended to become associated, as in Russia, with the old, the less educated, the disadvantaged, and those in occupations at the economic margin. More than that, even those who professed a faith tended to do so "in their own way" with diminished regard for ecclesiastical authority. And there appeared a large number of people equipped with neither religious faith nor ideological notions. This is a major development, paralleled in the West: the rise of the apolitical and the areligious. Many people now belong to the doctrineless center.

Yet there are also some interesting contrary indications, as Chapter 8, by Miklós Tomka, makes clear. Among the university educated, the small minority of believers has actually increased in recent years. This kind of religion is not supervised by priests, who are in any case aging and diminishing in number. It is based on religious self-education, often through *samizdat* (underground) literature passed from hand to hand, and it frequently draws inspiration from music. People committed in this way may well organize in cells outside the official church and concern themselves with social criticism or issues of war and peace. They create the Eastern European equivalents of the "base communities" and even of Western Christian campaigners against war and nuclear armament.

This Hungarian pattern is also present in the small Catholic community in East Germany, in Czech Lands, and in Moravia, and for that matter in Russia. It represents a revival of religion in small committed groups, often composed of highly educated young people. Such people may also, of course, link themselves to a traditional religiosity through a concern with the long-term roots of religion in their nation's culture, landscape, buildings, and artistic achievement.

The exceptions to this pattern of microreligiosity, as found today in Croatia, Slovakia, Lithuania, and above all in Poland, have to do with the way in which national resistance may be grounded in traditional religion. This does not imply obedience to church authority or to Catholic norms concerning, for example, contraception and divorce, but it does involve intense symbolic identification. This may express itself in pilgrimages to national shrines or in the kind of monument to national martyrs as that erected at Gdansk. It is sufficiently intense in Poland to engender an insistence on comprehensive religious socialization outside the state schools. Vocations are maintained or even increased, and the faithful provide more than enough resources to sustain the church. In such circumstances there even emerges a substantial Christian intelligentsia devoted to expounding the faith and to tracing and tending its roots in the national culture. The Croation Catholic intelligentsia, for example, has deep national loyalties as well as a vocal diaspora.

The faith that stimulates Poles, Lithuanians, Croats, and others is likely to be theologically conservative, given that boundaries cannot be blurred in times of intense external pressure. But if it is theologically conservative it can also be socially radical. As is well-known, Catholicism and Catholic workers were deeply involved in the brief emergence of free trade unionism in Poland, even though the church itself maintained a certain critical distance.

Catholics as Minorities in Protestant Cultures

A special situation exists where Roman Catholics are a minority in Protestant countries. This occurs either because part of the country remained Catholic at the Reformation, as in those countries lying at the European confessional border (the Netherlands, Switzerland, and Germany), or because of migration away from the Catholic heartlands into "Protestant" territory. The principal communities of the Catholic diaspora are to be found in England, Scotland and Wales, in Canada, Australia, and New Zealand, and above all in the United States. Communities have also recently been established in Scandinavia. Québec is a special case and will be treated separately along with other "peoples" who have a distinct territory, a consciousness of kind, and a language.

There are some general characteristics belonging to all Catholic communities in the Protestant (or post-Protestant) countries. First, they have not directly participated in the national myth of origins insofar as that was forged at the Reformation. The Netherlands, Germany, and England in particular, and by extension the United States, were forged in a Protestant crucible, and their foundation stories, their language and literature, have been impregnated by epic struggle. Indeed, in some of these countries, Catholics have participated in attempts to recover power and have therefore been regarded as treasonable. Even if that has not occurred there have been struggles between the dominant Protestant interest in the state (or in the federation) and the Catholic church. In Germany this led to the *Kulturkampf;* in Switzerland it resulted in the Civil War of the mid-nineteenth century. As a result Catholics have often been seen as second-class citizens; at any rate they have not been securely located in the national elite. In Germany, for example, the leading edge of German unification and the principal power after unification was Protestant Prussia.

Where Catholics have been in diaspora, as, for example, in Britain and the successor states of the British Empire, they have often been relatively recent migrants. In the United States they have been the Irish, and later still the Poles and the Italians and the German Catholics. In Australia and New Zealand they have been mainly the Irish, though there is now a sizable Italian community in Australia. In England and Scotland they have been the Irish, though there were also substantial Italian and Polish migrations after World War II. It is worth underlining these movements because they are part of a vast demographic expansion of Christendom, to which Catholic Christendom has been a major contributor. In the nineteenth century Europe exploded outward in terms of people as well as power. The present explosion of Islam is a parallel movement a century later.

Whether Catholics have been a historic minority lying at the confessional border or in diaspora, they had to find a way to join the national community without sacrificing the integrity of their church. This meant both trying to become first-class citizens and achieving some form of organization within a defensive ghetto, especially in the field of education. A great many tensions have arisen over this ghetto organization, especially in the Netherlands where it constituted a division running right through the society.[10]

The sense of partial exclusion, of being organized in a ghetto, of being concentrated in the lower strata of society, and (in the Irish and Polish cases) the memory of historic wrongs gave rise to a unique solidarity in the faith and an exemplary obedience to Rome. Moreover, because they were concentrated in the lower strata Catholics were not part of the conservative forces in their respective societies. In countries where Catholics were dominant their elites mostly ensured an association with conservatism or reaction, and thereby reinforced anticlericalism. But in Protestant countries a highly conservative form of religion had everything to gain by association with reformist movements or with movements for civil rights. In the twentieth century the Catholic party in Germany was the Center party, with an interest in welfare and reforms; in Britain Catholics supported the Liberal party and then the Labor party; in Australia they supported the Labor party (and even gave rise to a Catholic splinter group); in the United States they became associated with Democratic politics.[11] The first sizable break between conservative religion and conservative politics is of major significance.

Gradually over the last century Catholics moved closer to parity with Protestants. They had votes and used them.[12] In Australia, for example, they built a massive school system at all levels. They were sufficiently numerous in certain localities, in New York or Chicago, or Liverpool, to acquire a political preponderance or at least a major share of community power. In Germany they eventually became the majority due to a postwar division of the country, which placed part of Protestant Germany within the German Democratic Republic. They also tended to have higher rates of birth than Protestants, which gave them further democratic weight. Perhaps the most prominent symbol of the whole process was the election of John F. Kennedy as president of the United States. This is not to say that the tensions and difficulties have ended. Catholic politicans still have problems as to how they should translate Catholic moral norms in societies that are massively Protestant or just secular, as witness the problems of Mario Cuomo and Geraldine Ferraro in the United States. And it is still a matter of debate whether or not Catholic background and Catholic education provide comparable access to elite positions, especially in science.

Since the achievement of near-parity in the mid-twentieth century certain major changes have occurred affecting these Catholic minorities. The Second Vatican Council not only gave Catholics a chance to cooperate with Protestants and even to resemble them, but it also threatened the strong defensive boundaries that had been built up. In most of these countries Catholic practice had been uniquely impressive, with weekly mass attendance rising as high as 70 percent of the total community. But then in the mid-1960s and 1970s weekly mass attendance dropped, most dramatically in Québec and in the Netherlands.[13] It was as if the élan of these communities and their sense of historic solidarity had been unstrung. Institutional cohesion was damaged. People were worried by the loss of ritual markers, like the Friday abstinence. Secure bureaucratic governance to a minor extent dissolved in charismatic fervor. The priesthood and the religious orders lost many members in an atmosphere of existential confusion.

Of course, this was also a time of renewal throughout the church and an opportunity to review the founding charters of the community as a whole, and of all its subcommunities, notably the orders. The new sense of freedom stimulated some Catholics to adopt quite a loose ecclesiastical identity or to see the church more in terms of vital community than in terms of orders and of sources of authoritative doctrine. Indeed, the "service professions," the intelligentsia, and the religious orders increasingly took a structural and sociological view of the "social problem" and of the place of the church in the world. Certainly this happened throughout the whole church, among (for example) Belgians at Leuven (Louvain) and English Dominicans in Blackfriars, but it acquired a specific momentum in communities once highly committed to a Roman obedience. In America perhaps more than anywhere else the powerful solvents of Americanism with its origins in Protestant individualism had been quietly active for some time. These forces now became openly active, particularly in the sphere of feminism.

Nor were the bishops standing entirely on the sidelines. The Dutch episcopate, even though it eventually received conservative reinforcements, was involved with the other Dutch churches in social criticism. The English Roman Catholic episcopate took up a stance, along with the Anglican and other churches, that was close to the policy of the Liberal-Social Democratic Alliance. Catholic and Anglican bishops issued similar statements on war and peace. In America the Catholic episcopate issued documents on war and peace and on the economy, which subjected Western economic conservatism and Western foreign policies to critical scrutiny. In short, what had been a reformist inclination located at the level of Catholic voting behavior in Protestant countries now became a critical stance in the priesthood and the episcopate.

At the same time, of course, there had been nothing in these countries resembling the attempt in Latin Christendom to create Catholic political parties and unions. There was therefore less argument about how far such an explicitly political apparatus should be dismantled or reshaped. The Catholic presence in unions was largely on an individual basis, though the Catholic contribution to union leadership was considerable and merits further study. The only issue was, as always, the comprehensive nature of Catholic socialization, especially in the schools. These massive investments in religious solidarity (and in ethnic continuity) remained in place all over the "Protestant" world from Liverpool to Sydney and from Chicago to Belfast.

An Aside on Québec

It is here useful to touch briefly on micro-nationalism by reference to Québec. Québec belongs in one sense to the Catholic minorities in English-speaking Protestant cultures but it also exhibits the kind of micro-nationalism that is lodged in a territorial base within a larger entity, for example, Brittany in France, Wales in Britain, the Basque country in Spain, Flanders in Belgium. Of course, Québec is large enough to constitute a New France parallel to a New England, and allows us to examine an independent French culture without the traumatic schizophrenia over religion engendered by the French Revolution.

Québec is important both in itself and because it belongs to a group of cultural redoubts with a strong religious definition. Its remarkable evolution since 1960 enables us to indicate a distinctive path to modernization, one shared, for example, with Flanders and the Basque country. The following comments lean extensively on an article by Gregory Baum and on the information provided by Hans Mol (Chapter 13).[14]

Given the external pressure on the identity of Québec, the Catholic church acted as a cultural anchor and even defined the Québecois as a "holy remnant." Even when Québec was industrialized (by outside capital) and urbanized, the Catholic anchor held. As in Poland the cohesive network of Catholic associations in the rural areas was successfully transferred to the cities. The unions remained relatively tame under Catholic aegis, and even when they ceased to be tame they received extensive Catholic support, particularly from Catholic Action. The government of Québec deployed the Catholic church as careful guardian of its Québecois identity, as ideological guide, and as overseer of education, welfare, and health. The society in short retained organic unity over against external threat at a price in terms of a low level of social differentiation.

In 1960 Maurice Duplessis, the long-time "boss" of Québec, fell and with him the old order. A new Liberal government rapidly set about to introduce a long-delayed political modernization. It partly replaced the older classical education

designed for a professional and legal elite with a scientific and technological education. It also created ministries of health and welfare, and began to "nationalize"
industry by increasing French Canadian participation in the higher echelons. In this
process it was to some extent assisted by Catholic Action, which had a semi-lay character independent of the episcopate, the elite, and the government. Indeed the
church largely went along with the new Québec, and the Dominicans in particular
acted in critical solidarity with it. This evolution is the more remarkable since the new
nationalism had clearly constructed its base more in a linguistic and cultural renaissance than in the faith; and the process of disentanglement had affected the church
negatively in terms of practice and vocations. The falls were as dramatic as in the
Netherlands, perhaps more so.

The theoretical issue addressed by Baum (drawing to some extent on my own *A
General Theory of Secularization*) is why this rapid modernization did not produce a
violent Catholic "reaction" and a cultural schism along classic French lines. The
answer is that up to 1960 the Catholic faith in Québec worked as it had in Poland
and in Ireland. It sustained the culture against external threat at a price in terms of
priestly control and a certain nostalgic backwardness, as well as in terms of corporatist or rural images of how society operated or should operate. When this "bloc"
or blockage disintegrated in the 1960s it still remained unthinkable to repudiate the
ancient religious guardian of society. War over religion could not occur. In any case
the church universal was itself engaged in undoing the spirals of mutual repulsion
between itself and social change. What was "fed in" to Québec Catholicism from
outside was no longer militant defensiveness. So Québec followed the evolution of
Catholic Flanders (and for that matter the Catholic southern part of the Netherlands).
It simultaneously achieved equality with the wider society and quietly untied the tight
bands of ecclesiastical control to allow social differentiation and secularization to take
place, above all in health, welfare, education, and social legitimation.

Latin America

The condition of Catholicism in the twenty-three countries of Latin America is pecu-
liarly important because here lies the demographic weight of the immediate future.
By the year 2000 Latin America will probably have a population of well over 700
million.[15]

Chronological and social time are not identical in Latin America. The Second
Vatican Council came earlier in the social development of Latin America than in that
of Europe. Latin America presents both a past almost lost elsewhere and a future
that may be ahead of its time. There remain in Latin America layers of precolonial
cultures, of the Iberian union of faith and crown, and of the alliance of landowner
with bishop. At the same time Latin American Catholicism has been injected with
personnel from the universal church, and out of the conditions found in Latin America
has emerged a sophisticated social commitment. Where once the old-style military
could rely on the church, the new-style bureaucratic soldiery of the "National Security State" often find in the church the one institution able to maintain and develop
a critical independence. This newly found independence has not been universal. In
Argentina, for example, the hierarchy tended to maintain public silence during the

most recent dictatorship, whatever private protests were made by some, while those in the openly protesting minority were severely savaged.[16]

The Latin American church can criticize because it has a unique, long-term legitimacy and maintains humane symbols which it is difficult for the government publicly to repudiate. As in the last decade of Franco's regime in Spain the church can offer shelter, which is sometimes the church building itself. This does not mean that long-term legitimacy confers safety. There is a tradition of hostility to the very idea of priesthood, which can allow the representatives or agents of threatened interests to harass or kill protesting clergy without compunction, as witness the fate of Archbishop Romero in El Salvador and Bishop Angelelli in Argentina. Nor are such priests necessarily ideological radicals. They may simply take their stand on broad principles that reject expropriation, corruption, and intimidation. Romero was not appointed as a radical, but nevertheless he felt he had no option but to protest.

The main problem for the church in Latin America is how to be critical without becoming so identified with and submerged by Marxism that the role of moral legitimation is handed over to ideologues or to the rulers of the state. There is a theological problem here which relates to the maintenance of the existential universality of Christianity as salvation from the death of the soul and as the overcoming of mortality. The categories of liberation theology may on occasion empty salvation into utopian hopes of a social transformation. Liberation theology may also translate the "bias" toward the poor into the idea that a particular oppressed class *is* the church and may even allow itself to be subsumed in the crucible of radical nationalism. These are present dangers in Nicaragua. The danger of Christianity being subsumed by national solidarity is almost perennial, as the messianic history of Poland illustrates. The identification of a social stratum as ontologically privileged and as coextensive with the church is less frequent, though not at all novel.

The story of Catholicism in Latin America is one of the successive stages by which the strategies of an *integrista* Christendom have been partly abandoned and the bonds with conservative and privileged strata partly broken. So far as the abandonment of the strategies of Christendom is concerned, we observe a sequence that broadly parallels the experience of Europe. To begin with, the church saw itself as organic and still coextensive with the culture and it tried to manage social questions through Catholic Action or the kind of ambitious venture in the building of institutions as was represented by the Catholic trade unions of Colombia.

How successful the church might be in canalizing or at any rate maintaining some direction of new institutions depended to some extent on how severely it had been traumatized in its prolonged struggle with the radical bourgeoisie. In some countries, such as Uruguay, Guatemala, and Venezuela, it suffered an assault on a scale comparable to that mounted in the France of the later Third Republic.[17] The church emerged initially capable of doing little but look after its own diminished corner in an indifferent and largely secularized society. In Mexico the church was entangled in the issues of a prolonged civil war.

Indeed, the Mexican Civil War and the Spanish Civil War together may be viewed as the culminating struggles in the long history of warfare between clerical and anticlerical radicals. Catholic cultures in Latin America as in Latin Europe have been indelibly marked by clericalism versus anticlericalism. Anticlericalism arises through the massive participation of the clergy, especially the upper clergy, in the

structures of power and ownership, especially the ownership of land, and in the ecclesiastical oversight of the socialization of the next generation.[18]

The entanglement may be complicated by the fact that the state has steadily
taken over the church and eroded much of its essential character in the process.
Brazil offers the most dramatic instance of a church gutted from the inside by state
control. Of course, blatant state control of patronage was by no means unique in
Brazil. Indeed it was a continual source of tensions throughout the continent. But in
Brazil the influence of the orders was destroyed, the priesthood fell into indiscipline,
and the mass was neglected. The anticlerical "secular religion" of Comteanism came
to exercise a major role in the state and in the national intelligentsia. When eventually
church and state were separated in the early 1900s the church was weak and the
Brazilian people lived by a kind of syncretic folk Catholicism based on pilgrimages to
shrines and the invocation of the saints.[19] There was a free-floating unorthodox religiosity, which might become focused in a messianic movement or in a regional cult
like that of Padre Cicero in Joaseiro or in spirit mediumship such as is found today
in Umbanda.[20] Today Umbanda combines the invocation of the saints with the invocation of African deities and is practiced by millions of Brazilians.[21] The answer of
the church to diffuse superstition in the society at large and to internal slackness was
Romanization and the drafting of clergy from elsewhere.[22]

The general weakness of the Latin American church and its vulnerability to the
left means that it can often emerge more effectively and wholeheartedly as the partisan of justice and peace when the forces of revolutionary Marxism have been
silenced for a period or do not provide a widening channel for popular discontent.
As Madeleine Adriance points out (Chapter 15), the experience of the church in Chile
is highly instructive here. It is a key case of the relation of the church to revolution,
and it is therefore well worth retracing the historical background. Many developments occurred earlier in Chile than elsewhere.[23]

As always, the problem was one of extrication from alliances with the state and
with conservative strata which might involve the church in their own demise. In Chile
this was smoothly achieved by a separation of church and state in 1925 and the
ending of a long-term alliance with conservatives. The policy of the church required
political neutrality. Yet most Catholics continued to support the Conservative Party
and some provided an intellectual grounding for Catholic corporatism. As usual, this
corporatism was capable of traveling in several directions.

In 1957 the Falange National Party merged with several small Christian movements to form the Christian Democratic Party, which put forward Eduardo Frei as
its presidential candidate running on a platform of agrarian reform and profit-sharing.
Yet Catholic voters continued their support for the right. This identification may well
have arisen from Catholic weakness in the more modest sectors of society and its
exaggerated apostolate to the upper classes, especially through education. In any
case, the articulation of new social norms by the bishops remained quite general and
personalistic. It had not yet acquired a sociological edge.

On the other hand, the ground for change had been laid in the socially progressive programs of Catholic Action between 1935 and 1958. As middle and low income
voters experienced a loss of purchasing power in the early 1960s Christian Democracy rapidly gained ground in Chile generally, and practicing Catholics shifted toward
the center. Fear of communism, especially among Catholics, accelerated the shift to

the center. In this respect, and in the overlapping of the branches of Catholic Action and structures of the Christian Democratic party, the situation now resembled that obtaining in Europe. Moreover, the church was acting as a conduit for personnel and for resources directed toward change that came from the international church, and was itself engaged in a more structural analysis of social problems.

Clearly even an implicit alliance with Christian Democracy must pose problems. And under pressure Catholics might move again toward the right while a significant minority might move toward the left—as indeed happened in 1970. When the Popular Unity government took power in 1970 under the leadership of Salvador Allende the bishops sympathized with many of its objectives. For its part the Chilean left spoke of working within a democratic framework. It presented itself as aligned with Euro-Communism. In the event the church accorded a conditional legitimacy to the regime, and expressed strong criticism only over the proposal to control the curricula of Catholic schools. Throughout the period of strikes and rising tension in 1972 the relationship between church leaders and the government remained cordial. Several church apostolates adapted their programs to fit in with socialist objectives. And the Popular Unity party doubled its support among practicing Catholics between 1970 and 1973.

Yet when the coup came in 1973 the position of the church was ambiguous. Many bishops had privately believed that an armed intervention might be necessary to halt chaos; and they also supposed that the traditional respect shown for constitutional government would ensure that military intervention would be short and relatively bloodless. In the event there was a great deal of violence. The church denounced the bloodshed and also requested that the progress recently achieved by workers and peasants be maintained. Soon, however, all other institutions were either under surveillance or outlawed. At this point the church became the only legitimate channel of criticism.

By early 1974 the extent of repression under the new right-wing government was clear, and the local parishes became the focus of complaints and requests. In April 1974 the bishops published a major critical statement. Yet the growth toward corporate opposition was gradual and was not fully articulated until mid-1976 when repression touched the upper echelons of the church itself. Thereafter the church has constituted the main channel of opposition and of demands for human rights.

Something similar is evident from the situation in Brazil during the years from the coup in 1964 to 1984.[24] The Brazilian church has not been able to forge effective institutions to implement its policies and defend its interests, nor has it been able to influence voting. Yet a remarkable evolution has occurred. In the early part of the period the Catholic laity, clergy, and bishops were divided into progressives and conservatives. In 1965 conservatives gained control of the Secretariat of the National Conference of Bishops, which greatly facilitated a state purge of youthful militants in such para-ecclesiastical structures as the Young Christian Students, Young Christian University Students, and Young Christian Workers. But at the same time many Brazilian priests and nuns took to the streets against the arbitrary acts of the regime. Many indeed sought laicization, feeling badly frustrated by the collusion of the hierarchy with the military.

In 1968 a new era opened, marked by the attempt of Latin American bishops at Medellín to translate Vatican II for their own circumstances and by the violent opposition of Dom Hélder Câmara, archbishop of Olinda and Recife, to the regime. A civil rights movement began in the impoverished northeast and spread to the industrialized south, where the bishops had previously compromised with the military rulers. By late 1973 all the Christian churches of Brazil, with the exception of the Pentecostals, had condemned torture and launched a nationwide campaign for human rights.[25]

Gradually the church came to serve as a surrogate for civil society. The last steps in the evolution of church policy was the creation of base communities closely allied to "the People's Church" (cf. Chapter 15). The base communities and the People's Church acquired extraordinary influence within Brazilian Catholicism. (What their role and orientation will be now that Brazil has returned to civilian government and now that the policy of John Paul II is clear remains to be seen.)

Certain general points about the experiences of the Chilean and Brazilian churches as the main channels of political opposition apply all over Latin America, and indeed (mutatis mutandis) elsewhere. In the first place there is a difficulty in that Catholics have often been relatively less afraid of repressive governments of the right because governments of the left have so regularly expropriated the church. Second, there is an initial problem of securing episcopal unity. Third, the episcopate is concerned to prevent a pragmatic alliance with the forces of change from developing into a theological shift, spearheaded by the various groups of radical Christians existing all over Latin America. This shift would empty transcendence into social utopianism. Fourth, the church has to sustain attacks from the right, which take the form of upper class withdrawal of support, or accusations that the church acts as a shelter for Marxists, or physical violence against bishops and priests, or direct censorship, or—most effective—financial and other pressure on a critical apostolate such as education. And, of course, foreign priests can be expelled and overseas resources to some extent cut off.

These are the difficulties, yet the church has a public salience and legitimacy not easily insulted or ignored. Its agencies can quietly extend their sphere of operation, especially where people seek humanitarian rights rather than engage in armed rebellion. Moreover, it can focus international concern.

As Brian Smith suggests, when the vitality of church life increases, especially among the poor, the laity are brought into leadership positions, more communitarian modes of spirituality are developed, and faith is seen as including a commitment to justice and peace.[26] The key question relates to how far and how fast this process can go without causing institutional chaos in the church. The question also relates to the extent to which Christian symbols are being increasingly assimilated with Marxist discourse, losing that transcendent point of reference which is the source of human independence. Pressure for ecclesiastical decentralization causes organizational concern and strain; pressure for declericalization can be handled if radicals make haste slowly. The absorption of Christian symbols is, however, a quite different matter. When the church is seen as identical with "the poor" or with some entity called "the people" then the Catholic church faces dissolution.

The case of the church in Nicaragua is one where the church walks along a delicate edge, with on one side the threat of the subversion of its symbols and assimilation to the government (under the guise of the people), and on the other side the danger of identification with conservative forces and with their American backers.

The church was one of the main channels through which the Somoza dictatorship was rendered illegitimate in the eyes of the Nicaraguans. It contributed much by way of personnel to the revolution, including four priests who entered the new government. Yet the church is aware of a long history of interim governments tolerating the participation of democratic socialists—and others—only for a period and then emerging with an exclusively Leninist program. It is that awareness which first engenders a reserve toward the revolution. This in turn allows Marxist accusations of preventing the "people" to participate and begins a spiral of division. As everywhere else the revolutionary rulers seek to organize a church within the church, and in the Nicaraguan situation this means the "Church of the Poor" within the universal church. Its cadres are the cells created within the base communities. Many members are often devoted and generous people who may not be equipped with a knowledge of the tragic history of the first half of this century.

But the ultimate aim of revolution is to deprive the church of the national role of moral legitimation—and moral criticism. Criticism was correct before the revolution; it is inadmissible afterward. The ultimate weapon is a comprehensive resocialization achieved by combining the drive to literacy with government propaganda. Like the Catholic church of the Counter Reformation, totalitarian Marxism cannot conceive of any neutrality in education. It thereby becomes the functional equivalent of *integrista* Catholicism. That is a fundamental threat in that the church has been traditionally equipped with organicist models of society and has only recently considered individualist and pluralist models.

Whether the church can survive such a confrontation depends both on avoiding identification with reaction and achieving identification with the nation. If it is the case that the Sandinistas have succeeded in harnessing nationalism to their cause then the task of the church is indeed difficult. Conor Cruse O'Brien has argued that in Nicaragua the "Church of the Poor" is part of a movement that has harnessed religion to radical nationalism. It is therefore an open question whether even a deeply rooted national church can survive intact a deeply rooted national revolution.[27]

In Cuba, of course, the situation was very different, as Margaret Crahan points out (Chapter 14). Before the revolution the Catholic church in Cuba was unaffected by new theological understandings and it was very weak, especially in the rural areas. If it did not accept Batista it was nevertheless passively aligned with the social order. Moreover, it had continued to be dominated by Spaniards, and its schools were largely for the elite.

Thus it offered an almost united but ineffective opposition to Castro. Well over half the priesthood left Cuba in 1965, leaving the country even more understaffed with priests than before. Only recently have moves toward reconciliation, from the side of the government and of the church, borne fruit, and this change has support from the Vatican. What is interesting and significant is that the National Assembly of Catholics in Cuba in 1986 published a statement that affirmed the spiritual character of the message of the church! Its specific mission is "not of the political, economic or social order, but eminently religious."

Certain general comments about the Latin American churches take off from the more localized instances explored here and in Chapters 14–16. They can be set down quite summarily. In the twentieth century the church has emerged from situations in which it was taken over by the state, as in Brazil, and/or allied with conservative forces. That conservative alliance had been cemented in the struggle with radical middle class liberalism and with representatives of the state determined to remove the buttresses of ecclesiastical influence.

That struggle was at its most ferocious in Mexico, but it existed everywhere.[28] In countries like Venezuela and Uruguay the church was permanently weakened. In other countries, such as Colombia, it maintained its strength.[29] Perhaps the easiest transition was achieved in Chile, where the church succeeded in disentangling itself early on. In some areas, of course, elements of the old alliance remained. In Argentina, for example, in spite of early critical and radical initiatives, the episcopate did not emerge as a public critic of the military regime that existed prior to 1983. One way and another, however, one may say that the excesses of the National Security State have further stimulated the church to develop the critical stance elaborated at the Latin American bishops' meetings at Medellín and at Puebla.[30] Moreover, almost every country in South America has seen the emergence of a group of radical Catholics, among priests and among laity. Many of these may have taken an activism originally generated in organizations of Catholic cultural defense, such as the Young Catholic Workers, into the ranks of the left.

Apart from the problems of social radicalism and prophecy the church faces mere secularity. In some areas the church was always weak in terms of practice and/or orthodoxy. Catholic Christianity has often been assimilated to a folk religion based on the invocation of the saints, or has existed alongside spirit mediumship or voodoo. Now there are the added effects of large-scale urbanization and industrialization. Countries like Venezuela, Uruguay, Cuba, and the Dominican Republic are profoundly secularized.

Social changes, which have accelerated since the 1950s, have also stimulated the growth of Protestantism. The earliest shoots of Protestantism emerged in the late nineteenth century and were largely the work of missionaries from the mainline American denominations, for example, the Presbyterians. They were often encouraged by anticlerical, liberal governments. But since the 1950s these mainline denominations have been overtaken by Pentecostalism, so that perhaps half of the Protestant community is now Pentecostal or free evangelical. This challenge to Catholic hegemony now includes perhaps 25 million persons and is most advanced in Guatemala (25%), Haiti (15%), Honduras (15%), Chile (10%), and Brazil (8%).[31]

Africa

In Africa we have situations where the church has not had the monopolistic position prevailing until recently in Europe and Latin America, nor is it the kind of small minority found in most of Asia. In many cases it has a massive presence which has successfully survived the original attachment of Catholicism to European cultural forms. It is also surviving the reproduction of abrasive European conflicts between clerics and laity, church and state. It engages, more energetically in some countries, for example, Zaire, than in others, in giving Catholicism a fully African form, intellectually, artistically, and liturgically.

The Catholic church is strongest in Central Africa, especially in those areas previously colonized by the French, the Belgians, and the Portuguese. Catholicism is the majority religion in Burundi, Angola, Gabon, Rwanda, Congo, Uganda, and Zaire. It constitutes a large minority of between one-third and two-fifths in Togo, Cameroon, Mozambique, Tanzania, the Central African Republic, Malawi, Kenya, and Madagascar. It is somewhat weaker in Southern Africa (25% in South Africa, 20% in Namibia, 17% in Zimbabwe) and in Nigeria (13%), Ghana (25%), Chad (21%), and the Ivory Coast (21%).[32]

The main rival to Catholicism in the north is Islam, already implanted and shifting southward. There are several countries with a Catholic (or a Christian) south and an Islamic (or semi-Islamic) north, such as Togo, Cameroon, Chad, and the Sudan. As one goes further north on the west coast of Africa, the Catholic presence shrinks to a small minority. Sierra Leone has a Catholic minority of about 2.5 percent, Senegal a minority of 5 percent, and Upper Volta (Burkina Faso) a minority of 12 percent. There is also some rivalry with Islam in parts of East Africa, notably Tanzania, where Islam has advanced notably since the mid-century. Elsewhere the alternatives to Catholicism, apart from traditional religions, are various kinds of Protestantism, Anglicanism, and varieties of indigenous African Christianity. Anglicanism is strong in Uganda, Presbyterianism in Malawi and Togo, Lutheranism in Namibia, and indigenous forms of Christianity in Nigeria, Ghana, Zimbabwe, and Zaire (Kimbanguism, for example).

Catholicism in Africa faces Marxism and nationalism, as well as uncertain or confusing mixtures of the two such as are found in Cameroon. Perhaps the most difficult situation exists in formerly Portuguese Angola, where the intense conservatism of the Salazar regime and the conservatism of the Catholic church in the period 1860–1950 combined to help produce a radical reaction. In Angola we see the Marxist regime of a country once dominated by Portugal supported by troops from Cuba, where both the colonial approach and a conservative Iberian mentality were carried forward up to recent times by the Catholic church.

Catholicism in Cameroon is at a junction with Islam, though the north is only partly Islamicized. Catholic missions could not enter the north under the Germans, who, like some other colonial powers, preferred to deal with Islamic leaders and even to strengthen Islam. Since independence Cameroon has had an Islamic head of state, including the dictatorship of Ahidja. More than one head of state in Africa has been converted to Islam. For example, in the Central African Republic in 1975 Bokassa became a Muslim.

Christianity in Africa, like Islam, has expanded through conquest and commerce, and it has also been uniquely associated with education and medicine. In Togo in particular we see a country exhibiting an advanced degree of differentiation between church and society, which has been thrust forward by the influence of the French secularist model. The usual tensions between church and state associated with Catholicism have been exacerbated by a French background where historically such tensions have been at their most abrasive. The classic rivalry between church and state over the control of schools and the enmity between *curé* and *instituteur* are reproduced in Cameroon. The state itself is laicized and, as elsewhere in Africa, brotherhoods of various kinds exercise a visible role, for example, the freemasons and Rosicrucians.

Protestants and Catholics in Cameroon exhibit characteristic differences in their approach to the state. The Protestants are used to the notion of a lay state to which they relate as individuals. Many Protestants, or at any rate people of Protestant background and education, have been involved in the nationalist political party, the Union des Populations du Cameroon. The Catholic church, however, has acted in accord with its hierarchical and collectivist structure and deals directly with the government, engaging in the bargains and in the compromises inherent in politics.

On the African scene as a whole the Catholic church is slowly adopting a full African identity. Like all missions it was associated with European economic and political penetration, with the Bible sometimes preceding and occasionally following the flag. Some missionaries served Africans with devotion and criticized the conditions of employment enforced by their fellow countrymen. Others reflected the paternalism of their times and cooperated, more or less willingly, with "the civilizing mission." A paradox lies in the way in which both brought a metropolitan nationalism with them and provided the education that would stimulate African nationalism. Even now the influence of Africans in the Catholic church is weak relative to their numbers. As Meinrad Hebga points out in Chapter 18, 3 or 4 million Dutch Catholics make as much stir in the Catholic world as nearly 100 million African Catholics.

As everywhere, the international character of the Catholic church is at odds with the nation-state. We have an indication of that international character in the way the pope and some bishops elsewhere in Africa supported Bishop Ndongmo when he was accused of complicity with the Union des Populations du Cameroon. That international character has also been evidenced by the Catholic church's commitment to human rights when European and African successor governments have oppressed whole peoples or rival tribes. Catholicism often inserts itself within societies along tribal lines, and draws strength from identification with local or national cultures. There was, for example, some association between the aspirations of the Ibo to active independence in a new state, to be called Biafra, and Catholicism in that area. Likewise there is some association between Catholicism among the southern Sudanese and the movement for some degree of regional autonomy or even independence. The Sudanese situation is just one of many where religion follows cultural and geographical divides. (It inverts the situation in the Philippines where Muslims on Mindanao are the threatened and militant southern minority.)

The Middle East

Catholicism in the Middle East has a certain symbolic importance given that Christianity originated there and that the Crusades were fought over Jerusalem. But, of course, the whole of North Africa was Islamicized by the tenth century, apart from the Copts and Ethiopians; and continuous pressure was exercised against the Byzantine empire until Byzantium itself fell in 1453, giving Turkey over to Islam apart from Armenians, Greeks, and some Syrian Christians. They in turn departed, or were massacred, in the upheavals of the twentieth century. Modern nationalism barely tolerates ethnic diversity. The Turks had to leave Crete and Thrace even as the Greeks had to leave Smyrna and Alexandria.

A Christian presence remains along the eastern Mediterranean littoral, where east and west meet in Israel, Lebanon, and Syria. The historic junction was Beirut where Maronite Roman Catholicism and French influence mingled in a cosmopolitan atmosphere of trade, diplomacy, and intellectual exchange. This littoral is punctuated by reminders of ancient empires fighting for strategic control of the area, and by relics of the Latin counties and the Latin kingdom of Jerusalem. Indeed, everything in this region turns on historical roots, on attachments that are simultaneously ethnic, religious, and familial, and on long memories as to who slaughtered whom and when.

These areas have seen a long attrition of Christian influence and numbers resulting from second-class citizenship, social marginality, and intermittent violence. From time to time the remnants of Byzantine Christianity have endeavored to play a political role, particularly in the early stage of Arab nationalism. From time to time Rome has succeeded in attaching a group or a fragment of some ancient church to itself. But Christians are deeply divided by ethnic, linguistic, and theological differences, and even within Catholicism the mosaic of division is partly reproduced.[33]

The main Catholic presence is found among the Maronites of Lebanon, apart from a modest Catholic community in Iraq. The Maronites of Lebanon became prosperous and powerful during a brief interwar period which offered them the happy respite of partial secularization, the opportunities of economic liberalism, and the educational and political boosts of the French connection. Christian communities elsewhere also gained from liberal influences and economic freedom.

But the rise of Islamic fundamentalism and of an integrist nationalism fueled by anti-Western feelings has pulled the Christian communities back into an atmosphere of defensiveness and fear. As in the past, Western "protection" increases the long-term precariousness of their position. The Armenians relied on Western promises and experienced massacre and worldwide dispersion. Iraqi Christians likewise were used by the West in World War II and then abandoned to massacre. In Lebanon temporary assistance from the Israelis will also have deleterious consequences in the long run.

Of course, the Roman connection allows the life-blood of a universal institution to circulate freely where otherwise the veins might narrow fatally. The Maronite college established four centuries ago in Rome is a symbol of that wider universe of influences. Various initiatives have emerged in Lebanese Catholicism; the religious orders have been creative agents of culture and community and have even expanded. Only among the Egyptian Copts (Catholic and non-Catholic) has there been a comparable vitality. This has been maintained in spite of, and maybe because of, militant Islam.

In circumstances marked by multiple disadvantages, not unlike those once suffered by Jews in Christendom, various options have been open. Like the Jews, many Christians have assimilated to Islam or migrated to safer regions. In North Africa from the seventh to the eleventh centuries these two options eventually accounted for all Christians. Nowadays North African Christianity is almost entirely composed of ethnic enclaves (e.g., the Italians) or small remnants of European colonization. Today in Turkey and Egypt there is a perceptible assimilation of Christians to Islam, even though both states are among the most secular in the Middle East. Conversion to Christianity attracts legal penalties even in contemporary Egypt.

The more usual option for Christians is migration. Syrian and Lebanese Christians have gone to the Caribbean, Brazil, the United States, the Ivory Coast, and to Australia.[34] Thus the proportion of Christians in Syria has dropped from 14 percent to about 8 percent. Their absolute numbers may remain almost constant given high birthrates, but just as Catholics elsewhere outbreed Protestants so in the Middle East Muslims outbreed Catholics and other Christians. Christians often leave the areas where they have traditionally clustered, for example, in parts of Syria and Jordan, and these then become predominantly Muslim in character. In Lebanon Christians are once more clustering for safety around Mount Lebanon, abandoning their scattered villages and homes in the Chouf, and leaving Christian refugee towns like Jezzine dangerously exposed.

At the same time there is an extensive migration of Christians *into* the Middle East. Just as Turks and Algerians are entering Europe to provide manual labor, so Europeans are going to the Middle East to provide technical and other assistance. The Arab states contain migrant Filipinos and Indians, many of whom are Syrian Indian Christians. Kuwait and Saudi Arabia, where there has been no Christian presence since the ninth century, now contain sizable Christian communities. However, though non-Muslims are tolerated for the expertise they bring, they remain a restricted ghetto so far as religion is concerned.

These then are regions where the lines of ethnicity and religion have been almost coextensive. The Christians have suffered because they exist in semisubmerged rival minorities, most of them ethnically defined. The *"intégrisme"* that characterized European Catholicism a century ago now appears even more militantly in Islam. After all, Islam does not harbor even a residual distinction between faith and community.

The present situation prompts a reflection about the relation of religion to communal intolerance and the connection between the secular sword of state and holy war — *jihad* or crusade. Both Catholicism and Islam are organic. They are uniquely successful institutions rooted in repetitive ritual acts which offer powerful social definitions. They are demographically aggressive and will each soon encompass a billion persons. Under certain conditions of nascent nationalism and/or external secular pressure both can become intolerant. Catholicism became intolerant in the period of its association with expanding Spanish nationalism and during the church's crusade against liberalism in the nineteenth century. The same considerations apply to Buddhism and Hinduism, which are both thought of as tolerant religions. The association of war and intolerance with religion is brought about by the challenges religion faces and by its relationship to the society at large.

Asia

In Asia, leaving aside the Philippines, Catholics are very much in the minority. Catholicism has often faced organic societies, centered at least until recently on major religions such as Buddhism and Islam. Wherever that is the case it has gained little more than a toehold, often at geographical peripheries or in distinctive local areas, or among ethnic and tribal minorities.

In Buddhist countries we find the following percentages of Catholics: in Thailand 4 percent, in Burma 1 percent, in Kampuchea 1 percent, in Laos 8 percent, in Sri Lanka 6.5 percent, and in Vietnam 9 percent. South Korea and Japan are Buddhist countries to a rather lesser degree, but the Catholic communities are not large: 4 percent and .3 percent, respectively. In Muslim societies the same is true: in Pakistan

Catholics comprise .5 percent, in Bangladesh .3 percent, and in Malaysia (non-Malay) 2.8 percent. In Indonesia, where the density of Islam varies considerably, Catholics make up about 3 percent of the population, and in Brunei they are 3.2 percent. There may be about a million Catholics in China, split between those loyal to Rome and those not, but that number amounts to less than .1 percent of the population. In Taiwan Catholics have grown until they make up some 2.7 percent; in Singapore they comprise 4.6 percent mainly among the Chinese majority. Catholics in India number some 12 million, or 1.6 percent.

Certain general points can be made. The processes of organic solidarity and national integration around a faith that in Europe worked for Catholicism worked against it in Asia. Catholicism has had a presence in many Asian societies for centuries, often since the period of Portuguese exploration and the early Jesuit and Franciscan missions, but from time to time governments have seen Catholics as divisive or as likely to pose a political challenge or as prone to aid foreign powers. Catholics have been persecuted in most countries, and in premodern China, Korea, and Japan severely so. Moreover, expanding Protestant powers have sometimes seriously inhibited Catholic missions, as did the Netherlands in the former Dutch East Indies.

All this social pressure against Catholics has emanated from the solidary character of a particular religion within a particular society. In recent years that solidary character has been reinforced, as in the renewed insistence on Islam as the basis of the state in Pakistan and Malaya or as in the ideological monopoly demanded by communism in North Korea, China, and elsewhere. In Japan, the solidary character of the nation was shored up by a state-revived Shinto, and the "religion of Japan," that is, being Japanese, is powerful to this day.

Catholicism has suffered in Asia both because it has been anticommunist and because it is international, and in China for both reasons simultaneously, especially during the Cultural Revolution. Of course, the church has also gained from its anticommunism. In Taiwan, South Korea, and Hong Kong there were accessions of refugees, and also some increase in converts, though in Taiwan this was hindered by tensions between the newly arrived and powerful mainlanders and the local people. In Indonesia in 1966 when the government persecuted and massacred large numbers of "communists," it also demanded that all citizens acquire a religious label. At this juncture many Indonesians, including numerous marginal or "statistical" Muslims, chose to become Catholic or Protestant. In South Korea the anticommunist traditions of Catholicism reinforced Catholic groups, which sided with the semitotalitarian government established there. At the same time, Catholics began to prosper and expand in South Korea and their religion provided a notable element in the political opposition and in the campaign for human rights. Cardinal Kim played a role similar to that played by Cardinal Sin in the Philippines. It is important here to emphasize the considerable migrations enforced by the political upheavals of Asia: Catholics have fled from China, North Korea, Vietnam, and Kampuchea. The fate of those Catholics in North Korea who neither migrated nor were massacred is unknown.

So Catholicism is an organic religion vigorously repulsed by the ancient organic solidarities of Asia, by newly revived solidarities as in Islamic societies and Japan, and by the ideology of Marxism. Its organic character has had further consequences, some assisting survival, others making survival more difficult. In many parts of Asia, for example, in China, Thailand, and Vietnam, Catholics have grouped themselves in defensive villages or compounds. This both provides safety and generates hostility, as was particularly evident in Vietnam. There Catholics even created something approaching a statelet possessed of its own militia. In Vietnam Catholicism successfully aligned itself with a semifeudal peasant system. In other areas it included a strongly urban constituency as in areas of Portuguese influence, like Goa, Macao, and Sri Lanka. These areas of Portuguese penetration are mostly small enclaves and are relatively stagnant.[35]

As suggested earlier, Catholicism can often best find a toehold in an ethnic minority or tribe, or on the periphery, particularly where that periphery has been under a Catholic power. In Indonesia, for example, Catholicism is the majority religion on the islands of Flores and Timor. Indeed, it is to some extent implicated in the resistance of Timor to Indonesian "colonization" or "integration." In Thailand Catholicism has penetrated certain tribal groups, whereas in the rest of the society to be Thai is to be Buddhist. In Japan Catholics were traditionally concentrated in the area of Nagasaki, where they were decimated by the second atomic bomb. In Pakistan Catholics are most likely to be found in villages populated by ethnic minorities. In India Catholics are concentrated to some extent in Kerala and along the Konkan coast.

Catholicism tends to breed tension with governments especially by its attempt to provide inclusive and distinctive socialization through Catholic schools. Thus in Sri Lanka the shift of power toward the Buddhists brought about the confiscation of Catholic schools. Catholicism also sometimes breeds communism as well as offering inoculation against it. It is at any rate curious that the state of Kerala in India contains both the largest proportion of Catholics and an unusually high proportion of communists. It could be claimed that some of the classic European tensions between church and society have been replicated in Kerala.

Overall, the problem of Catholicism in Asia is one of indigenization. That has been the case for three centuries or so since the famous controversy over "Chinese rites." Latin in Japan probably constituted a barrier to expansion, yet it also provided a badge of identity in penal times. In China today that badge of identity is fiercely retained. Indeed, in some countries, such as India, those who strongly hold to their inherited Catholicism are anxious to retain signs, symbols, and customs that continue to distinguish them from the majority.

The case of Japanese Catholicism, so illuminatingly discussed by Jan Swyngedouw (Chapter 22), offers us insights into the basic problems of contemporary Catholicism outside its historic heartlands. Catholicism in Japan is, as Swyngedouw points out, more influential than mere numbers would suggest. This is frequently the case in Asia, as also in Africa, particularly where the Christian churches have created major educational institutions. It would be important to assess the way in which Christian influence has operated outside the walls of the church itself, as, for example, through the education of people who come from elites or go on to enter elites.

In Japan we see how foreign missionaries may be anxious both to achieve a closer relation to Japanese cultural forms and to exercise a prophetic mission. Lay Catholics, on the other hand, may not want to pursue either of these aims. They want to retain their hard-won identity, whether they are "old" Christians rooted in the penal period or new ones who have paid the costs of taking up a different faith. They may be reluctant to "inculturate" or to prophesy exactly because they are so Japanese in their respect for authority, especially male authority, and in their concern for harmony. If the radicals, foreign or Japanese, are also trying to exalt the role of the laity they run into a further paradox. The Japanese church is deeply clerical and the laity may mostly prefer it so. The clergy may have to teach the laity that the clergy would like to listen as well as teach. (This is true far beyond the coasts of Japan.)

Two further problems that emerge from Swyngedouw's analysis are of much wider application. One is the tendency of the Vatican to operate over the heads of local people. The obverse problem is that people are often attracted by a religion that looks powerful and exhibits power. Some Japanese Catholics compensate for weakness in Japan by a wholehearted identification with Rome. They wait obediently on what Rome has to say. It also means that the numerical progress of a religion may attend on the ebb and flow of material political power. The point is equally germane in the rest of Asia and in Africa, and poses problems for Christian theology. The resurgence of Japanese power and of confidence in the power of ancient religious paths, including the path of insularity, may go together.

The basic problem is insularity in the broadest sense of the word. All cultures are "insular," but some, like those of Britain and Japan, are literally islands. The Catholic church in Japan has to lose the taint for foreignness without submitting to pure insularity and the obfuscations sometimes generated by an emphasis on harmony. Japanese culture is often considered resistant to Christianity whereas Korean culture, at least in recent years, has been unusually open to it. But the Japanese community in Brazil of nearly three quarters of a million is almost two-thirds Christian. Perhaps it is not so much Japanese culture that is resistant as the sacred circle that frames and encloses the islands of Japan.

Characteristic Problems of the Different Niches

Surveying these kinds of niche in which the Roman Catholic church finds itself, we have identified certain problems characteristic of each. These need now to be drawn out in summary form. In the case of Latin Europe, above all France, the main problem is that of secularization. Previously the cohesion of the Catholic church was maintained by a siege mentality, which was at its most adamant in the Third Republic up to World War I and in Spain during the Civil War. Anticlericalism and clericalism mutually supported each other's existence, though the church was seriously ravaged by radical governments from time to time. But now almost all parts of Western Europe, including such ethnic enclaves as Flanders and Brittany, exhibit some decline in practice. This decline will have an impact on those political parties that rely to some extent on Catholic voters. The decline is also associated with a major erosion of obedience to the current rulings of official Roman Catholic moral theology, and with some discernible slippage in doctrinal orthodoxy.

In Eastern Europe the problem is one of manipulated secularization based on the compulsory privatization of religion and the removal of most supports that assist a religious socialization.[36] As in Western Europe, obedience to official moral rulings may be sharply eroded, leaving much residual Catholicism maintaining itself as a kind of symbolic identification. The church has to devise an approach that includes the free-flowering shoots of religiosity found in the new Christian cells. The old model of mass religiosity can survive where religion is anchored in national identity, as in Lithuania, Slovakia, and Poland.[37] But this anchor cannot be relied upon, particularly in places like western Czechoslovakia, where the church does not act as a guardian of the national myth. Moreover, the seeming power of religion when linked to feelings of repressed national identity, as in Eire and Poland, is not to be interpreted as proof of the eternal and inevitable role of faith in the psyche and in the community.

The last point is very important because the strongholds of Catholicism in Western and Eastern Europe that remain from the period of the Catholic monopoly of socialization occur mostly where national identity and Catholicism are commingled: the Irish and the Poles at home and in the United States, the nonrevolutionary French in Québec, the Croatians in Croatia and in diaspora, the Flemish, and the Bretons. This commingling of religion and national (or regional) consciousness can be strengthened by metropolitan pressure against religion and nationality and perhaps also against language directed from a semi-alien national center. The result has been a compact bloc of cultural resistance, often expressed in a regional party or maverick attachment to the right. But that bloc can dissolve over time, and with that dissolution there comes an erosion of religious practice, such as is observable in Brittany, Flanders, Québec, and elsewhere. Québec is important as the most dramatic instance of this process.

Another niche that exemplifies resistant characteristics and now undergoes parallel erosions is found in the Catholic ghettos set up in predominantly Protestant or post-Protestant societies. These ghettos are not confined to Protestant societies, since their creation followed from the fortress Catholicism of the nineteenth century. But they are certainly conspicuous in Protestant societies. This means that the current problem is how simultaneously to maintain distinctive socialization and engage in communication with the wider secular culture and with the other churches. As Roman Catholics have achieved basic civil rights and moved toward parity with regard to educational and social mobility, the ghetto has lost part of its raison d'être.

Since the battle for cultural survival in the past had been so hard and had led to such intense identification with Rome, the new signals coming from Rome after Vatican II were difficult to receive. Some people fell away because a key element in their identity had been rudely loosened; others fell away because the new freedom of conscience allowed them to slide at an accelerating speed into liberal indifference. This situation has now stabilized to some extent, but it has done so at lower levels of practice and with the signs of fallout still visible. It also has engendered potent ideological (and to some extent generational) differences in the priesthood. In short, these are cultures where the adage "Once a Catholic, always a Catholic" no longer holds. Of course, there is also explicit warfare between conservative and radical elites, and between a middle class critical Catholicism and a working class solidary Catholicism. There is further conflict between different sectors of the Catholic middle class, notably the teaching and service professions over against business avocations.[38]

The problems of Catholicism in Latin America are threefold: the challenge of Marxism, the rivalry of Protestantism, and the power of para-Christian and folk religion. So far as Marxism is concerned the pragmatic political decision is how far to cooperate with Marxists of various kinds in bringing about social change. Given the notorious capacity of hard-line Marxists to absorb allies once the joint task has been successful, it remains problematic to what degree the leopard has changed its spots. It may well be the case that the Catholic church finds social criticism easier where the threat of displacement by a powerful Marxist movement is absent.

Another pragmatic decision is how far to try to maintain ecclesiastical control of certain institutions, found above all in education but also existing in industry and political life. These institutions have sometimes been disbanded as outmoded relics of attempts to dominate society in the traditional manner of Christendom. Such disbanding often leaves large numbers of people without secure motivations or reference points. It may also set people on a trajectory toward a new activism on the left. There are, of course, general sociological processes of differentiation which will cut into this wider perimeter of Catholic organization as time goes on, whatever is decided. Men "decide" and processes "occur" in a complex dialectic. Organizations such as the Young Catholic Workers or the Young Catholic Students may slip away from priestly control and cease to assist ecclesiastical cohesion, and this happens through a combination of high-level policy decisions and the slow pull of social processes tugging people into other social or political orbits.

The problems of Catholicism in Africa are rooted in the need for a comprehensive adoption of African forms, without losing the rational cutting edge of theology or submerging the universal in local coloration. There are also difficulties associated with the need both to offer solidarity to African regimes and to criticize the drive to total power where that occurs. The Catholic church can be pulled into disputes over rival tribal bids for supremacy, and its role compromised by being a church overidentified with the interests and social solidarity of one ethnic group rather than another.

It is also important to recognize in Africa, as in Latin America, how far religion is viewed as a form of power and indeed treated as a manipulative device. The church is engaged in discriminating between the real, untapped sources of psychic and ritual power and mere magical manipulation.

Catholicism in Asia faces the mirror image of its *"intégriste"* role in Europe. It has to exist in societies that turn on the axis of another religion, be it Buddhism, Hinduism, nationalistic Marxism, or the religion of Japanese identity. Every attempt at expansion and every attempt at criticism may arouse accusations of foreignness. Yet it cannot become fully indigenous without adopting principles alien to itself. One possibility in this kind of situation is the development of a long-term and stagnant minority, trapped in particular ethnic groups, such as exists in Sri Lanka.

In the Middle East this problem is posed in even sharper form. Islam preempts the current of radical nationalism, and the Islam that does so is radically conservative. All non-Islamic communities are at best seen as second-class, and at worst they are bases for foreign intervention. Pressure grows to subordinate them entirely to the Islamic system or, if that is not achievable, to extrude them. The process of extrusion is in fact already happening in terms of demographic flight, and as the proportion of Christians drops the possibility of subordination grows. Though in Europe secularization may seem an enemy to Catholicism, in the Middle East—and perhaps in Asia also—it is a friend.

Secularization

There are certain general issues relating to secularization and the future of Catholicism. Full-scale secularization seems characteristic only of the European heartlands. In Brazil, we have seen that even the most sophisticated strata can simultaneously participate in a folkish Catholicism and join in services run by spirit mediums. Perhaps it is the very weakness of ecclesiastical organizations in Brazil that has resulted in a weak secular (and secularist) counterthrust.

But in Europe, where Catholicism has fought the modern world tenaciously, there has been both a vigorous political counterthrust and the slow erosion caused by large-scale urbanization and industrialization. The vigorous political counterthrust came from the radical bourgeoisie, and the long-term consequences of industrialization showed themselves in the alienation of the working class, particularly where people were massed together in large industries. The war between radical political elites and the church, begun by the French and Spanish revolutionaries, and continued even more ferociously by the communist elites later installed in Eastern Europe, resulted in a church pushed out of its organic identification with society as a whole, driven in the direction of the private sphere, and deprived in varying degrees of access to the means of self-reproduction in socialization and education. This war between ecclesiastical elites and political elites softened somewhat in the mid-twentieth century in Western Europe and in the late twentieth century in Eastern Europe. Outside Poland and Ireland the political elites controlled the metropolis and the church had various provincial and ethnic redoubts.

Other elements in secularization require the briefest possible recapitulation. There is first of all the process of rationalization operative in different modes: the reduction of social control to impersonal bureaucratic procedures and the erosion of local communal ties, and the shift toward "causal" conceptions of the natural and social worlds. There is also the process of structural differentiation whereby the church is partly eased out of the spheres of social legitimation, communication, welfare, and education.

This complicated and many-sided process had been present earlier in Protestant countries, but without so sustained a conflict between ecclesiastical and political elites. In spite of that difference the underlying question is how far the early evolution of Protestantism, and especially the emergence of liberal Protestantism, provides the paradigm of development to which Catholicism will in time conform. That paradigm can be summarized by a characterization of liberal Protestantism. It involves the diminution of external authority, especially priestly authority, the dissolution of dogma, a great increase in moral individuation, and the decline of any sense of obligation to attend worship and of the numinous objectivity of the transcendent. It can also involve, particularly in America, the adoption of a hedonistic attitude based on self-realization and may redefine Christianity in terms of social aspirations and perspectives.

It is not clear how far this pattern of secularization led by Europe is the pattern of the future. Europe may exhibit characteristics that are, in some degree at least, the product of its own specific history. In any case, the "lead" cultures are no longer European. Other patterns are emerging, not only in North America but also in other continents.

In these other continents, especially Latin America, we see both old shadows still cast from the European experience and influences still fed in from Europe, and unique and powerful new features, which could lead to very different outcomes. One of the most significant of these features is the rise of conservative Protestantism, which is buoyant in North America and extraordinarily dynamic in many Latin countries, above all Central America. This dynamism is, of course, part of a resurgence of conservative religion the world over, especially in Islam. Such a resurgence is important because it confounds the natural presuppositions of the European and American liberal traditions, at least for the time being, and it may therefore have implications for the future of Catholicism.

On the other hand, it may be that the developmental sequences are staggered quite differently in different areas but lead to similar ends eventually. It could be that the "fundamentalist" phase of Catholicism has already occurred in the period of the "ghetto organization," and that Islam is just passing *into* what Catholicism is just emerging *from*. Again, the dynamic of conservative Protestantism may be a partial repeat of the Methodist movement in English-speaking cultures, now transferred to Latin cultures, and likely to pass through a version of the liberal Methodist evolution.

The other striking emergent feature fits in with the notion that Catholicism is just now leaving the ghetto: It is the remarkable rapprochement of Catholicism with the proponents of political change. The organic traditions of Catholicism clearly enable it to achieve a mutation in the direction of socialism. Perhaps that mutation is almost too easily achieved, without the theological and social costs being fully canvassed. At any rate it is clear that the spirals of mutual repulsion between Catholicism and radical or revolutionary political elites are being greatly reduced.

Indeed, the present shifts in Catholicism seem to offer the church a renewed role in the mobilization of populations for political change. Clearly this role can be played in Brazil, Chile, El Salvador, Uganda, South Africa, and South Korea. It has been played most dramatically in the Philippines. It is remarkable how a church that at the beginning of the century was weak, ravaged by political opponents, in schism, and implicated in unstable rightist alliances could reorganize itself and eventually provide the master symbols to protect the advance guard of social change. Clearly the church can find a viable and creative stance in relation to social change. It is best able to do so when there are basic human rights at stake, since Catholic theology, loosed from the old alliances, can appeal vigorously to basic and humane principles of natural law. In other words, it is equipped with political principles at the broadest level.[39]

Beyond that, however, there are problems. In the Philippines, the alliance with President Aquino has to remain at the level of critical solidarity, not identification. In a similar manner the Portuguese church used its influence in northern Portugal to ward off the threat of communism during the post-Salazar revolution, but then withdrew from politics to some extent, and pointedly refused any connection with the self-styled "Christian" party.

The church is not adapted to enter into all the contingent twists and turns of economic and foreign policy without fatal compromises. The church can only be politicized in specific circumstances and only for an interim. To remain fully politicized means in the end alliances that tug the church in their wake. These are but a relic of the old organic relation to society that once sustained Catholic conservatism. The most interesting issue arises when the church simply encourages parties to adopt policies of the middle range, such as the Christian Democrats in Italy adopted to support small-scale enterprises.

The last question concerns the universality of the church, especially as it is currently located in Rome, and by extension in Italy. This question would properly require an analysis of the papacy in the Italian context such as was provided by Antonio Gramsci early this century. The only way the question can be raised here is by asking how far there is likely to be a geographical, that is, lateral dispersion of power, and to what extent the slope of centralized hierarchy may be made less steep. This leads directly to the issue of democratization and hence to fundamental questions of priestly function and episcopal oversight. Is the priesthood a survival of archaic forms of social power or is it central to the idea of communal "representation" and re-presentation? How long, in brief, can the church remain a federated empire under a powerful monarch? Does it gain strength from the worldwide demonstration of the papal icon and image?

The impact of the papal icon has been very strong in Brazil and Poland, controversial in Nicaragua, the United States, the Netherlands, and Germany, and marginal in Guatemala, Japan, and France. In Chile there was an explicit confrontation with the Pinochet government. A lot could be gained from a study of these variations in papal impact and from the undoubted sociological and political rationales underlying the planning and the sequence of papal visits.

Centralized direction does enable a constant redistribution of resources across national boundaries of the utmost importance for the vigor of the church. The church in the Philippines was reinvigorated by just such a redistribution.

The universal church seems to have survived the fissiparous pull of nationalism in all its forms. The present threat comes from a kind of union between national fervor and revolutionary ideology, which aims to suppress all voluntary associations and all independent socialization that is not totally subservient to the state. I mean such places as Cuba where "communism" is the militarized version of organic solidarity, where the party elite maintains its own control and legitimacy by invoking "the people," and where nevertheless certain basic advances are achieved in literacy, health, and the elimination of vice.

The most complex question posed for the universal scope of Rome is the same as that posed centuries ago by the matter of Chinese rites. At one level the Roman church has to deal with issues of local option such as have been resolved in Uniate churches by variations in the demand for priestly celibacy and relaxations of liturgical uniformity. The way such issues are resolved has obvious implications for ecumenical relations, especially with the Anglican and Lutheran churches. At another and more profound level the church has to try and enter into local cultural identities and forms. This is the prerequisite for possessing any influence at all. It prompts an extensive examination of the European cultural baggage, including Roman juridical concepts and the way in which some theologians have interpreted natural law in the sphere of sexual relations and the family. As ever, the issue for Rome must be what is *truly* of the essence, to be preached both "to the City and to the World."

NOTES

1. A theoretical background is provided in David A. Martin, *A General Theory of Secularization* (New York: Harper & Row, 1978).
2. See Giovanni Poggi, *Catholic Action in Italy* (Stanford, Calif.: Stanford University Press, 1967).

3. An excellent account of the layers of religiosity is provided in William Christian, *Person and God in a Spanish Valley* (New York: Seminar Press, 1974).

4. An account of the Catholic heartlands is found in Michael P. Fogarty, *Christian Democracy in Western Europe, 1820–1953* (Notre Dame, Ind.: University of Notre Dame Press, 1957).

5. Máire Nic Ghiolla Phádraig, "Religion in Ireland," *Social Studies* 5 (1976):129.

6. The results of the European Values Study are given in Mark Abraham, David Gerard, and Noel Timms, *Values and Social Change in Britain* (London: Macmillan, 1985), and Stephen Harding, David Phillips, and Michael Fogarty, *Contrasting Values in Western Europe* (London: Macmillan, 1986). There is still useful material in Hans Mol (ed.), *Western Religion* (The Hague: Mouton, 1972).

7. Suzanne Berger, "Religious Transformation and the Future of Politics," *European Sociological Review* 1 (1985):23.

8. Bohdan R. Bociurkiw and J. W. Strong (eds.), *Religion and Atheism in the USSR and Eastern Europe* (London: Macmillan, 1973).

9. Miklós Tomka, "Religious Change in Hungary." Paper presented at the Tenth World Congress of Sociology, Mexico City, 1982.

10. Major research on the creation of Catholic ghettos has been done by Hugh MacLeod. Cf. "Building the Catholic Ghetto: Catholic Organizations 1870–1914," unpublished paper, Department of Church History, Birmingham University, England; MacLeod, *Religion and the People of Western Europe, 1889–1960* (Oxford: Oxford University Press, 1981).

11. Mary T. Hanna, *Catholics in American Politics* (Cambridge, Mass.: Harvard University Press, 1979), and James M. Penning, "Changing Partisanship and Issue Stands Among American Catholics," *Sociological Analysis* 47 (Spring 1986):29–42.

12. John H. Whyte, "The Catholic Factor in the Politics of Democratic States," in Leo Mulin (ed.), *The Church and Modern Society* (London: Sage, 1977), and Whyte, *Catholics in Western Democracies* (Dublin: Gill & Macmillan, 1981).

13. John A. Coleman, *The Evolution of Dutch Catholicism* (Berkeley: University of California Press, 1979).

14. Gregory Baum, "Catholicism and Secularization in Québec," *Cross Currents* 36 (1986/87):436–458.

15. For an overview, see Edward L. Cleary, *Crisis and Change: The Church in Latin America Today* (Maryknoll, N.Y.: Orbis Books, 1985).

16. For an account of radical elements in the Argentinian church from 1966–1970, see Michael Dodson, "Catholic Radicalism and Political Change in Argentina," in Lyle C. Brown and William F. Cooper (eds.), *Religion in Latin American Life and Literature* (Waco, Texas: Markham Press Fund, 1980). For conservative tendencies in the hierarchy and further comments on the Third World Priests Movement, see *Latinamerica Press* 18 (1986) n. 42.

17. On Venezuela there is a useful account by Otto Maduro, "Le Catholicisme au Vénézuela," in *Amérique Latine* (Paris), July–September 1982. Guatemala is covered in Bruce J. Calder, *Crecimento y Cambio de la Iglesia Catolica a Guatemalteca, 1940–1966* (Guatemala City: Editorial José de Pineda Ibarra, 1970). For a brief overview of Uruguay, see *Latinamerica Press* 16 (October 18, 1984).

18. An excellent discussion of anticlericalism, together with an overview of Mexico, is found in José Sanchez, *Anticlericalism: A Brief History* (Notre Dame, Ind.: University of Notre Dame Press, 1972).

19. There is, of course, a massive essay to be written on the strategic role of shrines of the Virgin in mobilizing national sentiment and in issuing political warnings. Here I would simply draw attention to insightful articles by Rubem C. Fernandes, "Aparecida, our Queen, Lady and Mother, Sarava!" in *Social Science Information*, vol. 24,

no. 4, pp. 799-819 (Beverly Hills, Calif.: Sage Publications, 1985); William B. Taylor, "The Virgin of Guadalupe in New Spain," *American Ethnologist* 14 (February 1987):9-31; see also Penny Lernoux, *Cry of the People* (New York: Penguin, 1982).

20. Ralph della Cava, *Miracle at Joaseiro* (New York: Columbia University Press, 1970).

21. Diana de G. Brown and Mario Bick, "Religion, Class and Contexts: Continuities and Discontinuities in Brazilian Umbanda," *American Ethnologist* 14 (Spring 1987):73-89.

22. P. Ribero de Oliveira, *Religao e dominacao de classe: genese, estructura e funcao do catolicisimo romanizado no Brasil* (Petropolis: Vozes, 1985).

23. Here I rely on Brian H. Smith, *The Church and Politics in Chile* (Princeton, N.J.: Princeton University Press, 1982).

24. Here I rely on Thomas C. Bruneau, *The Church in Brazil: The Politics of Religion* (Austin: University of Texas Press, 1982), and Scott Mainwaring, *The Catholic Church and Politics in Brazil* (Stanford, Calif.: Stanford University Press, 1986). Mainwaring emphasizes the pioneering role of the hierarchy in the Amazon in defending the local population against what he calls "agribusiness."

25. I had the benefit of reading a privately circulated paper by Ralph della Cava, "The Church and the Abertura, 1974-1985."

26. Smith, *The Church and Politics in Chile.*

27. Conor Cruise O'Brien, "War of Two Faiths in Nicaragua," *The London Times* (Aug. 20, 1986). See also Michael Dodson's chapter in Daniel Levine (ed.), *Religion and Political Conflict in Latin America* (Chapel Hill: University of North Carolina Press, 1986).

28. See Denise Harriett Joseph, "Church and State in Mexico, 1931-1936," in Brown and Cooper, *Religion in Latin American Life and Literature.*

29. Sanchez, *Anticlericalism,* has a chapter on anticlericalism and "the violence" in Colombia. Yet the church in Colombia has remained strong. A comparison of Colombia and Venezuela is found in Levine, *Religion and Political Conflict in Latin America.* An account of the anomalous success of the Colombian church in co-opting a large sector of the trade union movement is provided by Kenneth N. Medhurst, *The Church and Labour in Colombia* (Manchester: Manchester University Press, 1984).

30. Otto Maduro, *Religion and Social Conflicts* (Maryknoll, N.Y.: Orbis Books, 1982), pp. 12-17.

31. Accurate figures are difficult to come by. However, the phenomenon is massive. I have found particularly useful discussions in Francisco Cartaxo Rolim, *Pentecostais no Brasil* (Petropolis: Vizes, 1985); Cornelia B. Flora, *Pentecostalism in Colombia* (Cranbury, N.J.: Farleigh Dickinson University Press, 1976); Jean-Pierre Bastin, "Dissidence religieuse dans le milieu rural mexicain," *Social Compass* 37 (1985):245-260; Stephen D. Glazier (ed.), *Perspectives on Pentecostalism* (Washington, D.C.: University Press of America, 1980); and Virginia C. Burnett, "Protestantism in Guatemala," unpublished Ph.D. dissertation, Tulane University, New Orleans, La., 1986.

32. In giving percentages throughout this chapter I have to rely on estimates of the Catholic community in David Barrett's *World Christian Encyclopedia* (New York: Oxford University Press, 1982). This is a marvelous source of material but in the nature of the case contains guesses and estimates.

33. Robert M. Haddad, *Syrian Christians in Muslim Society* (Westport, Conn.: Greenwood Press, 1970), and John Joseph, *Muslim–Christian Relations and Inter-Christian Rivalries in the Middle East* (Albany: State University of New York Press, 1983).

34. David Nicholls, *Haiti in Caribbean Context* (London: Macmillan, 1985).

35. I have relied in this section on Eric O. Hansen, *Catholic Politics in China and Korea* (Maryknoll, N.Y.: Orbis Books, 1980). See also Parig Digan, *Churches in Contestation: Asian Christian Social Protest* (Maryknoll, N.Y.: Orbis Books, 1984).

36. The most radical case of this has been carried out in Albania. See Janice A. Brown, "The Status of Christianity in Albania," *Journal of Church and State* 28 (Winter 1986):43–60.

37. Bogdan Szajkowski, *Next to God . . . Poland* (London: Frances Pinter, 1984).

38. Michael Hornsby-Smith and E. S. Cordingley, *Catholic Elites* (Guildford: University of Surrey, 1982).

39. An example is provided of Catholic defense of human rights in a chapter in Marjorie Hope and James Young's book, *The South Africa Churches in a Revolutionary Situation* (Maryknoll, N.Y.: Orbis Books, 1981). A lot of material is economically assembled in Daniel H. Levine, *Religion and Political Conflict in Latin America;* Philip Berryman, for example, contributes a useful chapter on El Salvador. See also, Bahman Baktiari, "Revolution and the Church in Nicaragua and El Salvador," *Journal of Church and State* 28 (Winter 1986):15–42.

2

Changing Vatican Policies 1965–85: Peter's Primacy and the Reality of Local Churches

Peter Hebblethwaite

Two decades in the life of a church that "thinks in centuries" is not a long time. But the twenty years covered by this chapter have been so crowded with fascinating incident, have aroused so many passions, and involve so many still open questions that any claims to omniscience should be given short shrift. It is difficult to arrive at even a moderately value-free judgment.

It might seem that the Extraordinary Synod of late 1985 provides a good starting-point for a consideration of "Vatican policies" after the Second Vatican Council since its purpose was to assess the implementation of the Council and apply it to new needs—as Pope John Paul II explained when he announced the event on January 25, 1985.[1] What bishops had to say about the course of the previous twenty years was not without interest or perspicacity. But they spoke not as historians so much as pastors who wanted either to commend Vatican II to their flock or warn them of its dangers.

If we consider the explanations offered for the state of the church in 1985, a great gulf yawned between the "pessimists" and the "optimists." The "pessimists" thought the church was in a state of grave crisis, which called for urgent remedies. They tended to be conservative nostalgics. Cardinal Joseph Ratzinger, prefect of the Congregation for the Doctrine of the Faith, became their natural spokesman with his book of interviews, *The Ratzinger Report*.[2] They held that since the Council the church had gone to rack and ruin, collapsing entirely "in certain countries" (of which the Netherlands was undoubtedly one). The blame for this situation was pinned on irresponsible theologians who upset the ordinary simple faithful with their anti-Roman speculations; and moral theologians were deemed particularly guilty of confusing Catholics on birth control, abortion, and homosexuality. This perception of a crisis led to measures taken against Hans Küng, Edward Schillebeeckx (more than once), Leonardo Boff, and Charles Curran. Thus pessimism was "institutionalized," and the first question to be asked about any theologian was not "Is he or she enlightening and showing the way forward?" but "Is he or she orthodox?" This was a major step backward.

Of course, the "pessimists" denied that they were pessimistic at all, and claimed instead to be "realistic." "Some people who live in never-never land wish the Catholic Church had no problems to deal with," said a Ratzinger aide, "but the church *has* problems. The church has constantly to defend her doctrines from distortion."[3] It was difficult to avoid the impression that although those obsessed with orthodoxy admitted—if pressed—that Vatican II had been a Good Thing, they could not find much to say about its fruits that was positive. What happened after the Council was *post hoc*, not *propter hoc*, they sometimes said, without sounding very convincing. Or they resorted to saying that the Council was good in itself, but had been wrongly, abusively, indeed wildly interpreted (the multilanguage review, *Concilium*, was regarded with particular mistrust, and most banned theologians had some connection with it). But in the pessimistic evaluation of the Council, one sees little trace of collegiality or the theological reality of the local church, and a certain hostility toward the episcopal conference that gives expression to them both.

So it is not surprising that the alternative "optimistic" vision of the church, prompted by Vatican II, should be kept alive chiefly in the local churches. The "optimists" said that it was not that the Council had failed, but that we had failed the Council. The submission of the English and Welsh bishops stood the pessimistic argument on its head: "Implementing the decrees of Vatican II has placed a heavy responsibility on bishops and priests. Where they have been open to change, this has enabled renewal to take place; where they have not been open to change, this has hindered the process of renewal."[4]

On this analysis, it is the conservatives who have proved an obstacle to the Council. Moreover, the English and Welsh bishops, far from blaming theologians for the confusion of the not-so-simple faithful, attribute it to defective early catechesis: "Because of the previous relative simplicity of expression of the church's teaching, present diversities in expression and also in pastoral practice have disturbed some of the faithful."[5] The "optimists" of 1985 had other common features that marked them off from the "pessimists." They remark that "traditionally the laity have been over-dependent on the clergy" and want to emancipate them for ministry; they greet pluralism, in the church and in society, welcomingly as an enrichment; they recognize that there has been "a failure to come to terms with the role of women in the Church" that must be remedied (they do not say how); and they state the social role of the church when they say that "effective evangelization today needs to recognize the hand of God in the world."[6]

However, the crucial difference between the "pessimists" and the "optimists" lies in ecclesiology, the doctrine of the church. The English and Welsh bishops quote a little noticed passage from *Lumen Gentium* which compares episcopal conferences to ancient patriarchal sees. The diversity "of liturgical usage and theological and spiritual patrimony" of local churches, "notably the ancient patriarchal Churches," is seen as displaying "all the more resplendently the catholicity of the undivided Church." *Lumen Gentium* then concludes: "In like fashion the episcopal conferences at the present time are in a position to contribute in many fruitful ways to the concrete realization of the collegiate spirit."[7] No new patriarchates can be created. (Venice and Lisbon are the only examples in the last millennium, and they have an air of artificiality.) But the episcopal conference has the task they habitually had: handing on the faith in their own cultural milieu and in a language that makes sense to the local people.

Now this is the judgment not of fractious "rebels" or "dissidents" but of very moderate and mainstream bishops. To stress the importance of the episcopal conference as the "incarnation" of a local church is not to deny the reality of papal primacy; on the contrary, it is to locate it more accurately. All authorized commentators agree that Vatican II, with its doctrine of collegiality, corrected the lopsided emphasis of Vatican I, which had time to deal only with the Petrine office before being interrupted by war. Vatican I therefore had a monarchical concept of the church. Vatican II made use of a collegial model in which the Bishop of Rome or Successor of Peter ("Pope" is not a theological title, and is used by neither Vatican Council) is seen as a member of the college, presiding over it in charity, but within it, not over and still less against it. But the two models were juxtaposed, and sat uneasily together. The *Nota Praevia* attached to Chapter 3 of *Lumen Gentium* can be interpreted as the ghost of Vatican I declaring that Vatican II had "really changed nothing."[8] Hence the problems of the postconciliar period stem directly from the Council itself. I will return to this after the next section.

The questions constantly recurred: how far could collegiality be allowed to go, and what would be its instruments? Would the papal monarchy reassert itself? It will be my contention that Paul VI strove manfully, almost in spite of himself, to keep both primacy and collegiality in balance, while John Paul II is happy to reassert the monarchical role of the papacy. Paul VI seems a tragic figure because he appears to oscillate. In a private note he wrote: "What is my state of mind? Am I Hamlet? Or Don Quixote? On the left? On the right? I don't feel I have been properly understood" *(Non mi sento indovinato)*.[9] John Paul II, who deals in certainties, proclaims without any Hamlet or Don Quixote-like tendencies "the joy of faith in a troubled world."[10]

The Role of the Media

In saying this I am well aware that the life of the church in any given period is infinitely richer and more varied than anything the pope or the Vatican can offer; and yet, as French theologian Henri Denis remarks, "there is something touching, rather pathetic and assuredly Catholic in wanting to sum up a particular period by the name of a pope."[11] But he adds the McLuhanesque remark: "The closeups of the television screen have a certain complicity with the ecclesiology of Vatican I."

I can bear witness to this from personal experience. During the papal visit to Britain in 1982—made dramatic by the Malvinas/Falklands conflict then raging—I spent most of my time in the Independent Television Network control room as adviser on matters papal. Whenever the pope sought to associate his fellow bishops with what he was doing, thus giving expression to visual collegiality, the transmitted images ignored the bishops and showed a solitary pope. This happened at Speke Airport, Liverpool, where he invited the bishops to join him in blessing the crowds. It happened again when he gave the sacrament of the sick in South London's South-wark Cathedral: seventy other priests, a biblical number, fanned out among the sick-beds, but once again the cameras obstinately followed the pope. He was the "star," the top of the bill, the one who "persuades by his presence," and the reason why television cameras were pesent in the first place.

So it is not without relevance for this chapter that Paul VI was a mediocre per-former in public, that his voice, never very robust, sounded increasingly strangulated with age, and that he came across as a rather querulous maiden-aunt.[12] Everyone who met him personally even briefly agrees that he was charming, sensitive, highly intelligent, remarkably well-read and well-informed. He rarely forgot names, was most reluctant to condemn, was deeply loyal to his old friends and quick at making new ones, and above all was "wholly present" to his interlocutors, whoever they were. They all say: he made you feel you were the most important person in the world.[13] But little of this was conveyed in his television appearances which, in any case, became infrequent after his last international journey to the Philippines and Australia in 1970. In the eight years that remained to him, he grew old, never left Italy, and lived in a *fin de régime* atmosphere in which curialists waited for his death with mixed emotions.

Thus in media terms, John Paul II won hands down. Youth—he was fifty-eight—replaced age (Paul died at eighty-one). He resolved the crisis that followed on the unexpected death of Albino Luciani, whose main contribution was to invent a double-barreled name and finally abandon the tiara. He had the advantage of surprise and novelty, as the first non-Italian pope since Adrian VI in 1521. He was actor, linguist, philosopher, poet, worker, swimmer, skier, globetrotter—in short renaissance man. He had a superb physical presence and a voice that was commanding when he wished it to be. At other times it was intimate and cajoling. He survived an assassi-nation attempt rather more serious than that on Paul VI in Manila, and went to prison to pardon his would-be assassin. Far from shunning international journeys, he has made them the mainstay of his pontificate. As of January 1987 he had made thirty-two international trips, and many more were scheduled. Cardinal Ratzinger, asked why the pope traveled so much, replied ingenuously, "because in that way he can get television coverage." No one bothers with stay-at-home popes—though John Paul II has made over fifty "pastoral visits" within Italy itself, all of them substantial affairs, rather like a three-day mission, and addressed every category of people.

Primacy and Collegiality at the Council

Yet in 1963, far away from the television cameras and indeed in conditions of super-secrecy, the seeds of future ambivalence on collegiality and primacy were being care-fully planted and nurtured. There are many different theories about what was the most "decisive moment," the hinge-point, of the Council. There is a *consensus* in

Xavier Rynne, René Laurentin, and Antoine Wenger that October 30, 1963, in the middle of the second session, was the day when the logjam was broken. On that day the results were announced of the voting on four propositions designed to "sound out" conciliar opinion. They were all accepted by large, though diminishing, majorities:

1. Whether episcopal consecration is the highest grade of the sacrament of orders: yes, 2,123; no, 34.
2. Whether every bishop, who is in communion with all the bishops and the pope, belongs to the body or college of bishops: yes, 2,049; no, 104.
3. Whether the college of bishops succeeds the college of the apostles and, together with the pope, has full and supreme power over the whole church: yes, 1,808; no, 336.
4. Whether the college of bishops, in union with the pope, has this power by divine right: yes, 1,717; no, 408.[14]

It looked as though the crisis of collegiality was over. This is the "turning-point of Vatican II," declared Bishop John J. Wright of Pittsburgh.[15] Cardinal Joseph Doepfner of Munich came out of a rather stormy meeting of the Council of Presidents saying, "After this, I hope there won't be any more spokes in the wheel." Pastor Roger Schutz, founder of Taizé, said the vote was "an answer to prayer." Paul VI himself went to the Lateran University the next day, October 31 — it was notorious for its hostility to collegiality — and cried, "No more polemics! no more polemics!"[16] Easier said than done. But it was undeniable that something had been achieved, and Chapter 3 of *Lumen Gentium*, "The Hierarchical Structure of the Church, with Special Reference to the Episcopate," began to acquire the form we know.

But collegiality was by no means home and dry. Recently published documents show what happened at the third session of the Council, and the intense pressures put upon Paul VI. The speeches made in Saint Peter's — which were all the press had to write about — had little effect on the inner story of the Council.

Those who had been defeated on October 30, 1963, came back again on September 13, 1964, with a violent diatribe against collegiality *secretly* addressed to the pope.[17] It was signed by Cardinal Arcadio Larraona, a Spanish Claretian, then prefect of the Congregation of Religious, and "about sixty" other Council fathers, whose names have not been divulged (except for that of the dissident traditionalist Archbishop Marcel Lefebvre).[18] According to Giovanni Caprile, S.J., it was signed by about twenty cardinals, all from the Roman Curia, and about ten major superiors.[19] It described "collegiality" as a "novel" doctrine that was not even "probable or solidly probable." The arguments used in support of this newfangled idea were said to be "strangely cavalier towards basic principles, even those derived from earlier Councils and solemn definitions." Moreover, the so-called arguments invoked in support of collegiality were pronounced "imprecise, illogical and incoherent, and therefore, if approved, would lead to endless discussions, crises, painful deviations, and deal agonizing blows to the unity, government and discipline of the Church."[20] It was a pretty formidable indictment, and one well calculated to alarm Paul VI. Was he squandering his pontifical birthright for a mess of collegial pottage?

What intensified the pressure on Paul VI even more was that this angry missive arrived on the eve of the third session, just as he was putting the finishing touches to his speech; because it was secret, no public reply was possible. Larraona urged that since the question of collegiality was not "ripe," it should be referred to a mixed commission, which naturally would exclude the present members of the Theological Commission.[21] No date should be fixed for the fourth session, so that the notion of "collegiality" could be fully explored by this putative body. The Holy Father should make this decision himself, and promulgate it as a *fait accompli*. Here is the key passage of this highly perfidious document, which sought to reverse by papal *fiat* the conciliar decisions of October 30, 1963:

> To avoid anything untoward, which might impede the exercise of the Holy Father's freedom in a decision of such importance, it seems to us opportune and even necessary that the decision should be taken authoritatively by the Holy Father himself, without asking the views of the Council, still less having any votes. Such an act of authority— longed for by many—would not only be a practical reaffirmation of papal primacy but would also help in the re-establishment of the balance needed to move ahead. . . .[22]

In short, Larraona wanted Pope Paul to disavow in one mighty act of primatial authority the Theological Commission and the vast majority of the Council Fathers. He even claimed that this would enhance and strengthen papal primacy. It would, in fact, have been suicidal for papal primacy. It would have meant setting aside the Council in its most striking achievement.

Paul VI knew this, and said as much in his reply.[23] But rather than quote the secret reply to a secret letter, I prefer to give the anguished "note" written by Paul VI about a week after receiving the Larraona letter. The translation is slightly expanded for intelligibility:

> 21-IX-64. On the Secret Note.
> 1) *Quadam amaritudine affectus sum* (I am afflicted with some bitterness): by the timing: on the eve of the Council; by the number of signatories: it looks like a maneuver; by what it hints at: the ruination of the Council, etc.; by its arguments—intransigently opposed, and not always well-founded.
> 2) Summary of the arguments.
> 3) *Quid faciendum?* (What is to be done?)
> 4) Reasons of convenience: the Council should end well; we need to profit from the good dispositions shown here; stress the advantages: collaboration is not a limitation on authority but a help to it; "communion" is charity and truth.
> 5) Pray, think; try to persuade in serenity.[24]

Paul VI did his best. The next day, another vote was taken on Chapter 3 of what would become *Lumen Gentium*, and the pope again confided in his quasi-diary:

> *Deo Gratias!* Has our assent: both on grounds of personal conviction, and because of the Council's decision. We have abstained from intervention, and yet done what was possible. . . . Collegiality is not contrary to the primacy (affirmed some 20 times?); the Church is monarchical *and* hierarchical; having collaborators is not a limitation. What would happen if this doctrine were not approved? (feudalism, ecclesiastical irresponsibility, etc.). Instead: solidarity, charity, unity; intrinsic and constitutional bonds with

the primacy; overcoming of Gallicanism and nationalism (cf. local episcopal conferences), and fears of papal aggression; obedience derived from it within; authority without jealousy or exclusiveness *(non rapinam arbitratus est)*. The living church: one single
heart, etc.; coordinated and articulated in a single college of charity (cf. Patriarchs,
etc.); honors and dignifies all living elements in the church; invitation to separated
brethren.[25]

These rather scrappy notes, jotted down late at night on September 22, 1964, take
us right to the heart of Paul VI's thinking about collegiality and primacy. They are
worth many an encyclical.

The snag, however, is that no one, not even Gérard Philips, secretary of the
Theological Commission, knew about this private note at the time. Paul VI continued
to behave mysteriously on the grounds that the Council must be free (unlike Vatican
I). At the same time, while rejecting in private the anticollegial position of Larraona
and his sixty, he tossed them a concession in the shape of the *Nota Praevia*. This is
the conclusion I draw from the private papers of Gérard Philips.[26]

Without going into all the details, in summary Philips felt that he had been tricked
by Pericle Felici, secretary of the Council. Working through Carlo Colombo, Paul VI's
personal theologian from Milan, the *"nota"* was first of all presented as a little *adden-
dum* to Chapter 3, which in no way modified its basic thrust but which would rally
the waverers and win over the doubters. But it was not that important. Imagine, then,
Philips's surprise when Felici read it out twice to the Council, and presented this
humble note as an authoritative interpretation of the entire dogmatic constitution.
Philips felt cheated. But the massive vote in favor of Chapter 3 (on November 17,
1964) helped to calm him down. At this penultimate stage there were only forty-six
non placet votes. That was a victory of sorts. Philips confided for posterity:

> So the Holy Father has achieved his aim of getting practical unanimity on this topic.
> Some of the minority claim that they have won a victory. Later on, some theologians
> would try to interpret the vote in a restrictive and anti-collegial way, exploiting the
> *Nota Praevia* to that end. This was only to be expected.[27]

Philips, who died in 1972, was prophetic on this point. The key passage in the *Nota
Praevia* stated:

> As Supreme Pastor of the Church, the Sovereign Pontiff can always exercise his
> authority as he chooses, as is demanded by his office [echo of an earlier phrase, *ex
> nature sua*]. While the college always exists, it does not always permanently operate
> through *strictly* collegial action, as the tradition of the Church shows. In other words,
> it is not always in "full act"; indeed it operates only at intervals, and only with the
> consent of its head.[28]

Up to 1985, all serious commentators on this passage refused to put the cart before
the horse. They took the conciliar text itself as the norm, and read the *Nota Praevia*
as a sop to soothe the wounds of bruised conservatives. The fact that the pope *could*
juridically exercise his office alone, said Bishop Christopher Butler in his final seminar,[29] did not entail that he *would* or indeed *morally* could. So for those who knew

only the public story of Chapter 3 of *Lumen Gentium* and its *Nota Praevia*, there was plenty of scope for positive expressions of collegiality.

Positive Collegiality

In his note written on the night of September 22, 1964, Paul VI said: "Collegiality is not contrary to the primacy; the church is monarchical and hierarchical; having collaborators is not a limitation."[30] So Paul VI was in favor of, or did not feel too threatened by, collegiality.

The Council had thus replaced the image of a pyramid with the pope at the apex with the image of interlocking churches in communion with each other. It is true that in his first encyclical, *Ecclesiam Suam*, Paul VI used the image of concentric circles wheeling round the center that was Rome; but this center–periphery image did not deny the reality of the local churches. As Monsignor Montini he had always encouraged episcopal conferences, and he aided Helder Camara Pessoa in setting up the Brazilian Conference in 1952.[31] As pope he encouraged the Italian Episcopal Conference to free itself from its centuries-old dependence on the Roman Curia, and made it an autonomous conference resembling those of France and Germany.[32] Though the pope remained Primate of Italy, and appointed the president of the conference, this was nevertheless an important historical development.

Moreover, there were fields in which Paul VI declared his incompetence and wanted episcopal conferences to take on full responsibility. The pope could not, and should not, substitute himself for the pastors of the local church. The best instance of this is provided by *Octogesima Adveniens*, a letter to Cardinal Maurice Roy, then president of the Justice and Peace Commission. It commemorated ninety years since Leo XIII's *Rerum Novarum*, but unlike Leo's encyclical it did not propose another stage in the development of "Catholic social doctrine": "In view of the varied situations in the world, it is difficult to give one teaching to cover them all or even to offer a solution that has universal value. Such is not our ambition, *or even our mission*." The task of discernment Paul VI felt unable to cope with on the universal level he assigned to "the Christian communities, with the help of the Holy Spirit, in communion with their bishops, in dialogue with their Christian brothers and all men of good will."

This illustrates a form of leadership that consists not in telling people what to do but in releasing and enabling them to do it. It was not that Paul VI was unwilling to think aloud on Catholic social doctrine: his Easter Sunday (significant day) encyclical in 1967, *Populorum Progressio*, proves the contrary. *Octogesima Adveniens's* remarks on Marxism, taken with his self-denying ordinance, made the development of "liberation theology" possible as an authentic Latin American version of Catholic social thinking. It was given great impetus at the 1971 Synod on Justice in the World, was still in the ascendancy (though criticized by, among others, Karol Wojtyla) at the 1974 Synod on Evangelization, and was basically accepted though with *nuances* in the apostolic exhortation *Evangelii Nuntiandi*, which responded to the Synod. It is enough to read paragraph 31 on "the profound links between evangelization and human development, between development and liberation" to be convinced that "liberation theology" was vindicated.[33] This provides the best example of the dialectical process going on between primacy and collegiality in which both the pope and the local churches progress together in dialogue.

If Paul VI came to mistrust universal solutions, why then did he not let the local churches decide on the ordination of married men to the priestly ministry? Many episcopal conferences, especially in the Third World, were pressing for this permission, and claimed that the future of the church in countries such as Indonesia was at stake. Alternatively, as in the Sudan, bishops warned that a new Bible-only church would come into being, in which the sacraments were rare, annual events. It could not be argued that priestly celibacy was a doctrinal matter *de fide divina,* for that was ruled out by the practice of the first centuries and the present practice of the Uniate churches. No doubt temperamental factors and Paul VI's highly developed sense of "precedent" played their part: shift one piece on the chessboard, and everything else has to move. But this was also compensating, since changes in themselves small could be of decisive importance for the future: thus the banning of cardinals over eighty from the conclave to elect his successor meant in effect that the college of cardinals was not sacrosanct, and that being a cardinal did not confer the "right" to elect the next bishop of Rome. He did toy with the idea of having the Extraordinary Synod (made up, therefore, of presidents of episcopal conferences, who were not necessarily cardinals) act as the electoral college, but the undisguised fury of elderly cardinals caused this project to be abandoned.

Yet Paul VI was reluctant to trust anyone else with the matter of clerical celibacy. In a letter to Cardinal Eugène Tisserant, dated October 30, 1965, he removed the question from the competence of the Council. Why? No one really knows. Paul Poupard, now a cardinal, then in the Secretariat of State, offered the following explanation:

> I well remember passing on to Paul VI letters from Council Fathers begging the pope to withdraw this question from the Council's competence. Their motive was the fear of a division of opinion being made public which would have the gravest consequences for priests; and they also feared that their freedom to speak would not be entirely free, given the pressure from the means of social communication.[34]

This principle ("divisions of opinion must never be made public") would, taken to the limit, have meant that no serious questions could ever be discussed in the Council. It also applied (as in practice it did) to women's ordination (when that question came up) and birth control. The other part of the argument, that they would be made to look foolish in the press, was no doubt true. Yet it seems regrettable that Paul VI tended to take more seriously the fears of those who did not have the problem than the pastoral needs of those who did.

Having clutched the question to his bosom, Paul VI then pronounced on it in his 1967 encyclical *Sacerdotalis Coelibatus.* Yet the problem did not go away, and the encyclical was not Paul VI's last word on the subject. In a letter to his Cardinal Secretary of State, Jean Villot, dated February 2, 1971, he said that the hypothesis of the ordination of married men could be envisaged *"in una situazione di estrema carenza di sacerdoti."*[35] This, it is true, was a reluctant concession that did not argue any great enthusiasm for the idea, but at least it left open the possibility that the topic would be publicly aired at the 1971 Synod by those bishops who felt themselves to be "in a situation of a great shortage of priests." It was discussed, but the majorities were insufficient and the question was shelved. So in this case we have collegial forces pushing for the consideration of a topic that the primacy withholds. When, finally, the collegial forces manage to get the question put on the agenda of the Synod, that supposedly collegial body throws it out.

In this instance we have a pattern that will become even clearer in the pontificate of Pope John Paul II. Though the function of the Synod is to give collegial advice to the primate—and some of it he may not want to hear—it is being transformed into a body that *rallies round* the primate against perceived troublemakers out there.

Primacy and Contraception

The issue that raised dramatically the problem of the relationship between primacy and collegiality was birth control. This, too, had been removed from the competence of the Council, as a famous footnote to *Gaudium et Spes* records:

> Certain questions which need further and more careful investigation have been handed over, at the command of the Supreme Pontiff, to a commission for the study of population, family, and births, in order that, after it fulfills its function, the Supreme Pontiff may pass judgement. With the doctrine of the *magisterium* in this state, this holy Synod does not intend to propose immediately concrete solutions.[36]

Few complained about this procedure *at the time*. Indeed a Council of 2,300 Fathers would not have been a very suitable forum for discussing such a difficult question. The majority at the Council welcomed the nonjuridical and "personalistic" treatment of marriage in *Gaudium et Spes,* and seemed content to leave to the Pontifical Commission the task of finding a formula that would somehow combine openness to the new with respect for tradition. The pope did not appear to be depriving them of their rights so much as relieving them of an embarrassing obligation.

1966 was the decisive year, and June the decisive month. The Pontifical Commission was supposed to conclude, but it was unable to agree. It had, therefore, in one sense "failed" to deliver. Perhaps what was asked of it was impossible. The four dissenting moral theologians on the commission questioned not so much the merits of contraception itself as the merits of *Casti Connubii*: did it retain its authority as it stood, or could a modified version of its teaching be acceptable as a "legitimate development"?

The consequences of the commission's failure to produce the hoped-for agreed statement meant that the whole question now reverted to Cardinal Alfredo Ottaviani at the Holy Office.[37] He had never liked this miscellaneous array of doctors and experts who served on the commission, and did not think them a competent body to decide what was, in his eyes, a doctrinal question. Thus, the final stage of the preparations of *Humanae Vitae* through 1967 and 1968 was dominated by men of the Ottaviani stamp (motto: *Semper idem*); and the result, therefore, was a foregone conclusion. All Paul VI could do was to make their drafts more "pastoral" in tone, and reintroduce some elements of the majority report (including the personalistic approach, the role of conscience, and the place of the Holy Spirit) but without their conclusion.[38]

But this was tinkering with the works. While *Humanae Vitae* was still being awaited, Cardinal Suenens published his book, *Co-Responsibility in the Church*.[39] It is legitimate to use the overworked word "bombshell" to describe it, and the detonations went on for another four or five years. It was a lament, polite, nuanced, "delicate" (as the Romans say) for the death of collegiality. The birth control commission had been Suenens's idea back in 1962. But now, by 1968, it was as though it had never existed at all. The waters closed in once more, and Ottaviani was back in charge. The very title, *Co-Responsibility*, was a program and a protest. It should be exercised at all levels of the church, but more particularly among the members of the college of bishops. Suenens speaks specifically of "*doctrinal* co-responsibility" within the college, and confidently declares that "if the primacy is in fact a prerogative of the sovereign pontiff, there can be no question of his governing the church without the collaboration of the episcopacy."

But that is precisely what Paul VI was on the point of doing. He had tried "doctrinal co-responsibility" (that was the meaning of the Pontifical Commission) and it did not work. Now he would have to act alone. Curiously, just a week before *Humanae Vitae*, when its imminence was being routinely and vehemently denied, Paul VI mentioned Suenens's book while addressing Belgian young people at Castelgandolfo and told them to trust their bishops:

> In this work [of justice and peace] be docile towards those who have been placed in the people of God as judges and teachers of faith. I refer to your bishops who, besides inviting you to play your role of "co-responsibility in the church," also have the task of guiding and giving you a sense of direction, and helping you to discern the "signs of the times" in the light of tradition.[40]

But that was not a very meaningful remark, and it reduced Suenens's slogan to banality.

What is most striking is that Suenens continued to complain of a lack of collegiality not simply before the encyclical, when he was trying to stop it, but also after it, when his cause was defeated. On May 15, 1969, there appeared in *Informations Catholiques Internationales* an "interview" in which Suenens came close to contesting the validity of *Humanae Vitae* on grounds of defective procedure:

> Vatican II did not say the last word on the subject of collegiality. In particular, nothing was said of *the consequences of collegiality for the pope in his relationship to the other bishops*. This is a major omission, and it is causing us *serious problems at the present time*. . . . It follows *the logic of Vatican II* that individual churches—through their bishops gathered in *episcopal conferences*—should be consulted publicly and collectively, and enabled to *collaborate in documents that vitally affect the whole church*. And that, merely by associating their strictly theological commissions in the work, but also by including *lay people qualified to speak* on the matter at issue. . . . I think, further, that it is of very great importance psychologically, in order to ensure the acceptance and internal loyalty of the People of God, that encyclicals and important documents from the Holy See should be *seen by everyone to be the result of a wide collaboration between Rome and the individual churches*.[41]

Twenty years later, these words still sear the page. This was not a Hans Küng or a Charles Davis speaking but a cardinal of the Holy Roman Church who remained head of the large and important diocese of Malines-Brussels until his honorable retirement at the age of seventy-five on October 4, 1979.[42] (He went early because he himself had proposed retirement at seventy-five, and thought he should obey his own rule.)

Invoking the Dialectic

A brave theologian ought not to flinch from the question: Was Suenens right and Pope Paul wrong? It is not enough to say that the pope should have the last word, for Suenen's complaint was about not being allowed even the last-but-one word. In any case, the underlying question turns on the meaning of the phrase used repeatedly by Suenens, "the logic of the Council." From this point of view, the nature of the debate has not changed between 1969 and Cardinal Joseph Ratzinger's interviews in 1985. If we now ask who, in 1968, had a better grasp of "the logic of the Council," I would have to come down on the side of Cardinal Suenens. He was not wrong to think that Paul VI's reluctance to hurt people, no doubt the main reason he left Ottaviani in place, was bound to sabotage not only the reform of the Roman Curia but the Council itself.

There is some evidence that Paul VI, without being able to undo *Humanae Vitae,* showed that he had accepted part of Suenen's case. The Extraordinary Synod of 1969 went over the primacy and collegiality ground yet again, but the problem was always more practical than theoretical. It produced the idea of an International Theological Commission made up of thirty non-Roman theologians. Karl Rahner was on the first team of the Commission, a gesture toward the "co-responsibility of theologians." Cardinal Franjo Seper replaced Ottaviani as prefect of the Congregation for the Doctrine of the Faith in January 1968, but he became effective only, and then not very, after *Humanae Vitae:* the reform of Holy Office procedures could at last begin. Suenens had said that the pope should not think of himself as a solitary Atlas bearing the whole church on his shoulders, and that documents should be collaboratively written. After *Humanae Vitae* Paul VI wrote no more encyclicals, and his best documents thereafter were the fruit of much collegial combined work.

This holds for *Marialis Cultus* (February 2, 1974), an important advance in sober ecumenically minded mariology, and even more for *Evangelii Nuntiandi,* which was a direct response to the 1974 Synod on evangelization. It illustrated what could happen when bishops tendered advice to the pope who listened to them respectfully and synthesized their discussions. This was the high point of episcopal co-responsibility. Paul VI published the text on December 8, 1975, exactly ten years after he had brought the Council to a close. This, therefore, was its mature, late fruit. It was the theoretical model the church had been looking for: primacy and collegiality were no longer at loggerheads, challenging each other like rivals: they were, on the contrary, in harmony, needing each other like the two sides of a Gothic arch.

Suppose that *Humanae Vitae* had been written along the same lines: discussions in the local churches feeding into episcopal advice to the primate who in consultation with theologians composes the document the whole church was waiting for. But it did not happen, and we cannot jump backward in time. I believe that Paul VI, having produced *Humanae Vitae,* did not want to go on obsessively about the topic. I do not mean that he changed his mind or thought himself mistaken, merely that he did not want this issue to be the defining feature of his pontificate.

This judgment is based on a little-known fact. The first meeting of the elected Synod Council (another aspect of co-responsibility) took place from February 29 to March 3, 1972. The most important question they had to decide was what should be on the agenda of the scheduled 1974 Synod. The debate was "long, lively, inconclusive," according to Caprile. He summarizes the discussion thus:

> There were links between the problem of democracy in the church and that of the *Magisterium;* the condition of women in the church, marriage and morality were interdependent matters. The problem of the *Magisterium* had already emerged with the utmost clarity *à propos* of *Humanae Vitae,* which also illustrated the influence of theologians on the decisions of episcopal conferences. The theme of the local church was not yet "mature."[43]

The last remark seems faint-hearted: a serious consideration of the local church, its relative autonomy, its structures (episcopal conference and so on), its relations to the primacy, all these questions would have merited attention from the collective mind of the Synod. To say a question is not "mature" is the ecclesiastical way of saying: we don't *want* to think about that.

Yet all the suggested topics are bathed, as it were, in the afterglow of *Humanae Vitae.* The church was in danger of becoming a post-*Humanae Vitae* church rather than a postconciliar church. To resolve the impasse, each member of the Synod Council was invited to write down not more than three proposals, giving the reasons for his choice. The first to finish was Cardinal Karol Wojtyla, archbishop of Cracow. He had two ideas:

> 1) family life—in practice linked with other themes: marriage, condition of women in the church, sexual morality and, to some extent, youth . . .
> 2) the relations between the *Magisterium* and theology need to be dealt with for a variety of reasons, not least because of the fall-out *(risonanza)* from *Humanae Vitae,* and the well-known attitude of some theologians towards this act of the *Magisterium.*[44]

Thus Cardinal Wojtyla envisaged a counterattacking Synod that would have knocked dissident theologians on the head and reminded bishops that they should not be dependent on (that is, listen to) unreliable theologians. Such a Synod would have rallied the church (that is, the bishops) around the pope. Pope Paul VI rejected this plan, perhaps partly because he could not count on that reassuring scenario.

But the main reason Paul VI rejected the idea was that it would needlessly reopen old wounds just as they were beginning to heal. The time from 1968 to 1974 was not a long period in the life of the church. The attempts to browbeat theologians into acquiescence had failed for the simple reason that the teaching of *Humanae Vitae* was "non-infallible" and therefore "not irreversible," as the Vatican spokesman said on the very day it was promulgated. The pastoral letters that had "interpreted" *Humanae Vitae* in a compassionate and pastoral way could not simply be explained away as the result of inordinate influence of theologians on bishops. Pastoral bishops close to their people knew that married couples had as much difficulty understanding the teaching of *Humanae Vitae* as obeying it. Concentration on contraception was impeding the development of other aspects of Catholic marriage teaching that were important. So Paul VI rejected the Wojtyla proposal, and chose instead the theme of evangelization in the world of today.

But the Synod-that-never-was on marriage in 1974 actually took place in 1980. In other words, at the first available opportunity, Karol Wojtyla, now pope, reached back to his 1972 idea.[45] The Synod concluded with forty-one "Propositions" summing up its advice to the pope. Joseph A. Selling remarks that "to read the Propositions is to encounter a spirit of enquiry and pastoral sensitivity to some of the more perplexing issues facing the church." But this sensitivity was not reflected in the ensuing document, *Familiaris Consortio,* even though it was allegedly based on the Propositions. Thus the appearance of co-responsibility here turns out to be a sham; and the Synod no longer represents a collegial balancing of papal primacy.

For proof of this, one need only turn to the discussion of primacy and collegiality in the final document of the Extraordinary Synod of 1985. Putting the cart before the horse, it makes the *Nota Praevia* the norm for interpreting Chapter 3 of *Lumen Gentium,* and explains that "a distinction cannot be made between the Roman Pontiff alone and considered together with the bishops, because the college exists with its 'head' and never without him, the subject of full and supreme power in the whole church."[46] Thus the victory of the third session of the Council, so painfully achieved, was casually thrown away. And now a revised and domesticated definition of collegiality may be proposed:

> From this first collegiality understood in the strict sense one must distinguish diverse partial realizations, which are authentically sign and instrument of the collegial spirit: the Synod of Bishops, the Episcopal Conference, the Roman Curia, the *ad limina* visits etc. All of these actualizations cannot be deduced directly from the theological principle of collegiality; but they are regulated by ecclesial law. Nonetheless, all of these other forms, like the pastoral journeys of the Supreme Pontiff, are a service of great importance for the whole college of bishops together with the pope, and also for the individual bishops whom the Holy Spirit has made guardians in the Church of God.[47]

I leave that in the rough-and-ready translation provided by the Vatican Press Office in the immediate aftermath of the 1985 Synod. It is astonishing—to use no stronger word—that collegiality should now be presented as including among its constitutive elements not only the Roman Curia but *ad limina* visits (where bishops are reminded of their failures) and papal visits round the world.

In all these cases the local churches are seen as *passive recipients* of centralized wisdom. It seems an awful pity that the "theology of the local church" never came to maturity. When is it going to be "ripe"? Cardinal Ratzinger's reduction of the episcopal conferences to "purely practical arrangements" of no collegial or theological significance suggests that we are going to have to wait yet awhile.[48] The new vocabulary creeps insidiously into minds and is reflected in the ordinary thought patterns of estimable American bishops. Thus Bishop Matthew Clark of Rochester, New York, accepted the papal verdict on Father Charles Curran, the Catholic University professor ousted in August 1986, "as the final word on the matter." More alarming was his reason: Bishop Clark accepted the decision "in recognition of the ultimate authority of the Holy Father . . . and in a spirit of collegiality with him."[49] Where "collegiality" becomes merely another word for submission, then the teaching of Vatican II has been utterly subverted.

This chapter began with reflections on "optimists" and "pessimists" — the optimists were those who believed that Vatican II still had something to say, while the pessimists suspected rather that it had been a source of error and a blow to Catholic vitality. But by 1987 optimism and pessimism had veered around in the wind. Or rather, pessimism had become more general. Ratzinger is pessimistic because the Council did not have the effects he desired, while Hans Küng, his former colleague at Tübingen, is pessimistic because the Council has been ignored and betrayed.[50]

One witness to the poignancy of the disenchantment is the English priest Michael Winter, who in December 1986 decided to "withdraw his labour" from the priestly ministry. He wished neither to marry nor to join some other church. He had just published a book significantly called *Whatever Happened to Vatican II?*[51] In a circular letter to well-wishers, he explained a move taken only after much heart-searching:

> The 1985 Synod confirmed my worst fears. Twenty years should have been enough to assimilate the Council, and the Synod should have been the next leap forward. If we are to assist the human race in its most challenging opportunities and problems, then we must be prepared to move forward courageously. That Synod put the ideals of the Council into "cold storage" for the foreseeable future.

One should not intrude on private grief. Yet Michael Winter, a founder-member of the English and Welsh Council of Priests in 1969 and co-founder in 1975 of Movement for the Ordination of Married Men (MOMM) is theologically interesting in that he has no intention of "leaving the church" (unlike Charles Davis, who in 1967 became a "disaffiliated Christian"), and even declares that "the documents of Vatican II contain, in germ, the solution to all the major problems of the human race." Personally I would not be so sweeping. Yet Winter is certainly no radical pessimist. He has hope, but it is hope deferred. The church's lapse from conciliar grace is temporary. There will be another swing of the pendulum, another twist of the dialectic. It must, however, be admitted that the trend over the last 200 years has been toward growing centralization, with the years 1962–1966 standing out as the timid and doomed exception. I remarked at the outset how difficult it is to be value-free on such matters.

But I would like, in conclusion, to offer a reason why one should not be too pessimistic about Pope John Paul II and the implementation of collegiality. He is Polish. But is that not precisely why, cry the groundlings, he is so conservative in theology, so obsessed by mariology, so fatally prone to misunderstanding the democratic West? Perhaps. But it is also the reason for what Halina Bortnowska, editor of some of his Polish works, calls his "sense of *cultural* collegiality." In his address to UNESCO in 1980 and in his 1985 encyclical, *Slavorum Apostoli,* John Paul II insists that the gospel can be preached only in a given language and culture. There is no abstract, overarching, ready-made, universally applicable nonmediated version of the gospel *anywhere.* It has to be incarnated anew in language, history, and culture. That is the Polish experience and, provided it is not imposed elsewhere, it is of the utmost importance for the universal church.[52] There will never be any final and perfect statement of the relationship between primacy and collegiality. *Solivitur ambulando.* We will find out what it means by keeping going. On our pilgrimage.

NOTES

1. See *l'Osservatore Romano,* January 25, 1985.
2. *Rapporto sulla Fede, Vittorio Messori a colloquio con Joseph Ratzinger* (Turin: Edizioni Paoline, 1985). English translation published by Fowler Wright and Ignatius Press, 1985.
3. See "The CDF and Its Mission," by Robert Moynihan, *National Catholic Register,* September 7, 1986.
4. See Peter Hebblethwaite, *Synod Extraordinary* (London: Darton, Longman & Todd, 1986), p. 70.
5. Ibid.
6. Ibid., p. 71
7. *Lumen Gentium,* 23.
8. See Joseph Ratzinger, in *Commentary on the Documents of Vatican II,* Vol. 1 (New York: Herbert Vorgrimler Herder, 1967). But that was before he had changed his mind.
9. *Notizario,* No. 9 (Brescia: Istituto Paolo VI, 1984), p. 50.
10. The phrase occurs in *Redemptor Hominis,* where John Paul II quotes his favorite text from *Gaudium et Spes:* "Christ, the second Adam, in the revelation of the mystery of the Father and his Son, fully reveals man to man himself and highlights his high vocation" (*Gaudium et Spes, 22*).
11. Henri Denis, *Eglise, qu'as-tu fait de ton concile?* (Paris: Le Centurion, 1985), p. 248.
12. The "gay community" had already claimed him as one of its own, especially in scurrilous works by Michel de Saint Pierre. The trouble with this judgment is that I do not quite know what it would mean. Montini had many friends, but his letters to Cesare Trebeschi, for example, have been published, and are totally innocent. However, it may be interesting and possibly relevant to note that *Personae Humanae,* December 29, 1975, speaks of "homosexuals whose condition is permanent and who are such because of some kind of innate impulse." *Vatican II, More Post-Conciliar Documents,* Vol. 2, ed. Austin Flannery, O.P. (Leominster, England: Fowler Wright, 1982), p. 491.
13. See the "cloud of witnesses" assembled by Daniel-Ange in *Paul VI, Un amour qui se donne* (Paris: Saint-Paul, 1979, pp. 47–51). They include Jacques Loew, Dominican priest-worker, and Yves-Marie Congar. On his memory for names, I have a letter from John Moorman, formerly Anglican bishop of Ripon, who was to have led an Angelican party to visit Montini in Milan in 1956. His mother died at the last moment. When he arrived at the Council as an observer in 1962 Cardinal Montini said: "I remember you, Dr Moorman, you were due to come, and then your mother died."
14. I have taken the translation from *A Blessing of Years: The Memoirs of Lawrence Cardinal Sheehan* (Notre Dame, Ind.: Notre Dame University Press, 1982), pp. 154–55.
15. Xavier Rynne, *The Second Session* (London: Faber & Faber, 1964), p. 171.
16. See Denis, *Eglise, qu'as tu fait de ton concile?*, pp. 74–75, for all these details.

17. Full text in Paolo VI, *Discorsi e Documenti sul Concilio—1963–1965* (Brescia: Istituto Paulo VI, 1986), pp. 340–46.
18. Lefebvre published an inaccurate version of the letter in his pamphlet *J'accuse le Concile* (Paris: Martigny, 1976), pp. 55–71.
19. Giovanni Caprile, S.J., *Paulo VI e il Concilio*, in *l'Osservatore Romano* (September 19, 1982), p. 7. Hereafter, *Discorsi e Documenti*. See footnote 17 above.
20. *Discorsi e Documenti*, pp. 340–41.
21. Larraona was a canonist and an early supporter of *Opus Dei*. He invented the notion of "secular institute" to cope with the peculiar problems of the new movement. See Giancarlo Rocca, *L'"Opus Dei", appunti e documenti per una storia* (Rome: 1986), pp. 27, 38.
22. *Discorsi e Documenti*, p. 345. The original was in French.
23. The Italian text was dated October 18, 1964. The French translation was done in the Secretariat of State. *Discorsi e Documenti*, pp. 347–49.
24. Caprile in ibid., p. 351.
25. Ibid., pp. 351–52.
26. Jan Grootaers, *Primauté et Collégialité, Le dossier de Gérard Philips sur la Nota Explicativa Praevia (Lumen Gentium. Chap. III)* (Louvain: Louvain University Press, 1986).
27. Ibid., p. 83.
28. Walter J. Abbott, S.J., *The Documents of Vatican II* (New York: Guild Press, 1965), p. 100.
29. At the Dominican *Studium*, Blackfriars, Oxford, October 1984.
30. *Discorsi e Documenti*, p. 352.
31. Dom Helder Camara, *Conversations with a Bishop: An Interview with José de Brouker* (London: E. T. Collins, 1979). As early as 1950, Montini said to him in Rome: "I am now convinced of the necessity, even the urgency, of setting up a Brazilian national conference of bishops."
32. See Giuseppe Alberigo, "Santo Sede e vescovi nello Stato unitario. Verso un episcopato italiano (1858–1985)" in *Storia d'Italia, Annali 9, La Chiesa e il Potere Politico* (Turin: Einaudi, 1986), pp. 857–79. Alberino asserts that "one must remember that the Italian bishops nominated under Pius XII were appointed at least until 1954 under the influence of Montini, and that therefore there was a sizable group of 'Montinians' already in the pontificate of John XXIII" (p. 868).
33. See Flannery, *More Post-Conciliar Documents*, Vol. 2, p. 724.
34. See Paul Poupard, *Paul VI et la modernité dans l'église* (Rome: Ecole Française de Rome, 1984), p. 292.
35. *The Month*, December 1971, p. 167.
36. Abbott, *Documents of Vatican II*, p. 256.
37. See Jan Grootaers, *"La Rédaction de l'encyclique Humanae Vitae,"* in *Paul VI et la Modernité de l'Eglise*, pp. 385–98.
38. It is not without interest that Karol Wojtyla also claims to have a "personalistic" approach while rejecting birth control. His *Love and Responsibility* (London: Collins, 1980, first Polish edition 1960), clearly influenced *Humanae Vitae*. The 1980 preface makes claim that *Humanae Vitae* has been "legitimized by experience" (p. 10). The author does not say whose experience.
39. London: Burns & Oates, 1968.
40. *Insegnamenti di Paolo VI*, Vol. 6 (Rome: Tipografia Poliglotta Vaticana, 1969), p. 321.
41. José de Brouker (ed.), *The Suenens Dossier* (Dublin: Gill & Macmillan, and Notre Dame, Ind.: Notre Dame University Press, 1970), pp. 12–13. Emphasis added.

42. About 1972–1973 Suenens changed his tone and became the virtual leader of the Catholic charismatic movement. There is a story that he went down on his knees to Paul VI and begged forgiveness for his earlier effrontery.

43. Giovanni Caprile, *Karol Wojtyla e il Sinodo dei Vescovi* (Rome: Libreria Editrice Vaticana, 1980), pp. 124–25.

44. Ibid., pp. 125–26.

45. The best account of the 1980 Synod is in Jan Gootaers and Joseph A. Selling, *The 1980 Synod "On the Role of the Family": An Exposition of the Event and an Analysis of Its Texts* (Louvain: Louvain University Press, 1983).

46. *Bollettino* of the Sala Stampa della Santa Sede, December 9, 1985, p. 8.

47. Ibid., p. 9.

48. *Rapporto sulla Fede,* pp. 59–61.

49. Peter Hebblethwaite, "Bishops as an Endangered Species," *National Catholic Reporter,* November 7, 1986, p. 15.

50. Hans Küng and Norbert Greinacher (eds.), *Katholische Kirche—Wohin? Wider den Verrat am Konzil* (Munich: Piper, 1986).

51. London: Darton, Longman & Todd, 1986.

52. I owe this insight in part to Joseph A. Komochak, in his essay "La réalisation de l'Eglise en un lieu" in Guiseppe Alberigo and Jean-Pierre Jossua, (eds.), *La Réception de Vatican II* (Paris: Cerf, 1985), pp. 124–26. Also relevant is Joseph P. Gremillion (ed.), *The Church and Culture Since Vatican II: The Experience of North and Latin America* (Notre Dame, Ind.: Notre Dame University Press, 1985).

PART
TWO

The European Heartlands

3

The Paradoxical Evolution of the French Catholic Church

Henri Madelin, S.J.

To speak about the evolution of the Catholic church in France requires analysis of a complex situation made up of numerous paradoxes. Two of these are of major importance and open the way to understanding the history of the French Catholic church from the time of Vatican II until the present.

First, Catholicism has always been closely linked with the whole country of France. For centuries it has been the dominant religion, exercising a virtual monopoly. During his pastoral visit in 1980, Pope John Paul II observed that "France is the eldest daughter of the church." That same French society, starting with the revolution of 1789, declared as its mission to keep religion separate from the secular workings of society as a whole. For two centuries, Catholicism and secularity have coexisted in merciless opposition. French Catholics see themselves forced to live in a society that is probably the most secularized in the world, in the sense that secularism represents an ideology that recognizes no religious dimension in human life and refuses to accept the social organization of religion. In this, the French reality is very different from the American experience, as Alexis de Tocqueville well recognized:

> I stop the first American I meet, either in his country or elsewhere, and I ask him if he believes that religion is useful to the stability of law and to the good order of society; he answers me without hesitation that a civilized society, and especially a free society, cannot subsist without religion. Respect for religion is, in his eyes, the greatest guarantee of the stability of the state and of the security of private citizens. Those who are the least knowledgeable in the science of government know at least this.[1]

One of the fruits of the Second Vatican Council has been to lessen the risk of war between these two antagonists on the French scene. Secularism has become weaker and polemical anticlericalism is no longer popular. The church, on the other hand, has renewed its own self-understanding by turning to the great conciliar texts on the church *(Lumen Gentium)*, the church and the modern world *(Gaudium et Spes)*, and religious liberty *(Dignitatis Humanae)*. But evolutions of this kind need time to produce effects and often take generations. In this respect, the Catholic church in France has demonstrated considerable wisdom in both its rhetoric and its practice, despite the temporary turmoil provoked by the events of May 1968.

A second paradox is that, at the time of the Council, the French Catholic church was both bold in its apostolic activity and profound in its theological reflection. It gave the Council three famous theologians: M-D. Chenu, Yves Congar, and Henri de Lubac, all of whom had earlier experienced trouble with the Vatican. Moreover, because of the Council, what the French had experienced and reflected on within their own country found wide ramifications elsewhere in the world. But as time went on, the differences between the French situation and the situation of other local churches became apparent, and France ceased to be a beacon of the church; no longer would its experiences serve as a model for the church in other parts of the world. France ceased to exercise the mission formerly attributed to it: "to bake the bread of Christendom." Its way of acting appeared more and more specific and iso-lated as inculturation progressed in other lands. The church in German- and English-speaking nations, in the Third World, and in Communist countries no longer accepted the pastoral models or missionary practices the church of France might offer them. This reticence was no doubt accentuated with the election of a Polish pope. What we have, therefore, is a church that remains unique, people with a predominantly Catholic mentality but little inclined toward religious practice, surrounded by large zones of indifference or atheism.

Its intellectuals and theologians have grown relatively silent and relief is slow in coming. The president of the French Bishops' Conference, Jean Vilnet, frankly rec-ognized such limitations in an interview with the editors of *Esprit:*

> I believe we are in the trough of the wave with regard to research, study and intellec-tual investment in the Catholic church. It is sufficient to note that influential intellec-tuals and those pastorally involved in intellectual activity are very few and have little following. . . . Formerly the clergy were by tradition involved in research work; they are less and less numerous. But the number of lay people who deepen their Christian culture increases markedly. The church must show it is capable of entrusting a mission of an intellectual order to priests but also to laity. We are devitalized in this domain, far from the kind of presence we should have. On this point I am categorical. It is high time we go forward. Christian culture needs to rediscover its full intelligence.[2]

Since 1965, in the wake of several waves of anti-intellectualism, the Catholic church in France has experienced a reduction and an aging of its intellectual poten-tial. It has had to confront a kind of "fundamentalism" of action, harmful to intellec-tual work no matter how indispensable it is at the present time. The militant members of Catholic Action who were the spearheads of the postwar apostolate in France have, in the end, little appreciated the results of the kind of intellectual research that might have brought some corrective to their commitments. Instead, they preferred to content themselves with rather hasty, often reductionist, theological studies capable of providing some justification for their choices.

For this reason any analysis of the paradoxical evolution of the Catholic church in France must combine several approaches. We will first consider the diversity of allegiance to French Catholicism, and then try to highlight the modifications worked out between bishops, priests, religious communities, and laity with regard to their distribution of tasks. Finally, we need to examine the political, social, and ecclesial orientations of this Catholicism in transition.

The Diversity of Allegiance to French Catholicism

Statisticians and centers of public opinion research have available a number of different instruments to measure Catholic practice in France. The impetus for this kind of study first came from historian and canonist Gabriel Le Bras in 1931. Observing the poor quality of religious statistics in comparison with the accumulation of data in social and economic matters, Le Bras remarked: "Oxen and horses are subject to a census, but who thinks of estimating the number of practicing Catholics whose place on earth is perhaps just as important?"[3]

Religious Practice

Le Bras classified religious practice into categories according to levels of decreasing attachment to the institutional church. His typology in effect included four categories: (1) the devout or committed Christians who do more than is required by the church; (2) regularly practicing Catholics who attend mass on Sunday, go to confession and Holy Communion at Easter; (3) the seasonal conformists who manifest their religion only at the time of baptisms, weddings, and funerals: "they enter the church only when the bell rings and in order to give a sign to their fellow parishioners that they observe the customs of their ancestors"; and (4) strangers in the life of the church characterized by strong withdrawal from the church's demands.

Le Bras's research among the rural population was eventually extended to the cities after World War II. The task of completing this work fell to Canon Fernand Boulard, who extended Le Bras's approach to the French rural communities to an analysis of different regions in the country. This led him to construct a scheme to chart religious practice at the level closest to rural reality that would allow for regional comparisons. The scheme included three categories: (1) "majority" regions in which 45 to 100 percent of adults make their Easter duty and generally attend mass on Sunday; (2) "minority" regions of Catholic tradition in which regularly practicing Catholics comprise a minority, while the population as a whole consists of "seasonal conformists" who attend church for religious "rites of passage" (baptism, weddings, and funerals); (3) "mission" regions in which at least 20 percent of the children are neither baptized nor instructed in religion. Applying these categories to the French situation since 1965, one finds a significant decrease in the number of practicing Catholics and a notable increase in the number of "mission" areas. The general picture has not changed much, although variations have become more extreme.

Available Statistics

Inquiries made by various survey institutes, especially those undertaken by the Société Française d'Enquêtes par Sondage (SOFRES), well document the changes in French religious practice in recent years.[4] As Table 3.1 reveals, religious practice declined between 1974 and 1983, even though the proportion of those identifying themselves as Catholic remained relatively stable.[5]

As for variations in religious practice by age, gender, and occupation (Table 3.2), one notices that religious practice regularly increases with age, while irreligion decreases. Religious practice is higher for those in certain occupations, such as farmers and retired people, while workers and clerical employees are much less likely to be involved in regular religious practice.[6]

These findings are confirmed by earlier studies, particularly those that have examined religious practice among the working class. About 5 percent of the workers in large cities regularly attend church, with the exception of a few metropolitan areas such as Lille and especially Saint-Etienne, where the percentage is even lower. People who locate themselves more toward the left of the political spectrum also report low religious practice, while the opposite applies to those belonging to political parties like the Union for French Democracy (U.D.F.) and for the Republic (R.P.R.), which lean toward the right. Some regions of the country show higher levels of religious practice than others because of the greater force of their traditional Catholicism. The figures in Table 3.2 offer a distant echo of this variation, but one knows that there are more regularly practicing Catholics in the Northwest (Brittany and the Vendée), the Northeast and East (Alsace-Lorraine), and in the region of the Massif Central. In addition, there are small regions where Easter communicants are still numerous: the Basque region, the mountains of the Lyons areas, and the lands of the Dauphiné, Aveyron, Anjou, Savoy, and Queyras.

By examining the significant sociodemographic variations among all regularly practicing French Catholics (Table 3.3),[7] one notices that the gender differences in religious practice are not great, although the decline in practice among women over the past six years has been sharper than for men. Even though communities of less than 2,000 inhabitants remain more practicing than people in the cities, the drop in practice since 1977 has been more rapid. It is the Paris basin, however, that shows the lowest rate of religious practice.

TABLE 3.1 Changes in Religious Practice in France, 1974–1983 (Percent)

RELIGIOUS GROUP	1974	1977	1983	PERCENT DIFFERENCE
Catholics (total)	86. 5	81	83	−3.5
Practicing regularly	21	17	14	−7
Practicing occasionally	18	14	17	−1
Not practicing	47. 5	50	52	+4.5
Other religions	3. 5	4	3	−0.5
No religion	10	15	14	+4

TABLE 3.2   Variations in Religious Practice (Percent)

Item	Regular Practicing Catholic	Occasional Practicing Catholic	Non-practicing Catholic	No Religion	Other Religion
All the French	14	17	52	3	14
Gender					
Male	11	13	56	3	17
Female	17	20	47	4	12
Age					
18–24 years	9	14	52	3	22
25–34 years	7	14	56	4	19
35–49 years	14	20	48	4	14
50–64 years	19	19	51	2	9
65 and over	24	15	52	2	7
Occupation					
Farmers	23	33	41	—	3
Shopkeepers, artisans	11	18	52	5	14
Major executives (industry, commerce), professionals	16	14	41	1	28
Middle-managers, civil administrators, teachers	10	15	48	5	22
Clerical employees	7	18	56	2	17
Workers	6	12	62	3	17
Unemployed, retired	20	17	49	3	11
Political party					
Communist	1	2	56	3	38
Socialist	7	15	59	3	16
Ecology movement	12	9	58	2	19
U.D.F.	27	19	47	2	5
R.P.R.	23	24	43	3	7
Region					
North	13	16	55	4	12
West	21	17	46	1	15
Southwest	11	21	55	1	12
Southeast	16	17	50	5	12
Center	10	15	59	1	15
East	21	18	51	4	6
Paris region	8	13	49	5	25

TABLE 3.3 Decrease in Regular Religious Practice, 1977-1983 (Percent)

ITEM	1977	1983	DIFFERENCE
Total regularly practicing Catholics	17	14	−3
Gender			
Male	13	11	−2
Female	21	17	−4
Age			
18–24 years	9	9	0
25–34 years	9	7	−2
35–49 years	19	14	−5
50–64 years	21	19	−2
65 and over	27	24	−3
Occupation (Head of family)			
Farmers	31	22	−9
Shopkeepers, artisans	15	12	−3
Major executives (industrial, commercial), professionals	23	24	+1
Middle-managers, civil administrators, teachers	14	10	−4
Clerical employees	9	7	−2
Workers	9	6	−3
Unemployed, retired	24	22	−2
Size of region			
Less than 2,000 inhabitants	27	18	−9
2,000–20,000	18	14	−4
20,000–100,000	12	13	+1
More than 100,000	15	15	0
Paris region	10	8	−2

On the occasion of Pope John Paul II's visit to France in 1986, SOFRES launched another survey which provides more refined information and, when compared with the 1983 data, indicates some stabilization in religious practice.[8]

Four French people out of five (81%) questioned by SOFRES in 1986 identified themselves as Catholic; 15.5 percent reported they had no religion. The other religions cited include Protestants (1%), Jews (1%), and Muslims (0.5%). In light of the changes in the Catholic church and in French society over the last twenty years, this affirmation may come as a surprise. But what kinds of religious practice correspond to calling oneself Catholic? On this the 1986 survey offers new information. In addition to the figures given in Table 3.4, the survey provided information on the importance given to baptism, Catholic marriage, and religious education. Only 51 percent of the French are interested in having a church wedding, 75 percent believe in the importance of baptism, and 61 percent think religious education is valuable. In other words, 40 percent of those people married in the church are no longer convinced it is important that their children also be married in church.

TABLE 3.4 Attendance at Mass (Percent)

Group	Frequency	Catholics	Total French Population
Regularly practicing	Several times a week	1	
	Every Sunday	13	16
	Once or twice a month	6	
Occasionally practicing	From time to time	19	15
Nonpracticing	Only for ceremonies (baptisms, etc.)	52	
			50
	Never	9	
No religion			15.5
Other religions			3.5

The Rise of Catholic Nonconformity

With regard to issues on which political parties, labor unions, and church leaders enunciate positions calling for popular support, the medley of French Catholicism reappears in strong relief (Table 3.5).[9]

Opposition to using violence to oppose injustices receives rather strong support across all sectors of public opinion, although this opposition is apparently contradicted by the relatively wide acceptance of class warfare. However, on all the other issues that are the subject of official church teaching (abortion, sexual relations before marriage, married priests, ordination of women, acceptance of papal declarations, and the possibility of change in Catholic doctrine), the rejection is fairly general. Even those who are regular churchgoers are unable to muster a majority opinion in support of the church's positions, despite the fact that these issues are widely discussed in the mass media and throughout French society.

The Importance of Irreligion

Between 1974 and 1986 those who reported they professed no religion increased from 10 to 15.5 percent, an increase of more than 50 percent.[10] This rise is particularly evident in the 18–34 age group. When Guy Michelat and Michel Simon studied two representative samples of declared Catholics and those with no religion, they found that each group revealed perceptions of the world, of politics, and of social relations quite at odds with one another.[11] This led these researchers to pay more attention to the type of culture and subculture to which different people belong, their networks of past and present allegiances. They realized that for their respondents religious affiliation or non affiliation expressed, in a more or less guarded way, a system of attitudes, consciousness, and feelings characteristic of specific individuals whose biographies, allegiances, and living conditions are quite unlike the other. And they tried to explore how these values, affective sentiments, social rules, and symbolic frameworks interiorized by the individual correlated with other perceptions and orientations.

The same kind of inquiry is needed to understand the gap separating "devout"

TABLE 3.5 Acceptance of Catholic Values

THE LEGITIMACY OF:	TOTAL POPULATION	TOTAL CATHOLICS	REGULARLY PRACTICING	OCCASIONALLY PRACTICING	NON-PRACTICING	NO RELIGION
Abortion						
Yes	51	50	25	52	58	57
No	40	42	68	38	34	31
No opinion	9	8	7	10	8	12
Sexual relations before marriage						
Yes	71	72	49	77	78	70
No	20	20	41	13	15	18
No opinion	9	8	10	10	7	12
Married priests						
Yes	69	69	47	71	76	72
No	21	22	43	17	16	15
No opinion	10	9	10	12	8	13
Ordination of women						
Yes	61	61	45	62	66	64
No	25	25	41	25	21	20
No opinion	14	14	14	13	13	16

Using violence to oppose injustice						
Yes	32	31	26	26	34	38
No	57	59	64	63	56	47
No opinion	11	10	10	11	10	15
Disagreement with official papal teaching						
Yes	56	55	43	56	58	65
No	28	30	46	30	25	18
No opinion	16	15	11	14	17	17
Class struggle						
Yes	54	52	34	53	57	65
No	26	29	47	27	24	14
No opinion	20	19	19	20	19	21
Change in Catholic doctrine						
Yes	61	61	52	62	64	63
No	19	21	31	22	17	13
No opinion	20	18	17	16	19	24

65

members of the church (to use Le Bras's term) and the bulk of French who call themselves Catholics (81%). The explanation must be sought in the way people construct their ideological universe, in the interplay of contrasting influences in which one's personal journey plays such an important role and one's personal identity develops apart from official churches, which no longer structure the totality of human consciousness the way they did before.

Taking this approach, J. M. Donegani studied a typical example of this period: Catholics who are active in the socialist party.[12] What emerges is a necessary relativization of church attendance (worship) as the unique criterion of Catholic allegiance. The study also shows that religious practice inclines people to give a certain coherence and order to the beliefs they receive from the church. Taking up the research of Le Bras and Hervé Carrier, Donegani develops in a more detailed study the necessity of using a psychocultural approach to better understand the varieties of French Catholic allegiance.[13] It is helpful in this regard to distinguish three different dimensions: (1) the "supernatural," which orients the person vertically to adherence to the truths proposed by faith; (2) the "communal," which orients the person horizontally toward fellow believers and deepens the individual's sense of belonging to a community or to the church; and (3) the "civic," which begins with a person's beliefs and personal biography but applies these to the nonreligious world of secular society, especially to the politcal sphere. These varied religious dimensions can remain stable in a Christian environment, as is seen, for example, in Yves Lambert's study of changing attitudes in the Breton village of Limerzel since the beginning of this century.[14] But when exposure to change occurs, these three dimensions do not evolve at the same pace; the civic dimensions adapt more quickly than the communal, and the communal, in turn, is more flexible than the supernatural. In short, even though allegiance to organized religion can be relatively fixed, the horizontal bonds to one's religious group may be relaxed; there is still room to relax the ties binding a person to his or her religious group and to accommodate changes in the larger culture and society.

Such hypotheses allow us to partially comprehend the changes in French religious practice since 1965. At the end of Vatican II, the level of practice in France generally reached 30 percent of the population, with even stronger bastions in rural areas where church attendance and adherence to Catholic beliefs remained relatively high. Twenty years later, the percentage of those practicing their religion has dropped by half, the number of priests in charge of parishes has declined, the liturgical changes inaugurated by the Council have provoked some dissatisfaction, and parochial organizations have been weakened by the wave of anti-institutionalism in the younger generation carried forward by the events of May 1968. There followed a period of intense politicization, which led certain militants to make a heavy investment in sociopolitical activities and desert the church for good. When the excitement diminished in the 1970s, the rate of religious practice did not increase. The situation stabilized, but many were converted to a religion à la carte, using religious sources to assist their own search for an identity that was wildly individualistic and freed from any allegiances and organizational affiliations. Only a minority reacted in a voluntary and personal fashion; with the encouragement of responsible church personnel they continued to work in comparative obscurity toward constructing a French Catholic identity capable of producing its own authentic praxis.

Catholic Action wished to "conquer the world" and "make our brothers and sisters Christians again," but it confronted a harsh reality. With considerable condescension, it looked upon Catholics baptized in France but now separated from any effective religious practice as practically pagan, while at the same time it fiercely defended its own allegiance to Catholicism. Worn out by a crushing task, fascinated at times by political sirens, Catholic Action showed a tendency to fall back on the certainties of former times, which are today more and more questionable. When it did not align itself completely with secular society, it began to work again in Christian institutions. But it now has trouble recognizing as Catholics those baptized people who maintain very loose ties with the institutional church. For now, the French remain attached to the symbols of Catholicism associated with the stages of human growth (baptism, first communion, weddings, and funerals) rather than with the regular practice of religious worship.

The other judgment one can make on the last twenty years has to do with the contrasting interpretations of what is "true" Christianity. As Emile Poulat observes:

> The truth lies neither in statistics nor in experience nor in the often awkward case which is brought against both of them. It lies rather in the conflict of interpretations which divide the French on what is *real* Christianity. The conflict . . . is between two concepts of Catholicism. One is the religion of authority, the other of mass opinion. Recognized Catholics, self-declared Catholics, I recognize that you are Catholic; I declare that I am Catholic . . . I recognize you, I recognize myself; the distance can be considerable.
>
> The first of these concepts claims the authority of the church, a confessing and committed church, alive to all the problems of its time, with styles that vary from the traditionalist to the reformist and missionary. By contrast, the second concept moves in the direction of a bourgeois distillation—reducing Catholicism to a spirit or an essence, a popular nebulous, laden with human existence and daily life, with sorrows, worries and hopes. The first concept is rich in value and new demands; the other finds its origin in rural and folk traditions, but is much wider in scope, following people in their migrations, finding a way between resignation and active revolt without excluding either attitude. Between these two concepts, within the Catholic institution with its own religious spirit, one observes a subtle interplay whose specific nature and historical impact are still very much unknown. Globally there appears a type of religion, a kind of perception, a way of understanding the human and life itself which in no way wants to appear church-oriented; to defend itself it is even willing to appear anticlerical. This anticlericalism would not have had such impact if it had been really atheistic or anti-Christian.[15]

The Distribution of Tasks Within the Church

As Vatican II neared its end, the church of France still represented an imposing social force, with well-defined tasks distributed among different groups. The Catholic Action movement enjoyed continual support from the hierarchy and tried to accomplish the missionary tasks it had been doing since before World War II. The work had been inspired by Henri Godin and Yves Daniel's book, *France—A Mission Country,* the exhortations of Cardinal Suhard, and the creation of priest societies such as Mission of France and Mission of Paris during the war. Into this situation came the "conciliar spirit," urging implementation of the insights of Vatican II. At the same time there was a felt need for fraternity and for simplicity in relations among the hierarchy, priests, and laity. Pomp diminished and lifestyles came closer together. But the task of renewal faced numerous obstacles.

A Conciliar Episcopate

The French bishops had made a notable contribution to the conciliar adventure and in this way forged contacts with other local churches, particularly those in French-speaking Africa. The Africans felt close to France because of their traditions, education, common language, exchanges of personnel, and financial assistance. A recent study provides a sociological profile of this episcopate, which now includes fewer than twenty bishops who participated in the deliberations of Vatican II.[16]

The average age of the French bishops is sixty-two. From a sample of 141, only fifteen bishops are less than fifty-eight years of age; eight out of ten range between fifty-six and seventy-five — which forecasts rapid replacement within the next several years, assuming retirement at seventy-five which the Council made possible.

Because of the small number of priestly vocations in France, the majority of French bishops come from traditionally very Catholic regions of the country: 20 percent were born or pursued major seminary studies in Brittany or the Vendée. Recruitment to the episcopate remains largely rural, since one bishop out of two was born in a village or a small town of less than 5,000 inhabitants. Only seventeen came from towns of more than 50,000, as shown in Table. 3.6.

As for social origin, the bishops generally come from rural backgrounds and the middle class. Gone is the time of recruiting bishops from great aristocratic families of the bourgeois elite. Out of 141 bishops, more than 110 have undergone traditional priestly formation: Catholic primary school, a secondary school seminary or religious college. Few have studied at state universities or *Grandes Ecoles*. Since the Council, however, the criteria for appointment to the episcopate have changed. Instead of looking first for good administrators of a diocese or men associated with Catholic Action, Rome now looks for men with pastoral experience, sympathy for Catholic Action, a concern for social problems, and suitable discretion in their political commitments. It is difficult to say whether or not John XXIII, Paul VI or John Paul II specially encouraged the appointment of a certain kind of bishop, since two bishops out of three are former vicars or pastors and half of them have served as chaplains to a college, a secondary school or hospital. More than two-thirds have also served at some time as chaplains for Catholic Action movements. Half of John Paul II's appointments are men of this background; in this he appears to be acting in much the same way as Paul VI (cf. Table 3.7). There is little reason to assert, therefore, that Catholic Action no longer finds worthy defenders in the Vatican.

But with the appointment of Cardinal Jean-Marie Lustiger as archbishop of Paris, it seems certain that a different set of qualities will be sought at least for some years to come: men more distant from the usual preoccupations of Catholic Action and with more understanding of intellectual debate, more concern for the needs of his diocese than for the functioning of the French Bishops' Conference, which has become overly anonymous and bureaucratic. Lustiger's appointment, in other words, presages future appointments for which some experience of university culture, an

TABLE 3.6 Rural or Urban Origins of Bishops According to Their Time of Episcopal Appointment

						DATE OF APPOINTMENT						
PLACE OF BIRTH	UNDER PIUS XII		UNDER JOHN XIII		UNDER PAUL VI (1963–70)		UNDER PAUL VI (1970–78)		UNDER JOHN PAUL II		TOTAL	
	N	%	N	%	N	%	N	%	N	%	N	%
Communities of less than 2,000	7	29.2	5	20	11	37.9	14	33.3	7	33.3	44	31.2
Communities of 2,000–50,000	9	37.5	15	60	8	27.6	14	33.3	8	38.1	54	38.3
Community of more than 50,000	8	33.3	3	12	8	27.6	12	28.6	5	23.8	36	25.5
Born outside France	0	0	2	8	2	6.9	2	4.8	1	4.8	7	5
Total	24	100	24	100	29	100	42	100	21	100	141	100

TABLE 3.7 Previous Responsibilities of Those Chosen Bishops According to the Time of Their Episcopal Appointment

| | | | | | DATE OF APPOINTMENT | | | | | | | |
| | UNDER PIUS XII | | UNDER JOHN XXIII | | UNDER PAUL VI (1963–70) | | UNDER PAUL VI (1970–78) | | UNDER JOHN PAUL II | | TOTAL | |
PREVIOUS EXPERIENCE	N	%	N	%	N	%	N	%	N	%	N	%
Local chaplain	3	12.5	5	20	9	31.0	17	40.5	1	4.8	35	24.8
Federal or diocesan chaplain	14	58.3	9	36	14	48.3	13	31.0	8	38.0	58	41.1
National chaplain	0	0	2	8	2	6.9	5	11.9	1	4.8	10	7.1
Unknown	0	0	1	4	0	0	1	2.4	2	9.5	4	2.8
No previous work with the laity	7	29.2	8	32	4	13.8	6	14.3	9	42.9	34	24.1
Total	24	100	25	100	29	100	42	100	21	100	141	100

understanding of nonecclesiastical structures, and previous experience with the laity will be important qualifications. Rome's concern in this regard is praiseworthy at a time when conflict grows on every side; the work of theological and pastoral reflection has been rather neglected, despite the increasing cognitive and critical level of believers and of all French society. Nevertheless, prestigious diplomas guarantee neither a genuine pedagogical ability nor pastoral sense. Similarly, familiarity with the university milieu does not enable one to deal successfully with those aspirations within that milieu that are concerned about the influence of Catholicism. Not long ago Guy Riobe, the bishop of Orleans, tried to mediate the differences between some of the positions taken by the Bishops' Conference and the allegedly "subversive" aspirations of progressive Catholics on issues of nuclear disarmament, priestly celibacy, and the culture of unbelief. To some Catholic intellectuals he was a hero; but his rather sentimental approach and his effort to play the role of avant-garde supporter succeeded only in marginalizing him from the French Bishops' Conference and from Rome. Since Riobe's untimely death at the beginning of John Paul II's pontificate, his position within the Bishops' Conference has been taken by the present bishop of Evreux, Jacques Gaillot.

Since 1965 the French bishops have faced a gradual deceleration of the dynamic forces generated by Vatican II, whether because of the inability of the traditionalists or integrists to adapt to new ways of thinking or because of the progressives' impatience with the pace of change in the church. Whether from the right or the left, assaults on the church have been strongly colored by both implicit and explicit political choices, and the bishops have spent considerable time in negotiation, discussion, and argument. What is surprising is that the bishops still remain generally open to the changes in the surrounding secular world. The 1905 law separating church and state brought them poverty and a lower social status. It also gave them freedom to speak and move within a democratic framework which they have learned how to use fruitfully.

Episcopal solidarity has been distinctly manifest in the work of the French Bishops' Conference and its numerous commissions, and during the annual bishops' meeting held in Lourdes. The bishops have produced a number of documents on responsibility in the church, openness to the Third World and the problems of immigrants, the risks of nuclear war and building peace, the economy, the mass media, new approaches to missionary activity, catechetics, and lifestyles. In this way they have helped to awaken French Catholics to their responsibilities and alert them to what has to be done. In the last few years, however, this work of "consciousness raising" has encountered major obstacles. There is question about the adequateness of followup to the bishops' statements; Rome has given strong encouragement to each bishop to become more responsible in his own diocese to the detriment of the collective action of the Bishops' Conference; problems of finance and personnel have hindered progress. Besides, severe tensions have arisen because of interventions beginning in 1982 with regard to the methods and publications of French catechesis. Catechists in France are overwhelmingly lay and mostly women. Although they exhibit various levels of allegiance to the church, their number (around 200,000) is all the more impressive because they work voluntarily. This diverse body is interested in new ways of teaching religion, and it remains the apple of the eye of the French church.

In a resounding lecture in Paris and in Lyons, Cardinal Ratzinger recently insisted on the importance of memorization with regard to religious instruction, the need to stress the dogmatic tradition of the church, and the need for prudence in using the results of critical biblical exegesis. The pedagogical innovation which had flourished for the past thirty years has now stopped; the main groups are now scattered. Many parents are now dissatisfied with the inadequacies of religious instruction and there are increasing pressures and public denunciations from traditionalist and integrist circles. More recently, however, these critiques of French catechists have been displaced by criticism over the use of funds raised during the Lenten campaigns of the Catholic Center against Hunger and for Development (CCFD); the CCFD is accused of providing financial support for "Marxist" and other "subversive" groups in several countries.

Since Vatican II, the role of the local bishop has been notably transformed. A recent book by Jacques Palard examines the distribution of power in the diocese of Bordeaux over the past twenty years. His analysis amply demonstrates how the organizational principles of centralization and hierarchy have been gradually weakened. The façade of unanimity has collapsed. The principle of democratic election has surfaced in the priests' senate, which advises the bishop, and new kinds of negotiation characterize the relationship of center (the bishop) and periphery (parishes, religious groups, etcetera). With this has come a significant increase in pluralism. "The bishop," writes Palard, "can from now on count only on the fidelity of priests and laity to the institution and on his own ability to persuade and reconcile if he is to successfully manage opposing groups. The game of legitimacy has been sensibly transformed."[17]

Declining Numbers and Increasing Age of the Clergy

The bishops' task today is made all the more difficult because of the declining numbers and rising age of the clergy, exacerbated by the low number of priestly recruits and an increase in men leaving the priesthood. Very soon after the Council, the French clergy experienced a great shock, greater perhaps than clergy elsewhere. The rise of new ideas generated by the Council (democracy, the notion of the "people of God," the expanded role of the laity), the moral liberalization proclaimed by secular legislation, feminist claims, an increase in the functionality of society as a whole, new opportunities offered by rapid economic growth—all these factors have helped to make the status of priests more precarious in advanced industrial society. The political events of May 1968 accelerated the process of change by developing a radical critique of all institutions including the church, by resurrecting the core of anarchist theory, by spreading a simplified version of the findings of social science and psychology, and giving a new chance to leftist tendencies by means of a slogan Marxism while in fact acting as a revolutionary minority.

Some priests entered this global contest in the 1970s, justifying this in terms of political commitment, the requirements of their professional job, or their so-called prophetic breakaway from clerical celibacy by openly contracting marriage. The bishops at the time experienced considerable difficulty with the priest group called "Exchange and Dialogue," which was composed of several hundred married priests either politically committed to the left or occupied in a secular job. These men claimed they wanted to escape the image of "pope," of the man presiding over the liturgy, spending his life administering the sacraments or celebrating mass for small groups of people; a large number of them found their self-fulfillment elsewhere—in work, sexuality, and commitment to secular society. Various writings and manifestos appeared one after another demanding that the priest be "a man like others," that he cease to be a person "set apart," but share the common fate of human beings including full human sexual expression. By giving up the outward signs of priesthood they felt they would become "more fully human" and in this way become "even more fully a priest."[18] In some cases this response also represented a way of breaking with their childhood and with a clerical past which they had generally borne with difficulty and which they considered dehumanizing. This fundamental repudiation was greeted with only minimal public acceptance and sparked the anger of traditionalists. A few "militant" lay people who were themselves liberated from church structures encouraged these developments. The media, following the scent of scandal that often surrounded the personal dramas of these men, exploited the situation.

Such a violent upheaval, so completely different from the traditional image of the priesthood, resulted in more departures. According to a study published in *Documentation Catholique* in 1969, 533 applications for dispensation from celibacy for diocesan clergy were sent to the Vatican between 1962 and 1968. The number of departures continued to increase until 1974, when it stabilized and then began to drop. The effects of this hemorrhage in the French clergy were especially severe since half of those who left were priests under forty years of age. As one priest noted in a recent study on the consequences of this decline:

> The clergy is getting gray-haired; there will be priests in France in the year 2000, but there will be no more "clergy." This great national body which one could see file past in my history book between the aristocracy and the Third Estate in 1789 is becoming extinct. I know that I am one of the last of this historic adventure.[19]

The figures speak clearly. Diocesan priests numbered 46,000 in 1960, 40,900 in 1965, 36,000 in 1975, 31,481 in 1981, and 28,695 in 1985. Ordinations nowadays number about 100 per year, compared with 1,000 per year in 1950—a rate similar to what existed at the time of the 1789 Revolution (a dark age for the church) when the French population was half what it is today. Between 1975 and 1985 the number of seminarians has varied little, remaining around 1,150. Replacement is not occurring since deaths are more numerous than ordinations. Julien Potel estimates that the openings created by this imbalance are the equivalent each year of the disappearance of all priests in the diocese of Rodez.[20] Priests from religious communities constitute only an auxiliary force since they number no more than 8,000, although the proportion of religious priests has remained more stable than that of diocesan clergy. The remaining clergy are also getting older: in 1965, 24.1 percent of the diocesan priests in France were under forty; this proportion fell to 12.8 percent in 1979, and in 1985 it was estimated that 10 percent of the diocesan clergy were under forty, while one-third were over sixty-five.

In order to fill the gap created by this loss of priests, the bishops, with the encouragement of John Paul II, tried to improve the quality of seminary training and to stimulate vocations. As a result, there has been a slight increase in seminary entrants from young people in the charismatic movement and, in some cases, young men with professional experience. At the same time, religious priests and sisters have been asked to become more involved in pastoral work, but they too have grown older and have been affected by the crisis of the 1970s. Young people, moreover, seem more attracted by monastic life than by priestly ministry in the world. The status of women in the church is still low and the training of sisters is too poor for them to play more than a helping role in parochial activities. Still, more sisters are now active in school chaplaincies and catechetical work. And, as with religious men, the location of their convents and their lifestyle often provide an opportunity for privileged contact between the church and the people in areas of poverty and joblessness and in places where immigrant families live.

For some years people have been searching for a new model for the diocesan priesthood since the present form, which mainly originated from the French school of spirituality, does not provide social support for a sufficient number of priests. Moreover, those who enter the priesthood generally come from traditional families and hence are more amenable to situations that combine classical religious formation, community life, a strong spiritual orientation, and an atmosphere of prayer.

A Changing Laity

In the 1960s, the most recognized and visible members of the French laity were those associated with Catholic Action. At Vatican II the French bishops defended the hierarchy's practice of "missioning" militant lay people to work in specialized milieux—a mode of operating that drew its inspiration from Pope Pius XI. Ten years later this model had lost much of its appeal, and in the 1980s the bishops gave up control of these movements, allowing them to take on a diversity of political options and social activities provided that these did not commit the hierarchy itself.

What then happened to Catholic Action? At the risk of oversimplification, several consequences can be listed: an abundance of political activities around 1968 especially in youth movements, a certain distancing from church structures, an extreme emphasis on action to the detriment of prayer and religious practice, an abortive clericalism—either from chaplains or militant laity—addressed to the bulk of supposedly traditional Catholics, and a lack of interest in the kind of openness to the world favored in the postconciliar period. Some also relied on a truncated social analysis that stressed one's social situation or social class differences and borrowed heavily from Marxist theory. Ironically, this came at a time when French society as a whole repudiated simplified dogmatic pronouncements and discovered a much more complex and changing structure of stratification.

Admittedly, these tendencies did not characterize the whole of Catholic Action, but they were sufficiently strong to divide those in charge from the hierarchy and to separate the staff of the Catholic Action movement from its grassroots base. While the sanction for these tendencies originated in a more militant spirit evident in all sectors of French society, it prevented the socialization of large numbers of young people into more specialized religious activities, as used to occur in the past.

Consequently, the bulk of anonymous Catholics, people in the parishes who simply practiced their religion, began to assert themselves, feeling they had a strong pontifical and episcopal support. The 1981 Eucharistic Congress in Lourdes was a spectacular manifestation of this spirit. It was a spirit more concerned with parish community and transmission of the faith: liturgy, catechism, strict religious discipline, renewal of prayer and the sacraments, preparation for the diaconate. A principal effort of the hierarchy looked to reinforcing a threatened Catholic identity and was helped by a sector of the laity who had hardly any right to speak in the 1960s. The clergy's cooperation in this effort was more or less strong, depending on their age and temperament. Because of their fewer number and increasing age, however, priests were no longer sufficient to carry out this task, and many still retained preconciliar clerical attitudes opposed to sharing power with the laity.

Another group slid rather easily into these church structures vacated of "permanent members." This movement may be called the charismatic renewal. It crossed the Atlantic from the United States and appeared in France in 1971. Its emphasis rests on reinforcing Catholic identity and hence it insists on spirituality, theological instruction, the experience of prayer and practice of the sacraments, sharing ownership among members, and fidelity to the hierarchy. The movement is young, solidly planted in several large French cities, and composed of married couples, single people, and young men preparing themselves for priestly ministry. The number engaged in this renewal, that is, those participating regularly in one of its activities, has recently been estimated at 50,000; but the number of Christians influenced by some element of this movement is closer to 100,000.[21]

A postconciliar episcopate that will experience considerable turnover in the next few years, an emphasis on the responsibility of the bishop in his diocese rather than on his contribution to the work of the Bishops' Conference, a continuing decline in numbers and increasing age among the clergy, a changing laity—these are the most important aspects of the evolution in French Catholicism over the last twenty years. Much hope is now focused on the new laity who are full of good will and concerned that the institution which has nourished them—and for which they feel responsible in the future—will not perish. It remains to ask what impact this church really has on the political life and social organization of French society.

The Sociopolitical Orientation of Contemporary Catholicism

What are the political and sociocultural orientations of French Catholicism today? How have they changed over the past twenty years?

The End of the Catholic Apocalyptic Approach to Politics

The postconciliar period in France is marked first by a more universal acceptance of the Republic and by a concern to avoid backsliding with regard to the more democratic tendencies legitimized by conciliar reflection. A key figure in this evolution was the charismatic Charles de Gaulle, who possessed a certain broad Catholicism and a wide-ranging vision capable of eliciting much support. Since de Gaulle the bulk of Catholics have ceased to indict any form of republican government, as they were tempted to do in the 1950s. Following Vatican II, they have insisted on the imperatives of conscience, human rights (rather than the "rights of God"), and the societal implications of religious freedom. A certain apocalyptic rhetoric began to disappear from the French church, as with John XXIII it had already vanished from the world church. A Christian democratic party had no chance of winning many Catholic votes and the Christian labor union (CFTC) abandoned its confessional reference as early as 1964, becoming simply the French Confederation of Workers (CFDT). Catholics no longer occupy a privileged position in political parties or unions. They are divided into several camps, and the bishops have refrained from using their authority to influence Catholics' political choices as they used to do.

Electoral Behavior

Voting patterns again show the cleavages we have already noted: Catholics who practice regularly, those who practice occasionally, nonpracticing Catholics, and those without any religion. Of all the variables explaining electoral behavior, the religious variable remains the most enlightening: religious affiliation and especially religious practice are both more predictive of voting differences than age, gender, or occupation. There is need, therefore, to relativize those one-sided analyses that seek to explain everything in terms of generation gap, gender differences, the struggle between social groups or social classes (orthodox Marxism), or differences between towns and countryside (the environmentalists). One comes then to the paradox, well-known among French political scientists, that top-level managers or civil servants without any religion are more likely to vote left than workers, if the latter practice their religion. This finding is the inverse of what one would expect from Marxian theory, which generally underestimates the impact of religion on social behavior.

Since 1945 and especially since the beginning of the Fifth Republic (1958), regularly practicing Catholics have massively voted for the right; the proportion hovers around 80 percent. The Marxist left in this sector of the population achieved its highest support in the presidential elections of 1974 when it attracted 23 percent of the vote, a proportion it has not regained since.[22] People who claim no religion (15% of the population) vote in exactly the opposite direction, giving 84 percent of its support to the left and 16 percent to the right. What we have, then, is a picture of two cultures rooted in very different perceptions of a religious universe, which carries with it considerable political antagonism.

Certainly "devout" (practicing) Catholics have participated in the renaissance of the French socialist party and have voted for it, but they remain a minority. In a 1972 document written in the wake of Paul VI's encyclical letter Octagesima Adveniens (1971) the French bishops admitted the possibility of political pluralism, but its echo finally reached only "militants" or an elite of believers; the great majority of Catholics continued to vote strongly for the right. The reasons for this preference—so different, for example, from the behavior of English Catholics—lie in the poor image of the Communist party in religious matters and the divisions in French society born of the 1789 Revolution, the 1871 Commune, and the 1906 separation of church and state. The motivations are also cultural: practicing Catholics are solidly integrated into the family of the church and its values; they identify with a system of political values that eschews violence and the warfare of competing interests. The values espoused by the left, in contrast, stress the importance of partisanship and labor unions, victories won only by conflict, and criticism of traditional leaders and the complicity of the church, in past and present social injustice. The political party or the labor union becomes a substitute for the church family, with its own sacred symbols, rituals, affective warmth, and feelings of comradeship. One can easily understand how people without any religion can find an almost natural refuge in them.

But the dominance of conservative politics prevalent among practicing Catholics over the last twenty years might need to be reassessed in the near future. As levels of religious practice continue their dangerous decline, Christian culture as well as the links to historical traditions will weaken; younger generations will not so easily find familiar points of reference; the continued rapid "marginalization" of the Communist party and the Socialist party's domination of the left (supported by some Catholics) could open a space for the left that is less virulent and turned more toward a social democracy along German lines. This development might well attract the support of Catholics who now vote with the right but who are deeply concerned about help for the Third World, peace, the search for greater social justice, and the need to humanize a savage capitalism that they do not really accept.

The Quarrel Over Schools

If the left wants to widen its appeal among Catholics close to the institutional church, it will have to radically revise its position on pluralism within the French school system, which it questioned during the debate that racked France between 1980 and 1984. The antagonism reached a high point in the impressive demonstration of June 1984—the largest since 1968—which forced the socialist president of the Republic to shelve the government's program. Since then, to everyone's satisfaction, the hatchet has been buried. With the right taking control of Parliament the debate is now concentrated on the school system's rigidities and on excessive union control of public school teachers. In this battle, significantly, the French bishops have encouraged moderation and avoided any direct confrontation with the socialist regime.[23] The majority of French people were more aggressive, not so much because they wanted to defend a religiously sponsored education but to salvage the popularity of a private system considered as a viable alternative (or safety valve) for those facing the institutional and bureaucratic rigidities of the public system. Trying to estimate the number of French people who want private instruction impregnated with authentic Catholic teaching, one finds only 15-20 percent, which corresponds to the percentage of regularly practicing Catholics registered by public opinion polls over the last ten years or so.

This chapter has tried to highlight the paradoxical evolution of the French Catholic church in the postconciliar period. The proportion of practicing Catholics and the number of priests have diminished considerably. A new kind of laity has emerged since the Catholic Action movement, after years of expansion, has declined. Pluralism in politics is now more widely accepted and, following the openness to the world fostered by John XXII and the debates and documents of Vatican II, the church's apocalyptic approach to politics has been muted. Nevertheless, regular religious practice continues to be associated with conservative politics. In spite of this, a greater diversity is evident within the church regarding questions of personal morality, the structure of the priesthood, and sexuality. Being a Catholic no longer signals a sharp separation from the rest of public opinion on global issues. One finds a certain resistance to these changes from Catholics whom Le Bras labeled "devout"; their number is diminishing but they continue to be more integrated into the institutional church. Theodore Zeldin observed in his book, *The French:*

> To say that a person is or is not religious in France is not to say a great deal. Only a person's personal history can explain what such a description means. Formerly the church was mainly an expression of communal identity, conformity, solidarity, humility before awesome forces. Today there are alternative ways of expressing those same sentiments. In the past there was a clear conflict between religion and modernity; now attitudes toward change are as varied among the religious population as among those who are not religious. Religious people probably disagree as much among themselves as they do with non-believers. Religion offers infinitely less certainty than it once did. It serves as a breakwater between anxiety and serenity that is never fully impervious to doubt; this has now become the norm for any "civilized" person.
>
> What this means is that the Christian community is not a minority but an ensemble of minorities split into atoms and molecules. More than it ever has been religion is a matter of reflection and personal choice, temperament and inheritance. And so a visitor from another country can never be sure what he will find when he enters a French church.[24]

Zeldin's humorous judgment corresponds rather well with what the use of sociological concepts and statistics in this chapter has been able to reveal about the outlines of French society and French Catholicism.

NOTES

1. Alexis de Tocqueville, *L'Ancien Régime et la Révolution* (Paris: Gallimard, 1952). *Oeuvres complètes,* Vol. II, Book III, Chap. 2, p. 205.
2. "Mgr Vilent: Les paradoxes de l'Eglise de France," *Esprit* 4-5 (1986):259.
3. Danièle Hervieu-Léger, *Vers un nouveau christianisme?* (Paris: Cerf, 1986), pp. 20-21.
4. J. Sutter, *La vie religieuse des Français à travers les sondages d'opinion publique,* Vol. 2 (Paris: CNRS, 1984).
5. SOFRES, *Opinion publique 1984* (Paris: Gallimard, 1984), p. 187.
6. Ibid., pp. 188-89.
7. Ibid., p. 190.
8. "Un sondage de la SOFRES sur les Français et la religion," *Le Monde* (October 1, 1986), p. 12.
9. Ibid., p. 13.
10. Ibid., p. 12.
11. G. Michelat and M. Simon, *Classe, religion et comportement politique* (Paris: Presses de la FNSPo et Ed. Sociales, 1977).
12. J. M. Donegani, "Itinéraire politique et cheminement religieux. L'exemple de catholiques militants au parti socialiste," *Revue Française de Science Politique* 45 (1979):693-738.

13. J. M. Donegani, "L'appartenance au catholicisme française: Point de vue sociologique," *Revue Française de Science Politique* 2 (1984):197–229.

14. Y. Lambert, *Dieu change en Bretagne. La religion à Limerzel de 1900 à nos jours* (Paris: Cerf, 1985).

15. E. Poulat, *L'Eglise, c'est un monde* (Paris: Cerf, 1986), p. 52.

16. G. Grémion and Ph. Levillain, *Les lieutenants de Dieu* (Paris: Fayard, 1986).

17. J. Palard, *Pouvoir religieux et espace social. Le diocèse de Bordeaux comme organisation* (Paris: Cerf, 1985), p. 115.

18. François Charles, *La génération défroquée* (Paris: Cerf, 1986).

19. Ibid., p. 139.

20. J. Potel, *Les Prêtres séculiers en France* (Paris: Le Centurion, 1977).

21. M. Cohen, "Le renouveau charismatique en France," *Christus* 131 (1986):265.

22. H. Madelin, *Les chrétiens entrent en politique* (Paris: Cerf, 1975).

23. SOFRES, *Opinion publique 1985* (Paris: Gallimard, 1985), pp. 31, 47.

24. Theordore Zeldin, *The French* (London: Collins, 1983), p. 501.

4

Secularization, Pillarization, Religious Involvement, and Religious Change in the Low Countries

Karel Dobbelaere

The Low Countries, Belgium and the Netherlands, split at the end of the sixteenth century over absolutism and religion. The Netherlands turned predominantly Protestant, and Belgium, which remained under control of the absolute king of Spain, became a stronghold of the Counter Reformation. While the two countries were once again united in 1815 after the downfall of Napoleon, the Belgian revolution of 1830 resulted in a definite split. From the beginning, Calvinism strongly influenced Dutch culture, although the population of the southern part remained predominantly Catholic. Consequently, the Netherlands is religiously mixed: in the mid-1960s more than 40 percent of its 12,200,000 people were Catholic and 35 percent were Protestant; 5 percent professed another religion and about 20 percent were registered as not religiously affiliated. In Belgium, the census does not register the religious affiliation of the population. However, based on registered baptisms, it can be estimated that about 93 percent of the nearly 9,500,000 people living in Belgium in the mid-1960s were Catholic, 1 percent was Protestant, and 2 percent professed another religion; the remaining were areligious. Culturally, Belgium is divided into three regions: Dutch-speaking Flanders in the north of the country, south of the Netherlands; French-speaking Wallonia; and bilingual Brussels. In the mid-1980s these regions represented, respectively, more than 57 percent, nearly 33 percent, and 10 percent of the almost 10,000,000 people living in Belgium. It should be noted that 2 percent of the population of Wallonia is German-speaking. By the mid-1980s, the population of the Netherlands had grown to nearly 14,500,000 people.

In 1985, the European Catholic Bishops' Conferences held a symposium in Rome on the evangelization of "secularized" Europe. Analyzing the European data assembled by the European Value Systems Study Group in 1981, Jean Stoetzel classed the Netherlands and Belgium, together with France, as a "région laïque."[1] Hence, it seems appropriate to analyze the evolution of the Catholic Church in Belgium and the Netherlands within a secularization framework.

Secularization is a descriptive concept which denotes a societal process in which an overarching and transcendent religious system is reduced to a subsystem of society alongside other subsystems and whose overarching claims have shrinking relevance. It is inconceivable that religious organizations making up the religious subsystem would not react to such a fundamental process. Not only will they fight secularization on the societal level, for example, through a process of pillarization, but they will also react organizationally and doctrinally.[2] Hence, we should study not only changes and conflicts on the macro-level but also changes on the meso-level: religious changes. Finally, since individuals will react to all those changes and adapt their religious involvement, we need also to study the micro-level. These three levels give us a frame of reference for our analysis. We will look at the conflicting processes of secularization and pillarization, the religious involvement of the people, and finally, some religious changes in the church. Before doing so, however, we need to analyze briefly the processes that lead to the secularization of societies.

Sociologists studying secularization implicitly or explicitly refer to functional differentation—sometimes called functional segregation, sometimes institutional or structural differentiation—and to the accompanying processes (in society and its subsystems) of rationalization, planning, specialization, professionalization, segmentation, fragmentation, mechanization, in a word, societalization or *Vergesellschaftung*, to explain the changing position of religion in modern society.[3] Some authors have stressed that so-called privatization of religion and not secularization is typical of modern society. According to Niklas Luhmann, the privatization or individuation of religion is a particular case of the individuation of all decisions, which is a consequence of the functional differentation of society.[4] Both aspects of modernization, namely, secularization and the individuation of decisions, are consequences of the same process of functional differentation, and are complementary processes. Indeed, the inclusion requirement, typical of modern society, can be met only, in each and every subsystem, if complementary roles emerge alongside the professional ones. But, functional segregation between complementary roles is also needed to prevent the destruction of functional differentiation. Because a strict segregation of complementary roles on the individual level is difficult to control and to enforce, the *Privatisierung des Entscheidens* (the privatization or individuation of decisions) serves as a functional equivalent. Through the individuation of decisions a statistical neutralization of certain individual role combinations is aimed at on the societal level.[5] It must be clear now that the individuation of decisions is *not* an individual option but a structural characteristic of the modern societal structure.

Secularization and Pillarization

In the 1950s the concept of pillarization was deployed in the analysis of Dutch society, and defined as "the organization of all kinds of social functions and activities on a religious basis." J. P. Kruyt strongly insisted on the religious basis of the pillars, suggesting that there were only two pillars in the Netherlands: a Protestant and a Catholic one, and that the Socialist organizational complex could not be called a pillar.[6] In the second half of the 1960s, political scientists also became interested in pillarization. They were intrigued by the political stability of ideologically fragmented societies like Belgium, Switzerland, Austria, and the Netherlands. Consequently, pillarization was no longer regarded as restricted to the Netherlands, and as not only based upon religion.[7] Pillars, then, may be defined as segmented and polarized organizational complexes that are religiously or ideologically legitimized and that strive toward autarky (self-sufficiency). Pillars promote social exclusiveness and an in-group mentality. The more services a pillar renders, the more autarkic it is. Hence, apart from a Catholic pillar we may refer in the Netherlands to a Protestant and a Socialist pillar, and in Belgium to a Socialist and a Liberal one.[8]

The Emergence of the Catholic Pillar

How is the emergence and the extension of such a process of pillarization to be explained? Historians and sociologists have put forward several theories to explain the emergence of pillarization in the Netherlands, Austria, and Belgium: the emancipation theory (W. Goddijn), the political mobilization theory (R. Steininger), and the preservation theory (J. Billiet).[9] Such a complex process can certainly not be explained by one single factor. However, H. Righart's comparative study of the Catholic pillars in Austria, Belgium, the Netherlands, and Switzerland convincingly demonstrated that the preservation theory—the establishment and extension of the pillar structure to insulate Catholics from a secularized world—is the most general explanation. In the last decades of the nineteenth and the twentieth centuries, the lower clergy was very active in building up and developing a Catholic pillar, which was partly also an adaptation of the church to modern society. "Protection through adaptation, this in a few words, is what pillarization was all about" is the last sentence of Righart's book.[10]

Pillarization was a radical reaction to the process of functional differentiation that accelerated in the second half of the nineteenth century and affected both Catholicism and Protestantism alike. It was a reactive policy: the clergy and part of the Catholic elite started creating a Catholic world segregated from the secularized world. In fact, they reverted to an older process of differentiation: segmentary differentiation, that is, the duplication of services in those sectors that were differentiated from the church, to check the impact of secularization and to preserve church control over the Catholic part of the population. If the state and the differentiated subsystems were no longer to be organized around a Catholic ideology, especially the schools and the professional world (trade unions, sick funds, political parties), then the new civic liberties provided the opportunity to establish Catholic organizations to protect believers from a secular, that is, an areligious or antireligious ideology. We may conclude then that it was the process of functional differentiation that provoked

Catholic pillarization: "dikes" were established to prevent the "secularization" of the church's flock. Once established, these different Catholic organizations were gradually organized into a more and more centralized pillar of which the Catholic party was the political expression. Hence, in Stein Rokkan's terms, we can speak about an institutionalized pillar, interlocking a political and a corporate channel.[11] By the 1950s, a comprehensive Catholic pillar was consolidated in Belgium and in the Netherlands.[12] But could they survive the ongoing secularization process resulting from functional differentiation?

Secularization and the "Tottering" of the Dutch Catholic Pillar

About a century after the emergence of the pillar structures in the Netherlands, studies have demonstrated that they had begun to "totter." This tendency to depillarize started in the political sector. Christian parties lost voters and the Catholic party merged with Protestant parties in the Christelijk Democratisch Appel (Christian Democratic Appeal). Federations and mergers were also registered between Catholic and Protestant, Catholic and neutral, and Catholic/Protestant and neutral organizations, for example, between trade unions, public servants organizations, officers organizations, and organizations of manufacturers. On the local level schools merged: Catholic with Protestant, and both with nonreligious schools. Such fusions also occurred among youth organizations and among local and regional hospitals. Many Catholic, Protestant, and neutral organizations for psychological well-being merged in the early 1970s. Catholic newspapers were deconfessionalized, and Catholic and Protestant radio and television broadcasting companies lost a large number of members.[13]

Factors responsible for the decline in strength of the Catholic pillar in Holland were: the crisis in the Catholic culture itself, which started among nuclear Catholics; the disorganization of Dutch Catholics under the pressure of the "permissive society" that surrounded them; the invasion of television in Catholic homes; social mobility; the integration of the elites at the top of the societal system; the slow permeation downward of objections to the pillar system from intellectuals; the successful conclusion of the emancipation process giving Catholics a greater self-confidence, which stimulated open-mindedness; the professionalization of social and psychological welfare services; financial needs, which, for example, stimulated mergers in the world of the media; legal regulations, for example, in the world of education; and an intensification of social and economic conflicts.[14]

Secularization and the Deinstitutionalization of the Belgian Catholic Pillar

In Belgium, the Catholic pillar did not appear to "totter" under the pressures that affected the pillar system in the Netherlands. It is true that regular Sunday mass attendance also dropped drastically at the end of the 1960s and the early 1970s in Belgium, indicating a crisis similar to that of the Netherlands. But in Belgium there were no mergers between Catholic and other organizations, nor in the long run was there any reduction in the membership of Catholic organizations or in the volume of services they provided, although there was a slight decline in the late 1960s and early 1970s. By the late 1970s, most organizations affiliated with the Christian pillar had recuperated. An example of this trend can been seen in Table 4.1 for the two Christian parties (C.V.P. and P.S.C.). There was, however, a definite crack in the Catholic pillar: Catholic Action groups for youth, that is, organizations for the apostolate of the laity, have seen a constant decline in membership since the late 1960s, and among the middle classes such groups have since completely disappeared. Neither was there any extension of pillarization into new fields. Rather, new types of social services are now provided by pluralistic organizations, such as the Federation of Neighborhood Centers. But the bulk of the organizations making up the Catholic pillar seem to be as strong as they were before the start of the crisis in the church if not stronger.[15] How can this be explained?

During the acute crisis in the church in the late 1960s and the early 1970s, the leadership of the Catholic pillar organized study sessions and conferences in which the following questions were debated: What is a Catholic school? a Catholic hospital? a Catholic youth movement? a Catholic trade union? They asked themselves whether they should go on providing pillarized services. It was in this period that a new legitimation of the pillar was developed: a new "collective consciousness," which J. Billiet and I have called "socio-cultural Christianity." The core values of sociocultural Christianity are: the legitimation of vertical pluralism on the basis of the constitutional freedom of assembly and choice, on the one hand, and the articulation of the Christian identity in so-called evangelical values, on the other: a humane approach toward clients and patients, or the *Gemeinschaftlichkeit* of Christian institutions; solidarity between social classes, with special attention to marginal people; rational economic use of available resources, that is, the elimination of luxury and the promotion of thrift; and the realization of social justice.[16] This "sacred canopy" is symbolized by a "C," referring more and more to Christian, that is, evangelical instead of Catholic, the latter considered to have a more restricted appeal and to be more confining. This collective consciousness is proclaimed externally and is used to attract clients and patients who are by and large not regular churchgoers. It should be stressed that all pillar services are subsidized by the state and consequently do not cost more for the clients than state-organized services. (This is true for both the Netherlands and Belgium.) The collective consciousness also functions internally to promote different programs, for example, a program for the humanization of Christian hospitals.

The "sacred canopy" is used externally. Indeed, on the basis of the new image of the "Christian" pillar—its openness, solidarity with marginal people, *Gemeinschaftlichkeit;* in a word, its "humane character"—the Catholic pillar still recruits, in

TABLE 4.1   Distribution of Votes for the Christian People's Parties at the National Belgian Elections for the House of Representatives in the Period 1965–1985 (Percent)

ELECTION YEAR	1965	1968	1971	1974	1977	1978	1981	1985
Percentage of total vote	34.5	31.7	30.1	32.3	35.9	36.3	26.4	29.5

SOURCE: J. Billiet, *Samenleving: Feiten en Problemen* (Leuven: Acco, 1986), part 1, p. 101.

a period of continuous declining church involvement, a large number of people, many of whom are only marginally Catholic. As a result, in so-called Catholic schools the number of liturgical services has been reduced. This is also linked to the declericalization of these schools, which resulted from a diminishing number of available priests and religious personnel, and a growing demand for professional teachers. This demand for professional personnel is, of course, a consequence of the democratization of education and the resulting need for state subsidies, which entail state requirements that regulate the qualifications of staff and the school curriculum.[17] This tendency was not limited to the schools. More and more lay people are working in the Christian pillar as economists, lawyers, social workers, therapists, psychiatrists, medical doctors, and nurses, and have secured a specialized domain of their own. As a result, in many Christian organizations religion has been latently marginalized. In Christian hospitals, for example, pastoral service is a mini-service, without administrative support, compared to medical and logistic services, and in Christian schools, religious classes are only one class among others, taught by a special teacher. It should also be stressed that those providing specialized services have difficulty in typifying the so-called religious, or Christian, character of their service; and professionals have difficulty in giving a typical religious answer to the problems with which they are confronted. Social workers of the Confederation of Catholic Sick Funds, for example, expressed a tension between the professional approach to clients and the Catholic worldview of the organization.[18]

The personnel of Christian institutions are also less involved in the church than a few decades ago. Mangers are preoccupied with this situation and often stress that employees of Christian institutions should be aware that their private life has implications for their mission. Should their private life situation openly contradict the values they are expected to demonstrate, some managers see in this a reason for discharging staff. In Christian schools, this has produced conflict. In 1977 a "Deontological Board" was established to solve such conflicts between teachers with tenure and managers. From the first cases that were brought before this board, it became clear that the board wished to protect the private lives of the teachers. In 1987, the highest administrative court of Belgium even decided that the regulations governing the professional life of teachers in Catholic schools had to protect their private lives against arbitrary decisions of the governing boards of such schools. Restrictions such as "aspects of their private life" that "affect their pedagogical relationships with their students or have an effect on school-life" could not be invoked for dismissal. In Christian hospitals, the discussion also ran in terms of "private–public": the choice between several formulations of a clause concerning the Christian character of institutions affiliated with *Caritas Catholica,* which was to be incorporated in their rules and regulations, was settled in a way that "respected the private life of the employee."[19]

The use of the terms "private–public" is an ideological translation of the process of functional differentiation. The so-called privatization of religion is typical of modern societies and is a particular instance of the individuation of decisions, which, as I pointed out in the introduction, is a structural consequence of the functional differentiation of society. By using the terms "private" and "public," members of society defend their rights to equal access to the subsystems of society, which are not to be restricted by the other roles that one occupies. This is what sociologists call "inclusion." In other words, by using the dichotomy private-public, people, in this case members of the Christian pillar, use ideological concepts that have emerged in a functionally differentiated society. By doing so they further promote the privatization of religion and the secularization of society.

The new "collective consciousness" of the Christian pillar is used not only externally but also functions internally. Let us take only one example. On the basis of its new values, primarily that of *Gemeinschaftlichkeit,* the Christian League of Caring Institutions, which represents the Christian hospitals and Old People's homes in Belgium, sets up programs to humanize its institutions. Human beings, not illness, should be the focal point of Christian care. This humane approach is stipulated as something the hospital management should ensure, but it is counteracted by economic and medical rationales. In practice the organization of hospitals follows the latter rationale, and social relations are strongly influenced by the professional model: they are specialized, segmental, hierarchical, and brief, the opposite of *gemeinschaftlich.* Repeated calls from the Subcommittee for the Humanization of Hospitals set up by the League of Christian Caring Institutions to implement its programs, to enforce the Bill of Rights of the patients, to ensure participation of patients and staff in the running of the hospitals, and to abandon the strictly medical model have not been heeded since they are not urgent or are dismissed as too expensive. A recent study came to the conclusion that in the current economic crisis the approach of the management of the institutions is rather inhuman. Most managers do not see a link between *Gemeinschaftlichkeit* and the organizational structure of their institution; they regulate it to the plane of informal, unorganized interpersonal relations. On this level it is defined as an *attitude* of patience, selflessness, availability, compassion, service, kindness, devotion, and so forth.[20]

As a consequence of functional differentiation, therefore, the organization of the services of the Christian pillar has become more and more specialized and *gesellschaftlich.* An increasing number of lay professionals have replaced a diminishing number of religious personnel. Organizationally, religion is not only latently marginalized, it is also privatized. Consequently, the control of the church over the membership and the clients is reduced to influencing their personal motives. On the other hand, control over the professionals was also greatly diminished because of the low visibility of the interaction between professionals and clients. (Indeed, the behavior of professionals in Christian hospitals, for example, is less and less exposed to the view of those who sustain Christian values—for example, religious sisters are no longer the nurses in charge of the operating theaters, and the registration of surgical interventions conceals in technical language religiously unacceptable behavior, for example, curettage instead of abortion.) The church tries to influence the personal motives of its members and its professionals, but its actual control is very limited. Indeed, all that remains is control over the orthodoxy of publicly proclaimed standpoints and the public formulation of ethical norms by the overarching organizations of the Catholic pillar.[21]

Confronted with a sharp decline of involvement in the Catholic church, the pillar has cast off its clerical character and replaced it with a Christian aura. In other words, in order to promote its services, the pillar adapted itself to the "secularization" of the Belgian population by promoting a process of "internal" secularization or religious change. But the Catholic pillar now promotes only values—*Gemeinschaft-*

lichkeit, solidarity, thrift, efficiency, and social justice—typical Western values which could also be claimed by groups outside the Christian pillar. In such situations the Catholic pillar loses its distinctiveness.[22]

Now, in the mid-1980s, a "secularized" collective consciousness has been able to maintain a flourishing corporate channel: The increase of clients made the pillar eligible for increased state subsidies, which enabled it to promote even better services. But, as Rokkan suggests, an institutionalized pillar has two channels: one corporate and the other electoral. Since the 1980s, the electoral channel has been crumbling (see Table 4.1). In a recent study, J. Billiet demonstrates that, after having recovered by the end of the 1970s their losses from the late 1960s and early 1970s, the Christian People's parties (CVP and PSC) abruptly lost more than 25 percent of their electorate in the 1981 election. This loss was to a large degree confirmed by the results of the 1985 election, and the polls of 1986–1987 give the joint Christian parties 26 to 27 percent of the Belgian electorate. Many people working in the corporate channel have also contested the privileged relationships between the Christian People's parties and the corporate channel. Consequently, the majority of clients and members of the Christian corporate channel and many of its executives reject the Christian People's parties as valid expressions of the Christian corporate channel. In a recent study of a Flemish town, V. Van de Velde clearly shows that members of the boards of the organizations making up the Christian corporate channel were related not only to the Flemish Christian People's party (CVP) but also to the Flemish Nationalist party and to Agalev, the Flemish Green party. Is this the beginning of the deinstitutionalization of the Christian pillar or will the Christian corporate channel be able to adapt to the new political preferences and affiliations of its membership and the members of the boards of its component organizations?[23]

Pillarization: A Conclusion

In the Netherlands and Belgium, the disintegration of the Catholic pillar proceeded according to different scenarios. In the pluralistic Netherlands, mergers and fusions were possible, but not so in duopolistic Belgium. In both countries, however, the Catholic pillar set up to support traditional Catholicism against secularization basically had to adapt to functional differentiation and its concomitant processes of rationalization, professionalization, individuation, and societalization. No longer able to enforce its overarching claims on the societal level, the church had vigorously promoted a "new state" within the state, a pillarized structure, to guide Catholics from

TABLE 4.2 Percentage of Catholics and Not-Religiously Affiliated in the Netherlands, 1947–1984

DENOMINATION	1947	1960	1971	1971	1984
Catholics	38.6	40.4	40.4	39.8	37.3
Not affiliated	17.1	18.3	23.6	23.7	31.3

SOURCE: The percentages for the years 1947, 1960, and 1971 are based on census data. Estimates for the 18–64-year-old population are based on one question without a filter; J. Oudhof, "Kerkelijke gezindten in 1984," *Sociaal-Cultureel Kwartaalbericht* 7 (1985):16.

TABLE 4.3 Frequency of Catholic Baptism (Related to Live Births), Catholic Marriages (Related to the Total Number of Weddings), Catholic Burials (Related to the Total Number of Funerals) and Regular Church Attendance (Related to Catholics Registered in the Parishes Seven years and Older) in the Netherlands (Percent)

Year	Baptism	Marriage	Burial	Weekend Mass Attendance*	Percent Decline*
1965	43.5	41.0	—	—	
1966	42.7	40.8	—	64.4	−1.1
1967	41.8	40.2	—	63.3	−4.9
1968	40.7	38.4	—	58.4/56.0	−4.8
1969	39.6	38.7	—	50.8	−3.9
1970	38.5	—	—	47.2	—
1971	—	39.6	29.9	—	4.9
1972	37.6	—	—	41.1	−3.6
1073	—	36.4	29.5	37.5	−2.4
1974	36.0	35.9	29.1	35.1	−2.5
1975	33.9	33.7	29.7	32.6	−1.5
1976	33.1	33.6	—	31.1	−1.3
1977	33.9	33.4	29.1	29.8	−2.0
1978	32.5		29.2	27.8	−1.4
1979	31.9	32.0		26.1	

Percent Decline braces: rows 1966–1969 → −4.3; rows 1972–1978 → −1.9

88

Year				
1980	31.2	30.8	29.3	25.0	$\left.\vphantom{\begin{array}{c}a\\b\end{array}}\right\}$ −1.2
1981	31.3	30.8	29.9	23.7	−1.3
1982	31.1	30.4	29.4	22.7	−1.0
1983	28.9	29.6	29.8	21.6	−1.1
1984	25.8	29.6	29.8	19.8	−1.8
1985	24.5	28.1	29.7	19.1	−.7
1986	—	—	—	17.5	−1.6
Mean decline per year	1965–72: −.1	−.8	none		
	1972–82: −.9				
	1982–85: −2.2				

*Based on mean number counted in two consecutive weekends: Jan. 1966–68; Oct. 1968–70; Jan. 1972–78; 1 April 1979, and March 1980–86.

SOURCE: Katholiek Sociaal Kerkelijk Instituut (KASKI), especially M. M. J. Van Hemert, *En zij verontschuldigden zich . . .: de ontwikkeling van het misbezoekcijfer 1966–79* (The Hague, 1980, Memorandum nr, 213), p. 9; Van Hemert, *Vijf jaar kerkontwikkeling in cijfers: de gegevens van de parochiestatistiek, speciaal vanaf 1975* (The Hague, 1981, Memorandum nr. 218), p. 62; *Statistieken 1986*, and *121 Informatiebulletin*, special edition containing yearly statistics of the Catholic church in the Netherlands.

the cradle to the grave. Now the pillars have succumbed to the same forces that have affected the wider society. Catholics have accepted the modern world and they now defend their inclusion, using a "private-public" dichotomy. They no longer want to be controlled by the pillar: they reject interferences from the pillar in their family life; they want freely to choose schools, newspapers, magazines, hospitals, political parties, sick funds, and trade unions for the quality of their services, not because they are part of the pillar. Catholics have moved toward pluralistic participation and away from segregation and controlled contact.

Religious Involvement

Basically, secularization is concerned with the operation of the social system: it is the system that becomes secularized. "Conceptions of the supernatural may not disappear, either as rhetorical public expressions—for example, American civil religion: "one nation under God," "in God we trust"—"or as private predilections, but they cease to be the determinants of social action."[24] As far as private religion is concerned, sociologists have even coined powerful phrases like "the social structure is secularized but not the individual."[25] Others have coined concepts that affirm this point: "invisible religion," "popular religion," "diffused religion," "implicit religion."[26] But is this correct? Did the secularization of the social system have no impact on the individual's religiosity?

The Dutch Situation

In the Netherlands, the number of people not religiously affiliated has been growing ever since the turn of the century.[27] Since the 1970s, this number has been growing not only at the expense of the Protestant churches, overwhelmingly the Dutch Reformed, but also vis-à-vis the Catholic church (see Table 4.2).

Radical changes in the Dutch Catholic population can be better determined by studying their participation in church rituals. Since the early 1970s, the number of people buried in the Catholic church in the Netherlands has been stable: 29 to 30 percent. This low percentage, compared to the percentages of church marriages and baptisms (cf. Table 4.3), is related to the fact that in the 1970s, Catholics were a relatively young population: they represented only one-third of the elderly population compared to 40 percent in the total population.[28] The stability of this percentage, compared to the decline in baptisms as related to live births in the Netherlands—.8 percentage points a year for the last twenty years—and an equal decline (.8 percentage points) in the number of marriages celebrated in the church as related to the total number of weddings (which has accelerated since the 1970s and especially in the 1980s) indicates that it is the younger generation of Dutch who are leaving the church. They no longer marry in the church or bring their children to church for baptism.

These figures also indicate that estimates of the total number of Catholics in the Netherlands based on answers to the question to which church or religious organization people belong overestimates the number of affiliated people.[29] Since the 1970s, when disaffiliation accelerated, a questionnaire using the question "Do you

TABLE 4.4 Estimates of the Number of Catholics in the Dutch Population of c. 18–64 Years, Compared to Catholic Baptisms and Marriages (Percent).

| | ETIMATES OF NUMBER OF CATHOLICS | | | |
| | WITHOUT | WITH | | |
YEAR	FILTER QUESTION	FILTER QUESTION	BAPTISMS	MARRIAGES
1971	39.8	37.7	—	—
1972	—	—	37.6	39.6
1977	39.6	34.6	33.9	33.6
1980	38.7	32.6	30.8	31.2
1983	37.7	30.2	29.6	28.9
1984	37.3	29.4	29.4	25.8

SOURCE: J. Oudhof, "Kerkelijke gezindten," p. 16.

belong to a church or religious organization?" before asking the interviewee "to which one he or she belongs," seems to have given a better estimate of the percentage of people belonging to a church (see Table 4.4). In the Netherlands in 1984, the number of Dutch without religious affiliation already amounted to 47.9 percent.[30] They are the Dutch majority: Catholics represent only 30 percent and Protestants 18 percent.

Of these Catholics, how many attended mass on weekends? Since 1966, not only did the number of people considering themselves as Catholics decline but the number of those going to church on weekends also dropped drastically (Table 4.3). This decline was very sharp in the period 1967–1973: 4.3 percentage points per year or one-fourth of all Catholics in six years. In the following years the percentage drop per year was lower, but even now, in the 1980s, attendance still drops by 1.2 percentage points a year.

These proportions are of course calculated on the number of Catholics registered in parishes. When people drop out of the church, they do not always inform the parish. Consequently, a number of people still registered in the parishes do not consider themselves Catholics. In Table 4.5, mass attendance on weekends was recalculated on the basis of the number of Catholics still defining themselves as Catholic

TABLE 4.5 Proportion of Catholics Seven Years and Older Proclaiming Themselves to be Catholic Who Attend Mass on Weekends

YEAR	PERCENTAGE	MEAN DECLINE PER YEAR
1977	34.4	
1980	30.6	−1.2
1983	28.1	
1984	26.2	

NOTE: The figures in this table are based on the data in Tables 4.3 and 4.4.

after a filter question (cf. Table 4.4). The mean decline per year does not change: there is a continuously growing number of Catholics—more than 1 percent a year— that is not celebrating the Eucharist on weekends: in the mid-1980s they numbered 75 percent of those defining themselves as Catholics.

The Belgian Situation

Turning now to comparative Belgian data, we may notice similar trends (see Table 4.6). Burial figures are constant, except in the Brussels region. This is due mainly to a heavy influx of foreigners belonging to other religions, especially Islam. The average decline in percentage points in the number of parents wanting their children baptized is identical in both countries. This figure is, of course, also influenced by immigration in both countries, which shows up very clearly in the differences in decline per region in Belgium. However, immigration does not explain the complete picture. A detailed study by A. Van den Bosch confirmed the average decline of baptisms in Belgium: in 1968–1979 it was twice the average decline in Belgian live births (.8 versus .4 percentage points a year).[31] In Belgium, the mean yearly relative decline in church marriages was sharper than in the Netherlands, but since the 1980s the decline has accelerated in the Netherlands. Again, regional differences in Belgium suggest the differential impact of immigration but also the growing number of remarrying divorcees. However, the number of people not prevented from marrying in the church because of a former marriage who are not now marrying in the church is growing steadily. In Belgium, it has nearly tripled since the mid-1960s, and continues to grow rapidly in the 1980s. These figures confirm the stability in church affiliation of the elderly people and the growing decline of church members in the younger generations, which suggests that the changes are probably generational changes.

As far as church attendance on weekends is concerned, the rate of decline was much sharper in the Netherlands than in Belgium; in the mid-1960s, of course, attendance rates were also much higher there than in Belgium. Indeed, the higher the percentage of people going regularly to church on weekends, the sharper the decline (see Table 4.7). The most drastic decline of church attendance on weekends occurred in the same period in the three cultural regions of Belgium (1968–1973); in the Netherlands, it started one year earlier. If, as in the Netherlands, we are allowed to use figures on baptism and marriage as crude estimates of the number of Catholics in Belgium, then we might suggest a figure of about 75 percent in the mid 1980s.[32] The recalculated number of Catholics going to church on weekends would then be about 28 percent. Again, we see that about three out of four Belgians who define themselves as Catholics are not going to church on weekends. The number is still somewhat higher in Flanders than in Wallonia; it is much lower in the Brussels region (Table 4.7). If there are three Catholics per four Belgians, only one of them goes regularly to church on weekends, then two out of four Belgians are *"des catholiques festifs"* ("festive Catholics") or "seasonal Catholics," indicating that they go to church for the "rites of passage" (baptism, confirmation, marriage, and burial). Some of them in addition go to church on special occasions, for example, at Christmas, at Easter, or on the Feast of the Assumption.

An Interpretation

From all these figures there emerge four questions: What is the orthodoxy and the ethical practice of these types of Catholics? How can we explain the decline of church attendance in the last two decades? Why was the decline so sudden and sharp in 1968–1973? What is the meaning of "rites of passage" for "seasonal" Catholics? Belgian data will be used to answer these questions; Dutch studies always include a high percentage of people belonging to other religions. This is not the case in Belgium: 96 percent of the Belgians are either Catholic or not affiliated to a religion, including former Catholics. The other 4 percent are Protestant (1 percent), Jewish (.5 percent), Islamic (2 percent), and members of other religions (.5 percent). Dutch data will be used to check if these explanations are confirmed for Christians in general.

People believing in a "personal God" overwhelmingly go to church on weekends. Nonpracticing Catholics believe in God, but conceive Him as a "spirit or life force, or do not really know how to 'conceive' Him." Those who doubt His existence or do not believe in Him overwhelmingly do not belong to the church. Among practicing Catholics several studies have also established a lack of orthodoxy as far as central Catholic beliefs are concerned (God, life after death, heaven, hell, soul, devil, and sin). This is especially the case among younger generations. And since studies have established that regular church attendance depends to a large extent upon one's beliefs, we may expect a further decline in church attendance in the near future. On ethics, differences between practicing, nonpracticing, and non-Catholics are well established in the field of bioethics and sexual morality, but not in other ethical fields. Practicing Catholics are more orthodox, non-Catholics are more tolerant, and nonpracticing Catholics fall in between. But the level of permissiveness in these matters is high among Belgian Catholics (in increasing order: suicide, extramarital relations, prostitution, homosexuality, sexual relations between minors, abortion, euthanasia, and divorce).[33]

R. de Moor, analyzing the European data collected by the European Value Systems Study Group in 1981, also established that the ethical permissiveness of Dutch Catholics is related to their church practice. Church orthodoxy is also higher among practicing Catholics but, in general, Dutch Catholics are more liberal in their beliefs than Protestants. Compared to Catholics in other European countries, Dutch Catholics are ethically the most permissive and the least traditional in their beliefs.[34]

Analyzing the Belgian data of the so-called European Value Study, one can look for social factors influencing religious practices, definitions, beliefs, attitudes, and morals of the Belgian people. Traditional social variables like social class, education, sex, ecology, deprivation, and migration did not produce significant variations. Only a combined index of age (as an indication of generational differences[35]) and domestic involvement (whether women were part of the labor force) produced changes in religious involvement on all of the levels mentioned: practices, self-definition, beliefs, attitudes, and morals.[36] Three social categories emerged: middle-aged and older housewives are most involved in religion; directly opposed are younger men and younger employed women. In between are middle-aged and older men, middle-aged and older employed women, and younger housewives. Do these social categories not

TABLE 4.6 Frequency of Catholic Baptism (Related to Live Births), Catholic Marriages (Related to the Total Number of Weddings), Catholic Burials (Related to the Total Number of Funerals) and Regular Church Attendance (Related to the Total Number of Inhabitants 5–69 Years Old) in Belgium (Percent)

Year	Baptism	Marriage	Burial	Weekend Mass Attendance	
				Percent	Decline
1964	—	—	—	44.7	
1965	—	—	—	43.9	− .8 ⎫
1966	—	—	—	43.4	− .5 ⎬ .6
1967	93.6	86.1	84.3	42.9	− .5 ⎭
1968	92.6	85.5	84.0	41.8	−1.1 ⎫
1969	91.4	84.4	84.0	39.6	−2.2
1970	90.2	84.1	83.7	37.4	−2.2
1971	90.9	83.2	84.4	35.4	−2.0 ⎬ 1.7
1972	90.2	82.6	84.1	34.0	−1.4
1973	89.3	82.0	84.3	32.3	−1.7 ⎭

Year	Belgium	Flanders	Wallonia	Brussels	(decline)
1974	89.4	80.9	84.5	31.5	− .8
1975	88.2	79.9	84.2	31.0	− .5
1976	86.7	77.8	83.7	30.2	− .8
1977	85.2	77.7	83.7	29.4	− .8
1978	84.5	77.0	83.3	28.5	− .9
1979	83.9	76.4	83.4	27.9	− .6
1980	82.4	75.7	83.0	26.7	− 1.2 ⎫
1981	—	—	—	25.8	− .9 ⎬ .8
1982	81.0	73.6	83.2	24.9	− .9
1983	80.6	72.4	83.3	23.8	− 1.1
1984	80.5	69.7	83.4	23.3	− .5
1985	78.6	69.1	82.1	22.4	− .9 ⎭

Mean yearly decline

	Belgium	Flanders	Wallonia	Brussels
Belgium	− .8	− 1.0	− .1	−1.1 (since 1967: 1.1)
Flanders	− .5 (96.1–86.6)	.9 (91.8–75.4)	− .1 (91.3–89.4)	since 1967: − 1.4 (52.0–26.9)
Wallonia	− .9 (92.8–77.4)	−1 (83.5–65.5)	− .05 (79.3–78.4)	since 1967: − .9 (33.9–17.7)
Brussels	−2.4 (81.6–39.0)	−2.5 (81.6–37.5)	− .6 (72.0–60.8)	since 1967: − .8 (24.3–10.6)

SOURCE: A. Van den Bosch, *Office of Church Statistics*, 1987.

TABLE 4.7   Frequency of Regular Church Attendance (Related to Total Number of Inhabitants 5-69 Years Old) in Belgium and Cultural Regions in Two Typical Time Periods (Percent)

YEAR	BELGIUM	FLANDERS	WALLONIA	BRUSSELS
1967	42.9	52.0	33.9	24.3
1973	32.3 (−1.7)	38.5 (−2.4)	26.9 (−1.2)	16.3 (−1.3)
1985	22.4 (− .9)	26.9 (−1.0)	17.7 (− .8)	10.6 (− .5)

NOTE: Figures in parentheses indicate mean yearly decline.
SOURCE: A. Van den Bosch, *Office of Church Statistics,* 1987.

suggest that different degrees of involvement in the secularized world are significantly associated with variations in religious involvement? How can we explain this?

Young adult employed women and young adult men have always lived and worked in a world that is considered controllable and calculable. The world of young adults is a world of the "here and now" in which interaction is based on role relationships that are planned and coordinated. A more and more rigorously applied functional differentiation, specialization, and rationalization of labor which mechanizes and fragments jobs results in work that seems less and less "meaningful" and in task relationships in which all "humane" contact gets lost. Relations are superficial, functional, hierarchical. Everyone is replaceable in his or her role. Communications are shallow and utilitarian: people relate to one another in a "segmented" way: as workers, clerks, employees, merchants, buyers, vendors, neighbors, functionaries. Personal, lasting relationships are very much reduced in our society, even outside the work sphere, and remain typical only of the family and friendship relations.

Middle-aged and older men and employed women have also become progressively caught in such an industrial and commercial world. But are *young adult unemployed women* not somewhat screened from this economic world? Important changes have also taken place in the family sphere during the last decades. Since the 1960s, the mechanization of domestic tasks has advanced much further, and even the most intimate, sexual relationships and their "consequences" are considered to be calculable and controllable. Not only can one better control the consequences but the sexual act itself is also presented in most modern "handbooks" as "technically improvable." In these books, love is almost reduced to a necessary orgasm which at best is of no "consequence" but which by its fleeting nature is very volatile.

The most "traditionalist" are *housewives of middle age and older.* They have known a different world where other values predominated: tradition, love, devotion, loyalty, humility, and service. The world in which personal, lasting relationships were still possible (a family undistrubed by the mass media), where the total person was implicated, and where attachment and reciprocity rather than competition dominated, offered a favorable substratum for monotheistic religions. Religions that offered total and personal salvation and could develop in a *Gemeinschaft* belong to the past, and today have become alien to more and more people.[37]

For many, a *jenseitige* God who controls a *diesseitige* world is, if conceivable, more and more unacceptable: human beings are thought to be capable of commanding and solving their own problems. And if individuals themselves cannot solve them, there are many specialists available to help them: medical doctors, psychiatrists, psychologists, social workers, family therapists, and so on. These days, people consult them rather than priests. In case of long-lasting infertility, people formerly went on a pilgrimage praying to a lovely, noble, and merciful Lady in white with a rosary in her hands; now people resort to a serene, noble, and competent man or woman in white with a stethoscope around his or her neck. What an older generation still saw as a "grace from the One above" now receives a natural explanation. What was thought to be under the control of a "creative God" is now commanded by human beings, within the domain of the medical profession.

For many people life no longer comes from God. Humans control it, command it in test-tubes, even experiment with it, while television cameras track the process and bring it into the livingroom. Couples are invited to "Play Doctor *and* God" through gender choice kits. Hence, life has lost its sacredness and people have taken control of it: suicide and euthanasia are more and more accepted and propagated, and abortion is increasingly regarded not as a "sin" but as a "solution" to contraceptive failure. Generally, the Christian notion of sin has disappeared from moral discourse or has, if it is still used, lost its Christian meaning: sin has become synonymous for guilt feelings or shame. It no longer implies repentance, penance, and reconciliation with God. Luhmann has stressed that the notion of sin has lost its traditional meaning in a modern society.[38] In a functionally differentiated society, which involves the individual only segmentally and where religion as a meaning-system has lost its overarching position relative to the different functional subsystems, only "partial" failures and technical defects can occur. Human beings in their "totality" are never involved in a functional subsystem. Consequently, a situational ethic is adapted to such a system. This ethic takes into account the particularity of the functional subsystem, the circumstances, those involved, and their motivation. The majority of the Belgian interviewees reject objective ethical norms and adhere to a situational ethic, which confirms the secularization of ethics.

When people take command of their world, God is more and more removed from it. And if the notion of God lingers on, He is more and more conceived of as a general power, a spirit, "something" vague and general, a "higher power" and not as a "personal God." How could He be thought of as a "personal God" if people experience fewer and fewer "personal relationships" in their social lives? In a society where control, calculation, and planning are the basis for success, where results are of utmost importance, where competition — even in families — is legion, where people do not have time for one another, but where role players have superficial encounters, there the belief in a "personal God," and consequently the celebration of the Eucharist, seems for many an anachronism. In the Eucharist one celebrates one's relationship with a caring, forgiving, and comforting Father, who is the Lord, Creator, King, and Savior, the Protector and Comforter of the oppressed.

My basic argument is that many people can no longer believe in God because not only the physical but also the psychological and social world are now seen as controllable and calculable. Consequently, human beings can manipulate these worlds: their actions become calculated, systematic, regulated, and routinized; they also become disconnected from religion and God. This not only has had an impact on church attendance and the desacralization of ethics but it has also desacralized for people the meaning of life, suffering, and death. Indeed, recent sociological studies in the Netherlands have documented the impact of the secularization of the social system on the meaning people give to life, suffering, and death. "An idea like Kluck-hohn's that there are 'sets of existential premises almost inextricably blended with values in the overall picture of experience' cannot be postulated any more."[39] Value orientations seem to vary independently from beliefs and interpretations of life, suf-fering, and death; nor is a relationship established between such interpretations and people's beliefs.[40] Therefore, these studies suggest that, since the organizing princi-ples of life have been detached from religious interpretations, they document a pro-cess of "secularization" on the level of the individual.[41] The differentiation of the personal life-world, which we can aptly describe as compartmentalization, results in the marginalization of religion in the personal life of the individual. This desacraliza-tion on the individual level often results either in the rejection of God or in His deper-sonalization. Indeed, if for some the notion of God lingers on, He is no longer con-ceived as a personal God but as something vague, a "higher power." And as Durkheim suggested, the more general and vague God becomes, the more removed He is from this world and the more ineffective He is. At the same time such a belief is very shaky. It is a belief in an abstract notion without real impact on people's lives, and can easily be disposed of.

Let us now turn to our third question: Why did we have this drastic acceleration of religious decline in 1967–1973? First, this cannot be explained solely by the Bel-gian or Dutch situation; it happened in the Catholic church all over the world. Second, as it was not limited to the Catholic church, it cannot be explained as a particular Catholic phenomenon.[42] Consequently, Andrew Greeley's explanation, that the dec-line was due to the papal encyclical on birth control of 1968, Humanae Vitae, is too simple; in the Netherlands, the decline started even before the publication of the encyclical (see Table 4.3)[43]

Several studies have established that social behavior is dependent upon social control, and consequently lingers on much longer than beliefs and opinions. In the Netherlands, for example, pillarized behavior was still very prominent when people's mentality was already depillarized.[44] In my research on the Catholic character of the Catholic University of Leuven, in the early 1970s, I observed that many professors were still going to church every Sunday, although their beliefs and moral attitudes no longer conformed with the church's theological and moral teachings.[45] Conse-quently, one might expect that under the growing impact of men's capabilities, belief in a "personal God" and in other articles of faith was already strongly undermined in the 1960s when Western civilization was in its "golden age," but that overt tra-ditional behavior simply continued under the impact of social control. Sunday mass became for many rather a duty, a tradition, not supported by belief in a "personal God."

When, by the mid-1960s, an internal church discussion started—in the United States in the form of "underground churches," internationally about John A. T. Rob-inson's Honest to God, and in Belgium with regard to the publication of Humanae Vitae (1968) and the refusal of the Belgian bishops to divide the Catholic University according to the language principle (1966)—one could for the first time, in social discourse and in the press, acknowledge that the religious understanding of ethics and church authority were very much undermined. Public discussion in the Nether-lands and in Belgium about the implementation of the conciliar resolutions of Vatican

II made this apparent as far as beliefs, church ethics, and church authority were concerned. All this also had an effect on the clergy, who in the same period massively left the church. This had further consequences for the beliefs, attitudes, and behavior of lay people.

The sharp decline in Sunday mass attendance at the end of the 1960s and the early 1970s may, consequently, be seen as the collapse of a traditional behavior that was no longer supported by the belief in a "personal God" and the traditional values that the church proclaims. It was the convergence of *public* behavior and the *personal* general disbelief in the doctrines and values of the church. Since then, social control has increasingly had a completely different impact: it has started to keep people out of the church, where before it had rather induced them to attend.

This behavior was also due to a structural change: an increase in leisure time and the development of leisure activities, of a "leisure culture." In the 1960s and 1970s, an increasing number of people got more and more leisure time: not only more vacation time but also the so-called English week: Saturdays were freed from work and school, and the total amount of work time each week was also progressively reduced from 48 to 38 hours. Consequently, in a period when for a growing number of people "Sunday mass" became a "sheer duty," an "obligation of little substance," it became more and more located in a period of extended leisure time. And the pleasure associated with leisure time—being primarily a time of "freedom," of "exemption from external pressures"—aggravated the feeling of "duty" associated with religious "obligations."[46]

The predilection for more freedom and less duty also became apparent in the increasing number of divorces. In Belgium, the number of divorces tripled from 1965 to 1985. In the same period the mean number of children per woman in Belgium also dropped sharply to 1.6 children.[47] In other words, the search for more individual freedom was general: more freedom from the bonds of marriage and greater freedom by having fewer children. This change was also associated with a growing number of women entering the work force. By the end of the 1970s, 70 percent of Belgian women aged 20–24 had a job, and the large majority remained part of the work force.

It seems then that after World War II parents introduced their children to a religion of "sheer duty," "obligations without substance." An empty tradition revealed parental doubts and could not be discussed for lack of time, as both parents were working. As a result children rejected behavior that they considered hypocritical. A new generation has come of age that is openly less attached to the church,[48] and the vanishing church-going elderly are not replaced. Consequently, we are still heading toward a possible "stabilization" on a lower level. It evokes the idea of the "Scandinavization" of the Christian world, Catholics included. In about a decade only about 10 percent of the Belgian population may be practicing Catholics. This of course will have its consequences on the Catholic pillar in Belgium, which could be more and more deinstitutionalized.

I have been arguing that people now think and act more and more in terms of insight, knowledge, control, and planning, and less and less in terms of the incidental, the random, or in terms of beliefs and magic. The application of science to technology has reduced the relevance of the supernatural, of God. This emerged very clearly in a recent study of Flemish farmers who were born in the 1930s.[49] In the 1970s about

35 percent of this sample had stopped putting "sacred palms" (distributed in the churches on Palm Sunday) in their fields. Some stopped doing it because they did not grow corn any more, but the vast majority stopped because this custom had become, in their own words, nothing more than "an outdated usage," a "tradition." Several added that it had become "useless": "artificial fertilizers are now much better than before" and "it doesn't bring rain." In other words "there is no need for it any more"; in the farmers' opinion the practice had lost its "instrumentality" and no longer had an "expressive" function.

The exodus from the church was also well documented in that study: the higher the farmers scored on a modernization index, the less they believed in a "personal God" or used "sacred palm." Does this not indicate that the more people think in terms of insight, control, and planning, the more difficult it is for them to believe in a "personal God"? And can we not hypothesize that in the long run a belief in God as a "vague, general power" could end up in unbelief, after a period when one was a "seasonal Catholic"?

We need to be careful with such predictions. In Belgium, according to the European Value Study, people believing in a "vague, general power" which they still call God, have not severed all relationships with the church: they still participate to some extent in rituals, at least in "rites of passage." Such people represent a middle position: to the right are those who believe in a "personal God" and who normally go to church on weekends; to the left are those who no longer believe in God and have mostly quit the church altogether. This middle category now represents the modal commitment to the church. In the 1950s, most Belgians were practicing Catholics. Now 50 percent are affiliated with the church only for the sacralization of some religious holidays (Christmas, Easter, the Assumption, All Saints Day) or of certain role transitions: birth or parenthood, adolescence, marriage, and death (the "rites of passage").

What is the meaning of such ritualization? This brings us to our fourth question. Are we observing a new way of being Christian, by simply ritualizing important moments of life without any consequences for the outlook on life and for values? Or is this new type of involvement in the church a transitory stage before becoming unchurched?

To get an answer, let us consider the motivations I registered form parents asking the parish priests to baptize their child. For nearly a year I was involved in observing a Flemish suburban parish, with a population of more than 10,000. Each month, parents wishing to have their child baptized meet with the parish curate. In a session of about two hours they talk together about the values they want to live for and what baptism means to them. Why do they want their child baptized? Since most of these people are young adults having their first, second, or third child, more than three out of four do not go to church on other occasions. They are a sample of those Belgians who demand only rituals from the church.

A first category of motivation that emerged was instrumental. They want to be good parents and want the best schools for their children. It is very common for Belgians to consider the Catholic schools as providing a better education than public schools. Indeed, most children go to Catholic schools for primary and secondary education. Consequently, some parents who are unchurched want to send their children to Catholic schools and raise them as Catholics until they are twelve years old and confirmed. As Catholic schools are fully subsidized by the state, they will not have additional payments to make. Consequently, baptism is, in their eyes, a "cheap" price for a "better" education.

Other parents want their child baptized for family reasons or because it is a Belgian tradition. They do not want tension with their own parents or they do not want to defend their position—not having the child baptized—with their neighbors or friends. They might even add: "We are not religious, but we are not fanatical about it." This is a typical attitude of compliance, but also has an instrumental aspect to it. Some parents will indeed say: "If it doesn't do the child any good, it doesn't harm him either." Other parents will say, "We were raised Catholic and it was not that bad after all! It teaches children how to achieve a better world! In catechism they will learn about important values like honesty, justice, dedication, commitment, devotion, fidelity, amiability, love, care, charity, humility, and friendliness, which, after all, promote a civic attitude!"

A third type of parent will say: "After all, we are Catholics, even if we do not go to church on Sunday! We believe in God and we want our child also to be a Catholic!" These people refer not only to the civic values taught in catechism. They especially refer to Christ and suggest that He is after all a good example: Someone to look up to, someone who gives meaning to life. For these people, religion is a meaning system, and baptism is a dedication to that meaning system. It is the solemn expression of their adhesion to the Christian meaning system.

Sociologists and anthropologists have pointed out that meaning systems serve a dual function. First, there are the emotional adjustments required by disappointment, death, and disaster. As the contingencies of human life occasionally force people to ask fundamental questions about meaning and purpose, meaning systems have been built, of which religion is one type. We can scientifically explain natural disasters; an illness can be medically analyzed and the prospects given, death can be explained scientifically. But a person is then left with "his" illness, not "an" illness, with "her" death or the "death of a loved one" and not the objectified deaths of the statistics or of science; "his" experience of sorrow and contingency. This leaves us with a problem-area where, for many, science cannot bring comfort and where psychiatry can give only counsel. It is a domain where the individual must give *meaning*.

However, modern man looks not only for meaning, he also needs wholeness. In modern society, new questions have emerged. As functional subsystems are based on rational norms that are not only segregated but quite often incongruent with one another—we need only consider the norms governing the family and those guiding our economic activities—the individual has to accommodate himself to them. Moreover, as Luckmann states, "the 'meaning' of such performances is 'rational'—but only with respect to the functional requirements of a given institutional area. It is, however, detached from the overarching context of meaning of an individual biography."[50] To cope with this compartmentalization, individuals will have to choose their meaning systems from a pluralistic assortment that is available, or they will have to construct their own. Consequently, meaning systems function to "integrate the discrete realms of life" *and* to "provide a larger frame of reference in relation to which personal meaning can be perceived."[51] Meaning systems can provide wholeness or unity and meaning.

For many, these functions are the continuing "expressive functions of religion."

People ask the church for meaning: the meaning of life, suffering, and death; the meaning of the contingencies in life, the good and the bad. It is at such moments that people return to religion. They ask for baptism to solemnize life and for a religious burial to cope ritually with sorrow. It is also on the occasion of religious festivals, which celebrate goodness or the symbolic triumph over evil, that they especially go to church: at Christmas and Easter, at Pentecost and All Saints Day. There they celebrate life and ritually overcome disaster. There calamity is symbolically changed into salvation.

But religion can also offer unity, wholeness. Especially during transitions in life, "unity" must be pointed out. This is what some "rites of passage" do. For parents and grandparents the unity of the family is celebrated at baptism and even extended through the special roles of godfather and godmother. The family and the community celebrate the adulthood of a child at his confirmation. He is now ready to fulfill roles with often conflicting demands. It is suggested to him that he can integrate these. He can unify his life by living according to the great values of his culture: honesty, justice, commitment, dedication, care, humility, charity, and friendliness. At marriage, the union of man and wife, of the two families, of different generations is celebrated. Here also cultural values are proposed to solidify the union: fidelity, love, care, and devotion. With the help of these rituals, which bring together kin and friends, a new *élan de vie,* a new life force, is given, as Durkheim so forcefully described.

Thus, the pattern of secularization on the individual level can be simply summarized: (1) a sharp decline in the number of nuclear Catholics: in the mid-1980s still 25 percent in Belgium, and 7 to 8 percent in the Netherlands (i.e., 25 percent of Dutch Catholics); (2) a rapidly growing number of people only marginally integrated in the church: in the mid-1980s about 50 percent of the Belgians, and more than 20 percent of the Dutch (i.e., 75 percent of Dutch Catholics)—most of them interested in the expressive function of religion; others, on their way out, staying only for the services the church and its pillar still can provide; and (3) a still growing number of people leaving the church and becoming unchurched: in the mid-1980s about 25 percent of the Belgians, and nearly 50 percent (especially former Protestants) of the Dutch. In the long run, the survival of the Catholic church and its power seem to depend to a large extent upon its future capacity to maintain and improve its "expressive function." This will also partly depend upon its capability to adapt its theology, and to fit the demands of the growing number of people who are interested only in the "expressive function," which brings us to the third problem of our study: religious change.

Religious Change

Many changes have been noted in the Catholic church since Vatican II: use of the vernacular in the liturgy, institutionalization of collective confessions, changing rules on Lent and Friday abstinence, easing of the Sunday mass obligation to Saturday, etcetera. One of the most dramatic changes, however, is the graying of the clergy.

This aging is due to a decline in recruitment and an increase in departure. Since 1967 in the Netherlands and at about the same time in Belgium, the number of ordained diocesan priests have no longer "compensated" for the deceased. In 1986, there were 2,377 diocesan priests in the Netherlands, or 57 percent of the 4,173 in 1965; the number of religious-order priests declined by 50 percent. Since 1967 the number of religious sisters has declined by 36 percent. In Belgium in 1980, there were 6,819 religious-order priests and 7,785 diocesan clergy, 30 percent fewer than in 1961; the number of religious sisters declined 31 percent from 1967 to 1984. The age distribution clearly shows the graying character of priesthood and religious personnel. In Belgium in the mid-1980s, the modal age for diocesan priests is about 65–70; 55 percent of the religious-order priests are older than sixty, and half of the religious sisters are older than sixty-five. In the Netherlands in 1982, nearly 60 percent of the religious-order priests were fifty-five or older; in 1985, this percentage was 55 for active diocesan priests, and only 7 percent were younger than forty.[52]

In the Netherlands, this change gained momentum in 1967: the total number of ordained priests in that year dropped to under 200, and the total number of men leaving the priesthood was then already at two thirds of its highest point (1969–1970) (see Table 4.8). By 1972, the total number of ordained priests was only 11 percent of the number ordained in 1965. Since then, a total number of thirty ordinations a year has been exceptional. In the 1980s, an average of twenty-two men a

TABLE 4.8 Number of Ordinations and of Men Leaving the Priesthood in the Netherlands in 1965–1985

	ORDINATIONS			DEPARTURES		
YEAR	DIOCESAN PRIESTS	RELIGIOUS-ORDER PRIESTS	TOTAL INDEX	DIOCESAN PRIESTS	RELIGIOUS-ORDER PRIESTS	TOTAL INDEX
1965	81	156	100	16	29	18
1966	73	154	96	25	49	30
1967	60	133	81	42	113	64
1968	48	95	60	56	146	83
1969	28	82	46	87	157	100
1970	4	43	20	96	147	100
1971	13	36	21	64	157	91
1972	6	21	11	66	98	67
1973	7	28	15	34	122	64
1974	15	14	12	39	95	55
1975	8	21	12	24	70	39
1976	4	12	7	25	33	24
1977	9	7	7	22	28	21
1978	7	8	6	7	19	11
1979	12	9	9	10	13	9
1980	9	7	7	8	8	7
1981	18	8	11	3	12	6
1982	11	9	8	6	16	9
1983	17	15	14	5	13	7
1984	12	3	6	4	5	4
1985	10	2	5	5	10	6

SOURCE: KASKI, *Statistics 1986*.

year were ordained: thirteen diocesan and nine religious-order priests. By the late 1970s, the number of those leaving the priesthood again reached the level of the early 1960s.

In Belgium in 1968, the number of those entering diocesan seminaries was only about 55 percent of the number entering in 1965. The decline stabilized by the end of the 1970s at a level of 25 percent of the 1965 entrances (see Table 4.9). Ordinations of diocesan priests declined from about 1969 on and since the 1980s has fluctuated at 20 to 25 percent of the number of ordinations in 1965. This low figure is due not only to the decline in seminary entrances but also to the fact that in the 1980s only 50 percent of those entering seminary were ordained.[53] This figure was, however, already an improvement: in 1973-1974, in Flemish dioceses, the rate of successful completion of the seminary was less than 30 percent.[54] Table 4.9 also shows that in Flemish dioceses priest departures reached their peak in 1971.

All these data confirm the crisis in the Catholic church. Figures on lay involvement and changes in the composition of the clergy suggest that the Low Countries

TABLE 4.9 Number of Ordinations, Entrances in Diocesan Seminaries, and Men Leaving the Presthood in Belgium in 1965-1986

YEAR	DIOCESAN PRIESTS		SEMINARY ENTRANCES		DEPARTURES IN FLEMISH DIOCESES	
	NUMBER	INDEX	NUMBER	INDEX	NUMBER	INDEX
1965	143	100	264	100	6	16
1966	124	87	201	76	12	32
1967	128	90	154	58	17	45
1968	140	98	138	52	19	50
1969	103	72	94	36	29	76
1970	113	79	—	—	34	89
1971	99	69	92	35	38	100
1972	70	49	88	33	31	82
1973	51	36	60	23	23	61
1974	—	—	53	20	26	68
1975	—	—	64	25	—	—
1976	40	28	67	25	—	—
1977	48	34	69	26	—	—
1978	38	27	71	27	—	—
1979	28	20	61	23	—	—
1980	33	23	60	23	—	—
1981	30	21	77	29	—	—
1982	27	19	76	29	—	—
1983	33	23	82	31	—	—
1984	37	26	68	26	—	—
1985	34	24	70	27	—	—
1986	—	—	63	24	—	—

SOURCE: Liliane Voyé, "Aspects de l'évolution récente du 'Monde Catholique'," *Courrier Hebdomadaire du CRISP* 925-26 (June 26, 1981), p. 15, supplemented with data from P. Delooz and K. Dobbelaere, *Radioscopie de l'Eglise Catholique en Belgique*, May 1985, p. 78; *Kerk en Leven*, June 12, 1986, p. 6 and February 19, 1987, p. 4.

and the Catholic church went through a period of rapid social change from 1967 to 1973, and that the church could not recuperate its losses. To the contrary, it stabilized, as far as personnel is concerned, in the late 1970s at a much lower level.

The church can adapt to but it cannot control social change. The response to a similar decline in church involvement of lay people and clergy was very different in Belgium and in the Netherlands. In the period from 1966 to 1972, the Dutch church explicitly tried to analyze the problems and to ease the supposed sources of dissatisfaction by institutionalizing new collective structures.[55] The Belgian church did not manifestly attack the problems. It latently accommodated to the world, minimizing internal tensions, and thus produced less polarization than the Dutch church. Indeed, as John Coleman suggests, in several national settings the Roman Catholic church has adapted to functional differentiation. The rapidity and thoroughness with which Dutch Catholicism adapted, not the general direction of change, sets it apart from the Catholic churches in other national settings.[56]

A more thorough sociological reflection, however, allows us to suggest why the *outcome* of the Belgian and Dutch endeavors was so similar, except for the polarization within the church. The factors producing a secularized world and the impact of the secularized world on church members is the same all over the Western world, and the church cannot control these processes. Indeed, churches have no impact on the process of functional differentation and its complementary processes of individuation, rationalization, professionalization, planning, and societalization. Most people living in societies where these processes operate either become areligious or restrict their church involvement to a minimum, sacralizing positional changes through church rituals. Only a minority — in the statistical and the social meaning of the term (elderly people and housewives) — is still involved in the church.

Losing social control over the people by becoming a subsystem alongside other subsystems and as a consequence of the deinstitutionalization of the pillar, church authorities can only adapt to this situation and must resort to motivating individual persons to promote religious behavior. Can the church learn something from the manifest accommodating process of the Dutch church to improve its motivating power? I will restrict my analysis of the changes within the Dutch church to this question, since there is enough descriptive and analytic material available about its recent evolution.[57]

John Coleman makes it very clear that the bishops were the "change agents" in the Dutch Catholic church: they were "permissive yet decisive," "holding channels of communication open to dissatisfied parties," trying "to guide them along reformist lines, while showing a firm resistance to revolutionary movements."[58] They sensed a growing degree of incongruence between the "official" church model and the priorities of individuals, and they wanted to accommodate the church to the life situation of Catholic people. But they were caught in the middle, between their local church and Rome, partly because certain contesting groups sent petitions to Rome.[59] In these disputes,

> the Dutch position sought procedures of collegial dialogue between bishops, theologians, and catechists which would allow new formulations of faith for a searching church, a legitimate pluriformity in theology, and open procedures for judgment in the church. Rome seemed to fear that an unresolvable pluralism was being introduced into

the church which needed to be checked by stern, even authoritarian, measures.[60] Consequently, Rome used all available methods to defend the Roman scholastic position.[61]

Rome not only defended its theological positions, it also opposed the projected decision-making structure of the Dutch church. For example, it did not accept the charter for a Dutch permanent National Pastoral Council that was meant to be a policy-forming organ, co-responsible for pastoral policy with the bishops' conference. In 1973, a national pastoral dialogue began based on the model used in the Dutch-speaking dioceses of Belgium. In 1984 the Landelijk Pastoraal Overleg (National Pastoral Council) was put in place. It is convoked by the Dutch episcopal conference to advise them on a theme set by the bishops. The chairman of the episcopal conference is president of the council. Consequently, it is not a policy-forming organization and it can only advise in matters asked for by the bishops' conference. Even the episcopal conference lost power vis-à-vis individual bishops. The collective power of the Dutch bishops was strongly diminished. In a communiqué of January 6, 1984, about the Landelijk Pastoraal Overleg, the Dutch bishops stated that, in accordance with canon law, "the dioceses in the Catholic church in the Netherlands are to a large extent independent."[62] The bishops meet only "to inform each other," "to assist each other in the execution of their task," and "to map out a common policy where needed."

It is clear that Rome has brought the Dutch church in line by appointing bishops of its liking: Adrian Simonis became archbishop of Utrecht, and two more conservative bishops have been appointed since the mid-1970s. Coleman's expectations that the changes in the Dutch church were consolidated by the early 1970s and that now bishops would be forced to be responsive to the entire Dutch Catholic community because of the institutionalized democratic structures of the Dutch church was disconfirmed. The Roman policy has also strongly aggravated the polarization in the Dutch church. The low-key reception of the pope in 1985 in the Netherlands clearly demonstrated this.

Some people will argue that this Roman policy was provoked by the Dutch "revolution" and was a logical consequence of the policy of the Dutch bishops in the late 1960s and early 1970s. However, those well informed about the situation of the Belgian church know that the Belgian primate had to lobby intensely in Rome to prevent the nomination of conservative bishops in open positions, who in his eyes would have polarized the Belgian situation. Thus, even in a country that follows a cautious policy, Rome wants to support the conservatives. Consequently, a manifest adaptation of the church seems possible only within the limits set by canon law and insofar as it is promoted by the local bishop. A strong progressive episcopal conference would of course stimulate such a policy, but this can no longer be expected because of the conservative presence in most national conferences.

What could be some characteristics of a manifestly adaptive policy by the local bishop? He could promote an adaptation of the catechetic approach to the pluriformity of social life, informed by a pluriform theology. Such a policy cannot be carried out by a bishops' conference, as the new Belgian Geloofsboek (Book of Beliefs) clearly demonstrates. This publication simply confirms, under the impact of conservatives, the traditional beliefs and ethics of the church, even if it is written, in the terms of its contributors, in a context of "deep mercifulness" and "rapprochement toward the people." This is a typical pastoral approach: you are "wrong," but we "understand" and "we hope that one day you will repent."

However, certain intellectual problems confronting Catholics cannot simply be resolved by a "pastoral approach." Catholics, like others, live in a world they are helping to build: "we have the world in our hands," they presumptuously sing. Consequently, they have problems with the root metaphors of traditional Catholic cosmology and certain doctrinal points that contradict recent scientific discoveries. They look for a cosmology and a reformulated theology that accept secularization as legitimate. How can one do justice to the creativity and responsibility of humans, on the one hand, and to their dependence upon God, on the other? How does one rethink certain basic principles of religion and ethics without returning to the notion of natural law, which is typical of Greek cosmology and scholastic theology? How can the basic religious insights in human nature be reformulated without contradicting the findings of science? By reaffirming, again and again, the old basic principles, which do not give credit to human autonomy and responsibility, which neither offer a credible theodicy nor integrate the basic insights of modern science and cosmology, the church betrays the intelligence of modern men and women and allows them to fall into unbelief. Indeed, the crisis of religion is due not only to the fact that modern man refuses to believe in God but also, and to a large extent, because the church does not speak about God in a way that modern people can understand and accept. To say the least, it is unintelligible to many theologians, catechists, sociologists, and anthropologists that, for example, the new insights of process-theology were not used to reformulate some basic problems of Catholic theology and ethics in the new *Geloofsboek*.[63]

Of course, both the Belgian and the Dutch church are in a precarious position. They not only lack a numerically strong priesthood but there are also indications that the intellectual level of the church's recruitment is much lower than three and more decades ago. This may have made them less vigorous and intellectually dynamic churches in recent times. On the other hand, a new dynamism is demonstrable: permanent deacons are now ordained, sisters and lay people are becoming more and more engaged in pastoral work. The latter are sometimes called pastoral workers, pastoral helpers, or catechists. The situation differs from diocese to diocese. In the Netherlands, in six out of seven dioceses, the bishop has nominated pastoral workers; in Belgium, there are pastoral workers in only a few dioceses. In 1986, 392 pastoral workers were engaged by the Dutch bishops, 2.5 times more than in 1976. Of these, 21 percent were women, compared to only 8 percent in 1976. In 1984, nearly 60 percent were younger than forty. In 1986, thirty-six permanent deacons were also working in the Dutch church; the first was ordained in 1974.[64]

In Belgium, permanent deacons have been ordained since 1970; in the last fifteen years 304 were ordained and 95 are still in training.[65] Three out of four permanent deacons are engaged in pastoral work in parishes. A large number are engaged in pastoral activities in their workplace, for example; in schools; and some work in familial and charismatic groups or do pastoral work in hospitals and prisons.

In all dioceses, sisters and lay people help in parishes (as members of the parish council, a catechetic team, a liturgical work group or a meditation group, in youth movements), and in pastoral teams in hospitals, old people's homes, and schools. In several dioceses, special education programs were set up to give them some pastoral and religious training and theological schooling. These programs run from one and a half to two years, and are regionally organized. In the diocese of Ghent, for example, more than 200 people have participated in such programs since 1983; in the diocese of Bruges, more than 1,200 people have participated in five different programs organized since 1976.

But it seems that the church is still not using the full potential of its constituency. Although the number of priests and seminarians is down, a large number of people still study theology or religion. The number of these people also declined in Catholic and Protestant colleges in Belgium in the critical period 1967-1973, but since then it has grown higher than before that period.[66] Since 1975 the number of students enrolled in religious studies at the Catholic University of Leuven has been three to four times higher than in the mid-1960s (see Table 4.10).

We may hypothesize that, since the number of seminarians has remained at about the same level since 1973, many of these students in religious studies would likely have entered the seminaries or religious life in another sociocultural and church climate. Indeed, in a colloquium organized by the Theological Circle of the Catholic University of Leuven, these students expressed the desire to do pastoral work.[67] Until now, they were mostly employed in secondary schools to teach religion. The sudden reduction of the enrollment in 1986-1987, suggests that for lack of pastoral jobs, the enrollment figures follow the actual downward trend of the market for all teaching positions.

In the Netherlands, the number of students studying theology in Catholic colleges was 1,225 in 1970 and 1,216 in 1985. However, the number of women enrolled went up in the same period from 6 to 44 percent. In 1985, 611 additional students were enrolled in programs preparing for a teaching position, and 48 percent of these were women.[68]

The above data suggest that new forms of involvement in the church are viable: pastoral workers and lay people engage in parish work. This type of voluntary work, as compared to the United States, is largely underdeveloped in all sectors in Belgium. In some parishes, priests still do not work with lay volunteers; either they are psychologically not ready for it or they have difficulty in recruiting people to help them, especially in those parishes where not even 10 percent are practicing Catholics.

This points up again the enormous problem of professionally supporting lay volunteers. Why does the church not use more of those university students who studied religion and theology in other than teaching positions? Are some bishops and priests afraid of their more critical attitude and greater independence? Or is "tradition" so important that it can outweigh the "spiritual and religious needs" of the people? One

TABLE 4.10   Number of First-Year Students in the Religious Studies Department at the Catholic University of Leuven

PERIOD	NUMBER	PERIOD	AVERAGE NUMBER PER YEAR
1975-76	84	1975-79	110
1980-81	124	1980-85	113
1985-86	109		

wonders if there is any surviving organization that has neglected the professional support of volunteers to the same extent as the Catholic church has up to now.

These and similar problems have often been formulated in different councils. But as pointed out when discussing the Dutch *Landelijk Pastoraal Overleg,* such structures are not policy-forming organs: they are places of deliberation and dialogue. Indeed, the church has always confirmed its hierarchical structure and the difference in competence between lay people, priests, and bishops. In Belgium, such councils exist on the level of the parish, the deanery, and diocese, and the regions. They were established to underscore the co-responsibility of members of the church. On the diocesan level there is a pastoral and a presbyteral council. H. De Wachter and L. Voyé have studied the councils on this level and have analyzed their regulations, functions, and the topics discussed. The so-called co-responsibility was understood by bishops as purely advisory, although, especially in the initial period, members tried to extend this limited interpretation. Unsuccessful, many members felt deceived and quit. De Wachter also indicates that no specific domain for advice was reserved for these councils: they were merely added to already existing diocesan bodies. Moreover, as Voyé makes clear, no rule determined the respective attributions of the presbyterial and pastoral councils, so most of the time they discussed the same themes, although the presbyteral councils were more interested in internal church matters and the pastoral councils looked at the relations between church and world.[69]

Typical for Belgium is the existence of regional councils. The *Conseil Général de l'Apostolat des Laïcs,* until the autumn of 1985 a representative organ of the French-speaking apostolic movements in Belgium, was reorganized to become more like the Flemish council, *Het Interdiocesaan Pastoraal Beraad* (Interdiocesan Pastoral Deliberation). In 1970, the IPB was institutionalized as the highest organ of deliberation and dialogue of the Flemish church community. It meets three weekends a year, and is qualified to discuss all matters of pastoral policy and the relations between church and world. It advises the church hierarchy and sensitizes the Flemish Catholic community about important problems. Recent topics of discussion have included the catechetic support of the adults, politics and church, the cooperation between men and women in church and society, tendencies of polarization in the church and their pastoral implications, pastoral care for the sick and dying, requirements for a vital Europe, peace and détente, marriage and the family, youth and faith, co-responsibility in the church, and new functions and services in the church.

According to an internal IPB working document, the crucial problems IPB faces are "its competence and its exact position within the church."[70] IPB sees positive but also negative indications as far as the "openness and confidence" of the bishops are concerned. Cardinal Godfried Danneels has always taken seriously the suggestions and recommendations of IPB on the theme of the bishops' synods in his written and oral reports. On the other hand, the bishops sometimes publish "pastoral letters" that "take IPB completely by surprise" and that attest to a lack of consideration for the work already done by IPB on the topic, especially the letters on "crisis and employment" (1980) and "the new evangelization" (1985). Many important recommendations the IPB sends to the bishops never receive a reply, for example, those about a new catechetical approach for adults, the position of women in the church, and the pastoral support of divorced parishioners.

The attitude and answers of the bishops to these critical comments reveal the precarious juridical position of IPB within the church. IPB relates to the conference of the Flemish bishops but, according to the regulations of the church, episcopal conferences have only limited power. Individual bishops take pastoral options, and juridically they depend directly on Rome. For the bishops, IPB serves as a barometer of what lives in the church, but for all important questions, they refer to their own special committees and experts.

It is clear that certain problems exceed the jurisdiction of the local church: the position of women in the church, married priests, and the position of an organ like IPB, which considers itself co-responsible for the church. Relations between IPB, diocesan councils, and "other" advisers in the church are ill-defined. Finally, the bishops seem to expect unanimous decisions from lay representatives. This suggests that they still do not take pluriformity in the church seriously. Such an attitude is strange from persons who themselves are not in agreement on all matters. This became patently manifest in IPB itself, when one bishop left IPB as it started discussing *Humanae Vitae,* and the other bishops stayed. The only acceptable function of councils that church authorities will accept seems to be to inform them about problems and issues in the church. Once these are "detected," the authorities make decisions, using recommendations taken from "secret" experts and committees. Such secret consultations may even go on until the recommendations fit the "tradition" of the church. How long will seriously concerned lay people continue "playing barometer"?

Conclusions

In the first part of this chapter I argued that functional differentiation and its concomitant processes have secularized society and that pillarization, as a defensive mechanism, could not withstand the same processes. The changes were written according to different scenarios in the Netherlands and in Belgium, depending upon the social circumstances: religious pluralism versus religious duopoly. The Catholic pillar either was eroded through mergers or church religiosity became marginalized within the pillar and was replaced as a sacred canopy by a new collective consciousness. Both types of pillar were desacralized. The personnel of the pillar also progressively protected their individual freedom with concepts typical of a functionally differentiated society: the so-called private–public dichotomy, which stands for "inclusion." Consequently, structurally and culturally, the Low Countries became more and more secularized, even in their "Christian structures" (the pillars).

In the second part of the chapter we analyzed Luhmann's hypothesis: "the social structure is secularized, but not so individuals." The available data do not confirm this hypothesis in the Netherlands and Belgium. Human consciousness has also changed in response to the increasingly rational and societalized patterns of behavior in the different societal subsystems. Consequently, on the individual level, life is increasingly compartmentalized and religion is marginalized. A growing number of people have become less and less involved in the church, even if they stayed in it. They attend church only on religious holidays and when taking up important positions. For them, religion is a meaning system, giving meaning and unity to their compartmentalized lives. Others have become unchurched. Since this change is generational, we may expect the decline to go on for about another decade.

Both churches have accommodated differently to this new situation. The Dutch church has manifestly tried to adapt to the secularized and pluriform world, whereas the Belgian church has done so rather latently. It is clear that Rome has used all its power through canonical rules, regulations, and appointments to confirm traditional teachings and church hierarchy. Even "pastoral" bishops cannot mend the intellectual problems raised by such a policy; neither are they in a position to take lay people seriously. Certain reactions of "progressive" bishops even suggest their own fear of lay co-responsibility in pastoral service and councils.

It is my conviction, however, based on an analysis of current research data, that the crisis of religion is also partly due to the fact that the church does not speak about God in a way modern people can understand and accept. Modern people take seriously their God-given mission to create culture. They seem to expect that the church should do the same in its teachings and its decision-making structures. They do not understand the sole importance of "tradition" if the future of humankind is at stake. They cannot work in an "aristocratic" church where only the nobility (bishops and priests) decide, since they are used to democracy. If Rome cares only for "tradition" and "power," then it seems to have forgotten that religion is about people and their God, about a Christian praxis and not about "sacred texts" and "hierarchy." Are local bishops ready to accept this challenge and to become "permissive yet decisive" reformers?

NOTES

1. Jean Stoetzel, *Les valeurs du temps présent: une enquête européenne* (Paris: Presses Universitaires de France, 1983).
2. Franz-Xaver Kaufmann, *Kirche begreifen: Analysen und Thesen zur gesellschaftlichen Verfassung des Christentums* (Freiburg: Herder, 1979); and Karl Gabriel and Franz-Xaver Kaufmann (eds.), *Zur Soziologie des Katholizismus* (Mainz: Matthias-Grünewald Verlag, 1980).
3. Karel Dobbelaere, "Secularization Theories and Sociological Paradigms: Convergences and Divergences," *Social Compass* 31 (1984):119-219.
4. Niklas Luhmann, *Funktion der Religion* (Frankfurt: Suhrkamp Verlag, 1977), pp. 232-48.
5. For a more detailed exposition of Luhmann's ideas, see, e.g., Karel Dobbelaere, "Secularization Theories and Sociological Paradigms: A Reformulation of the Private-Public Dichotomy and the Problem of Societal Integration," *Sociological Analysis* 46 (1985):378-83.
6. See, e.g., J. P. Kruijt et al., *Verzuiling* (Zaandijk: Heijnis, 1959), pp. 9-12.
7. See, e.g., H. P. C. M. Van Schendelen (ed.), "Consociationalism, Pillarization and Conflict-Management in the Low Countries," *Acta Politica* 19 (1984):7-178.
8. In Belgium the Catholic Pillar is the most autarkic. It embraces the majority of schools (from kindergarten to university), hospitals, old people's homes, youth movements, cultural associations, sports clubs, newspapers, magazines, book clubs, and libraries. It also has a health insurance fund, trade union, and political party, the Christian People's Party (*Christelijke Volkspartij,* or C.V.P.). Although since 1945 this party has officially been nondenominational, it continues to play a central role in organized Catholicism. The Catholic pillar provides almost all possible services

from the cradle to the grave. A Catholic can be born in a Catholic hospital, attend Catholic schools, organize his vacation through a Catholic travel agency, have dental care in a Catholic clinic, save in a Catholic bank, be informed by Catholic newspapers. Socialist and Liberal pillars provide fewer services, do not have their own schools, and have only few hospital facilities, relying rather on state schools and state hospitals. But they have their own mass media (newspapers and magazines), health insurance fund, trade union, and political party.

9. Walter Goddijn, *Katholieke minderheid en Protestantse dominant* (Assen: Van Gorcum, 1957); R. Steininger, "Pillarization *(Verzuiling)* and Political Parties," *Sociologische Gids* 24 (1977):242-57; Jaak Billiet, "Beschouwingen over het samengaan van secularisatie en verzuiling," *De Nieuwe Maand* 19 (1976):244-57.

10. Hans Righart, *De katholieke zuil in Europa: Een vergelijkend onderzoek naar het ontstaan van verzuiling onder Katholieken in Oostenrijk, Zwitserland, België en Nederland* (Meppel: Boom, 1986), p. 274.

11. Stein Rokkan, "Towards a Generalized Concept of 'Verzuiling': A Preliminary Note," *Political Studies* 25 (1977):563-70.

12. For a description of pillarization in the Netherlands in the 1950s, see John A. Coleman, *The Evolution of Dutch Catholicism, 1958-1974* (Berkeley: University of California, 1978), pp. 67-77.

13. J. M. G. Thurlings, *De wankele zuil: Nederlandse katholieken tussen assimilatie en pluralisme,* 2nd ed. (Deventer: Van Loghum Slaterus, 1978), pp. 210-18.

14. Thurlings, *De wankele zuil,* pp. 182-209 and 218-25; F. Van Heek, *Van hoog kapitalisme naar verzorgingsstaat: Een halve eeuw sociale verandering, 1920-1970* (Meppel: Boom, 1973); David Martin, *A General Theory of Secularization* (Oxford: Blackwell, 1978), pp. 115, 189-90; Coleman, *The Evolution of Dutch Catholicism,* pp. 80-86; Leo Laeyendecker, "Soziologie des Katholizismus in den Niederlanden," in Gabriel and Kaufmann (eds.), *Zur Soziologie des Katholizismus,* pp. 191-92.

15. Karel Dobbelaere, "Religious Situation of Catholics in Belgium: The Secularization of Flanders," and Liliane Voyé, "Situation des Catholiques en Belgique: De l'adhésion ecclésiale au catholicisme socio-culturelle en Wallone," *Actes 15ème Conférence Internationale de Sociologie Religieuse: Religion et politique* (Lille: CISR, 1979), pp. 273-92 and 295-322; Karel Dobbelaere and Jaak Billiet, "Les changements internes au pilier catholique en Flandre: D'un catholicisme d'église à une chrétienté socioculturelle," *Recherches Sociologiques* 14 (1983):141-57; Jaak Billiet and Luc Huyse, "Verzorgingsstaat en verzuiling: een dubbelzinnige relatie," *Tijdschrift voor Sociologie* 5 (1984):131-38.

16. For a discussion of the recent developments of sociocultural Christianity and a comparison with American civil religion, see Karel Dobbelaere, "Sociaal-culturele Christenheid en publieke religie: een vergelijking," *Tijdschrift voor Sociologie* 7 (1986):653-79; translated "Chrétienté socio-culturelle et religion civile: essai d'étude comparative," in Roberto Cipriani and Maria I. Macioti (eds.), *Omaggio a Franco Ferrarotti* (Rome: Ed. SIARES, 1987).

17. For a more elaborate argumentation, see Karel Dobbelaere, "Professionalization and Secularization in the Belgain Catholic Pillar," *Japanese Journal of Religious Studies* 6 (1979):49-55.

18. Ibid., 55-58.

19. See for a discussion of these problems ibid., 54-55; Karel Dobbelaere, "Contradictions Between Expressive and Strategic Language in Policy Documents of Catholic Hospitals and Welfare Organizations: Trials Instead of Liturgies as Means of Social Control." *The Annual Review of the Social Sciences of Religion* 6 (1982):117-18 and 121-23; Dobbelaere, "Het kristelijk karakter van de verzorgingsinstellingen: konfessionele definitie of utopie?" *Kultuurleven* 51 (1984):237-43.

20. Karel Dobbelaere, "Organizing Christian Values in Social Organizations: The Case of Catholic Hospitals in Belgium," *Social Studies: Irish Journal of Sociology* 2 (1973):475-83; Dobbelaere et al., "Secularization and Pillarization: A Social Problem Approach," *The Annual Review of the Social Sciences of Religion* 2 (1978):108-111; Dobbelaere, "De crisissituatie is eerder deshumaniserend want veelal bureaucratisch en commercieel," in Verbond der Verzorgingsinstellingen (ed.), *Verzorgingsinstellingen doorheen de crisis* (Brussels: Licap, 1984), pp. 169-73.

21. Dobbelaere and Billiet, "Les changements internes," pp. 175-79; Karel Dobbelaere, "De katholieke zuil nu: desintegratie en integratie," *Belgisch Tijdschrift voor Nieuwste Geschiedenis* 13 (1982):151-57; Dobbelaere, "Contradictions," p. 125.

22. Ibid., pp. 124-26.

23. Jaak Billiet and Karel Dobbelaere, "Vers une désinstitutionalisation du pilier chrétien?" in Liliane Voyé et al. (eds.), *La Belgique et ses Dieux* (Louvain-la-Neuve: Cabay, 1985), pp. 136-48.

24. Bryan Wilson, "Secularization: The Inherited Model," in Phillip E. Hammond (ed.), *The Sacred in the Secular Age* (Berkeley: University of California Press, 1985), p. 19.

25. Luhmann, *Funktion der Religion*, p. 172.

26. Karel Dobbelaere, "Some Trends in European Sociology of Religion: The Secularization Debate," *Sociological Analysis* 48 (Summer 1987):107-137.

27. H. Faber and T. T. Ten Have, *Ontkerkelijking en buitenkerkelijkheid in Nederland, tot 1960* (Assen: Van Gorcum, 1970), p. 28.

28. J. Oudhof, "Kerkelijke gezindten in 1984," *Sociaal-Cultureel Kwartaalbericht* 7 (1985), p. 16.

29. J. Oudhof and G. C. N. Beets, "Kerkelijke gezindten in Nederland, 1971-'81," *Sociaal-Cultureel Kwartaalbericht* 4 (1984):12.

30. Oudhof, "Kerkelijke gezindten in 1984," p. 16.

31. Karel Dobbelaere, "La religion en Belgique," in J. Kerkhofs and R. Rezsohazy (eds.), *L'univers des Belges: Valeurs anciennes et valeurs nouvelles dans les années 80* (Louvain-la-Neuve: Ciaco, 1984), pp. 78-82.

32. I arrived at similar figures using data from surveys. See Karel Dobbelaere, "Vrijzinnigheid, kerkelijkheid en kerksheid in een geseculariseerde wereld: grensvervaging of nieuwe grenzen?" *Tijdschrift voor de Studie van de Verlichting en het Vrije Denken,* 14-15 (1986-1987):283-311.

33. For more details, see Dobbelaere, "La religion en Belgique," pp. 70-75 and 86-96; Dobbelaere, "La Dominante Catholique," in Voyé et al. (eds.), *La Belgique et ses Dieux,* pp. 200-203.

34. Ruud De Moor, "Religieuze en morele waarden," in Loek Halman et al., *Traditie, secularisatie en individualisering: Een studie naar de waarden van de Nederlanders in een Europese context* (Tilburg: Tilburg University Press, 1987), pp. 31, 38-39, and 45.

35. My interpretation that age refers to "generational differences" and not to the impact of the "life cycle" is based on successive data on church attendance in Belgium (Dobbelaere, "La religion en Belgique," p. 106), confirmed by data from Dutch studies: W. Goddijn et al., *Opnieuw: God in Nederland. Onderzoek naar godsdienst en kerkelijkheid ingesteld in opdracht van KRO en Weekblad De Tijd* (Amsterdam: De Tijd, 1979), p. 70 and A. Felling et al., "Gebroken identiteit: Een studie over christelijk en onchristelijk Nederland," in Katholiek Documentatie Centrum (ed.), *Jaarboek 1981* (Nijmegen: KDC, 1981), p. 71.

36. For more details, see Dobbelaere, "La religion en Belgique," pp. 103-108.

37. See also Bryan Wilson, "Aspects of Secularization in the West," *Japanese Journal of Religious Studies* 3 (1976):273; Wilson, *Religion in Sociological Perspective*

(Oxford: Oxford University Press, 1982), pp. 27-32; and Martin, *A General Theory of Secularization,* pp. 160-61.

38. Luhmann, *Funktion der Religion,* pp. 227-28.
39. Mady A. Thung et al., *Exploring the New Religious Consciousness: An Investigation of Religious Change by a Dutch Working Group* (Amsterdam: Free University Press, 1985), p. 147.
40. Ibid., pp. 112-13; 157-59, and 194-95; Felling et al., "Identitätswandel in den Niederlanden," *Kölner Zeitschrift für Soziologie und Sozialpsychologie* 34 (1982):26-53; Felling et al., *Burgerlijk en onburgerlijk Nederland: Een nationaal onderzoek naar waardenoriëntaties op de drempel van de jaren tachtig* (Deventer: Van Loghum Slaterus, 1983), pp. 144-47.
41. A. Felling et al., *Geloven en Leven: Een nationaal onderzoek naar de invloed van religieuze overtuigingen* (Zeist: Kerckebosch, 1986), p. 76; De Moor, "Religieuze en morele waarden," p. 47.
42. M. M. J. Van Hemert, *"En zij verontschuldigen zich ...": De ontwikkeling van het misbezoekcijfer 1966-79* (The Hague: KASKI, 1980), pp. 10-11.
43. Andrew M. Greeley et al., *Catholic Schools in a Declining Church* (Kansas City: Sheed & Ward, 1976), pp. 103-154.
44. Thurlings, *De wankele zuil,* pp. 210-18.
45. Karel Dobbelaere et al., "Dimensies in de houding van professoren tegenover het katholiek karakter van hun universiteit," *Kultuurleven* 43 (1976):880.
46. For a revealing discussion of this cultural change, see Paul Yonnet, *Jeux, modes et masses: La société française et le moderne, 1945-1985* (Paris: Gallimard, 1985).
47. K. Matthijs, *Hertrouw in België: Een sociaal-demografisch profiel van recente ontwikkelingen* (Leuven: Sociologisch Onderzoeksinstituut, 1986). For a broad discussion of these trends, see Louis Roussel, "Uue nouvelle révolution démographique," in S. Feld and R. Lesthaeghe (eds.), *Demografie en toekomstverkenning* (Brussels: Koning Boudewijnstichting, 1984), pp. 143-57.
48. R. Rezsohazy, "Le religion des jeunes," in Voyé et al. (eds.), *La Belgique et ses Dieux,* pp. 278-79.
49. Walter Van Trier, *Een sociologisch onderzoek naar enkele facetten van de moderne landbouw* (Leuven: Departement Sociologie, 1986), pp. 195-211.
50. Thomas Luckmann, *Invisible Religion: The Problem of Religion in Modern Societies* (New York: Macmillan, 1967), pp. 95-96.
51. Robert Wuthnow, *The Consciousness Reformation* (Berkeley: University of California Press, 1976), p. 77.
52. KASKI, *Statistics 1986; 121 Informatiebulletin* 14 (1986); H. F. Van Zoelen, *Analyse van het actieve Nederlandse priesterbestand (seculier zowel als regulier) per 1 januari 1982* (The Hague: KASKI, 1983). Liliane Voyé, "Aspects de l'évolution récente du 'Monde Catholique'," *Courrier Hebdomadaire du CRISP* 925-26 (June 26, 1981), pp. 11-25; Pierre Delooz, "Vocations sacerdotales et religieuses," in Voyé et al. (eds.), *La Belgique et ses Dieux,* pp. 221-31; and Karel Dobbelaere, "Enkele demografische en sociologische bedenkingen bij het dalend aantal priesters in de Vlaamse bisdommen," *Collationes* (1976):91-114.
53. Delooz, "Vocations sacerdotales," p. 242.
54. Dobbelaere, "Enkele demografische bedenkingen," p. 98.
55. Coleman, *The Evolution of Dutch Catholicism;* W. Goddijn, *The Deferred Revolution: A Social Experiment in Church Innovation in Holland 1960-1970* (Amsterdam: Elsevier, 1974).
56. Coleman, *The Evolution of Dutch Catholicism* pp. 260, 297.
57. For a broader historical analysis, see also Laeyendecker, "Soziologie des Katholizismus."

58. Coleman, *The Evolution of Dutch Catholicism,* pp. 99-101.

59. Ibid., pp. 232-37, 247-59.

60. Ibid., p. 251.

61. Ibid., pp. 257-59.

62. See also R. G. W. Huysmans, "1964-1984: Twintig jaar structurering van de leiding der kerkprovincie in Nederland: Een rechtskroniek—ook een tragiek?" in Philippe Stouthard and Gerard Van Tillo (eds.), *Katholiek Nederland na 1945* (Baarn: Ambo, 1985), pp. 49-50.

63. Many theologians and philosophers have introduced process-thinking in Catholic theological, catechetic, philosophical, and cultural journals and magazines all over the world. In Flanders: J. Van der Veken in *Tijdschrift voor Theologie* 18 (1978), *Collationes* (1978), and *Kultuurleven* 45 (1978); A. R. Van de Walle, Wim Thys, en Michel Van Bosstraeten in *Korrel* 8 (1986): "God!? Wie bedoel jij?"; G. De Schrijver in *Communio* (1979) and M. Wildiers, *Wereldbeeld en theologie van de middeleeuwen tot vandaag* (Antwerpen/Amsterdam: Standaard Wetenschappelijke Uitgeverij, 1973). See, worldwide, *Concilium; Process Studies;* the studies of Charles Hartshorne and A. N. Whitehead; and introductory and systematic studies by Joseph A. Bracken, D. Brown, John B. Cobb, Jr., E. H. Cousins, David R. Griffin, J. and G. Reeves, I. Leclerc, Robert B. Mellert, Schubert Ogden, etcetera.

64. KASKI, *Statistics, 1986; 121 Informatiebulletin,* December 5, 1986; and M. M. J. Van Hemert, *Permanente diakens en pastorale werkers en werksters per 1 Januari 1984* (The Hague: KASKI, September 1984).

65. A. Vanden Avenne, "Les diacres permanents en Belgique," in *Radioscopie de l'Eglise Catholique en Belgique* (Brussels: Licap, 1985), p. 90.

66. Dobbelaere, "Enkele demografische en sociologische bedenkingen," p. 110.

67. J. Kerkhofs and L. Steppe (eds.), *Laat mijn volk gaan, kerkopbouw van onderuit* (Antwerpen/Amsterdam: Patmos, 1975).

68. Marie-José Angenent-Vogt, *Enkele tendenzen met betrekking tot de kerkelijke participatie van de vrouw in Nederland* (The Hague: KASKI, 1981), pp. 13-14, and H. F. Van Zoelen, *Statistiek Priester- en Diakenopleidingen, Katholieke Theologische Faculteiten en Hogescholen, Opleiding Godsdienstleraar in Nederland per 1-1-1985* (The Hague: KASKI, 1986), p. 5.

69. Hilde De Wachter, "De pastorale raden in de Vlaamse bisdommen: Een overzicht (1968-1976)," *Collationes* (1977), pp. 461-477; De Wachter, "Tien jaar werking van pastorale raden in de Vlaamse bisdommen," *Politica* 27 (1977), pp. 331-63; Liliane Voyé, "Les conseils presbytéraux et pastoraux diocésains," in Voyé et al. (eds.), *La Belgique et ses Dieux,* pp. 233-54.

70. Interdiocesaan Pastoraal Beraad, *De dialoog tussen bisschoppen en leken georganiseerd door het IPB: Een evaluerende studie* (Contribution of IPB to the European Forum on "The dialogue in the church, 20 years after Vatican II," Paris, July 1986).

5

Authority, Change, and Conflict in Italian Catholicism

Paul F. Furlong

In 1962 Italian Catholicism had already undergone recent profound change, and was about to undergo more; but the face it presented to the outside observers bidden to Rome for the Second Vatican Council was that of a powerful conservative institution which so far had successfully withstood the political, socioeconomic, and cultural change of the postwar period. Both through the number of Italian bishops in attendance and through its weight in the Roman Curia, the Italian church was widely expected to ensure that the Council's proceedings would reinforce the prudence, firmness, and confident authority that were its outward characteristics. Neither the public image, if such it was, nor the expectation of future success was accurate. In this as in some other features, the Italian church was similar to Italy's political institutions with whose development it had been closely involved.

The Italian Church Before the Council

The basis for the parallel development of Italy's political and religious institutions was laid down even before the end of World War II, when the Italian church successfully disengaged itself from its record of cooperation with the discredited fascist regime and established itself as the major if not only domestic obstacle to the forward march of communism in Italy. Apart from the ideological conflict with the communists and the left, the Vatican had important interests to protect in the shape of the privileges and guarantees enshrined in the Lateran Pacts agreed to in 1929 with the fascist regime. The Pacts resolved the long territorial dispute between the Holy See

116

and the Italian state; they also gave the Vatican immunity from taxation on share-holdings in Italy, and gave legal recognition to the church's enormous resources in welfare and education. The protection of these gains was a central objective for the Vatican in the immediate postwar period.[1]

The church also sought in various ways to strengthen its positive impact in Italian political and social development, and to ensure that such development occurred in directions that were at least consonant with the church's teaching. Part of this political strategy relied on maintaining close relations with the Christian Democratic Party (DC), in government uninterruptedly since 1945, but another important aspect was the support of the Vatican for the Western alliance. Neither of these two components in the general pattern should be regarded as inevitable or uncontested. The Vatican came to support the emerging DC party only after Pope Pius XII and the Curia's senior officials had been persuaded that a more unambiguously anticommunist and conservative grouping than the DC would have little chance of immediate success and might split the Catholic electorate. Papal support for the DC and for its first leader, Alcide de Gasperi, was fraught with conflict, particularly over the issues of lay independence and coalition strategy. The relationship between Pius XII and Gasperi, far from ripening into the mature mutual respect that some might have hoped for, worsened rapidly after the elections of 1948, so that in 1952 Pius XII came close to a complete break with the DC. This was the occasion of "Operation Sturzo," when the Vatican and right-wing Catholic interests in Rome planned to have the former leader of the Popular Party, Don Luigi Sturzo, appointed mayor of Rome with the help of votes from the neo-fascist Italian Social Movement (MSI) and from the Monarchist party. The authoritarian right-wing coalition favored by Pius XII was not a realistic option either politically or numerically, but the pope remained thoroughly dissatisfied with the centrist policies followed by de Gasperi.

Vatican support for NATO and for United States policy in Europe was initially hesitant both because of the established neutrality of the Holy See in modern international affairs and because of well-founded fears for the effect of the church's international strategy on Catholics in Eastern Europe and the Soviet Union. Here once again the strategy that emerged was formed by a variety of factors ranging from the parochial to the international. Pope Pius XII appears to have been seriously concerned for the future of the city of Rome under supposed threat from Italian or foreign communist forces, and at the more general level was appalled by the wartime devastation of Western Europe, which he feared also offered fertile ground for the church's opponents. The traditional rhetoric of the papacy has emphasized that the only true and lasting peace in international affairs lies in following Christian teachings, that this applies to all countries and regions, and that the church stands above all regional and national power groupings precisely because its message has to be accessible to all. While this theme remains a constant feature of papal diplomacy, it was mitigated in practice in the later years of Pius XII by formal and informal support for the Western alliance as a bulwark against international communism, support first elicited by President Harry S. Truman in an exchange of letters with Pius XII in 1949. Though there was significant support on the left of the Italian Christian Democratic Party for more neutralist policies, the combined impact of U.S. aid, Vatican pressure, and domestic coalition demands were sufficient to quell dissenters at least during the crucial period in which the structures of postwar politics were being laid down.

But the Vatican has never in modern times been the sole arbiter of developments in Italian Catholicism. Though now it may be a commonplace to emphasize the plurality of cultures and practices within and among national Catholic churches, it has not always been so, and the Italian Catholic church has been misinterpreted more widely than most on this account. Italian Catholics in the early 1960s could claim vigor, imagination, and a wide diversity of views; what they could not claim was institutional expression of their diversity or free rein for their creative energies. Development since the ending of the Council has been characterized by the gradual breakup of the old institutionalized certainties and their replacement by the de facto recognition of differing expressions of Catholic morality. The development has taken some perhaps surprising turns and has often left progressives and conservatives alike dissatisfied, even bemused by the unexpected results of changes they have initially welcomed or spurned.

The most obvious expression of diversity in Italian Catholicism throughout the postwar period has been in its regionalism. The cultures and practices of Catholicism differ widely between that of the less developed south and those of the other areas, and in the other areas the levels of religious practice vary not only between regions but also between city and countryside. In its forms of religious practice, the *Mezzogiorno,* Italy's south, has often been regarded as both more traditional, more Tridentine in its formal appearances, and more prone to anarchic populism than the wealthier, more industrialized north and center.

The relationship of religion to politics in the south is complex, and has fundamentally affected the development of party politics because of the social authority of the clergy and their role in the patronage networks of politics.[2] In the postwar period, none of the political parties and associational groups that are the accoutrements of modern industrialized democracies have found it easy to organize in the conventional manner in these areas. Gross underemployment, land hunger, unstable landholding patterns, the traditional localism, and suspicion of national politics and national institutions of all kinds have militated against the integration of the south into the developing national culture. On the other hand, the extension of compulsory national insurance and nationwide health schemes, the use of public resources to encourage industrial investment and modernization of agriculture, and the development of a social infrastructure in the 1950s and 1960s gave rise, among other things, to the phenomenon of more modern forms of clientelism. These were based primarily on mass benefits, mediated through national politicians as well as or even instead of the local notables. The crucial role of the local clergy in presenting a substitute state structure in the south was therefore diminished both by the extension of the welfare capacity of the national state and by the development of a mass centrist party, the DC, which was able to mobilize alternative sources of support as well as that of the church in the south.

In the south, therefore, the extraordinary economic growth of the immediate postwar years certainly affected levels of religious practice and altered the relationship of the clergy to the laity, but it did so in ways that allowed and even encouraged the fragmentation of institutions and communities. Elsewhere in Italy also, the nationalization of politics associated with economic development did not erode the localisms of which religion was such an important part; rather it could be said to have adapted and integrated them into a national culture, which for the reasons already described has remained loose-knit and far from uniform. The associational strength of the DC relied particularly on the traditional Catholicism of the Veneto in the Northeast, of the northern areas of Lombardy such as Bergamo, and of the border region of Trentino-South Tyrol. In regions such as these, the church provided a ready-made social base for the new Christian Democrats after the war. Under the Lateran Pacts, Catholic Action (*Azione Cattolica,* henceforth AC) had been allowed to operate during the fascist period, albeit with strict limitations, and its graduate section, FUCI, was the initial springboard for many of the younger leaders of the DC such as Aldo Moro and Giulio Andreotti. The principle of collateralism meant that lay Catholics were encouraged to involve themselves in associations and groups that had an explicit Catholic identity, preferably operating directly within the organizational structure of the church through Catholic Action. As well as the numerous AC groups active in a wide variety of social, educational, and welfare fields, other Catholic organizations developed to meet particular occupational needs.

Immediately after the war the Catholic Association of Italian Workers (ACLI) was established to give Catholic trade unionists and their organizations a discrete identity within the single, communist-dominated trade union confederation CGIL, but this was not sufficient to allay the fears of many Catholic activists and of the hierarchy; by 1949 there were three separate confederations, among them the Italian Confederation of Free Trade Unions (CISL), dominated by Catholic trade unionists. In agriculture in particular Catholic organizers were active in establishing occupational associations, cooperatives, and pension funds to take advantage of the extension of welfare benefits and subsidies provided by the state. The most influential of these in this period has undoubtedly been a small farmers group, the Association of Direct Cultivators (*Associazione Nazionale dei Coltivatori Diretti,* usually known simply as Coldiretti). The financial and organizational muscle of this group was such that it was regularly able to secure the election of significant numbers of DC deputies and senators and to dominate the Ministry of Agriculture and the permanent commissions on agriculture in Parliament. In the 1963 election Coldiretti was estimated to have helped elect over eighty deputies and over thirty senators, including its own long-serving national president, Paolo Bonomi. Though its scope has declined in recent years, it retains important influence within several DC factions; the "Friends of Coldiretti" group numbered twenty-eight deputies in the 1979–1983 legislature, and twenty-five in the 1983–1987 legislature.

These Catholic organizations fulfilled important functions both for the church and for the Christian Democratic Party in its early years of existence. For the church, they ensured that the Catholic population, which previously had lacked experience of mass organizations, were enrolled safely in ways that insulated them from communist influence and that gave the church grounds for expectation that the hierarchy and the Vatican would have direct leverage in the democratic development of Italy. For the DC, these subsidiary or collateral interest groups provided a ready-made source of party activists and potential candidates, organized at elections in the umbrella groups known as the Civic Committees. On the whole, the Vatican and senior Italian hierarchy were able to retain authority over the collateral organizations, but the extent of this control posed repeated problems for Christian Democratic politicians and leading lay Catholics, many of whom had been drawn into political and social activism not only by the encouragement of the papacy but also by the spread of newer Catholic social thinking about democracy and human rights. Associated in general with the development of neo-Thomism as a perhaps surprisingly fertile theological orthodoxy and in particular with the work of writers such as Jacques Maritain, these new trends allowed lay Catholics to see in political and social activity their own apostolate, and gave to such work a dignity and independence that had previously been largely absent. But between the doctrinal certainties of the later years of Pius XII and the pragmatic ambiguities of the DC party leaders, the lay apostolate found little room to flourish.[3]

The divisions beneath the surface, therefore, were not only due to regional imbalances or to occupational distinction but were also the result of profound disagreement about the scope and direction of Catholic activity in a rapidly changing society. The conflict showed itself most obviously in the emerging factionalism of the DC, where integralists and liberals came into conflict repeatedly with one another over the applicability of Catholic doctrine to the new political problems. Integralists were themselves divided over the proper extent and modes of papal involvement. Those on the left such as Amintore Fanfani wanted to be free to apply Catholic social doctrine integrally but according to their own best judgment, while others on the right such as Flaminio Piccoli and Antonio Segni regarded the most important aspects of the church's teaching as those requiring obedience to established authority and respect for traditional Catholic morality. Among the liberal Catholics could be found politicians who favored a return to free-market principles, such as Giulio Andreotti, and those who leaned toward more Keynesian strategies, such as Aldo Moro. The church hierarchy remained firmly in the grip of the traditionalists, in particular Cardinal Ottaviani, secretary of state to Pius XII, and Cardinal Siri, archbishop of Genoa and first president of the Italian Bishops' Conference, which was founded in 1958. With this leadership the bishops resisted the development of political dialogue with communists and socialists, and supported, albeit unsuccessfully, the rigorous application of the Papal Bull of 1949 excommunicating all members and supporters of these parties.

At times the Vatican and the senior bishops seemed to take an inordinate, even exclusive, interest in political aspects of their Italian pastoral activity. Certainly their perspective, which extended to papal concern for the results of local elections in major cities, was dominated by their concern to preserve the unity of Catholics within a single party and to keep the chosen instrument pliable to the demands of the church. In the first of these objectives they were successful only at the price of imposing an extraordinary heterogeneity on the DC, and in the latter the bishops found themselves competing with many other pressures, often unsuccessfully. But of course other issues did meet their attention, and found the same inflexible and sometimes self-defeating response, as the parochial clergy, the religious orders active in education and welfare, and the newly assertive laity sought to make sense of their role in a highly mobile, increasingly affluent industrialized society. Among such issues postponed rather than resolved were liturgical reform, reform of seminary education, the mission of worker-priests, and improvements in the administration of dioceses. The Italian church that faced the Second Vatican Council in 1962 was less than united, and had good reason for concern over its possible impact.

Secularization and Maturity

The Council marks a turning point in the development of the Italian church, but it should not be regarded as solely responsible for the painful changes that followed it. Perhaps the most direct way to demonstrate the extent of the changes would be to note the changes in religious practice. It is impossible to give a national average for Sunday observance, and the most that can be said is that all commentators concur in acknowledging a serious decline in religious practice. In this as in more public and obvious ways, Italy is no longer a Catholic country: the majority of the adult population no longer attends mass on Sundays with any significant degree of regularity, though many of the nonattenders would continue to describe themselves as Catholic, and baptism was until recently still almost universal for the newborn, whatever the religious status of the parents. Regional differences, reluctance of clergy and laity to cooperate, and profound disagreement over the proper way of measuring religious practice all make the assessment of even such an apparently simply matter as Sunday attendance difficult. No thorough and reliable national survey of attendance at Sunday mass is available: most surveys until recently have relied on estimates by the local clergy or head-counting at the church door by researchers, and even the 1973 national survey by the Bishops' Conference was unable to provide systematic evidence. Local surveys have found enormous disparities even within individual regions, and the most thorough of these, that by Burgalassi in the 1960s in communist-dominated Tuscany, found levels of Sunday observance ranging from 60 percent of the adult population in the "white enclave" of the province of Lucca to levels below 10 percent in the cities of Florence and Pisa.[4] Though reliable data are now beginning to become available, the lack of earlier records makes comparison over time hazardous, and one is compelled to rely, perhaps not too unhappily, on "harder" indirect data such as levels of civil marriage, separations, divorce, abortion, and, more directly, numbers of ordinations and numbers of priests.

The numbers of civil marriages as a proportion of all marriages remained static for many years after 1945 at about 4 percent.[5] For much of this time, the use of civil matrimony alone had been widely regarded as a form of militant anticonformism restricted to principled anticlericals. The use of religious matrimony was a symptom of a widespread secular conformism, and like the similarly extensive use of other religious rites of passage did not of itself seem to imply any commitment—formal, intellectual, or moral—to the community of the church. As in other Western European countries, the high levels of these very restricted forms of religious practice had little effect on the social influence exercised by nonreligious groups, foremost among them the Communist party. An anthropological study of a communist suburb of Bologna in the 1970s described this phenomenon in these terms: "the success of the church in retaining a near monopoly on rites of passage in the Communist *quartiere* [suburb] is not duplicated in the rites of the community. The traditional ritual expressions of local solidarity have largely been usurped and transformed by the Communist Party."[6] In many areas of course neither the Communist party nor the church had continuous influence of the kind implied in this description, and the widespread recourse to religious ceremonies was not matched by any countervailing or alternative collective moral symbols.

The point at which even this minimal religious practice began to decline seems to be about 1970 in the official statistics. In 1972 civil matrimonies stood at 7.8 percent of all matrimonies, and there has been a gradual increase in proportional terms since then, so that in 1985, the latest year for which figures are available, the equivalent figure was 14.2 percent. The regional levels vary considerably, from 5.6 percent in Puglia and Basilicata in the south to 24.7 percent in Liguria, the region around Genoa. At the same time, marriage ceremonies have diminished both in absolute numbers and as a proportion of the adult population (from about 750 per 100,000 inhabitants in 1972 to about 520 in 1985). During the same period the number of legal separations increased from 24.8 per 100,000 inhabitants in 1972 (13,493 in total) and now appears to be steady at about 59 per 100,000 (33,860 in 1985, 59.5 per 100,000 inhabitants); the availability of divorce since 1971 undoubtedly contributed to this increase, since the divorce procedure requires in virtually all cases a considerable period of legal separation. After an initial period in which the divorce courts had to settle many long-standing cases, the number of divorces also appears to have stabilized, at about 25 per 100,000 inhabitants.

The other major indicator of an increasingly secularized society is, of course, the occurrence of legal abortion. The abortion law, passed in 1978, contained a conscience clause which has been widely used by Catholics in the medical profession. A report to Parliament by the Minister of Health in 1986 estimated that 50.2 percent of all doctors in the appropriate specialties had used this provision. For this reason, as well as because of the shortage of funds for its application, the impact of the law has been extremely variable in different parts of the country, with higher levels of legal abortion in the regions of Liguria, Emilia Romagna, and Tuscany, and lower levels in the Veneto and in hinterland regions of the south. The number of legal abortions peaked at about 234,593 in 1982 and has diminished every year since to an estimated 210,192 in 1985. The same report gave approximate figures of 100,000 illegal abortions in 1985.

It would be hazardous to read large conclusions from these numbers. They can be interpreted restrictively in two ways. First, they indicate how much the formal structures of the state have been secularized, largely through the efforts of alternative elites which challenge the domination of the DC and of the church. These new elites are not generally inspired by antireligious motives as such, but rather are bent on the laicization of both society and the state, and include in their number significant proportions of active dissenting Catholics, both clergy and laity. Second, whereas in preconciliar Italy these apparent acts of overt disobedience to the institutional church were acts of defiance of a small minority, symbols of militant anticlericalism, they have now lost this heavy layer of meaning and are much more part of the generally accepted resources of a pluralist society. As is often the case, the confidence and militancy of the secularizing elites have stimulated opposition from some Catholic groups and have therefore served not to banish religious issues from the political agenda but to heighten their salience and encourage the formation of new religious alliances and groupings. These processes and groups will be considered later.

Numbers of ordinations and numbers of priests are more difficult to assess since official figures are not released. All may concur that the general trend is downward, but this is hardly illuminating and usually is based on little more than impression and hearsay. From a prewar base of 51,364 secular clergy in 1931, the church has been consistently unable to replace losses from death and laicization, and the survey by the Bishops' Conference previously referred to found that the number of secular clergy in Italy had declined from 43,071 in 1965 to 42,215 in 1971.[7] *Annuario Pontificio*, with less reliable data, lists a total of 41,711 for 1976, which is one for every 1,335 inhabitants.[8] This slow downward trend has certainly continued since then, but the Italian church is not yet at a stage where the numbers give cause for concern about the adequacy of the church's pastoral capacity in absolute terms. The trend is significant rather in relative terms as part of a general questioning of identity among the Italian clergy. For the conservative Italian church prior to the Council, the priest's activity had been restricted to his sacramental role, and formal teaching posts represented the major outlet for pastoral work. The emphasis on the ministry within the community that emerged from the Council therefore represented a radical change from accepted practice: much of the work that in Northern Europe or North America was assumed to be part of the priest's life had in Italy been left to the female religious orders and lay organizations. This was particularly so in the south, where the priest was traditionally a figure of authority set apart from the community and could not achieve closer involvement without the risk of scandal. Hence in the 1960s the church did not have a well-developed pastoral organization, and the implementation of recommendations on such matters as pastoral councils caused many priests to see themselves in a new light; the Council challenged Italian priests to take up tasks for which the narrow, highly theoretical, and rigid training of the seminary had not suited them.

The survey to which we have already referred was commissioned in 1971 by the Bishops' Conference, in an unprecedented effort that reflected the widespread concern about the weaknesses of the pastoral structures of the church. Though the survey was much criticized on methodological grounds, it provides a degree of insight into Italian pastoral practice, and its general conclusions represent the beliefs of an influential and authoritative section of the hierarchy at a period of great change for the church. These may be summarized as follows:

1. Italian pastoral practice was not sufficiently evangelical, and was too much directed toward practicing Catholics.
2. The content of pastoral teaching was too theoretical and did not try sufficiently to make Catholics aware of the demands of their faith in a "secular world."
3. Pastoral activity concentrated too much on three sectors, which were youth, the family, and the sacraments, to the exclusion of other sectors.
4. In general, pastoral practice was undoubtedly in a period of great experimentation, but at the time of the survey it was tied too closely to the parish, with little effort made outside the parochial structure (for example, in the workplace).[9]

The final paragraph of the report was gloomily emphatic:

Through the data collected in the investigation . . . it is not difficult to come to the conclusion that *the extent to which Italian pastoral practice effectively reaches adults and effectively deals with problems that concern the mentality and life of adults is small.*[10]

While the Italian bishops, some more reluctantly than others, were attempting to meet the demands of the Council in a society that was now more explicitly non-Christian, other members of the church's structure were under similar pressures and coming to sometimes very different conclusions.

The Papacy and the Emerging Pluralism

The policies of Pius XII in the Italian arena had been characterized by a traditional integralism, claiming a universal scope for his authority, using laity and clergy as direct instruments of his intentions, and expecting their obedience. Those of Paul VI were more modest in their expectations and more limited in their objectives. Though Paul VI was well acquainted with the inner workings of the Christian Democratic Party, during his reign the Vatican refrained from close involvement in Italian politics, and the pope's public interventions tended to occur in the form of statements of support for positions already adopted by the Italian Bishops' Conference. The Conference itself, though still organized on oligarchic principles, developed an independence of implementation under its new president, Cardinal Poletti, who as vicar-general of the diocese of Rome was also a close associate of Paul VI. Its statements on political issues were altogether less frequent, and showed a greater emphasis on the substantial issues of faith and morals than on the previous concerns of disciplined political unity and rigid lines of authority.

But though the Council was followed by great changes in Italy, these were not always in direct line with the Council's teaching. The institutional church was not suddenly opened up and revivified: the old structures were resilient and adaptive, and if outright opposition to *aggiornamento* was limited, there were many more in the Vatican and among Italian pastoral bishops whose priority was to restrain the processes of change and direct them toward less sensitive areas. The postconciliar church in Italy appeared beleaguered by the threats from internal dissent and external militancy. It was a church in the process of slow ideological adjustment, suffering assaults on its authority, increasingly aware of its minority position in Italian society, poorly organized to adapt to its new position, determined both to retain the institutional privileges that remained from its previous majority position and to maintain its political authority over the practicing Catholic faithful. This was not so much a church in crisis as a church detached from the crises of others around it and responding with the reflexes of a heavyweight brought out of retirement.

For laity and parochial clergy, the period immediately after the Council was one of great movement but also of great opportunity; it resulted in the emergence of a wide variety of responses to the conciliar recognition of pluralism and to the increasing confidence of the secularizing elites. More prosaically, the traditional lay groups were suffering continual loss of membership. Catholic Action claimed over 3 million members in 1960 but by 1970 was claiming 1,657,000, and by 1975 it had declined to 630,000. With branches in over 16,000 parishes in 1970, by 1975 AC was present in only 9,400 parishes.[11] In part this was the result of a deliberate attempt to narrow the scope of AC's work and to redirect it away from direct involvement in politics. In 1969, AC adopted new statutes, with the approval of the Vatican. These formally ended the collateral relationship with the DC and directed Catholic Action explicitly toward a more pastoral and less political mission. The Association of Catholic Workers (ACLI) declared itself "politically nonaligned" in the same year, and the Catholic Trade Union Confederation (CISL) began to work more closely with the other confederations in a manner that previously would have been unthinkable but that owed at least as much to the "hot autumn" in industrial relations in 1969 as it did to directly religious developments. The decision of Catholic Action to adopt a more neutral political position did not reflect a lack of concern about political issues. It was rather a consequence of a greater freedom of political expression among the laity, which with or without the consent of the local bishops allowed Catholics, clergy and laity, to find political outlets other than through the church's organizations and through a Christian Democratic party that could make little claim to have made Italy a more Catholic country in its long period of government.

The period produced the movement known as the *Comunità di Base,* "grass-roots" churches that occupied an uneasy position within the church as community but outside the institutional church. They were often closely involved in local political campaigns against the DC and local bishops. They were radical in their orientation not only toward society but also toward the church, challenging the church's attitude to contraception, to celibacy, to women's rights, to communism, and to social problems such as drug abuse and poverty. One of the best-known and longest-surviving of these was the Isolotto community in Florence, which came into constant conflict with the local hierarchy and which was evicted with the parish priest from the parish church. Another gathered around Don Giovanni Franzoni, the abbot of St. Paul's Outside the Walls in Rome, whose radical view of his responsibilities to the poor and homeless incurred the wrath of some of the more traditional clergy and local DC politicians. He was deposed from his seat in 1973, and after a series of further political conflicts during the divorce referendum campaign in 1974 and the general election campaign in 1976 was reduced to the lay state in June 1976.

These *causes célèbres,* though highly visible and unwelcome to the church, were by no means isolated examples of dissent. The development of genuine radical and collective alternatives within the Italian church in the 1970s, restricted as it was to relatively small minorities, was still a new phenomenon for the postwar period and must be distinguished from the isolated and usually sterile gestures of priests who refuse to move from parishes where they are well settled—a time-honored and relatively frequent occurrence, particularly in the South. The *Communità di Base* helped sustain the weekly periodical *Com-Nuovi-Tempi* through difficult times, and perhaps reached its organizational peak in its third national congress, held in Florence in 1975, which attracted over 2,000 participants representing 235 groups.[12]

In the new pluralism, it was not only on the left that dissatisfaction with the DC stimulated new groupings. By far the most consistent and influential of the conservative lay groups to emerge after the Council was "Communion and Liberation" (*Communione e Liberazione,* usually known as CL). CL began as a student group in Milan in 1966, and soon established itself with a combination of modern methods and traditional message; its appeal was and is predominantly to the more affluent Catholic youth, to whom its verbal radicalism is not only acceptable but even attractive when linked firmly with loyalty to papal authority and traditional social policy. CL is particularly strong in Lombardy and in the Veneto; it now has an overtly political subsidiary organization, Popular Movement (*Movimento Popolare*), which CL uses as its electoral agent. Despite their generic expressions of loyalty to established authority within the church, the willingness of these groups to criticize individual members of the hierarchy and specific policies which they hold to be tainted by liberalism puts these groups in a direct line of descent from the social integralists of the immediate postwar period rather than the more authoritarian traditional integralists. Despite their initial expressions of contempt for the DC, both CL and MP now organize as a faction within the DC and (with some reluctance on the part of *Movimento Popolare*) have deputies and councillors elected on the DC list. Unlike the left-wing groups, they do not usually have to concern themselves about episcopal displeasure.

The process of development of which these groups were some of the components had its mainspring in religious beliefs and responses, but it was also marked by a constant interaction with politics, by a discovery and exploitation of the fact that the secular does have its autonomy and its own worth. This means, of course, that political events have their own meaning and can induce changes in other areas; the crucial examples of this in the postconciliar church have been the two referenda—the first on divorce in 1974 and the second on abortion in 1981.

The Divorce Law was originally passed in December 1970; its proposers in Parliament were a Socialist and a Liberal, and it was treated as a nongovernmental issue. The Vatican protested against the divorce bill with a diplomatic note in January 1970, which argued that the bill would constitute a violation of the 1929 Concordat. This note occurred during difficult negotiations for the formation of a new government, and had the counterproductive effect in the short term of making it impossible for the DC to make withdrawal of the bill one of the conditions for a new coalition, since they would have seemed to have been bowing to Vatican pressure. But it did have the effect of forcing the issue onto the political agenda and compelling the DC to decide how to respond to it. In the event, though the Christian Democrats opposed the bill, as did the neo-fascist MSI, its success did not bring down the Christian Democratic government of the day, and there are grounds for arguing that both the Vatican and the DC were not generally inclined to pursue the matter further through their own actions[13]; as part of an apparent if unspoken compromise between the DC and the lay parties, parliament also passed a law that implemented the previously dormant clause in the Constitution referring to popular referenda. In the debate on the referendum bill, the view that clearly emerged was that with the required number of signatures set at 500,000 and with complex procedural obstacles to be overcome, only the major parties would be able to organize a successful campaign to call a referendum. This assumption has been proved radically incorrect on at least nine occasions since then. As in other instances, the political classes showed themselves deficient in grasping the significance of wider changes occurring in society, and set in train or gave unwitting assistance to processes that would cause them major problems in the long run.

The signatures for the referendum against the Divorce Law were collected by ad hoc groups of Catholic laity and clergy, whose national leaders had previously had no known political career. The DC had not been directly involved in collecting signatures but maintained its passive opposition to the divorce law in Parliament; it proved impossible to reach a compromise in Parliament that would have rendered the referendum unnecessary even though all the major parties exhibited considerable nervousness at the prospect of this unprecedented political event.

Others were less nervous. The Radical party *(Partito Radicale)*, a previously insignificant anticlerical group, established itself as the market leader in civil liberties with an aggressive campaign in favor of divorce when the referendum was finally held in May 1974; but more important than the public displays of the Radicals were the deep divisions among Catholics. Among the laity, attempts to recreate the climate of the 1948 election by resuscitating the defunct Civic Committees were unsuccessful, and the antidivorce groups employed widely differing arguments, which reflected the divisions of principle among them: the traditional integralists such as Agostino Greggi, a former DC deputy who later was elected for the neo-fascist MSI, argued with frank simplicity that divorce should be rejected because it was "against God's Law"; social integralists such as Amintore Fanfani, Christian Democratic Party secretary, were more concerned to argue against what they held to be the social and political consequences of divorce, sometimes in lurid terms; and liberal Catholics such as Giulio Andreotti, DC boss of the region around Rome, pitched their rather more elegant debate at the individual consciences of Catholics.

For the first time in the postwar period there was a sustained and substantial revolt by Catholic intellectuals in favor of religious tolerance. A group made up mainly of trade unionists, university professors, and leading journalists formed "Catholics for a No vote" *(Cattolici per il "No")*, arguing that Catholics did not have the right to restrict the availability of divorce to those who did not share their views. For the mobilization of the Catholic vote, if such an entity existed, the policies of the Catholic associations were crucial; of the three major organizations, Catholic Action gave formal support to the referendum only after pressure from the Vatican, the Graduates Group (FUCI) asserted the right to freedom of conscience, and the Workers Association (ACLI) could only find agreement in an ambiguous declaration of respect for the views of the Bishops' Conference.

The dispositions of the Vatican and the Bishops' Conference were highly revealing. The Vatican was distinctly more reluctant to engage the church's forces in a referendum campaign than was the Permanent Commission of the Bishops' Conference, and the Permanent Commission, which has on it all noncurial Italian cardinals, was also distinctly more hawkish than the General Assembly of the Conference, in which all pastoral bishops in Italy participate. The General Assembly on this occasion reflected more closely the concern of the parochial clergy at the possibility of a divisive crusade against divorce, and under pressure from the Permanent Commission was split between those who sought to limit the Conference to a firm and moderately worded denunciation of the law and those who wanted active participation in the campaign against the law.

Pope Paul VI no doubt could have stopped the campaign if he had wished; that he did not do so owed more to his "hands off" approach to domestic politics than to enthusiasm for the cause. On the other hand, his public restraint was certainly significant in ensuring that the hierarchy on the whole did not involve itself in mobilizing Catholic support in a religious crusade, and with some obvious exceptions (among whom was Cardinal Luciani of Venice) those who did involve themselves were drawn into the fray by those activities of Catholic dissenters that were interpreted as direct challenges to their own authority. Several bishops spoke publicly in favor of liberal interpretations of the Bishops' Conference's statements; the most senior representative of this wing of the hierarchy was Cardinal Pellegrino of Turin, who issued a pastoral letter in March 1974 emphasizing the importance of preserving unity even in the face of disagreement over what he referred to in typically coded language as "contingent political judgments." Also quite typically for the modern church, he was later to modify his position in the face of "manipulation" of his views by the prodivorce camp.

The result of the referendum apparently came as a surprise to the prodivorce parties, who had consistently preferred to describe themselves as ahead of majority opinion in the country rather than as giving expression to vigorous popular demand. Cardinal Poletti showed greater realism and frankness than many on both sides when he said after the result was announced, "I thought that it would rain but not that it would pour." Nationally, those in favor of divorce were 59 percent of valid voters, those against 41 percent, but 11 percent of the total electorate did not vote or spoiled their ballots, an unusually high figure for Italy. In thirteen out of the twenty regions the antidivorce vote was higher than the DC vote at the parliamentary elections two years previously. The antidivorce vote varied from 30 percent of voters in Piedmont to about 60 percent in the small rural region of Molise, and the south (excluding the islands) produced a majority against divorce in all its regions, though here as elsewhere in Italy the differences within regions between city and countryside were comparable in size to the differences between the regions themselves.

There can be little doubt that divisions within the church and the greater priority given by senior church leaders to maintaining unity and authority had a major effect on the result of the 1974 referendum. The circumstances of the abortion referendum in 1981 were very different, and the attitude of the church, particularly of Pope John Paul II, made the 1981 referendum resemble more closely the "Census of obedient Catholics" which some apparently wanted both to be. The abortion law, passed in 1978, did not reflect any great enthusiasm on the part of secularizing elites in Parliament, as had the divorce law. Indeed, the main impetus behind the passage of the law came from the prospect of a referendum organized by the Radical party, which would have removed all existing legal restraints on abortion if successful.

The Bishops' Conference successfully mobilized a campaign of conscientious objection against the abortion law, and might well have been satisfied with this. But their hands also were forced by the militant secularizers in the Radical party, who collected signatures for a referendum whose effect would have been to liberalize further the conditions for abortion and to restrict conscientious objection to it. Despite this initial reluctance, once the campaign was under way the church was deeply and unambiguously involved, and much of the responsibility for this must rest with Pope John Paul II. The pope has consistently used his position as bishop of Rome to gain an entrance into Italian politics which neither John XXIII nor Paul VI ever claimed. The involvement of Pius XII, on the rare occasions when he appeared concerned to justify it, based itself on the grounds of the universality of the church's moral teaching, and that of John Paul II marks a return to this doctrine and an updating of it. But the DC is no longer the favored instrument of papal politics in Italy, and the pope on this occasion as on others gave positive support to single-issue Catholic pressure groups such as Movement for Life (Movimento per la Vita) and to the broader-based organizations such as Communion and Liberation whose loyalty is to the church's authority rather than to more complex governmental responsibilities.[14]

Whether despite the papal involvement or because of it, the results of the abortion referendum showed a considerable decline in the church's capacity for mass mobilization even since 1974. The low turnout (79.6 percent) did not help the anti-abortion cause, but the proportion of valid voters in favor of the "Movement for Life" proposal was 32 percent, 9 percent below the equivalent vote in 1974. At least by comparison with 1974 there was a uniformity about the vote between regions: only in Trentino-South Tyrol was there an anti-abortion minority, and the regions of southern Italy that in 1974 had surprised few observers by returning antidivorce majorities surprised many in 1981 with consistent majorities in favor of the existing abortion law. The 1981 vote also indicated definitively that the DC could no longer be described as completely reliant on the church's support, if this had ever been arguable: the DC vote in 1979 was higher than the 1981 anti-abortion vote in every single region. But none of this should be interpreted to mean that an overwhelming majority of the population is completely outside the church's reach on nonpolitical matters, and the bishops might have consoled themselves in private with the even more decisive rejection of the Radical party's proposal on the same ballot paper which achieved 11 percent of the vote. Rather, it indicates the extent to which the autonomy of the secular has been firmly established and affects the church's role in society in radical ways.

Because of its majority position, its moral authority, and its historical strength, the church in Italy has traditionally taken on itself the responsibility of close involvement in the affairs of the state. If the state was not fully Catholic in its policies, this was so, in the church's view, because of the unwarranted interventions of non-Catholic minorities such as liberals or socialists. The church has now relinquished this general responsibility, in implicit recognition of its new minority position. It may be that a similar realization on the church's part lay behind the agreement of a new Concordat in February 1984, which excludes any suggestion that Catholicism is in any sense the religion of the state, and which has removed most of the anomalies resulting from the 1929 Concordat in the fields of marriage law and rights of the clergy. The new Concordat leaves to future negotiation the rights of the church in religious education, taxation, and welfare services. In 1986 Franca Falcucci, the DC Education Minister and a member of the Fanfani faction, demonstrated that she at least still remembered her origins when she finalized the religious education details in a form so favorable to the church that it left the lay parties in the coalition wondering what they had actually gained from the Concordat.

The church in Italy still has great political, financial, and moral powers, but it should no longer be seen (if ever this was correct) as a substitute state, unitary and disciplined, making up for the weaknesses and failings of a fledgling democracy and often fulfilling functions that properly were those of the state, such as family law and education. The way the church now operates is much more clearly that of a predominant interest group, which itself has an articulated and complex structure and which competes with other groups for the attention of the electorate.

The role of the papacy is crucial for an understanding of the church's position in this new political context, as it was in previous periods of intense development. In April 1985, ten years after the "Evangelization and Sacrament" Convention organized by the Bishops' Conference had called on the church in Italy to treat Italy as a de-Christianized society in need of its missionary effort, the church met again in convention, this time with the theme "Christian Reconciliation and the Community of

Man." The first convention had revealed an inward-looking church concerned particularly with its failures in pastoral reform and its incapacity to get its message across. In the 1985 convention, held at Loreto, this church could still be discerned, but another church was also determined to have its say; in Italy as elsewhere, the Church of Reform and the Church of the Restoration were in increasingly open conflict with one another. In the late 1980s the pressures for public unity are not as great as in past times, and the battle lines are therefore less easily obscured by coded language and generic appeals to fraternity. The Loreto Convention revealed a church in which the fragile pluralism of the Pauline period had hardened into segregation and into intolerance of the views of other Catholics.

One of the few unifying features is the underlying assumption that the church has been badly served in politics by the Christian Democrats, but in what way they have failed the church and how to remedy the failures is not at all clear. Particular problems that are the immediate cause of division are the role of women in the church, the treatment of priests who wish to be laicized, and the pastoral care of divorced Catholics. Within the church the distinction appears to be between Christians of presence and Christians of mediation, between those who seek the restatement of traditional values without compromise and those who want the church to mediate for the modern world. In general, the distinction applies to Communion and Liberation, the Christians of political presence, and Catholic Action, the pastoral Christians. This distinction is so reminiscent of the Gramscian distinction between the war of position and the war of maneuver that it can hardly be coincidental. The distinction implies two profoundly different perceptions of the problem, and two different strategic responses. The CL perceives the problem as that of an unredeemed world in need of clear leadership from the church, while the perception of the pastoral Christians is that of a society which needs to be engaged in dialogue, again in line with the Gramscian distinction between domination and hegemony.

The intervention of the pope at the Loreto Convention was much awaited, and it proved characteristically uncompromising. It was also largely ineffective in bringing the "mediationists" into line. John Paul II called on the Italian church to unite around established teaching "particularly at moments of responsible and coherent choice," and to resume its role as leader and guide of the whole of society. He had no words of comfort for dissident Catholics, and he made it clear that the term "reconciliation" should not mean a softening or dilution of the church's teaching.

But part of the reason for the failure of this assertion of authority to achieve genuine unity can be found in other parts of the papal speech: the traditionalist movements, which otherwise the pope clearly supported, were also invited by him to refer constantly to their own bishops and to avoid antagonism and conflict. But while the reference to episcopal authority appears fully coherent with the pope's general policy of enhancing the scope of national hierarchies, in Italy as elsewhere the pastoral bishops are not fully in sympathy with the practical measures the pope supports, and Communion and Liberation often appeals over the heads of the local bishops, whom they are not reluctant to criticize. Indeed, the support of many of the bishops for the pluralist political stance of Catholic Action was quite clear at Loreto. If the pope is relying on the Italian Bishops' Conference to mobilize Catholics for his crusade, it is difficult to envisage his success unless he is able to appoint and promote sufficient numbers of new bishops who are more in harmony with his approach. This problem is not unique to Italy. But one of the striking features of the church in Italy is how it has joined the mainstream of the international church, and is treated by the papacy appropriately.

In conclusion, it must be observed that the church in Italy still has an immense wealth of cultural and moral influence, even though it is no longer able to rest on the old certainties and the unity of past times. The church is involved as it always has been in many of the problems that confront Italian society, but it appears to have difficulty getting used to the diversity of views that has undoubtedly always been present but now is clearly revealed. This diversity gives the church a flexibility of response and a scope for intervention that previously it lacked, but it also appears to raise problems for those who place a high priority on static notions of authority within the church. The processes of secularization have certainly diminished the numbers of practicing Catholics. What is less often recognized is the extent to which they have also weakened the social basis of the closed Catholicism on which the church previously relied. As a result, practicing Catholics can now be found exercising their apostolate in a wide variety of different social and political groups. The political unity of Catholics, whether within or outside the DC, cannot be rebuilt once demolished.

The future development of Catholicism in Italy will therefore follow a much less linear route than its leaders have enjoyed in the past. The church will also have to accept a permanent demotion from the center of the international stage: Italy is an important national church in the papal grand design, and will benefit from the fact that the pope is a member of its national hierarchy, but it will have to learn to live with its reduced dimensions in international affairs. The unwinding of the certainties, unities, and authority of the Italian church promises to be difficult and complex.

NOTES

1. On the relationship between the Vatican and Italy in the postwar period, see G. Poggi, "The Church in Italian Politics 1945–1950," in S. J. Woolf (ed.), *The Rebirth of Italy* (London: Longman, 1972), pp. 133–35; S. Magister, *La Politica Vaticana e L'Italia 1943–1978* (Rome: Editori Riuniti, 1979); D. Settembrini, *La Chiesa nella Politica Italiana (1944–1963)* (Milan: Rizzoli Editore, 1977).

2. The *locus classicus* of the debate on this issue is A. Gramsci, *La quistione meridionale*, 3rd ed. (Rome: Editori Riuniti, 1971), particularly pp. 90–94; but see also by the same author, *Quaderni del Carcere*, vol. 3, *Edizione critica dell'Istituto Gramsci a cura di Valentino Gerrata* (Torino: Giulio Einaudi Editore, 1975), pp. 2280–81, and vol. I, pp. 66 and 151–52.

3. See G. Baget-Bozzo, *Il Partito Cristiano al Potere, la DC di De Gasperi e di Dossetti* (Firenze: Vallecchi Editore, 1974); P. Scoppola, *La proposta politica di De Gasperi* (Bologna: Il Mulino, 1977); and a Marxist who tries to agree with both these two, G. Chiarante, "A proposito della questione democristiana: democrazia, valori cristiani, societa borghese," *Critica Marxista* 15 (1975):27–42; also M. R. Catti De Gasperi, *De Gasperi, Uomo Solo* (Milan: Mondadori, 1965); on the organizational strengths of the church, see C. Falconi, *La Chiesa e Le Organizzazioni Cattoliche in Italia 1945–1955* (Torino: Giulio Einaudi Editore, 1956).

4. S. Burgalassi, *Italiani in Chiesa* (Brescia: Morcelliana, 1967); by the same author, *Il Comportamento Religioso degli Italiani* (Firenze: Vallecchi Editore, 1968), particu-

larly pp. 188–90; see also C. Falconi, *La Religiosita* (Rome: Editori Riuniti, 1963). The most reliable of the later studies have been carried out by the opinion polling agencies Demoskopaea and Doxa, but these show consistenly high levels of "don't knows."

5. All statistics relating to separations, divorces, civil marriages, and legal abortions were aggregated by the author from *Annuario Statistico Italiano* (Rome: ISTAT, 1970 onward).

6. D. I. Kertzer, *Comrades and Christians, Religion and Political Struggle in Communist Italy* (Cambridge: At the University Press, 1980), p. 143.

7. "Situazione pastorale alla luce dell'indagine CEI," *Sociologia e Statistica Religiosa* 2/3 (1973):6; *Evangelizzazione e Sacramento: Rapporto di ricerca sulla situazione pastorale oggi in Italia, a cura della Conferenza episcopale Italiana* (Rome: Conferenza Episcopale Italiana, 1975).

8. *Annuario Pontificio 1976* (Rome: Tipografia Poliglotta Vaticana, 1976), my elaboration.

9. *Evangelizzazione e Sacramento 1975*, pp. 125–32.

10. Ibid., p. 155. Emphasis in original.

11. Statistics from S. Cova, "I movimenti cattolici: ecco le loro forze," *Il Settimanale* 17 (1976):28–31.

12. On Catholic dissent in this period, see G. Baget-Bozzo, *La Chiesa e La Cultura Radicale* (Brescia: Editrice Queriniana, 1978).

13. On the attitudes and behavior of the Vatican and the DC on this issue, see P. F. Furlong, "On Millstones and Milestones: The Catholic Hierarchy and the Divorce Referendum in Italy, May 1974." Paper presented at the ECPR Joint Workshop Sessions, Brussels, 1979.

14. See P. F. Furlong, "The Changing Role of the Vatican in Italian Politics." In *Italy Today: Changing Patterns of Life and Politics,* ed. L. Quartermaine and J. Pollard (Exeter: Exeter University Press, 1985), pp. 59–75.

6

Spanish Catholicism in Transition

Aurelio Orensanz

Since 1950 the population of Spain has shifted dramatically from a predominantly rural and agricultural society to an industrial and urban one. In the 1950s Spain departed from a basically nineteenth-century model of political and social organization, and from then on the economic, demographic, political, and cultural contours of the country began to resemble the other nations of Europe.

The Church in a Suddenly Industrial Society

With regard to its demographic composition, Spain's active working population remained much the same between the 1950s and 1980s, comprising 37–38 percent of the total; but the sectorial distribution of this population reflected drastic changes (see Table 6.1). In terms of political and technical design, the main impetus for social change came from the vision of a large group of technocrats who drew up the main outlines of four economic and industrial development plans. This was the first time a Spanish government had ever been involved in active economic and industrial planning. The people who brought about that transformation or who caught up and embodied the spirit of massive national change were a generation of highly educated, efficient, and well-connected professionals. They were, for the most part, members of *Opus Dei,* a religious organization that I will discuss later in this chapter. The new vision of the country bolstered the creation of twelve major industrial parks outside the traditional industrial regions of Catalonia and the Basque country.[1]

Although in 1940 only one out of five Spaniards lived in cities of more than

TABLE 6.1   Distribution of the Spanish Work Force

SECTOR	1950	1960	1970	1980
Agriculture	48.8	41.3	29.2	18.9
Industry	25.1	31.4	38.1	44.6
Services	26.1	27.3	32.7	36.5

100,000, by 1965 that proportion had risen to 33 percent and to 53 percent in 1980. This transfer from agricultural and rural to industrial and urban occurred in less than two decades, in contrast to the much longer period of industrialization and urbanization that unfolded in Great Britain, or for that matter in Catalonia and the Basque country where such mutations took almost 100 years. This massive displacement proved disruptive for a people organized for centuries into differentiated cultural settings in the basic eighteen regions into which the country is divided. The Spain of the 1960s and 1970s, however, did not turn into a wasteland of anomie like nineteenth-century France, England, and northern Italy, or even the slums of Barcelona and Bilbao. The fact that such anomie did not materialize is due in part to two very specific factors. On the one hand, migrating masses were supplied with modern means of transportation and communication unthinkable decades before. These enabled the extensive dislocations to be much less dramatic than they otherwise might have been. To understand this we need merely compare the reports of witnesses of the Barcelona and Bilbao slums of the 1890s and the accounts of the slums of Madrid, for example, in the 1960s. On the other hand, the Catholic church in Spain manifested a very different presence from the one offered seventy years before during the industrialization of Bilbao and Barcelona.[2]

With regard to transportation, in 1960 there were 300,000 automobiles in Spain; in 1970 there were 2.4 million; and in 1980, 7.3 million. As for mass communications, Spaniards had five television sets per 1,000 inhabitants in 1960; 70 per 1,000 in 1970 and 400 per 1,000 in 1980. Similar increasing proportions apply to radios, newspapers, books, magazines, videos, and films. The availability of transportation and communication stimulated a reverse inner process in the Spanish mind. The mass dislocation to the cities was accompanied by an ever deeper mental repossession of the world left behind. The automobile made possible a widespread, temporary exodus back to the countryside, allowing people to forge strong links with the original soil. Communication made possible a constant revisitation of one's roots, bringing to the living rooms of the destitute modern slums enhanced visions of the rural past in documentaries, soap operas, and newscasts. Some of the best novels of the 1950s, 1960s, and early 1970s were based on rural themes, for example, Jesús Fernández Santos's *Los Bravos*, Jesús López Salinas's *Central Eléctrica*, and José Caballero Bonald's *Dos días de septiembre*. The rural world—a somber counterpoint to the official hype of industrialization—also produced some of the most readable material in modern Spanish literature in travel books such as Juan Goytisolo's *Campos de Níjar*, Armando López Salinas's *Caminando por las Hurdes*, Antonio Ferres's *Tierra de Olivos*, and Alfonso Grosso and Armando López Salinas's *Por el rió abajo. Bien-*

vendio Mr. Marshall and *Los jueves, milagro* by José Luís Berlanga are only two of the most celebrated films from the 1950s with a rural theme.

At the same time, both the tourist explosion and tourist advertising deeply affected Spain's self-consciousness. The number of tourists visiting Spain annually jumped from 6 million in 1960 to 24 million in 1970 and to 49 million in 1980. Tourism became Spain's first industry, bringing in $297 million in 1960, $1.6 billion in 1970, and $3.7 billion in 1980. That outpouring of foreign currency, together with the remittances of hundreds of thousands of displaced farmers and menial workers who had emigrated to France and central Europe, made it possible for Spain to become the tenth largest industrial nation in the world. Besides these economic consequences, massive tourism had an enormous social and cultural impact on the country. "Spain is different," the popular slogan in international tourist markets, appeared on millions of posters and in brochures all over Europe and in Spain as well. The rural image with its landscapes, flowers, foods, crafts, festivals, and costumes became the main attraction Spain had to offer to the overindustrialized, bored, overurbanized masses of central and northern Europe. What the average Spaniard had left behind now had become the trendiest, most fashionable tourist product. The backward was made instantly chic. Soon every restaurant and coffee shop in the centers and the slums of industrialized Spain were stuffed with rural decor.[3]

During the time of Spain's first industrial revolution, the church moved into the slums very late, if it moved at all. Its distance was not only physical but also spiritual. In Catalonia, for example, the church had kept itself entrenched in defending the nationalist ideals of the middle class as well as its own privileges. Entire urban areas of Barcelona were served by only one priest, as was the case in the *barrio* of Pople Nou which in the early 1900s was inhabited by over 41,000 people. When in 1909 during the anticlerical riots of the Tragic Week eighty churches, parochial schools, and other church related premises were burned down, the church of Pople Nou was the first to be destroyed.

At the turn of the century the Spanish church became highly urbanized, despite the predominantly rural mood of the country. New religious orders, such as the Sons of the Immaculate Heart of Mary founded by St. Anthony Mary Claret in Barcelona, took it upon themselves to missionize the countryside. Thousands of religious men and women returned to their homeland from former Spanish colonies when the Philippines, Cuba, and Puerto Rico were lost to the United States. The religious orders in the cities catered for the most part to the educational and pastoral needs of the middle class and did little for the masses of people living in the slums.[4]

During the late 1950s and 1960s, however, the Spanish church developed a wholly new attitude toward the new neighborhoods. Zaragosa can serve as an example of the new situation. It had a population of 236,300 in 1960 and was on the threshold of industrialization. That population climbed to 429,697 in 1970 and to over 600,000 in 1980. The archdiocese of Zaragosa established twelve new parishes in 1961, six in 1962, six in 1964, and twenty-three between 1965 and 1972. A new parish in the Spain of the 1960s and 1970s meant, besides a parish church, social services such as a kindergarten and youth center, a cluster of associations, and a few movements of religious inspiration. It was precisely in these neighborhoods of the old and new industrial areas that the first glimpses of a democratic civic life in Franco's

Spain could be discerned. From the early 1960s on, the Franco regime very cautiously allowed the establishment of associations of local interest catering to the needs of neighborhoods. These were the *asociaciones de barrio* (neighborhood associations), which grew up around a single issue or set of consumer complaints about transportation, housing, traffic, schools, or sanitation and then moved on to issues of wider interest such as education, local elections, autonomous government for the regions, use of local languages in the schools, urban planning, and disarmament. These associations represented the first steps toward democratic participation in the public life of postwar Spain and were allowed to form only during the very last years of the Franco regime. The associations rallied all the opposition forces around common goals, and both the local church and the Communist party provided active support to these civil movements. The movements used a wide variety of creative pedagogies to convey their requests and protests during the countercultural years when street theater, graffiti, performance, and mime were aggressive tools for social change.[5]

New parishes were always considered a battleground and were staffed by young priests from both the diocesan and the religious clergy. People interested in social change were well aware of the worker-priest movement in France and Spain. These were people eagerly concerned about the unfolding reforms of the Second Vatican Council. The new parishes were the first to embrace these reforms and experiment with them. The atmosphere of urgency, incompleteness, and transition of the industrial neighborhood provided an ideal setting where young clergy and committed laity could reinvent the church, responding to the biblical experience of the early church and the demands of a secular, freedom-loving, expectant Spanish society.

The 1980s mark the saturation point for Spain's industrialization. The international industrial crisis in steel, energy, garments and other branches of manufacturing put a halt to the drive of the 1960s and early 1970s. Nor had Spain been particularly successful in adapting its obsolete plants to new technologies. In addition, it faced increasing export competition from the Far East and the European Economic Community, to which it now belongs. Its unemployment rate of about 20 percent is among the highest in Europe. At the same time, the church has lost several thousand priests through the normal process of aging and over frustration with the slow pace of change since the end of Vatican II. The consolidation of democracy under a socialist government has required that the church thoroughly reassess its role in contemporary Spanish society. Areas that before were its privilege—education, the new family civil code that allows for divorce and abortion, a state-owned television that actively fosters an increasingly secularized culture—now have become arduous battlegrounds.

Practices, Beliefs, and Resources

Data collection and systematic reflection on religious trends and practices, beliefs, and resources are recent phenomena in the Spanish church. There has never been a national survey of religious practices, and studies in the sociology of religion go back only to the late 1960s. The church's own data collection methods seem rather unreliable, and the Spanish university system, where sociology is a recent arrival, has traditionally paid little attention to religion. Spanish religious practices and beliefs have been the subject of many surveys, opinion polls, and essays of varied ideological biases. However, throughout the last three decades numerous institutions such as the Institute of Sociology and Applied Pastoral Research (IPSA) in Barcelona have amassed enormous amounts of information, and Madrid's *Instituto Fe y Secularidad* has fostered pioneering reflections on the relationship between religion and society.

In general, religious practice is higher in rural than in the urban centers of northern Spain. In southern Spain, practice is higher in the cities than in the countryside. The deep transformation of the northern cities accounts for much of the loss of religious practice in the north. On the other hand, the rural south has a Muslim tradition dating back over 800 years. Lower religious practice is also associated with smaller numbers of priests and religious, and fewer schools and assistance centers. It could be that the south was never intensively socialized into church mores and practices, such as Sunday mass, reception of early baptism and first communion, and no delay of canonical marriage. Nevertheless, those rural masses, mostly from the south, were the people who fed the slums of Barcelona and Bilbao from the beginning of Spanish industrialization and, during the second industrialization of the 1960s and 1970s, the poorest sections of Huelva, Seville, Valladolid, Granada, Cordoba, Zaragosa, and Madrid.[6]

Table 6.2 presents a regional profile of religious practice in Spain at the height of its industrialization and urbanization (1972). After ten years of democracy with all the upheavals in public images and counterimages offered by various political and cultural groups, Spanish religious practice displays remarkable stability. Table 6.2 was composed by the International Conference for the Sociology of Religion (ISPA) of Barcelona after a thorough analysis of most sources available. In 1982 the *Centro de Investigaciones Sociológicas,* a state institution, published an opinion poll which indicated that almost 12 million Spaniards eighteen years of age and older attended mass with some regularity (see Table 6.3).[7] Throughout the decades of deep dislocations and intensive religious reforms, Sunday mass has continued to be a permanent form of worship and personal religious identity. A parallel study conducted by the Office of Statistics and Sociology of the Church concluded that geographical mobility was probably the main reason for loss of religious practice. Of those sampled in the church survey, 58.6 percent were born in the locality in which they now lived; 24.2 percent had come from another town within the same province or county, and 17.2 percent had come from another county or region.

The beginning of industrialization was accompanied by the state appropriation of enormous land and real-estate holdings which the church had accumulated since the Middle Ages. That state initiative brought about the collapse of thousands of churches, convents, and monasteries and a consequent decline of the clergy. Actually, the Spanish clergy had been on the decline since the end of the eighteenth century. In 1776 the country had 65,823 priests and 83,118 religious; by 1833 there were 50,507 priests and 56,893 religious; by 1900 the number of diocesan clergy had dropped to 33,403 and religious clergy to 54,738. In the mid-1980s Spain had about 23,000 diocesan priests and 29,000 religious priests. The heavy casualties in church personnel reflect the influence of several factors: the cumulation of massive shifts in the population and their geographical displacement, long-term changes in people's lifestyles, and a new theological emphasis on the vocation of the laity. Nothing shows the impact of these changes on Catholic religious consciousness as clearly

TABLE 6.2 Religious Practice in Spain, 1972

Region	Population	Percent of Total Spanish Population	Number of Practicing Catholics	Percent of Population	Percent of All Practicing Catholics in Spain
Andalusia	5,906,730	17.1	1,311,858	22.4	12.9
Aragon	1,096,112	3.2	518,989	61.2	5.1
Catalonia	5,457,441	15.8	1,004,769	21.7	9.9
Baleares	522,500	1.5	258,981	58.3	2.5
Canary Islands	1,244,720	3.5	274,337	22.4	2.7
New Castile	5,492,165	15.9	820,275	17.6	8.1
Old Castile and Leon	3,392,000	9.8	1,882,283	65.3	18.5
Extremadura	1,225,809	3.5	278,632	26.7	2.7
Galicia and Asturias	3,547,008	10.3	1,230,274	40.8	12.1
Valencia and Murcia	4,264,958	12.3	1,093,270	30.3	10.8
Basque country and Nararre	2,455,643	7.1	1,489,101	71.3	14.7
Total	34,585,382	100.0	10,162,767	29.4	100.0

TABLE 6.3 Religious Practice in Spain, 1982

	NUMBER	PERCENT
Attend mass at least every Sunday	4,822,998	18.5
Attend mass almost every Sunday	3,309,135	12.7
Attend mass but not every Sunday	3,608,781	13.8
Attend mass some Sundays in the year	6,300,384	24.2
Never attend mass	8,014,889	30.8

as the trends in priestly vocations. During the 1950s Spanish diocesan seminaries averaged about 8,000 students per year; this number rose to 8,500 during the 1960s. Behind these numbers stand decades of a very public and intense Catholicism. By the end of the 1960s, however, diocesan seminarians declined to about 6,000 per year, dropping to a low point of 1,500 in the mid-1970s. That number has increased slightly in the 1980s.

During the years immediately following World War II, many of the clergy tried to recreate a Spain identifiable with fierce orthodoxy. Severe moral standards and intense public practice were not only encouraged but often implemented by civil authorities. Catholic rituals and festivals defined the official worldview for both individuals and institutions. The horrors of the civil war were too fresh in the memory of most Spaniards, the fears and rigors of the dictatorship too strong, the stagnation of economic and industrial life too evident. Contacts with the outside world were strictly limited and censored. Catholic fervor was the only viable alternative—or complement—to the ideology and rituals of the Franco regime.

The Second Vatican Council brought a halt to this internal optimism, and the clergy began to develop some sense of historical purpose. A generation of young men came upon the scene who had no experience of the civil war and its accompanying persecutions and strictures. It was a generation who eagerly welcomed the small liturgical and pastoral reforms initiated by the Council, such as participatory celebrations, use of vernacular languages, and limited input from the laity. The Spanish clergy—both diocesan and religious—soon became acquainted with the new theological horizons and pastoral experiments underway in France, Germany, and Italy. Priests, religious, and laity began to advocate a new religious language, poetry, art, and more open self-confident lifestyles.

These horizons radicalized in the late 1960s. On the one hand, the documents of Vatican II appeared; at the same time, books like Bishop John A. T. Robinson's *Honest to God* and Harvey Cox's *The Secular City* were widely circulated and discussed. New theological treatises about secularization and the "death of God" seemed to accept almost any modern ideology as a substitute for a traditional religious framework. On the other hand, the planned economic and industrial growth as well as Spain's opening to European tourism produced more disappointment than the prospects of increased prosperity promised by the technocrats. A deep technological transformation had occurred but no maturity or democratic freedoms had arrived. The early humanistic breath of existentialism was altered by a stark Marxist analysis.

The year 1969 marked the climax of a bittersweet atmosphere of expectation and frustration. A national conference of bishops and clergy met in Madrid to approve the conclusions of several years of grass-roots analysis and nationwide reflection. Nowhere, expect perhaps in the Netherlands, had there developed such an atmosphere favorable to secular and religious change based on the spirit of Vatican II. After a highly charged exercise in democratic participation and progressive conclusions regarding crucial points of church discipline and practice, a chill settled over Madrid in the form of half-endorsements and caveats sent from Rome. Back in 1965, 130 priests in Barcelona had staged a protest march criticizing political repression. Those were the years when Camilo Torres, a young priest recently graduated from the University of Louvain, died in the guerrilla sierras of Colombia—the same year as Ernesto "Che" Guevara. Scores of priests left the active ministry; dozens of priests were sent to jail because of their political activism, and hundreds of them were fined because the police found that their homilies expressed political dissent.[8]

These traditional years of Spanish Catholicism were characterized by the emergence, consolidation, and sometimes the disappearance of many movements, groups, and associations. Three of them deserve particular mention because of their impact on the Spanish church and on Catholicism worldwide: *Opus Dei*, the *Cursillo de Cristiandad*, and the Neocatechumenal Way.

Opus Dei began as a college religious movement founded in the 1930s by a diocesan priest from Aragon, Josemaria Escrivá de Belaguer. From the beginning it attracted young college graduates and professionals, and when it later established headquarters in Rome it became a renewal movement with an international outlook. Its impact on Spain was profound. It embodied and explored many of the seeds of Vatican II, such as a serious acceptance of the modern world as the real arena of human beings' sanctification and a genuine appreciation of the values of professional and ordinary life.[9] For many centuries, the church had not witnessed such a strong endorsement of everyday life and a person's secular profession as the locale for baptismal fulfillment. Hundreds of businessmen, bankers, university professors, doctors, civil administrators, and people in the media joined *Opus Dei* in the 1950s and 1960s, linking the traditional religious values of private prayer, religious devotion, spiritual direction, and high moral standards with successful professional dedication. Large sectors of the public administration, particularly those in charge of economic and industrial planning, were for many years considered *Opus Dei* territory; this made it possible for the Franco regime to bring about a profound structural change in the country without altering its ideological and political base. *Opus Dei* has contributed many puzzling and dazzling accomplishments to the Spanish religious scene. Never before nor after had anyone in the country proclaimed and implemented such a program of rationality, efficiency, and planning, such an espousal of the accoutrements of modernity tied to an uncompromising commitment to traditional religious values. Indicative of this accomplishment, two books were jointly awarded the national prize for literature in 1949: Pedro Lain Entralgo's *España como problema* and Rafael Calbo Serer's *España sin problema*. Lain Entralgo advocated a mutual acceptance of the two traditionally warring Spains: the liberal, open-minded republican and the Catholic, orthodox monarchist in an inclusive common national unified project. He personified the liberal yet compromising side of the Spanish mind. Calvo Serer, a member of *Opus Dei*, personified the technocratic point of view of many in *Opus Dei*: Spain would be saved through adherence to its strict orthodox religious heritage and through the technology of modernity. The following decades of Spanish history have demonstrated that subsequent events conformed first to Serer's vision, then to Entralgo's in a play of discontinuities and continuities.

The *Cursillo de Cristiandad* movement (A Short Course on Christianity) began in 1949 as an outgrowth of the spiritual retreats conducted by the traditional *Acción Católica* (Catholic Action) in Palma de Mallorca. The *Cursillo* revival embodies a search for the true Christian lifestyle and a reaction against the folksy, gregarious religious experiences prevalent at the time. Its name derives from a short (three-day) encounter in which the candidate absorbs a committed new religious worldview. The thrust of the revival resides in the experience of God's grace achieved and lived on the basis of a daily commitment to honesty, piety, and an awareness of one's personal call in Christ. The *Cursillo* departs from anonymous, external, and massive expressions of orthodoxy, stressing instead individual assertiveness, commitment, and the relevance of faith to everyday life. Almost 1 million Spaniards have participated over the years in the *Cursillo* movement. In the beginning the *Cursillo* was a male movement, and it has preserved its masculine distinctiveness. A few years after the first Palma de Mallorca retreat, the movement spread to various countries and became a worldwide Catholic revival under lay initiative.

The third movement that played a significant role in Spanish Catholicism's transitional years is the Neocatechumenal Way. It originated in the early 1970s, growing out of the personal religious experience and conversion of a middle-class artist and musician, Kiko Arguello, and a handful of unexpected companions in the Palomeras slums of Madrid. Like *Opus Dei* and the *Cursillo,* this revival movement has spread to all corners of the globe and boasts several hundred thousand followers. The Neocatechumenal Way possibly encapsulates many of the best features of the reforming spirit of Vatican II. It expresses dissatisfaction both with the religious experience of the common Catholic churchgoer and with the dangers of a secularized society. As a countermeasure it tries to reenact the long, probing years of teaching and training catechumens underwent in the early church. This involves close familiarity with biblical texts and themes, a permanent experience of the church as a small welcoming community, recovery of the Easter Vigil as the central feast of the Christian calendar, and participation in Sunday evening Eucharist and the sacraments in a way that goes far beyond the predigested rituals of the post-Vatican II liturgy. It envisions a church that is small in numbers but strongly communitarian, with an important role for the lay catechist and a vigorous missionary zeal that seizes every member. The Neocatechumenal Way does not sponsor any particular social or political project or set of programs.

While these streams of revival and renovation have given Spanish Catholicism a strong personalized religious accent, they have by no means eroded the pervading popular religion of traditional Spain. The *Romería de Rocío* in Andalusia (the annual pilgrimage to the shrine of Our Lady of the Dew) still draws over half a million participants, and the monasteries and shrines of Montserrat, Aranzazu, El Pilar, Guadalupe, Santiago de Compostela, and Covadonga are thriving with pilgrims, festivals, and renewed popularity. In a country that has devoted its last fifteen years to an excruciating process of soul-searching regarding its various regional identities, roots, and imageries, the religious heritages of its different autonomous groups have emerged stronger and revitalized. Finally, the socialist government has actively encouraged popular festivals, all of them of religious origin, and has helped to foster new levels of participation, excitement, and enjoyment in both small towns and large cities. Through the unexpected channel of a socialist cultural revolution, Spain's traditional cults have achieved even higher prominence.

Church and State

In his analysis of English religion, David Martin has applied to France, Britain, and the United States a two-part interpretive model of the relationship between church and state.[10] The British and American model can be identified with the Anglo-Saxon political and religious arrangement in which an undisputed form of state more or less smoothly persists for some two hundred years. The spasms of the industrial, social, and urban revolutions that have characterized the modern Western world have been weathered by timely, partial, and rather peaceful reforms, adaptations, and trade-offs. The state, therefore, appears as a solid, consensual, unchallenged embodiment of the civil society at large. Churches, denominations, and sects cannot claim to represent the soul of the country as compactly as the state itself. Britain, in spite of retaining an established national church, first conducted its own Reformation and then allowed channels for alternative religious bodies and recognized religious dissent within a broad pluralistic universe of values.

The French model represents the situation not only in France but also in other Latin countries, especially Italy and Spain. In this model, the modern state emerges in a series of syncopated, convulsed, and even violent and bloody disruptions. In France the church crushed the Reformation and associated itself with an increasing exercise of central royal authority that allowed little scope for social change. Since there were no pluralist or working democratic models available, alternative structures had to be elaborated, sometimes in a rather abstract way, by individuals progressively alienated not merely from a particular church but often from religion itself. As soon as the church hierarchy initiated the process of change, forces built up within the system exploded more and more violently.

> The question of religion was posed in terms of all or nothing, and the political system developed in a way which placed the forces of tradition and change in dramatic opposition with the church largely aligned with tradition. Eventually, those high tensions were fed into the channel of the Communist party and other forces of radical change, proclaiming their own version of total, imminent change in the secular order.[11]

The emergence of the modern state in Spain is part of a dramatic saga that includes three royal abdications, three dethronements, eleven constitutions, and ten revolutions in just about a century and a half. To buttress the country against such endemic instability the state surrounded itself with a rhetoric and a culture that amounted to a civic religion. That rhetoric and culture includes a mythology of the origins of the state; an architecture and decor that pervades the buildings of the state bureaucracy, schools, military, and police establishments; statues commemorating both large and small wars and their heroes; a well as street parades, festivals, and music. State rhetoric reminiscent of a religion is more subdued in Anglo-Saxon coun-tries and more blatant in Latin and Hispanic countries.

In the case of the Spanish state, religion is at different times a strong ally and the quintessential enemy. The liberal tradition in general establishes a state deeply antagonistic to the Catholic church. This antagonism reached its climax in the 1930s and took one of two forms, both of which sought to override the Catholic culture of the country in order to bring into existence a modern nation endowed with the civic freedoms, progress, and pluralism associated with modernity. The first form corre-sponded to a republican, idealized Spain driven by secular-minded intellectuals and large segments of the urban middle class. The second followed the path of openly anticlerical anarchism, communism, and certain brands of socialism. The anticleri-calism of these political forces was not merely a feature of their respective ideologies. A deep anticlerical sentiment has typified the mentality of ordinary Spaniards for the last century and a half and is reflected in a popular language of profanity, blas-phemy, and irreverence perhaps unparalleled in any other Western country today.

Historically, Spanish anarchism brought about the only long-term experiment in large-scale social arrangements and, together with the Spanish communists during the heyday of the civil war, waged a bloody persecution of the church: some 5,000 priests were killed and a similar number of churches were destroyed or severely damaged. After the civil war a forced exile kept anarchists, communists, and social-ists out of sight for almost forty years. An organized, aggressive anticlericalism was unthinkable during the Franco regime, but popular, profane anticlericalism mani-fested itself in many ways. The reconstitution of the state after Franco climaxed in 1978 with a constitution that enshrined the secular nature of the state. The simple mention of the Catholic church was an exercise in tedious filibustering, simply a concession of the major power brokers of the time.

The new constitution that makes Spain a conventional Western democracy was soon implemented by a socialist government that sought affirmation not in terms of specifically socialist economic programs (which were not even attempted) but in terms of political, social, and cultural issues. It is here that the church faces its most serious challenge. Public education, divorce and abortion, use of an exclusively state-run television system, the use and control of the country's artistic and historical patri-mony are only a few of the main areas of contention. What is puzzling in the contem-porary sitaution is that only socialism—and a very moderate socialism at that—survived after Franco as the mainstream political mood of the country. The collapse of the anarchist tradition can be interpreted within the context of the collapse of anarchism worldwide, or at least its eclipse. But it is still difficult to understand its absence from the Spanish scene today given its central role in Spain's early indus-trialization and trade union movement. The collapse of the Communist party is a second enigma of contemporary Spain. Spanish communists' active involvement in civic movements and the cultural revival of the 1960s and 1970s, its strong repre-sentation among the educated classes, and, above all, its important role in today's labor movements would have led one to expect that it would exercise considerable influence on the reshaping of the democratic Spanish state.

The new constitution also formally recognized Spain's various historical regions and nationalities. As a result, the country today appears divided into eighteen autonomous governments. Navarre, Galicia, Aragon, Andalusia, and especially Catalonia and the Basque country had long-standing claims to their autonomy. Other regions now see themselves virtually forced to define themselves as autonomous territories as well. Once again the church is driven to relate to a state with a new face. Local and regional governments tend to be more leftist than Madrid, but proximity makes it easier to smooth away rough edges. In the search for local identity in which regional governments are involved the church is often at a loss to provide alternative communal symbols and images of deep cultural distinctiveness.

Conclusion

The last forty years in Spain have witnessed an interrupted series of transitions that fit perfectly within the country's last 150 years of continual political and cultural mutation. These last years encompass, on the one hand, the violent establishment of fascism, the advent of technocratic rule under the aegis of *Opus Dei*, the end of the Franco era, the transition to a covenanted democracy, and the establishment of democratic socialism. On the other, Spanish Catholicism began in the 1940s to implement the farthest public and private consequences of a confessional state. Following a decade of intense personalist and existentialist fermentation and another decade of dramatic post-Vatican II expectations and frustations, the church ended up with a defensive, adaptive stance toward the secularist culture of democratic socialism. The result of this long march seems to be a far-reaching reconciliation with modernity, democracy, and a rather artificial cultural and religious pluralism. The society as a whole has moved away from its embrace of an authoritarian, repressive, and rightest culture toward a conventional democracy within the European Common Market. Moreover, the church no longer claims to impose an ultra-orthodox religious and social order but has accepted the challenges of secularization, liberation theology, and the culture of unbelief; it has moved from a predominantly rural, traditional setting to an urban, postindustrial, and pluralistic one.

The two major hinges of this transition are the urban-industrial transformation of the 1960s and early 1970s, and the political-cultural transformation of the 1980s. At the end of both transformations, Spaniards for the most part seem wedded to the religious beliefs and practices that have long held the population together. In the long run, the infrastructural transformations of the 1960s and 1970s appear to have had a greater impact than the political and cultural changes of the 1980s. If urbanization and industrialization strongly affected the church's resources, personnel, practices, and beliefs, the cultural and democratic transformation seems more to have influenced the inner texture, mood, and internal sway of those beliefs and practices. If the dislocations of the 1960s moved Spain toward a kind of *"L'Espagne, pays de mission,"* then the mutations of the 1980s could produce a kind of "Anglicanization" of Spanish Catholicism. In other words, external factors such as geographical dislocation (caused by urbanization) and professional readaptation (caused by advanced industrialization) seem to affect the patterns of religious practice and belief differently than political and cultural change. The first are more lasting and dramatic, the second less dramatic but quite intense in terms of the inner texture of religion.

But if Spanish society at large and the Catholic church in particular appears to have negotiated a settlement with modernity and democracy once and for all, a settlement with the past has not occurred. In the Spanish mentality the past always seems to outweigh the present. Collective memory encompasses too long a stretch of centuries for anyone to feel comfortable with the present. Salvation comes through the past, and obscure and distant struggles can be sensed in the way businesses and relationships are conducted at all levels. Except for the tourist image, Spain—unlike Great Britain—has never developed an aesthetic, sanitized version of its heritage.

The last forty years have thus witnessed two major embodiments of the haunting weight of the past over contemporary affairs. On the one hand, the Franco regime couched its most appealing slogans in terms that recalled the golden age of the sixteenth and seventeenth centuries, the heyday of Spanish imperial discovery, conquest, literary and artistic achievement, and the implementation of a strict Catholic orthodoxy. Franco's rhetoric extolled a popular, unitarian Spanish soul above and beyond regional histories and peculiarities. The Fascist political project looked back to the empire and saw the present as the arena where the best features of that empire would be recreated not geographically but politically and culturally. The Spain of the late 1970s again searched the past for salvation and inspiration in formulating a new democratic constitution. The centralized structure of the authoritarian state should be dismantled and the eighteen autonomous regions or nationalities, some of them ostensibly created *ex machina,* would now supply an alternative identity, immediacy, and plurality for everyone. The new Spain has forged its future out of a composite of socialism, progress, and a host of vernacular langauges, flags, emblems, boundaries, heritages, and differentiated mythologies.

By the late 1980s the Spanish church seems dispossessed of the coercive, authoritarian countenance with which it previously had handed down its teachings and beliefs. It also appears as a space for dialogue between the ever-contending forces of nationalism, supranationalism, and internationalism. The church played a significant role in bringing Franco into power and in eroding that power, in bringing about socialism and in criticizing it. Few churches in Western Europe keep a similar check against the megalomania and mythology of the state. The fragmentation of the Spanish church into various tendencies, movements, theological schools, and sensitivities will always be a safeguard against its own errors and the errors of Spanish society at large.

NOTES

1. *III Plan de Desarrollo Económico y Social* (Madrid: Imprenta Nacional del Boletín Oficial del Estado, 1971).
2. Regarding industrialization in the Basque country, see Juan Pablo Fusi, *Política Obrera en el País Vasco, 1880–1923* (Madrid: Ediciones Turner, 1973); industrialization in Catalonia is treated in Jaime Vicens Vives, *Cataluña en el siglo XIX* (Madrid: Ediciones Rialp, 1962). The social atmosphere in the slums of Madrid in the 1950s and 1960s is well reflected in contemporary novels, e.g., Antonio Ferres, *La Piqueta* (Barcelona: Destino, 1959), and Luis Martin Santos, *Tiempo de silencio* (Barcelona: Seix Barral, 1962).
3. José Luis Febas, *Semiología del Lenguaje Turístico: Investigación sobre los folletos*

españoles de turismo (Madrid: Instituto Español de Turismo, 1978). For an overview of Spanish tourism, see J. Cals, *Turismo y Política Turística en España: Una Aproximación* (Barcelona: Editorial Auriel, 1974).

4. Joan Connelly Ulman, *La Semana Trágica: Estudio sobre las causas socio-económicas del anticlericalismo en España, 1889–1912* (Barcelona: Esplugas de Llobregat, 1972).

5. "La lucha de barrios: Barcelona, 1969–75," *Construcción, Arquitectura y Urbanismo* 34 (November-December, 1975); Aurelio Orensanz, "La Semiótica Beligerante: Cultura y Contracultura en los Movimientos Urbanos," *Comunicación* (Madrid), no. 33 (1972).

6. Rogelio Duocastella et al., *El Cambio Religioso en España* (Barcelona: Publicaciones IPSA, 1975); Table 6.2 appears on page 130.

7. Table 6.3 is taken from Francisco Azcona, "El Catolicismo Español en cifras: Panorama sociográfico de lay Iglesia Española," *Ecclesia* (Madrid), no. 2,098 (October 23, 1982).

8. For an interpretation of the dilemmas of Spanish Catholicism in the 1960s and 1970s, see Alfonso Alvarez Bolado, *El Experimento del Nacional-Catolicismo* (Madrid: Cuadernos para el Diálogo, 1977).

9. For a systematic view of the values of *Opus Dei* and their impact on Spanish society, see José Vincente Casanova, *The Opus Dei Ethic and the Modernization of Spain* (New York: The New School for Social Research, 1976), unpublished. An important book on Spanish Catholicism in the 1950s is *Catolicismo y Protestantismo como formas de existencia* (Madrid: Revista de Occidente, 1952).

10. David Martin, *A Sociology of English Religion* (London: Heinemann, 1967), pp. 77–85.

11. Ibid., p. 82.

7

Catholicism in German-Speaking Central Europe

Karl Gabriel and Franz-Xaver Kaufmann

The German language is spoken in central Europe, where the lines of communication and transport between north and south, between east and west have crossed since the high Middle Ages. In the southernmost regions Christianization had already begun with the Roman occupation. It progressed during the early Middle Ages, especially under the influence of the Franks and of Irish and English monks. In the north Christianization first consolidated itself as a result of the train of conquests by Charlemagne. The result was to extend the boundaries of the German-speaking world toward the east, above all as a consequence of the German propensity toward colonization. Today the German-speaking world consists essentially of four individual nation-states, West Germany, East Germany, Austria, and Switzerland.

The Catholicism of these four states is our topic of discussion. Their territories all belonged to the Holy Roman Empire until the end of the Thirty Years War (1648), out of which Switzerland then emerged. Austria became dominant in the course of defending itself against the Turks; its regent remained hereditary heir to the imperial throne. During the nineteenth century, after the Congress of Vienna (1815), which more or less established the present-day map of Europe, a rivalry developed between Catholic Austria-Hungary and Protestant Prussia. After a brief war in 1866 this rift led to German unification (1870) exclusive of the multilingual Austrian Empire. Austria lost possession of Hungary and its Slavic territories as a result of World War I. It became thereafter a relatively minor state in German-speaking Central Europe. Simultaneously, the German and Austrian empires ceased to be monarchies and assumed republican forms of government. These were replaced in Germany (1933) and in Austria (1938) by the dictatorship of Adolf Hitler. As a result of World War

II the German empire was divided into two separate states (1949), the Federal Republic of Germany and the German Democratic Republic, under the influence of the victorious powers. Today the Federal Republic of Germany is a member of the European Economic Community and NATO while the German Democratic Republic remains a member of COMECON and the Warsaw Pact. Switzerland (since 1815) and Austria (since 1955) have dutifully committed themselves to political neutrality. During the recent past a strong rapprochement between the two countries ("Alpine culture") has taken place.

As regards the religious orientation of this German-speaking world, its history has been stamped by the common experience of the Reformation and the Counter Reformation. Within the whole of Europe only here did the long political and religious struggle for stabilization result in a bi-confessional structure which can still be seen today in the active exchanges between the theologies of both confessions. Moreover, in all four countries (with restrictions in the GDR) religious freedom has a constitutional guarantee. This guarantee protects the right of religious associations to exist and the right of individuals to practice the religion of their choice, to change their religion, or to renounce their faith entirely.

Historical Assumptions: Catholicism in the Reformation

From the Reformation to the French Revolution

Inclusive of recent history, no other set of events or experiences has been as decisive for German Catholicism as the Reformation. The breakup of a unified Christian Church in the West moved from the middle of Europe outward, forming three confessions (Catholicism, Lutheranism, and Calvinism). Now there remain two great religious traditions—Catholicism and Protestantism—whose further development can be understood only in terms of their changing relations with one another.

A good hundred years before the Reformation, demands for the reform of the medieval church had already risen in German-speaking Central Europe. As attempts at reform advanced only hesitantly and then only to be suffocated in a web of political interests, the Reformation came to pass at the expense of Western Christianity's institutional unity. The result was that reform of the Christian tradition took its specific form and dynamic from opposition between the confessions. While both Protestant and Catholic reforms reached broad masses of people, the resulting religious revival remained the self-contained heritage of the respective denominations. Both churches succeeded in stabilizing themselves only by accepting the help of political authorities. In this respect it must be remembered that within many areas of the German-speaking world Catholicism was established from top to bottom by a specifically trained Catholic elite and the massive assistance of political means that had been set in motion by the Counter Reformation. In this sense the price of success was quite high. In service to the stabilization of feudalistic territorial states, the movement of confessionalization put a lasting imprint on the Christian tradition. In this regard the Catholic principalities, Josephine Austria, and the Catholic cantons of Switzerland were only negligibly distinguishable from the territorial churches under Protestant administration.[1]

The Peace of Augsburg (1555) and, almost a hundred years later, the Treaty of Westphalia (1648) rendered the "German Empire" conclusively proportional as far as the sizes of the confessions were concerned. This proportionality, however, was founded upon the principle *ubi unus dominus, ibi sit religio,* out of which came the well-known later formula *cuius regio, eius (et) religio,* and it made for a confessional church of the territory. Until 1815 the boundaries of the confessional church and those of the territorial state more or less coincided. The coexistence of confessions was solely a phenomenon of the imperial cities. These political boundaries of German Catholicism lastingly influenced its later history. This holds true not only for those territories in which the unity of church-state boundaries remained coextensive but also for those Catholic territories that later came under Protestant rule and where Catholicism had to find new social boundaries of its own.

Catholicism's involvement in reform in German-speaking territories also resulted in a special, often ambivalent relationship with the central authority of Rome. As inheritance from the Counter Reformation, an especially dependent, weakened form of Catholicism peculiar to the Germans persisted because of the splintered nature of the territorial states. Thus throughout the phase of baroque, state-sponsored churches the influence of Rome remained noticeably greater in Germany than it did, for example, in France. The nationalist tendencies of the church in the German empire usually associated with the name of Febronius was an especially critical theory, but politically weak and without a chance of being implemented. In Switzerland the confessional differences remained a constant element of domestic politics until relatively recent times. Austria remains an exception here insofar as, unified confessionally, it has won its conscious identity as a result of having successfully defended itself against Turkish invasion.

The relationship of Catholicism to nation-building addresses the last important historical factor relevant to the foundation of Catholicism in the German-speaking world.[2] Germany's confessional split and that of Switzerland ruled out the possibility of any unified religious and nationalistic movement. Nationalist ideas and interests found no support in the religious aspirations of the day, and Catholicism was unable to refer back to any connection with the national idea for the sake of stabilizing and anchoring itself in a culturally based church of the masses. In this regard the starting point for Catholicism in Germany and Switzerland differs considerably from the situation in Austria.

The Formation of German Catholicism in the Nineteenth Century

In the German-speaking territories of Central Europe modern Catholicism assumed a unique character during the course of the nineteenth century. It received its specific form through its confrontation with the development of modern society and the revolutionary upheavals in politics, economics, and culture that were a part of that development. We begin our presentation by focusing on German Catholicism, and will then treat specific developments in Austria and Switzerland.[3]

The collapse of the feudal church in Germany in 1803 was the prelude to far-reaching changes in the social form of Catholicism. Secularization (through the expropriation of all church assets during Napoleon's intervention in 1803) in a single blow all but destroyed the material basis of the church in Germany as well as the prevailing church hierarchy. In Germany alone eighteen reasonably well-endowed Catholic universities were lost because of this intervention. Left in their place was a telling educational, organizational, and developmental deficit that would persist into contemporary times. The fact that something like 3 million people fell under the jurisdiction of a new ruler proved equally consequential. Previously, many Catholic churches had prospered under the rule of Protestant princes; because of this any unified form of church–state relations was frequently precluded. In the course of the nineteenth century the reorganization of the Catholic tradition upon the ruins of its medieval and feudalistic form of social organization brought forth a specifically modern brand of Catholicism.

On the basis of concordats between the Holy See and the majority of German states a new form of church administration came about in the first half of the nineteenth century with an episcopacy no longer bound to the nobility. As in Napoleonic France, secularization created the necessary conditions for a strongly centralized, rational/bureaucratic form of organization in the hands of the bishops. The organization's spine came from a clergy that had been established upon the basis of reforms decided by the Council of Trent and that wielded authority as an instrument of church/pastoral interests. If in the old empire the bishops feared the demands of papal authority more than those of the territorial state, then in the course of the nineteenth century this situation changed fundamentally. Papal authority became the churches' primary support in the struggle for freedom and independence from state power and its demands for a controlling voice in church affairs.[4] The new "ultramontane"-oriented German churches entered into the oppositional structure of the total church vis-à-vis state authority and, without the counterweight of feudal social and political conditions, became hierarchically subordinate also in an organizational sense. Thus, the theological principle of *hierarchia ordinis* became both an ecclesiastical fact and a profane social reality.

The second no less important factor in the formation of Catholicism was a new kind of binding relationship for the reorganized churches and their clergy with the masses. The strong religiosity of the people—ever since the Reformation the special heritage of confessionalism—was challenged by the mingling of confessions within one state, and the identity of the two confessions was threatened by the impositions of authority, especially by the Protestant houses. These circumstances lent to the efforts of a revitalized clergy that was working toward the awakening of a specifically Catholic piety among the masses an unexpected and sweeping success in the form of a pilgrimage mentality and the worship of saints and reliquaries. The ability of the churches to mobilize the faithful became a politically effective factor in German Catholicism.[5]

In close relationship with these considerations is a third factor: German Catholicism as a quickly organizing social movement. In 1848, that year of endemic revolution, Catholic initiatives and organizations mushroomed everywhere in Germany. As a rule, the clergy played no small role in their establishment, but their legal foundation was the right to free and open association. Above all, the crystallization of these organizations formed a defense of the rights of the church within the emerging systems of liberal government. The basic idea was to give independent status to the church without political control but with a right to become a political force within the public realm. The Catholic movement was differentiated on three dimensions: politics, associations, and welfare. All three, however, remained closely related, the same Catholics often being organized within more than one sector.

Political Catholicism was an answer to the loss of the church's official public status and the means of state control as much as it was an answer to the political and social discrimination of a Protestant majority against a Catholic minority in states like Prussia. This tendency finally found expression in the establishment of a Catholic party, the Center Party, which by realizing the newly emergent possibilities for democratic action pursued the public interests of the Catholic church as institution as well as the interests of the Catholic portion of the population, in particular that population's political and social emancipation.

Social Catholicism was an answer to the plight of the masses during the nineteenth century. It came about as a result of the liberal, capitalistic modernization in Europe. Civic associations and unions formed the organizational basis of social Catholicism out of the circumstances in which Catholics found themselves. The circumstances of the movement's origins, overwhelmingly those of peasants and artisans, found their expression in precapitalistic forms of orientation. At first the reestablishment of state-sponsored guilds and ranked forms of organizations prevailed as ideal solutions to the "social question." Only in the course of lengthy debates among the widespread branches within organized social Catholicism did the church in Germany establish a social and political position that, by adhering to what was essentially a critique of capitalism, sought to tame and limit the sociopolitical consequences of industrial capitalism while grounding itself in that self-same system. Within this context political and social Catholicism became the staunchest promotor of the German welfare state.

In the network of its charitable organizations the Catholic church also developed another significant external side. In a long accelerating process comparable to developments on the Protestant side, these welfare associations consolidated themselves by the end of the nineteenth century on the national as well as the diocesan level as organized charities for Catholic Germany.

The specific formative processes of Catholicism were thus a part of the molding of a comprehensive milieu whose effects left their mark upon the conditions of everyday life. After the victory of Prussia over Austria the defensive character of German Catholicism was strengthened. The denominational character of the institution served as a social basis for all areas of everyday life. The reasons for interacting with non-Catholics were reduced to a minimum. With a high degree of self-awareness these fundamentals of the "Catholic milieu" formed a fully endowed Catholic world and worldview, which gained plausibility by deliberately demarcating and contrasting its boundaries from those of the "fallen" Protestant, civil-secular, and socialistic environment of the modern world. The church's monopoly over interpretation guaranteed the unity, superiority, and self-contained nature of the Catholic worldview in every instance of relevance, as well as in those instances where difficult questions overstepped the boundaries of the religious sphere. The legitimacy of this worldview as the ultimate reality valid for all areas of life drew Catholic thinking out of the context of scholastic thought about natural law, which nowhere retained the prominence and significance that it did for German Catholicism.[6] There was also a uniform structuring of interests within the "Catholic milieu" due to political discrimination and the economic backwardness of its overwhelmingly peasant and artisan constituency. German Catholics experienced the modernization of the German empire as the product of a state that discriminated against them and disregarded the rightful interests of their church. The struggle with a state coined by Protestants, with its high point in the *Kulturkampf* of 1870-1887, became the crucial basis for the interest-oriented alignment of the "Catholic milieu."

Through its orientation toward the leadership principle embodied in the pope the social milieu of German Catholicism retained an especially emotional tone as a symbol of its strong sense of solidarity. Based upon traditional forms of piety and a confessionally specific morality, there came to pass what until then was a never-before achieved degree of religious and moral permeation of everyday life. This permeation of everyday life by religion spread among disparate groups of people and not only through religious elites.

In the form described here, the developmental process of German Catholicism reached its high point around the turn of the century. Within the Catholic intellectual elite a minority called for escape from the "tower" of the Catholic milieu, which had become too claustrophobic well before World War I. After the collapse of the empire in that war the new constitution of the Weimar Republic dismantled what had been the prevailing evangelical bias of church-state relations. At the same time it established a special public status for both the Catholic church and the evangelical territorial churches, which guaranteed their total independence from state supervision, their legal and tax status, their right to carry out religious instruction in state schools, and other privileges. After an interval of strife and struggle with the National Socialists, this status for the church was reproduced in the constitutional law of the Federal Republic of Germany and further strengthened through numerous conventions with both churches.[7]

In regard to the spiritual aspect of the church, the period between the wars broke with more than just the liturgical movement. A break with the past came also from the impulse behind the Youth Movement which definitely aimed for something beyond the kind of "milieu Catholicism" discussed here. However, it was the epoch after World War II that proved decisive as far as a spiritual outlet for Catholicism was concerned. Flight and migrations led to a pronounced mixing of what had been extremely homogeneous confessional territories. This intermingling of denominational areas led to generally intensified contacts with alternative forms of thought. It formed an essential condition for an emerging ecumenical consciousness. Greatly impressed by the threat of totalitarianism, the confessions drew closer together. This process resulted in the formation of a broadly based political party that appealed to both confessions, the Union of Christian Democrats (CDU). With the separation of the almost totally Protestant German Democratic Republic from the Federal Republic, West Germany achieved approximate numerical parity between the two confessions, and the long term in office of the Catholic chancellor Konrad Adenauer contributed to the disappearance of what had been an awareness of minority status. The great authority of both churches in postwar Germany concealed the process that was dissolving the old confessional cultures. Since the middle of the 1960s, however, the deep-rooted changes in the social form of Catholicism have been obvious.

Specific Constellations of Catholicism in Austria

The Austria of today was until 1806 a part of the Holy Roman Empire and until 1866 belonged to the empire's German Federation.[8] Until the end of the nineteenth century Vienna and Innsbruck were naturally counted among those places where German Catholics met with other Catholics in open assembly. One can begin to understand Austrian Catholicism only by understanding the close relationship between Austrian Catholicism and its German counterpart. Despite this fact, Catholicism in Austria was imprinted again and again by a series of historical constellations that distinguish it clearly from the rest of German-speaking Catholicism. These constellations relate to the special role played by Catholicism for the ruling House of Hapsburg and for the general process of state formation in southeastern Europe.

In the beginning, the Reformation found fertile ground in Austria. Its load was carried by a nobility struggling for independence as well as by the common masses of people whose actions were influenced by the fact that most of them were tired of the monastic rule dominant since the time of Austria's Christianization. As of about 1570 Austria was close to being totally Protestant. During the Counter Reformation, which set in after 1590, however, the fate of Austrian Catholicism became intimately associated with that of the Imperial House of Hapsburg itself. Vienna became the emporium for the forces of Catholic reform in southern Europe during its struggles against the Protestantism of the north. The establishment of numerous new religious orders such as the Jesuits, the Capuchins, the Cistercians, and the Servetians give persuasive evidence of this. The imperial house and Catholicism alike saw themselves engaged in a war on two fronts: on the one side, the Protestant stronghold and, on the other, from the southeast, the advancing forces of the Turks. The victory over the Turks in 1683 also paved the way for a specifically baroque form of Catholicism, one marked by triumphalism and anchored in the masses.

Between 1750 and 1850 Austrian Catholicism received another special stamp upon its character, one that has carried over into present times through the effectiveness of so-called Josephinism. As with the Prussian kings who had united Protestantism by force out of Lutheranism and Calvinism, from Maria Theresia onward the rulers of Austria established Catholicism as the means for modernizing the absolutist state and maintaining their domination of it. Particularly with regard to the way in which society was to be controlled, the church was given a key position. This required a rational form of organization right down to the level of the parish. The conditions for this turn of events were laid by a newly trained clergy emerging from the state-sponsored seminaries founded by Joseph II. In fact, this situation brought about a state-sanctioned Catholic church in Austria with only loose ties to Rome. The traditional liaison, however, between the Holy See and the Austrian empire prevented a possible break.

The surmounting of Josephinism began at its weakest point, with a lack of support from a devout people. The intellectual circle of the Viennese Romantics under the leadership of Clemens Maria Hofbauer found a bridge to the baroque piety of the masses. The strengthening of the church in the first half of the nineteenth century and the simultaneous weakening of the monarchy expressed itself in the concordat of 1855, which brought about a break with Josephinism and granted the church—

without breaking all ties between throne and altar—a new degree of autonomy. When disputes arose between the church and the liberal government in power during the second half of the nineteenth century the kind of crisis represented by the *Kulturkampf* in Prussian Germany proved conspicuously absent. Thus the impulse toward self-organization and association was also correspondingly weaker among Austrian Catholics.

The influence of German Catholicism became especially apparent through the early Catholic general assemblies *(Katholikentage)* of which five took place in Austria. The Christian social movement in Prussian Germany grounded itself in industrial capitalism. However, the Vienna school stood firmly behind what was for all practical purposes a precapitalistic social form with a sharply critical stance against "Jewish" capital and an equally sharp position against the "godless" proletariat. In this way the movement carried with it the potential to polarize these two fronts, the socially and politically organized *petite bourgeoisie* of Catholicism and the proletariat, a potential that finally showed itself with full intensity after 1918.

In contrast to developments in Germany, Austrian Catholicism blossomed during the period between the wars. Political Catholicism—organized and led by clerics in the case of the Christian Social Party—took pride of place. Its natural enemy was an intentionally anticlerical Austro-Marxism. Unfortunately, political Catholicism in Austria proved unable to meet its two main challenges: to create a new identity for "the Austria which remained" and to attain the support of a democratic system from the anxious Catholic masses.[9] The headlong rush into an authoritarian Christian-based state in 1933 ended in 1938 with the power grab of the National Socialists. The hierarchy of the church saw these developments as the lesser of two evils, greeted them openly, or only half-heartedly fought against them. The National Socialists broke the concordat agreed upon in 1933, in their struggle against the church effectively shattering the historically grown structure of Catholicism in Austria.

Catholicism in Switzerland

Next to the German Martin Luther, John Calvin and Ulrich Zwingli are the most significant reformers of the early modern period. The effectiveness of both was manifested in territories that today are a part of Switzerland, that is, Geneva and Zurich.[10] The two men were separated less by theological than by political ideas. The Reformation and its aftermath, the painful and sometimes violent disputes between those for and against reform deeply influenced the way in which Switzerland conceived of itself culturally. Furthermore, the Reformation played the role of antagonist during the process of political unification.

At the time of the Reformation, Switzerland comprised a league of thirteen territories (today cantons) to which were attached a number of other subject regions. Five of these territories (above all, the cities, with the exception of Lucerne) embraced the Reformation, seven remained by the old faith, and one was divided by the issue. Until the French Revolution, the history of Switzerland was determined by confessional opposition. The territories formed separate leagues on the basis of confession and conducted their own foreign policy. The opposition between the confessions often led to civil war. Switzerland was united and centralized by Napoleon into the "Helvetian Republic" in 1798 only to return to the status of the territorial league after the Congress of Vienna in 1815. In 1848, after a renewed and comparatively bloodless civil war, which was waged along confessional lines and was resolved in favor of the Protestant and liberal cantons, a confederation (federal republic) of twenty-two cantons was established, predominantly Protestant but with 8½ Catholic cantons and five of mixed denomination. Clearly, politics were weighted in favor of the numerically superior Protestants and their Liberal party. The federal constitution contained clauses that discriminated against Catholicism and provisos against an autonomous politics on the behalf of Catholicism which were not formally removed until 1973.

The history of Catholicism in Switzerland must be understood against the background of this hardening confessionalism. However, the opposition between faiths is only one among several antagonisms that fill Switzerland with social and political tension. In addition, one must take into consideration the tension between city and countryside, between the entrepreneurial economy and the workers movement, and between the linguistic minorities (especially the French-speaking "Romands") and the German-speaking majority. Where these opposing forces overlap—as between the Catholic, rural-oriented, French-speaking Jura and the Protestant, urban, German-speaking canton of Bern—the differences between the two can assume powerful forms even today. In the case of the Jura only the revision of the constitution in 1978 and the acknowledgment of the Jura as a separate canton could resolve the deep-rooted conflict.

First and foremost, then, the formation of Swiss Catholicism has its roots in the opposition between the Catholic and the evangelical "states" and their political alliances and agreements. A good portion of Swiss territory belonged to dioceses whose see lay outside the political boundaries of Switzerland. These arrangements facilitated the primarily political (and not the ecclesiastical) organization of the Catholic church in Switzerland. Nevertheless, one cannot speak of a state-sponsored church here as can be done in the case of the Protestants. Efforts by Swiss Catholics in the nineteenth and twentieth centuries to bring the diocesan boundaries into agreement with existing political boundaries and to create their own provincial church foundered upon resistance both from Rome and from the individual self-governing cantons. Still today four cantons are not affiliated to a Swiss bishopric but are only administered by the bishop of Chur.

Only gradually in Switzerland did Catholicism become a mass movement and only then as a result of the so-called *Kulturkampf* (1848–1888), that is, as a result of the systematic oppression of Catholics by a Protestant-liberal majority. In a way similar to the German example, political Catholicism in Switzerland allowed for a distinction in terms of the organizational forms of its parent organizations: on the one side, the political party (the Catholic-Conservative Populist Party) and on the other; the federative or associative form of organization.

Strong ties always bound political Catholicism and associational Catholicism (which divides into a multitude of different binding alignments), and only recently have they slackened. The influence of the church upon this brand of Catholicism was, first, spiritual: "Unity and unanimity" counted as the leading motif under which oppositions between hierarchy, elites, and church membership could hardly develop. To conclude from election returns and other statistics, organized Catholicism succeeded over the long term in binding more than half of all Swiss Catholics to it. Thus a kind

of Catholic subsociety arose in Switzerland that acted as a homogeneous and polem-
ically distinct confessional block, not least in respect to the politics of the federation.
Along with the liberals and social democrats who gained political weight as the twentieth century wore on, Catholics represented the third important political force in
Switzerland until 1970.

State-church relations in Swiss law remain different from canton to canton even
today. Over the last ten years the pronounced mixing of confessions in any given
area has led to a situation in which the cantons, along with their conventionally dominant confessions, have increasingly acknowledged other religious communities as
legitimate territorial churches. Thus in many cantons until this very day the old—or
Christ-centered—Catholic church plays a role alongside that of the Roman Catholic.
This religious community separated from the Roman Catholic church as a consequence of the doctrine of papal infallibility defined at the First Vatican Council of
1870.

In comparison with the Federal Republic of Germany, the influence of the state
upon the internal organization of the church remains comparatively great. No concordat between the Holy See and the Swiss Confederation exists today because the
conception of church-state relations is at odds and because the influence of Rome
provokes a notable degree of apprehension on the part of all those concerned. The
strong democratic tradition in Switzerland has also permitted the attitudes of Swiss
Catholics to prosper in a way that is difficult to reconcile with Rome's centralism and
its hierarchical way of thinking. Thus the old Roman saying *"Bisogna lasciar gli Sviz-
zeri negli loro usi ed abusi"* ("One has to leave the Swiss with their uses and abuses")
still fits the situation.

Relevant Aspects Today: Catholicism in the Light of an Unfolding Modernity

Common Lines of Development in Church and Society since World War II

It is difficult to describe the epoch since World War II because its social and
cultural modernization arrived at different times but with similar force in the countries
in question here as well as in their Catholicism. While in the Federal Republic the
rapprochement between confessional groups was already underway before the end
of the war, and while in Austria a set of legal discriminations against the rights of
Protestants was abolished in 1961, in Switzerland the confessional tendency to think
as a solid block persisted well into the 1960s. Here the Second Vatican Council led
eventually to a break out of the "ghetto mentality." The most important developments can be outlined as follows:

1. The church increasingly disengaged itself from politics.
2. Catholic thinking gained more sway over public affairs in general although it
   lost some of its distinctive character.
3. Ecumenism and rapprochement between the denominations increased.
4. Individualization of the understanding of the meaning of faith also increased.

The tendency to loosen or dissolve the institutional entanglements of the church with politics after World War II is obvious in all of the German-speaking territories. This tendency expressed itself in the form of a withdrawal from direct, party-organized political engagement. While during the interwar period clerics not infrequently held positions of leadership within Catholic parties, after World War II they recognized that the roles of cleric and party activist were clearly incompatible. The church's relations with the liberal and socialist parties generally improved, although an effective "equidistance" between the players was never fully realized. Only the relationship to the SED (the German Socialist Unity Party) in East Germany remained tense. Appropriately, the traditional Catholic parties put aside their distinctive confessionalism and opened themselves to Protestant membership. The primary goal of political Catholicism—to secure the interests of the church in a state with a neutralized worldview and to hasten the emancipation of Catholics—was essentially fulfilled. The specific tradition of political Catholicism came to an end after the war. In recent years the increasing independence of politics in general and the growth of Christian parties into large, conservative, bourgeois, culturally integrative political parties has only served to further secure the disentanglement of the church from politics.

The disengagement of the church from politics, however, ran up against another tendency: the increasing influence of the church upon public life in general. Before World War II Catholicism more or less exercised its importance and influence as a distinct but particular and somewhat marginalized cultural entity. After the war a new phase began in which the Catholic tradition was taken seriously as an element of a pluralistic culture. Everywhere in evidence, this stepping outside the boundaries of the church's traditional milieu coincided with the withdrawal of its most distinctive features as a religion.

Thus a third line of development needs to be considered: the ecumenical rapprochement of the confessions. Sooner or later the boundaries between the confessions lost their significance everywhere in German-speaking Europe. Shared experiences like the struggle during Hitler's dictatorship and the exponential growth in everyday contact caused the specific denominational models of reality, with their reciprocal stereotypes, to lose their plausibility. At the same time weighty impulses toward ecumenical dialogue came from German theology. In the light of the decrees of Vatican II these impulses received a most impressive legitimacy. Although rapprochement between the confessions has slowed down in the last decade, the identity of Catholicism and Protestantism became more rooted in a common Christian tradition than in their polarized confessionalism. In view of the mutual stabilization of the churches since the Reformation as confessional opposites, the importance of these developments can hardly be overestimated.

Last but not least, the increasing individualization of one's understanding and acceptance of faith belongs to developmental lines common to both church and society. Culminating in the 1970s, modernization pushed those social groups that had been molded by tradition (and had remained traditional) toward a form of socialized consumerism. Catholics especially were affected by the economic development of the rural regions, expansion of the educational system, and the tremendous increase in mobility. Consequently, the "Catholic milieu" in German-speaking Central Europe partially disintegrated. The dissolution of the Catholic milieu furthered this individualizing process, which encompassed not only one's understanding of faith but also one's ties to the church, and which was magnified by a growing standardization of consciousness by the mass media.

The Catholic Church in the Federal Republic of Germany

After World War II, the Catholic church found itself in a unique situation in the Federal Republic of Germany.[11] For the first time Catholics were no longer in the minority. Moreover, the collapse of the Nazi dictatorship left in its place a spiritual and institutional vacuum which gave the Catholic church the opportunity to be very effective socially. Thus, until the mid-1960s, Catholicism enjoyed high standing and little contested authority, which offered ample opportunities to influence social development in the Federal Republic.

The church–state relationship fixed by the Weimar constitution was resurrected in the new constitution of the Federal Republic and was generously enlarged upon through a series of territorial concordats. The organizational structure of the Catholic church, however, changed only slightly within the Federal Republic. Several dioceses included within their sphere of administration certain areas of the German Democratic Republic. As of today the boundaries of the bishoprics have not been coordinated with the boundaries of the two states. Only in the area of the Ruhr was a new diocese founded, in Essen in 1957, from parts of the dioceses in Cologne, Paderborn, and Münster.

While the Nazi dictatorship had left the administrative structure of the church largely unmolested and while its continuity with the past had been secured during the period following the war, associational group Catholicism did not survive the crushing defeat of the National Socialists. In their new surroundings Catholics saw neither the ubiquitous threat that had again and again animated the old confessional organization nor did many bishops show any special interest in rejuvenating an autonomously organized lay movement. Catholicism as a whole thus underwent a kind of "internal reorganization" in the sense that the official church and its administration of confessional identity grew in importance.[12] This tendency is clearly discernible in the changed composition of the "Central Committee of German Catholics" insofar as members of particular diocesan councils were now drawn from the representatives of the various Catholic associations. The Catholic General Assemblies also changed face as a result of this train of events. Previously, these assemblies had chiefly consisted of interest groups drawn toward a thematic social position; now they became—as did the evangelical assemblies—great meeting places, especially for young Catholics.

After the war participation in religious, church-oriented life was exceptionally high. The number of regular churchgoers continued to rise until the middle of the 1960s. For the Catholics this percentage rose from 51 percent in 1949 to 55 percent in 1963.[13]

Between 1965 and 1973, participation in religious life came to a sudden and revolutionary break, one that still influences German Catholicism today. A process of social modernization along with a transformation in values came together with the church's own attempts at reform to construct an intense and inextricable network of reinforcing social and cultural factors.

The struggle waged during the 1960s over the role of the church in state schools mirrored this new situation. Strengthened by these new surroundings, Catholics did not want to stand on the sidelines while the educational system was being reformed. The stamp of confessionalism upon the state educational system—once the pride of the church's social politics—now occasioned alarm on the part of Catholics, who suspected it to be the cause of an existing educational deficit among Catholics. For the first time modern Catholicism's characteristic relation between clergy and laity was broken. The bishops stood alone in the struggle to retain state-sponsored confessional schools and saw themselves forced to abandon their old position. Like everyone else, Catholics were taking part in the fruits of the unique economic prosperity of the 1960s and 1970s in the Federal Republic and were important supporters of the new conditions of material well-being.

As a consequence, the boundaries of the Catholic milieu broadened to include a far wider range of alternative courses of action than had ever before been recognized, and this development confronted Catholic masses and elites alike. A new disassociated and differentiated relationship of Catholics to their church emerged and was stabilized in the course of the further development of the Republic. Empirical data make clear that this break in fact occurred over very few years. Thus the percentage of regular churchgoers declined suddenly between 1968 and 1973 from well over 50 percent to 35 percent.[14] As a 1970/1971 poll detected, the perception of the church by Catholics and the perception of the church by the general public were surprisingly close.[15] Many Catholics also saw themselves in tension with the value system represented by the church as against society's values. At the center of this value conflict lay the society's push toward individualization, which the sudden dissolving of the Catholic milieu further facilitated.[16]

During this same period in the Federal Republic the labor movement experienced a similar process of dissolution and push toward liberation.[17] This fact bespeaks a need for caution when bringing together the changes outlined above with the renewal of the Second Vatican Council and the attempts at reform of the church within the dynamic context of the Federal Republic. The conciliar opening up to the world corresponded to a level of consciousness and a set of interests that, in the context of a relatively sudden break with traditional forms and concepts of life, confronted Catholics in exceptional ways.

This explains the enthusiasm with which Vatican II was greeted by the majority of Catholics in the Federal Republic. However, the concurrence of conciliar renewal with the far-reaching push toward the modernization of society created an additional set of circumstances whereby church reform, especially within a large segment of the episcopate, met with suspicion, endangered the stability of the church, and yielded counterproductive results. Thus a surprising picture emerged: the same German bishops who had headed the forces for reform during the conciliar movement were now cautious and skeptical toward church reform in their own individual dioceses.

The Joint Synod of Bishops in the Federal Republic of Germany conducted from 1971 to 1975 makes plain the basically ambivalent constellation of the elements just described. On the one hand, the synodal process made it possible for bishops, priests, and laymen alike to undergo a common learning experience unique in the history of German Catholicism, a process reflected in the series of foundational, future-directed "working papers."[18] On the other, the Synod's legal form made certain that the functional control of the episcopate was not at risk. Contrary to proceedings in Austria and Switzerland, the German Synod remained more clearly a continuous process of communication without institutional anchoring. An obvious symptom of this state of affairs is seen in the fact that despite the recommendation of the Council and the Synod's own working papers and despite the wealth of the church in the Federal Republic, the funding of a "German Pastoral Institute" has not come to pass.

Consolidating this new form of Catholicism has been the task of the permanent organizations of the German Conference of Bishops. Twelve commissions for specific issues have been created, in addition to agencies, institutes, and task forces that are expected to cooperate with them. The permanent head and organizational core of this structure is the Secretariat of the German Conference of Bishops. Its influence is important because it also manages the Association of German Dioceses to which, in 1968, the dioceses in the Federal Republic attached control of their legal and economic affairs. The newly established Joint Conference, comprised of representatives of the Conference of Bishops and the Central Committee of German Catholics (representing lay organizations), originates from a resolution of this Joint Synod. Until the present, however, its influence over the evolution of the church has been meager.

Parallel with the emergence of these interdiocesan structures one can also observe an organizational differentiation and professionalization on the level of individual dioceses. This growth of personnel is due mainly to the increasing employment of lay people in the service of the church and affects not only pastoral and charitable services but also the administration of the church itself. The creation of such an administrative ecclesiastical structure is unique in the Catholic world and could not have been accomplished without the substantial wealth that flows from the tax privileges of the German churches.

The most salient feature of the contemporary religious situation in the Federal Republic is a breakdown in the transmission of the faith to the adolescent generation. The decrease in the number of churchgoers originates with the fact that the young no longer assume the obligations of their elders to participate in the life of the church. The result is a sharp rise in the ratio of elderly to the total number of churchgoers including a self-reinforcing tendency to exclude the young.[19] The increasing responsibility of democratically legitimated church councils for pastoral work has hardly led to the differentiation and multiplication of participatory forms called for by the greater openness of today's youth toward religious issues. Besides a few specific group initiatives, there are only the *Katholikentage*, which offer social forms of faith appropriate for today's young people. Moreover, now as before, men as against women, and white collar workers as against blue collar workers, along with today's youth, remain clearly underrepresented among those Catholics most intimately associated with the church.

Religious orientations, at least as far as they are accessible to empirical research, demonstrate similar tendencies.[20] There is widespread disassociation from traditional forms of dogmatism and institutionalism without the appearance of new forms of religiosity. At the same time, only a relatively small minority of individuals in the Federal Republic designate themselves "atheists." The strength of the churches and their religiosity is due to the nonexistence of viable alternatives.

The Catholic Church in the German Democratic Republic

The minority status of Catholics in the German Democratic Republic distinguishes their situation from Catholics in West Germany.[21] According to official statistics issued in 1983, there are 1.2 million members of the Catholic church and 7.7 million members of the evangelical church out of a total population of 16.7 million. Since the end of World War II the percentage of Catholics has shrunk from 11.9 percent in 1947 to 8.01 percent in 1964, and to 7.2 percent in 1983. Indeed, the high percentage of Catholics immediately following the war is accounted for by the immigration and escape from the east of many Catholic refugees who passed through East Germany. Today the percentage of Catholics is again something like it was in 1939.

Without being able to refer back to any sociological research on the subject, one must begin with the assumption that the number of church members more than likely constitutes an overly optimistic image of the situation of church and religion in the GDR. Even more clearly here than in the other German-speaking areas, those groups closely involved with the church can be divided along lines of age, profession, and community structure, into a group of people who are rather marginal to the society in which they live.

The basic situation of the Catholic church over and against the state and society was determined by stressing the separation of the church throughout every phase of the development of the GDR. Even as the period of sharp conflict between the founding of the republic (1949) and the building of the wall (1961) was winding down and the evangelical church in the GDR was, by degrees, introducing a reorientation, defining that position as one between conflict and cooperation as a "church in a socialist society," the Catholic church held fast to its position of withdrawal. It put forth in especially accentuated form what was the typical strategy of Catholic survival prior to the Second Vatican Council: its basic delimitation as a tightly organized church over and against culture and society. With a relatively large context for freedom of action that it was able to maintain because of its minority status, the Catholic church was able to strengthen itself. It managed to establish many charitable organizations, many training sites for social workers who would address spiritual problems, and programs for the training of medical specialists as well as programs for youth and adults such as the Philosophisch-Theologische Studium Erfurt for the training of priests.

The reorganization of the church administration has amounted to a step-by-step process of rapprochement between state and church. The western portion of the diocese of Breslau (now Wroclaw) lies within the boundaries of the German Democratic Republic, as does the eastern portion of the dioceses at Osnabrück, Paderborn, Fulda, and Würzburg. These territories are now administered by the diocese of Görlitz and by the bishops of Schwerin, Magdeburg, and Erfurt-Meiningen. Since 1976, together with the diocese of Dresden-Meissen and the eastern portion of the diocese of Berlin they have formed the Berlin Bishops' Conference, comprising eleven dioceses with the status of a regional conference. The Vatican has never recognized the intent of the East German government to have diocesan boundaries determined within the context of the GDR.

The Catholic church's emphasis on its distance from state and society has not remained uncontroversial within the church itself. In the course of conciliar renewal and strengthened by various ecumenical contacts, discussion began about a more worldly, more strongly dialogical and diaconal church within the context of a socialist society. The pastoral synod of Meissen (1967–1970) formulated a new orientation of these relations only to have its approach corrected by the pastoral synod in Dresden (1973–1975), which had jurisdiction over all the areas in question. Dresden took a more reserved position, a "wait-and-see" kind of attitude. In recent years, though, signs have multiplied of a cautious willingness to open the Catholic church toward socialist society. Roused by John Paul II, the bishops of East Germany drafted a pastoral letter on the question of Christian responsibility for peace. The concrete and critical position taken by the Catholic bishops has been an irritant to the state. The state has made it clear that any move away from a traditional posture of restraint where questions of social relevance are concerned carries risks for the Catholic church. The bishops' pastoral letter of October 1986 offered no new answers to the question of Catholic retreat or advancement from positions of social responsibility, although it did give more attention to the notion that society is the proper context for faith. Now as before, and more clearly than is the case with the other German-speaking areas of Catholicism, the Catholic church in the GDR is characterized by the defensive subcultural Catholicism of the period between the two Vatican Councils. Even new religious impulses, which surprisingly emerge within socialist society, do so differently in the East German church than they do in, say, Hungary.

The Catholic Church in Switzerland

As already mentioned, World War II and its consequences represent a lesser watershed for Swiss Catholicism than for the rest of German-speaking Catholicism.[22] The territorial boundaries of Switzerland, as a neutral state, remained unchanged; the country possessed an intact industrial base and peaceful relations between management and the work force, and quickly achieved what is today the highest standard of living in the world.

Although the confessional polarization in Switzerland after the war took more moderate forms than before, it was not until the Second Vatican Council that Swiss Catholicism began to move forward. The Council broke down the prejudices of the dominant Protestant groups and within Catholicism as a whole stimulated concern for strengthening the influence of those who wanted to transcend the conditions of the "confessional ghetto." The decisive change came with "Synod '72," which concerned all of Switzerland as well as each and every diocese. The bishop of Chur announced as early as 1966 that a diocesan synod would be held for the express purpose of implementing the proposals of Vatican II. The other Swiss bishops decided to take part as well; as a result, the synod instantly became a synod of all Swiss dioceses (1972–1975). These diocesan synods were paralleled by committees all over Switzerland which, together with the Conference of Swiss Bishops, made pronouncements for Switzerland as a whole. This "federalistic" synodal model addressed the Swiss conception of the state and led to exceptionally broad participation among Catholics in the "internal" workings of the church. For the first time emphasis upon the interests of Swiss Catholics shifted from the political arena to that of the church. "The Church in Switzerland" became the slogan of a program that produced increasingly transdiocesan coordination and a common set of directives (for example, concerning fasting, charity, a pastoral sociological institute, and the Catholic University of Fribourg). The Vatican Congregation of the Clergy did not agree to regulation by a pastoral council, which should include laymen as well as bishops and priests. Instead, the Swiss bishops placed considerable value upon the participation of laymen in the decisions of the church. This emphasis found expression in the form of occasional interdiocesan pastoral forums called by the Conference of Swiss Bishops.

The strong position of the cantonal organizations within the Swiss church is a characteristic unique to the Catholicism of Switzerland and is due to the conditions set by public authorities for the exercise of the churches' public status. Thus, the right to raise taxes for its support is, in most cantons, bound up with the existence of cantonal church bodies with strong lay participation. Because the majority of dioceses include several cantons the organizational structure of the church is doubled: the Conference of Swiss Bishops is paralleled by the Central Conference of Swiss Roman Catholics, which exercises a decisive influence wherever questions of finance are concerned. In contrast to Germany, fiscal and other activities remain very decentralized.

As the organized church of Swiss Catholics was being strengthened after Vatican II and lay participation was made more effective, an apparent dissolution of the old block-politics and confessionalism as well as changes in the politics of Catholic associations also took place. Not the least of these changes is expressed in the fact that since 1954 the *Schweizerischer Katholikentag* has not taken place. Interestingly, that was the first "Catholic Day" where a woman was allowed to take the podium. In 1970 the conservative, Christian-social *Volks* party, the political arm of Swiss Catholicism, changed its name to the "Christian Democratic Volks Party of Switzerland" and thereby opened itself to Protestant participation. For the time being, championing specific confessional interests has retreated into obscurity. Within the various Catholic associations noticeable changes have taken place: youth groups, traditionally segregated along gender lines no longer appear so attractive and have had to be restructured. The organizational forms of Christian motivation, such as the "Hungerdrive," appear rather weak.

However, Catholics have gained intellectual weight in the public arena as a result of the disappearance of the block-forms of confessional organization. Today, the Catholic University of Fribourg is fully integrated with the other universities in Switzerland. Catholic efforts to climb the social ladder are no longer stymied. Indeed, in Switzerland as a whole the importance of religious ties seems to be lessening. In 1960, 52.7 percent of the population was Protestant and 45.4 percent Catholic. As of the 1980 census, 45.4 percent of the population designated themselves as evangelical and 47.6 percent as Catholic. The increase among Catholics relates specifically to the steady influx of foreign workers from the Catholic countries of southern Europe, while the percentage of nondenominational designates and designates of another denomination increased from 1.4 to 7 percent. Participation in the life of the church varies strongly from region to region, as well as by social position. No reliable data exist for the whole of Switzerland, but participation in the church seems to have regressed over the last twenty years. In particular, the ties of the young to the church have grown weaker. The prevalent outlook seems to be that advanced by 80 percent of Swiss Catholics in a 1980 opinion poll: "To be Christian one need not necessarily attend church."

The Catholic Church in Austria

The path followed by Catholicism in Austria after World War II was carved from the anguishing experience of the First Republic and the government of the National

Socialists.[23] Improvement in the relations between the Catholic church and the social-ists made possible a coalition of socialists with the Austrian *Volks* party, which has lasted for years. Both forces joined together and finally succeeded in stabilizing the identity of postwar Austria. They succeeded in developing a form of state that takes its character from its federal structure and contains an extensive basis in the idea of "social partnership." In particular, societal consensus, with its ethical foundation rest-ing upon Christianity, on the one hand, and socialism, on the other, has found hard-won expression in the creation of an Austrian welfare state.

In the forefront of the first Catholic assembly in Austria after the war in 1952 was the "Mariazeller Manifesto," formulated by Austrian Catholics as a new stan-dard, one that clearly renounced the traditional alliance of throne and altar, the "state-ordained church" and the "political church" of the era between the wars. It called for all of the forces within society to work together. Although today Austrian Catholics still remain closely associated with the Austrian *Volks* party in unusually high numbers, the Catholic church, especially at the urging of the Viennese arch-bishop, Cardinal Franz König, has extricated itself from every one-sided political rela-tion to the state. The foundation of the relation between the Catholic church and the state remains the concordat finalized in 1933, which since 1957 has been acknowl-edged by the socialists and supplanted and enlarged upon through a long list of amendments.

The legal and institutional position of the Catholic church in Austria more or less matches the situation in the Federal Republic. The church enjoys a "qualified status in law" insofar as it has been granted the status of a public corporation. The common efforts of church and state extend chiefly to questions of education, vocational train-ing, charity, health, the schools, and the media. The church receives both direct and indirect assistance from the state. The Austrian system of cooperation between church and state has been given concrete form in a number of ways: religious instruc-tion in the schools is mandatory, although the right of abstention does exist; the state assumes the costs for personnel in Catholic schools; there are theological faculties at each state university; the state provides pastoral care to the military and other insti-tutions associated with the state; and Sundays and religious holidays are protected by law. The Catholic church obtained its present organizational structure through articles of amendment in 1964 and 1968. There are now two provincial churches, one at Vienna and the other at Salzburg, and nine dioceses, among them the newly established dioceses of Innsbruck and Feldkirch.

Eighty-four percent of the Austrian population belong to the Roman Catholic church. During the course of the century, however, the percentage of Catholics among the total population has diminished about 10 percent while the percentage of Protestants has almost doubled. The receding numbers of Catholics relates directly to the number of people leaving the church. Before the war these numbers changed with the swings of political movements, while today something like 30,000 Austrians a year express their distance from the church by formally leaving it altogether.

That the church of the majority is clearly the Catholic church and that this facil-itates leaving the church—especially in Vienna and other large cities—is evident when comparisons are made to the Federal Republic. As Zulehner's representative figures from 1980 make clear, one can in fact start with what was previously a stable "basic ecclesiasticality" in Austria. Indeed, this base has lessened by 15 percent through the loss of a minority of members with weak ties to the church.[24] As far as religious practice is concerned, a certain polarization has developed. And the respective extremes have become stronger: on the one hand, "very intensive" religious practice; on the other, "no practice whatsoever." The changes of the last ten years are better demonstrated through matters pertaining to one's orientation toward the church, as expressed in family rituals and weddings, than by the numbers of people who attend church services. As always, the majority of Austrians consider themselves religious (71 percent). They all share the notion that faith in God is important for a happy and meaningful life (73 percent).[25] Seventy-nine percent believe in the existence of God; 58 percent believe in life after death. Using Peter Berger's terminology, Zulehner characterized the "people's religion" as a "sacred canopy" which is supposed to provide protection, comfort, and reassurance. Its social compass favors the values of the simple life, marriage, and family, while the world of professionalism and affluence are little affected by one's faith. Now as before, however, connections between religious affiliation and party preference are strong. Also, in Austria the "aging of the flock" and gulf between the generations so evident in the Federal Republic of Germany have not yet manifested themselves.

Doubtless Austria belongs among those countries where the foundation put down by Vatican II looks back upon a long-established tradition. The ideas—already circulating before 1848—of the Catholic reformer Bernhard Bolzano need only be remembered to establish this fact; and Vatican II itself received significant impetus from Austrian professors Karl Rahner and Ferdinand Klostermann. After Vatican II, readiness for change was especially evident in Austria because this conciliar opening of Catholicism toward the contemporary world corresponded so effectively to the situation in which Austrian Catholics found themselves. The pastoral constitution on the church and the modern world (*Gaudium et Spes*) offered an outstanding opportunity for Catholics to tear down long-standing walls of confrontation between themselves and others and to openly cooperate with other social groups in forming contemporary social life.

Even in Austria, however, the long-term institutional transformations introduced by Vatican II remained far behind the level of enthusiasm for change and the charisma in the period immediately following the council. But more than in the Federal Republic, the church in Austria succeeded in developing a lasting foundation for church reform and in institutionalizing circumstances that continue to reflect the situation of the church in the modern world.

Synods took place in almost every diocese that joined in the so-called Austrian Synodal Proceedings. The Conference of Austrian Bishops reports regularly on the state of the church's social effectiveness in "Five-Year Reports."[26] The Institute for Pastoral Social Research in Vienna is another of the accomplishments of the Bishops' Conference. This institution has put together an accurate pastoral-sociological data base and has developed an empirically supported image of pastoral theology valued as highly as its counterparts in the Federal Republic.

The postconciliar reform movement has also increased the diversity within Austrian Catholicism. Along with the Catholic associations and "Catholic Action," new groups generated by the charisma of reform, such as "Family Circle," the "Meditation Circle," and Christian "basic communities," all function as a kind of Catholic "third column." But the Catholic assemblies of the 1980s, especially the Jubilee Assembly of 1983 which included a visit from the pope, have made plain the difficulties ahead for taking conciliar renewal any further along the path of reform or of expanding the intellectualism of the post-Vatican II period. These assemblies have demonstrated the strength of traditional forms of piety among the masses while introducing new elements into the traditional ceremonies of the church.

The recent appointments of bishops which the Vatican chose without consulting either the respective dioceses or the Austrian Conference of Bishops have disappointed the majority of Austrian Catholics and may lead to new tensions between pre- and postconciliar trends in Austrian Catholicism.[27]

Sociological Interpretation

In conclusion, we must ask one question: Which theoretical perspective might best interpret the development of Catholicism in German-speaking Central Europe? It should already be clear that what is going on is hardly a unilinear process of secularization at the institutional, societal, and personal levels which will continue into the foreseeable future. During the second half of the nineteenth century, ostensibly one high point of the secularization process, the influence of the church upon the various Catholic social classes was greater than at any other time in its history. The fact that Catholicism in German-speaking Europe had never before exercised an influence upon the development of the state as great as that in the development of the Federal Republic is also seriously at odds with this interpretation. What was true in the past remains true today: the various forms of religiosity in the German-speaking nations— with the exception of the GDR—belong to the sociocultural self-conception of the German-speaking public.

So what other interpretation can be offered as a basis for understanding the development and contemporary situation of Catholicism in the countries we have been discussing? In characterizing the whole of the developmental process one can say that Catholicism, on the basis of the political confessionalism of the Reformation and the development of autonomous social alignments during the nineteenth century, has yielded a specifically modern social form of the Christian tradition. This modern social form developed in tandem with the nineteenth-century model of industrial society in which elements of tradition and modernity converged and in a reciprocal manner fell out of balance.[28] The ultimate triumph of modernity after World War II has once again set free the tensions always inherent in processes of modernization only to have this development rob the specifically modern form of Catholicism of its social base. Catholicism today faces an alternative: as a social factor it either retreats to a reservation for a dwindling amount of traditional lifestyles or, on a new plain, it works with the other social forces at large to produce again a balanced form of modernity.[29] On the basis of a desire to develop a humane society one can only hope for the success of the latter alternative. Indeed, properly understood, it establishes the tasks ahead for church reform and the necessity of Catholicism's search for new social forms, which have as a foundation a sufficient relationship between institutions, individuals, and the circumstances of contemporary life.

NOTES

1. See H. Schilling, *Konfessionskonflikt und Staatsbildung* (Gütersloh: Mohn, 1981); E. W. Zeeden, *Konfessionsbildung: Studien zur Reformation, Gegenreformation und katholischer Reform* (Stuttgart: Klett-Cotta, 1985).
2. See A. Langner (ed.), *Katholizismus, nationaler Gedanke und Europa seit 1800* (Paderborn: Schönigh, 1985).
3. For more extensive analysis, see K. Gabriel and F. X. Kaufmann (eds.), *Zur Soziologie des Katholizismus* (Mainz: Grünewald, 1980). For good overviews of the history of German Catholicism, see H. Hurten, *Kurze Geschichte des deutschen Katholizismus, 1800–1960* (Mainz: Grünewald, 1986); C. Bauer, *Deutscher Katholizismus: Entwicklungslinien und Profile* (Frankfurt: Knecht, 1964); A. Rauscher (ed.), *Der soziale und politische Katholizismus: Entwicklungslinien in Deutschland, 1803–1963* (Munich: Olzog, 1981); K.-E. Lönne, *Politischer Katholizismus im 19. und 20. Jahrhundert* (Frankfurt: Suhrkamp, 1986).
4. E. E. Y. Hales, *Pio Nono: A Study in European Politics and Religion in the Nineteenth Century* (London: Eyre & Spottiswoode, 1952).
5. J. Sperber, *Popular Catholicism in 19th Century Germany* (Princeton, N.J.: Princeton University Press, 1984).
6. F. X. Kaufmann, *Theologie in soziologischer Sicht* (Freiburg: Herder, 1973), pp. 78–92.
7. F. X. Kaufmann, "Secular Law and the Form of Religious Organization in the Federal Republic of Germany," *Acts of the 19th International Conference for the Sociology of Religion*, Tübingen, 1987.
8. See N. Leser (ed.), *Religion und Kultur an Zeitenwenden: Auf Gottes in Österreich* (Vienna: Herold, 1984); J. Lenzeneger, P. Stockmeier, K. Amon, and R. Zinnhobler (eds.), *Geschichte der katholischen Kirche* (Graz: Styria, 1986).
9. A. Diamant, *Austrian Catholics and the First Republic: Democracy, Capitalism and the Social Order, 1918–1934* (Princeton, N.J.: Princeton University Press, 1960).
10. See U. Altermatt, *Der Weg der Schweizer Katholiken ins Ghetto* (Zurich: Benziger, 1972); Altermatt, "Der Schweizer Katholizismus von 1948 bis zur Gegenwart," *Historisches Jahrbuch der Görres Gesellschaft* 103 (1983):76–106; P. Stadler, *Der Kulturkampf in der Schweiz* (Frauenfeld-Stuttgart: Huber, 1984); J. Müller (ed.), *Katholische Kirche Schweiz heute* (Fribourg: Kanisius, 1981).
11. For overviews, see the literature cited in note 3, as well as H. Maier (ed.), *Deutscher Katholizismus nach 1945* (Munich: Koesel, 1964); K. Forster (ed.), *Katholizismus und Kirche: Zum Weg des deutschen Katholizismus nach 1945* (Studien und Berichte der Katholischen Akademie in Bayern, vol. 28, Würzburg, 1965); N. Greinacher and H. P. Risse (eds.), *Bilanz des deutschen Katholizismus* (Mainz: Grünewald, 1966); G. Gorschenek (ed.), *Katholiken und ihre Kirche* (Munich: Olzog, 1976). The monthly review *Herder-Korrespondenz* is the main forum for discussing current trends in German Catholicism.
12. One may speak about a "churchification" *(Verkirchlichung)* of Catholicism; cf. F. X. Kaufmann, *Kirche begreifen* (Freiburg: Herder, 1979).
13. See R. Köcher, "Religiös in einer säkularisierten Welt: Eine religionssoziologische Analyse der internationalen Wertestudie." (Unpublished paper, Allensbach, 1985).
14. Ibid.
15. Kaufmann, *Theologie in soziologischer Sicht*, pp. 111–16.
16. See G. Schmidtchen, *Zwischen Kirche und Gesellschaft* (Freiburg: Herder, 1972); K. Förster (ed.), *Befragte Katholiken—Zur Zukunft von Glaube und Kirche* (Freiburg: Herder, 1973).

17. See J. Mooser, "Auflösung der proletarischen Milieus: Klassenbindung und Individualisierung in der Arbeiterschaft vom Kaiserreich bis in die Bundesrepublik Deutschland," *Soziale Welt* 34 (1983):270-306.

18. Cf. *Gemeinsame Synode der Bistümer in der Bundesrepublik Deutschland: Offizielle Gesamtausgabe*, 2 vols. (Freiburg: Herder, 1976-1977).

19. Cf. R. Köcher, "Abwendung von der Kirche: Eine demoskopische Untersuchung über Jugend und Religion," *Herder Korrespondenz* 35 (1981):443-46; Köcher, "Religiosität Jugendlicher ohne Kirche?" *Religionsunterricht Heute* 1-2 (1985):6-10.

20. *Zur pastoralsoziologischen Situation im Bistum Essen: Daten und Überlegungen* (Mimeographed report of the Institut für kirchliche Sozialforschung des Bistums Essen, 1986); R. Köcher, "Religiös in einer säkularisierten Welt"; Zentralarchiv für empirische Sozialforschung zu Köln, *Allgemeine Bevölkerungsumfrage der Sozialwissenschaften*, Cologne, 1983.

21. See W. Knauft, *Katholische Kirche in der DDR* (Mainz: Grünewald, 1980); M. Albus, "Kirche in der DDR," in M. Albus and P. M. Zulehner (eds.), *Nur der Geist macht lebendig: Zur Lage der Kirche in Deutschland nach 20 Jahren Konzil und 10 Jahren Synode* (Mainz: Grünewald, 1985); Th. Mechtenberg, *Die Lage der Kirchen in der DDR* (Miesbach: Hanns-Seidel-Stiftung, 1985); F. Neubert, *Reproduktion von Religion in der DDR-Gesellschaft* (Frankfurt am Main: Lembeck, 1986).

22. Besides the literature cited in note 10, see A. Stoecklin, *Schweizer Katholizismus: Eine Geschichte der Jahre 1925-1975 zwischen Ghetto und Konziliarer Öffnung* (Zurich: Benzinger, 1978); *L'Eglise catholique de Suisse* (Brussels: Pro Mundi Vita, 1982); H. P. Röthlin, *Einheit und Vielfalt der Kirche in der Schweiz* (Mimeographed document of the Informationsstelle der Schweizer Bishofskonferenz, Fribourg, 1984). The *Schweizerische Pastoralsoziologische Institut* at St. Gall publishes *Kirchenstatistische Hefte* (reports on church statistics) and reports on various issuses in Swiss Catholicism. A recent assessment of the situation has been given by Leo Karrer in a series of articles in the *Schweizerische Kirchenzeitung* 155 (1987):97-102, 113-19, and 129-31.

23. Besides the literature cited in note 8, see Th. Piffl-Percevic (ed.), *Kirche in Österreich: Berichte, Überlegungen, Entwürfe* (Graz: Styria, 1979); *Die katholische Kirche in Österreich* (Brussels: Pro Mundi Vita, 1985).

24. See Zulehner, *Religion im Leben der Österreicher* (Vienna: Herder, 1981), p. 61.

25. Institut für kirchliche Sozialforschung (Essen), p. 21.

26. *Österreichischer Synodaler Vorgang—Sekretariat: Fünfjahresberichte über den Stand der gesellschaftlichen Wirksamkeit der katholischen Kirche in Österreich, 1977-81* (Vienna, 1982).

27. Cf. H. Erharter, "Bischofsernennungen unter Missachtung der Österreichen," *Orientierung* 51 (1987):74-78.

28. See K. Gabriel, "Die neuzeitliche Gesellschaftsentwicklung und der Katholizismus als Sozialform der Christentumsgeschichte," in K. Gabriel and F. X. Kaufmann (eds.), *Zur Soziologie des Katholizismus*, pp. 201-225.

29. See F. X. Kaufmann and J. B. Metz, *Zukunftsfähigkeit—Suchbewegungen im Christentum* (Freiburg: Herder, 1987).

8

Stages of Religious Change in Hungary

Miklós Tomka

For about a thousand years, from the beginning of the eleventh century until 1948, Hungary considered itself a Christian country. By tradition it has a large Catholic majority, and Catholicism was the established state religion.[1] Before World War II the church owned large amounts of land[2] and operated a great number of schools,[3] hospitals, and printing houses; there was a large network of church organizations,[4] and the church exercised significant political influence.[5] Religion's institutionalization and integration into the social system was similar to other European countries with a Catholic majority until the advent of industrialization, urbanization, and secularization, and is similar to most countries in present-day Latin America.[6]

In the new situation following 1945, attempts to build a socialist society brought about radical changes in the form, location, and function of the whole religious system. By "religious system" we mean: (1) the place and role of religion in the social structure; (2) the role religion plays in one's personal motivations and way of life (including individual religiosity and religious practice); and (3) the institutional and organized expressions of religion. The socialist experiment has produced different types of religious system. Historically these changes involved much more than simply a shift in the politics of the church; dramatically different forms were given to the whole religious system. Three distinct stages of religious change can be discerned: the immediate post-1948 period when the church lost its lands, its schools, its welfare bodies, and its hospitals; the decade after 1956 when sociopolitical stabilization made religion uninteresting and the church slipped into the background; and the economic and political changes inaugurated in 1964–1965, which eventually led to a religious revival beginning at the end of the 1970s.[7] Analysis of these periods is important not only for understanding the evolution of Catholicism in Hungary but also for studying potential social forms of religion.

Confrontation

In essence, Hungarian politics after World War II sought to create a perfect new society. One aspect of this effort was the reconstruction of the whole sociopolitical system, with both cultural and social consequences. The former elite or leading social stratum was "de-classed." Upward mobility was now effected by administrative means; the onward mobility of the former lower and middle classes continued; and the entire institutional structure of society was rebuilt. The expressed political goal was the rapid replacement of the former social system with one imagined to be ideal. But replacement is not a natural process; in Hungary it was imposed by political power and achieved at a high social cost.

Termination of the bond between state and church was one of the most important changes. The political slogan justifying the division of church and state rested on the results of civil development and early secularization; the differentiation of sacred and profane was declared an unavoidable stage in social progress. In contrast, the process of political change—the suppression of political parties and nationalization—did not lead to differentiation but to the cultural predominance of political centralization and a unified ideology and culture. The nationalization of church-sponsored schools, hospitals and welfare organizations, and printing houses and press centers occurred within this framework, after an earlier nationalization of church estates. The church was also deprived of its religious activities in public hospitals, reform schools, prisons, homes for the elderly, and the army (with religious training in elementary schools the only exception). In sum, the church lost not only its partnership in the organization of the state but also the bulk of its political and economic power.

Obviously the cultural importance and influence of the church diminished. The autocratic political structure allocated it a new function: to be the opposition.[8] The church became a reservoir for the unsatisfied, who sometimes were the majority. Struggle on behalf of the outlawed was nothing new for the church; nevertheless, what a difference compared to earlier times! It was now the church that reclaimed the acceptance of democratic principles and the will of the majority, as with the question of land distribution and nationalization. The state was able to determine the outcome of this political struggle only by the decapitation of the church.[9] This produced a profound cultural controversy in Hungary, especially at the level of values and ideas. The earlier triumphalism of the church was replaced; the church was cornered and obliged to fight.

At the same time, despite the church's changed political location, its profile was actually heightened because of its opposition to what was happening in the larger society. Changes in political function were, of course, a direct result of the shift in the relationship between state and church. The ensuing confrontation weakened the stability of the centralized, totalitarian political system. Long-term tension between religion and the state created pressure for change. The church partly denied the legitimacy of the sociopolitical system and thus decreased its influence. In this way religion became the bearer and institutional source of a culture different from and in opposition to the official one.

The integrating function of religion affected only one part of society, namely, the opposing part, even as the new political system altered religion's place in the social structure. Until the end of World War II religion had penetrated the whole population, although its roots were stronger in the peasantry than among workers. In the postwar period until 1956 the church's relation to political power became the decisive factor for religious practice. The powerless majority maintained its contacts with religion; those who possessed or sought to acquire power distanced themselves from religion. This situation also shaped social expectations. Informal social control was a force in favor of religion, while formal control opposed it. The ideological polarization of Hungarian society thus determined both the image of religion and people's relation to it. On the one hand, religion was understood as persecuted but able to exercise some opposition; on the other, it was a force that supported tradition and the former social order.

Clearly this political and ideological confrontation was not the same for everyone. It became important only for those touched by power and its changes or, to be more exact, only those whose personal situation was bound up with political change. For those affected, however, religiosity and church adherence, which formerly were inherited qualities and largely unreflected, now became a matter of decision and courage. Religion assumed a higher value in personal life, especially for the younger, mobile, and educated sector of society. This was followed by a clarification in the personal role of religion. The great majority of Hungarians understood religion as a persistent basis of their worldview in an age of confrontation. The challenge coming from holistic Marxism did not weaken this perception but stimulated reflection and increased the intellectualization of religion. Religion was now accepted as a measure of morality, despite the opposition of government officials who tried to establish a different foundation for ethical behavior. In contrast to former times, religion grew in importance as a regulator of individual and communal life and as a valuable source of social relations and community, but only for that part of society with religious self-understanding. Finally, although more people practiced religion than before and religion itself became more conscious and personal, religious practice rested on more than purely religious motivation.

During the immediate postwar period, the position of the church also changed. As part of the process of political centralization, the church faced not only the loss of its property and institutions but also the dissolution of important parts of its organization—the religious orders, lay movements, and congregational groups. The remaining networks of diocesan clergy, parishes, and dioceses specialized exclusively in sacramental and liturgical services. Activities outside of worship and preaching were prohibited. The state, ironically, thereby strengthened the centralized and clerical disposition of the church. This simple church organization had sufficient personnel. Replacements were guaranteed not only by a large number of new recruits but also by former members of the dissolved religious orders.

Given the acknowledged determination of the ruling political group, however, even this organization could not be maintained as an absolutely certain sphere for the church's life. Many felt that guarantees to survival must be sought outside the accepted framework. Members of the dissolved religious orders tried to stay in contact with one another despite considerable pressure. Private prayer and study groups, small communities, and religious instruction (up to high school standards) developed in secret. These isolated efforts did not constitute an underground church, but perhaps only the seeds of one. In all of this, the members of the dissolved religious orders were decisive. They were accepted by the state neither as priests nor as members of an order, but worked in a way similar to the French worker-priests in a variety of places. In this way there emerged, alongside the officially permitted church structure, a parallel structure, more informal than formal, with the same identity and same aims as the official church. A certain division of labor was worked out within the prescribed limits. Forbidden activities like youth work, religious education, social work, and political involvement had to find their own channels of expression. The government, of course, had not foreseen such solutions; when they were noticed they were labeled as a conspiracy against the state and condemned. By making martyrs for this semi-underground church, the judiciary in fact strengthened it. And since these activities and communities were carried on independently of the official church, it was difficult for the state to condemn the church itself. It is important to note the integrating and unifying role the church played under these circumstances. It was able to preserve unity between the official church and the plurality of spontaneous groups lacking any formal ties with it. Further, the state's efforts to divide the church by establishing a movement of so-called "peace priests" brought no success; the church remained united against it.

The functions performed by the church during this period were obviously influenced by the general political framework. The church understood its mission in universal terms: the gospel encompassed everyone. The practice of confrontation, however, worked to divide. The preservation and transmission of the faith was a task for Christians; representatives of antireligious policy were opposed and excommunicated. Although the church's political and cultural role in fighting for fundamental human rights and moral values (e.g., for the family or the rights of the unborn) lent it new authority, its structural onesidedness became a source for later loss.

Nor could the organized church sufficiently provide either for evangelizing or for renewing Christianity, though this lack would only later become visible. Rapid industrialization, urbanization, revolutionary growth in education, and, in consequence, an extreme mobility, destroyed both the strongly traditional religious culture and its interconnecting relationships based mostly on kinship and neighborhood, which had formerly sustained the religious culture. A crippled church could not substitute for this loss with a single hour of religious instruction and another hour's religious service per week; nor could it fully guarantee adequate religious socialization.

Two forms of evangelization were typical in this period of confrontation. Both were independent of the regularly organized activities of the official church. With the migration of a large number of peasants to the cities, the proportion of people practicing religion grew faster in the working class than among white collar workers. A more conscious but private evangelization was performed by members of the abolished religious orders who found themselves in very different surroundings. Certainly both ways of transmitting religion were impermanent. Migration from the villages slowed down in the early 1960s. The number of former religious priests and nuns engaged in secular occupations diminished, partly because of the absence of replacements, aging, emigration, and the incardination of some of them in dioceses. Evangelization in effect ceased to exist, since the official church was not allowed any activity outside the church building (apart from carefully defined religious instruction in elementary schools), and because it accepted this regulation.

Such a religious system possessed no potential for renewal. All its energies were absorbed by its confrontation with Marxism and a hostile state. It was compelled to withdraw into tradition, insisting on practices and beliefs that had formerly proved effective. Church and religion behaved in a traditional fashion and the religious system was on the defensive. Even renewal efforts in other countries could not be utilized: the Iron Curtain effectively isolated Hungary from the universal church. The church lost its capacity to reproduce itself. Soon after World War II church authorities decided that doctors of theology should leave the country. The nine high schools sponsored by religious orders were liquidated and diocesan seminaries were reduced from twelve to five. The absence of an assured replacement of intellectual forces and scientific staff prepared the way for decades of devastating consequences. Since autonomous reflection and conscientious attitudes were made difficult if not impossible, the church's incapacity for renewal endangered its own survival.

This religious system, however, turned out to be provisional. The effort of the ruling communist party to create a totally new and ideal society, as well as the cult of personality characteristic of the immediate postwar period of dogmatism, could not endure forever. The strategy of the church and of the religious half of the population was to weather the storm and hope for political change. The state's continuing affronts to human rights and the public good for the sake of abstract goals created serious moral obstacles to any cooperation by the church. Moreover, such cooperation would have been seen as inexcusable collaboration. Confrontation and withdrawal cannot be practiced without limitations. The postwar religious system was in a certain way a response to the intolerable. When socioeconomic conditions became acceptable, that is, when the majority of the population accepted the political order as the basis of present and future life, the church's response lost its justification. At the same time, the church's own inability to renew itself prevented preparation for the time "after." The consequences of this tardiness became manifest in the years following 1956, when the church faced a new set of sociopolitical conditions and expectations.

Isolation

The next stage of religious change in Hungary began with the recovery of 1956 and continued for a decade. Political dogmatism passed into limbo, and Hungary commenced to construct a new type of socialism supported by the majority of the population. Party and government rejected the former politics of confrontation. Instead, they strove for understanding by all social forces, one of which was the church or groups of religious people. While politicians differed in their estimates of the numerical strength of Hungarian religiosity, they recognized that religion and the church would not disappear in the short term. The politics of national unity led both the state and the church to search for agreement about a *modus vivendi,* which, after the previous period of confrontation, had to encompass the pragmatic regulation of coexistence. The rearrangement of these relationships served to clarify some questions but neither reversed nor corrected the restrictions on the organizational presence of the church.

The characteristic feature of this period was to safeguard a living space for religion and the church that would create an opportunity to integrate them within the whole social and political organism under appropriate state control. The evolution of a sociocultural alternative or even of a "counter" or "contrast-society" was impossible because the church lacked its traditional organizations and was prevented from developing new ones.[10] The door of progress did not lead toward a counterculture but toward a sectarian existence. No publicity was given to this new stiuation. The church simply accepted as a self-limitation that it had nothing to do with the concerns of secular life, the public affairs of the non-church-goer, or with social problems. Undoubtedly the church's withdrawal from public life contributed to a stabilization of the political order. In turn, the institutional church remained outside the process of sociopolitical change, with no chance to influence its evolution. Since its different role remained hidden, the church's activity did not render Hungarian society explicitly more complex. For this reason, the new politics of national unity was in fact built on false pretenses.

The church's new relationship to the state was mirrored in other aspects of the social structure. The expression of religious values in social and public matters was not desired, yet private religiosity was not forbidden. So long as religion remained a purely individual affair, religious practice was accepted as a human right. After all, religiosity and social status stood in inverse relation to each other.[11] As for the public sphere, religiosity was effectively marginalized.

This situation posed a difficult choice for religious people. One option was to renounce all rights and privileges with which the society did not, in any case, provide all its members. This meant accepting a low social position without power and with little money. That this option was feasible at all demonstrates that the state did not have sufficient power to enforce an overall rejection of religion. At the same time, the defenseless and semimarginal groups, with no social influence, hardly posed a threat to the political equilibrium. Hence the authorities felt no need to undertake direct repression of these "nonconformists." Put another way, insofar as someone was willing to renounce the rewards and gratifications offered by the state, he or she was able to transgress state expectations by publicly practicing religion.

A second option was relevant only for people who strove for higher goals: a qualified job, improving their intellectual or other skills, an occupation in direct contact with people, such as education. Such people were forced into a kind of double-dealing: on the one hand, a privately practiced and otherwise secret and hidden religiosity, on the other, behaving in public without any reference to religion. Such conduct in fact produced an artificial social schizophrenia. It was not easy to preserve one's real self and authentic religious adherence in this atmosphere.

The number of believers started to fall during this post-1965 period. A curious optical illusion caused this decline to appear greater than it was in reality. The semimarginal groups were only slightly reflected in public opinion polls; nor were they represented among those seeking higher positions. On the other hand, religiosity in the middle and upper classes remained mostly hidden. The filter between the religious ghetto and profane public life worked well. The division of society into two well-isolated parts temporarily reestablished the self-evident religiosity of the lower classes and the nonreligiosity of the middle and upper classes. The middle and upper classes, of course, were less organically structured and more vulnerable to explicit state pressure; both formal and informal social controls, therefore, strengthened their nonreligious attitudes.

The close connection between groups unable to express their interests or their religion, the option to practice religion secretly and retain its concealment under certain circumstances, the separation of open religiosity and everyday life, and the self-accepted withdrawal of the church from public and socially relevant issues—all of these separate social facts had a common result: the almost total disappearance of religion from Hungarian culture and society. Religion was understood less and less as a basis for one's worldview and morality. Its integrating role worked, if at all, only among religious people. Even in the private sphere there was a decline in religious belief and practice (see Tables 8.1 and 8.2).

The main distinctive feature of the religious system in this period is its double-track nature. The official church believed that, despite its absence from the public sphere, its situation had improved compared to the confrontation of the immediate postwar years. It also believed that the lack of church leaders could be recovered, the continuity of the hierarchy protected, and the administration of the sacraments guaranteed.[12] To safeguard these rights and possibilities, the official church condemned every religious activity and all communal movements of which the state disapproved. There were, however, a large number of priests and lay Catholics who took it upon themselves to substitute for the church's neglect of such areas as religious education, cultivating religious communities, and promoting spirituality, despite

TABLE 8.1 Catholic Religious Practice and the Number of Priests and Seminary Students Between 1948 and 1985

Year	Baptisms (%)	Church Weddings (%)	Religious Burials (%)	Priests per 10,000 Catholics	Seminary Students per 10,000 20-24-Year-Old Catholic Men
1948	—	—	—	82.7	46.4
1951	102.8*	86.3	90.8	61.1	—
1955	—	—	—	—	15.6
1961	99.9	83.5	90.2	55.9	8.3
1971	89.6	68.0	88.2	48.3	7.5
1974	—	—	—	—	6.8
1976	—	—	—	—	6.0
1978	—	—	—	—	5.3
1980	—	—	—	—	6.5
1981	71.1	57.1	83.8	40.9	6.6
1983	—	—	—	—	6.8
1984	73.0	58.4	83.0	37.0	7.4
1985	—	—	—	—	7.5

*In 1951 the birthrate of Catholics was higher than the national average; it is also possible that some children of non-Catholic parents and/or orphans were baptized as Catholics.

TABLE 8.2 Religious and Nonreligious Self-Identification in Hungarian Polls Between 1972 and 1976

| YEAR | "Are You Religious or Non-Religious?" | | | "Which of the Following Statements Best Reflects Your Position?" | | | | | |
	RELIGIOUS	NON-RELIGIOUS	UNDECIDED AND NO REPLY	I Am Religious... I Follow the Teachings of the Church	I Am Religious... In My Own Personal Way	I Cannot Really Say Whether or Not I Am Religious	I Am Not Religious... and I Am Not Interested in Things Like That	I Am Not Religious... Since It Is My Conviction That Religion Is Wrong	Other Replies and No Reply
1972	46.0	46.6	7.4						
1974	47.2	50.6	2.2						
1975	44.8	53.2	2.0						
1977	38.9	57.8	3.2						
1978	36.3	62.2	1.5	8.1	36.2	10.9	17.3	23.5	4.0
1979	38.6	60.1	1.3						
1980	37.7	60.7	1.4	10.6	40.9	8.2	19.3	19.0	2.0
1981	39.3	59.1	1.6						
1983				9.5	44.4	9.5	17.2	16.1	3.3
1984				14.6	44.8	7.6	15.0	14.1	3.9
1985	40.7	57.5	1.7	10.9	42.6	5.3	14.5	11.4	15.3*
1986				12.0	47.7	7.2	16.3	12.6	4.0

NOTE: These poll data were collected by the author and have not yet been published.
The sample sizes for the first question are as follows: in 1972: 9,000; 1974: 1,200; 1975: 6,000; 1977: 500; 1978: 10,000; 1979: 10,000; 1981: 6,000; 1985: 4,000; for the 5-item scale: in 1978: 500; 1980: 1,000; 1983: 1,000; 1984: 9,000; 1985: 8,000; 1986: 9,000.
*Instead of a 5-item scale the 1985 poll contained a 6-item scale. The added item ("I am not religious, but I am interested in religion") was chosen by 13.1 percent of the respondents.

rebukes from official church authorities. A great gulf thus appeared in the church; two strategies of action opposed each other. Each had a different relationship to the secular political power. Each understood differently the goal of the church, and in different ways each met the religious needs and aspirations of the people.[13]

As the official church more clearly defined its relation to the state, its integration into the state progressed. The "parallel church" possessed no organization and tried to function unostentatiously. The state considered it to be a strange body, a grain of sand in the machine, and tried to remove it. Thus, while the official church moved into a position of public isolation with regard to the state, the "parallel church" continued in a stage of confrontation. The official church's program consisted of preserving and protecting Christianity in the social space permitted to it—among church members and in the sphere of private religiosity. The "parallel church" eschewed such limitations, striving instead for the totality of Christian life and witness. In fact, all the activities of the official church pertained to worship and preaching (often in an abstract, nostalgic manner unrelated to the present). The "parallel church," in contrast, undertook efforts of conscientization, promotion of religious culture, and the augmentation of religious education, simultaneous with the sacramental practice provided by the official church.

The objective of the official church was to create Christians with strong ties to the church. To provide for them, it maintained a network of parishes covering the whole country. The "parallel church" of this time consisted of engaged Christians who accepted in principle a general and unlimited vocation to all people, but who were able to realize it first among students and intellectuals. With its declining resources the official church was unable to guarantee the transmission of the faith. Beginning in this period, we witness a diminution even of the rites of passage: a large number of babies were not baptized; only two-thirds of the baptized proceeded to first holy communion and only one-third to confirmation; at most, 5 percent of young people attended Sunday mass. To preserve the continuity of the faith, the "parallel church" organized religious instruction, small communities, and spiritual retreats with considerable success.

Under the influence of the official church, then, there was no renewal during this period. The preparations for the Second Vatican Council did not touch the Hungarian church. Even the participation of some of its bishops in the Council brought no change for many years. It was too early to speak about the "parallel church" as an agent of renewal. Its strong commitment and acceptance of responsibility and its growing maturity and autonomy on religious questions were fundamental and perhaps functioned as conditions for—and precursors of—a later religious renewal.

The typical characteristic of the post-1956 religious system, therefore, was the absence of a unifying and integrating church. The official and parallel churches consisted mostly of the same people. Yet each carried on its own life, sometimes without any communication with the other. At other times, unavoidable contacts escalated into conflicts and condemnations of each other's ways of thinking and acting. Because of this neither could reach the rapidly growing numbers of people who lived outside the church. Religious people within and outside the church had neither contact nor communication with one another.

Until now the official church had been the accepted representative for all religious people in questions of morality, worldview, and politics. Whenever the state wished to negotiate any matter with the religious half of society, it did so with representatives of the official church, even though the government knew the official church no longer represented the majority of religious people. The official church was also considered the norm against which any other form of religious expression (ranging from the "parallel church" to nonchurch religiosity) was judged deviant. This left the social image and influence of the official church in a position of considerable ambiguity.

A religious system of isolation manifests important deficiencies in all its relationships. Perhaps the most important is an absence of concern for public affairs and social problems. What remains is a certain social "egoism," which is adequate neither to realize the central goal of the church's mission nor to sustain committed Christians. Nor is the church respected by the state or the society at large, since neither receives any support from it.

Dialogue

The third stage of religious change in Hungary began in the mid-1960s and coincides with the development of what has been called the Hungarian model of socialism. This model is characterized by relative political and economic stability and includes the acceptance of certain elements of a market economy—an emphasis on efficiency and opening up private initiatives. It is a socialism that allows for greater social differentiation and a political system that strives to reconcile different social interests. The church—and religion—initially played no part in this general development. The accent lay on economic growth and the struggle for wealth. The inner logic of this evolution, however, pushed toward a redefinition of the relationship between state and church, the sacred and the profane.

In the first decade of this period (1965-1975) economic growth was continuous. Two aspects of this growth are particularly important. The first was an increased autonomy for economic, cultural, and other organizations. The second related to the social costs and consequences of growth itself. On the one hand, economic factors were judged to be more important for progress than either ideology or politics, and this change in emphasis produced other shifts in the social structure. The organizational complexity of the state expanded; the degree of freedom for all organizations increased. Space was created for new initiatives, which also affected the church. On the other hand, the stress on efficiency created a diabolic circle that destroyed communities and social values. Women were moved into the sphere of work; two wage earners per family became the norm and in most cases was unavoidable. Legal permission was granted for second, third, or even more jobs. This made the shortening of official working hours senseless: real working time became longer since the second shift of three, four, or five hours began for the same person after his or her regular eight-hour working day. Housework, however, remained the woman's task. Children were left in kindergartens and dayschools. Crime, divorce, and suicide were on the rise. Neither increased freedom nor increased wealth guaranteed more personal happiness, and public opinion polls revealed a revitalized desire for nonmaterial values.

Since 1975 economic growth has slowed, social services have been reduced, and social tensions have increased. At the same time, there is pressure to solve these problems by engaging the participation of all levels of society. The need to share burdens emerged just when official policy was moving closer to religion and when articles appeared in the nonreligious press about the possibility of a larger social role for the church. Two religious printing firms began new life after apparent death, a house for retreats opened, theological correspondence courses for lay people (including women) were permitted, and the church was allowed to operate a home for the elderly and homes for mentally and physically handicapped children, and take the first steps toward establishing a religious order for women to increase the personnel involved in social work. A readiness on the part of the state to accept pragmatic solutions appeared stronger than historical prejudice and ideological reservations.

The chance of a slow organizational renewal of the church has increased the value of religion in society at large, whether people want it or not. This development represents a curious contradiction both to the irresistible decline of traditional religion and to its meager presence in the official culture. All the religious concerns of the former culture had been forgotten through decades of antireligious socialization and the obvious disadvantages of admitting religious adherence. A whole generation has grown up without any knowledge of Hungary's Christian cultural heritage. Yet when dissatisfaction rose against the state's emphasis on efficiency as well as a desire for more transcendent values, the conspiracy of silence about religion fell under sharp criticism. In the last six to eight years books and programs about religion have reappeared, and the Bible as literature is now taught in schools. In marked contrast to former practice, the role of religion is now seen to have great value. Official Marxist and Christian representatives have begun a dialogue. One part of this dialogue is the acceptance of each other's position, perhaps a relationship of partnership, but in any case the cessation of mutual excommunications and moral disqualifications.

Despite this progress, the transmission of elementary knowledge and the slow rehabilitation of religious culture is severely hindered by a lack of available literature and religious specialists. The long period of silencing the religious voice has produced a hiatus in official culture, and it is not clear how this will be overcome. Religion and the church have assumed a more visible sociopolitical function. They contribute to stability by accepting the evolution from centrism to democracy and by their willingness not to make exaggerated demands. This attitude legitimizes the political system, and neither the state nor the church fails to emphasize this fact. Such legitimation, however, is not a support for the status quo but for an ongoing politics and an expanding institutional system. In this sense, the church has become a mobilizing force, strengthening and supporting recent developments.

While a semblance of social unity had been achieved in the previous period by a withdrawal of religious people from public affairs, the present struggle for cooperation has made social integration an explicit goal of the religious half of society. This struggle has not led to uniformity but the preservation of pluriformity in which religious people, groups, and organizations seek to be accepted as autonomous alternatives. The effort for such an emancipation is surely rooted in the changing social situation of contemporary Hungary. Traditional religiosity is mostly associated with the old, the less-educated, the disadvantaged, the rural population, and those in occupations at the economic margin. The challenges of the past decade have been grasped mainly by urban youth and intellectuals, among whom the number of believers has actually increased in recent years. The center of gravity in the religious system has moved from the villages to the cities, from the older to the younger generation, from the less educated to groups with high school and university education. This movement is likely to continue and will exercise a growing influence on the changing place and prestige of Catholicism and on changes within the church.

This period of dialogue is characterized both by pressures toward greater efficiency in the workplace and by broadening personal freedom. More and more, however, this freedom is associated with a disregard for rules, structures, and self-control, leading to anomie: it becomes senseless and empty. For some people social and political freedom is destroyed by the hopelessness of their aspirations, by the feeling that their activities have no meaning, by a sense of unprotectedness and loneliness amid the anonymity of their fellow human beings. Religion is still not particularly obvious—partly a hidden tradition practiced by a declining and marginal minority, partly the intensely personal choice of a few. The majority remains informally antireligious, although, with the spread of anomie, religion is more and more seen to hold out an exotic promise and vision. Rejecting religion and at the same time attributing extraordinary capacities to it are not contradictory tendencies, but reflect a common attitude toward oracles, magic, witches, and secret societies. The religious part of society is separated as an obscure minority, independent of its numerical strength. But this means that the characteristic features of religion are accepted. Moreover, the politics of consensus and the effort to integrate all social forces in the society obliges the representatives of the official culture to maintain a dialogue with religion. Such dialogue encourages honesty, has opened channels of self-description that were nonexistent in the periods of both confrontation and isolation, and creates a dynamic that changes opinions about the image and social function of religion.

Formerly, religion was the basis for a closed worldview. People's conviction that other ideologies are not sufficiently useful in everyday life underlines the stability of the religious worldview. Current uncertainty about moral values, structures, and practices is confronted by the value, practicability, and factual realization of a religiously based ethics. In contrast with other ideologies or strategies of action, religion seems more able to regulate everyday behavior in harmony with its principles. Finally, religion is seen to provide the most effective institutional base for building communities. Today more people seem to take for granted that religion can give answers in such fields as ontology, ethics, everyday life, sociability, solidarity, and communality—fields in which secular society has created only anomie. Despite these advances, however, religion remains a distant reality for most people. It is difficult to build a bridge from anomic decomposition, from a lack of consistency, to stable structures of thinking and behaving.

One sign of the change now taking place can be found in data about religious practice. In the former period of isolation and even more during the first half of the period of dialogue, religious practice declined rapidly. This trend was reversed in 1978: the proportion of practicing Christians stabilized and then slowly began to rise. Most significantly, the data about religious identification moved in a direction opposite to what the theory of secularization had predicted.

In summary, there is reason to predict a further increase and strengthening of religion both on the individual and on the social levels. As yet, this process has not found institutional expression. The forms of "religious organization" that exist are those inherited from the 1948-1965 period. The forms of organization that exist today can more accurately be called "islands." The official church remains weak; not even in its own sphere of influence can it guarantee authority, communication, and working discipline. The effectiveness of the church does not depend on organizational factors but on personal qualities, that is, on the existence of capable people. This means that the official church is more a latent principle and juridical form than a real functioning structure. It provides merely the background for the real kernel of Christian life. This kernel can be found in religious orders, well-functioning parishes, a retreat house, a youth pilgrimage, church shools—all without a common conception, division of labor, or systematic interconnections. These activities, together with the work of "base communities," the charismatic movements *Focolare* or *Regnum Marianum* (founded in Hungary), prayer and study groups not dependent on any of these movements, all constitute separate islands whose relationship to one another, to the official church, and to the institutions of the larger society remain unclear.

As yet these islands are too undeveloped to enable them to merge into any organic unity. While the sum of these various initiatives may contain the possibility of a multidimensional, complex church of the future, the movement presently contains many dysfunctional features. This kind of religion eschews centralization and clerical manipulation, preferring to remain flexible to meet varying social needs in different situations.[14] It ascribes to a new concept of the church and its mission, one that reaches out to all people and whose tasks are determined by specific circumstances. The church is a reality to be born and this birth occurs in different stages. The inner circle is composed of those truly committed to transmitting the Good News and the Christian way of life. Those interested in the Good News, those who need to be reached, are the outer circle on the way to the church: they are interested but not yet Christian. This "church to be born" is still traditional, but it presumes people to be actively engaged in its creation—people with initiative and imagination. People committed in this way are principally found among young adults, students, city dwellers, and intellectuals. The logic of recent religious change in Hungary thus appears to be moving the center of religious gravity in the same direction as efforts toward democratization in the society at large.

NOTES

1. The Hungarian People's Republic comprises an area of almost 56,000 square miles and a population of 10,646,000 (1986). Some 3-4 million Hungarians live in neighboring Czechoslovakia, Rumania, and Yugoslavia in the territory of pre-World War I "Great Hungary." Hungary still has an important and continually growing Catholic majority; see J. Kovacsics, *Magyarország történelmi demográfiája (Historical Demography of Hungary)* (Budapest: Kossuth, 1985).

	1910	1930	1949	1972	1985
	CENSUS DATA FOR THE TERRITORY OF PRESENT HUNGARY			POLL DATA	
RELIGIOUS AFFILIATION				N = 4,500	N = 25,000
Roman Catholic	65.0	67.2	70.5	71.0	71.5
Reformed/Calvinist	21.4	20.9	21.9	22.8	21.1
Evangelical/Lutheran	6.4	6.2	5.2	3.6	4.6
Jewish	6.2	5.1	1.5		0.4
Other (Orthodox and "Free Churches" such as Baptist, Seventh-Day Adventists)	1.0	0.6	0.9	1.1	0.2
Nonreligious	—	—	—	1.5	2.2

Poll data for 1972 and 1985 are based on registered baptisms in the community, not on opinion surveys. Differing data published in Donald B. Barrett, *World Christian Encyclopedia* (Oxford: Oxford University Press, 1982), pp. 363–67, are empirically unfounded.

2. Of the 35,520 square miles of agriculturally cultivated land, the churches owned 2,236 square miles and the Catholic church owned 1,949 square miles. This land financed both cultural and social institutions and church organizations, See Andor Csizmadia, *A magyar állam és az egyházak jogi kapcsolatainak kialakulása és gyakorlata a Horthy korczakban (The Evolution and Practice of Juridical Relations of the Hungarian State and Churches in the Horthy Era)* (Budapest: Akademiai, 1966).

3. The ratio of Catholic schools in pre-World War II Hungary is given below; see *Dokumentumok a magyar közoktatás reformjáról (Documents About the Reform of Hungarian Public Education)* (Budapest: Akademiai, 1966).

SCHOOLS	NUMBER	CATHOLIC
Elementary (grades 1–4)	6,899	40.5%
Civic schools (grades 1–6)	398	23.6
Secondary (grades 5–12)	173	27.4
Nurses' and kindergarten teachers' training colleges and higher schools for teacher training	59	52.2
Commercial and agricultural high schools and colleges	53	15.1

At the time of their dissolution in 1950, the religious orders provided 75 hospitals, 46 homes for the elderly and destitute, and 50 other welfare institutions; see Jenö Gergely, *A katolikus egyház Magyarországon: 1944–1971 (The Catholic Church in Hungary: 1944–1971)* (Budapest: Kossuth, 1985), p. 243.

4. In 1950 when religious orders were dissolved, 23 male and 40 female orders worked in Hungary and maintained 632 religious houses. The church personnel numbered 2,582 religious priests, 8,956 nuns, and 3,583 diocesan priests (Emmerich András and Julius Morel, *Bilanz des ungarischen Katholizismus: Kirche und Gesellschaft in*

Dokumenten, Zahlen und Analysen [Munich: Heimatwerk, 1969], p. 121); 1,779 men studied in theological seminaries, and 390 students in high schools and colleges were preparing for the priesthood (*Statistics on Hungary's Church* [Vienna: Hungarian Institute of the Sociology of Religion, HIS Press Service, no. 19, March 1981]). In the context of the 1946 proscription against religious organizations, some 1,500 different organizations appear to have existed at that time. Cf. *Uj Ember (New Man,* the Catholic weekly newspaper), August 4, 1946. Among them were the Agrarian Young Men's Catholic Association (KALOT), numbering about a half million members in the 1940s, and the Congregations and Confraternities of the Blessed Virgin Mary, with 700,000 members in 1945 (cf. András and Morel, p. 136). It can be calculated that 15 percent of the adult Hungarian population belonged to one or more religious associations.

5. Different positions in public administration were reserved for representatives of the church. Among the 259 members of the Upper House of Parliament in the 1940s, churches were represented by 42 priests and six laymen. One of the seven members of the Council of State was the archbishop of Esztergom, primate of Hungary (Csizmadia, p. 399).

6. "Integration" is probably not the correct word to describe this organic unity of social and religious systems; a better term might be "undifferentiated oneness." See Maria Raksay, "The Blurring of the Distinction Between Church and State in Hungary Before the Second World War," *Concilium* 174 (April 1982):1-5.

7. Miklós Tomka, "Le Rôle des églises instituées dans un contexte de changement," *Social Compass* 28 (1981):93-111.

8. The oppositional role of the church determined the views of the state; see Sándor Orbán, *Egyház és állam 1945-1950 (State and Church 1945-1950)* (Budapest: Kossuth, 1962). The centralized political structure, however, ignored that the source of church-state polarization was centralization itself and the unlawful measures of official policy (cf. Gergely, p. 211).

9. The primate of Hungary, Joseph Cardinal Mindszenty, was sentenced to life imprisonment in 1949. His successor as head of the Hungarian Bishops' Conference, Archbishop Joseph Grösz, who signed the first agreement between church and state in 1950, was sentenced to fifteen years in prison in 1951. Other bishops were held in detention camps for years.

10. Gerhard Lohfink has proposed that the original idea of Christian community was a "contrast society"; see *Wie hat Jesus Gemeinde gewollt?* (Frieburg: Herder, 1982).

11. Statistical evidence is available only for the period after 1972; cf. Tomka, "The Religious-Non-Religious Dichotomy as a Social Problem," *Annual Review of the Social Sciences of Religion* 3 (1979):105-37.

12. Some observers suppose that the argument of Vatican diplomats at this time was basically the same; see Hansjakob Stehle, *Eastern Politics of the Vatican 1917-1979* (Athens: Ohio University Press, 1981).

13. Foreign observers noted the existence of two competing pastoral concepts several years ago; see Emmerich András, *Conflicts in Hungary's Church over Two Different Pastoral Concepts: The Episcopacy and the Base Communities* (Vienna: Hungarian Institute of the Sociology of Religion, HIS Press, no. 22, January 1982). György Kozma's content analysis of the Hungarian bishop's pastoral letters reaches the same conclusion; see *Das Kirchenbild der ungarischen Bischofe im Spiegel der bischoflichen Rundschreiben* (Vienna: UKI-Berichte über Ungarn, 1978 and 1979).

14. If any influence of the Second Vatican Council can be detected in Hungarian Catholicism, the growing responsibility, the formation of an adult Christianity, and the social influence of the "islands" are its only indicators.

9

Polish Catholicism in Transition

Barbara Strassberg

This chapter will attempt to explain both the relative persistence of religion in post-World War II Poland and recent changes in Polish religious culture. Most discussions of religion in Poland stress either the role of the church as a political opposition to the ruling Communist party or the importance of religion for Polish national identity. While both emphases are justified, at least one related question also needs to be explored: Why has the Roman Catholic church not functioned as a political force and source of national identity in other East European countries as it has in Poland? As a frame of reference for considering the postwar Polish situation, it will be useful to begin by briefly reviewing several facts about the history of Christianity in Poland and some traits of Polish national culture.

Poland became a political entity in the tenth century. To meet the dangers arising when the Germans began to penetrate the barrier formed by other pagan and mostly Slavic tribes, Poland's first ruler, Mieszko I, conceived a policy of deliberately adopting Western civilization. This was also the chief object of his successors for the next several centuries. Mieszko secured his state from the aggression of his new neighbors by acknowledging himself as a tributary of the Holy Roman emperor Otto I and removed all danger of hostile crusades by accepting Christianity for himself and his people in 966 with the help of the Czech Princess Dubravka, whom he had married a year before. He also placed all his lands in the hands of the pope, thus inaugurating a close relationship that gave Poland the special protection of the Holy See. By the thirteenth century Poland's Christianization was complete and the Catholic church's dominance was secure.

The Protestant Reformation exerted little lasting influence in Poland. At their best, the various forms of Protestantism never won more than a scanty noble and intellectual elite of the nation; they never took root among the peasants or petty

184

bourgeoisie (except in the cities of Royal Prussia). Only one dissident movement orig- inated in Poland—the so-called Polish Brethren, who prompted both religious and social reform. This group demanded liberation of the peasants, equality of rights, and equal access to education; they also operated their own publishing house. When in 1565 the Jesuits, the vanguard of the Catholic Counter Reformation, appeared in Poland, the Polish Brethren were soon expelled and the ideas of the Reformation banished. The king accepted the decrees of the Council of Trent and the Catholic church again stood on firm foundations.

During the period of division of the kingdom into autonomous principalities (twelfth–fourteenth centuries), when the supreme princely power did not have much authority, or in the period following the eighteenth-century partitions of Poland, when the nation was deprived of its own statehood, the Polish people were linked together only by the church. Between the two world wars the church's influence over all aspects of political and social life remained exceptionally strong. In 1921 the teaching of Catholicism was made mandatory in all public schools, and in 1925 the Polish government signed a concordat with the Vatican. World War II, however, ushered in the separation of church and state, thus opening a new chapter in the history of Catholicism in Poland.

Finally, Polish Catholicism has experienced two major schisms. The first was the mystical sect of Mariavites founded by the Franciscan nun Maria Felicja Kozlowska in 1806. Spreading rapidly (with upward of 200,000 members by 1911), the Mar- iavites aimed at a religious, moral, and social renewal of the clergy and people; they stressed the veneration of the Eucharist and the Blessed Virgin Mary; they rejected the authority of the pope, introduced the Polish language into the liturgy, and allowed women to be ordained priests and bishops. The second was the formal establishment of the Polish National Catholic Church by Bishop Francis Hodur of Scranton, Penn- sylvania, in 1907. It is the only schismatic sect to have sprung from the soil of Amer- ican Catholicism. Founded because of nationalism rather than doctrinal dissent, its origins go back to the turn of the century when thousands of Poles arrived in the United States and, like most national groups, tended to settle among their own coun- trymen. They wanted to have their own priests and to run their own parishes on a trustee basis. The resulting conflict between the non-Polish clergy and some strongly nationalistic Poles led eventually to the formation of a separate and distinct Polish sect. During the 1920s and 1930s the group undertook missionary activities in the motherland so that now it also functions in Poland as the Polish Catholic Church of Poland. The traditional religious culture of Poland, however, has been exclusively determined by Roman Catholicism.

Traditional Polish Religious Culture

The overwhelming majority of Poles (nearly 94 percent) belongs to the Roman Cath- olic Church. Before World War II, the Polish Protestant Church, the Polish auto- cephalous Orthodox Church, and the Jews accounted for almost 30 percent of the total number of citizens. Because of the German extermination of Jews, voluntary or forced migrations, and the shift of national borders after the war, non-Catholics now comprise only about 3 percent of the population. The awareness of belonging to the

Polish nation linked with Catholicism is a consequence of historical processes through which the Polish people have passed during the last thousand years. When Poland was endowed with its own church hierarchy in 1000, and with the Gniezno archbishopric depending entirely on Rome, the Polish Catholic church became an equal member of the European community of Christendom. Since that time the church hierarchy has played a significant role in Polish history.

At the same time, as in every other sociocultural context, Poland developed its own Catholic "dialect." As used here, "dialect" refers to one of the many variants of the supranational Roman Catholic culture. Since it is impossible in this chapter to enumerate all the specific characteristics of this Polish Catholic dialect,[1] we will focus on only two, probably the most important: the ontological and the ethical. The ontological trait is composed of Polish perceptions of the divine; the ethical trait refers to the way in which Poles conceive of the relationship between God and human beings.

If one classified religious cultures along a continuum from exclusively theocentric to exclusively anthropocentric, then surely the Polish religious culture lies much more in an anthropocentric direction. With regard to the prevailing perception of the divine, this anthropomorphism reveals itself, first of all, in the intensity of the cult of the Virgin Mary and the saints. Although Poles venerate all members of the Holy Family, the Virgin Mary is considered most important. She is also the agent through whom religious culture has become "nationalized" in Poland. When, in the eighteenth century, the Polish Parliament declared Catholicism the country's state religion, it also "enthroned" Mary as "Queen of Poland." The cult of the saints runs very deep. Saints are believed to take special care of particular parishes, particular spheres of everyday life and, above all, individuals who have been given their names at baptism. Poles do not celebrate birthdays but "name days," the liturgically designated days on which particular saints are venerated. Traditionally, Poles avoid giving their children the names of saints whose feast day precedes the child's day of birth; otherwise, the child would have no name day during his first year of life (a very bad omen).

Love, goodness, forgiveness, compassion—these are traits attributed first of all to the Virgin Mary and then to the saints. God is perceived more as an "angry father," primarily evoking feelings of awe and fear. Every Polish child knows that thunderstorms, a frequent phenomenon in the Polish climate, are manifestations of God's anger. In the Polish culture, the Virgin Mary and the saints have acquired such a level of sanctity that traditional Polish religion can almost appear "polytheistic." The explanation for this situation partly derives from the process of Polish Christianization from the tenth to the thirteenth centuries, when statues of the pagan deity were destroyed and replaced by a "new" God who was ready to punish the people for worshipping their former God.[2] The image of an "angry god"—remote and fearsome—became strongly rooted in people's consciousness. The loving pagan deity was gone and the lesser deities were replaced with the good saints and motherly Virgin Mary—human beings enjoyed God's favor, more accessible to the people than the transcendent God of Christianity. As a consequence of the persistence of pre-Christian folk beliefs, these holy people were begged for favors of health or wealth, and promised a cross, a chapel, or a shrine if they granted the petitioner's request.

Besides the Virgin Mary and the saints, another key figure in traditional Polish religious culture was the wandering pilgrim or beggar who attended religious rituals in the name of a particular community that supported him financially. Although the church's calendar of religious rituals was adapted to the cycle of agricultural work, in case of conflict these "secular" religious experts were to pray or participate in pilgrimages for the benefit of the community. Interestingly, they were usually considered more effective than priests or members of religious orders. Initially, of course, Catholicism in Poland was the religion of the upper class, and until the mid-nineteenth century most of the Polish clergy was recruited from this class. Hence, a priest or member of a religious order was esteemed but considered by the common people as "one of them" rather than "one of us." Both socially and culturally, pilgrims and beggars were much closer to the people than church functionaries. "A Polish peasant bows before a priest and goes to him to ask for Mass or other services. He listens to a beggar."[3]

Within traditional Polish religious culture not only special people (such as pilgrims and beggars) but also certain places, times, objects, and formulae were perceived to possess "magical power." Prayers had to be recited according to prescribed formulae; otherwise they would have no power. Representation of holy persons (the Virgin Mary and the saints) appeared to function as if separated from what they represented. People believed these representations had lives of their own: they bled, wept, talked, disappeared, and reappeared in different places. One picture of the Virgin was considered less or more powerful than another; the national shrine of the Virgin in Czestochowa is the most powerful of all.

Religious rituals, too, serve instrumental purposes and reveal an anthropomorphic character. Since in traditional Polish culture the doctrinal aspect of religion has never been very important, religiosity is reduced to its ritual dimension and these rituals are expected to serve the everyday needs of the individual and the group. Moreover, in the Polish context, the social dimension of religion has always been more important than the individual. Even the family unit is less important for rituals than in other cultures. Every member of the family is expected to participate in a ritual first as a representative of his/her demographic category (sex, age, marital status) and then as a member of a parish. Individual devotion is less significant, and hence mysticism has been relatively scarce in Polish religious history.

The anthropocentric character of the Polish religious culture can also be observed in the sphere of ethics, where horizontal relationships (person-to-person) have always played a more important role than vertical relations (human beings-to-God). People follow certain patterns of behavior not because they are prescribed by God but because that is the way in which their forebears acted. At the same time, however, secular, traditional morality has acquired a religious dimension. The entire local community shares collective responsibility for the moral behavior of its members. To avoid collective punishment, various forms of group control, including ostracism, are applied to individuals who dared to violate the norms.

In short, traditional Polish Roman Catholic culture is secular, humane, and social. It rests on a symbolic-mythical tradition more than on dissemination of the church's teaching. Thus it is part of the everyday life of individuals, but is relevant only for membership in given social categories. Obviously the Catholic culture of the elite and the religious culture of non-Catholic groups living in prewar Poland differed from this dominant folk Catholicism; but it was the folk religion that exerted most influence on the shape of the national religious profile.

Religion and National Identity in Prewar Poland

The relationship between religion and national identity in Poland needs to be distinguished in terms of three different levels: religious culture and national consciousness, religious and national identity, and religiosity and patriotism. With the first of these, the religious "dialect" and national consciousness comprise the given cultural potential with which people grew up. Each generation modifies this potential in some way, but it remains as a basic framework within which people form their identities. People may know their national religious dialect and be conscious of their nationhood, but they may not fully identify themselves with either. For pragmatic reasons they may fashion their identity on the basis of only selected elements of this cultural potential linking them with other outside points of reference or they may select completely different ones. Religiosity and patriotism serve as manifestations of religious and national identity and may be used to measure the intensity of both.

Identity, then, seems to be the crucial concept, and both religious and national identity possess at least three components. For religion these components are doctrine, ritual, and the institutional church. For national identity they are the national culture, society at large, and the state. While full identification with all these components occurs rarely, the necessary condition for it seems to be the development of a broad cultural central zone that constitutes "the center of order of symbols, of values and beliefs, which govern the society . . . and which is intimately connected with what the society holds to be sacred."[4] In addition to the cultural central zone, however, every society has "cultural peripheries," so that the relative social and cultural integration of a whole society depends on the extent to which the peripheries approach the center. This, in turn, depends upon the degree to which the economic system is unified, political democracy is accepted, urbanization and education are developed.

In Poland, for several reasons, the cultural center has always been rather small with a great distance between it and the cultural peripheries. Polish society has always been relatively closed to social mobility. Moreover, from the time of the third partition (1795) of its territory by Russia, Prussia, and Austria, there was no Polish state, no nationwide market, and no uniform system of education; none of the conditions necessary for developing a central cultural zone had been fulfilled. What center existed was constituted by a common language and common territory, both threatened by foreign powers, and some common features of everyday life. But since the partition times, central symbols and ideas reflected no empirical national reality. Strong local identities were constructed along the cultural peripheries: regional, ecological (towns and villages), and especially occupational. But in the nineteenth century, the cultural values of the center were obviously not espoused by the ruling foreign authorities. In the absence of a network of nationwide social structures, the only institution capable of expressing the ideas and values of the cultural center was the church.

It is clear, then, why Polish national identity has been so strongly related to religious identity in a way quite different from what occurred in other sociopolitical contexts not exposed to the experiences of partition. Religiosity in all its dimensions became the manifestation of patriotism. And this patriotism was in no way diminished by giving up the empirical reference of the central culture, that is, by leaving Polish territory. What Polish patriots felt a passion to retain were the supra-empirical symbols and values of Polish culture. Obviously, different social strata did not internalize these symbols in the same way: folk culture was not identical with elite culture. Nevertheless, one can formulate certain generalizations with regard to the culture of Polish society as a whole.

First, because of the specific character of traditional Polish religious culture, the different components of religious identity never fully harmonized. The dogmatic (or belief) component has never been particularly important in Poland. There has been strong identification with the institutional church; but the social and ritualistic dimensions of religion have always assumed the greatest importance. Hence, participation in religious festivals and attendance at religious services in fact constitute the principal manifestations of religious identity.

Second, during the times of the partitions (beginning in 1764), there was little balance between the three components of national identity. There could be no identification with the state since the country had lost its independence; identification with the society at large remained quite strong but was peripheral. The Polish culture itself remained the only point of reference for national identity. National identity, as a consequence, became unidimensional and referred primarily to symbols, ideas, and ideals that had no empirical equivalents.

Third, the absence of a Polish state did not destroy the potential for national consciousness. Among the elite, this consciousness was composed of the traditional Polish political principles expressed in the 1791 constitution. Polish masses also retained an image, a dream, of a Polish independent state. Thus, in addition to its strong cultural component, Polish national identity was supplemented by the vision of a country in which people could live better lives than they did in Polish territories under foreign occupation. The only institution still able to function on a national level and help them hold firmly to their national consciousness was the church. The church, therefore, became a reservoir of both religious and state identity, and it began to serve as a surrogate of an independent "state." The relationship between religion and nationalism was reinforced; religious and national symbols merged.

Factors Contributing to Change in the Religious Culture

The factors contributing to religious cultural change in Poland fall into two broad categories[5]: (1) factors that in themselves neither promote nor inhibit religion, whether these are (a) unrelated to religion (e.g., the development of science and humanistic ethics; sociopolitical motivation for action; changes in secular institutions; geographical, social, and "intellectual" mobility[6]) or (b) are directly related to religion (e.g., increasing pluralism, the internal secularization of religious systems, or the church's inability to adapt to modern life); and (2) factors related to conscious, intended, planned activities undertaken by various institutions or organizations to directly influence religious culture either (a) by hindering secularization or attempts to "re-sacralize" society (e.g., the movement of "pillarization" within the Catholic church in the Netherlands[7] or the activities of the Protestant right in the United States), or (b) by accelerating secularization (e.g., the creation of completely secular societies in communist countries).

Factors Not Related to Religion

Let us begin by considering the development and dissemination of science in Poland after World War II; its impact can be gauged by looking at the level of general education in Polish society. After the war, compulsory elementary education was strongly promoted and illiteracy almost completely disappeared. In 1937, only 13.5 percent of the 14–17-year-olds attended school; by 1956 this figure had risen to 46 percent and, by 1962, to 72.8 percent.[8] The character of education is also important, since people with technical education appear to be generally more religious than those educated in the humanities.[9] From 1849 to 1964 Poland witnessed a tenfold increase in its number of engineering students, whereas the number of students in the humanities increased only fourfold. In 1975, whereas 32.5 percent of the students were enrolled in technical courses, only 9.2 percent were studying the humanities.[10]

This rise in general education was hardly a threat to Polish religious education, since there is very little strictly religious education in the country. Although the church continues to sponsor a few elementary and secondary schools and one university, their impact is extremely limited. In 1978, only 2.5 percent of all Polish university students attended the Catholic University in Lublin. Moreover, the teaching of religion does not appear very effective. According to a 1971 survey, 75.3 percent of the rural population were aware of the church's teaching about Jesus Christ, 43.8 percent knew about the resurrection, and 49.4 percent about the sacraments; 35.9 percent were unaware that the church does not permit divorce and remarriage, and only 25.2 percent had "used" the Bible.[11] Since the religious culture does not rest on a knowledge of church teaching, it is undisturbed by the dissemination of a scientific approach to the natural and social world; caring little for dogma, people do not apply scientific knowledge to religious beliefs.

Another factor contributing to change in the religious culture is the development of a humanistic ethics—what the government promotes under the name "socialist ethics." Hardly anyone really knows the contents of this ethics, but people feel that it promotes ideals that contradict the accustomed rules of conduct, which, they believe, are rooted in their Catholicism. The "national" ethics, although neither genetically nor logically related to religion, is very strongly related to it psychologically. In Poland moral values have always been transmitted together with religious beliefs.[12] This does not mean that people obey them because they are religious; they follow them because they are traditionally accepted ways of doing things. In fact, some of the values of the prewar Polish elite seem very popular in society at large. The two values at the top of the contemporary hierarchy are "individualism" and "democracy." In the context of the government's promotion of group interests over individual interests, of "collective responsibility" for political views and decisions, of a centralized political and economic system, the tendency to esteem what is individual is increasing. In 1978, 56 percent of the students in Warsaw, asked about the conditions needed for a "good social system," replied "the influence of all citizens on the way society is governed"; only 3 percent answered "obedience of the citizens to the decisions of authorities."[13]

The popular morality today thus appears countercultural both to socialist and to traditionally religious Polish morality. When, in the mid-1970s, Poles were asked what played the most significant role in shaping their moral values, 49 percent of them cited Polish classical (i.e., pre-World War II) literature, and 63 percent, Polish historical movies. Only 22.1 percent said they were influenced by postwar Polish writers and 5 percent by movies recreating the postwar reality. Only 26 percent felt that school had influenced their ethical values.[14] On the other hand, Piwowarski's 1971 study of rural religiosity revealed that only 26.7 percent looked to religious principles to resolve moral conflicts.[15] These data support the view that the source for contemporary moral values is neither religion nor socialist ethics.

The promotion of sociopolitical motivation for action is another source of change in Polish religious culture. This motivation is especially stressed by the government. In 1974, however, only 7.5 percent of the students in Warsaw, when asked about their plans for the future, intended to become involved in social or political activities.[16] And an international comparison of occupational prestige rankings revealed that in 1975 jobs perceived as "state-related" were ranked much lower in Poland than in other countries.[17] While it might seem that young Poles do not want to involve themselves in activities judged negatively by the government or little esteemed by Polish society, the events connected with the Solidarity movement in the late 1970s and early 1980s demonstrate that, if political activity is aimed against the government, the Polish people are willing to be deeply involved.

What about the influence of the organizations and institutions created to satisfy various human needs? The government has sponsored many of these institutions, but the existing data confirm that people do not trust them.[18] If people need advice on marital or legal matters or on problems with their children, instead of relying on religious or state organizations, they prefer to consult family and/or close friends.[19] The only institutions relatively accepted by the society at large are schools and hospitals, although even here there is some distrust. While these institutions provide free services, some people believe they would be better served if the institutions could reward the doctors, nurses, and teachers who work in them.

Geographical and social mobility have also affected changes in the religious culture.[20] Because of the shift in Polish national boundaries after World War II, people from the eastern part of the country resettled in the western territory, which had been inhabited by Germans. Moreover, 7 million people (from a total population of 30 million) moved from rural to urban areas. The proportion of people employed in nonagricultural occupations rose from 52.9 percent in 1950 to 76.6 percent in 1978. Since the mid-1970s, however, lagging technological development has slowed the pace of social mobility: fewer new positions requiring specific qualifications and skills have become available. At the same time, neither geographical nor social mobility has increased people's readiness to reject traditional values. Possible changes in group consciousness were hindered, for example, by a shortage of housing in the newly developing cities. Hostels or whole housing districts of familial neighborhoods were constructed for the workers, and these often united people fron one rural area. Hence, rural folkways have persisted and the new Polish working class has maintained its peasant character.

Factors Related to Religion

In the Polish context, three factors directly related to religion have contributed to changes in the traditional religious culture: the church's inability to adapt to modern life, the interplay between religion and national (state) consciousness, and the election of a Polish pope.

Among the most serious problems the church faced after the war were the aging of the clergy and their relatively homogeneous composition. Most priests had come from rural areas, and from large, poorly educated families; they found it difficult to provide a proper ministry for an increasingly urban, heterogeneous population. In 1977, only 36.8 percent of urban parishioners felt attached to their local church, only 6.8 percent reported that they considered the priest an authority in resolving moral conflicts, and as many as 73.8 percent expressed some criticism of the clergy.[21] On the other hand, in comparison with other West European countries, the number of recruits for the priesthood is relatively high; yet socioeconomic motivations appear to play a stronger role in this choice than religious ones. The church has undertaken numerous efforts to introduce new approaches to ministry and to the teaching of religion but, as we shall see later in this chapter, these have not produced much change in Polish religious life.

What, then, may be said about the interplay between religion and national identity in the postwar period? The political system that the Soviet Union imposed on Poland after World War II has no popular support. Contrary to its theoretical proclamations, the system is characterized by an absence of popular democracy, political liberty, and equality of rights. Communist ideology provides the foundation not only for politics but also for an economic system unfavorable to the healthy development of industry and urbanization. Both these developments have not succeeded in neutralizing deep social inequalities. Since everyone has a right to work, work is not considered a value in itself; the absence of competition for employment produces growing ineffectiveness and low productivity, since greater efforts do not bring greater rewards.

The political and economic systems, in turn, shape the country's social stratification. Polish society is still relatively closed, and intergenerational mobility is slow. The social hierarchy is well defined, with great distances separating the lowest and highest rungs of the social ladder. Although in theory all people have equal access to education and the curricula are uniform for every level of schooling, the better schools give preference to children from the higher classes. The mass media, carefully controlled by the central government, favors the elite over the folk and national culture. Other institutions that might fill the gap between the family and the nation do not evoke respect and hence are unable either to pursue or to affirm the values that might constitute a central cultural zone. Only the church is accepted as a legitimate mediating structure for the values of the center.

In this context, the interplay between religion and national identity acquires a specific character. To be defined as a Roman Catholic, to participate in religious practices, and above all, to declare respect for the church, is to be a Polish patriot. Without any other point of reference for national identity, patriotism means defending the church against communist attempts to minimize its influence and maintaining the Polish religious dialect. The expression of national consciousness has thus changed little since the times of the partitions.

Against this background it is easy to discern the significance of the election of Cracow's Cardinal Karol Wojtyla to the papacy in 1978. Poles began to believe that since they have "their own pope," John Paul II will not allow the communists to destroy them. They began to hope that the wider world would recognize that they needed external assistance to alleviate their political situation. Poles also recovered their pride—a member of their nation was chosen for the highest religious leadership position in the world. On the religious level, a Polish pope could protect the Polish church against government interference; this expectation was confirmed when, between 1978 and 1980, Polish authorities granted the same number of permissions to erect new church buildings as they did between 1945 and 1978.

Activities Against Religion

In addition to the objective factors discussed above, the government has consciously undertaken a number of activities specifically designed to inhibit religion and reduce its influence. These factors can best be presented in chronological order.

During the first period (1945–1955), by a government decree in 1947 and the constitution of 1952, the separation of church and state was formally introduced in Poland. No information about religious affiliation could be given on any application form, the teaching of religion was withdrawn from all public schools, and people were allowed to contract purely civil marriages. Between 1949 and 1950 all church property and all but a few church-run schools were nationalized. In 1953 the state took over responsibility for appointing bishops and pastors and determining the territorial boundaries of parishes and dioceses. From 1953 to 1956 Poland's primate, Cardinal Wyszynski, was imprisoned for refusing to cooperate with the government.

The second period in postwar church–state relations began in 1956 with the signing of an agreement between church and state authorities. Religion was permitted to be taught in public schools as an elective; state and church authorities together were to cooperate in the selection of bishops, pastors, and chaplains for the army, prisons, and hospitals; bishops were to declare their loyalty to the state, and the activities of church-sponsored organizations such as KIK (Club of Catholic Intellectuals), *Wiez* (The Bond), and *Znak* (Sign) were regularized. The church also agreed to apply for state permission to erect new church buildings, chapels, and religious houses. In 1958, civil marriages were proclaimed the only form acceptable to the state, with an additional religious ceremony a matter of choice.

During the early 1960s, permission to teach religion in public schools was once again withdrawn, and since then has been taught only in the churches. Members of religious orders were forbidden to be teachers. No extrareligious organizations (e.g., for sport, cultural, or educational activities) were allowed to function at the parochial level. The church had to apply for permission to hold any religious functions outside church buildings (e.g., pilgrimages, processions), and censorship of religious books was strictly enforced.

In 1966 Poland celebrated one thousand years of Christianity. Once more, church–state relations became antagonistic. One reason was the letter the Polish bishops had sent the year before to the bishops of Germany expressing their forgiveness of all the "sins" which the Germans committed against Poland during World War II. The government was outraged; it severely restricted the church-organized celebration of the millenium and in 1967 revoked Cardinal Wyszynski's passport, thus preventing him from attending the first bishops' synod in Rome following the Second Vatican Council.

Another chapter in church–state relations opened in the 1970s. Since the end of the war until 1972, the western territories of Poland were under the direct jurisdiction of the Holy See. When Pope Paul VI recognized that these territories in fact belonged to the Polish state, the state transferred jurisdiction over them to the Polish church authorities. Subsequent efforts were made by representatives of both institutions toward more peaceful coexistence, and Polish state authorities began to establish more direct links with the Vatican. In 1978, Cardinal Karol Wojtyla became Pope John Paul II, and in 1979 he paid his first visit as pope to his native country.

What can be said about church–state relations in Poland since 1980? During July and August 1980, when people initiated work stoppages, slowdowns, and strikes, the Catholic hierarchy made no official statement, although groups of Catholic laity (publishers, writers, etcetera) were strongly involved in the newly developing movement for human rights and social justice. Cardinal Wyszynski appeared on television to appeal for peace and work, and on August 26 the main council of the Polish bishops met at Jasna Gora in Czestochowa to discuss the reasons for social discontent, the issue of civil rights, and the question of social and moral revival in Poland. On August 31 representatives of Solidarity and the state signed the so-called Gdansk Agreement, which allowed more religious freedom, including the broadcasting of Sunday masses. In early September Cardinal Wyszynski met for the first time with Solidarity's Leader Lech Walesa, and from September 24 to the end of the year, a joint commission of the bishops and the government met eighty-one times. During the spring of 1981, after the riots in Bydgoszcz, the social tensions in Poland dramatically increased. Upon receiving a letter from the pope requesting that every possible effort be undertaken to solve the existing problems in a peaceful way, Cardinal Wyszynski met first with General Wojciech Jaruzelski and, two days later, with Lech Walesa. As a result of these meetings, the so-called Warsaw Agreement was signed on April 1, 1981, as the foundation for a peaceful compromise.

Cardinal Wyszynski died on May 28, 1981, and was succeeded by Cardinal Jozef Glemp. It soon became obvious that the Polish church under his leadership would function more as a neutral force than as an explicit supporter of Solidarity. At the first national convention of Solidarity held on September 5, 1981, in Gdansk, Glemp appealed to both the leaders of Solidarity and the state to strike a lasting compromise. In November, Glemp, Jaruzelski, and Walesa met for the first time and agreed to create a Front for National Agreement. At the December 4 Solidarity convention in Radom, however, some of the movement's leaders expressed sharp criticism of the government and they found support among representatives of the church. Social and political tensions mounted and martial law was declared on December 13, 1981.

From that time on, it was evident that since Glemp's appointment and despite his desire for neutrality, a more radical wing within the church had become strongly involved in the underground activities of Solidarity. Special masses were held for Solidarity and on behalf of a free Poland, with many priests as guest speakers. The importance of religious symbols increased: Walesa himself made frequent use of the pictures of the Virgin Mary and John Paul II as representatives of "sacred people" on whom the Polish nation could rely. In 1983 there was a political battle over displaying crucifixes in public school classrooms. In October 1984, after the assassination of Father Jerzy Popieluszko—one of the priests deeply involved in the fight for human rights—candlelight processions were organized in the churches. The symbol of the cross was also reinforced, and began to be erected at street intersections to protect demonstrators from militia or army intervention.

Vatican II, Existential Personalism, and the Ethics of Solidarity

The church's efforts to hinder secularization and to respond to the rapid changes affecting modern societies need to be considered at the level of the universal church and within Poland itself. On the first level are the reforms introduced by the Second Vatican Council and the papal encyclicals issued since 1965; for Poland mention needs to be made of the philosophical reflections on existential personalism developed by Karol Wojtyla when he was professor at the Catholic University of Lublin, as well as the ethical principles of solidarity articulated by Cracow's Father Josef Tischner.

In Poland, the church confronted serious problems in trying to implement the reforms of Vatican II. Traditionally oriented Poles, following patterns developed by their forefathers, were neither ready nor willing to welcome changes into "their" church. Especially in a context where the national religious dialect is the only stable frame of reference, any attempt to alter the status quo seemed a betrayal. In the years immediately following the Council some Poles expressed the view that "communists must have managed to force the church to make these changes." Even today, more than twenty years after Vatican II, Poles still complain about the changes. Such dissatisfaction, however, has not had any noticeable impact on religious or church involvement. Dissatisfaction is neutralized by the common suspicion that the church cannot be blamed for these reforms because they were introduced in response to other external forces, as well as by the extra religious role the church plays in Polish national identity and by the election of the Polish pope.

On the national level, the church "re-sacralizes" all aspects of social, economic, and political life by its involvement in the postwar struggle for freedom and social justice. Moreover, the intellectual foundations for this struggle are, to some extent, provided by people related to the church. There are, for example, Wojtyla's philosophical writings, which take the orientation of an existential personalism with strong emphasis on the matter of individual dignity. Some of these ideas have found expression in his encyclical *Redemptor Hominis* in which the issue of human rights is central. In addition, Jozef Tischner's writings on the ethics of solidarity have exercised considerable influence, as have the intellectual contributions of Tadeusz Mazowiecki, Adam Wielowiejski, and Lech Bedkowski.[22]

At the same time, the church in Poland did not develop any movement comparable to the liberation theology articulated in Latin America. Church intellectuals responded to socio-political trends that were developing spontaneously in Polish society. They were not the leaders in the fight for liberation, but their support for the struggle has been both significant and impressive.

All of the factors influencing religious change discussed in the preceding pages, except for geographical and social mobility, have operated continuously in postwar Poland. Three of them—"socialist ethics," institutions and organizations founded by the state (except schools and hospitals), and secular ideology—have been rejected by Polish society at large. The Catholic church has also made serious efforts to overcome the side effects of its previous slowness to adapt to the conditions of modern

Poland. Only education has continually operated with the consent of society. As we have seen, however, scientific, technological, economic, and political rationalism do not have an "opponent" in religious dogma, since dogma is not a strong component of Polish religiosity; hence, the foundations of the religious culture cannot be shaken by an increase in the scientific approach to natural and social reality. The new Polish ethics differs from traditional folk ethics principally with regard to the way in which the relationship between individual and group is perceived. In the traditional model, an individual could be "corrected" by a group; for the prewar elite and now in Polish national ethics, a group—even the whole society—can be "corrected" by an individual. It is interesting that this approach finds considerable support among postwar church intellectuals.

An additional observation is called for regarding Polish society's acceptance of education and rejection of socialist ideology. Research carried out in Cracow at the end of the 1970s showed that Poles suffered from "reiterated illiteracy," that is, they did not fully comprehend what they read and about 89 percent of the population appeared not to understand news on television.[23] Subconsciously or unconsciously people become accustomed to nationalized property, centralized administration, free education, and medical service, and it is difficult for them to conceive alternative arrangements. In the struggle for greater democracy and respect for human rights, private property, private schools, or hospitals are not mentioned among the demands. Even when they migrate to the United States, for example, most Poles keep at a distance from the systems of education and medical service, not checking what options might be available to them.

The Religious Life of Postwar Poland

For most of this chapter we have focused on the concept of Polish religious culture. It will be helpful at this point to present some statistical information about religious life and practice. Unfortunately, there are no reliable data that would allow generalizations with regard to the whole society. What studies there are have been conducted with limited samples and according to categories suggested years ago by the French sociologist Gabriel LeBras. These data are, in addition, limited by the fact that Poles tend to be inconsistent in answering questions about religion, and responses obtained by church versus state researches vary widely. Knowing the expectations of both these institutions, people try to present themselves as either less or more religious than they really are.

Nevertheless, the information we have provides sufficient justification for the statement that Polish society is evolving from the stage of traditional religiosity (which, in the Polish context, we have seen already means some kind of "selective" religiosity) to a stage of even more selective religiosity. People believe in only some elements of dogma, participate in religious practices in a more and more irregular way, and accept the church's authority only in some matters. In 1980, 93 percent of the population had been baptized Roman Catholic, and it was estimated that between 80 and 90 percent were Catholics in fact. Information from the best studies conducted so far—both in rural and urban areas—are summarized in Tables 9.1–9.5.[24] Although the statistics are not recent and were conducted in only one region of Poland, they still reveal some interesting general trends.

TABLE 9.1 Religious Beliefs of the Polish People at the End of the 1960s

BELIEFS	RURAL POPULATION	URBAN POPULATION
Deeply believing	16.7%	21.7%
Believing	79.4	66.3
Less religious now	18.3	31.8
Believe due to tradition	79.2	52.4
Believe due to conviction	17.8	35.6
Believe in the Trinity	92.9	85.6
Believe in Christ as God's Son	87.6	70.3
Believe in the Resurrection	60.0	55.6
Belief is important for being religious	13.7	18.7
Loss of belief is a sin	8.9	7.8

TABLE 9.2 Religious Practices of the Polish People at the End of the 1960s

PRACTICES	RURAL POPULATION	URBAN POPULATION
Regularly practicing	39.3%	57.2%
Irregularly practicing	43.0	25.4
Attend mass every Sunday	34.6	51.6
Individual prayer every day	54.7	32.3
Family prayer every day	1.7	5.7
Communion once a month	25.2	6.6
Communion only at Easter	23.5	23.4
Attend processions	80.3	72.8
Attend pilgrimages	19.3	4.9
Religious practices are important for being religious	59.7	51.1
Not attending religious practices is a sin	2.0	4.0

TABLE 9.3 Opinions on Moral Issues of the Polish People at the End of the 1960s

MORALITY	RURAL POPULATION	URBAN POPULATION
Premarital sex is wrong	72.3%	49.7%
Extramarital sex is wrong	92.0	76.1
Divorce is wrong	74.6	47.3
Artificial means of birth control are wrong	63.2	34.4
Abortion is wrong	83.8	54.2
Morality is important for being religious	25.0	29.1
Immoral life is wrong	67.1	78.8
Ten Commandments are important	49.4	38.6
Confession is important	89.5	69.3

TABLE 9.4 Polish Attitudes Toward the Church at the
End of the 1960s

THE CHURCH	RURAL POPULATION	URBAN POPULATION
Interested in church life	76.9%	—
Help church financially	12.9	6.0%
Help church personally	48.2	21.8
Would like a priest in family	84.9	64.6
Criteria of Church membership		
Baptism		88.2%
Moral behavior		78.2
Following Ten Commandments		75.4
Prayer to Virgin Mary		73.1
Brotherly love		72.9
Sunday mass		72.2
Following church's teaching		70.5
Church marriage		70.3
Following clergy's teaching		61.5
Communion		60.9
Financial support of the church		57.1

Both rural and urban Poles consider belief as the least important component of being religous, morality somewhat more important, and ritual most important. Although fewer people from urban areas define themselves as religious, those who maintain their faith do so in a more conscious way, based on personal conviction rather than tradition (Table 9.1). Urban Poles also appear to attend Sunday mass more regularly, while other religious practices seem to them less important (Table 9.2). It is interesting to note, however, that the ritual of daily family prayer is somewhat more evident among them than in the rural population. In the face of the increasing privatization of urban life, participation in religous practices becomes more attractive. On moral matters (Table 9.3) urban Poles seem to care less for the church's teaching than those in rural areas; they do not consider the Ten Commandments or confession so important. Yet for those in the city, praying to the Virgin Mary is a more significant criterion of church membership than church marriage, Sunday mass, following church teaching, receiving communion, brotherly love, or financial support of the church (Table 9.4).

Table 9.5 reveals levels of belief, practice, and attitude toward religion among different occupational groups. If we agree that peasants, peasant-workers, and unskilled workers represent traditional occupations, and nonmanual workers more modern ones, and assuming a continuing rise in the proportion of nonmanual workers in contemporary Poland, the number of believing and practicing Catholics is declining, but those who remain religious consider belief, ritual, and morality almost equally important components of religion. Comparing the attitudes of peasants and nonmanual workers, the importance of belief increases from 12 to 27.1 percent, the importance of ritual decreases from 63.3 to 31.3 percent, and the importance of morality increases from 21.3 to 36.8 percent.

TABLE 9.5 Polish Religiosity at the End of the 1960s, by Occupational Categories

Categories	Deeply Believe	Believe	Now Less Religious	Regularly Practicing	Irregularly Practicing	Divorce Is Wrong	Important for Being Religious		
							Belief	Ritual	Morality
Peasants	27.4%	68.4%	—	—	—	81.0%	12.0%	63.3%	21.3%
Peasant-workers	17.3	73.2	—	—	72.4%	67.1	12.6	62.6	23.5
Unskilled workers	25.7	63.3	24.8%	46.8%	33.0	67.7	22.3	52.3	22.9
Skilled workers	25.6	62.8	31.4	39.5	40.7	52.2	31.5	44.5	21.0
Craftsmen	26.6	62.4	29.4	43.1	26.6	70.0	28.6	52.2	16.8
Nonmanual workers	16.9	66.9	41.7	37.0	35.7	59.1	27.1	31.3	36.8
Housewives	30.9	64.0	28.7	60.3	24.3	70.0	16.0	58.9	23.7
Students	14.8	77.0	39.3	42.6	42.6	40.9	28.9	55.4	14.5
Retired	43.3	46.7	20.0	53.3	23.3	85.8	9.3	53.5	37.2

These changes in religious attitude and behavior follow more general structural and cultural changes in Polish society and mean something more than a decline in the salience of religion or attachment to the church. The content of Polish religiosity is also changing. So too is the traditional Polish religious dialect. The cult of the saints has sharply declined, and pilgrims and beggars as "experts" in religious matters have almost disappeared. The cult of the Virgin Mary and belief in the "magical" power embedded in particular places, times, and sacred formulae have shifted from the level of the individual and local community to national aims and issues. Religious symbols and values, as well as participation in religious rituals, continue to be used instrumentally, even with greater intensity since the late 1970s; but they now also serve extrareligious purposes—social, economic and political—of the entire nation.

Participation in religious practices not only has changed at the level of its instrumental function but also no longer occurs according to demographic categories. Especially in urban areas, people now participate in rituals by occupational categories rather than by age, sex, or marital status. Representing a group of parishioners is no longer important; today, Polish Catholics see themselves as representing the whole nation through their occupational circles. Although some still criticize the clergy as "one of them" (in the context of aristocratic versus peasant culture), more and more priests are considered "one of us" anticommunists.

Finally, there has been some limited development of the charismatic movement in Poland. Initially, this movement received no support from the official church. Nevertheless, younger generations have become interested in it, and even though the movement remains small, it represents another change in the Polish Catholic culture.

We spoke above about the basic change in Polish Catholicism from one form of selective religiosity to another. Does this mean that Poles are becoming less religious? If "being religious" means accepting all elements of dogma, regular participation in religious rituals, and unquestioning obedience to church teaching, then Poles have become less religious. But if "being religious" means attachment to religion and the church, considering them both as a principal reference point for individual and social identity, then Poles seem no less religious today than they were during the nineteenth-century time of partition. Certainly any decline in religious practice over the last twenty years is offset by an increased relevance in the political, social, and national dimension of Polish Catholicism. On the political level, the church functions as a surrogate for the state; on the social level, the ethics of solidarity developed by church intellectuals supports current social programs and activities, and religious myths remain an integral part of Poland's national myths. Moreover, religion and the church act strongly on behalf of the oppressed.

The patterns of change in religious culture presented in this chapter support the view that Poland represents a very special situation. The sociological process of differentiation in Western countries has meant the functional separation of religion as an overall agent of social legitimation. In response to this differentiation, churches have concentrated more and more on answering strictly "religious" needs. A drop in religiosity has generally been interpreted as a gradual weakening of religious needs altogether and a slow withdrawal of religious influence. In the Polish context, declining religious practice does not mean the same thing. In the postwar period, the church has not become separated from the social, economic, and political life of the nation. On the contrary, its involvement in extrareligious national issues is more intense. Despite the absence of its own educational system, religious socialization deeply penetrates the culture and strongly correlates with all aspects of national identity.

The fact that in other East European countries changes in religion have not followed the Polish pattern is not merely a consequence of the church's support for the "oppressed" or its institutionalized opposition to the ruling communist government. Neither of these roles is a sufficient condition for the church's persistent significance in Poland. The analysis presented in this chapter suggests that the church will be able to exercise continuing influence in social and political matters if a nation's overall religious dialect is very strongly anthropocentric, even to the point of blurring the borderline between what is "divine" and what is "human." "Nationalizing" the Virgin Mary by a purely political act of Parliament is exceptional. So too is the tendency to "sacralize" people who have played an important role in history. National heroes in Poland are venerated in a way quite comparable to the veneration of religious persons, and Poles perceive "sacred" persons—God, the Virgin Mary, and the saints—as much more human than transcendent in solving various everyday problems. If secularization can be understood as a process of the detheocentrization and simultaneous anthropocentrization of cultures, in a sociocultural context in which religion itself is anthropocentric, change leads to a deeper penetration of religion into the entire culture of the nation rather than its functional separation, individualization, or privatization. The entire Polish culture is impregnated with religion, and religious beliefs and values seem to be legitimated as much by the overall Polish tradition as by the Gospel or the teaching of the church.

NOTES

1. See W. I. Thomas and Florian Znaniecki, *The Polish Peasant in Europe and America,* 2 vols. (Chicago: University of Chicago Press, 1918-1921); J. S. Bystron, *Folk Culture* (Warsaw: Trzaska, 1947); S. Czarnowski, "Folk Culture of the Polish People," *Dziela 1* (1956); L. Krzywicki, "Articles and Dissertations 1888-1889," *Dziela 4* (1960); P. Super, *The Polish Tradition: An Interpretation of a Nation* (London: Allen & Unwin, 1939).
2. M. Kowalczyk, *Pagan Beliefs of the Past Era* (Lodz: Wydawnictwo Lodzkie, 1968), p. 38.
3. Czarnowski, "Folk Culture," p. 106.
4. Edward Shils, *The Center and Periphery* (Chicago: University of Chicago Press, 1982), p. 9.
5. See Barbara Les, *Religiosity of Industrial Societies: A Comparative Study of France and Great Britain* (Warsaw: Panstwowe Wydawnictwo Naukowe, 1977).
6. See D. B. Clark, "Local and Cosmopolitan Aspects of Religious Activity in a Northern Suburb," *A Sociological Yearbook of Religion in Britain* 3 (1970):45-64.
7. See K. Dobbelaere, J. Billiet, and R.Creyf, "Secularization and Pillarization: A Social Problem Approach," *Annual Review of the Social Sciences of Religion* 2 (1978):103.
8. D. Lane and G. Kolankiewicz, eds., *Social Groups in Polish Society* (New York: Columbia University Press, 1973), pp. 20-21.

9. A. Aver, "Une Enquête aupres d'étudiants parisiens," *Archives de Sociologie des Religions*, No. 22.

10. *Statistical Yearbook 1980* (Warsaw: Glowny Urzad Statystyczny, 1980).

11. W. Piwowarski, *Rural Religiosity and Urbanization* (Warsaw: Weiz, 1971).

12. M. Ossowska, *Sociology and Morality* (Warsaw: Panstwowe Wydawnictwo Naukowe, 1969).

13. S. Nowak, "Values and Attitudes of the Polish People," *Scientific American* 245 (1981).

14. K. Wenta, *The Personality Ideal of a Polish Citizen* (Warsaw: Panstwowe Wydawnictwo Naukowe, 1978).

15. Piwowarski, *Rural Religiosity*.

16. S. Lewicki, *Customs* (Warsaw: Ksiazka i Wiedza, 1976).

17. H. D. Nelson, *Poland: A Country Study* (Washington, D.C.: U.S. Government Printing Office, 1984).

18. Wenta, *The Personality Ideal*.

19. Piwowarski, *Rural Religiosity, and Urban Religiosity and Industrialization* (Warsaw: Wiez, 1977).

20. J. Van Brabant, *Reflections on Poland's Economic Policies in the 1960s* (Berlin: Osteuropa Institut, Wirtschaftswissenschaftliche Folge, no. 32, 1973).

21. Piwowarski, *Urban Religiosity*.

22. See Josef Tischner, *The Spirit of Solidarity* (New York: Harper & Row, 1984).

23. See T. Borkowski, Unpublished Research Report on the Impact of Mass Media Among the Polish People, Institute of Sociology, Jagiellonian University, Cracow, 1983.

24. The data presented in these tables are drawn from the 1971 and 1977 studies by W. Piwowarski.

PART
THREE

The English-Speaking World

10

Ireland: The Exception That Proves Two Rules

Máire Nic Ghiolla Phádraig

Ireland occupies a unique position in religiopolitical history: It is the only predominantly Roman Catholic country in the English-speaking world. It was, to varying degrees, a colony of Britain from the twelfth until the present century. It exhibits, in its northeast region (Northern Ireland) a continuing colonial situation and a continuation of the religious wars Europe experienced around the time of the Reformation. In some ways, Ireland is insular and oblivious to influences of other cultures, particularly in matters pertaining to family life, in 1983 and 1986 taking unique referendum decisions against abortion and divorce. In other ways, it is a very open society, steeped in foreign mass media, highly dependent economically on trade and loans from wealthier members of the European Economic Community (EEC) and with renewed high levels of emigration in response to the current recession.

The population composition of Northern Ireland fits David Martin's category of countries with a Protestant majority and substantial Catholic minority of 60:40,[1] yet sectarian divisions have intensified rather than diminished since the 1960s, in contrast to other European countries of this composition.

The Republic of Ireland, by contrast, is comprised of over 90 percent Roman Catholics and seems to correspond to the category "Catholicism in its historic heartlands"[2]; agnostic liberalism and radicalism, and class and regional divisions, have until recently been lacking in the Irish situation. As late as 1974 the Catholic church in Ireland claimed a regular Sunday mass attendance of over 90 percent of the Catholic population.[3] Its ethics in family and health matters have been dominant, and it has control of primary and postprimary education. While widely believed to be a major influence on government policy, the church has rarely needed to inter-

205

vene in such matters.[4] The last twenty years have brought about some erosion, but by and large the Republic of Ireland may be characterized as an unself-consciously Catholic state.

Indeed, the position of this chapter is itself problematic. Ireland, with 1,550 years of unbroken allegiance to Catholicism, might well have been categorized as part of the "European Heartlands." And yet, in its recent history, its pattern of emigration, and mission it has related mainly to the other countries in "the English-speaking world." The style of Catholicism adopted in Ireland since the mid-nineteenth century has been aptly characterized as Tridentine Victorianism, combining Roman ultramontanist legalism with British Victorian prudery,[5] so it would seem to be a hybrid of European and Anglo-Saxon countries to which the Irish emigrated in large numbers. Further, response of Irish clergy and religious in exiling themselves in large numbers with their flocks left a disproportionate mark on the style of the Catholic church in these countries, particularly on the Australian, Scottish, and American churches, at least until the mid-1960s.

Martin has explained the anomaly of the Irish situation in the context of recent colonial history, because the colonizing country—England—was of a different religion.[6] Although this explanation seems plausible, it may not completely account for the position of the Irish Republic. The manner, extent, and explanation of the departure of the Irish case from the two religiopolitical categories to which its demographic composition would seem to consign it will constitute the structure of the present chapter.

Historical Content/"Crucial Event"

Beginning in 432 Saint Patrick evangelized most of the island of Ireland in just under thirty years. In the seventh and eighth centuries, Irish monks reclaimed much of Europe for Christianity and classical scholarship. The reform of the Irish church (despite its recently having reformed itself) formed the rationale for the invasion of Ireland by Henry II of England, equipped with a Papal Bull from Adrian IV. In later centuries religious reform was interwoven with imperialist designs in the final conquest and plantations of the country. The earlier plantations of the Normans and Old English were largely assimilated within Gaelic culture. But, following the Reformation the native Irish largely retained their allegiance to Rome and castelike divisions arose between them and the English and Scottish Protestant settlers introduced in great numbers in the seventeenth century. The major Irish ethnic marker had been Gaelic culture; it now became adherence to Roman Catholicism. The law ensured the concentration of property in Protestant hands and the Anglican church was the established church until 1870. The plantations were concentrated in the area that now forms Northern Ireland.

Fear of their dispossessed Roman Catholic neighbors and abhorrence of their religion formed the basis for Loyalism and Unionist opposition to nationalist aspirations for independence. These barriers were temporarily breached in an attempted rebellion in 1798, when some sections of the Roman Catholic population made common cause with Presbyterians—who also suffered some degree of discrimination—and some liberal Anglicans. Britain subsequently was careful to favor the Presbyterian minority and to rekindle their suspicions about Catholics. This division was confirmed by the political mobilization of Catholics under Daniel O'Connell, whose two great aims were repeal of the Union and Catholic Emancipation (equality under the law). Priority was given to Catholic Emancipation (achieved in 1829). The movement was organized through Catholic parish units led by Catholic bourgeoisie/petty bourgeoisie. The institutionalization of politics and the upward mobility of the middle class Catholics was carried out in coordination with the reconstruction of the Catholic church in Ireland in the mid-nineteenth century. In this triangle we find the basis of Irish society as we know it today.

The Irish Catholic church had lacked clergy, churches, seminaries, and an effective episcopacy for the better part of two centuries, relying for its transmission largely on private prayers, pilgrimages, local holy places, and folk devotions. Regular mass attendance would have been possible for at most 42 percent of Catholics as late as 1840.[7] A massive program of church building, recruitment and formation of clergy, introduction of Roman style saints and devotions, a strict Victorian sexual ethic, and legalistic ritual practice combined with the social transformations (population fall through famine and emigration) to help bring about a remarkable institutionalization of a "late Tridentine Victorian" Catholicism, which continued to flourish up to the early 1960s.

The penchant of Victorians for institutional solutions to social problems also assisted the consolidation of the Catholic church. Universal primary education was introduced in the 1830s and in response to Presbyterian demands was soon organized along denominational lines, giving Catholic clergy control over the education of Catholic children. Fear of proselytization led to the formation of women's religious orders to set up hospitals and orphanages for Catholics leading to the partial pillarization of health and child-care services to the present day. The reorganization of farm inheritance to preserve and consolidate holdings meant that only one son and one daughter remaining at home could expect to marry, and then often at an advanced age. Other members of the family could look forward only to a life as celibate "assisting relatives" or emigration unless there were sufficient funds to give them an education or a business. The strict sexual ethic newly emphasized by the church was embraced as a means of achieving this reorganization. A high positive value on celibacy and religious life was also a product of this strict sexual teaching, and helped to boost vocations. The clergy acted as brokers and mediators in the local community between the ordinary people and state officials, businessmen and professionals.[8] The clergy also largely supported the late nineteenth-century land reform movement and were thus viewed to stand on the side of the oppressed. For these reasons, alienation from power structures in Ireland has not usually meant alienation from the church.

The Catholic church in Ireland was so taken up with erecting buildings and servicing the population that these means of evangelization became ends in themselves to the exclusion of intellectual pursuits or the development of Catholic thought in the Irish context. There was no real challenge to church teaching from within the church, although the condemnation of militant nationalism was largely ignored; in matters of sexual conduct, family life, and education there was almost total acceptance. A childlike faith, strict adherence to the sexual code and sacramental duties, together with the rote learning of the catechism, was considered ample equipment to lead a good Catholic life at home or in exile. This anti-intellectual approach was carried through in the work of Irish clergy and in the structures they established throughout the English-speaking world. The impact of their work was often disproportionate to their numbers. For example, in the United States in 1970, 17 percent of Catholics, 34 percent of the clergy, and 50 percent of bishops were estimated to be of Irish origin or descent.[9] The postindependence period also saw a flourishing Irish missionary movement to the Third World, largely to British colonies, and the same formula was applied without due consideration of local cultural conditions.

Martin has observed: "At certain crucial periods in their history, societies acquire a particular frame . . . subsequent events persistently move within the limits of that frame."[10] The establishment of the Irish Free State and of the Northern Ireland State in 1922 continued the administration that had been negotiated between the churches, the Catholic bourgeoisie, and the British government. The formula of the state paying the piper and the churches calling the tune remained unchanged. Unionist control of Northern Ireland was threatened by the large Catholic minority whose allegiance was to Dublin rather than to Belfast. To retain control, discriminatory employment practices, housing policy, and the "organization" of constituency boundaries were practiced on a wide scale. The Protestant minority in the Irish Free State (later Republic of Ireland) was too small to pose a threat and was not a target of systematic discrimination, but neither were their views and needs given special consideration, and they made few efforts to alter this.[11] There was, however, no attempt to establish Catholicism as the state church of the Republic of Ireland.

Sociocultural Changes in Ireland Since 1965

In 1981 the population of the Irish Republic stood at 3,537,195 and that of Northern Ireland at 1,558,000 (mid-term estimate).[12] Both states have been characterized by heavy emigration levels at times of economic recession and political unrest. This, together with the large average family size, has brought about a situation of unusually high percentages of population in the dependent age groups. The ecomonic boom of the 1960s in the Republic brought a large-scale return of emigrants, helped to increase the birth rate, and resulted in an unusually youthful population. As the demand for labor has been very low at most points, immigrants from lesser developed countries are very few in number. Until the 1960s, the Republic was a mainly rural population. This has since reversed, and now about one-third of the population live in the greater Dublin area.

Typical of many neocolonial states, although more affluent, agriculture and agribusiness are still important for the Irish Republic's economy. Industrial growth has been chiefly achieved by inducements to multinational companies to set up plants in designated areas. Their main activity has been light assembly work on imported components, involving no real interface with the local economy. This strategy worked well for some years, but recently emigration and unemployment levels have soared again (19.2 percent of the work force were unemployed in March 1987). The situation is likely to deteriorate further in the foreseeable future. Unskilled workers have the highest levels of unemployment and in some working class areas, crime, marital breakdown, and drug abuse have shown corresponding increases. Alienation in these areas includes low voter turnout, which in turn contributes to the neglect. This section of the population is the only one to show a major drift from religious practice.

The 1960s mark a watershed in Irish life. Greater openness to other cultures and links with other societies were developed. The protectionist policy of the Irish government gave way to free trade with Britain and later with the EEC. The decline of agriculture went hand in hand with growth in the service and industrial sectors, an increased level of urbanization, and greater social differentiation between different sections of the population.

At its foundation in 1922 Northern Ireland was a much more urbanized and industrialized state than the Irish Republic. Ghettoization on the basis of religion has increased with the violence of the last seventeen years. Belfast was a major shipbuilding and engineering center and textiles were also an important industry. The rise of more competitive centers in Asia has contributed to the virtual collapse of these industries despite grant assistance. Attempts to induce multinational companies to establish factories have been less successful than in the Republic mainly because of the "Troubles." Unemployment levels stood at 19.3 percent (adjusted downward) in January 1987 and, as in the Republic, mainly affected the unskilled classes, particularly Roman Catholic; it is in the most depressed areas that paramilitaries—both Republican and Loyalist—have flourished.

Irish politics do not fall into the usual Western European pattern of a left–right continuum. While class divisions and class issues form part of the background of Irish political life, this is a secondary element in the mobilization of voters and in party policies. The "National Question" on issues relating to the sovereignty of the Republic and the possibility of reunification with Northern Ireland and the relationship with Great Britian provides the main ground of political divisions in both the Republic and the North.

Internal Changes in Irish Catholicism

In Ireland the implementation of Vatican II decrees on the liturgy was carried out by the bishops in obedient conformity on a gradual basis from 1964 onwards. Certain ecumenical events were introduced as a regular occurrence. Both changes were accomplished without opposition, but were changes in the letter of the law, rather than in the spirit of the council.[13]

Certain elements of the teachings of the Second Vatican Council were ignored or implemented only in an emasculated form. This is particularly true of the involvement of the laity in church affairs which was done in a very limited manner: certain minor tasks were delegated to "safe" Catholics, some parish councils were established, and the National Council for the Apostolate of the Laity was established in 1968. These bodies were generally more conservative than the clergy themselves, although some organizations such as the Society of Saint Vincent de Paul showed signs of renewal.

The main changes introduced by the council, as far as the laity was concerned, were liturgical. The old pious trappings of the "devotional revolution" were discarded or drew smaller crowds. For example, between 1968 and 1973 attendance at the Redemptorist annual retreat in Limerick—a major stronghold—dropped from its usual level of 6,200 to 2,500.[14] Mass attendance has become the main or even sole public expression of religiosity for the majority. Benediction, devotions, and recitation of the rosary are only infrequently organized by the clergy. Most churches that offer a weekday evening mass have their coteries of lay people who start the rosary immediately after mass, retaining a "captive" congregation. Mildly subversive efforts like this show dissatisfaction with conciliar changes among mainly older sections of the laity and ironically achieve the lay initiative the Council proclaimed and the Irish bishops stifled.

The major impact of Vatican II in Ireland was on the clergy and religious. This was manifested first in a negative fashion by declining vocation levels, to about one-third of their former number, particularly to religious orders, and an increase in those leaving before and after profession or ordination.[15]

The religious orders were directed by Vatican II to undertake chapters of renewal, to discover their original spirit, and to simplify and democratize their structures. This initially produced a great deal of insecurity and dissension and contributed to the dropout rate. However, this stage has largely been replaced by a renewed sense of responsibility and mission. The pattern of recruitment to the priesthood and religious life had mirrored the class divisions in Ireland. With exceptions, recruits to the national and diocesan seminaries were drawn from the sons of the bourgeoisie and well-to-do farmers who could pay their fees and outfit themselves. Poor aspirants were sponsored and ordained for British or American dioceses or swelled the ranks of missionary orders (up to 1965, approximately half of those ordained in Ireland each year were to go abroad[16]).

Ireland was a happy hunting ground for juniorates for Irish and American religious orders; parents of large families were often relieved to have one child fed and educated. The religious orders themselves were usually internally stratified into choir and lay members. There was a hierarchy of status between orders depending on the class identity of the section of the population to whom they ministered. This was carefully reproduced by the dowry levels demanded and by recruiting from schools run by the order. Reform of the recruitment process, democratization within orders, return of missionaries with a raised consciousness about issues of justice have all helped to bring about a new ideological climate. Many orders have taken an "option for the poor" and are reorganizing themselves to work with marginalized groups and to highlight major inequalities. Whereas the main thrust of the work of religious orders had been to underpin the state's control of the poor through the educational, health, and welfare systems—even to running juvenile prisions—the future direction seems to lie in challenging inequities in such systems and in work among local communities. The growth of the educational system and the decline in numbers of religious personnel have forced orders to rethink and develop new priorities. The Conference for Major Religious Superiors, the coordinating body for the orders working in Ireland, has established a Justice Office, which promotes reflection and action on issues such as poverty, women's rights, unemployment, housing policy, and budgetary allocations and which occasionally issues public statements on political matters.[17]

There has thus been an alliance with the left on welfare and human rights issues. In this the bishops have also had some involvement by setting up pilot projects and issuing statements and pastoral letters on such topics as justice, unemployment, and prison conditions. But the most remarkable evidence of a shift in the thinking of Irish bishops was perhaps the occasion of the state visit of President Ronald Reagan, which provoked many protests, often spearheaded by religious, against U.S. involvement in corrupt Latin American regimes. Irish bishops absented themselves from the special functions organized in connection with the visit; this contrasts with their boycott of any events that included people suspected of being communists in the 1950s.

Alongside its alliance with the left on human rights and welfare issues has been an alliance with the right in holding the line against liberalization in relation to sexuality, evident in the referenda on abortion in 1983 and divorce in 1986. The image presented by the church is thus somewhat confusing, although issues of justice receive little media coverage compared with issues of sex and family life. It should be pointed out, however, that the same personalities are not usually involved in both left- and right-wing issues, and by and large the constituencies for both messages are predominantly from the lower classes.

Martin has observed that where religion is an important ethnic identifier against an imperialist power, levels of religious adherence are very high.[18] This is still true in Ireland, although some decline has occurred recently. In Northern Ireland in 1968, 95 percent of Catholics attended mass at least weekly; by 1984 a community study in Derry found that 84 percent attended at least weekly.[19] South of the border, two national samples of Catholics may be compared. The first, carried out in 1973–1974, found that 91 percent attended mass weekly or more often; in 1984 this percentage had dropped to 87 percent.[20] These studies also chart a drop in at least monthly confession from 47 percent to 26 percent, but a rise in monthly confession plus communion from 28 percent to 38 percent. The levels of belief are lower than levels of practice, showing the influence of social pressures to conform. There was a slight decline in firm acceptance of church doctrine and moral teachings over this ten-year period, but this represents a greater tendency to doubt or partially reject rather than a growth in unbelief. Legalism was evident in both samples as the most frequent reason for religious practices and for condemning moral transgressions. The prediction made on the basis of the earlier study seems to have been borne out: there has been some increase in polarization among Irish Catholics, with some moving away from legalism to spirituality, on the one hand, and secularism on the other.[21] However, the group with a personal spiritual commitment to Catholicism is still very much a minority, and the overall future is different to predict.

The rates of religious belief, practice, and assent to values vary in relation to social and cultural factors. The lowest levels of adherence are found among the more "modern" sections of society—the young, urbanized, those using foreign media, and males in particular. The rural population, farmers, older people, and women are generally most religious. Class has a mixed impact, with higher levels of belief but lower levels of practice among blue-collar workers.[22] There is also some evidence that the unemployed have only a minority adherence to the church.[23]

Over half of the population of Ireland attended at least one of the ceremonies presided over by Pope John Paul II on his 1979 visit. This was greeted as a sign of renewal and was followed by a small increase in vocations, but it did not seem to have a lasting impact. Similarly, signs of revival were read into a collective behavior phenomenon, involving many thousands of people in 1984–1985, when reports from all over the country told of public statues of the Virgin Mary moving and sometimes being transformed into images of Christ. Clergy and bishops were careful to distance themselves from the cult, and it gradually evaporated. Others viewed such occurrences as symptoms of a crisis of faith as people struggled for concrete signs of the beliefs that no longer seemed so convincing.[24]

Bill McSweeney has claimed that the Second Vatican Council sowed the seeds of division within the monolith that was Catholicism, by introducing relativity into matters of faith and morals, a flexibility that has resulted in four broad groupings: political Catholicism, charismatic Catholicism, traditionalist Catholicism, and theological individualism.[25] What evidence is there for these divisions in Ireland? Political Catholicism is as yet mainly confined to certain members of religious orders. Where lay Catholics have espoused such views, they have lived out their beliefs in nondenominational rather than Catholic Action organizations. There are approximately nine associations of Christian feminists in Ireland, most of whom have a political commitment. Charismatic Catholicism peaked in enthusiastic, large-scale ecumenical gatherings in the mid-1970s and since then has been found mainly in small prayer groups and Scripture groups attached to parishes or religious houses. It has contributed to the growth of personal spiritual commitment, but it has had little social impact. Traditionalist Catholicism attracted very few to breakaway groups, although there are two small congregations of such groups in Dublin. Theological individualism is a growing but still minority position, if this means qualified assent and selective dissent to tenets of faith and morals; it is a position increasingly adopted by urban, middle class, and younger Catholics. The bulk of Irish Catholics still lies outside these groupings in a legalistic fidelity to a preconciliar Catholicism, which, given the style of the current papacy, may well return in abbreviated form.

Changes in the Relationship of Church and State

"The Irish Catholic church professes a social doctrine, but no longer entertains a coherent social project."[26] In the 1940s Eamon de Valera, then *taoiseach* (prime minister), made a speech in which he painted a vision of Ireland that was rural, traditional, and simple in its way of life, where families could be brought up "in frugal comfort." The vision matched that of the Irish church, whose main social involvement lay in promoting rural development, cooperatives, small factories, and which rejected socialism in favor of small-scale benevolent capitalism and the family firm. This was not in conflict with the state's policy of protectionism, which sought to encourage native Irish capital.

In 1958 the state's policy radically changed. Michael Peillon claims that at this stage it adopted the "project of the bourgeoisie," placing priority on economic growth. The main thrust of industrial policy then was to induce multinational companies to set up factories and to orchestrate growth in the service sector. This policy was successful to the extent of transforming Ireland from an economy composed mainly of self-employed (farmers and others) to a wage-earning work force. All other bodies, including those such as trade unions whose interests might clash with the goal of economic growth and the church which might view such a goal as dangerously materialistic, have been coerced into accepting this as the major aim and criterion for Irish policies. Through content analysis of official statements, journals, and newspapers, Peillon concludes that the church largely abandoned its Catholic program for the reconstruction of society after the 1950s. While the church has abandoned its corporatist position, no coherent project for society has replaced it. The church has maintained its concern for the poor and its involvement in education; the conservatism underlying these efforts testifies not to an enthusiasm for the status quo but to a reluctance to question the accommodation to the established social and political order, which, in turn, looks after the essential needs of the church.[27]

There is support for this view from other analysts. At the macro-level, John Whyte assesses the stance of the church as condemning state intervention on the basis of the principle of subsidiarity, and as promoting the vocational organization of society. The shift away from this approach during the late 1950s and early 1960s led in the 1970s to a position to the left of center of the political parties on issues of deprivation and poverty. Whyte quotes Liam Ryan's suggestion that the best model to use for the hierarchy's current role is to see it as seeking to be "the conscience of society." The Catholic social movement focused on issues of poverty. The role of the state was viewed as necessary for the elimination of deprivation.[28] One might add that the church has increasingly applied the principle of subsidiarity in reverse fashion by setting up pilot schemes for marginalized groups not covered by state provisions and by using these to lobby for more comprehensive state aid to such groups.

At the micro-level, Chris Eipper's study of church, state, and business in Bantry (a medium-sized town on the south coast) confirms a decline of clergy influence at the community level. In many cases they needed to have the support of business people and politicians to get a scheme going, while managing to enlist ordinary people as their lieutenants.[29] Business people were by far the most influential and powerful in seeing schemes they advocated implemented.

The state's embrace of the "project of the bourgeoisie" has had major secularizing effects in many areas. Entrance into the EEC in 1973 has led to the legal subordination of the Irish constitution to the laws of that body. This has led to changes, for example, in the implementation of equality legislation, which has improved employment conditions and prospects for all women in theory and some women in practice. Various aspects of family law are being challenged in the European Court of Justice with varying success. Irish society has become more open to influence from outside given the popularity and availability of foreign media, on the one hand, and the extent of leisure travel and temporary emigration on the other. With more disposable income than in the mid-1960s, Irish people have a more individuated and consumerist approach to living. This new approach has spilled over from the purely economic sphere to the sphere of sexuality and family life. The economic growth project of the bourgeoisie demands the removal of obstacles to the free movement of capital and labor. Restrictive Irish family law is one such obstacle, and hence the backing of liberalization moves by bourgeoisie and intellectuals is understandable.

The way in which the changes in society and the changes in the Irish church have interacted to produce a new configuration of church, state, and business on the ideological map of the Republic may be illustrated by looking at the area of family law.

There was almost total acceptance of Catholic sexual ethics in the first few decades of the Republic; this is understandable in the light of the system of delayed family farm inheritance and the consequent late marriages of the heirs and often lifetime single status of the siblings who did not migrate. Nonmarital sexual relations posed a threat to the whole fabric of society and the viability of the farm family. In precontraception days, this was also the prudent ethic of the urban Irish, and the labor market conditions for women made it almost impossible to rear a family alone.

The social changes from the 1960s onward combined to alter this situation. On the economic front, agriculture declined in significance in relation to industry and services. There was increased demand for female labor and the equality legislation made it impossible to dismiss a woman on marriage or pregnancy. Contraceptives were illegal until 1979 and were available only through illegal family planning clinics or by prescription as "cycle regulators." There are still rural areas in which pharmacists are unwilling to sell contraceptives, but by and large pregnancy is in theory a matter of choice rather than accident. In this transformed situation the traditional Catholic sexual ethics is no longer perceived as quite so relevant. Sexual activity is increasingly viewed as a matter of individual choice rather than communal concern, and aspects of legislation that inhibit its expression are yielding to attacks by pressure groups. This has put the entire relationship of church and state under review.

The process of sexual liberalization and the church–state tension this has unleashed have brought about a new polarization in Irish society. In 1983 a conservative lay Catholic lobby succeeded in having a referendum held to add an article to the national Constitution that would prohibit the enactment of legislation permitting abortion. A long and bitter debate preceded the vote. Religious minorities, most of Fine Gael, left-wing groups, feminists, and many Dublin media personnel and intelligentsia opposed the amendment. The prolife group drew direct support from the Catholic church, Fianna Fail (the largest party with 45–50 percent of the vote), and especially from people in rural areas. The outcome was 60–40 in favor of the prolife amendment.

The Irish constitution, adopted in 1937, also contains a provision prohibiting divorce. The *taoiseach,* Dr. Garret Fitzgerald, had agreed to hold a referendum allowing the introduction of divorce when opinion polls showed a clear majority in favor. In the spring of 1986 the polls gave a 20 percent lead to those who favored divorce in certain circumstances. The referendum date was set for June 26 and a brief campaign ensued. The prodivorce campaign had been geared up to fight the issue on church–state lines; they faced instead the church's reaffirmation of the indissolubility of marriage without a firm directive on voting. The antidivorce campaign concentrated on pointing out the lack of clarity on economic and legal issues in the proposals. The government was ill-prepared to answer these questions, and much of the final stage of the debate focused on the economic disutility which divorce might introduce, especially in the case of the farming community and middle income groups. The prodivorce campaign was supported, to varying degrees, by all parties, with the exception of Fianna Fail, who remained "neutral." In other ways, the opposing groups were a mirror-image of the 1983 referendum. The result was an almost perfect correspondence in each constituency with the earlier referendum and a 63–37 overall defeat of the amendment. The fact that such questions were raised at all is an indication of increasing distance between church and state. The impact of Northern Ireland may also be seen as sections of the population began to view issues in a pluralist context. As recently as 1967 both Church of Ireland archbishops joined the cardinal archbishop of Armagh's rejection of a proposal to allow of divorce.[30] A few Dublin constituencies narrowly favored the introduction of divorce, but elsewhere the proposal was rejected.

Changes in church–state relationships in Northern Ireland have taken a form different from that in the Republic and must be viewed mainly in relation to the conflict situation. The civil rights movement in the United States evoked a comparison between blacks and Catholics and resulted in a similar movement in Northern Ireland. This put the demands of the Nationalist community on a new plane of human rights, uncomplicated by questions of sovereignty. The demands became impossible for the British government to oppose, especially as the world's press paid great attention. However, research pointed to continuing levels of discrimination, particularly in the employment field.[31] Some progress toward reform fueled Nationalist desires for more progress, on the one hand, and aroused the insecurity and anger of Loyalists, on the other. This tension culminated in the "Troubles" in 1969. Since then, both British and Irish governments have been increasingly involved in defending the status quo against the threat of militants from both communities and in staging talks to attempt at least an interim solution. So far, attempts at solutions have not received consent from most sections of the community, and the only likely alternatives are a British withdrawal or continuation of the current situation. The fabric of everyday life is marked by the "Troubles." Special powers were enacted to arrest and try those suspected of involvement, and nonjury trials were held for suspected paramilitaries. Expenditure on security has escalated. Population movement to areas perceived as safer for a given religious affiliation has been widespread. In both the Republic and Northern Ireland it is unlikely that a "normal" politics in terms of left–right divisions will emerge without a resolution of this question.

Peillon has described the Irish Catholic church as speaking with a "plurality of languages."[32] Nowhere is this more clearly illustrated than in relation to the conflict in Northern Ireland. An interesting aspect of Catholicism in Ireland is that, as with all the other denominations, it has one organization covering both states. It thus operates in a "state of monopoly" and a "state of minority" simultaneously. The mixture of strategies employed in each situation gives rise to a certain amount of tension and contradiction. No divorce is available in the Republic, but in Northern Ireland couples seeking a church annulment of their marriage need first obtain a civil divorce. To some extent this contradiction is avoided by the diocesan structure itself. Although some dioceses straddle the border, those serving the most urban and populous areas of Belfast and Derry in the North and Dublin and Cork in the South are exclusively within one state. With the exception of the Primatial See of Armagh, which includes sections of both states, it is these dioceses that have the most vocal incumbents. The statements from the Northern bishops usually involve a message of condemnation of violence mixed with a call for greater fairness in the administration of justice and restraint on the part of the security forces. At the same time, the plight of political prisoners and their families receives attention. Certain priests work quite closely with those associated with paramilitary organizations, keeping the lines open to such groups. Others forbid any military symbols at funerals and barely conceal their hostility. This mixture of pastoral approaches works reasonably well in maintaining affiliation of different sections of the population.

Taking both states, Catholics form an overall majority and are located in all classes. Their allegiance to the church has been successfully retained by its populist "plurality of languages." As class divisions and inequalities become more apparent, the new poor—that large section of long-term unemployed—and the new rich find such a message increasingly implausible. In colonial times, the church functioned as protector of the oppressed against the British, and it retained this aura throughout the period of independence. There was a reluctance to take sides or go beyond a mediation role, as the church sought to keep the flock intact. Given renewed concern with the poor and marginalized, gradual detachment from this position seems less tenable. The challenge of the Gospel in relation to social concerns is replacing the preoccupation with individual salvation.

NOTES

1. David Martin, *A General Theory of Secularization* (Oxford: Blackwell, 1978), p. 113.
2. David Martin, "The Religious Condition of Europe," in Salvador Giner and Margaret S. Archer (eds.), *Contemporary Europe: Social Structures and Cultural Patterns* (London: Routledge & Kegan Paul, 1978), p. 244.
3. Máire Nic Ghiolla Phádraig, "Religion in Ireland," *Social Studies* 5 (March 1976):129.
4. John M. Whyte, *Church and State in Modern Ireland, 1923–1979*, 2nd ed. (Dublin: Gill & Macmillan, 1980), pp. 363–64.
5. Desmond Fennell, *The Changing Face of Catholic Ireland* (Washington: Corpus Books, 1968), p. 187; Louis McRedmond, "The Church in Ireland," in John Cummings and Paul (eds.), *The Church Now: An Inquiry into the Present State of the Catholic Church in Britain and Ireland* (Dublin: Gill & Macmillan, 1980), p. 39.
6. Martin, *A General Theory of Secularization*, p. 107.
7. Emmett Larkin, "The Devotional Revolution in Ireland, 1850–1875" in *Historical Dimensions of Irish Catholicism* (New York: Arno, 1976), p. 636.
8. Chris Eipper, *The Ruling Trinity: A Community Study of Church, State and Business in Ireland* (Aldershot: Gower, 1986), p. 96.
9. Andrew M. Greeley, *The American Catholic* (New York: Basic Books, 1977), p. 159.
10. Martin, *A General Theory of Secularization*, p. 15.
11. Whyte, *Church and State in Modern Ireland*, pp. 57–59.
12. Central Statistics Office, *1986 Census Preliminary Report* (Dublin: CSO, 1986), p. vi; Central Statistics Office, *Monthly Digest of Statistics* (London: HMSO No. 494, February 1987).
13. McRedmond, "The Church in Ireland," p. 42.
14. Personal communication from Rev. G. Reynolds, C.S.S.R.
15. John Weafer and Ann Breslin, *Irish Catholic Clergy and Religious, 1970–1981* (Maynooth: Council for Research and Development, Report No. 17, 1983).
16. Fennell, *The Changing Face of Catholic Ireland*, p. 139.
17. Sean M. Healy and Bridget Reynolds, *Social Analysis in the Light of the Gospel and Ireland Today: Reflecting in the Light of the Gospel* (Dublin: Conference for Major Religious Superiors, 1983 and 1985).
18. Martin, *A General Theory of Secularization*, p. 152.
19. John Hickey, "Religion in a Divided Society," in Patrick Clancy et al. (eds.), *Ireland: A Sociological Profile* (Dublin: Institute of Public Administration, 1986), p. 269.
20. Ann Breslin and John Weafer, *Religious Beliefs, Practice and Moral Attitudes: A Comparison of Two Irish Surveys, 1974–1984* (Maynooth: Council for Research and Development, Report No. 21, 1985), p. vii.
21. Máire Nic Ghiolla Phádraig, "Alternative Models to Secularization in Relation to Moral Reasoning" (16th Biennial Conference of the International Conference of the Sociology of Religion—Lausanne, 1981. Published in the Acts of the Conference).

22. Máire Nic Ghiolla Phádraig, "Religious Practice and Secularization," in Patrick Clancy et al. (eds.), *Ireland: A Sociological Profile,* pp. 151–53.

23. Breslin and Weafer, *Religious Beliefs, Practice and Moral Attitudes,* Appendix C.

24. Peadar Kirby, "On Moving Statues: A People's Cry for Spirituality," Part I, *Doctrine and Life* 36 (April 1986):171–81.

25. Bill McSweeney, *Roman Catholicism: The Search for Relevance* (Oxford: Blackwell, 1980), pp. 165–232.

26. Michel Peillon, *Contemporary Irish Society: An Introduction* (Dublin: Gill & Macmillan, 1982), p. 99.

27. Peillon, *Contemporary Irish Society,* chap. 10.

28. Whyte, *Church and State in Modern Ireland,* chap. XI.

29. Eipper, *The Ruling Trinity,* p. 106.

30. Fennell, *The Changing Face of Catholic Ireland,* p. 188.

31. Robert Miller, "Social Stratification and Mobility," in Patrick Clancy et al. (eds.), *Ireland: A Sociological Profile,* pp. 227–30.

32. Peillon, *Contemporary Irish Society,* p. 90.

11

Into the Mainstream:
Recent Transformations
in British Catholicism

Michael P. Hornsby-Smith

This chapter will review recent transformations in British Catholicism as a result of postwar social change and in the light of the Second Vatican Council. We will use the analytical framework suggested by David Martin, who aimed to construct an empirical theory about changes in "the role, power, and popularity of religious beliefs and institutions."[1] In spite of his earlier criticisms of the concept of secularization, Martin later admitted that religious institutions are adversely affected by heavy industry in homogeneously proletarian areas and by high levels of geographical and social mobility.[2] Secularization should be seen as a relativization of perspectives and the differentation of religion from other institutional spheres. These processes are molded by crucial historical events, especially the path taken by the Reformation, but also, for example, in the British case by the outcome of the English Civil War in the seventeenth century.[3] Of the six resultant historical patterns Martin identifies, the British pattern involves a *partial* dislodgment of the politicoreligious establishment by substantial dissent.[4] Religion as such is politically unproblematic, though certain partial alignments of denominations and parties occur. Religious institutions are attenuated but beliefs remain widely disseminated, albeit in a somewhat amorphous manner.[5]

Later Martin suggested that the Anglo-Saxon pattern was characterized by institutional erosion and erosion of religious ethos, and by the maintenance of amorphous religious beliefs. More specifically, he described the English pattern as one with a medium degree of religious pluralism and a fairly low level of anticlericalism. Clerical status tends to be medium and cultic participation fairly low. Internal religious conservatism is fairly high and intellectualism in religion medium. The stability of democracy is said to be high and communist influence low. The political orientation of Catholics is center-left and civil religion is religiously toned. The church–state nexus is retained (with the Established Church of England), and the school system, originally religious, now tends to be semisecular. The intelligentsia are both more and less religious than status equivalents and there are no religous parties. In a typology of political power relationships, Britain is regarded as having a system of institutionalized tolerance with stable tolerance limits, and in these circumstances the evidence strongly indicates the stabilizing effects of Catholicism where it is a dispersed and fairly small minority.[6]

This chapter will explore the evidence for a number of Martin's propositions relating to Catholicism in such a structural position, mainly on the basis of empirical data about English Catholics collected in the 1970s and 1980s. Martin suggests that one must be aware of four distinct cultural layers that are encapsulated in Catholicism: para-Christian and pre-Christian manipulative magic; semi-Christianized systems of mediation, expressing local loyalties and providing sources of personal consolation and assistance; the religion of the Council of Trent; and the religion of the Second Vatican Council. In our review we will follow Martin's major concerns with the founding myths of the nation and processes of differentiation; the impact of the industrial and urban revolutions; the migration of religio-ethnic groups (such as the Irish); and transformations in religious meanings, belonging, and authority relationships in the light of the Second Vatican Council.

National Differentiation

It is necessary at the outset to recognize something of the complexity of the relationships between the three nations that go to make up Great Britain. Briefly, the principality of Wales has been governed by the English since its conquest by Edward I at the end of the thirteenth century. The union with Scotland was not achieved for another four centuries. After the uniting of the crowns of England and Scotland in 1603 with the accession of James I, there followed the Cromwellian period and the restoration of the monarchy. The 1701 Act of Settlement required future sovereigns to be members of the Church of England, and the Act of Union of 1707 finally joined the Parliaments of Scotland and England.

These crucial historical events explain the fact that, for the purposes of Roman Catholic ecclesiastical administration, there are two separate hierarchies for England and Wales and for Scotland. (Catholicism in Northern Ireland, which is juridically part of the United Kingdom, is administrated ecclesiastically by a unitary Irish hierarchy and is considered separately in Chapter 10.) This reflects their different historical, legal, and religious traditions and the different forms taken by the Protestant Reformation and the subsequent emergence of Roman Catholicism after centuries of persecution and hostility to political emancipation in the nineteenth century, as well as their gradual social and religious acceptance in the second half of the twentieth century. While in England and Wales the hierarchy of bishops was restored in 1850, it was not until 1878 that it was restored in Scotland.[7] In general, easing the hostility toward Catholicism in Scotland, with its strong Presbyterian form of Protestantism, has tended to lag behind the more tolerant situation in England.[8] Catholics in peripheral Wales, with its strong dissenting tradition and its politics of cultural defense vis-à-vis the dominant political and religious English center and its disestablished church, form a tiny minority concentrated around the old centers of Irish immigration.[9]

It is necessary to emphasize the heterogeneity of the two Catholic communities. In both a large part of the increase in the Catholic population from the 1790s on is attributable to Irish migration. In Scotland other significant contributions have been made by people of Italian, Lithuanian, Ukranian, and Polish descent, and the deep divisions between native Scots and Irish immigrants have lessened since the restoration of the hierarchy.[10] Estimates derived from opinion surveys suggest that the proportion of self-defined but not necessarily practicing Roman Catholics may be around 16 percent of the population (1.8 million) in Scotland and 11 percent (5.4 million) in England and Wales.

In England and Wales, where there is a stronger research base on which to interpret recent changes, it is possible to distinguish at least four distinct groups.[11] First, presently around 650,000 "recusant" Catholics can trace their Catholicism to pre-Reformation days. Martin notes their concentration in remote areas such as the Fylde district in Northwest England and in some of the Scottish Western isles.[12] Second, about 460,000 English Catholics are converts. Third, in the late 1970s there were some 590,000 first-generation and 700,000 second-generation Irish immigrant Catholics. Fourth, apart from the Irish immigrants, around 670,000 Catholics were born in countries outside the British Isles. Of these, the largest groups came from Italy and Poland but there are also over 100,000 Catholics from African, West Indian, and Asian countries.

It has also been estimated that there are about 460,000 second-generation immigrants with origins outside the British Isles. The balance of around one-third of English Catholics has a variety of other backgrounds, but the bulk of them will likely have an Irish ancestry that originated three or more generations ago. Analyses of 1971 and 1981 Census Country of Birth tables suggest that nearly one English Catholic in four was born outside Great Britian, over four times the proportion of first-generation immigrants among the rest of the population.[13] The immigrant origins of many Catholics is reflected in their lower age and social class profiles, but the signs of their assimilation are found in their social and geographical mobility. Gallup omnibus data suggest that by the late 1970s, while the proportion of Catholics in the general population was still the greatest in the Northwest, two-fifths of English Catholics were to be found in London and the Southeast.[14]

The impediments of being a Roman Catholic in the British Protestant State have gradually been reduced: in recent years Catholics have held such posts as secretary of the Cabinet, leadership of both Houses of Parliament, the editorship of The Times, and general secretary of the Trades Union Congress. The gradual realization that international Catholicism poses no threat to Protestant Britian is reflected in ending a long-standing imbalance in its diplomatic relationships with the Holy See. Whereas British diplomatic representation at the Vatican has existed since World War I, it was not until 1938 that an apostolic delegate was appointed to London. While diplomatic privileges to the pope's representative were gradually extended in the postwar years, it was not until 1982, shortly before the successful visit of Pope John Paul II to Britian, that the apostolic delegate was accorded ambassadorial status as apostolic pronuncio.

Three developments in particular have manifested the coming of age of British Catholicism. First, the National Pastoral Congress held in Liverpool in 1980 and attended by 2,000 priests, religious, and lay delegates from all dioceses and Catholic organizations in England and Wales generated some prophetic reports and, in the bishops' response, *The Easter People,* drew forth a major commitment in principle to "The Sharing Church."[15] Second, the pope's visit to both communities in 1982 was generally regarded as a diplomatic and ecumenical success, the result of careful preparation and much tact at the time of the Falklands War. For many Catholics it signified a final emergence from the fortress church. Third, leadership style has significantly changed since the time when Cardinal Heenan boasted of his ability to pick up the telephone and speak to the prime minister. The unassuming and charismatic Cardinal Hume commands wide respect throughout Britian, and the eased ecumenical climate, which manifested itself especially at Canterbury during the pope's visit, continues to be expressed in the remarkable collaboration between the Catholic archbishop and Anglican bishop of Liverpool.

The Mobility Disruption Hypothesis

In his essay on "The Unkown Gods of the English," David Martin drew attention to the need to investigate empirically the relationship between social and geographical mobility and the condition of the churches.[16] Later, in his review of a variety of religiocultural identities, he hypothesized that:

> sub-cultural identity is loosened where there is an antecedent long-term loyalty to the nation as a whole and where processes of social and geographical mobility blur frontiers and lower inter-group antagonisms. . . . Sub-cultural loosening also occurs where political aims are achieved and identity [is] recognized. In other words the achievement of substantial autonomy and recognition may weaken those sources of identity, more especially religion, which were previously so necessary to survival.[17]

It is possible to test Martin's propositions in the case of English Catholics. Given the low status and immigrant origins of many Catholics, some upward mobility momentum relative to the rest of the population might have been anticipated in the affluent years after World War II.[18] The evidence is not at all clear-cut. A study of Catholic and non-Catholic electors in four English parishes in the 1970s provides no support for the proposition; the same conclusion can be drawn from the national survey of Catholics in 1978.[19] In fact, a comparison of the mean mobility movement of Catholic men with the national data from the Oxford mobility study of 1972 showed that Catholic men born in Great Britian showed a higher level of intergenerational upward social mobility than all men in the Oxford study. However, the average rate for Catholics was reduced by the fact that Irish-born Catholic men had much lower levels of upward mobility, while those Catholics born outside the British Isles were on average downwardly mobile. Other data indicate that by the second generation Irish immigrants, though not other immigrants, had substantially converted to the national average in terms of mean mobility.[20]

Martin suggests that experiences of either social or geographical mobility are likely to disrupt traditional religious practice and belief, particularly for those migrants who have come from relatively high-practice areas like Ireland. Welch and Baltzell have suggested an "integration-disruption" hypothesis, that geographical mobility inhibits church attendance indirectly by disrupting an individual's network of social ties and bonds of community attachment[21]; Luckmann and Berger suggest that in a "mobility ethos" one of the functions of the churches is "social maintenance and repair services" for a precarious private universe in "a world of radical subjectivism."[22]

In the study of four English parishes, contrary to the original suppositions, variations in social mobility were not significantly related to religious practices.[23] On the basis of data from the 1978 national survey of English Catholics, one can infer that significant variations in social mobility occurred only with regard to doctrinal orthodoxy, adult religious behavior, new-style activism, and liturgical traditionalism. Geographical (mainly immigrant) mobility was significantly associated with only five factors: doctrinal orthodoxy, adult religious behavior, prayer, sexual orthodoxy, and the weight attached to papal authority.[24]

Although few of these variations in social mobility were large enough to be statistically significant, on eleven of the fifteen measures the stable middle class recorded the highest scores. These people are clearly the most institutionally involved in terms of orthodoxy of belief, religious practice, organizational involvement (both tradtitional and innovative), social and personal morality, awareness of papal authority, and a concern about religious sanctions. Those with other mobility experiences, that is, the upwardly or downwardly mobile or the stable working class, are remarkably similar. There was little evidence overall for the emergence of a committed and institutionally involved new middle class—the upwardly mobile—though their innovative potential was reflected by the fact that they scored highest in supporting new types of ministries. They were also the least orthodox group in terms of sexual morality and had the highest proportion of nonpracticing Catholics. The disruption hypothesis receives some support from the fact that downwardly mobile Catholics scored lowest on ten of the fifteen measures considered. It is possible that both the upwardly and downwardly mobile jettison some elements of their original religious culture. In the case of the downwardly mobile there is some loss of both practice and belief though not sexual orthodoxy. In contrast, the upwardly mobile have largely ceased to conform to the institutional identity, which is strongest among the stable working class; more than the other three groups, they have also rejected the sexual orthodoxy of the church.

Irish Catholics exhibit a large measure of assimilation to the norms of English Catholicism by the second generation. First-generation Irish Catholics retain many of the traditional aspects of Irish Catholicism. On nine of the fifteen measures investigated they recorded the highest scores. They showed the highest levels of religious practice, doctrinal and sexual orthodoxy, liturgical traditionalism, support of papal authority, awareness of religious sanctions, and conformity to institutional identity. Conversely, they were least likely to emphasize world justice or support new styles of ministry. In general, they reflected a pre-Vatican institutional model of the church. By the second generation, however, there were signs of a considerable degree of convergence to the norms of English Catholicism: assimilation to local church norms (e.g., in doctrinal and sexual orthodoxy), liturgical traditionalism, attitudes to priests, and new styles of ministry. There was also an increase in the proportion of nonpracticing Irish Catholics in the second generation, although this was balanced by a high proportion of involved orthodox attenders. Thus, while the first-generation Irish Catholic immigrants tend to remain near the periphery of institutional parish life, their children are disproportionately to be found among the core membership of parish organizations.

Finally, there is strong evidence that the higher the level of lay leadership attained within the institutional church, the greater the amount of intergenerational mobility. This finding is consistent with Musgrove's explanation of the compensatory functions of leadership in voluntary associations for the disruptive effects of both social and geographical mobility.[25]

The Decline of the Politics of Cultural Defense

Among the issues raised in Martin's alternative formulation of his thesis about religion in Europe are the salience of national or regional cultural awareness and the tension between elite power in the nation-state and independent structures of religious loyalty or criticism.[26] These issues are particularly relevant for British Catholics. At least until the 1950s, there was a strong sense of a separate religious and cultural identity especially among the Irish working class in the inner cities, so it was possible to specify key elements of a distinctive Catholic subculture in British society.[27] This led to the politics of cultural defense and a strategy of segregation, particularly with regard to the religious and moral socialization of young Catholics. In the period of postwar reconstruction the leadership of the English Catholic community was initially suspicious of the collectivist trend in social policy and of the social reforms proposed under the general rubric of the welfare state, but their main efforts were addressed to the construction of a "dual system" of education and the right to state aid for schools that remained under the control of the Catholic authorities.[28]

It was the protracted battle over the financial implications of the 1944 Education Act that led to the mobilization of the Catholic community in defense of the right to a separate school system and control over the religious curriculum and moral teaching. As in other societies, the Catholic–secular antagonisms which Martin addresses were worked out in conflicts with the state over the control of schooling and the socialization of the younger generation.[29] The financial burden of the school building programs in the 1960s and 1970s was considerable in a period of unprecedented inflation and high interest rates. In order to ease this burden the government grant for school building programs was raised from 50 percent to 85 percent in a number of stages as the bitter religious antagonisms of the years up to 1944 gradually declined.[30] Arguably, these battles consumed almost all the available energies of the Catholic community and diverted attention from competing claims for limited financial resources. In many ways the building of Catholic schools was regarded as an end in itself, and little attention was paid to their quality or effectiveness. In the more tolerant or indifferent religious climate of the 1980s, it is doubtful if the Catholic community could again be mobilized for a major defense of the dual system.

There are good reasons for thinking that, in spite of a measure of upward social mobility, British Catholics are not a significant political force. Indeed, Bishop (later Archbishop) George Beck, at the time of the centenary of the restoration of hierarchy, gloomily observed that Catholic influence had declined since the time of the Liberal Government of 1906 and the subsequent withdrawal of the Irish members of the House of Commons and the creation of the Irish Free State.[31] Thus the proportion of Catholic Members of Parliament is only about half the proportion of Catholics in the population generally—a situation that has remained unchanged for decades. Several explanations can be offered: the defensive mentality forged in the penal years, which generated a low-profile political strategy; a general "other-worldly" religious style; and a residual and covert anti-Catholicism.[32]

The major test case of Catholic political power was recent abortion legislation. Any attempt to claim that Catholics consititute a politically powerful interest group in British society must address their failure to prevent the passage of the 1967 Abortion Act or of the nine parliamentary attempts subsequently to amend it. Roman Catholic Members of Parliament were prominent in all these efforts; Catholics also comprised a large part of the two main pressure groups: the Society for the Protection of the Unborn Child (S.P.U.C) and Life. An analysis of the failure points to the "fundamentalist" stance of the extraparliamentary lobby and hence a failure to determine priorities and seek the appropriate political compromises, which might pragmatically have resulted in more restrictive legislation.[33] In the light of this example it may tentatively be suggested that the conflict between a fundamentalist stance on moral principle and a pragmatic need for political compromise in pluralist democratic societies has produced a weak Catholic contribution to political decision making.[34]

For historical reasons, largely grounded in differences between the political parties with respect to the Irish question, Catholics have disproportionately supported the Labor Party.[35] However, survey data indicate a substantial degree of convergence between Catholics and the rest of the population on a wide range of social, economic, political, and moral issues.[36] There is a contrast between support in general terms, especially among young Catholics, for a greater involvement of the church in issues such as housing, poverty, and race relations, and a slight majority against the church taking active steps to promote social justice if it means becoming involved in politics. On balance, British Catholics appear to prefer a "domesticated Gospel" to a "political Christianity."[37] These findings support Martin's conclusion about "the stabilizing effects of Catholicism where it is a dispersed and fairly small minority."[38]

There are some signs, however, that radical Catholics are beginning to overcome the deep suspicion among many Catholics of the church meddling in politics and to contest its traditional other-worldly orientation as well as existing social and economic relationships. Thus the report of the Justice Sector at the National Pastoral Congress confessed: "We regret our failure as a church to combat the prevailing national mood of insularity, to identify with the poor in our midst and to work vigorously for a more peaceful world.[39] A growing minority of Catholics has challenged the image of the "domesticated denomination" and has urged that the preferential option for the poor be adopted in the praxis of the church and not just in its rhetoric. The resolution of this conflict will depend upon questions of relative power and the role of competing elites in their pursuit of hegemony. In any event, it seems that, encouraged by the mass media, the processes of both economic "embourgeoisement" and cultural normative convergence with the general population have lessened the politics of cultural defense.[40]

Religious Transformations

Martin concludes his alternative formulation of religion in Europe by suggesting that:

> in general the disorientations of industrial society in terms of conceptual, geographical and social mobility, all militate against the roots and the sense of the familiar and familial which support Christian images of the world. But certain fundamental facts stand out: insofar as work takes place in a personal setting where people own their own homes . . . or their own individual skills and professional abilities in contexts which are familiar and on a human scale they are more likely to practice Christianity and be sensitive to it. Insofar as they are submerged in a mass, dominated by vast enterprises and large scale private or state undertakings, subject to a soulless process based on mechanism, they are less likely to practice Christianity or to be aware of its meaning.[41]

The 1978 national survey of English Catholics provided some support for these propositions. Not only was there evidence of considerable heterogeneity of belief and practice but it also showed that the post-Vatican church was disproportionately attractive to the educated middle classes and older Catholics.[42] There was also some evidence for the disruptive effects of both social and geographical mobility.

The effects of migration on maintaining religious identity and practice depend upon a variety of factors. In the case of the Irish in Britain these include the extent of social mobility and the breakdown of norms of ethnic and religious endogamy. Recent survey evidence suggests that Martin may have underestimated the mobility of Irish Catholics, at least over two generations, and also the amount of intermarriage. The net effect has been a substantial convergence toward the norms of English Catholicism by the second generation.[43] Where religion remains a major element of an immigrant group's identity or where processes of assimilation to a nonpracticing culture have been inhibited, for example, by maintaining group endogamy, fairly high levels of religious practice and identity will most likely be retained.

Martin's conclusion that the church is distinctly unsuccessful with the male, the postadolescent, the worker, and the inhabitant of the vast impersonal housing complex finds substantial support in the case of English Catholics in the late twentieth century. Luckmann's hypothesis that the degree of involvement in the work processes of modern industrial society correlates negatively with the degree of involvement in church-oriented religion is also supported.[44] Women who do not define themselves as housewives show a strong tendency to heterodoxy or departure from traditional belief and practice patterns.

In several analyses Martin refers to subterranean theologies—the paradox of strong approval for recent liturgical changes accompanied by increasing numbers of Catholics ceasing to practice regularly; the existence of a vague, unformulated, inarticulate faith; the notion that religion is not simply to be equated with church practice; a religion without direct ideological expression; and a generalized tendency toward an apathy that shrinks from explicit institutional religion.[45] Empirical support for these themes can be found in the focused interviews with random samples of Catholics in four English Roman Catholic parishes carried out in the mid-1970s. A variety of heterodox beliefs and practices made up the customary religion of these Catholics. These derived from "official religion" but were not under its control; they were also the product of formal religious socialization but subject to trivialization, conventionality, apathy, convenience, and self-interest. Customary religion therefore tends to be unstructured and heterodox. The researchers noted that:

> it appears that there has been very little coherent ideological opposition to [the post-Vatican] renewal. This is not to say, however, that its absence betokens a widespread commitment to renewal. We suspect that the official functionaries within the institutional church have too often assumed that lay Catholics have been effectively socialized, are ideologically committed, have a coherent belief structure, and are responsive to direction by the institutional leadership and that they have interpreted the absence of a widespread and coherent negative reaction to the post-Vatican changes as a sign that they have been substantially accepted. The prevalence of customary religion . . . suggests that all these assumptions are problematic.[45]

Martin considers that processes of differentiation have penetrated deeply into the areas of social morality so that official Catholic social morality concerning the family is often disregarded, especially by educated and student Catholics and this is congruent with widespread moves to separate the norms of Christianity or the church from the legal norms governing family life. This again makes familial life a matter of Christian conscience not external regulation. Broad ideas of personal fulfillment replace rigid legal and social categories and prohibitions.[47]

The attitudes of English Catholics on such matters as contraception, divorce, and abortion have been well documented.[48] By the mid-1970s Catholics in general had in large measure transferred judgment about the morality of contraception from the religious authorities to their personal conscience.[49] Further evidence of the transformation of Catholic attitudes to religious authority was found in the responses of lay people attending the public events held during the pope's visit in 1982. While there were overwhelmingly positive evaluations of the pope as a person, even mass-attending Catholics varied widely in their responses to his teaching: from unconditional acceptance to outright rejection. Most Catholics felt entitled to make up their minds and put greater reliance on private judgment than on church orthodoxy in many areas of their lives.[50]

In a study of the delegates to the National Pastoral Congress, however, the ordinary lay delegates were much more traditional than Catholics generally on the birth control issue.[51] A subsequent analysis of progressive tendencies among British Catholics suggested that three overriding dimensions, each with lower-order elements, might be distinguished: progressive ecclesiology (including theology of the church, orientation to church rules and authority, liturgical orientation, openness to ministerial innovation, and community emphasis); this-worldly religious involvement (including a sociopolitical religious involvement and antinuclear defense stance); and progressive morality (including an emphasis on liberation from sinful structures and a rejection of traditional personal, sexual, and marital proscriptions).[52]

It remains to consider David Martin's interpretation of the transformations in Catholicism in recent decades. In this connection it is helpful to compare his observations of responses to social change in Methodism and Catholicism:

> The ghetto, particularly separate education, maintains cohesion, although at enormous financial cost and maybe also at some cost in the acceptability of the community and the social mobility of its members. The "total environment" held together by ecclesi-

astical authority as well as by ethnic identity protects its members, even attracts out-siders who feel the pull of this protective security; but it can also build up tensions to the point of explosion, as well as encouraging extremism among radicals. Such an explosion will occur whenever a *single* point of doctrine is undermined simply because a hole in the dyke undermines the complete defensive system. And of course if some limited social mobility creates a Catholic middle class in closer contact with Protestants and humanists of similar status, then this is where the explosion is audible. What becomes audible dissent at this level is often unspoken divergence from Catholic norms at lower levels. Intellectuals begin by inventing verbal subterfuges and, when they can bear these no longer, erupt against authority; the working class either obeys or silently pursues its way in the usual manner of erring humanity. The Catholic system can cope with large-scale divergence, but it cannot brook overt disruption and challenge, and it is precisely this that occurs as more and more climb out of the overlapping ghettos of class and religious separatism.[53]

This interpretation needs to be modified in at least three respects in the light of the research of the past twelve years. First, the dyke metaphor is empirically inaccurate and misleading with regard to the likely consequences of a breach in the doctrinal system. Rather, the research evidence suggests considerable heterogeneity and a complexity of progressive tendencies. In general, British Catholics retain high levels of creedal beliefs alongside widespread divergence as far as the moral teachings of the church are concerned.[54] Second, there is no evidence of an inevitable process from "verbal subterfuges" to "audible dissent" and finally "eruption against author-ity." Rather, there has been "a *transformation* and new interpretation of authority which enables the contestants to co-exist with the other members of the institutional church."[55] Third, there is no evidence that "overt disruption and challenge" has been an inevitable consequence of social mobility and religious ecumenism. Martin himself offers one possible explanation when, in a comparison between English and Dutch Catholicism, he notes that in England innovations succeeded each other slowly enough not to cause confusion.[56]

Into the Mainstream

The biographer of Cardinal Hinsley has written that in the period immediately before World War II "never had the English and Welsh Catholic body seemed so secure, *so united, so insulated.*"[57] In the mid-twentieth century, English Catholics

constituted a subculture by virtue of their specific norms and values in sexual, marital and familial morality, their allegiance to Rome, the importance attached to the Mass, their belief in life after death and their numerous distinguishing symbols such as Friday abstinence. Catholic social teaching . . . was consistent with the endeavour of English Catholics to develop "subsocietal institutions" to preserve their subculture by segre-gating the young in educational terms through the maintenance of a separate denom-inational education system. Similarly group endogamy sought to provide an all-Catholic milieu within the family. Such educational segregation and marital endogamy in com-bination with an array of other Catholic associations . . . were designed to protect the Catholic subculture.[58]

A review of the research evidence of social change in English Catholicism since World War II and religious change since the Second Vatican Council leads to the clear conclusion that this once distinctive subculture had largely dissolved by the mid-1980s. Mary Douglas could bemoan the fact that "now the English Catholics are like everyone else."[59] The process was not cataclysmic—the dramatic collapsing of the fortress walls as a result of a single explosive attack from without. It was, rather, a gradual dissolving of the walls in the solvent of rapid external social change after the global trauma of World War II and the internal *aggiornamento* encouraged in the 1960s by Pope John XXIII. The elements of the religious transformations that characterized this process were:

> the gradual assimilation through education and mixed marriage, the dissent over traditional teaching in birth regulation, the questioning of the limits of papal authority, the gradual substitution of English for Latin in the liturgy, the tentative movements towards ecumenism, the softening of traditional disapproval of mixed marriages and the abolition of Friday abstinence.[60]

The research evidence from the 1970s and the 1980s points clearly to the conclusion that structurally British Catholics were rapidly becoming socially and religiously assimilated to the norms of British society. In the three decades after World War II they experienced a process of economic embourgeoisement. The data also reveal a high level of convergence between Catholics and the rest of the population on a wide range of social, moral, political, and religious issues. It would be misleading to regard this as a process of assimilation to a clearly identifiable static model of "Protestantism." Certainly a strong emphasis on making up their own minds about aspects of Catholic teaching, so evident at the time of the papal visit, suggests a strong element of private decision making, which is one mark of Protestantism. The reality, however, is clearly more complex. Catholics have retained many aspects of a customary religion with identifiable components of an earlier Catholic upbringing learned in the socializing institutions of family, school, and parish. In general terms, although they retained some distinctive features, Catholics have largely entered the mainstream of British society and have become an accepted and acceptably domesticated denomination. Accommodation has been slow and nonthreatening; there has been no sudden trauma to disturb the lethargy of British Catholicism. Only in the new justice and peace movement are prophetic voices emerging to challenge a prevailing comfortable passivity. To call this process secularization, however, distorts the reality that there never was a golden past and neglects the signs of new life and growth in the contemporary church.

NOTES

1. David Martin, *A General Theory of Secularization* (Oxford: Blackwell, 1978), p. 12.
2. David Martin, "Towards Eliminating the Concept of Secularization," in *Penguin Survey of the Social Sciences*, ed. Julius Gould (Harmondsworth: Penguin, 1965).
3. Martin, *A General Theory of Secularization*, pp. 2–4.

4. In his influential study, Bossy regards English Catholicism as linked with this tradition of dissent. See John Bossy, *The English Catholic Community 1570–1850* (London: Darton, Longman & Todd, 1975).

5. Martin, *A General Theory*, pp. 5–6.

6. Ibid., pp. 7–8, 59, 108–111, 119.

7. George Andrew Beck, ed., *The English Catholics: 1850–1950* (London: Burns Oates, 1950); David McRoberts, ed., *Modern Scottish Catholicism: 1878–1978* (Glasgow: Burns, 1979).

8. Steve Bruce, *No Pope of Rome: Anti-Catholicism in Modern Scotland* (Edinburgh: Mainstream, 1985).

9. Martin, *A General Theory*, pp. 148–49; John Hickey, *Urban Catholics: Urban Catholicism in England and Wales from 1829 to the Present Day* (London: Geoffrey Chapman, 1967).

10. See, for example, Anthony Ross, "The Development of the Scottish Catholic Community 1878–1978," and James Darragh, "The Catholic Population of Scotland 1878–1977," in *Modern Scottish Catholicism,* ed. McRoberts. Estimates of the Catholic populations of both England and Wales and Scotland from the eighteenth century are given in Robert Currie, Alan Gilbert, and Lee Horsley, *Churches and Churchgoers: Patterns of Church Growth in the British Isles Since 1700* (Oxford: Clarendon Press, 1977), pp. 23–32, 153–55.

11. Michael P. Hornsby-Smith, *Roman Catholics in England: Studies in Social Structure Since the Second World War* (Cambridge: At the University Press, 1986).

12. Martin, *A General Theory*, p. 141.

13. Michael P. Hornsby-Smith, "The Immigrant Background of Roman Catholics in England and Wales: A Research Note," *New Community* 13 (Spring–Summer 1986):79–85.

14. Hornsby-Smith, *Roman Catholics in England,* chap. 2.

15. Both the *Congress Reports* and *The Easter People* are published in *Liverpool 1980: Official Report of the National Pastoral Congress* (Slough: St. Paul Publications, 1981).

16. David Martin, *The Religious and the Secular: Studies in Secularization* (London: Routledge & Kegan Paul, 1969), p. 105.

17. Martin, *A General Theory*, p. 80.

18. J. G. Bode, "Status Mobility of Catholics Vis-à-Vis Several Protestant Denominations: Some Evidence," *Sociological Quarterly* 11 (1970):103–111.

19. Michael P. Hornsby-Smith, Raymond M. Lee, and Peter A. Reilly, "Social and Religious Change in Four English Roman Catholic Parishes," *Sociology* 18 (August 1984):353–65.

20. Hornsby-Smith, *Roman Catholics in England,* chap. 4.

21. Michael R. Welch and John Baltzell, "Geographical Mobility, Social Integration, and Church Attendance," *Journal for the Scientific Study of Religion* 23 (March 1984):75–91.

22. Thomas Luckmann and Peter Berger, "Social Mobility and Personal Identity," *European Journal of Sociology* 5 (1964):331–44.

23. Hornsby-Smith et al., "Social and Religious Change in Four English Roman Catholic Parishes."

24. For details, see Hornsby-Smith, *Roman Catholics in England,* Section 4.5.

25. Frank Musgrove, *The Migratory Elite* (London: Heinemann, 1963).

26. Martin, *A General Theory*, p. 100.

27. This is most clearly articulated in Peter Coman, *Catholics and the Welfare State* (London and New York: Longman, 1977), especially p. 15f.

28. Ibid., chaps. 5 and 6. See also Michael P. Hornsby-Smith, *Catholic Education: The Unobtrusive Partner* (London: Sheed & Ward, 1978), chaps. 1 and 2.

29. See, for example, John H. Whyte, *Catholics in Western Democracies: A Study in Political Behaviour* (Dublin: Gill & Macmillan, 1981), pp. 36–37. He writes: "A denominational education system could be seen as an important underpinning to a closed Catholicism, because it ensured that Catholics shared an experience which set them apart from the wider society" (p. 65).

30. James Murphy, *Church, State and Schools in Britain, 1800–1970* (London: Routledge & Kegan Paul, 1971), pp. 121–29.

31. Beck, *The English Catholics*, pp. 602–603.

32. Hornsby-Smith, *Roman Catholics in England*, Section 8.2.1.

33. See David Marsh and Joanna Chambers, *Abortion Politics* (London: Junction Books, 1981), especially pp. 131, 144, 162.

34. Hornsby-Smith, *Roman Catholics in England*, Section 8.2.2

35. In the 1978 national survey, 57 percent of English Catholics claimed to have voted for the Labor Party at the previous general election, compared to 47 percent among the population as a whole. See Michael P. Hornsby-Smith and Raymond M. Lee, *Roman Catholic Opinion* (Guildford: University of Surrey, 1979), p. 38.

36. Hornsby-Smith, *Roman Catholics in England*, Section 8.3.

37. Hornsby-Smith and Lee, *Roman Catholic Opinion*, p. 55.

38. Martin, *A General Theory*, pp. 119–24, 203.

39. *Liverpool 1980*, pp. 290–95.

40. A useful analysis of the effects of this decline of the Roman Catholic subculture in England is given by Coman, *Catholics and the Welfare State*, pp. 100–106.

41. Martin, *A General Theory*, p. 160.

42. Hornsby-Smith, *Roman Catholics in England*, chaps. 3 and 7. See also Michael P. Hornsby-Smith, Raymond M. Lee, and Kathryn A. Turcan, "A Typology of English Catholics," *Sociological Review* 30 (August 1982):433–59. In his analysis of power relationships, religion, and legitimacy, Martin notes that in Britain the working class is separated from both aristocratic and liberal styles of religion by their cultural distinctiveness (see *A General Theory*, p. 113). This seems to have emerged clearly in English Catholicism as the distorting impact of Irish working class immigration has declined.

43. Hornsby-Smith, *Roman Catholics in England*, chap. 6.

44. Thomas Luckmann, *Invisible Religion* (New York: Macmillan, 1970), p. 30.

45. Martin, *The Religious and the Secular*, pp. 108–110; Martin, *A General Theory*, pp. 63, 82, 92, 304; David Martin, *The Dilemmas of Contemporary Religion* (Oxford: Blackwell, 1978), p. 13.

46. Michael P. Hornsby-Smith, Raymond M. Lee, and Peter A. Reilly, "Common Religion and Customary Religion: A Critique and a Proposal," *Review of Religious Research* 26 (March 1985):249.

47. Martin, *A General Theory*, p. 158.

48. Hornsby-Smith and Lee, *Roman Catholic Opinion*, pp. 52ff, 192, 195; Hornsby-Smith, *Roman Catholics in England*, especially Section 5.4.

49. A moral theologian, the late Eric Doyle, O.F.M., in a video comment on the 1978 national survey *Roman Catholic Opinion*, noted that there had been a dramatic change in the attitudes of Catholics on the question of contraception over the previous twenty-five years and interpreted this change in terms of the development of doctrine.

50. Michael P. Hornsby-Smith, Jennifer Brown, and Joan O'Bryne, "Second Thoughts on the Pope's Visit," *The Month* 16 (April 1983):131–33.

51. Michael P. Hornsby-Smith and Elizabeth S. Cordingley, *Catholic Elites: A Study of the Delegates to the National Pastoral Congress* (Guildford: University of Surrey, 1983), p. 31.

52. Michael P. Hornsby-Smith, Michael Procter, Lynda Rajan, and Jennifer Brown, "A Typology of Progressive Catholics: A Study of the Delegates to the National Pastoral Congress," *Journal for the Scientific Study of Religion* (1987); see also Hornsby-Smith, *Roman Catholics in England,* Section 7.5.

53. David Martin, "Church, Denomination and Society," In *A Sociological Yearbook of Religion in Britain,* ed. Michael Hill (London: S.C.M., 1972), pp. 184–191. (Quote from pp. 187–88).

54. Hornsby-Smith, *Roman Catholics in England,* chaps. 3 and 7; Hornsby-Smith et al., "A Typology of English Catholics."

55. Mary C. Mansfield and Michael P. Hornsby-Smith, "Authority in the Church: The Interpretation of Lay Members of the Bishops' Commissions in the mid-1970s," *New Blackfriars* 63 (November 1982):450–60, especially p. 459. This article attempts to apply the analysis of F. Houtart, "Conflicts of Authority in the Roman Catholic Church," *Social Compass* 16 (1969):309–25.

56. Martin, *A General Theory,* p. 194. A related point is made by Peter L. Berger in his discussion of *aggiornamento,* "that is of limited, controlled accommodation" to secularization (as an alternative to an entrenched intransigence) in *A Rumour of Angels: Modern Society and the Rediscovery of the Supernatural* (Harmondsworth: Penguin, 1971), p. 36; see also Berger, *The Social Reality of Religion* (Harmondsworth: Penguin, 1973), p. 171. A valuable treatment of religious transformations in Liverpool in the 1970s is to be found in T. Koopmanschap, *Transformations in Contemporary Roman Catholicism: A Case Study,* unpublished Ph.D. thesis (Liverpool: University of Liverpool, 1978).

57. Thomas Moloney, *Westminster, Whitehall and the Vatican: The Role of Cardinal Hinsley 1935–43* (Tunbridge Wells: Burns & Oates, 1985), p. 242 (emphasis added).

58. Coman, *Catholics and the Welfare State,* pp. 4–5.

59. Mary Douglas, *Natural Symbols: Explorations in Cosmology* (Harmondsworth: Penguin, 1973), p. 67.

60. Coman, *Catholics and the Welfare State,* p. 105. Indicators of the decline of group endogamy and assimilation of English Catholics include the increase in the proportions of Catholics entering mixed marriages from under one-third up to the end of the 1950s to two-thirds in the 1970s, and entering canonically invalid marriages from just over one-tenth to over one-third over the same period; see Hornsby-Smith and Lee, *Roman Catholic Opinion,* p. 232.

12

American Catholicism

John A. Coleman, S.J.

American Catholics are as American as they are Catholic. Historian Jay P. Dolan, in his magisterial social history of American Catholics, *The American Catholic Experience,* notes that "by 1815, two schools of thought were manifest in the American Catholic community. One desired to fashion an indigenous church, an American Catholicism; the other wanted to transplant to the new nation a continental European version of Roman Catholicism."[1] These two positions constitute the opposing sides in an ongoing dialectic which has posed a challenge to Catholicism in the United States until the present. As we shall see, they constitute alternative visions for the church among liberal and conservative Catholics.

In order to illuminate the social portrait of American Catholics, it will be useful to focus on the following topics:

1. the historical planting and evolution of Catholicism in a Protestant America;
2. the present demographic portrait of American Catholicism;
3. selective Catholicism: American Catholic beliefs, practices, and commitment;
4. the new "Catholic moment" in American culture.

The Historical Planting and Evolution of Catholicism in Protestant America

A British-American Republican Ethos

The first American Catholic settlers were wealthy English plantation owners in Maryland and Kentucky. In all things except religion they mirrored rather closely the educational background and class bias of their fellow English transplanted gentry.

232

Like Counter-Reformation English Catholics, the early settlers and leaders of the church—with the exception of questions regarding religious liberty—entertained few explicit quarrels with English culture, laws, or institutions. These first Catholics brought with them an English Catholic animus against "going against the grain" of their surrounding culture.[2]

These British-American early Catholics such as the first bishop, John Carroll, and his cousin, Charles Carroll, a signatory of the Declaration of Independence, were deeply imbued with Enlightenment thought, as were the Founding Fathers. They encouraged the ideals of egalitarianism, ecumenism (Protestants and Catholics regularly visited each other's churches during the period 1776–1910), and democratization (the first three American bishops were elected by the lower clergy; parishes were controlled by boards of lay trustees). Bishop Carroll urged the practice of a vernacular liturgy. He inaugurated Catholic academies (often with a sizable student population of Protestants) modeled on the Enlightenment idea of science. An early lay trustee in Charleston, South Carolina, could argue that "American Catholics should rear a national American church with liberties consonant to the spirit of the government under which they live."[3]

Jay Dolan notes that "the Revolution had given Catholics a sense of belonging to and being an integral part of the new nation. One concrete result of this sense of belonging was their political involvement; another equally visible result of this new mentality was a prolonged period of cordial relations between Catholics and Protestants."[4] A third impact was enthusiastic Catholic support for the First Amendment provision of separation of church and state, a Catholic stance unbroken in American history.

This "first liberty," as William Lee Miller calls it, of religious freedom meant that, even from its beginnings, the "founding act" of America—its identity myth—was only ambiguously Protestant. Unlike England, no religious tests could be allowed for public office; no church could be estabished, given favored privilege, or persecuted. Although after 1820 evangelical revivals fostered needed community building on the frontier to establish an informal Protestant cultural establishment, the ideal of a "Christian America" (read this term always as a code-word for "evangelical Protestant) was disputed from the very first. American Catholics effectively broke a Protestant monopoly of defining America religiously.

The Rise of the Immigrant Church: 1810–1960

The first wave of American Catholic support for an Enlightenment republican ethos crested in the early decades of the nineteenth century. The anticlerical bias of the French Revolution prompted a Vatican reaction against the principles of reason, liberty, and democratization which Bishop Carroll espoused. With the arrival of the first waves of foreign Catholic immigrants—mainly Irish and German—American Catholics, originally ethnically and culturally similar in all ways but doctrinal religion to their Protestant British counterparts, increasingly began to seem a foreign implant. Foreign-born clergy brought with them a more conservative traditionalist spirit inimical to the American Enlightenment. They distrusted the democratization of the church and Carroll's insistence on the virtues of the republic within the life of the church community itself.[5]

Yet, when, in the 1840s, nativist reaction to the waves of new immigrants took a nasty anti-Catholic tone (anti-Catholicism has deep roots in British and the original American political culture), New York Bishop John Hughes organized his Catholics into counterattack. Hughes successfully challenged an implicit Protestant control of the public school system by insisting on the letter and the spirit of the First Amendment: no prayer or Bible reading or religious instruction in the public schools. Hughes armed his Catholic flock to protect Catholic property and churches from nativist crowds intent on burning convents and parishes. Following the pattern set by Hughes, the church's stance toward the recurrent anti-Catholic movements of the nineteenth and twentieth centuries has been, simultaneously, to protect Catholic culture, life, and institutions and to defend its integrity as a rightful expression of American life. As the largest and first "minority," Catholics had to break the exclusionary vision of a Protestant convenant with America to make room for what Will Herberg has referred to as the "triple melting pot" of an America legitimately Catholic, Protestant, and Jewish. As a recent sociological study of American Catholics aptly notes, "America is a far more tolerant society than it might otherwise be because of the contributions of American Catholics."[6]

By the end of the Civil War in 1865, Catholics were the largest American religious denomination. The Catholic community continued to receive sizable blocs of immigrants after 1880, mostly from Italy and eastern Europe, especially Poland. Debates within the Catholic community until the latter part of the nineteenth century centered on the tempo and desired amount of assimilation and Americanization and the extent to which an indigenous American Catholic culture and church life were desirable.

The Americanist Agenda

Toward the turn of the century, as Dolan demonstrates, Irish and German immigrants were already rapidly ascending the social ladder into the middle class.[7] Catholics began to enter fully into national political life as mayors of large cities such as New York, Boston, Chicago, and San Francisco. They sided with the machine politics of ticket-balancing, pragmatic compromise, and the beginnings of the welfare state against the Tory white Anglo-Saxon Protestant reformers in the Progressive movement or the Protestant politics of cultural defense of a now receding rural America. The leadership of the American episcopacy at this time—the so-called Americanist bishops: Cardinal James Gibbons, Archbishop John Ireland, Bishops John Keane, Denis O'Connell, and John Lancaster Spalding—desired full integration of American Catholics into national life. They urged interfaith discussion, participation by Catholics in the Chicago Parliament of World Religions, and the amalgamation of Catholic and public schools. The Americanists also urged a vigorous Catholic participation in civic life, reform movements, and the associational life of the nation. Gibbons and Ireland gave counsel to presidents. Spalding was called upon by President Theodore Roosevelt to mediate a national strike of coalminers.

Another Americanist, Isaac Hecker, founder of the Paulist Fathers, himself a convert from Unitarian transcendentalism and an alumnus of Brook Farm, called for an active, this-worldly, pragmatic, and experiential Catholic spirituality. Cardinal Gibbons, an ardent champion of the incipient national labor movement (in which Catholics held and continue to hold disproportionate leadership positions), became a trusted counselor to presidents. Gibbons's leadership kept the American church from losing the working classes as had the Catholic church in Europe.

With the condemnation of the heresy of Americanism in Pope Leo XIII's encyclical letter to American Catholics in 1899 *(Testem Benevolentiae)* and Pius X's chilling antimodernist encyclical *Pascendi Dominici* in 1907, "the lights went out for American Catholic intellectuals" and for the Americanist agenda of a major Catholic contribution to American life and institutions.[8] The suppression of this Americanist surge was all the easier to achieve since important elements of the American hierarchy— the German bishops, for example, and conservative Irish bishops such as Corrigan of New York and McQuaid of Rochester—felt that the Americanizers were premature in sounding a death-knell for the immigrant church.

Entering what Dennis McCann has called "the long dark night of its largely self-imposed exile from the mainstream of American culture" in 1910, an exile that would last almost until 1960, Catholic America focused its talent, money, and energy on institution-building (for example, establishing the National Catholic Welfare Conference in 1919) as an edifice for the erection of parish plants and parochial schools.[9] World War II and its aftermath brought profound change as Catholics achieved higher economic status. David Leege, the director of the University of Notre Dame study on Catholic parish life, sagely observes that in the United States "the GI bill (providing free college tuition for veterans after World War II) may have had more of an impact on the Catholic church than the Second Vatican Council."[10]

Protestant Cultural Influences

Historians of American Catholicism note the subtle and more obvious ways in which the ethos of the dominant, voluntaristic, evangelical Calvinism, which has traditionally set a cultural frame for American life, has also had its impact on Catholicism. Quintessentially American patterns of religious praxis include: (1) the voluntary character of American religion; (2) pragmatism; (3) a congregational style of parochial government; (4) evangelical devotional styles.

As noted, Catholic Americans have rarely doubted the institutional wisdom of separation of church and state. Through John Courtney Murray's theological opus, American Catholics contributed decisively to the Vatican II document, *On Religious Liberty,* which endorses voluntarism in religion and religious liberty.

Pragmatism stresses the important role of learning from experience in new settings. Early on, Isaac Hecker endorsed an experiential, pragmatic sense of the ongoing direction of the Holy Spirit. In Hecker's view, Catholicism would be God's instrument for bringing to perfection the exercise of that "intelligence and freedom" that characterizes American culture. He boldly stated, "I have the conviction that I can be all the better Catholic because I am an American; and all the better American because I am Catholic."[11] More recently the American bishops in their pastoral letters on nuclear arms and on the economy, "consistent with the earlier Americanist agenda . . . are remaining open to the experience of people in this country, Catholics and non-Catholics alike, and are allowing that experience to reshape the contours of traditional Catholic social teaching."[12]

More than most national churches, American Catholicism has been extraordinarily parish-centered. The American parish is a strong community-forming institution. The Catholic parish remains, as well, the fundamental locus of catechesis, religious education, and moral formation. Unlike French and other European Catholicisms, the "milieu" Catholicism of American Catholics is their parish life. In this, Catholics follow the congregational style of American Protestants.

Dolan has shown that the immigrants came to America with a very low level of Catholic practice and devotional life. More than mere sustenance of Catholic identity was needed. A genuine Catholic revival was called for. Unlike the wider American revivalist movements, however, the Catholic revivals and "parish missions" lacked any specific social content, although they did reinforce the moralism, individualism, and experiential bias of wider American religion. These revivals helped lead to unparalleled levels of American Catholic religious practice and commitment when compared to statistics for other Catholic churches in Europe or Latin America or to other American religious groups.[13] In the post-Vatican II period, significant new revival movements in American Catholicism (the Cursillo movement, Catholic Pentecostalism, the parish-based Renew movement, Marriage Encounter) continue to reinforce an American bias toward evangelical, devotional styles of personalist and experiential religion.

After over three centuries in American soil, Catholic Americans now represent far and away America's largest denomination, three times as large as the next largest denomination, the Southern Baptists. Catholics are statistically overrepresented in politics (as members of the House of Representatives, in holding state governorships, and so on) and in the highest reaches of corporate America. A 1986 *Fortune* magazine study revealed that more Catholics and Episcopalians (the highest status Protestant group in the United States) now head the nation's top corporations.[14] American Catholics lead Protestants in indices of educational achievement, social status, economic wealth. This Catholic combination of commanding size and favorable social location and relatively strong inner religious discipline and church commitment has led a number of cultural critics to postulate a "Catholic moment" in American culture or "the Catholicization of American culture." Before inspecting this notion of a "Catholic moment," however, we need to explore the present demographic profile of American Catholics.

The Demographic Portrait of American Catholicism Today

Catholics represent approximately 28 percent of the American population, minimally 53 million Americans (the estimate of the 1986 *Catholic Directory*) and possibly as many as 67 million (a self-identification exhibited by Gallup poll data, including a significant number of nonpracticing or unchurched Catholics who, nevertheless, still identify with their communal Catholic upbringing). Historically, Catholics have been overwhelmingly urban and located in the Boston–Washington, D.C. corridor along the East Coast and the famous German triangle of the Midwest (St. Louis, Chicago, Detroit, Cincinnati, and Cleveland). Currently, one out of three Catholics lives in the suburbs. An amazing 39 percent still live in central cities. Forty-four percent live in the eastern part of the United States, 26 percent in the Midwest, 16 percent in the South, and 26 percent in the West.[15] Because of the overall population shift to the sunbelt, the proportion of Catholics in the South and West continues to grow apace. About one in five of those born Catholic no longer affiliates with the church.[16]

Geographical Spread

As the *Yearbook of American and Canadian Churches 1986* makes clear, Catholics are found everywhere throughout the land. Nevertheless, inspection of a religious map of the United States shows that Catholics are particularly concentrated in large urban areas in the northeastern part of the country and in the Great Lakes region.[17] Catholics represent a clear majority of the population in many counties of New Mexico and in southern Texas where the Spanish-speaking church is strong, in the Delta country of Louisiana, and in the heavily populated states of Massachusetts and Rhode Island. In the Northeast and the Great Lakes states there are scores of counties where Catholics represent from 30 to 50 percent or more of the population. In most large American cities in the Northeast, Midwest, and Southwest, Catholics are the largest denomination. They are poorly represented, however, in much of the South and in Oklahoma, northern Wisconsin, northern Minnesota, and the Dakotas, as well as in the Northwest. In all but two counties of California, on the other hand, Catholics represent the largest single religious grouping. Two other important points about American Catholics emerge from a careful inspection of a religious map. First, in many cities and counties and in some states Catholics represent a clear majority of the population. There exist distinctively Catholic cultural enclaves in the United States. Second, in some locales (Iowa, South Dakota), Catholics vie primarily with Methodists as the largest two denominations; in others (for example, Minnesota, Wisconsin), Catholics and Lutherans dominate the religious center; in still others (Louisiana, West Texas, South Florida), Catholics compete or cooperate with Southern Baptists and evangelical fundamentalists. New York is primarily a Jewish-Catholic city. As a national denomination, Catholics enjoy a more significant geographical spread and concentration than any mainline Protestant or evangelical group. This geographic spread promises wide cultural impact. As Mary Hanna has put it, Catholics "by residence, have become a kind of middle people. They are the small-town life of many white northern Protestants, the big-city experience of Jews and blacks, and the suburban lifestyles of, especially, white northern Protestants and Jews."[18]

The Diversity of the Immigrants

Catholic immigrants came to America in different waves and assimilated to the larger population in different rhythms. The earliest wave, before the Civil War, included mainly German, French-Canadian, and Irish Catholics. With the exception of the French-Canadians, the first wave of immigrants (1820–1880) assimilated well into American society. As the research on Catholic ethnicity of Andrew M. Greeley and his associates at the National Opinion Research Center at the University of Chicago has shown, after Jews "Irish Catholics have the best education and the best income in the country and their educational and income mobility advantage of Protestants is substantial."[19] The Irish are the most financially successful of the white gentile ethnic groups in the United States. They are followed closely, among Catholic groups, by Germans and Italians.

The ethnic composition of today's American Catholics is as follows: Irish (8.3

million, 16%); Germans (7.6 million, 14%); Italians (10 million, 19%); Polish (5.3 million, 9%); French-Canadians (5 million, 8%); other Eastern European-Yugoslavian, Hungarian, Czechoslovakian, Austrian, Lithuanian, etcetera (3.6 million, 6%); black and Asian American (1.4 million, 2%); Hispanics (16–20 million, c. 20%).[20] Because of the presence of nondocumented aliens and language difficulties, the actual Hispanic population is difficult to estimate. Gallup and Castelli, in a statistic that is surely too conservative, estimate that Hispanic Catholics number 10.5 million or 16 percent of the American Catholic population. Other estimates, perhaps inflated, postulate more than 20 million, or more than a third of the Catholic population.[21] Italians, Poles, Lithuanians, and other Eastern European Catholics came later than the Irish and Germans, mainly in the period between 1880 and 1920. They have shown remarkable economic, educational, and occupational mobility. While they lag behind the Irish and German Catholics, they approach or slightly exceed the current national average in educational achievement, income, and occupational placement. Their generation rates of cohort mobility, however, far exceed the national average. In that sense, American Catholicism is overwhelmingly a middle class church. At present, 17 percent of American Catholics are college graduates.

The Hispanic Catholics

Hispanic Catholics are themselves internally divided: Cubans in Florida, Puerto Ricans in New York, Mexicans in the Southwest. A significant proportion of the Hispanic population in Arizona, California, and Texas originates from Central America (El Salvador and Guatemala). The Cubans in Florida have rapidly ascended to middle class status (they were originally of middle class origin with language skills and entrepreneurial experience in Cuba) and political power through the Republican party. Other Hispanic groups are still lower class.

Hispanic Catholics are geographically located in different patterns than other American Catholics: 29 percent live on the Pacific coast; 30 percent in the Rocky Mountains, and Southwest areas; 10 percent in the Midwest; 10 percent in the Southeast and 21 percent on the east coast.[22] Fifty-six percent of those with Hispanic origin usually speak Spanish at home. The so-called new immigrants to the United States in the 1970s—Cubans, Central Americans, Haitians and others from the Caribbean area, Filipinos, Koreans, and Vietnamese—have also been disproportionately Catholic. They lag behind middle class America. Thus, Hispanics have considerably lower incomes than other Catholics. In 1978 one Hispanic Catholic in five had an income over $15,000 a year. This represents half of the average income for a national sampling of Catholics at that time.

Two remarks need to be made about the clear splintering of the American Catholic population into a church that is three-fourths middle class and one-fourth poor. There is the danger of a cleavage based on class differences into two churches radically disjointed in terms of attitudes, desires, hopes, and aspirations. During Pope John Paul II's visit to the United States in 1979, this cleavage was dramatically illustrated by back-to-back statements to the pope. One, by Sister Teresa Kane, S.M., pointedly confronted the pope in Washington, D.C., with the unsolved, festering issue of women in the church. The second, delivered by Fr. Louis Olivares, president of *Padres* (an association of Spanish-speaking priests and sisters) remarked, "The Hispano-Catholic relates to the family, not affluence. Ordaining women is trivia. Birth-control or married priests are non-issues."[23]

On the other hand, a significant presence of poor Catholics skews the attention span of the leadership of the national church to keep a social justice agenda, concern for welfare, and immigrants' rights on the front-burners of church policy and thought. Because at least one-fourth of American Catholics remain on the margin of poverty, the largest middle class church makes "an option for the poor." This option—clearly articulated in the rhetoric of the American bishops' pastoral letter on the U.S. econ-omy—takes flesh in Catholic commitment to inner-city parochial schools, which serve the black population. While only 3 percent of American Catholics are black (1.3 million), 9 percent of the students in Catholic elementary schools are black.[24] The leadership of the U.S. Catholic Conference urges an increase in the minimum wage, a more liberal immigration policy, a more generous health care policy for the poor and elderly, a different American stance in Central America. Through its Campaign for Human Development, it financially supports self-help businesses in poor areas and champions both community-organizing efforts among the poor and the trade union movement.

A recent sociological profile of the American Catholic population shows wide-spread support for this episcopal leadership.

> American Catholics are in substantial agreement with the bishops on broad economic themes: a strong role for the government in economic matters, the role of circum-stances in forcing people into poverty, the need for tax reform and the redistribution of wealth and income in more equitable fashion. Catholics have remained liberal in economic matters, even though they have become entrenched in the middle class.[25]

Thus, by a 5 percent margin Catholics exceed the general population in their support for increased spending on Medicare and social programs. They are more likely than other Americans to support vouchers to help the poor relocate to new jobs and to accept the need for wage and price controls.

Political Affiliation

Traditionally Catholics have served as one of the major constituencies of the Democratic party. Robert Axelrod notes, "Catholics have formed a large and reliable segment of the Democratic coalition. They have always provided more than a third of the Democratic votes . . . even though they are only a quarter of the population."[26]

Since the 1970s Catholic support for the Democratic party has begun to erode. There has been an increase in Catholics preferring to call themselves independents rather than Democrats and in those who vote Republican. At the level of congres-sional elections, Catholics still vote 55 percent for Democratic candidates, but in pres-idential elections there has been a sharp erosion of Catholic support for the Demo-cratic party since 1972, as the statistics in Table 12.1 demonstrate.[27] But Catholic Republicans tend to be more liberal in their political leanings than other Republicans. As Hanna notes, "Young Catholics with party preferences are nearly three times as likely to call themselves Democrats as Republicans while young Protestants who express a party preference tend to divide evenly between the two parties.[28]

TABLE 12.1 Percentage of the
Catholic Democratic Vote for U.S.
Presidential Candidates

Year	Candidate	Percent
1928	Smith	85%
1932	Roosevelt	73
1948	Truman	66
1956	Stevenson	51
1960	Kennedy	78
1964	Johnson	73
1968	Humphrey	59
1972	McGovern	48
1976	Carter	57
1980	Carter	44
1984	Mondale	44

Selective Catholicism: American Catholic Beliefs, Practices, and Commitment

American Catholics exhibit selective allegiance to church doctrines. Large majorities state that Catholics should be allowed to practice artificial birth control (73%), that a divorced Catholic who remarries is not living in sin (60%), and that abortion should be legal in cases of pregnancy resulting from rape or incest (66%). Only 33 percent say that premarital sex is wrong. Sizable groups of American Catholics support the proposal of a married clergy (63%) and the ordination of women (39%).[29]

Yet it is unlikely that Catholics will turn away from the church because of their disagreements on sexual ethics. More likely, they will reject the church's teaching and go to church or not for other reasons. Andrew Greeley has postulated an intervening variable he calls "loyalty" to explain how a selective style of Catholicism (picking and choosing which church teachings to accept) does not lead to decreased adherence to the church or to apostasy.[30]

Catholics markedly differ from American Protestants in style of religiosity (49% of Catholics see themselves as religiously liberal versus 40% of Protestants), tolerance of other faiths (Catholics are 25 percentage points more likely than Protestants to say that a person who does not accept Jesus can have eternal life), and on choosing belief items on evolution. Catholics are more likely to believe in evolution while Protestants are more likely to believe in creationism.[31]

Gallup and Castelli aptly characterize the Catholic belief system as: (1) *intellectual:* the Catholic worldview is more likely to reconcile faith and reason than the Protestant worldview, which relies more heavily on faith alone; (2) *accepting:* American Catholics take a more understanding attitude toward sinners and those who hold different religious views; thus, they are more likely than the general population to be accepting of homosexuals and atheists; (3) *pragmatic:* Catholics give a relatively low priority to personal salvation as a value and a higher priority than Protestants to love of neighbor and action to solve the problems of the world; (4) *communal:* Catholics are more likely to rank broader social concerns over personal evangelization and less likely to give an individualistic reading to social problems and issues; (5) *nonconversionist:* American Catholics are relatively indifferent to evangelization; thus, only 12 percent of Catholics (versus 31% of Protestants) say that a person trying to follow Jesus should tell other people about Jesus.[32] A sociological study of Catholic converts shows that personal contacts with friends rather than evangelizing witness is the characteristic style of Catholic presence to potential converts.[33]

Practice and Commitment

In the post-Vatican II period weekly mass attendance among Catholics plummeted from a high of 74 percent in 1958 to 53 percent in 1985 (against a 1985 Protestant weekly attendance of 39%). The precipitious declines in Catholic mass attendance have leveled off since the mid-1970s. Moreover, if weekly attenders are added to the 78 percent of American Catholics who attend mass at least once a month and the 71 percent who attend at least twice a month, it is apparent that American Catholic mass attendance remains comparatively very high. Forty-four percent of these weekly attenders are male, an average higher than the percentage of male Protestant attenders. Confession practice among Catholics has slightly increased in the past decades. A "homecoming effect" can also be observed among the baby-boom generation, who now as young adults return to the church as they marry and begin to raise families. The full measure of church commitment is weaker among this generation of returnees when compared to their parents' generation, but sizable percentages of the baby-boomers are now rejoining the church.[34]

Sixty-eight percent of Catholics versus 53 percent of all Protestants and only 38 percent of evangelical Protestants do no volunteer work within the church. A notable difference between Catholics and Protestants involves financial contributions to the church. Protestants average a yearly church contribution of 2.2 percent of their annual income while Catholics contribute a meager 1.1 percent. Both groups give about the same percentage of their annual income to nonreligious charities. The Catholic percentage of annual income as a contribution to the church has declined since the 1960s when Catholic giving was about the same as Protestants. One explanation for this discrepancy may be that "Protestants since they are more deeply involved in the finances of their congregations are more likely to be aware of the increased costs of administering a full-service local church than are Catholics and, hence, more realistic in making decisions about contributions."[35]

Hispanic Catholics hold looser institutional ties to the church. Only 36 percent attend weekly mass, 64 percent claim that religion is very important in their lives, although only 57 percent see themselves as "good Catholics." At least 10 percent of originally Catholic Hispanics have converted to Protestant evangelical sects. Seventy-four percent of American Catholic Hispanics claim that they have been approached by evangelicals for conversion. Hispanic Catholics turn to the church primarily in search of community; 78 percent would like to see more emphasis on Hispanic culture and traditions in church liturgy and ministry, and 76 percent desire more Hispanic priests and deacons. Hispanics give the church lower grades for meeting their needs than do other Catholics.[36]

The selective adherence to certain church teachings needs to be seen in a context that Catholics "do not necessarily want the church to change all of the teachings with which they disagree. They just want those teachings viewed as ideals which may seem impractical in the real world."[37] Selective Catholicism—as Andrew Greeley who coined the term, notes—points mainly to areas of authority relations in the church. In a recent overview of American Catholicism, Patrick H. McNamara mirrors Greeley's point: "The basic question of authority, 'Is anyone out there listening, pondering and heeding?' will not go away quickly. It is certainly among the central questions facing the American Catholic church in the mid-1980s."[38]

Despite declines in some areas since the early 1960s, stability and growth—not decline—are the benchmarks of American Catholic religious life in the 1980s. Looking at the level of religious belief in core doctrines (the divinity of Christ, the efficacy of prayer, life after death) rather than at more peripheral teachings about sexuality would uncover a portrait of American Catholicism considerably less selective in its belief system than popular stereotypes suggest. Moreover, there has been a veritable explosion of nonordained lay ministries with lay people trained in liturgy, social justice, parish administration, and pastoral care. Two-thirds of American Catholics show "a great deal" or "a lot" of confidence in the church and 80 percent give high approval to local parish priests. Gallup and Castelli observe that "Catholic participation in religious practices may not be as widespread as it was in the 1950s but it is more widespread and vital than it has been for at least a decade—and seems likely to continue to grow."[39]

Other areas of American Catholic life should be noted: its impressive organizational structure with a network of hospitals, schools, welfare services, a vigorous Catholic press. Catholics maintain 235 colleges and universities across the nation, far and away the largest Catholic effort in higher education anywhere in the world. Catholic parochial schools enroll 2.7 million students, down from a high point of 5.6 million in 1964. The number of Catholics in parochial and church-run high schools holds steady, but elementary enrollments have been sharply curtailed. Catholic charities constitute the largest relief service in the United States. In view of the evidence of steady practice and strong adherence to core beliefs and the vibrant organizational life of Catholics, Gallup and Castelli sum up their interpretative understanding of the statistics for contemporary American Catholicism: "The fact is American Catholics are in the middle of a religious revival."[40]

American Catholics' Sociocultural Agenda

With the definitive end of the immigrant church and the closure of their lower class status, "Today's Catholics no longer worry about being accepted—they worry about how to lead."[41] American Catholics exhibit a unique profile on social attitudes.

We have already seen the prevalence of liberal Catholic attitudes on economic issues. American Catholics are also a tolerant people, supportive of civil liberties for minorities and outcast groups: 47 percent support interracial marriage versus 43 percent of American Protestants. A significantly higher percentage of American Catholics than Protestants declare their support for Protestant–Catholic and for Jewish–Christian intermarriage. In practice, three-quarters of white Catholics are married to spouses of their own faith. This percentage is not as high as the percentage of endogamous marriages among white northern Protestants (85.4%). Among younger Catholics the rate of out-marriage is dramatically increasing. Young Catholics (age 18–29) are two-and-a-half times as likely to have married non-Catholics (36% have non-Catholic spouses) as are Catholics fifty years of age and older (14.4% have non-Catholic spouses).[42]

American Catholics are significantly more likely to declare that they would vote for a qualified Jew or woman, even a qualified atheist, for president than are American Protestants. Fifty-four percent of Catholics support the hypothetical candidacy of a qualified atheist for president as compared to 64 percent of American Protestants who say they would not. Again, Catholics are more likely to support civil liberties for homosexuals (67%) than Protestants (59%). White Catholics are more likely than Protestants to attend an integrated church (60% versus 40%) and to say they would like to have more blacks in their churches (72% versus 62%). It seems likely that America is more racially tolerant and more respectful of civil liberties because of the presence of its Catholics.[43]

Since the Vietnam war, American Catholics have been doves for a generation. With 43 percent of Catholics answering yes, they are more likely than Protestants (35%) or the general population (41%) to argue that the nation is spending too much on defense. While the majority of American Protestants (56%) supported President Reagan's handling of Central American and military policy, only 28 percent of Catholics supported it. Catholics also show less eagerness for the "Star Wars" initiative and a stronger support for a verifiable bilateral nuclear freeze than any other religious group in America. Clearly the American bishops' pastoral letter on nuclear weapons influenced Catholic attitudes on peace, defense spending, and war. Still, Catholic objections to defense spending predate the pastoral. Indeed, during Vietnam, Catholics represented the largest single denominational group among conscientious objectors to the war.[44]

In recent years the American bishops have espoused a social agenda of a "consistent ethic" for prolife issues: anti-abortion and anti–capital punishment; pro–gun control, arms control, and government activism to care for the poor; against military escalation in Central America. They have placed highest priority on four issues: abortion, peace, Central America, and social justice for the poor. And they receive strong support from their people on all of them:

- Six in ten American Catholics support a constitutional amendment to restrict legal abortions.
- Eight in ten support a verifiable bilateral nuclear freeze.
- Six in ten support cuts in military spending.
- Seven in ten believe Central America could become another Vietnam and thus oppose a military solution to Central America's problems.
- More than seven in ten American Catholics support increased federal spending on social programs.

The majority of American Catholics, following their bishops, tend to see life as a "seamless garment," a value to be preserved and protected from cradle to grave.[45] Nevertheless, in opposition to the bishops' perspective, a well-organized intergralist group of conservative Catholics maintains its own network of conservative journals and orchestrates an alternative vision of an excessively ultramontane church. The ongoing dialectic in American Catholic history between those who desire an indigenous church, an *American* Catholicism, and those who want to transplant to America a continental version of Roman Catholicism remains. These conservative Catholics complain to Rome about liturgical impropriety and doctrinal unorthodoxy. They appear to have good contacts with some members of the Vatican Curia. Groups like Catholics United for the Faith and the Wanderer Forum serve as watchdogs of orthodoxy. They have claimed credit for the Vatican censure of Seattle's Archbishop Raymond Hunthausen and the moral theologian Charles Curran.[46]

Like their bishops, American Catholics are conservative on some key social issues: abortion, school prayer, pornography. But, "Catholics clearly come down on the 'liberal' side of other key social issues: most notably women's rights, gun control, civil rights for minorities and homosexuals. . . . In fact, the strong Catholic support for women's rights and minority rights is one of the most overlooked social phenomena in the nation today."[47] Although Catholic attitudes somewhat overlap with the "moral majority" on issues of family and sexual concerns, the thrust of the "seamless garment" puts them at odds with the social agenda of evangelical Christians. Since both groups are in a cultural ascendancy—Daniel Bell has spoken of the aggressive moralism among evangelical Protestants—the Catholic and evangelical social agendas will likely clash. Both benefit from the precipitous decline of liberal Protestantism as a social force.

The decline of liberal Protestantism in America—represented by the United Church of Christ, Presbyterians, Methodists, Episcopalians—is especially dramatic. Mainline Protestantism—the cultural mainstay in America from 1880 until 1960—has lost much of its energy, nerve, and cultural creative abilities. Paul Chalfant captures the statistics. "In the period from 1965–1970 Methodists, United Presbyterians, Episcopalians, Lutherans and the United Church of Christ began to suffer declines in membership. In the next five years, 1970–1975, other mainline churches followed suit." Among the large American denominations only Southern Baptists and Roman Catholics have held their numbers or increased membership. The 1970–1980 losses are especially staggering: United Presbyterian Church, 19 percent; Disciples of Christ, 17 percent; Episcopalians, 15 percent; United Church of Christ, 11 percent; United Methodists, 9 percent.[48]

The liberal Protestant decline is as much a matter of ethos as of numbers. Protestantism in America today presents an anomoly of a strong majority group with a growing minority consciousness. The reasons for this eclipse are multiple. Dean Kelley points to the lack of internal church discipline and appropriate community mechanisms in liberal churches.[49] Lutheran author Richard J. Neuhaus, in *The Naked Public Square,* argues that the liberal churches have sold out to prevailing fashions and accommodated too much to a secularity that is itself in considerable disarray. Dean Hoge, in a careful statistical study of church growth and decline in the 1970s, focuses on an emphasis on evangelism, a distinctive lifestyle and morality, and insistence on orthodox beliefs as three important predictors of church growth.[50] Churches prosper when they are successful in providing clear identity symbols and a vivid sense of belonging. Liberal Protestant churches are especially weak in maintaining the children of church members. They lack decisive criteria for church membership or belief. Catholics and evangelicals have better score cards on these items.

In the political elections of 1980 and 1984, for example, evangelical and Catholic prelates had voice and impact in defining the moral issues. Liberal Protestants—the most articulate religious voice for American cultural values for a century—fell strangely silent. As Benton Johnson notes, "many of the symbolic resources of the liberal churches have been depleted and cannot be renewed."[51] As that center could not hold, many commentators have begun to speak of "a Catholic moment" in American culture.

A Catholic Moment in American Culture

A number of thoughtful commentators on American culture and religion—Martin Marty, Robert Bellah, Richard Neuhaus—have suggested just such a new Catholic moment in American history. They argue that the Roman Catholic leadership has changed position with earlier mainline Protestants with respect to articulating a social vision for the nation's future and point to the American bishops' recent pastoral letters on arms control and on the U.S. economy. But as we have seen, Gallup poll data and Greeley's studies also show that Catholics are well placed geographically and in terms of social class position to function as a kind of middle people in American life and culture. Moreover, they hold a distinctive social agenda, surprisingly similar to the agenda of historic Catholic social teaching. Finally, although post-Vatican II Catholicism reveals several symptoms of important institutional decline, Catholic weekly church attendance, adherence to core doctrinal beliefs, and an inner sense of disciplined integrity remain higher than for liberal Protestantism.

Will this Catholic center in American culture hold into the 1990s? Much will depend upon structural adaptations to address the precipitous decline in ordained ministers, the church's ability to hold women and the new Hispanic immigrants, and some decentralization in decision making. Will Rome and the American bishops permit institutional and cultural adaptation to American religious patterns of voluntarism, pragmatism, a congregational style of parochial government, and evangelical devotional styles? As the latest in a long line of Americanizers, Dennis McCann, observes, the American Catholic church continues to "struggle with the tension between its institutional loyalty to Rome and its inescapable involvement in our national experience."[52] The American bishops are caught in a cross-fire between the pastoral and cultural needs of their own situation and directives from Rome.

The success of a new Catholic moment in American culture will also depend on combining new programs of personal renewal, focused on an adult lay spirituality, concentrating religious education on the religious imagination. Greeley especially has stressed the issue of religious imagination for the renewal of American Catholicism. Joe Holland, chairman of the American Catholic Lay Network, speaks eloquently to the question of an adult lay spirituality.

In recent pastoral letters and in statements defending life at every level, Holland argues, the Catholic bishops challenge the present direction of American culture. A consistent ethic of life is a new voice being heard in our land. But to bear fruit, he suggests, this consistent ethic must meet two conditions. First, the bishops' concern for life needs to be restated, not as moral conclusions ordering life from the outside but rather as arising from within an authentic lay spirituality rooted especially in the ordinary experience of family and work. Second, such an authentic lay spirituality will be possible only if we grow beyond the modern reduction of spirituality to privatized psychological experience.

Holland notes that American Catholics "are nearly 60 million, a quarter of the nation, rooted in an ancient tradition, maturing in our post-European immigrant phase, being renewed after Vatican II, contributing a new wave of artists and intellectuals, and providing leadership across America's institutions." He seeks for this population "an authentic and public lay spirituality rooted in family and work, in service of the evangelical healing and renewal of American culture."[53]

What Holland and others calling for a new Catholic moment desire is a profound *resourcement* of the substance of our culture, to see that substance come alive through vital church engagement as "communities of memory" and hope.[54] They seek a renewal of religious presence to the culture—a presence of discernment both of its spiritual vitalities and its deflections from truth. In short, they envision the kind of cultural vitality and public church that liberal Protestants once provided.

Some doubt that evangelical Protestantism has sufficient substantial depth to provide this public church. Holland sees the monolithic views of evangelical Protestantism as a repetition of earlier pleas for a Christian America. Harvey Cox, on the other hand, has argued that evangelicals might provide essential resources for a postmodern culture.[55] Richard Neuhaus, who applauds the evangelicals' attack on secular humanism, feels that they substitute private revelation for public reasoned discourse. Catholic public policy rhetoric, for its part, has become more Bible-based without sacrificing its traditional natural law appeals to reasoned discourse and a pluralistic consensus beyond revelational or confessional argument. The American Catholic public is very reluctant to legislate its morality into law. The new Catholic public stance represents a new synthesis of the three major strands of American culture: biblical religion, Enlightenment concern for human rights and freedom, and the tradition of civic republicanism.

William Lee Miller eloquently states the case for this new Catholic moment:

> The immense, historic, worldwide "Catholic" institution has within it resources that American Protestantism has lacked, and that the sort of government and society which was the original American project—let us call it again a Republic—requires.
>
> "The Common Good," the central term—the *res publica*—is a theme running down through the Catholic ages. Catholicism, like Judaism in a different way, may bring to this excessively individualistic American Protestant culture that sense of life being bound up with life, of "solidarity," as say not just the Polish but other trade unionists and French Catholic thinkers and many others—the awareness, as part of the fundamental religious insights and commitment, of the interweaving of human beings and community. All of that—a personalistic communitarianism, let us call it, may be distinguished both from the collectivisms of our much denounced world adversaries and from the all too individualistic libertarianism created by the forces—very much including our sort of Protestantism—that have combined to build a prevalent form of American culture. Something like such a personalistic communitarianism is the necessary base for a true republic in the interdependent world of the third century of this nation's existence. And the Roman Catholic community is the most likely single source of it—the largest and intellectually and spiritually most potent institution that is the bearer of such ideas.[56]

The dangers that American Catholicism faces in this moment of cultural possibility are twofold. First, institutional pressure from the Roman center about pastoral innovations and doctrinal orthodoxy may force American Catholic energies inward in polarizing fights between liberals and conservatives, as it has done to the Dutch Catholic community. Second, Rome may not understand the "Catholic moment" for American culture as in anyway related to the mission of the church. In the final analysis, a Catholic contribution to the renewal of American culture along the lines Miller suggests means that the present challenge to Catholicism consists in its willingness to risk, to permit American culture and its democratic ethos to become much more the form of its acculturated religion, without losing church discipline and Catholic identity. Statistics about the American Catholic people as a people sure of their identities as both American and Catholic suggest that this risk might well pay off.

NOTES

1. Jay P. Dolan, *The American Catholic Experience* (Garden City, N.Y.: Doubleday, 1985), p. 124.
2. See also James Hennesey, *American Catholics: A History of the Roman Catholic Community in the United States* (New York: Oxford University Press, 1981), pp. 84–86.
3. Cited in Jay P. Dolan, "Catholicism in America," *The Wilson Quarterly* 5 (Fall 1981):453.
4. Dolan, *The American Catholic Experience*, p. 102.
5. Portions of this chapter are adapted from my chapter, "The Fall from Innocence," in John A. Coleman, *An American Strategic Theology* (Ramsey, N.J.: Paulist Press, 1982), pp. 167–83.
6. George Gallup and Jim Castelli, *The American Catholic People* (Garden City, N.Y.: Doubleday, 1987), p. 189.
7. Dolan, *The American Catholic Experience*, pp. 127–57.
8. For more information on the Americanizers, see Gerald P. Fogerty, *The Vatican and the Americanist Crisis* (Rome: Gregorian University Press, 1974).
9. Dennis McCann, *New Experiment in Democracy: The Challenge for American Catholicism* (Kansas City, Mo.: Sheed & Ward, 1987), p. 20.
10. Cited in Joseph Berger, "Being Catholic in America," *The New York Times* (August 23, 1987), p. 64.
11. Cited in David J. O'Brien, "An Evangelical Imperative: Isaac Hecker, Catholicism and Modern Society," in *Hecker Studies: Essays in the Thought of Isaac Hecker,* ed. John Farina (Ramsey, N.J.: Paulist Press, 1983), p. 106.
12. McCann, *New Experiment in Democracy*, p. 30.
13. Jay P. Dolan, *Catholic Revivalism* (Notre Dame, Ind.: University of Notre Dame Press, 1977).
14. Cited in Berger, "Being Catholic in America," p. 25.
15. These demographic data are taken from Gallup and Castelli, *America Catholic People*, pp. 1–9.
16. Catholic defection rates are taken from a New York Times-CBS poll quoted in *The New York Times* (September 10, 1987), p. 14.
17. *Yearbook of American and Canadian Churches 1986* (Nashville: Abington Press,

1986). A religious map of Catholic population distribution appears in Jackson Carroll, Douglas Johnson, and Martin Marty, *Religion in America 1950 to the Present* (New York: Harper & Row, 1979), p. 64.

18. Mary T. Hanna, *Catholics and American Politics* (Cambridge, Mass.: Harvard University Press, 1979), p. 103.

19. Andrew M. Greeley, *The American Catholic: A Social Portrait* (New York: Basic Books, 1977), p. 63.

20. Cited in T. William Bolts, *The Catholic Experience in America* (Encino, Calif.: Glencoe Publishers, 1980), p. 17.

21. Gallup and Castelli, *American Catholic People,* p. 140.

22. Ibid., p. 143.

23. Cited in Erik Hanson, *The Catholic Church in World Politics* (Princeton, N.J.: Princeton University Press, 1987), p. 163.

24. Cited in Berger, "Being Catholic in America," p. 64.

25. Gallup and Castelli, *American Catholic People,* p. 67.

26. Robert Axelrod, "Where the Votes Come From: An Analysis of Electoral Coalitions 1952-1968," *American Political Science Review* 66 (June 1972):16.

27. Compiled from Gallup and Castelli, *American Catholic People,* pp. 126-29.

28. Hanna, *Catholics and American Politics,* p. 118.

29. These statistics appear in Gallup and Castelli, *American Catholic People,* pp. 50-55.

30. Regarding this notion of loyalty and selective Catholicism, see Andrew M. Greeley, *American Catholics Since the Council: An Unauthorized Report* (Chicago: Thomas More Press, 1985).

31. Cf. Gallup and Castelli, *American Catholic People,* p. 227.

32. Ibid., p. 17.

33. Dean Hoge, *Converts, Dropouts, Returnees: A Study of Religious Change Among Catholics* (New York: Pilgrim Press, 1981).

34. Statistics on the baby-boomers returning to church were presented by David Roozen of Hartford Seminary at the annual meeting of the Society for the Scientific Study of Religion, 1986.

35. Andrew M. Greeley and William McManus, *Catholic Contributions* (Chicago: Thomas More Press, 1987), p. 54.

36. For these statistics on Hispanic Catholics, see Gallup and Castelli, *American Catholic People,* pp. 139-48.

37. Ibid., p. 183.

38. Patrick H. McNamara, "American Catholicism in the Mid-1980s: Pluralism and Conflict in a Changing Church," *The Annals of the American Academy of Political and Social Science* 480 (July 1985):74.

39. Gallup and Castelli, *American Catholic People,* p. 42.

40. Ibid.

41. Ibid., p. 2.

42. Hanna, *Catholics and American Politics,* p. 106.

43. Gallup and Castelli, *American Catholic People,* pp. 59-65.

44. Ibid., pp. 76-90.

45. Ibid., p. 102.

46. For a profile of the conservative Catholic agenda, see T. Lincoln Iglesias, "CUF and Dissent: A Case Study in Religious Conservatism," *America* (April 11, 1987), pp. 303-307.

47. Gallup and Castelli, *American Catholic People,* p. 115.

48. Cf. Paul Chalfant, Robert Beckley, and Eddie Palmer, *Religion in Contemporary Society* (Palo Alto, Calif.: Mayfield Publishing Co., 1981), pp. 455-60.

49. Dean Kelley, *Why Conservative Churches Are Growing* (New York: Harper & Row, 1977).

50. Dean Hoge and David Roozen, *Understanding Church Growth and Decline* (New York: Pilgrim Press, 1979), and Richard J. Neuhaus, *The Naked Public Square* (Philadelphia: William Eerdmans, 1984).

51. Benton Johnson, "Liberal Protestantism," *The Annals of the American Academy of Political and Social Science* 480 (July 1985):96.

52. McCann, *New Experiment in Democracy,* p. 20.

53. Joe Holland's remarks appear in the newsletter of The American Catholic Lay Network, Vol. 1, n. 3 (October 1986).

54. The term "communities of memory" comes from Robert N. Bellah et al., *Habits of the Heart* (Berkeley: University of California Press, 1985).

55. Harvey Cox, *Religion in the Secular City* (New York: Scribner's, 1984).

56. William Lee Miller, *The First Liberty* (New York: Alfred A. Knopf, 1986), p. 288. Portions of the last part of this chapter have been adapted from my article, "The Substance and Forms of American Religion and Culture," *New Catholic World* (May/June 1987):106-108.

13

Canada, Australia, and New Zealand

Hans Mol

Catholicism in Canada, Australia, and New Zealand began in rather different ways. In Australia, the first officially acknowledged Roman Catholic priests were reluctantly appointed to restrain Irish convicts, and their salaries came from the Police Fund budget. In the middle of the seventeenth century, Canada was virtually the preserve of the Jesuits and it showed in very interesting ways. Yet in the second half of the twentieth century, all three ex-British colonies have reacted similarly to the changes brought about by Vatican II. We begin with Canada for two reasons: (1) in both absolute and relative figures it has a much larger Catholic population than either Australia or New Zealand: at the 1981 census 11,392,000 Canadians (47.3% of the population) identified themselves as Catholic, whereas in the same year the comparable figures were 3,787,000 (26%) for Australia and 235,000 (14.4%) for New Zealand; and (2) Catholicism in Canada has a much longer history.[1]

Canada

French Catholicism

Catholicism in Canada was closely intertwined with the founding of the nation. At the beginning of the seventeenth century the Recollects, and after 1625 the wealthier and better-organized Jesuits, carried out energetic missions to the natives. Under the Jesuits, New France became a virtual preserve of the Society of Jesus, so much so that the Jesuit missionary Paul Le Jeune could write in 1636 that the church

250

in Québec imposed and carried out penalties "for blasphemy, drunkenness, failing to attend Mass and divine services on Holy days."[2] The punishment consisted of both fines and being placed on a wooden horse for a fixed time near the church.

After the British conquest of New France in 1760 Catholicism began to function as the main support and defense of French culture in an increasingly Anglo-Saxon environment. Until the second half of the twentieth century the church vainly attempted to halt the exodus from the rural areas. In 1950 the archbishops and bishops of Québec published a pastoral letter in which they expressed their concern for the disruptive influence of industry and city on family life. They attacked not only the frivolous use of leisure time and materialism but also the conditions that made for family breakdown, such as inadequate housing and the lack of opportunity to develop satisfaction in one's job.[3]

The church's involvement in trade unions was closely related to this concern for good family life. However much *La Confédération des Travailleurs Catholiques du Canada* (C.T.C.C.) "was a negative response: it was anti-socialist, anti-communist, anti-international, anti-American, anti-Protestant and anti-neutral,"[4] it also positively championed decent wages for good Catholics with large families. In Québec the relation between the working classes and the church had always been close. The reason for this was not simply that the clergy generally came from these classes but also that the church was suspicious of the rich and powerful and their penchant for hedonism. Secularism, liberalism, and anticlericalism prevailed more among the educated middle classes. By contrast, the church found that the poor manifested some of its own most cherished values: a Christ-like powerlessness, the austere life (albeit not by choice), and a developed sense of sin. It was because of this close relation that neither socialism (as protest against capitalist exploitation in Europe) nor sectarianism (as protest against establishment religion in the United States) got any foothold in Québec. Some Catholic lay organizations, such as Catholic Action, were usually most militant in the lower class parishes and least so in the richer suburbs.[5]

Until the Quiet Revolution in 1960, when the Liberal, socially sensitive, Lesage regime took over from the Conservative, big business oriented, Duplessis government, there had been extensive consultation between the ecclesiastical and political spheres—so much so that "no government would consider submitting a bill of any importance without first being assured that it would receive the favor, or at least the tacit approval of the episcopate."[6] This cozy arrangement had already begun to crumble in 1949 when the Duplessis government used every legal, and less than legal, means at its disposal to quell an asbestos strike. At that time both Bishop Roy of Québec and Bishop Charbonneau of Montréal backed the workers in no uncertain terms. Charbonneau justified his intervention by calling the workers victims of a conspiracy and by forcefully pointing to the church's duty to give priority to the human factor over financial interests.[7] Since the 1960s the political and religious spheres have become much more widely separated, so that French-Canadian consciousness seems now more closely associated with politics than with religion.

It was also in the 1960s that the June 24 celebrations of French-Canadian nationhood changed from being very Catholic (St. Jean Baptiste day) to being secular (la Fête Nationale). The St. Jean Baptiste Society was founded in 1834 by the *Patriotes* (who a few years later were to instigate the 1837 uprising) to defend and promote French institutions and language in North America. The parades had been purely political (the church had come out against the Patriot party), but after 1840 they began to include a carriage on which John the Baptist was represented by a young boy with a sheep slung over his shoulder and a cross in his hand, symbolizing Christian leadership of the flock (Québec). The parades led to the local church, which all the people were required to attend on that day. After the service the parade was reformed and proceeded to the city square for public speeches. It was the largest annual parade in Québec. In 1968, however, the separatists used this same parade as a protest against Prime Minister Pierre Trudeau who had opposed any special status for Québec and who stood on the reviewing stand. After this confrontation it reverted back to its original political purposes and became la Fête Nationale. During its heyday the parade expressed the unity of French-Canadians supremely guided by a Catholic saint.[8]

The close alliance between Catholicism and French-Canadian nationalism during that period, says Fernand Dumont, was the only means for survival of the latter, as apart from the church there were no institutions powerful enough to support the patriotic sentiment. It was the church that provided the skeleton and the consciousness to an otherwise powerless society. However, the present secularization means that the church has to yield control over secular institutions. Therefore the question arises as to whether each of these separate entities can produce sufficient effervescence to bolster its internal unity.[9] This is the situation of the 1980s. The profound changes registered in the severe drop in French Catholic attendance in the last twenty years suggest that the erosion of its national sacralizing function has not been altogether painless for the church. Yet the Catholic church continues to have a firm hold on the way most French-Canadians shape their personal and family identity even when there are now non-Catholic and non-Christian alternatives for self-definition.

English-Speaking Catholicism

In 1971, 42 percent of the Catholics in Canada (representing 4,200,000 individuals) came from non-French origins. Nevertheless, the 70,000 who lived in Canada in 1766 were almost all French. After the English conquest, the immigration of the French came to a standstill. By contrast, Catholics from the British Isles and from the United States arrived in increasing numbers.

In the nineteenth and twentieth centuries Catholic immigrants also came from non-British lands. The 1971 census amply demonstrates the multi-ethnic components of Canadian Catholicism. Thus, apart from the French (94% of whom listed themselves as Catholics), the Catholics comprised 93 percent of the Canadians of Italian origin, as well as 71 percent of the Polish, 56 percent of the Indians and Eskimos, 26 percent of the Germans, 23 percent of the Dutch, 21 percent of the British (including Irish and Scots), 19 percent of the Asians, 15 percent of the Ukranians, 13 percent of the Russians, 8 percent of the Scandinavians, and as much as 50 percent of the immigrants from other European countries. Since for most of these groups being Catholic was closely associated with ethnic loyalties, the church had to face the formidable problems of coordinating the various Old World allegiances with an emerging Canadian way of thinking. Much commotion and maneuvering went on behind the scenes, and only occasionally does the outsider get a glimpse of the friction between the church and its ethnic components. The Polish National Catholic Church came into being as a protest against what the Poles felt to be inadequate support for their native distinctiveness by the Mother Church. Although this church originated in the United States, some disgruntled Canadian Poles formed affiliates.

Yet this was the exception rather than the rule. Catholic bishops were often elevated to high office because of their tact and diplomacy. They generally managed to juggle personnel and building requirements so that unassimilated immigrants did not have to go elsewhere or start an independent religious organization. When a specific ethnic group was sufficiently large, they often promoted an ethnic parish for the area. When numbers did not warrant such an expense they often attached Polish, Italian, Lithuanian, and other priests to local parishes, encouraged social affairs for specific native groups and, after Vatican II, offered masses in the Old World language. By combining foreign and English masses in the one parish, the hierarchy also kept a hold on the younger generation, which too often tended to become disenchanted with an un-Canadian (as they thought) parental tradition.

Social Justice

Catholic bishops were also concerned with social justice. The hardships of the Great Depression led Pope Pius XI to publish *Quadragesimo Anno* in 1931. This encyclical had a profound effect on Catholic policy in Canada. When in 1933 the Cooperative Commonwealth Federation or C.C.F. (which in 1961 allied itself with the Canadian Congress of Labour to form the New Democratic Party) was founded in Calgary, the Canadian bishops echoed the papal statement by warning against new parties that undermined the principles of private property, provoked class struggle, and defended a materialist philosophy. This had the effect that in Canada (like Europe, but unlike Britain, Australia, and New Zealand) Catholics felt that they could not in good conscience join or vote for a socialist party such as the C.C.F. They felt quite certain of this when in 1934 Archbishop Gauthier of Montréal pronounced the C.C.F. program irreconcilable with Catholic teaching. In the same year the Catholic bishops in Saskatchewan warned against socialist solutions to the moral problems of greed and materialism represented by the depression. Nevertheless some prominent Catholics, such as Henri Bourassa in Québec and Henry Somerville, editor of the Catholic Register in Toronto, found the C.C.F. policies much more to their liking.

Since World War II the Catholic church has decidedly softened its opposition to socialism. In his letter *Octogesima Adveniens* (1971) Pope Paul VI allowed much more leeway to Catholics who were also socialists. He drew the line at those forms of socialism that claimed to provide an all-encompassing worldview. The Canadian Catholic bishops traveled in the same direction. In the 1970s they showed little inhibition in exposing social injustice and locating Canadian problems, such as the development of the Canadian North and the liberation of native peoples in the structures of international capitalism.[10]

In 1983 the Canadian Catholic bishops released a report, "Ethical Reflections on the Economic Crisis," in which they expressed concern for the unemployed and the basic moral disorder unemployment created in Canada. First priority, the bishops said, should not go to fighting inflation but to alleviating the misery of the poor, the pensioners, the natives, and those who are threatened with the loss of human dignity because there is no work in which they can meaningfully express themselves. The report was attacked by government and business alike for its "idealism." Yet the bishops were also widely praised for their courageous stand against the excesses of the profit motive. Many Canadians seemed to agree that the salvation of the country was advanced more through better work opportunities than through the accumulation of profits and technology. During his visit to Canada in 1984 Pope John Paul II expressed the same views.

Vatican II and Secularization

After World War II Catholic church attendance remained uniformly high until about 1965. Gallup polls showed that both in 1946 and in 1965 as many as 83 percent of the Catholic population in Canada had been to church in the previous seven days. After 1965, however, the percentages began to decline rapidly: they dropped to 65 percent in 1970, to 61 percent in 1975, and to 50 percent in 1980. English-speaking Catholics had never been as loyal to the church as French-speaking ones, but after 1965 the former too began to attend much less.

A secondary analysis of three Canadian electoral studies (1965, 1974, and 1984) provides details about this decline. The percentage of regular attenders (defined here as individuals who went to church at least twice a month) dropped over these years from 73 percent to 55 percent to 51 percent for English-speaking Catholics, and from 92 percent to 59 percent to 48 percent for French-speaking Catholics. The decline is even more severe for persons with more than secondary education: from 71 percent to 57 percent to 36 percent for English-speaking Catholics, and from 89 percent to 40 percent to 39 percent for French-speaking Catholics. Similarly for the youngest age brackets (21–30 years in the 1965 electoral study and 18–30 years in 1974 and 1984): here the decline was from 66 percent to 48 percent to 38 percent for English-speaking Catholics, and from 90 percent to 38 percent to 30 percent for French-speaking Catholics.

What caused these pronounced changes? Some Catholics put the blame squarely at the feet of the Second Vatican Council (1962–1965). That Council opened the windows to the world, but in doing so it introduced the secular air inside its hitherto carefully nourished Catholic identity. It abolished the Latin mass and replaced it with the language of the people. Archbishop Levèbre of France continued to say mass in Latin and was consequently suspended by Pope Paul VI. In Canada Father Yves Normandin and others continued to celebrate Latin masses, but they did so without the consent of the local bishops, and their communicants knew about it only through word of mouth or newspaper advertisements. Vatican II also began to stress "collegiality" at the expense of papal authority. When in 1968 Pope Paul VI published the encyclical *Humanae Vitae* (which condemned artificial birth control) the Canadian bishops weakened its impact by stating that in final resort the individual conscience was the arbiter of moral matters.

Yet it is a mistake to blame internal, organizational decisions on the weakening of Catholic boundaries. Pressures to use the vernacular for the mass and to relax proscriptions of artificial birth control existed long before the 1960s. The secular individualism of urbanized societies had infiltrated many Catholic circles, and Vatican II merely recognized the change taking place. In a survey of twelve parishes in metropolitan Toronto on behalf of Archbishop Pocock in the early 1970s, 73 percent of practicing Catholics favored the changes brought about by Vatican II. Yet in the exuberant opening of windows the innate Catholic hankering for the stable frame of reference was underrated. Decline in church attendance shows a continuing disillusionment with the changes.

For at least some Canadian Catholics "Catholicism is like a city destroyed by war."[11] In previous times when Catholic education depended more on rote learning than on developmental psychology, external authority for one's actions was taken for granted. The confessional enforced the idea that evil was to be eradicated and forgiven rather than discussed and personally mastered. Good was excitingly demonstrated in the lives of the Christian martyrs in the beginning of the Christian era and was rewarded in heaven rather than regarded as variable with time and circumstance. The consequences of ambiguity for church attendance are described by the example Anne Roche gives of her father who was a millwright in Newfoundland:

> I was never so shocked in my life as when my father told me, several years before he died, that he was no longer going to mass. . . . My father, whose faith through the poor times, and through my mother's agonizing death, had remained so innocent, cheerful and trusting, who until then would have rather died than miss mass intentionally, who took Holy Communion so seriously that he wouldn't receive it if he had so much as laughed at a blasphemous joke in the mill—now for him, the miracle had departed. They had taken away his Lord, and he didn't know where they had laid Him.[12]

Roche concludes (somewhat excessively) that the heart of Catholicism has been broken. One cannot live the Catholic life unself-consciously any more. One can go to church out of love, "but it is love among the ruins." Gutted masses with antic priests, manufactured excitement, and cafeteria casualness at Holy Communion are all she can see. Clearly her opinions are not shared by many other Catholics.

Vatican II also affected divorce, or better, annulment. To the Catholic church marriage is a sacrament and therefore permanent and indissoluble. Before the 1960s, in rare cases and after expensive and long, drawn-out procedures a marriage could nevertheless be declared null and void. The church then declared that a true marriage had never existed. Vatican II's *Pastoral Constitution on the Church in the Modern World* insisted that marriage was not primarily ordained for begetting and educating children (as the church had maintained in the past) but that its provision of a communion of life, a covenant relationship based on trust, self-giving, and sacrificial love, was equally important. This new definition proved to be the mechanism for streamlining annulment procedures; now the validity of a marriage could be attacked on the grounds that either partner was incapable of mutually supportive human relationships or that mental problems, selfishness, homosexuality, alcoholism, extramarital affairs, or plain immaturity had prevented a marriage from being what it should be. As a result, annulments increased fifty-fold. The problem with this pastoral/psychological view was that it weakened the indissolubility of actual marriages: the sacred bonds strengthening any family could now be broken by the very factors that had made the institution of marriage increasingly precarious in the first place. The new exalted view of marriage weakened the antidote for the breakdown of actual marriages, however realistic its insights into what had gone wrong.

Over the last twenty years the stigma of mixed marriages has also become much less potent. Numerous were the stories of Catholic girls deeply in love with Protestant boys who remained spinsters all their lives because the thought of marrying outside the church was abhorrent. Catholicism forcefully realigned its own denominational identity with that of its families and emphatically minimized the potential for divided loyalties. In some instances Catholic priests even succeeded in persuading Catholic husbands to leave their non-Catholic wives.[13] All this has now changed. In 1967 joint counseling by Catholic priests and Protestant ministers of couples planning mixed marriages was begun.[14] The excommunication penalty has been abolished and Protestant ministers are now permitted to join in prayers with the priest during a Catholic marriage ceremony. No longer is it necessary for the Protestant partner in a mixed marriage to guarantee in writing that children will be baptized in a Catholic church and educated in a Catholic school.

Australia

Denominational Proportion and Church Attendance

Catholicism began rather inauspiciously in Australia. A large number of convicts were Irish (42% in 1827) and Catholic (39% in the same year). Yet priests to serve them were barred from 1788 until 1820. In that year they were reluctantly introduced primarily to improve control, and it was only natural that their salaries were paid from the Police Fund.[15] Even so, weekly attendance at mass was relatively poor until the second half of the nineteenth century. In Victoria it rose from roughly 20 percent of the Catholic population in 1861 to 54 percent in 1901, and in New South Wales from 23 percent in 1861 to 31 percent in 1901.[16] The establishment of Catholic schools in that era was not altogether foreign to this development. By the end of World War II weekly attendance of Catholics in Australia as a whole was by far the highest of all denominations. In 1954, 75 percent of Catholics attended church weekly as compared with 19 percent of Anglicans, 33 percent of Methodists, and 21 percent of Presbyterians. Yet in the second half of the twentieth century, weekly attendance dropped to 55 percent in 1962, 51 percent in 1970, 42 percent in 1976, and 37 percent in 1981, at which point it seems to have leveled out.[17]

Immigration and birthrate are the two major factors accounting for the fluctuations of the percentage of Catholics in the Australian population. In both 1851 and 1981 Catholics formed 26 percent of the population, but in between the proportion dropped to as low as 20 percent in 1933 and rose as high as 27 percent in 1971. The comparatively lower influx of Irish immigrants around the turn of the century is responsible for the percentage decline in that period. Conversely, the increase after World War II is mainly due to the large numbers of settlers from Catholic countries in eastern and southern Europe.

Fertility and Contraception

Prior to 1933 the ratio of 0–4-year-old Catholic children per 100 Catholic women over the age of fifteen was lower than the national average. The reason was not that Catholic women practiced birth control more but that fewer Catholic women were married. Once they were married, they would generally have more children.[18] Over the last fifty years the Catholic ratio has exceeded the national average and therefore contributed to an increase of the Catholic proportion in the Australian population. In 1961 there were as many as 38 children aged 0-4 per 100 Catholic women over the age of fifteen, compared with 26.8 for Anglican women of the same age group.

Yet over the last fifteen years the Catholic fertility ratio (number of 0-4-year-old children per 100 women aged 15-45) has diminished dramatically. In the 1966 census the ratio was 57.2. In 1981 it was 33.8. But the Anglican ratio (Anglicans formed the largest denomination in Australia until the 1981 census when the percentage had declined to the same 26% as the Catholic proportion of the population) has also diminished (from 44.4 to 27.2) over the same fifteen years. Because the Catholic ratio is still higher, one can confidently assume that now the Catholic proportion of the Australian population is larger than the Anglican one.

The dramatic drop of Catholic fertility ratio since 1966 was presaged by attitudes toward the contraceptive pill. My religion survey in that year asked whether the respondent approved, disapproved, or did not worry about a Catholic who used the contraceptive pill.[19] Of the Catholics who were regular churchgoers (at least once a month) 60 percent disapproved; of the irregulars only 25 percent disapproved. But this percentage dropped for the regulars who were in the 20-40 age bracket (51%) and had lived less than ten years in the area of interview (43%). In spite of the encyclical *Humanae Vitae* two years after the survey there is good reason to believe that, as in other countries, Catholic objection to the use of the contraceptive pill has continued to erode.

Catholic Schools

In the final quarter of the nineteenth century the Catholic archbishops and bishops turned fiercely against the public schools in Australia. In their joint pastoral letter of 1879 they observed that secular education leads to "practical paganism . . . to corruption and loss of faith, to national effeminacy and to national dishonour."[20] Although this was an overstatement, the subsequent effort to build alternative schools proved to be a boon for Catholicism in Australia. A costly and elaborate system of denominational schools galvanized laymen and religious orders into action, producing a bunker mentality among Catholics and increasing their loyalty to the church. In the diocese of Melbourne alone, for example, enrollments at Catholic primary schools increased between 1885 and 1905 almost ten times as fast as enrollments at state schools.[21] By the middle of the twentieth century approximately 80 percent of all Catholic children attended Catholic schools.

However, beginning in 1950 the baby boom together with European immigration strained the resources so much that in 1976 Michael Mason estimated that "barely half of Catholic school-age children were attending Catholic schools."[22] Yet the denominational schools received a new lease on life. In 1963 the federal government began to finance new science laboratories and other facilities in private schools. Subsequently it increased its grants to 20 percent of the standard public school cost for each child attending a private school. At present, 13 percent of the Commonwealth education budget goes to private schools. Since these schools provide for close to 25 percent of Australian children, the federal government pays in actual fact about half what it pays to educate a child at a government school. And in Australia, by far the greatest majority of these private schools are Catholic.

The religion-in-Australia survey also asked a question about parochial schooling and found that 80 percent of Catholics with at least some denominational school education went to church regularly as compared with only 48 percent who had never been to such a school. When parental church attendance was held constant, the effect of Catholic schooling was still evident.[23] Sister Marion Carmel Leavy and Marcellin Flynn support the latter finding.[24] Yet the large increase of lay teachers in the Australian Catholic school system may obviate this effect somewhat, since one has the impression that the religious effect of Catholic schools was primarily due to the teaching and example of Brothers and Sisters.

Class and Politics

In Australia Catholics have usually been overrepresented in the blue collar occupations and underrepresented in the professions. In the 1901 census, for instance, Catholics represented only 8.2 percent of those working in banking and finance but 40.8 percent of those working on roads, railways, and earthworks, and as much as 43.0 percent of those under legal detention.[25] During the Great Depression they were also more likely to be out of work. Of late, however, these differences have disappeared: according to the 1981 census the number of university graduates is 22 per 1,000 for both Catholics who were born in Australia and for Anglicans who were traditionally overrepresented in the professions.

The Australian Catholic hierarchy has also been quite openly involved in politics. A number of highly influential prelates expressed sympathy for the Labor party because it was the party of the wageworkers. Nevertheless, when in 1955 the Catholic and communist tensions within the Labor party came to a head, the Catholic group formed what later became the Democratic Labor party. Support for this party has now dwindled, and presently more Catholics than Protestants tend to vote for Labor. Even so, this support is more evident among non-churchgoing Catholics than for those who attend mass regularly. Both the 1966 religion survey and more recent polling data clearly reveal that, on the whole, Catholics favor the Australian Labor party more than non-Catholics. Still, church attendance more strongly influenced party preference than did denominational affiliation, and this influence moved people in a conservative direction. This, of course, was also the finding of the European value systems survey.[26]

New Zealand

Denominational distribution in New Zealand accurately reflects the comparative strength of regional migrations. In contrast with Australia and Canada neither the Irish nor southern and eastern Europeans are strongly represented. The Catholic proportion of the population, therefore, has always been much lower. It was 11.1 percent of the population in 1858 and slowly rose to 14.3 percent in 1906. It dropped to 12.9 percent in 1926, increased to 15.7 percent in 1966 and dropped again to 15.6 percent in 1971 and to 14.4 percent in 1981. The Irish felt attracted to the mining fields on the west coast of the South Island and hence Catholics are overrepresented in Westland (22.4% in 1981).

The fertility ratios were generally higher for Catholics than for the population at large. They were 53.2 (1921), 42.1 (1936), 52.6 (1945), 88.7 (1961), and 70.8 (1971). The corresponding ratios for the population at large were 52.5, 39.4, 50.9, 74.3, and 59.1 for the same years. (All figures indicate number of 0–4-year-old children per 100 women over fifteen.) These ratios reveal that both the depression and advanced contraception since 1961 affected all parts of the New Zealand population (including Catholics), with the latter still maintaining higher fertility levels.

As in Australia, the government of the day collected church attendance data in the second half of the nineteenth century. In New Zealand this practice extended well into the twentieth century. By dividing these figures by the number of those who, according to the census of that year, stated that they belonged to each of those churches, one can arrive at some rough estimate of church attendance. The percentage of Catholic regular attenders increased from 27.2 percent in 1874 to 28.1 percent in 1881, 35.0 percent in 1891, and 36.5 percent in 1896; it then decreased to 32.7 percent in 1906 and increased again to 34.3 percent in 1911, 56.4 percent in 1921, and fell to 53.0 percent in 1926.[27] Until 1921, Methodist attendance was always higher than Catholic, whereas attendance for the other two major denominations (Presbyterians and particularly Anglicans) was always lower. From 1926 onward, however, Catholic attendance has always exceeded the others. From surveys carried out in some of the major cities after World War II, it appears to have generally hovered around 70 percent of the population. Yet there is no reason to doubt that after Vatican II church attendance has dropped as much as it has in Australia and Canada.

In New Zealand Catholics have usually been underrepresented in the farming population, among those employed in medical and hygienic services, and in banking, finance, and insurance. By contrast, they were overrepresented among those engaged in the liquor trade, hotel work, fishing, trapping, forestry, sports, and entertainment.[28] In both Christchurch and Wellington, Anglicans and Presbyterians were disproportionately present in the wealthier and professional classes, Catholics in the working class.[29]

As in Australia, Protestant anti-Catholic feelings and Catholic anti-Protestant feelings were strongest when the inner solidarity of Catholicism (as measured, for instance, by high attendance figures) was at its height. In the early days of the colony the Catholic Bishop Pompallier encountered strong antagonism.[30] Much later, toward the close of the term of office of the Catholic prime minister, Sir Joseph Ward, a virulent Protestant political association attempted to discredit him and his government "on religious grounds."[31] Since Vatican II, however, interdenominational rivalry has substantially abated. Catholics have become more open toward other Christians and Protestants feel less threatened by the Catholic fortress mentality, discovering to their surprise how diverse Catholicism is. The wall that held it all together was much weaker than they had imagined.

Concluding Observations

There is more to religion than churchgoing. Nevertheless, attendance is a fascinating measure of membership loyalty. It says something about the strength of the boundary around, in this case, Catholicism. As a bounded system the Catholic church has enjoyed almost undivided loyalty in those countries where it stood on the ramparts of a beleaguered nation, one with that nation and the symbol of its determination to persevere against all odds. Poland and Ireland come to mind, but also Québec. An almost unbelievable 92 percent of the adult French-speaking population of Canada went to church regularly until the mid-1960s. The Catholic church in Québec had become the embodiment of patriotic sentiments and opposition to the British conqueror.

In other countries where the Catholic church was the national church the opposite happened. It tended to be taken for granted, or worse, to be associated with an outmoded establishment. It had little to set itself against. The low church attendance in such traditionally Catholic countries as France, Italy, Portugal, and Spain are cases in point. Church attendance here appears to be much more strongly determined by such internal divisions as class boundaries or regional traditions.

English-speaking Catholics in Australia, Canada, and New Zealand belong to a third category. Here Catholics are, or at least were, in the minority. Catholic identity could not be taken for granted. Competing with a variety of Protestant denominations, it had to defend itself. Until the mid-1960s church attendance was somewhat below the Irish and Québec figures, in the neighbourhood of 60–70 percent of adults going regularly, but considerably above the Mediterranean nations. Apart from Australia, Canada, and New Zealand, the United States, England, the Netherlands, and South Africa are in this category.

Yet denominational competition is not the only variable strengthening Catholic boundaries. The upturn of Catholic attendance in Australia and New Zealand since the final quarter of the nineteenth century appears to coincide with the far-reaching policy of the Catholic hierarchy to set itself strongly against the secular school. It inaugurated an expansive and expensive parochial school system and activated laymen and teaching orders alike. There is good evidence that this policy paid dividends in increased church attendance.

Vatican II proved to be a decisive watershed. In one fell swoop the bunker mentality disappeared. The windows to the secular world were opened, but the secular air streaming in corroded inner solidarity. Catholic church attendance dropped severely everywhere, if only because institutional authority took second place to the rather Protestant emphasis on individual conscience. Usually, however, things were a bit more complicated: when regular church attendance in French-speaking Canada dropped from 90 percent of the young adults (21–30 years of age) in 1965 to 30 percent in 1984, the urbanization, industrialization, and secularization of Québec society (the Quiet Revolution) in the 1960s also played a significant role.

There is no doubt that Vatican II has been interpreted by many Western-thinking Catholics as embodying the fear that too much stress on personal identity might endanger the institutional and social system. Politically this means a resounding endorsement of democratic institutions, which assume that a reasonable degree of individual independence is compatible with tolerable social cohesion. It can be safely predicted that too much exuberance about private conscience in some Catholic quarters at present will slowly lose its edge, if only because John Paul II seems to be committed to restoring a balance between institutional and private authority.

It is ironic, however, that at the very time Catholicism has moved away so decidedly from institutional autocracy, the most successful sects and new religions have traveled in the exact opposite direction and have created islands of belonging and havens of meaning by setting themselves apart from society at large. At least in Australia, Canada, and New Zealand this had been the Catholic stance until the Second Vatican Council came on the scene.

NOTES

1. This chapter uses materials from the following books by Hans Mol: *Faith and Fragility: Religion and Identity in Canada* (Burlington, Ontario: Trinity Press, 1985; *Religion in Australia* (Melbourne: Nelson, 1981); *The Faith of Australians* (Sydney: Allen & Unwin, 1985); *The Fixed and the Fickle: Religion and Identity in New Zealand* (Waterloo, Ontario: Wilfrid Laurier University Press, 1982). With the exception of *Religion in Australia,* these works apply the "identity" model or dialectical approach to religion set out in Mol, *Identity and the Sacred* (New York: Free Press, 1977), and Mol, *Meaning and Place* (New York: Pilgrim Press, 1983).

2. John S. Moir, *Church and State in Canada, 1627–1867: Basic Documents* (Toronto: McClelland & Stewart, 1967), XIV, p. 3.

3. Samuel H. Barnes, "Quebec Catholicism and Social Change," *Review of Politics* 23 (1961):68.

4. Sheilagh H. and Henry Milner, "Authoritarianism and Sellout in Quebec in the 1930s," in *Religion in Canadian Society,* ed. Stewart Crysdale and Les Wheatcroft (Toronto: Macmillan, 1976), p. 165.

5. Everett C. Hughes, "Action Catholique and Nationalism: A Memorandum on the Church and Society in French Canada." In ibid., pp. 182–83.

6. Jean-Charles Falardeau, "The Role and Importance of the Church in French Canada," in *French Canadian Society,* Vol. 1, ed. Marvel Rioux and Yves Martin (Toronto: McClelland & Stewart, 1971), pp. 356–57.

7. Mason Wade, *The French Canadians 1760–1967,* Vol. 2 (Toronto: Macmillan, 1968), p. 1109.

8. Miriam Chapin, *Quebec Now* (Toronto: Ryerson Press, 1955), p. 145.

9. Fernand Dumont, "Sur notre situation religieuse," *Relations* 25 (1966):36–37.

10. Gregory Baum, *Catholics and Canadian Socialism* (Toronto: Lorimer, 1980), pp. 213–14.

11. Anne Roche, "Love Among the Ruins," *Today Magazine,* April 10, 1982, p. 10.

12. Ibid., pp. 10, 16.

13. Moir, "Canadian Protestant Reaction to the Ne Temere Decree," *Sessions d'Etude (La Société Canadienne d'Histoire de l'Eglise Catholique),* 1981, p. 86.

14. Edward L. Bader, "New Approaches to Interfaith Marriage: A Report, " *The Ecumenist* 6 (July–August, 1968):172–74.

15. Patrick O'Farrell, *The Catholic Church in Australia* (Melbourne: Nelson, 1968), p. 16.

16. Mol, *The Faith of Australians,* pp. 53–54.

17. Ibid., p. 56.

18. Mol, *Religion in Australia,* p. 250.

19. Ibid., pp. 253–57.

20. C. M. H. (Manning) Clark, *Select Documents in Australian History,* Vol. 2 (Sydney: Angus & Robertson, 1955), p. 722.

21. K. S. Inglis, "The Australian Catholic Community," in *Catholics and the Free Society: An Australian Symposium,* ed. Henry Mayer (Melbourne: Cheshire, 1961), p. 11.

22. Michael Mason, "Pastoral Leadership for Tomorrow," *Australasian Catholic Record* 60 (1983):33.
23. Mol, *The Faith of Australians,* pp. 112–13.
24. Marion Carmel Leavy, *Religious Education, School Climate and Achievement: A Study of Nine Catholic Sixth Form Girls' Schools,* Ph.D. thesis, Australian National University, Canberra, 1972, p. 340; Marcellin Flynn, *Some Catholic Schools in Action* (Sydney: Catholic Education Office, 1975), p. 286.
25. Mol, *The Faith of Australians,* pp. 170f.
26. Jean Stoetzel, *Les Valeurs du temps présent* (Paris: Presse Universitaire de France, 1983).
27. Mol, *The Fixed and the Fickle,* pp. 82–83.
28. A. J. Nixon, *Divorce in New Zealand* (Auckland: University College, 1954), p. 19.
29. Mol, "Church Attendance in Christchurch, New Zealand" (Christchurch: Department of Psychology and Sociology, Canterbury University, 1962), p. 11; John D. Malcolm, *Survey* (Christchurch: National Council of Churches, Christian Education Committee, 1969), p. 25.
30. Patrick Francis Moran, *History of the Catholic Church in Australia* (Sydney: Oceanic Publishing Co., 1894), p. 897.
31. John A. Lee, *Socialism in New Zealand* (London: T. Werner Laurier, 1938), p. 267.

PART

FOUR

The Third Church

14

Cuba and Nicaragua: Religion and Revolution

Margaret E. Crahan

Over the past three decades the Catholic church in Latin America has increasingly been identified in the public's mind with revolution.[1] Yet the Nicaraguan bishops have recently leveled some of the same charges against the Sandinista revolution that the Cuban hierarchy used against the Castro revolution in the early 1960s. These include encouraging massification of society at the expense of pluralistic politics, using a nationwide literacy campaign and primary and secondary education to inculcate Marxism/Leninism, unjustly nationalizing private property, and employing universal military service to create a standing army that is a partisan force. In addition, the leaders of the Catholic church in both Cuba and Nicaragua have evinced deep concern over what they regard as the revolution's undercutting the church's role as the prime moral legitimator in society. It was precisely to strengthen this role that, in the post-World War II period, the Catholic church undertook extensive reforms. These were given expression at the Second Vatican Council (1962–1965) and the Latin American bishops' conference in Medellín, Colombia, in 1968.

In the aftermath of World War II, and in the face of increasing pressures for socioeconomic and political change, particularly in areas—like Latin America—characterized by substantial levels of poverty and repression, the Catholic church engaged in extensive reevaluation. There was a sense that the church had been remiss by not responding more strongly to problems such as the rise of European fascism and the resulting Holocaust. In addition, surveys undertaken in Latin America in the 1950s indicated a worrisome decline in lay participation in the face of a growth in Protestantism and secular competitors such as socialist movements.[2] The upshot was a thoroughgoing attempt to reform the church theologically, pastorally, and administratively in order to respond more adequately to the challenges of the modern world.

As a consequence, at Vatican II and Medellín the church emphasized active participation in the struggle to create societies characterized by that level of socioeconomic justice and respect for human rights conducive to societal concord and, hence, peace. In Latin America this stance propelled the church into a political and ideological struggle over how best to accomplish change. While the church as an institution claimed it favored no particular strategy or system, individual church people increasingly involved themselves in partisan struggle. This resulted in their becoming targets of repression by those elements opposed to substantial change. It also prompted even stronger ecclesial denunciations of human rights violations and stimulated church unity in the face of authoritarian governments.

Such was the case in Nicaragua when in June 1979 the Nicaraguan hierarchy issued a pastoral letter asserting that the insurrection against Somoza was moral and legitimate in the face of the government's long-term gross violations of the full spectrum of human rights. This endorsement, however, did not offer a carte blanche to whatever government succeeded Somoza. Hence, upon the establishment of the Sandinista government in July 1979, the bishops issued another pastoral in which they urged the new Government of National Reconstruction to encourage political pluralism and popular participation and to avoid the importation of foreign "imperialisms." The promised revolution should be Nicaraguan in its political and social structures and free of state idolatries. Finally, belief in God should be at the epicenter of the revolution, since only with this focus could authentic liberation be achieved.[3]

Developments in Nicaragua since 1979 indicate that, while the leadership of the Catholic church is willing to support insurrection in the face of highly repressive regimes, it is no more disposed to support Marxist revolution than it was in Cuba in 1959. The clergy and laity within Nicaragua, however, are not so united in favor of this stance as were their counterparts in Cuba in the face of the Castro revolution. What has happened since 1959 is that the theological, pastoral, and administrative reforms undertaken in the 1960s and 1970s have encouraged greater pluralism within the Latin American church, particularly with respect to how best to achieve socioeconomic justice and greater observance of human rights. As a consequence, while the Nicaraguan hierarchy has sharply criticized the Sandinista government, the latter includes four clerics at the ministerial level. In addition, the Sandinista revolution retains vocal support of a cross-section of Catholic clergy and laity.

Such diversity has raised tension and conflict within the Nicaraguan Catholic church and has made it the focus of an intense political and ideological struggle. Today, therefore, the Catholic church in Nicaragua is not as united an institution as the Cuban church was in the early 1960s. This is in spite of the fact that, at the outset of the Sandinista revolution, the Nicaraguan church was institutionally far stronger than the Cuban church at the outset of the Castro revolution. This strength was in large measure the result of the reforms promoted by Vatican II and Medellín. These are the same reforms that paradoxically contributed to the political and ideological pluralism that divides the contemporary Nicaraguan church.

In order to better understand the origins of this paradox, as well as the nature, extent, and limits of the transformation of the Catholic church over the past thirty years, this chapter will analyze the strength of the Catholic churches in Cuba and

Nicaragua, their identification as national institutions, their public image, the origins of ecclesial criticisms of revolution, links to the counterrevolution, the role of the Vatican, ties to foreign actors, and relations with the revolutionary governments. The conclusion will suggest some possible directions of the Cuban and Nicaraguan Catholic churches in the future.

Institutional Strength of the Catholic Churches in Cuba and Nicaragua

Historically the Catholic church in Cuba was weak.[4] In the 1950s it had the lowest percentage of nominal (72.5 percent) and practicing Catholics (5–8 percent) in Latin America. Cuba also had the highest percentage of non-church members (19 percent). As indicated by a 1957 survey of 400 heads of families, rural Cuba remained relatively unevangelized. Only slightly over one half identified themselves as Catholics, 88.8 percent never attended services, and only 4.3 percent attended three or more times a year. This low level of religious practice was due largely to the absence of church personnel in rural areas. Only 53.5 percent of those surveyed had ever laid eyes on a priest and less than 8 percent had ever had any contact with one. More telling was the fact that only 3.4 percent of those surveyed believed that the Catholic church would help them improve their lot. The vast majority (85 percent) of priests and religious were concentrated in Havana teaching in private schools rather than engaged in pastoral work. This meant that even some urban neighborhoods were without pastors.[5]

Prompted in part by these statistics, the Catholic church in Cuba in the 1950s increased its rural programs and encouraged social welfare activities by lay activists. Catholic Action, intent on combating the appeal of socialism, initiated a series of projects aimed at identifying the needs of rural workers. The Young Catholic Workers attempted to compete with labor unions for the loyalty of workers and claimed 20,000 members. Both groups injected some vitality into the church, but their activities were concentrated primarily in Havana. Hence, the institutional church was not a major barrier to the ideological inroads of Castro's revolution after 1959, particularly in rural areas.

Catholic Action and the Young Catholic Workers movement aimed at maintaining traditional Catholic cadres drawn from the bourgeoisie within the church in face of increasing societal pressures. In so doing they tended to insulate lay people from secular organizations, thereby limiting their influence over movements like Castro's. While some Catholics did participate in the insurrection against Batista, overall the Catholic church did not play a major role. Although Catholics were generally anti-Batista, there was little feeling that their faith required them to participate in his overthrow. Rather, there was a strong desire to appear neutral. According to an official of the Cuban bishops' conference, the hierarchy in prerevolutionary Cuba essentially accepted the existing political, economic, and social system, if not Batista.[6] In contrast to the Nicaraguan hierarchy, the Cuban bishops in December 1958 rejected a request from the clergy to issue a pastoral letter concerning the insurrection. That same month a handful of Agrupación Católica members, including Manual Artimé who was subsequently to lead the Bay of Pigs invasion, joined Castro in the mountains.[7] The church's image, consequently, was one of passivity and acceptance of the status quo.

This passivity was partly due to the absence in Cuba in the 1950s of any theological basis for justifying participation in the insurrection. The "preferential option for the poor" had not been enunciated, nor had the church begun to take a prophetic role in the denunciation of human rights abuses. While some Catholics did participate in the 26th of July Movement, their objective was to reform, not restructure the existing system. Hence, when the Castro government initiated a revolutionary program, most Catholics who had supported the insurrection felt duped.

Twenty years later the Catholic church in Nicaragua was stronger institutionally, theologically, and pastorally than the Cuban church had been in 1959. Historically, Nicaraguans had identified more closely with the Catholic church, with well over 90 percent claiming to be Catholics and 98 percent believers.[8] Secularism had made fewer inroads in Nicaragua in 1979 than in Cuba in 1959. While Protestants were and are active, most of the mainline denominations reflected some of the same changes as the Catholic church. Marxist/Leninist political parties and labor organizations incorporated a very small percentage of the population and were not perceived to be a threat to the predominant position of the Catholic church.

In contrast to Cuba, the Nicaraguan Catholic church was present in rural areas, particularly in the 1960s and 1970s. While as in Cuba the majority of priests and religious were based in the capital, there were greater efforts to maintain a Catholic presence in the countryside. This was facilitated by extensive use of lay preachers known as Delegates of the Word and Christian Base Communities (CEBs), which were introduced even before the Medellín Conference.[9] Both served to disseminate the church's growing support for socioeconomic justice and human rights. Priests, brothers, and nuns who previously had taught in secondary schools in Managua became involved in grass-roots social welfare work, particularly after the 1972 earthquake. This experience tended to politicize them by making them more aware of the extent of poverty in Nicaragua and the corruption of the government. Their growing awareness coincided with an overall strengthening of the opposition to Somoza and the intensification of armed struggle spearheaded by the Sandinista Front for National Liberation (FSLN). In response, the National Guard increased repression, sometimes targeting church people. As a result, the bishops declared in January 1977 that a "state of terror" existed, particularly in the rural areas. While the bishops did not endorse the FSLN, increasingly priests were approached by youths seeking advice about the morality of taking up arms and joining the Sandinistas.[10]

Meanwhile a number of priests and Catholic lay leaders had incorporated themselves into the FSLN, most notably the Maryknoller Miguel D'Escoto, the Jesuit Fernando Cardenal and his brother Ernesto, and Uriel Molina. At the grassroots, Catholic parishes, schools, and CEBs served as sanctuaries and communications networks for the guerrillas. By 1978 the Catholic church was by and large identified with the insurrection. Hence, when the bishops issued their June 1979 pastoral stating that participation in the insurrection was moral and legitimate, they were essentially recognizing the existence of extensive involvement of church personnel and laity in the movement to overthrow Somoza. In addition, while some Catholics hoped for a liberal, reformist regime, the majority, including the bishops, expected that the new government would undertake substantial structural change.[11]

Image of the Cuban and Nicaraguan Churches

At the outset of the revolution in 1959, the image of the Catholic church in Cuba was of a somewhat marginal institution, dominated by Spaniards who cultivated local elites in pursuit of institutional interests. Although Christianity was a pervasive cultural presence in Cuba and helped mold national identity, the Catholic church retained the aura of a missionary operation of the Spanish church. This image was supported by the fact that approximately three-quarters of Catholic priests and male religious were Spaniards.[12] Allegations of elitism and depreciation of Cuban culture were common. The low number of Cuban vocations was frequently attributed to the supposed lack of opportunity for nationals to rise in the church, particularly in those institutions controlled by the religious orders.

While the majority of priests and male religious in Nicaragua in 1979 were also foreigners, the Catholic church was very much identified as a national institution. This was due largely to the widespread presence of church personnel throughout the country and the utilization of popular religiosity to reinforce the church's identification with nationalist sentiment. While some tensions have arisen between foreign clerics and Nicaraguan priests, they have not been as serious as in Cuba. What strains exist flow largely from the fact that the foreign priests are generally members of religious orders and hence have had more advanced education and greater access to resources through their international contacts. Non-Nicaraguan clerics are more likely to be engaged in nonpastoral work, and are less politically conservative. This situation markedly contrasts to the profile of Spanish clerics in pre-1959 Cuba. Because of their backgrounds the foreign priests in Nicaragua have more contact with the international press and with scholars. They also have been exposed to new theological and pastoral developments and tend to be innovators.

As a postconciliar institution, the Nicaraguan church in 1979 was more open to lay participation both pastorally and in decision making, than the Cuban church in 1959. In fact, the Cuban hierarchy resisted pressures to increase lay input for twenty years after Vatican II. This resulted in an exodus of lay persons, particularly young people, from the Cuban church up through the mid-1970s.[13] It also meant that, at the outset of the Cuban revolution, the church's image was of a strongly hierarchical institution with limited lay input—an image that contributed to the low levels of practicing Catholics and lay activism. In contrast, the Nicaraguan church in 1979 was regarded as an institution more dependent on and responsive to the laity. It is not surprising that the level of practicing Catholics and their loyalty to the institution were higher and that Catholics in Nicaragua were less susceptible to hierarchical control. In fact, the Nicaraguan Catholic church was a far less monolithic institution with a greater diversity of opinions within it. Hence, it had more potential for internal conflict in the face of a revolutionary challenge than the Cuban church.

In Nicaragua in 1979, the Catholic church's image was populist, largely as a result of its efforts to implement the preferential option for the poor enunciated at Medellín. These efforts resulted in channeling church resources to grassroots evangelization, conscientization, and social welfare activities. While one-quarter of Nicaraguan students attended private Catholic schools, these schools tended to be less elitist than those in Cuba. A good number were located in poor neighborhoods and received part of their financing from surpluses generated by wealthier schools.

All the Cuban church people I have interviewed agree that their church in the prerevolutionary period had limited concern for socioeconomic justice and was largely preoccupied with institution building. Humanitarian programs were used to avoid confronting the structural bases of poverty and exploitation and there was a real failure to condemn repression and corruption. There was criticism of the traditional dependence on foreign and domestic elites and lack of identification with the poor. The church was also seen as somewhat racist and paternalistic.[14]

Such an image contrasts dramatically with that of the Nicaraguan church. The latter was the object of greater loyalty from its members and exercised strong moral leadership with Nicaraguan society. As a consequence, it should have possessed greater capacity to mobilize the general populace than the Cuban church. Nevertheless, in November 1959 a National Catholic Congress attracted an estimated 1,000,000 Cubans to Havana where chants of "Cuba sí, Comunismo no!" filled the air. The only comparable gathering in revolutionary Nicaragua was the March 4, 1983, open air mass celebrated by Pope John Paul II in Managua. There the crowd was obviously deeply split between pro- and counterrevolutionary Catholics.[15]

In reality, the church in Nicaragua today is severely divided. It is not the strong, vital institution committed to revolution that was frequently presented in the press and in some scholarly literature. This suggests that the postconciliar Catholic church has not been as profoundly transformed as has been thought.

Issues in Church–State Relations

At the crux of church–state tensions in post-1959 Cuba and post-1979 Nicaragua was the hierarchy's fear of a consolidated Marxist revolutionary government inimical to the interests of the church. While Fidel Castro did not proclaim the Cuban revolution to be Marxist/Leninist until April 1961 in the aftermath of the Bay of Pigs invasion, as early as February 1959 disquiet was expressed over communist influence in the government. In that month Monsignor Enrique Perez Serantes, archbishop of Santiago, cautioned the government against "utopian egalitarianism," a catchword for Marxism. On November 17, 1979, Nicaraguan episcopal preoccupation over possible Marxist inroads found expression in a pastoral letter that warned of the "massification" of society through the creation and expansion of Sandinista organizations. The bishops also feared that the projected national literacy campaign would be used to spread materialist atheism. Nevertheless, the hierarchy supported the revolutionary process although they insisted that Nicaraguans recognize "freedom of expression and criticism as the only way of indicating and correcting errors in order to perfect the achievements of the revolutionary process."[16] Throughout the letter the bishops made clear they reserved to themselves the right to determine the moral legitimacy of the revolutionary process. These cautionary words, coming as they did at a time of increasing criticism of the government by the newspaper La Prensa and the Superior Council of Private Enterprises (COSEP), were interpreted by some as support for opponents of the revolution.

Something of the same ambiguity characterized the position of the Cuban Catholic church in the early months of the Castro revolution. In March 1959, while Bishop Evelio Díaz, in the name of the hierarchy, expressed approval of a proposed agrarian reform law, some leaders of the lay organization Agrupación Católica publicly opposed it. In June the Jesuits organized a meeting of sixty-two clerics at Fidel Castro's alma mater Belén to discuss the legislation, as well as the general direction of the revolution. The majority were critical of the agrarian reform program and suspicious about communist influence in the government.[17] In the aftermath of the meeting increasing numbers of priests began to denounce the government from their pulpits. This stimulated counterrevolutionary sentiment among the laity and attracted some individuals who previously had not been involved in the church.

Another concern was a draft education law that proposed a unified curriculum for public and private schools. Many Catholics feared this curriculum would diminish the quality of private education and allow the government to inculcate Marxism. They were also disappointed that the new government was not willing to reintroduce religious education into the public schools and increase financial support for parochial schools. Some regarded failure to do the latter as proof of the government's antireligious bias. The 1961 literacy campaign was regarded, with some justification, as a government attempt to increase its influence over Cuban youth and mold them ideologically. The right of Catholic parents to fully determine the nature of their children's education hence became a rallying point for opponents to the revolution and was a prime motive for emigration abroad.[18]

Control over education also became a contentious issue in Nicaragua and was the focus of one of the two addresses that Pope John Paul II delivered during his 1983 visit to the country. In it he asserted an absolute right for parents to choose the type of education they desire for their children and for confessional schools and teachers to freely discharge their responsibilities.[19] At root was a fear that a standard curriculum for all primary and secondary schools would foster Marxist indoctrination of students. The issue is complicated because approximately 10 percent of Nicaraguan primary students and 25 percent of secondary students attend Catholic schools, most of which receive financial assistance from the government.[20] Catholic school students and parents have, in a number of cases, been in the forefront in organizing antigovernment protests, some of which have been disrupted by Sandinista youth.

Agrarian reform in Nicaragua has been less controversial than in Cuba. This reflects a liberalization on the issue of private property and state-controlled economies within the Catholic church as a whole. In its November 17, 1979, pastoral the Nicaraguan hierarchy stated that a species of socialism was acceptable if it did not usurp the free will of individuals and societies. What the bishops had in mind was a system that would guarantee that the resources and economy of the country would ensure the meeting of basic needs. The prelates warned against any approach that encouraged class hatred.[21] There has not, however, been any official statement from the episcopacy about the Sandinista agrarian reform program, partly because of differences of opinion among the bishops concerning it.

Cardinal Obando y Bravo of Managua in his frequent trips to the countryside in 1985 and 1986 appealed to rural discontent over inefficiencies in the agrarian reform apparatus and the fears of some small and medium-sized farmers that their independence was being usurped. At the grassroots, Catholic sentiment about agrarian reform reflects whether or not local communities have benefited from it. Overall, it has not become the major issue it was in Cuba.

What has become a critical issue in Nicaragua is universal military service. In

August 1983 the government announced a draft for all men aged 17 to 50, in response to the upsurge in contra warfare. Nicaragua had never had universal military service and there was general consternation. On August 29, 1983, the Nicaraguan Episcopal Conference sharply criticized the proposed draft on the grounds that it created an army identified with a political party, rather than the state, which the bishops judged to be an illegitimate mixing of the legal rights of the state with the desire of the FSLN to indoctrinate Nicaraguan youth. Hence, the bishops concluded that draftees could refuse to serve.[22] This position has encouraged draft evasion, as well as an upsurge of Nicaraguans declaring themselves seminarians. While the latter are not legally exempt from military service, the government's practice was not to draft those officially enrolled in seminaries. However, many youths who were seminarians have been denied exemption by the government. The extensive coverage of this dispute in the first issue of the church's publication *Iglesia* was probably one reason for its suppression in October 1985.[23]

Univeral military service in Cuba also became a bone of contention in the early years of the revolution, but not to the same extent as in Nicaragua. Since many Cuban youths opposed the draft, the Cuban Council of Evangelical Churches in 1964 requested that a program of alternative service be instituted. This resulted in the drafting of a number of church people into forced labor battalions known as Military Units to Aid Production (UMAP).[24] UMAP was disbanded in the late 1960s under public pressure, but some Cuban church people continued to be imprisoned for draft evasion, most notably Jehovah's Witnesses.

Charges are made repeatedly that the Cuban and Nicaraguan governments are intent on creating docile national churches. In the fall of 1959 two Cuban priests in Miami mounted a campaign charging that Castro planned to create a national church. This was strongly denied by the Bishop of Pinar del Río, Evelio Díaz, on behalf of the Cuban hierarchy.[25] Ironically, when the Cuban church attempted to implement some of the reforms of Vatican II in the late 1960s, particularly the use of the vernacular in the liturgy and optional use of clerical garb, some Cubans resisted on the grounds that it was actually an effort by Castro to create a national church.[26] More recently some Cuban exiles have alleged that the February 1986 National Cuban Church Encounter, the first island-wide Catholic meeting since 1959, was another effort to create a national church.[27]

In Nicaragua charges that the Sandinistas are intent on creating a national church have centered on the alleged existence of a potentially schismatic, "popular" church. What is referred to is the prorevolution sector within the Catholic church, which incorporates a good portion of the intellectual elite among the clergy, some CEBs, the ecumenical Antonio Valdivieso Center, student groups, and others. On June 29, 1982, Pope John Paul II publicly criticized the "popular" church on the grounds that it was too ideological and radical. In particular, he alleged that it encouraged class hatred and violence, rather than the church's ideal of a nonconflictual society. He also stated that the "popular" church undercut the teaching authority of the pope and the bishops as the ultimate interpreters of church doctrine.[28] Prorevolution Catholics replied that discord within the Nicaraguan church was the result of differences over politics, not over faith or doctrine, and they had no intention of undercutting the unity of the church.[29] This, however, did not resolve the problem, and allegations continue that the Sandinistas and their allies within the church are intent on creating a schismatic church.[30]

The problem appears to arise from increasing heterodoxy within the Catholic church in Nicaragua and elsewhere regarding the means for accomplishing socioeconomic justice, as well as the degree to which theological orthodoxy and hierarchical discipline must be maintained. These issues do not lend themselves to rapid resolution. That they will result in the establishment of a national church in Nicaragua, however, appears unlikely.

Churches and Counterrevolution

In both Cuba and Nicaragua the Catholic church has been charged with serving as the institutional base for counterrevolution. The emergence of the Cuban church as the institutional base for the opposition was amply demonstrated by the one million-plus turnout at a National Catholic Congress in Havana in November 1959. This gathering assumed considerable importance in the face of the disintegration of most Cuban political parties. The significance of the meeting was confirmed by Castro's attendance at the opening session. While many of the speakers avoided political topics, the gathering came alive when the Agrupación Católica leader, José Ignacio Lasagna, ended his speech with the exhortation "Social justice yes; redemption of the workers and the farmer yes; communism no!" The crowd responded "Cuba sí, Communismo no!"[31]

One month later, Manuel Artimé, another Agrupación Católica leader, left for Miami after having made contact with the CIA through a Jesuit priest. While still in Cuba he had begun organizing the counterrevolutionary group Movement of Revolutionary Recuperation (MRR).[32] Eventually, he commanded the Bay of Pigs invasion force which incorporated many Catholic lay leaders and three Spanish priests.

The year 1960 witnessed a spate of pastoral letters from the Cuban bishops attacking the government. In May 1960, Fidel Castro's former defender Archbishop Enrique Pérez Serantes declared, "We cannot say that Communism is at our doors, for in reality it is within our walls, speaking out as if it were at home."[33] This resulted in a series of progovernment demonstrations in front of churches at which the revolutionaries shouted "Cuba sí, Yanqui, no." Catholics replied "Cuba sí; Rusia, no."

During this period the Cuban bishops issued a series of pastoral letters attacking the legitimacy of the government and the revolution. They also stated that in any conflict with the United States and the Soviet Union over Cuba, they would support the former.[34] The hierarchy emphasized their belief that since the majority of Cubans were Catholics, a Marxist revolution was inappropriate. A multiparty system was strongly urged and the revolution was criticized for lacking a spiritual conception of life and a recognition of the dignity of the person, and for attempting to impose ideological orthodoxy.[35] These are all charges that have been made by individual Nicaraguan prelates, particularly Cardinal Obando y Bravo and Bishop Pablo Vega of Juigalpa.

Similar phraseology was used in the Nicaraguan bishops' April 1984 call for a national dialogue of all the contending parties including the contras. In that pastoral letter they criticized the government for promoting:

Materialistic conceptions of the human being [that] distort the person and teachings of Christ, reduce human beings to merely material categories without supernatural content, with the result that the human person is left subject to material forces called the "dialectic of history." Alienated from God and from themselves, people are left disoriented, without moral and religious reference points, without transcendental content, insecure and violent.[36]

They also charged that a "materialistic and atheistic educational system is undermining the consciences of our children and young people." Particular condemnation was leveled at a sector of the church that the prelates alleged had "abandoned ecclesial unity and submitted to the orders of a materialistic ideology. It is sowing confusion inside and outside Nicaragua through a campaign extolling its own ideas and slandering the legitimate pastors and the faithful united with them." Foreign economic and ideological exploitation was also condemned.[37]

Between 1981 and 1986 clerics were charged with counterrevolutionary acts and expelled from the country by the Nicaraguan government. The most senior of these is Bishop Pablo Vega, who was expelled on July 4, 1986, on the grounds that he had repeatedly encouraged support for the contras. The government cited his attendance at a forum sponsored by the Heritage Foundation in Washington in March 1986 when he met with the contra leaders Adolfo Calero and Arturo Cruz. On June 5, 1986, Bishop Vega also participated in a conference sponsored by PRODEMCA, a Washington-based organization that supports U.S. aid to the contras. At that meeting he was reported by two pro-Sandinista newspapers to have said, "In Nicaragua there is a totalitarian Marxist-Leninist regime. Armed struggle is a human right. What remedy is left to a repressed people?"[38]

The chief spokesperson for the domestic opposition to the Sandinista government has been Cardinal Miguel Obando y Bravo. In early 1986 he met with the United Nations' secretary general, Javier Pérez de Cuellar, and the secretary general of the Organization of the American States, Jõao Clemente Baena Soares, to present a list of charges against the Nicaraguan government. These included allegations of harassment of church personnel and institutions, censorship of the religious media, and expulsions of foreign clergy. These charges he reiterated in an article in the *Washington Post* and an interview in *Newsweek*. Obando's action was followed by a letter from the Nicaraguan bishops' conference to all national bishops' conferences, making similar allegations.[39] Such activities and statements have convinced the Sandinista leadership of the counterrevolutionary sentiments of the episcopacy. Not all the Nicaraguan Catholics share Obando's and Vega's opinions and hence the church as a whole cannot be characterized as counterrevolutionary.[40]

The passage of time in Cuba has allowed for greater clarity concerning the role of the Catholic church in the counterrevolution. In 1970 the rector of the Catholic seminary of San Carlos stated that

> many priests actively supported the counterrevolutionary movements that arose, especially after the summer of 1960, and that culminated in the Bay of Pigs invasion in April 1961. I don't know how much, but I am certain that counterrevolutionary meetings were being held on church property, and that some priests urged Catholics to take part in counterrevolutionary activities and to go into exile.[41]

At the Latin American bishops' conference in Puebla, Mexico, in 1979 a report from Cuban Catholics stated that in the early 1960s the hierarchy "supported . . . counterrevolutionary tactics, and at other times . . . was indifferent to them. These tactics oftentimes incorporated the use of religious symbols in an effort to penetrate the popular conscience. The right wing also used many clergy, primarily foreign, and lay leaders."[42] Mateo Jover, the president of Catholic Action in 1959, who subsequently left Cuba, characterized the conflict as not between church and state but rather between "revolution and counterrevolution, and this latter kept making religious freedom one of its battle cries—at least for reasons of propoganda."[43] The principal difference between the Cuban and Nicaraguan situations is that in Cuba the counterrevolutionary stance was shared by the vast majority of Catholic clergy, religious and laity. In Nicaragua, Catholics are much more divided in their attitudes toward the revolution.

The unity of the Cuban church did not, however, translate into a long-term threat to the government, since over one half of priests, religious, and lay leaders had left the country by 1965.[44] Of the more than 2,500 priests and religious who left approximately 8 percent were expelled.[45] By 1965 some had begun to return, but to date the Catholic church in Cuba remains seriously understaffed. In contrast, the clergy and religious in Nicaragua have not left in great numbers irrespective of their political stances.

Relations with the Vatican

Another difference between the Cuban and Nicaraguan experiences has been the role of the Vatican. At the outset of the Cuban revolution Pope John XXIII counseled the Cuban episcopacy to try to avoid conflict with the government. In 1961 he appointed a Florentine diplomat, Monsignor Cesare Zacchi, as the papal representative in Cuba. Over the next fourteen years Zacchi worked to improve church–state relations in the face of strong opposition from within the Cuban church.[46] The strength of this opposition made any efforts at rapprochement highly suspect. Hence it was not until the late 1960s that the first steps were taken with the issuing of two pastoral letters, the first opposing the U.S. economic embargo of Cuba and the second urging Catholics to cooperate with Marxists for the common good.[47]

The process of rapprochement was closely controlled by the bishops, who limited themselves to improving relations with the government rather than attempting to assert any influence over Cuban society. The latter is only now being contemplated after a five-year process of reflection and evaluation that resulted in a national assembly of Catholics in February 1986. A prime emphasis of the meeting was integration into Cuban society through dialogue with nonbelievers and participation in building a better society. The meeting concluded this was possible, since

> the Christian faith which is not an ideology, can live in any political system or in any historical process. The church in Cuba knows its specific mission is not of the political, economic or social order, but eminently religious, even though that which is religious-Christian always has a social and political dimension.[48]

The Vatican encouraged the meeting at which Cardinal Eduardo Pironio, president of the Pontifical Council of the Laity, represented Pope John Paul II.

Such developments are the result not only of changes in attitudes and behavior within the church but also within the Cuban government. At a 1972 meeting with Christians for Socialism in Chile, Fidel Castro raised the possibility of strategic alliances between Marxists and Christians since, he asserted, "both wish to struggle on behalf of man, for the happiness of man."[49] Given the Cuban government's official position that religious beliefs are a private matter and that freedom of conscience and worship are guaranteed by the Cuban constitution (Article 54), there has been increasing space for church people and institutions to operate, so long as they do not adopt a counterrevolutionary stance.

In recent years the Cuban government has consciously sought to improve relations with churches in Cuba as well as with the Vatican. This appears to have been promoted by a desire to eliminate pockets of dissent within Cuba, improve the government's image internationally, and build alliances with progressive church people worldwide. Given the Vatican's interest in promoting Catholicism in Cuba, there has been an increasing degree of cooperation between Havana and Rome.

The same cannot be said about Rome and Managua. Since 1980 Pope John Paul II has generally supported critics of the Sandinistas, particularly Cardinal Obando y Bravo. The pope's March 4, 1983, visit to Nicaragua served not only as encouragement of the cardinal but also of the Sandinista opposition. As one Nicaraguan businessman phrased it:

> The Pope helped us a hell of a lot. That's the best thing that could have happened to us. His comment reflected a widely held assessment that the church hierarchy increasingly could become the focus of political opposition in this overwhelmingly Catholic country. Under Obando y Bravo's uncompromising leadership, it is considered more able to attract mass following than the alliance of conservative parties and business groups that constitute the Sandinistas' tolerated political opposition.[50]

There is evidence that the Vatican's Secretariat of State under Cardinal Agustín Casaroli has sought to reduce tensions, as has the Sandinista leadership. It appears, however, that there is not sufficient flexibility either in Rome or in Managua for any substantial advances.

Foreign Influences

The influence of the Spanish Catholic church in Cuba at the time of the 1959 revolution was substantial. In particular, it inclined church personnel to conceive of the Cuban situation in terms of the 1930s struggle in Spain in which the Catholic church supported Francisco Franco out of fear of communist influences in the republican forces. The deeply rooted anti-Marxism of the Spanish clergy colored the perceptions of Cuban Catholics and gave fervor to their counterrevolutionary sentiments. It also stimulated the tendency of church personnel to leave Cuba for Spain, Latin America, or the United States, where they were assisted by local churches. The exodus helped defuse church–state tensions and, with the elimination of some of the strongest opposition elements, facilitated the consolidation of the revolution.

The high degree of identification of the Cuban bourgeoisie with the United States inclined a good number of Cuban Catholics, including the bishops, to side with the United States as tensions grew between the two countries. The proximity of the United States encouraged Cuban Catholics to take refuge there, at least until the expected U.S. invasion overthrew the Castro government. When in 1961 the Bay of Pigs failed and the Cuban government closed all private schools and the head-quarters of Agrupación Católica, there was a virtual hemorrhage of Catholics leaving the country. A 1969 survey of Havana parishes estimated that 50–70 percent of their members had left Cuba.[51] Of 723 priests in Cuba in 1960, 220 remained in 1965. Nuns declined from 2,225 in 1960 to 191 in 1965.[52] The chief consequence of the international links of the Cuban church was to predispose Catholics to resist the revolution and abandon the island out of fear of Marxism. By the mid-1960s the Catholic church had lost most of its leadership and had become a refuge primarily for those who opposed the revolution but did not emigrate abroad. It became a church for the disaffected and, as such, was marginal to the revolutionary process and Cuban society as a whole.

While the Second Vatican Council encouraged Marxist/Leninist Catholic dia-logue and groups of Christians for Socialism sprang up in Latin America in the late 1960s, the profundity of anti-Marxist feeling within the Catholic church, especially at the level of the hierarchy, has not appreciably diminished over the last thirty years. There is also strong evidence of anti-Marxist feeling among rural Catholics. In addi-tion, identification with the United States has caused some church people to support this country's Nicaraguan policy. The Reagan administration has used the issue of religious persecution to justify contra aid, and recent revelations indicate that some Nicaraguan church people have been assisted by the U.S. government in organizing resistance to the revolution. According to the *Washington Post,* the U.S. embassy in Managua has assisted anti-Sandinista clerics by expediting

> multiple exit visas, normally hard to obtain, and assist[ing] in their ticketing to the United States. One minister said the embassy helped him attend a meeting in Califor-nia addressed by presidential hopeful Marion G. (Pat) Robertson and Gen. Efraín Ríos Montt, former president of Guatemala, who is an evangelical and a fierce opponent of the Sandinistas.[53]

Dissident ministers also reported that the embassy has helped a national organization of pastors drawn from the Baptist church, the Assembly of God, and the Archdiocese of Managua to defray the costs of ecclesial communities, leadership training, and overhead, according to testimony before Congress by former Assistant Secretary of State for Inter-American Affairs Thomas O. Enders and former AID official Otto Reich.[54]

Prorevolution church people in Nicaragua also have extensive contacts in the United States, including groups opposed to Reagan administration policy. These links are used to obtain funds for their projects, such as those sponsored by CEPAD, an ecumenical organization that represents over forty churches. It has been very active in cultivating support abroad for the Nicaraguan revolution through its counterpart churches. It also engages in social welfare projects. Religious orders like the Jesuits, Maryknoll, and Capuchines have used their international networks largely in support of the revolution. Hence the Catholic church's foreign links cannot be said to support one particular position and reflect the diversity of views within the church itself.

The Church and Revolution

This brief comparison of the reaction of the Cuban and Nicaraguan churches to revolution suggests that Catholicism has been less changed at its institutional core than many analysts have presumed. The changes stimulated by Vatican II and Medellín, together with generalized pressures in post-World War II Latin America, have resulted in some transformations in the church's theology, pastoral forms, political behavior, and decision-making processes. Many traditional political beliefs and practices, however, have not been abandoned. Rather, as it has traditionally done, the church has adapted to its existential situation to the degree that it believes it can without jeopardizing itself as an institution. To date, the leadership of the Catholic church, as well as a fair proportion of the faithful, perceive Marxist/Leninist governments as a threat to its existence. It is notable that while the Catholic hierarchy in Nicaragua is determined to prevent the consolidation of a Marxist revolution, the Catholic bishops in Cuba are engaging in a dialogue with a Marxist government to deepen the rapprochement initiated in the 1960s. The Cuban hierarchy has taken this position in spite of the fact that of all the Latin American churches theirs was the least affected by Vatican II, Medellín, liberation theology, and related developments. This suggests that while the initial reaction of the Catholic church to revolution may be determined largely by general institutional characteristics, external reality will eventually determine its specific stance.

The Cuban and Nicaraguan experiences also suggest that the likelihood of a unified Catholic response to political developments is increasingly unlikely. While institutionally the Cuban church in 1959 was relatively weak, it was able to focus and mobilize counterrevolutionary sentiment largely because of its traditional role as the prime moral legitimator within Cuban society. Although the Nicaraguan church appeared eminently stronger institutionally in 1979, its increasing theological and political heterodoxy has diminished its capacity to mobilize members to support or oppose the Nicaraguan revolution. Hence, while both pro- and anti-Sandinistas look to the church to legitimate their stances, the church as an institution does not speak with a single voice.

This further suggests that the exercise of hierarchical authority within the Catholic church has become more difficult, reflecting the increased decentralization of decision making since the 1960s. There are some who see in this, and in the growing pluralism within the church, an increase in ecclesial democratization. It is doubtful whether such a process will be consolidated in the near future, particularly given Pope John Paul II's emphasis on reasserting orthodoxy and hierarchical authority.

Some have attributed the divisions within the Nicaraguan church to Marxist penetration, which has promoted the creation of a schismatic church. The current situation of the Nicaraguan Catholic church is more the result of the redefinition of the church's role, which has been underway since the 1960s. In its efforts to be more responsive to critical problems of the modern world, the church has increasingly emphasized identification with the struggle for socioeconomic justice, human rights, and peace. It has also enunciated a preferential option for the poor. This has forced the church into political and ideological struggles in regions such as Africa and Latin America and has placed strains on its traditional elite alliances. While it was never the church's intention to abandon these alliances, it has been difficult to maintain them, particularly in the face of such developments as liberation theology.

In the midst of the ferment generated by the church's commitment to a preferential option for the poor, it has been difficult for it to continue promoting its objectives of salvation for all and the development of nonconflictual societies. General unanimity about broad-based goals has not translated into agreement over how to achieve them. Hence the multiplicity of strategies supported by church people to achieve socioeconomic justice, greater observance of human rights, and peace tend to conflict. Until the church transcends this disparity, it is unlikely that internal debate and discord will diminish.

Such ferment has not, however, caused any substantial exodus from the church. Rather, the church's image of vitality and hence its appeal, particularly to the young, have increased. This suggests that the strife within the Nicaraguan church will not necessarily diminish its influence. Furthermore, conflict within the church has not weakened loyalty to it from all sides. Rather, there appears to be a shared belief that through the action of grace in the church such earthly conflicts will be overcome. The prevalence of this belief in Nicaragua suggests the unlikelihood of a schismatic or national church.

That such a church did not emerge in Cuba even in the face of its tremendous loss of human and material resources in the 1960s further indicates the unlikelihood of such a development. In fact, the attitude of the Cuban church leaders at the recent National Cuban Church Encounter was one of optimism, particularly because of the progress made since the late 1970s in developing a theology adequate to the situation. Theology in Cuba prior to the revolution had been created in Europe or North America and had limited relevance to Cuban conditions. Pastoral forms suffered from the same deficiency. What has occurred since 1959 in Cuba has been the Cubanization of the Catholic church, not the creation of a national church dominated by the government. Today Cuban church leaders regard that as the key to institutional resurrection. In Nicaragua a nationalist Catholic church is an integral part of the current political and ideological struggle.

In both Cuba and Nicaragua the fate of the Catholic church is unclear. What is clear is that neither institution is monolithically in favor of the status quo or of radical change. Rather, they are seeking nonviolent change without opting for specific systems. Such ambiguity generates both flexibility and tension. Both have characterized the Catholic church since its origins.

NOTES

1. Due to space limitations this chapter will deal exclusively with the institutional Catholic church.
2. A 1954 survey undertaken by Agrupación Católica Universiteria in Cuba indicated that only 72.5 percent of the population identified themselves as Catholics. Protestants had increased to 6 percent from 1 percent in 1940. Those claiming no religious affiliation constituted 19 percent of the population, spiritists 1 percent, and Jews 0.5 percent. While Cuba had the lowest level of Catholic identification in the 1950s, declines in the number of practicing Catholics and increases in Protestants and secularism were preoccupations throughout Latin America. Agrupación Católica Universiteria, "Sobre el sentimiento religioso del pueblo de Cuba, 1954," in Manuel Fernández, *Religión y Revolución in Cuba (Veinte cinco años de lucha ateista)*

(Miami: Saeta Ediciones, Colección Realidades, 1984), p. 22; J. Merle Davis, *The Cuban Church in a Sugar Economy* (New York: International Missionary Council, 1942), pp. 52, 62-63.

3. Conferencia Episcopal de Nicaragua, *Presencia Cristiana en la Revolución: Dos Mensajes—Momento Insurrectional 2 de junio 1979; Iniciando la Reconstrucción, 30 de julio 1979* (Managua: Cristianos en el Mundo, Comisión Justicia y Paz, Documentos, 1979).

4. Luis Aguilar, *Cuba, 1933: Prologue to Revolution* (New York: W. W. Norton, 1974), pp. 21-22; Davis, *The Cuban Church in a Sugar Economy*, p. 49; Leslie Dewart, *Christianity and Revolution: The Lesson of Cuba* (New York: Herder & Herder, 1963), pp. 93-99; François Houtart and André Rousseau, *The Church and Revolution* (Maryknoll, N.Y.: Orbis, 1971), pp. 113-14; J. Lloyd Mecham, *Church and State in Latin America*, rev. ed. (Chapel Hill: University of North Carolina Press, 1966), pp. 423-24; Lowry Nelson, *Rural Cuba* (New York: Octagon, 1970), p. 268; Ramón E. Ruiz, *Cuba: The Making of a Revolution* (Amherst: University of Massachusetts Press, 1968), p. 162.

5. Houtart and Rousseau, *The Church and Revolution*, p. 115; Agrupación Católica, "Sobre el sentimiento religioso del pueblo de Cuba," p. 22; Oscar A. Echevarría Salvat, *La agricultura cubana, 1934–66: Regimén social, productividad y nivel de vida de sector agrícola* (Miami: Ediciones Universal, 1971), pp. 14-16, 25; René F. de la Huerta Aguiar, "Espiritismo y otras supersticiones en la población cubana," *Revista del Hospital Psiquiátrico de la Habana*, II, 1 (1960):45-47.

6. In 1973, 1974, 1976, 1979, and 1984 I conducted some sixty interviews of Cuban church people on the island, in Spain, and in the United States.

7. Dewart, *Christianity and Revolution*, pp. 3, 108; Alfred L. Padula, Jr., "The Fall of the Bourgeoisie: Cuba, 1959-1961" (doctoral dissertation, University of New Mexico, 1974), pp. 438-39.

8. *Anuario Pontificio, 1970, 1975, 1980, 1985; Statistical Abstract for Latin America; World Christian Encyclopedia.*

9. In the northeastern province of Zelaya alone the Capuchins trained Delegates of the Word. Phillip Berryman, *The Religious Roots of Rebellion: Christians in Central American Revolution* (Maryknoll, N.Y.: Orbis Books, 1984), pp. 59-60, 70.

10. Berryman, *The Religious Roots of Rebellion*, pp. 72-73.

11. Conferencia Episcopal, July 30, 1979.

12. Dewart, *Christianity and Revolution*, p. 95.

13. Pablo M. Alfonso, *Cuba, Castro y los Católicos (Del humanismo revolucionario al Marxismo totalitario)* (Miami: Ediciones Hispanamerican Books, 1985).

14. It should be noted that all of the Cuban church people I interviewed, clerical, religious, or lay, in Cuba or abroad, agreed on these criticisms. The former Latin American secretary of the World Council of Churches, Theo Tschuy, reported similar findings. G. Rivas, Minutes of the Cuba Sub-Group, Latin American Methodist Task Force, March 1, 1971, p. 4; United Methodist Board of Missions, Minutes of May 14, 1971 Meeting, Cuba Sub-Group, Latin American Task Force.

15. Edward Cody, "Tension Grows in Nicaragua: Sandinistas Take Harder Line," *The Washington Post* (March 5, 1983), pp. A1, A10.

16. Nicaraguan Episcopal Conference, "Christian Commitment for a New Nicaragua" (11/17/79), Managua, p. 2.

17. Houtart and Rousseau, *The Church and Revolution*, p. 119; Padula, "The Fall of the Bourgeoisie," pp. 143, 449-54; Claude Julien, "Church and State in Cuba: Development of a Conflict," *Cross Currents* II (Spring 1961):187.

18. Padula, "The Fall of the Bourgeoisie," pp. 441-45.

19. Juan Pablo II, "Laicado y Educación," (March 4, 1983), León, Nicaragua.
20. In 1986 there were 247 private schools in Nicaragua of which 173 were religious. Government financial assistance was received by 188 private schools of which 152 were Catholic and 21 were Protestant. The remainder (15) were nonconfessional. Universities are free and largely supported by the government. Statement of Ambassador Carlos Tunnerman, Nicaraguan minister of education, 1979-1985, New York University Law School, April 19, 1986.
21. Conferencia Episcopal Nicaragüense (CEN), *Compromiso Cristiano para una Nicaragua Nueva* (11/17/79), Managua, pp. 8-9.
22. Conferencia Episcopal Nicaragüense, *Comunicado* (8/29/83), Managua, pp. 1-3.
23. "Clero granadino protesta: Por reclutamienito SMP," "Capituran seminaristas de Río San Juan," Otros seminaristas reclutados, *Iglesia*, 1, 1 (10/12/85):6-8; Margot Hornblower, "Ortega in N.Y., Defends State of Emergency," *The New York Times* (Oct. 21, 1985), p. A17.
24. Raimundo Garcia Franco, "Pastores en la U.M.A.P.: Diálogo en la U.M.A.P.," Manuscript (Feb. 10, 1966), pp. 1-8.
25. Padula, "The Fall of the Bourgeoisie," p. 466.
26. Piero Gheddo, "What I Saw in Cuba," *LADOC 'Keyhole' Series*, 7 (Washington, D.C.: United States Catholic Conference, n.d.), p. 13.
27. Wilfredo Ramírez, "The State of the Church in Cuba," *Express News* (3/2/86), San Antonio, Texas, pp. 1F-8F.
28. John Paul II, "Letter to the Nicaraguan Bishops" (June 29, 1982), Rome.
29. Católicos de Nicaragua, "Carta a Juan Pablo II" (15 de Agosto de 1982), Managua, Nicaragua, *Informes CAV*, 15-16 (Sept. 1982), p. 7.
30. Alvaro José Baldizon Aviles, "Nicaragua's State Security: Behind the Propaganda Mask," The Institute on Religion and Democracy, *Briefing Paper*, 6 (Sept. 1985), pp. 1-6.
31. Julien, "Church and State in Cuba," p. 188; Padula, "The Fall of the Bourgeoisie," pp. 458-59.
32. Julien, "Church and State in Cuba," p. 188; Padula, "The Fall of the Bourgeoisie," p. 466.
33. Enrique Pérez Serantes, as quoted in Julien, "Church and State in Cuba," p. 188. For the full Spanish text, see "Por Dios y Por Cuba" (May 16, 1960), Santiago, in Ismael Teste, *Historia Eclesiástica de Cuba*, V (Barcelona: Artes Gráficas Medinacelli, 1975), pp. 562-68.
34. Conferencia Episcopal de Cuba, "Carta Abierta del Episcopado al Primer Ministro" (Dec. 4, 1960); Enrique Pérez Serantes, "Ni Traidores, Ni Parias" (Sept. 24, 1960), "Roma o Moscu" (Nov. 1980), "Con Cristo o Contra Cristo" (Dec. 24, 1960); Teste, *Historia Eclesiástica de Cuba*, pp. 569-77, 585-90, 603-606.
35. Dewart, *Christianity and Revolution*, pp. 298-309.
36. Nicaraguan Episcopal Conference, "Pastoral Letter on Reconciliation" (4/22/84), Managua, p. 2.
37. Nicaraguan Episcopal Conference, "Pastoral Letter on Reconciliation."
38. *Barricada* and *Nuevo Diario* (6/6/86). See also Marjorie Muller, "Dissident Catholic Bishop Expelled from Nicaragua," *Los Angeles Times* (7/5/86), pp. 1-1, 27.
39. Cardinal Miguel Obando y Bravo, "Statement to U.N. Secretary General Pérez de Cuellar" (Jan. 21, 1986), New York; "Statement to OAS Secretary General João Clemente Baena Soares" (Jan. 23, 1986), Washington, D.C.; Conferencia Episcopal de Nicaragua, "Carta del Episcopado Nicaraguense a las Conferencias Episcopales del Mundo" (July 7, 1986), Managua, Nicaragua.
40. E.g., "A Word of Freedom and Christian Love Regarding the Recent Pastoral Letter

by the Nicaraguan Bishops' Conference: Declaration of the Jesuit Delegate in Nicaragua with his Council of Advisers" (May 5, 1984), Managua, Nicaragua.

41. Carlos Manuel de Cespedes, quoted in Antonio Benitez Rojo, "Fresh Air Blows Through the Seminary," *LADOC 'Keyhole' Series,* 7 (Washington, D.C.: United States Catholic Conference, n.d.), p. 53.

42. Maria Teresa Bolívar Arostegui et al., "Cuban Christians and Puebla," *LADOC 'Keyhole' Series,* 17 (Washington, D.C.: United States Catholic Conference, n.d.), pp. 42–43.

43. Mateo Jover, "The Cuban Church in a Revolutionary Society," *LADOC* IV, 32 (April 1974):21.

44. *Annuario Pontificio.*

45. Houtart and Rousseau, *The Church and Revolution,* p. 124.

46. Alfonso, *Cuba, Castro y los Católicos,* passim.

47. Episcopal Conference of Cuba, "Pastoral Letter, April 10, 1969, *LADOC 'Keyhole' Series,* 7 (Washington, D.C.: United States Catholic Conference, n.d.).

48. Eve Gillcrest, "Cuban Catholic Encuentro Calls for Evangelism, Dialogue," NC News Service (2/27/86), p. 2.

49. Fidel Castro, "There Are No Contradictions Between the Aim of Religion and the Aims of Socialism," *Granma,* XII (Nov. 20, 1977), p. 5.

50. Edward Cody, "Tension Grows in Nicaragua: Sandinistas Take a Harder Line," *The Washington Post* (March 5, 1983), pp. A1, A10.

51. Jover, "The Cuban Church in a Revolutionary Society," p. 27.

52. *Annuario Pontificio.*

53. James A. Gittings, "U.S. Link to Nicaraguan Churches Seen," *The Washington Post* (8/30/86), p. B7.

54. Interview with an official of the United States Catholic Conference (8/4/82), Washington, D.C.

15

Brazil and Chile:
Seeds of Change in the
Latin American Church

Madeleine Adriance

In recent years the Latin American Catholic Church has become known as a source of social and pastoral innovations. Among these are the basic ecclesial communities, new roles for lay people, and a sociopolitical position on the side of the oppressed classes—phenomena collectively referred to as the preferential option for the poor.[1] Nevertheless, some social scientists have expressed skepticism as to whether the official church is really an agent of change, since the majority of bishops do not advocate any drastic structural transformation of either the church or the larger society.[2]

These seemingly contradictory views of Latin American Catholicism result from different aspects of institutionalization, which in the present context refers to establishing a new ecclesial policy that profoundly affects religious belief and practice. The option for the poor originated in essentially conservative efforts, that is, in social and pastoral programs encouraged by bishops who aimed to restore the church's influence in the face of competing belief systems, particularly Marxism and evangelical Protestantism.[3] The paradoxical consequence of these defensive measures was that once they became institutionalized they would open the church to new courses of action. These would allow lay people, women religious, and priests to move in the direction of a greater openness toward the modern world, criticism of established political powers, solidarity with the poorer classes, and cooperation with some of the very elements the bishops had been opposing.

This chapter traces the institutionalization of the preferential option for the poor in Chile and Brazil, where the first stirrings of religious renewal appeared. A brief and general analysis of those aspects of the process that have been common to both countries will be followed by an examination of specific developments in each.

General Analysis

Industrialization and urbanization create profound alterations in all aspects of people's lives, not the least of which is the weakening of the bonds of kinship and community. In the semifeudal context of preindustrial Latin America, religious devotion had been closely tied to the life of the rural village. Industrialization not only undermined this religious culture but also served to relativize the whole social order. Peasants who had previously believed that their subservience to the local landowner was the will of God discovered a different world when they left the rural estates and sought work in the growing cities. Those who remained on the land also experienced a demystification of the old order as they received information from relatives and neighbors who had migrated to the urban areas. The resulting transformation in social consciousness eventually led poor people to become open to the organizing efforts of leftist groups in both the urban and the rural areas. Furthermore, the loss of community ties left many urban migrants in search of new bonds, which some of them found in the small congregations of the evangelical Protestant sects.

As religious leaders became concerned about the apparent lessening of church influence over the masses, they tried various means to restore that influence: Catholic trade unions and associations of Catholic workers; Catholic Action movements to strengthen the piety of the laity; social programs to rival those of the left; changes in pastoral methods; attempts to recruit more priests; and an eventual reliance on lay people and women religious in ministerial roles. In both Brazil and Chile the process of development of these innovations was not smooth but rather was characterized by conflict between the conservatives among the bishops and other people in the church who were pushing for radical changes. Eventually, some new religious practices did become institutionalized as a result of phenomena that were both regional and global: collective pastoral planning by national conferences of bishops, the Second Vatican Council, and the Second General Conference of the Latin American bishops held in Medellín, Colombia, in 1968.

Chile and Brazil were ahead of other Latin American countries in collective pastoral planning. The episcopate in both countries was already organized into national conferences by the early 1950s. Meetings of these episcopal conferences were coordinated by some of their more forward-looking members, such as Bishops Manuel Larraín of Chile and Hélder Câmara of Brazil. In the 1960s these progressive bishops were involved in writing official documents that would give encouragement to priests, sisters, and lay people who were inclined toward social and pastoral experimentation.

The Vatican Council further legitimized religious renewal and concern with social problems. It is important to point out, however, that this influence was not unidirectional, since Chilean and Brazilian bishops provided input into conciliar documents, particularly those concerned with issues of social and economic development.

Bishops Larraín and Câmara were instrumental in organizing the Medellín Conference, the purpose of which was to implement the guidelines of Vatican II within the Latin American social and ecclesial context.[4] The documents produced at Medellín expressed the need for social reconstruction and committed the Latin American church as a whole to the preferential option for the poor. Once institutionalized, the option for the poor met a challenge from outside the church: the military juntas that took over Brazil in 1964 and Chile in 1973. In the face of extreme repression, the bishops began to take increasingly strong prophetic stands on behalf of the victims of that repression.[5] The bishops' opposition to abuses by military regimes strengthened the church's alliance with the oppressed classes.

Although church people from both Brazil and Chile took the lead in the transformation of Latin American Catholicism, the process of religious change developed along different paths in those two countries. Let us now examine each of those paths.

Early Innovations

Chile

The seeds of ecclesial change were evident very early in Chile. As far back as 1921 bishops wrote pastoral letters that showed an awareness of social problems. Even before, the church was involved in social action, as indicated by the societies for Catholic workers already in existence before the turn of the century. By 1915 trade unions were organized by priests.[6]

There were specific political-economic factors associated with this concern within the church for the problems of the working classes. Chile had undergone industrialization and urbanization long before other Latin American countries as a result of the mining boom in the nineteenth century. Along with these societal changes came the political mobilization of workers. The first signs of union organizing began to appear in the 1870s. In 1909 the Chilean Workers' Federation was established; it was followed in 1912 by the Socialist Workers' party (which was later to become the Chilean Communist party). The organization that eventually had the strongest impact on electoral politics, however, was the Socialist party founded in 1933. Among its founders was Salvador Allende, who began running for president in the 1950s.[7]

The growth of socialism was a cause for concern among the bishops, who feared that a leftist government would persecute the church.[8] As early as the 1930s they warned Catholics against cooperating with Marxist movements. The bishops also began to develop structures through which the church could deal with the changing social context. The structure which the Vatican particularly favored at that time was Catholic Action, which extended church influence into secular spheres by indirect means, that is, small groups of lay persons who would study Catholic social doctrine and apply it. The form of Catholic Action urged by Pope Pius XI (sometimes called general, or Italian, Catholic Action) was highly clerical in its authority structure and did not encourage much initiative from the laity. This would eventually be replaced by the French model of movements, which were specialized according to milieu and encouraged a higher degree of lay autonomy. In any case, general Catholic Action did have some success in Chile, where it was begun in 1931. Within five years the movement had been established in almost every diocese, and its members and chaplains helped make the Chilean church the most progressive at that time in all of Latin

America.[9] However, the most significant element in the defense system of Chilean Catholicism came to be Christian Democracy.

The Christian Democratic party (PDC) was begun in 1957 by a group of Catholic laymen, including Eduardo Frei, who became its presidential candidate. The founding of the PDC coincided with the growing concern among the hierarchy that, with the increasing strength of the Socialist party as well as of socialist unions, the election of a Marxist president was a real possibility. The bishops employed various means to help promote the PDC as an alternative to socialism. In September 1961, the Pastoral Advisory Commission of the Chilean Episcopal Conference proposed backing Frei's candidacy through all church organizations, as well as generating grassroots support through community development projects. In 1962, the bishops published a pastoral letter, "The Social and Political Duty," which stated that communism was diametrically opposed to Christianity. This letter was reprinted and widely circulated during the 1964 presidential campaign, very likely contributing to the victory of Frei over Allende.[10]

Although the bishops' public statements never mentioned specific candidates or parties, it was clear that they had moved away from their policy of political neutrality and now supported Christian Democracy.[11] While the consequences were positive for the party, they were negative for the church, for several reasons: (1) the PDC drained off personnel and other resources from Catholic Action and other church programs, which may have been one reason why Catholic Action in Chile was not as strong in the 1960s as it had been in the 1930s; (2) the PDC took over many of the church's social programs, thus lessening its direct contact with the poorer classes[12]; (3) the eventual failure of Christian Democracy (which will be discussed later) not only led to the collapse of those social programs but also left the church identified with a party that had apparently failed in its promise to improve conditions for the poor.

In the meantime, the Chilean bishops participated in the Second Vatican Council, where they became known for their progressive leadership.[13] It is very likely that their insights, derived from their experience of the social and ecclesial context of Chile, influenced the writing of *Gaudium et Spes,* the pastoral document concerned with the church's relationship to the modern world. It was also at Vatican II that the progressive leadership of the Brazilian bishops became visible.

Brazil

The development of progressive Catholicism in Brazil began approximately thirty years later than in Chile. Again the political-economic context contributed to the timing of ecclesial change. The industrialization of Brazil started in the 1930s, when import substitution resulting from the Great Depression stimulated the growth of domestic industry. For at least three more decades, however, agriculture remained the occupation of the majority of Brazilians.

During this time the rural people's view of the social order was altered not only by the stories told by urban migrants who returned to visit their home villages but also by economic transformations that were going on in the rural areas themselves. At the same time that industry began to develop in the cities, sugar plantations in the rural northeast were becoming modernized.[14] The semifeudal structure of land use, which had allowed peasants a certain autonomy in growing crops on the plots of land allotted to them, was replaced by a capitalist system in which maximization of profit required replacing the peasants by landless laborers who would work long hours for low wages. Peasants gradually became mobilized to establish their right to remain on the land. The growth of critical social consciousness in the rural areas did not, however, strengthen political parties of the left since rural people were not accustomed to gaining power by this means, particularly with the domination of national politics by the large landowners. Instead the "Communist threat" in Brazil mainly took the form of peasant leagues.

Not surprisingly, the church's first efforts at social reform were in the countryside. In the 1940s, a group of priests in the archdiocese of Natal organized a multifaceted program which eventually included rural trade unions, political education, religious instruction, and literacy lessons transmitted by radio. The union element was imitated by priests in other dioceses, and the radio courses in literacy and political education were later utilized by the Basic Education Movement (MEB), a nationwide program organized by the bishops' conference and funded by the government.[15] Members of the episcopate also sought and received financial assistance from the government in setting up regional development projects. All of these programs were staffed to varying degrees by members of Catholic Action.

Catholic Action had had a poor start in Brazil. The Italian version, which was introduced in the 1930s and which emphasized individual piety, appealed mainly to upper class people and did not become a vital force for renewal within Brazilian Catholicism. By the 1940s, however, there were priests in different regions of the country who began to facilitate the organization of specialized movements according to the French model, which emphasized the development of lay leadership.[16] The rapid growth of Brazilian Catholic Action during the 1950s not only produced a generation of lay persons who became a force for change in the church but also helped produce a new breed of bishops. In the 1960s, those members of the episcopate who encouraged pastoral and social experimentation were most frequently former Catholic Action chaplains.[17] These were the bishops who influenced the pastoral plans that made critical social consciousness and a strong role for the laity important elements in ecclesial renewal.

The social and pastoral innovations encouraged by the Brazilian bishops did not include the formation of a Christian Democratic Party. Although a group of laymen founded a PDC in Brazil in 1948 (nine years earlier than the founding of its Chilean counterpart), it never received any tangible support from the majority of the bishops.[18] A possible reason for this may have been that the leftist threat in Brazil did not take the form of electoral politics, as it did in Chile. Consequently Brazilian bishops sought to defend the church against Marxism by concentrating their main efforts where the threat appeared the greatest—in rural movements. In addition, they gave some attention to evangelization efforts in the cities, where they were concerned that people who had left their rural roots would be drawn into either socialist or Protestant groups. In both rural and urban areas, the clergy continued to encourage formation of specialized Catholic Action movements, which flourished in Brazil during the late 1950s and early 1960s (the same period when Christian Democracy was gathering strength in Chile).

Progressive policies of church people in Brazil and Chile might have remained

mere defensive adaptations had it not been for an important factor: the institutionalization of ecclesial innovation at the Second Vatican Council. Since the Chilean
bishops maintained a defensive posture (manifested in their support of the PDC)
longer than the Brazilians, the following section on developments after Vatican II will
begin with Brazil.

Developments After Vatican II

Brazil

Even at the time of the Council, the majority of Brazilian bishops were not prepared to make drastic changes in the church. Members of University Catholic Action
(JUC), however, who apparently were moved by the spirit of Vatican II and by the
radical movements that were proliferating in Brazil during the early 1960s, had a
different viewpoint. They developed an increasingly critical analysis, producing documents concerning both the political-economic causes of widespread poverty and the
church's implicit compliance with structures of oppression. Of even greater concern
to the hierarchy was the involvement of members of JUC in the National Student
Union (UNE), which had a communist image. The bishops took various steps to curb
the new direction of JUC: verbal reminders that Catholic Action was supposed to be
an extension of the hierarchy, expulsion from JUC of a student who became national
president of the UNE, reorganization of Catholic Action to restore episcopal control,
and finally, in 1966, dissolution of JUC altogether.[19] Meanwhile, many members of
JUC had already slipped out from under episcopal authority by forming a new movement called Popular Action (AP). This movement, which advocated the revolutionary
mobilization of peasants, workers, and students, provided for middle class Catholic
leftists a means of unifying their religious and social commitments. Although AP was
not officially part of the church, many of its members were active in the Basic Education Movement (MEB), which was a church organization. Through MEB, AP activists were able to influence the way in which many lay persons, religious sisters,
priests, and even some bishops defined the unity of faith and social action. Meanwhile, an unexpected event in the larger political milieu eventually compelled the
episcopate as a body to take a prophetic position.

The military coup of 1964 met with very little resistance and, initially at least,
there was little or no bloodshed. Most of the bishops who had been concerned about
the leftist direction of the popular movements were apparently relieved when the
generals took over the government. The episcopal conference issued an official statement, thanking God and the armed forces for delivering Brazil from the communist
peril.[20] Nevertheless, during the late 1960s and early 1970s, when government
repression became increasingly severe, the church was not spared from persecution.
Countless priests, seminarians, and lay church workers were arrested, tortured, or
expelled from the country. Five priests were assassinated and nine bishops were
arrested or detained.[21] At the same time that the repressions fell on people identified
with progressive elements within the church, the bishops became aware of the
increasing economic hardships suffered by the majority of the people.

Although the first collective pastoral document criticizing the military regime was not published until 1973, individual bishops began speaking out in the 1960s.[22] By this time a new pastoral form had emerged within the Brazilian church—the basic ecclesial community (CEB). Although many of these groups are now viewed as a force for religious and social change, it is likely that some of the bishops initially encouraged their formation as a defense against the proselytizing efforts of evangelical Protestants, whose numbers had been rapidly increasing since the early 1950s.[23] A story frequently told in connection with the origin of the CEBs concerns one of the more conservative members of the hierarchy, Dom Agnelo Rossi.[24] This bishop became concerned about a complaint from a devout woman who told him that her local Catholic church, which was without a priest, had been closed at Christmas, while three nearby Protestant churches had been full of light and music. Dom Rossi subsequently organized a program to train lay catechists who could gather people each Sunday for prayers, hymns, and Scripture readings. Although it is sometimes disputed whether this program really represented the origins of the CEBs, it must be acknowledged that many bishops did support new religious roles for the laity in order to counter the efforts of the evangelicals.

Meanwhile, progressive bishops in both Chile and Brazil carried the institutionalization of religious renewal one step beyond Vatican II. In the mid-1960s, Bishop Manuel Larraín decided to organize a conference of the Latin American bishops to discuss the implications of the Vatican Council for their continent. He was assisted in this effort by Dom Hélder Câmara.[25] The documents from the Medellín Conference encouraged development of basic communities as instruments of both evangelization and social-economic development. They also advocated some social change, including land redistribution and the participation of poor people in developing new structures. Although the Medellín documents were more reformist than revolutionary, they provided encouragement for women religious, lay people, and priests who were inclined to work for social change.[26] Some of these people pushed the implications of Medellín far beyond the liberal-reformist intentions of the bishops, providing a basis for synthesizing Christian and Marxian perspectives on the levels of both theory and practical action.[27]

During the years of the military regime (1964–1984), the Brazilian bishops acquired a progressive reputation because of the prophetic voice some of them raised against the repression. As the repression eased in the late 1970s and early 1980s, the church became increasingly active in organizing poor people around issues of land, labor, and housing. However, with regard to the structure of the church itself, fewer bishops have been willing to implement concrete changes. At the present time, only about thirty out of 300 members of the Brazilian episcopate have made a commitment to incorporating lay input from basic communities into their pastoral planning. Nevertheless, this 10 percent constitutes an influential minority that is setting the tone for church policy. They have placed their national bishops' conference in the foreground of ecclesial change, leading some observers to refer to Brazilian Catholicism as the church of the future.[28]

Chile

At the time of the coup in Brazil, the Chilean bishops, along with many priests, women religious, and lay people, still supported the Christian Democrats. By the late

1960s, however, there was no longer consensus on this matter. At the time of Eduardo Frei's election campaign (in 1964), the PDC had proposed to alleviate poverty through reform programs, particularly land reform and the "Chileanization" of the copper mines. However, Frei's land reform program accomplished only about 20 percent of the property transfers that he had promised, and resulted in peasants receiving only the poorest lands. As for the copper industry, the Chilean government paid so much for the shares that it purchased from foreign corporations, and gave them such large tax breaks, that the greatest benefits went to the corporations, rather than to the people of Chile.[29]

Furthermore, after the middle of Frei's presidency (1967) there was some evidence that he was moving toward the right, as he began to abandon reform programs and to create incentives to attract even more foreign investment. Because the expectations of the poorer classes were not being met, there was considerable social unrest, evidenced particularly in labor strikes and land occupations. Several of the workers' demonstrations were countered by police violence.[30] As a result of these developments, Frei began to lose the support of sectors of the church, of the majority of the Chilean people, and of some members of his own party.

By the late 1960s the Chilean bishops began to see the error of their involvement in electoral politics. Their pastoral documents once again affirmed that the church was not allied with any particular party. At this time the bishops also attempted to implement the recommendations from Medellín. They began to encourage the development of basic ecclesial communities, both as a means of evangelization and as a vehicle for social action. Meanwhile, the failure of Christian Democracy and the continued growth of socialism split the progressive elements in the church. On the one hand, there were the liberal reformists, including several of the bishops, who still saw social programs as a means of preventing Marxism from taking hold among the masses. On the other hand, increasing numbers of lay Catholics, women religious, and priests had moved beyond the fear of communism and tried to carry their efforts in social milieus beyond mere reform.

The first public sign of this new conflict appeared in August 1968, when a group of 200 lay people and nine priests (who were later to call themselves the Young Church movement) occupied the Santiago Cathedral. This group demanded that the church take a stand in solidarity with the poor and in opposition to capitalism. Cardinal Silva responded by suspending the nine priests involved in the occupation. Although the cardinal later reinstated them in conjunction with a mass of reconciliation, he made no concessions to the group's demands.[31]

Another manifestation of the deepening cleavage between Catholic reformists and Catholic radicals originated within the PDC, in a faction whose members advocated an alliance with parties of the left. In 1969, when it became clear that the sector of the PDC supportive of Frei was moving toward an alliance with the right, the radical faction left the party and started the Movement for United Popular Action (MAPU).[32] Although MAPU never gained political strength comparable to that of the PDC, it served an important function for radicalized middle class Catholics by providing a vehicle through which they could combine their religious beliefs with a Marxian analysis.[33]

The best known movement combining Christianity with Marxism emerged after Salvador Allende became president. His government offered hope to people both within and outside of the church who saw in socialism the only realistic means for altering structures perpetuating poverty. The bishops, however, while accommodating to the presence of a democratically elected socialist government, still preferred to maintain a clear distinction between Catholic belief and Marxism. So in November 1971, when a group of priests and lay persons organized a Chilean branch of the Christians for Socialism movement, the stage was set for conflict with the hierarchy.

One source of conflict was the movement's use of a more explicitly Marxian analysis than the bishops were inclined to accept (for example, the assertion that ecclesial unity was impossible as long as the church tolerated class divisions within itself). Even more problematic was that some of the documents published by Christians for Socialism criticized documents of the Chilean Episcopal Conference, thereby undercutting the bishops' traditional teaching authority. It was not surprising, therefore, that by 1973 the bishops were preparing an official statement prohibiting priests and members of religious orders from actively participating in Christians for Socialism. In the meantime, the movement was gaining influence. Between 1971 and 1973 it had an active membership of several hundred lay people, Protestant ministers, Catholic priests, and religious who established local chapters in almost every province of Chile, published monthly bulletins and pamphlets, and worked with basic communities.[34]

The impact of the bishops' prohibition against Christians for Socialism was weakened by its inclusion in a document that was published after September 11, 1973. The extremely violent military coup on that date resulted in repression against all persons and organizations that appeared even mildly leftist, including numerous church people. This bloody event drew different responses from various ecclesial sectors. Within the episcopate the reaction was mixed. Individual bishops publicly thanked the military for saving the country from Marxism. However, the permanent committee of the Chilean Episcopal Conference made a more moderate response. Although these bishops encouraged the Chilean people to cooperate with the new regime, they also decried the bloodshed and pleaded for moderation by the military and respect for previous gains made by the poor.[35]

Clearly there were differences in the responses of the Chilean and Brazilian episcopates to the military coups in their respective countries. In 1964, the Brazilian bishops had been almost unanimous in their relief at the military takeover, in contrast to the mixed reaction of the Chilean bishops in 1973. These differences are likely related to the sociopolitical contexts of these two periods. There had been virtually no resistance or bloodshed in the initial phase of the military takeover in Brazil. In Chile, however, there was considerable resistance, and thousands of people were killed. In Brazil in 1964 the fear of communism was still visible in many sectors of the church. By 1973, however, most of the Chilean bishops had not only accommodated to a socialist president but some of them even appreciated the gains made by people of the poorer classes as a result of Allende's policies. Furthermore, as a result of the institutionalization of religious renewal there was also an important change in the ecclesial context. At the time of the coup in Brazil, the Vatical Council had not yet ended and the Medellín Conference had not even been conceived. In contrast, the coup in Chile occurred eight years after Vatican II and five years after Medellín. In other words, the preferential option for the poor had already been institutionalized. Nevertheless, because the Chilean bishops assumed that the army's intervention would be temporary, their initial criticism of the junta was relatively mild.

There were clergy and lay Catholics, however, who did not have the luxury of offering mild responses, since many of them were arrested, tortured, killed or exiled. Those who survived informed the bishops of the real consequences of the coup, specifically human rights violations and the increased poverty suffered by the majority of the people as a result of the junta's economic policies.

An important source of such information was the Committee of Cooperation for Peace (COPACHI). This represented an ecumenical effort begun one month after the coup as a vehicle of advocacy for prisoners arrested by the military government. By 1975 COPACHI had expanded its services to include a broad range of community self-help projects. The activities of this organization brought women religious, priests, and lay church workers into daily contact with people who were suffering from the worst consequences of the repression. These church people began to put pressure on the bishops to speak out.[36] Meanwhile, COPACHI presented a sufficient threat to the military regime that Augusto Pinochet, the leader of the junta, put pressure on Cardinal Silva to end it. In December 1975, the cardinal used his influence to shut down the organization, appearing to comply with Pinochet's demands; shortly afterward, however, Silva instituted the Vicariate of Solidarity, which continued the work of COPACHI but now under the control and protection of the Catholic bishops. This vicariate established regional offices in twenty provinces and published a biweekly bulletin for circulation in parishes throughout the country. It became particularly significant as the vehicle by which the institutional church in Chile placed itself on the side of the poor and other victims of the repression.

Nevertheless, for the first three years after the coup, the bishops' criticisms remained mild. Apparently they continued for some time to believe that they could influence the government to act more humanely. A change in their approach occurred with the beginning of attacks on prominent Catholic laymen and on bishops themselves. In 1976 two lawyers who had been closely associated with the PDC were expelled from the country after they presented a paper expressing criticism of conditions in Chile at an assembly of the Organization of American States. That same year police allowed demonstrators to hurl stones at three bishops who were returning from a pastoral meeting in Ecuador (which had been shut down by the military government there under the charge of subversion).[37] As a result of these and similar incidents, the hierarchy began to voice stronger criticisms of the Pinochet regime. The government retaliated with attacks on the bishops through the mass media.

At the same time that it became clear that the church–state alliance had disintegrated, there were also rearrangements of alliances within the church itself. As basic communities and lay leadership programs increased in strength and numbers, wealthy Catholics and political reactionaries began to express criticism of the church's increasing identification with the poor. Meanwhile, other persons who had previously been alienated from the mainstream of the church (such as members of MAPU) became staff members of its human rights projects.

In spite of these changes, it is difficult to define the present position of the Chilean church. On the one hand, some bishops appear progressive because of their opposition to the continuing repression of the Pinochet regime. On the other hand, the majority do not appear to encourage the degree of lay initiative that would be consonant with a progressive *ecclesial* policy. Moreover, there is evidence that the Vatican intends to replace retiring bishops with those who are relatively conservative in both social and religious viewpoints.[38] Since the bishops do not constitute the entire church, perhaps one should instead look to the laity, women religious, and priests for innovative leadership. But how far will these people be able to take the preferential option for the poor if their bishops actively oppose these efforts? Because the church in Chile is much smaller than its Brazilian counterpart, with only one-tenth of the number of bishops, there is less prospect in Chile for the development of the small but influential progressive minority characteristic of the Brazilian episcopate.

The Paradox of Institutionalization

The cases of Brazil and Chile provide examples of the paradox of institutionalization. They illustrate how measures taken by some members of the hierarchy to restore the church's influence in the context of a secularized, pluralistic society unleashed a potential for both social and ecclesial change that may eventually prove far more radical than the bishops ever intended. Furthermore, these cases show how specific defensive measures used by church leaders—for example, the strong support by Brazilian bishops for Catholic Action, in contrast to the Chilean bishops' support of Christian Democracy—may be attributed to differences in political-economic contexts. The different pace of social-historical developments in each country also affected the timetables for ecclesial change. The earlier emergence of social consciousness in the church in Chile related to the earlier industrialization in that country. By the 1960s, however, two political factors pushed the leadership of the Brazilian church to develop the preferential option for the poor: the emergence of socialism on the level of electoral politics in Chile and the timing of the military coup in Brazil. The Chilean episcopate had just moved away from Christian Democracy at the time that Brazil entered into the worst phase of government repression in its recent history. Consequently, the Chilean bishops were slower than their Brazilian counterparts to become aware that right-wing authoritarian regimes might pose a greater threat to both religion and humanity than the Latin American variety of socialism.

Beyond differences in the church in Chile and Brazil is an important common contribution: the initiative to organize the Medellín Conference in 1968. At Medellín the preferential option for the poor received ecclesial legitimation for all of Latin America. Once this new ecclesial position became institutionalized, it enabled the church to serve a relatively autonomous, prophetic function in relation to military regimes. This prophetic role led church people to speak out against government policies resulting in human rights violations and economic hardships, even at the risk of persecution of the church itself.

As a further result of institutionalization at Medellín, the option for the poor has spread throughout the Latin American church, particularly manifested in liberation theology and the basic ecclesial communities. Since the unity of the spiritual and the social is central to both the theology and the CEBs, it is not surprising that the option for the poor has produced sociopolitical consequences. These have varied among individual countries, according to their societal contexts and the internal life of the local church. Where they have been visible on the level of concrete action, these consequences have ranged from Catholic participation in nonviolent social activism in Chile and Brazil to their involvement in revolutionary struggles in Nicaragua and El Salvador.[39] Thus, innovations that were approved by bishops for the purpose of defending the faith against secular doctrines such as socialism produced a new role for the church in relation to socialist movements.

It is difficult to predict at this point what will be the impact on religion and society of this new social role of the church. Much will depend on Vatican policies, which in recent years have not appeared to favor social or ecclesial innovation, and on the degree of intervention by foreign governments (such as the United States) into the affairs of Latin American countries. Both of these factors suggest that lay people, women religious, and priests who engage in the struggle to help people of the oppressed classes to attain a stronger voice in church and society may continue to come into conflict with religious and secular powers. One can only hope that the eventual resolution of those conflicts will be conducive to social justice and human development.

NOTES

1. Basic ecclesial communities are small groups within a parish. They are often characterized by the study of Scripture, mutual aid, and an orientation to social action.
2. I am grateful to Hannah Stewart and to Kenneth Aman for calling my attention to conservative directions among the Chilean episcopate, and to people who provided similar information in interviews and conversations during my field research in Brazil. I am also grateful to Helen Rose Ebaugh and Brian Smith for their helpful criticisms of an earlier draft of this chapter.
3. This statement is not intended to imply that all religious innovators in Latin America have acted out of defensive motives. However, there is ample evidence in the literature to indicate that this was the case on the level of church policy through the 1960s. See, for example, David Mutchler, *The Church as a Political Factor in Latin America with Particular Reference to Colombia and Chile* (New York: Praeger, 1971); Thomas Bruneau, *The Political Transformation of the Brazilian Catholic Church* (New York: Cambridge University Press, 1974); Brian Smith, *The Church and Politics in Chile* (Princeton, N.J.: Princeton University Press, 1982); Hannah Stewart, "Toward a Framework for Examining the Socio-Political Role of Latin American Churches with Special Reference to the Chilean Case" (Paper presented at the annual meetings of the Society for the Scientific Study of Religion, Savannah, Ga., 1985); Madeleine Adriance, *Opting for the Poor: Brazilian Catholicism in Transition* (Kansas City, Mo.: Sheed & Ward, 1986).
4. Boaventura Kloppenburg, "A Segunda Conferencia Episcopal do Episcopado Latinoamericano," *Revista Eclesiastica Brasileira* 23 (Sept. 1968):623; Luiz Alberto Gomez de Souza, *Classes Populares e Igreja nos caminhos da Historia* (Petropolis: Vozes, 1982), p. 291.
5. In this context, "prophetic" refers to a socially critical position, in the tradition of the biblical prophets.
6. Henry A. Landsberger, "Time, Persons, Doctrine: The Modernization of the Church in Chile," in *The Church and Social Change in Latin America*, ed. Henry A. Landsberger (Notre Dame, Ind.: University of Notre Dame Press, 1970), pp. 78–79.
7. Gary MacEoin, *No Peaceful Way: The Chilean Struggle for Dignity* (New York: Sheed & Ward, 1974), pp. 9–11.
8. It is interesting to note that this concern focused on the cities where the threat from the left was most visible. Pastoral letters on land issues did not emerge in Chile until

thirty years after the labor pastorals. In the meantime, the bishops were encouraging priests to organize unions among urban laborers at the same time that they were suppressing the rural unions that had been organized by other priests. See Virginia Marie Bouvier, *Alliance or Compliance: Implications of the Chilean Experience for the Catholic Church in Latin America* (Syracuse, N.Y.: Maxwell School of Citizenship and Public Affairs, Syracuse University, 1983), pp. 24–25. A further discussion of the interaction between the Chilean political context and church policy regarding rural workers is in Stewart, "Toward a Framework," pp. 9–21.

9. Smith, *The Church and Politics in Chile,* pp. 95, 105.

10. For a more detailed account of the process by which the Chilean bishops worked against the election of Allende, see Mutchler, *The Church as a Political Factor,* pp. 248–53, 308–311.

11. Admittedly this political neutrality was relatively new, since the Catholic church in Chile had traditionally been identified with the Conservative party.

12. Smith, *The Church and Politics in Chile,* pp. 137–38.

13. Ibid., p. 121.

14. An explanation of the process of transformation of agricultural production from a semifeudal to a capitalist form is given in Fernando Azevedo, *As Ligas Camponesas* (Rio de Janeiro: Paz e Terra, 1982), pp. 43–53.

15. The Natal Movement and the Basic Education Movement are described in more detail in Adriance, *Opting for the Poor,* pp. 25–28, 43–52.

16. Marcelo Cavalheira, "Momentos historicos e desdobramentos da Acao Catolica Brasileira," *Revista Eclesiastica Brasileira* 43 (March 1983):18–19.

17. This was also true of the Chilean bishop, Manuel Larraín.

18. Bruneau, *The Political Transformation of the Brazilian Catholic Church,* p. 101.

19. Ibid., p. 177. The students did maintain JUC for a few more years without episcopal support.

20. The full text of the bishops' statement has been reprinted in Luiz Gonzaga de Souza Lima, *Evolucao Politica dos Catolicos e da Igreja no Brasil* (Petropolis: Vozes, 1979), p. 147.

21. These cases have been documented by the United States Catholic Conference in *Repression Against the Church in Brazil, 1968–1978* (LADOC Keyhole Series, Number 18, 1978), pp. 20–27, 31–33.

22. See Adriance, *Opting for the Poor,* pp. 147–51.

23. According to an article by Boaventura Kloppenburg ("O Fantastico Crescimento das Igrejas Pentecostais no Brasil," *Revista Eclesiastica Brasileira* 26 (Sept. 1966):653), between 1952 and 1956 the membership of Protestant sects in Brazil had increased from fewer than 100,000 to over 3 million.

24. Helena Salem, *A Igreja dos Oprimidos* (São Paulo: Brasil Debates, 1981), p. 155.

25. Bishop Larraín died as the result of an automobile accident on his way to a planning session for the Medellín Conference, leaving the guiding power to the Brazilian bishops. In addition to Dom Hélder, the most influential Brazilians at Medellín were Dom Avelar Brandao Vilela, who succeeded Bishop Larraín as president of the Latin American Bishops' Conference, and Dom Eugenio Sales (one of the main organizers of the Natal Movement), who, as chair of the Committee on Justice and Peace, would influence the social statements to come out of the conference.

26. I have termed Medellín "reformist" because in the final documents the bishops reaffirmed their opposition to socialism and proposed the reform of capitalism as a solution to the problems of poverty and underdevelopment. See *The Church in the Present-Day Transformation of Latin America in the Light of the Council* (Medellín Documents), Volume II (Bogota: General Secretariat of CELAM), pp. 36–37.

27. This synthesis of Christianity and Marxism would be evident in the theology of liberation.
28. Penny Lernoux, "Brazil: The Church of Tomorrow" (Lucha, July–August, 1977), pp. 11–16.
29. MacEoin, *No Peaceful Way*, pp. 50–52.
30. Bouvier, *Alliance or Compliance*, pp. 30–31.
31. Franz Vanderschueren and Jaime Rojas, "The Catholic Church of Chile: From 'Social Christianity' to 'Christians for Socialism'," LARU Studies, Number Two (Toronto: Latin American Research Unit, 1977), pp. 23–24.
32. Frei's move toward the right is described below.
33. Vanderschueren and Rojas, "The Catholic Church of Chile," p. 25. With regard to providing a vehicle for combining Christianity with radical politics, MAPU may have served a function similar to the AP movement in Brazil.
34. For a more detailed description of the Christians for Socialism movement, see Smith, *The Church and Politics in Chile*, pp. 231–58.
35. Bouvier, *Alliance or Compliance*, p. 44.
36. Information in this paragraph and the next two is derived from Smith, *The Church and Politics in Chile*, pp. 305–318, 333–34.
37. A more detailed account of these incidents is given in ibid., pp. 305–306.
38. This Vatican policy seems evident in the recent replacement of Cardinal Silva (archbishop of Santiago) and Dom Hélder Câmara (archbishop of Olinda and Recife) by more conservative prelates.
39. For an account of the participation of Christians in struggles for change in Central America, see Phillip Berryman, *The Religious Roots of Rebellion: Christians in Central American Revolutions* (Maryknoll, N.Y.: Orbis Books, 1984).

16

Too Weak for Change: Past and Present in the Venezuelan Church

Juan Carlos Navarro

The purpose of this chapter is to describe and analyze the Venezuelan church and to define the particularity of Catholicism as it has developed in Venezuelan society, with special reference to recent developments.

My main premise is that a full understanding of the church and contemporary Catholicism in Venezuela can be gained only from a historical perspective, since it is the highly particular historical development of both that explains their interesting and somewhat unusual present-day characteristics. We begin, therefore, by describing the historical evolution of the church and Venezuelan Catholicism from the period of the Spanish Conquest up to the middle of this century. Second, we need to examine the church in the context of the democratic regime that has existed in Venezuela since 1958, pinpointing some of the main dynamics of Venezuelan Catholicism in recent times. The final section draws together some of the more pertinent results from the preceding analysis.

Throughout this chapter the case of the Venezuelan church will be periodically compared or contrasted with that of other Latin American countries, notably Colombia. It should be clear, however, that a comparative analysis is beyond the scope and purpose of this chapter, and that the relevant comments are merely intended to direct the interested reader toward avenues of further inquiry.

The Weight of the Past in the Venezuelan Church

Let us begin this historical account by focusing on some of the distinctive characteristics of the Venezuelan church in the period immediately preceding the War of Independence at the beginning of the nineteenth century.

First, in the area today known as Venezuela, the church had, from the outset,
been a decentralized organization. The main cause of this was the role of religious
orders in the process of evangelization, a role far more prominent than in most other
Latin American countries. Second, in organizational terms, the church at the time
was poorly developed; its needs outstripped its resources, which meant that its foothold in the area was precarious. Third, the church had inherited a long history of
conflict between religious authorities (which regularly fulfilled civil functions, especially in the missions), civil officials, and the "Cabildos."[1] Fourth, in spite of its prominent role in the colonial sociocultural order, the church never managed to carry out
a full program of evangelization. In fact, because of the difficulty and the late arrival
of the Spanish Conquest in the area, the extent and depth of Venezuelan Catholic
culture were never very great.

With this sad legacy, the church reached the end of the colonial period and had
to endure the turbulent war of Venezuelan emancipation (1810-1824), one of the
most prolonged and violent in Latin America. As a result of this war, Venezuelan
society in its entirety was thrown into a state of upheaval in the form of racial and
class tensions, to such an extent that it proved impossible to rebuild a sociopolitical
order of any stability whatsoever, at least until 1870.

The church's role in this process was only secondary. Decentralization led to an
absence of unity or, rather, an absence of any clear dividing line between the clergy
on the Republican side and those who supported the Spanish crown, and the church
made no decisive contribution to the conflict's final outcome. Nevertheless, the
church bore the brunt of these events in a very unusual way. The war devastated
the church's infrastructure throughout the country, leaving religious posts vacant
everywhere and, more important, decisively altering the legal status of the church.
In 1824 the Law of Ecclesiastical Patronage introduced under Venezuela's new
Republican government gained the right to appoint religious officials (notably bishops), which had previously been the sole prerogative of the Spanish crown. The Law
of Patronage remained in force until 1964 and proved to be the main source of
conflict between religious authorities and civil elites in Venezuela, just as in most
other Latin American countries.

The pattern of conflict between religious and civil powers was remarkable in one
significant respect. Every dispute was invariably settled in favor of the republican
government and against the church's interests. A detailed account of the many conflicts lost by the church in the nineteenth century is beyond the scope of this chapter,[2]
but what is particularly striking is how each new government from 1830 to the end
of the nineteenth century held more or less the same attitudes and took similar steps
to subject the church to the will of the state. In contrast to the situation in Colombia,
there were no Catholic loyalties among the Venezuelan elite. Liberals as well as conservatives shared a marked antagonism toward the church, leaving it devoid of any
significant political support. The roots of this particular situation are of course to be

found in the influence of the French Enlightenment, which played an important role in the emancipation, but also in the traditional disagreement and lack of understanding between civil and religious authorities during the colonial period.

An interesting case in point was the church–state conflict during the presidency of Guzmán Blanco (1870–1888). Guzmán was the first Republican leader to succeed in rebuilding a stable—albeit only temporarily stable—political and economic order in Venezuela since the beginning of the century. He defeated most of the "caudillos" (military leaders who represented the main force of anarchy in society at the time) and forged strong alliances with other caudillos, which led to a short-lived period of calm in the country. He introduced innovations into public administration and communication, created incentives for foreign investment, and promoted the development of a nationalist consciousness. Guzmán was an autocratic leader who combined strong authoritarianism with an equally strong adherence to French liberal thought; he was, consequently, a man who thought that the church was a source of social ills and an obstacle to his political goals of modernization. For this reason, Guzmán closed convents and seminaries, banned the immigration of clergy, introduced civil marriage, and gave it priority over its ecclesiastical equivalent. He expelled the archbishop of Caracas and put an end to the by now precarious financial independence of the church. His attempt to create his own enlightened church was thwarted only through direct intervention by the Vatican, which negotiated an agreement in terms markedly unfavorable to the church.

Without doubt Guzmán almost totally destroyed the Venezuelan church. In 1881, only 393 priests remained in the country; in 1810 there had been 547 in Caracas alone. The church's cultural influence had dwindled to the point of near insignificance, and a weakened popular Catholicism survived beyond any institutional control. Earlier we defined the principal characteristics of the Venezuelan church as its organizational decentralization and lack of solidity. At the end of the nineteenth century decentralization had become disastrous and decline was at its lowest ebb. Never was the social influence of the church weaker than at this time.

In these circumstances, it is understandable that the principal goal of the Venezuelan church in the twentieth century has been reconstruction. The strategy for accomplishing this reconstruction has included accepting the rules imposed by the state, strengthening religious practice within the church, and dependence on the Vatican. Each of these will be dealt with in turn.

In 1908, Juan Gómez seized power by force and retained it until his death in 1935. Venezuelan society was on the threshold of development. Having been until then a static, rural society, almost totally incapable of generating any economic surplus, it would henceforth begin to undergo the transformation caused by oil production. The state income gained from this production would allow it to expand and play an increasing role in all aspects of Venezuelan life.

Gómez, the most powerful dictator in the history of Venezuela, showed a benevolent attitude toward the church. Allowing it to coexist with the state so long as it refrained from involving itself in politics, he availed himself of the existing Law of Patronage. From the closing years of the last century, some religious orders had entered the country after the end of the Guzmán period. In 1890 a Catholic newspaper, *La religión*, appeared, and in 1900 the seminary of Caracas reopened. Under the Gómez regime, four new dioceses were established, and public debates even began to take place between positivistic scientists and newly surfaced Catholic intellectuals.

However, the main instrument through which the church regained prominence in society—as well as in politics—was education. Most of the recently arrived religious orders made strong and systematic efforts in the educational field, establishing numerous and important schools. A substantial part of the emerging urban middle class attended these schools and absorbed religious values. Although we will return to this matter later, for the moment let us examine the other elements in the church's strategy of reconstruction: the consolidation of local religious practice and the strong dependence on the Vatican.

The pastoral statement of 1904 throws these characteristics into relief more effectively than anything else. The first Latin American Council, held in Rome in 1899, had adopted measures designed to preserve and defend the Catholic faith in Latin America from socialism, freemasonry, and superstition. These measures were implemented in each country by local bishops, and in Venezuela the outcome was a pastoral statement that retained much of the apologetic and defensive tone of the Council; its main features were an ecclesiocentric perspective and an emphasis on orthodoxy and hierarchical relations. The document embodies a sense of nostalgia for the medieval relationship between church and society, a nostalgia for the rule of Christendom, even though it concedes the duty to obey the political leadership "even in the most unjust circumstances."

The statement provided the main normative guidelines for developing the church and training Venezuelan clergy until at least the middle of the 1960s. Let us return to education, however, the main instrument of reconstruction. Catholic schools had been responsible for educating a large proportion of the rising middle class. During this time Venezuelan society underwent a complex and rapid process of development: new elites appeared, modern institutions such as trade unions and (most important) political parties proliferated, the state expanded, and the economy, dominated by oil, began to diversify.

The efforts of the church were beginning to bear fruit. In 1936 a group of students from Catholic colleges founded the National Union of Students (UNE), an organization directed at defending Catholic institutions and values in the political arena in opposition to the previously founded Federation of Venezuelan Students (FEV). The FEV was strongly influenced by Acción Democrática (AD), an emerging political party that, although not actually communist, was strongly Marxist in origin and whose educational philosophy was emphatically opposed to any religious influence over education. Later the UNE became a political party of its own known as COPEI (1946).

From 1935 to 1940, Venezuela was governed by López Contreras, and between 1941 and 1945 by Medina Angarita. Both were military officers who had supported Gómez; but during their respective leaderships they made attempts to democratize the country, attenuating the more repressive characteristics of the Gómez regime and opening up restricted but new channels of participation. These efforts, however, were seen as inadequate by the rising political leadership, especially that of AD, which accused the government of not going far enough in its reforms and demanded a completely open electoral campaign. As soon as it became clear that the government would impose its own candidate in the subsequent presidential period, a civilian/military coup installed a new government in 1945, with political power shared between AD and a group of young officers; this government lasted for three years during the period known in Venezuela as "el Trienio" (1945-1948).

The chuch-state relationship during this period is particularly important, given that for the first time since the birth of the republic, a conflict with the government had a favorable outcome for the church. For the first time also, the conflict involved the mass of the population, and broad social forces participated both for and against the church; in fact, a political party with wholly Catholic interests and values became involved. The conflict centered on the right of the state to supervise examinations in Catholic schools. For the AD government, the possibility of limiting and increasingly reducing the influence of the church in education was at stake; for the church, it meant the defense of what was proving to be its most successful instrument of influence and reconstruction for half a century. Street demonstrations, parliamentary debates, and intense campaigns for public opinion took place, and the conflict had still not been resolved when a military coup displaced AD from power in 1948, heralding a period of military dictatorship during which political opposition was prohibited. In this way, the church was one of various social forces that contributed to the downfall of the AD government.[3]

At the same time, however, the church was still a weak social organization; there was still a major shortage of clergy, and the Catholic faith of the masses remained beyond control. But the strategy of reconstruction had been successful. Catholic loyalties were forged in certain sectors of the elites, and in the years to come it would no longer be possible to attack the Venezuelan church directly.

During the military dictatorship (1948-1958), church organization grew. The laws preventing the immigration of clergy were revoked, six new dioceses were established, and the military government's lack of concern over public education was exploited by the expansion of the Catholic educational system, including the founding of a Catholic University under the responsibility of the Jesuits. In the meantime, the church hierarchy lent its tacit—and sometimes overt—support to the dictatorship.

Church and Democracy in Contemporary Venezuela

The year 1958 was one of the most important in contemporary Venezuelan history. In that year, the military government of General Pérez Jiménez was overthrown by the action of a broad-based social movement which included unions, political parties (mostly clandestine), business groups, sections of the army, and, surprisingly, the church. The church had, of course, made considerable headway during the decade of military dictatorship. There were no apparent reasons for antagonism between the church and the government, so long as they both recognized that politics was not a legitimate area of concern for the church. In fact, the regime pursued a strongly repressive policy against members of political parties and against any citizen who publicly expressed criticism or undertook any form of opposition. Meanwhile, the church turned a blind eye to these proceedings and concentrated on its own organizational growth.

Suddenly, toward the end of 1957, the church acquired a reputation as a critic of the government when the archbishop of Caracas, Rafael Arias Blanco, issued a pastoral letter on the subject of unemployment which the government considered unacceptable. In all probability, this pastoral letter was not specifically oppositional in intent, and it is likely that the government exaggerated its importance. When, however, in January the dictatorship was overthrown, the church was in fact viewed as one of the forces that had contributed to political change. In this way, during the democratic period begun in 1958, the Venezuelan church achieved its strongest position in Venezuelan society; insofar as democracy has shown great stability and durability, this position has been a lasting one. It is important to consider the nature of this position and how it was achieved.

After the fall of the dictatorship, an open electoral campaign was organized in which political parties competed for parliamentary seats and for the presidency. Prior to this, a broad agreement, known as the Pacto de Punto Fijo (Fixed-Point Pact), had been reached and included not only political parties but also other social groupings (unions, businessmen, students, the armed forces). The pact committed its signatories to abide by the election result, and committed the winning party to form a coalition government with the losers. In the event, Rómulo Betancourt, the AD's presidential candidate and head of the government during the Trienio of 1945–1948 won the election, respected the agreement, and initiated a regular sequence of freely elected governments and a political system that has continued to the present. The church quickly adjusted to the new regime, and the process was facilitated by the AD government in various ways. It is worthwhile focusing briefly on this period, since it sheds light on the subsequent political and organizational policy of the Venezuelan church.

First, a decisive change had taken place in the attitude of the AD leaders toward the church and in particular toward its educational role. Since the educational conflict with the church had been one of the crucial factors weakening the AD government in 1948, Betancourt opted for a policy of toleration in this area, with a view to avoiding any conflict with the church. For this reason, he began to negotiate an agreement with the Vatican aimed at abolishing the Law of Patronage, which was achieved in 1964 when the *modus vivendi* came into operation. The Law of Patronage, it will be recalled, had been instrumental in the state's subjugation of the church since 1830, and its abolition was thus enthusiastically received by the church hierarchy.

Apart from this, the inclusion of COPEI in the government gave the church additional grounds for trusting the regime and, in particular, guaranteed that its educational interests would be safeguarded. Meanwhile, the coalition as a whole sharply distanced itself from leftist parties, and AD in particular cut all its possible remaining ties with Marxism. Last, the government committed the state to financing church activity, a sensitive move in view of the economic weakness of the Venezuelan church.

During this time, the church committed itself to unconditional support of the democratic regime. Specifically, this support entailed the dissemination of a political discourse in which the church placed itself above any political position and ideology, while at the same time affirming its refusal to compromise in day-to-day politics and its faith in the supreme virtues of democracy as this existed in the country. As Donald Levine has noted, for the hierarchy, political noninvolvement consisted in abstaining from open support for any particular party, but this did not preclude its lending general support to the regime in itself.[4]

There are nevertheless two ways in which the church's apolitical stance has been inconsistent. First, it has openly rejected all Marxist movements or parties in Venezuelan politics. This factor is important given that, particularly in the 1960s, the leftist parties adopted guerrilla tactics as the main route to power and succeeded in posing a serious threat to the Betancourt government, taking measures that were strongly condemned by the bishops. Second, COPEI, which had originated in the 1940s from the activity of students in Catholic colleges, received unofficial but substantial support from almost every priest or religious minister in Venezuela, at least until the end of the 1960s.

These, in summary, were the terms of understanding between the church and the democratic regime, and this understanding has proved to be both strong and stable. There have, indeed, been no conflicts between the two sides since 1960, and it can be said with some certainty that the church has achieved credibility under the democratic regime and has completed its process of reconstruction. The church, and the hierarchy in particular, have developed a strong attachment and loyalty to the democracy and a strong sense of gratitude toward a regime that has allowed it to regain a place in Venezuelan society. This factor exercised a major influence on the development of the institutional church; I will try to define the nature of this influence in what follows.

An initial glance at purely quantitative indicators shows that the 1960s were a period of expansion for the church. In 1970 there were eight more dioceses, 182 more parishes, and 728 more priests than in 1960. Such figures indicate that the formal structures of the church were rapidly expanding, a process that was taking place all over the country, including certain regions and places from which the church had long been absent. At the same time, the Venezuelan church's traditional decentralization was counteracted by new organizations such as the Venezuelan Episcopal Conference and the Venezuelan Federation of Religious.

However, if the growth of the clergy is studied in more detail, some interesting characteristics become apparent. Only a small minority of the clergy (18.4%) were actually born in Venezuela, and more than half of these belonged to religious orders. The first characteristic indicates that the expansion of the clergy was due to an intensive process of clerical immigration—mainly from Spain, Italy, Belgium, and France; it also indicates that a large proportion of those responsible for running the church at the local level were newcomers to Venezuelan society and culture. In sharp contrast with Colombia, there was a marked dearth of vocations, and the bishops opted for a massive injection of European clergy in preference to the alternative of stagnation. A second characteristic should be interpreted from a historical perspective. The process of reconstruction had been carried out principally by religious orders whose starting point was a situation in which ecclesiastical structures were weak and in total disarray. Consequently, the orders maintained their quantitative and qualitative importance in relation to the diocesan clergy even after the process of reconstruction was complete. The Venezuelan bishops thus lacked any direct control over the majority of clergy in the country, and what control they did have was at best tenuous. The bishops were aware of this. In the meantime, the Second Vatican Council had taken place. On the one hand, newly arrived young European priests had been trained in—or were at least well disposed toward—the spirit of *aggiornamento*, while on the other, the bishops were in principle open to change and reform. Nevertheless, as soon as the immigrant clergy began to get acquainted with the country and to take initiatives with regard to social action or the renewal of the church, the bishops reacted negatively, thus preventing any possibility of renewal. To understand this process better, it is necessary to look more closely at the currents at work in the Venezuelan church.

We have already seen how the main preoccupations of the hierarchy during the 1960s were to maintain a working relationship with the democratic regime and to increase the number of clergy working in the country. However, Venezuelan Catholicism was in need of far more. The only systematic survey carried out in the country on popular religion during this time concluded that

> 78 per cent of those interviewed described their religious practice in terms of traditional norms and customs, while only 7 per cent used metaphysical terms, 16 per cent utilitarian terms, 26 per cent terms of obedience to practical norms and customs. A full 52 per cent described their religious faith as one which really had no explanations at all, or where tradition was regarded as paramount.
>
> The sense of belonging to the Catholic church is, consequently, broadly distributed but at the same time very diffuse and flexible. It is clear from all this that religious practice is undoubtedly Catholic in nature (at least implicitly), but this does not mean that the Catholic church as an institution exercises any control over these practices. The church is a reference point rather than something which is genuinely belonged to.[5]

For the hierarchy, however, the Venezuelan people were by definition Catholic; belonging to the church was synonymous with belonging to Venezuelan society itself. As a result, the problems outlined in the above quotation—the need for a pastoral program aimed at promoting religious belief rather than consolidating it—lay outside the bishops' immediate concerns. Pastoral activity was directed first toward cultivating Catholic values in the middle and upper classes—the main focus of the much-vaunted strategy of reconstruction to which most available resources were undoubtedly aimed. It was also directed toward a widespread administering of the sacraments, the main purpose of which was to demonstrate and to confirm the supposed breadth and solidity of Venezuelan Catholic culture.

Significantly, however, some priests became aware of the problems: increasingly dissatisfied with the existing state of affairs, they began to seek illumination for their practices and to promote change in line with the teachings of the Council. By the time of the Second Latin American Episcopal Council held at Medellín in 1968, certain clerical and lay communities in Venezuela were already beginning to adopt a more questioning attitude.

A survey carried out in 1966 among the clergy of Caracas revealed a wide range of Catholic identities among the priests, including a significant number of groups at either end of the radical-reactionary spectrum. It concluded:

> it may be said that all the different attitudes described, even the most radical, nevertheless remained within the institutional church. The position of each (especially at the level of the two most extreme groups, groups 1 and 2 classed as traditional and groups 7 and 8 classed as reformist), is sufficiently consistent for the groups to argue among themselves and to mutually challenge each others' positions, each believing that it has adopted a more authentic form of Christianity.[6]

Indeed, during the second half of the 1960s and at the beginning of the 1970s, a conflict of a rather different sort took place within the Venezuelan church in which sections within the church itself were opposed to each other rather than to the state. The conflict did not involve a protest movement organized on a large scale and coherent in its diverse aspects and activities; it can best be understood as a series of skirmishes and episodes that were not always closely interconnected but that were related inasmuch as they highlighted the existence of conflicting viewpoints concerning the Catholic church's mission in Venezuelan society.

In this way, lay groups without much substance and almost invariably composed of young people, organized church sit-ins and public demonstrations to pressure the hierarchy to adopt a firmer social commitment. Groups of priests in various cities of the country identified with innovative ideas from the Council and from Medellín. They even succeeded in organizing a national congress, although a clerical movement on the scale of the ONIS in Peru or the GOLCONDA in Colombia was never formally established. Open letters were sent to the bishops demanding a clearer commitment to social justice and to the poor and challenging their unconditional support for the existing regime. At a more official level, some teachers sought to introduce new theological perspectives in seminaries, while others pressed for a pastoral program of renovation and for an end to discrimination against foreign clergy. Even the normally placid Catholic University was shaken by a major conflict that led to its temporary closure, a denunciation by the authorities, and a parliamentary inquiry.

It is impossible to discuss the mechanics of the conflict in detail, but it should be noted that after its initial indecision and surprise, the hierarchy's response was to close down all channels of dialogue and to put an end to any possibility of reform. The clerical movement was dismantled and its members dispersed if not actually expelled from the country; seminaries were purged of teachers in favor of reform, and the implementation of the joint pastoral program was indefinitely postponed. To understand the force and the unanimity of the hierarchy's response, it is important to bear in mind that the push for reform came at the worst possible time as had Medellín itself in the context of the church's position in Venezuelan society.

It should be remembered that the protests and attempts at reform at the grassroots level, together with the notions of liberation elaborated at Medellín, reached Venezuela at just the moment when the Venezuelan church leaders thought they had realized the principal goal of all their efforts of the previous 150 years, namely, the recovery of a respectable and secure place in Venezuelan society and politics, which would allow them to operate without constraint. The bishops had of course inherited a long history of humiliation by the state and saw the excellent relationship which the two had achieved under the democratic regime established in 1958 as their main historical achievement. In a context such as this, any disruption of the internal harmony of the church tended to be interpreted, first of all, as imperiling its unity, which was seen as its indispensable bastion in a world that until recently had been hostile to it, and second, as a disruption which could lead the Venezuelan elite to revert to its former opinion that the church was a source of problems for the political order.

In addition to this general position it should also be said that the internal conflict of the Venezuelan church developed at the very time when President Rafael Caldera, the first member of COPEI to become president, was in office. In this way, just when many church people could see their dream of a man from a Christian party achieving power come true, the unanimity over choice of party, which until that point had prevailed among Catholics, was called into question.

The result was complete mutual incomprehension between factions and an almost complete recovery by the bishops of control over every single aspect of church organization, particularly the training of new priests. Given the low number of native vocations, the prospects of promotion were relatively high for the small number of indigenous priests; it was, after all, illegal for a foreign priest to become a bishop, and this, together with the tight control over training, clearly tended to produce conformity.

This conclusion, however, requires some qualification because of an additional element: most of those in favor of change did not choose to leave the institutional church, but tacitly retained their convictions while remaining within it, for the most part engaged in social work with the poor, while at the same time keeping up with the progress of liberating Christianity in Latin America. Recent evidence shows that this involvement is still minor and relatively undeveloped compared with the activity of the church as a whole, which continues to be primarily directed toward the middle and upper social classes.[7] This should not detract, however, from the very significant progress that has taken place in the opposite direction.

Toward the Future

The picture we have drawn of the Venezuelan church has shown it to be a church marked by a precarious and chaotic past that is finally at peace with the prevailing political system and at the same time relatively backward in most pastoral and organizational respects. What becomes clear from this social and historical analysis is that conservatism can arise not only in situations where the church wields vast social power and is deeply involved in the system of social domination (as, for example, in Colombia) but also in situations where the church is extremely weak in both sociocultural and political terms. Not only the first but also the second form of social context can produce, albeit by different routes, factors that strongly inhibit change and renewal in the church.

It should be added that the social context experienced by the Venezuelan church exhibits certain features which, to say the least, make it atypical of Latin America as a whole. The society is one of late socioeconomic development in which social organizations, apart from political parties, are weak. There is little tradition of social involvement and there are great variations in the standards of living among different classes. The society has been accustomed to living in recent decades with a certain material abundance made possible by oil resources, an abundance that, while it has not been primarily used for the benefit of a privileged elite, has certainly not been used for the benefit of the underprivileged masses. From a political point of view, since 1958 the country has enjoyed a democracy that is open and tolerant of any political opposition. Although in many cases the state does restrict participation by its citizens to voting every five years, the regime has achieved a high degree of credibility, which has enabled it to govern the country peacefully (apart from the guerrilla conflict of the 1960s) and which seems to assure its continuation into the future.[8]

In this way, the absence in Venezuela of a strong movement of popular Catholicism—along the lines of the base communities in Brazil, for example—should in no way be attributed only to the very specific characteristics of the Venezuelan church's organization and to the political bias of its leaders. The elements outlined above have also had a great effect on the way the Catholic church in Venezuela has developed.

The specificities of both Venezuelan society and of the church, and the brand of Catholicism within it, collectively provide a topic of sufficient interest to justify study and further exploration in the future.

NOTES

1. The "Cabildos" were decision-making bodies for local government during the colonial period. Their members belonged to the wealthier groups of landowners and traders in colonial society, known as "Criollos" (creoles), and provided the only official representation of local interests against the authorities that came directly from Spain, and with which they frequently came into conflict.

2. For an informative and complete study of the situation of the Venezuelan church during the republican period, see Mary Watters, *A History of the Church in Venezuela: 1810–1930* (New York: AMS Press, 1971).

3. An excellent description and analysis of the church–state conflict during the Trienio, together with the appropriate sociopolitical contextualization, can be found in Donald H. Levine, *Conflict and Political Change in Venezuela* (Princeton, N.J.: Princeton University Press, 1973).

4. See Donald H. Levine, "Democracy and the Church." In *Venezuela, the Democratic Experience*, ed. J. Martz and D. J. Myers (New York: Praeger Publishers, 1977). See also Levine, *Religion and Politics in Latin America* (Princeton, N.J.: Princeton University Press, 1981).

5. CISOR, *Religiosidad Popular e Iglesia como Institución* (Caracas: Mimeo, 1970), pp. 13–14. CISOR (Centro de Investigaciones Socio-Religiosas) is a social research center which the Venezuelan church helped to found in the 1960s. This center, and in particular its director, Fr. Alberto Gruson, have been responsible for most of the sociological research into Venezuelan Catholicism.

6. CISOR, *Consulta a los Sacerdotes sobre Renovación Conciliar en Venezuela* (Caracas: Mimeo, 1966), pp. 6–7.

7. See M. Parra and M. G. Ponce, *Renovación y Opción en la Vida Religiosa: Semántica de la Opción Social de los Religiosos a partir de una Encuesta en Caracas* (Caracas: Mimeo, Universidad Católica Andrés Bello, 1986).

8. For a detailed study of the links between the peculiarities of contemporary Venezuelan society and the church, see Otto Maduro, "La Spécificité politique du catholicisme vénézuélien" (Mexico: Mimeo, presented at the Tenth World Sociology Conference, 1982).

17

East, Central, and Southern Africa

Adrian Hastings

The Second Vatican Council's impact upon Africa can be understood only in the context of two other processes already well developed when it began: one religious, the other political.[1] The modern Christian history of black Africa goes back, depending on the part of the continent one is considering, only to the middle of the nineteenth century, its final decades, or even the first decades of the twentieth century. It is by and large a history of response to the nineteenth-century missionary movement, which got going earlier in the Protestant than in the Catholic world. The presence of the Catholic church in Africa at the close of the nineteenth century was still extremely limited, though it was beginning to grow quite rapidly in the context of a new colonial order imposed on most of the continent between 1880 and 1900.

It was only in the wake of World War II that the scale of religious change, occurring within the context of the rapid colonial modernization of other aspects of social life, above all education, became fully evident. The 1950s were the high point of a new, mostly benign, colonialism endeavoring to get the young nations of Africa onto their feet in a Western sort of way as quickly as possible. That was also the decade when the Catholic missionary movement was at its most confident, most innovative, and most numerous in personnel. The Catholic church in black Africa in the 1950s advanced rapidly in numbers, in the range of its institutions, and in the competence of its ministry. It was still, undoubtedly, overwhelmingly led by whites. There had never before been nearly so many foreign missionaries in Africa. They came from more and more countries and from more and more different religious orders and societies, including a quickly growing number of lay people. The appeal of Africa in the 1950s was very great and the response within the Catholic church was unprec-

308

edented, often to the bewildered alarm of Protestant churches and mission societies who were unable to field so many. But it was also, and increasingly, a black-led advance. The Catholic missionary effort in Africa had long been authoritarian, and in most places it had been distinctly slow to look for any black initiative above the level of catechist. Only in a few areas, most notably the White Father missions around the great lakes, was there an African clergy of any considerable number in 1950. Only in the vicariate of Masaka in Uganda was there, at that date, a black bishop, Joseph Kiwanuka. By the death of Pius XII in 1958, he had been joined by just twenty more, of whom half were auxiliaries. In 1958, of over 200 Latin dioceses and vicariates, only eleven were ruled by an African. Not one of the latter was in Zaire (then the Belgian Congo), the giant of Catholic Africa, though there were by then over 300 African priests in that country.

Everywhere major seminaries were enlarged, new minor seminaries opened, just as new congregations of African Sisters were founded, new secondary schools established. There was nothing very radical or in wider Roman Catholic terms unconventional in these developments. Neither black nor white in Catholic Africa at that time was theologically or pastorally creative or radical. Seminary teaching was conventionally neoscholastic in the extreme. It is true that in 1956 a small group of young black priests in Rome and Paris published a challenging collection of essays, *Des prêtres noirs s'interrogent*. They had been stimulated while abroad by the *nouvelle théologie* of France and Belgium as well as by the new winds of black nationalism. But little indeed of this had got back to the general run of an African diocese by the day Pius XII died. January 1959 saw the start of an important new quarterly, *The African Ecclesiastical Review,* for the whole of English-speaking Africa, edited from the seminary of Katigondo, Uganda. Its spirit represented all that was best in the upsurge of the Catholic church in Africa: a new openness, certainly; a new concern for the lay apostolate, for an adapted catechetics, for a more participative liturgy; but nothing very radical, certainly nothing to disturb the sleep of the Roman Curia. For many years the *African Ecclesiastical Review,* despite the genuine efforts of its White Father editor, Joop Geerdes, was almost entirely written by white people. Clearly any sort of ecclesiastical renaissance had far to go.

Nevertheless, the material was very much there, together with a cautious but increasingly widespread sense of need for more radical change — a genuine Africanization of this, in all sorts of ways, still terribly Western, Latin, unadapted church. The missionary movement to Africa had developed in the decades after Vatican I, in the highest period of ultramontanism, and the missionary societies were almost to a man ultramontanist in their theology. It was a Roman church they were bent upon establishing in the utterly different world of Africa with its thousand languages and tribal division, its poverty and illiteracy, its marriage practices so very far away from those of canon law, its endless network of little villages largely inaccessible in the rainy season, its own amorphous but powerful world of beliefs in ancestral spirits, witches, rain-makers, all integrally related to the cycle of season and human development. The growth of the church did not necessarily mean the decrease of all these things. Indeed, as the church grew faster and faster, the tight early clerical control over its functioning and the lives of its members was inevitably relaxed, so that a new existential mix — Catholic and traditional — became more apparent. Hence the 1950s, if an era of great achievement, was also an era in which the problems of the young church were becoming more and more obvious. Therefore, there was an obvious need for new approaches, for an Africanization of Catholic Christianity instead of a mere inposition of forms long developed elsewhere.

That was, clearly enough, the point reached when John XXIII became pope and, almost simultaneously, the *African Ecclesiastical Review* appeared from Uganda to call, mildly but insistently, for an African *aggiornamento*. But, of course, all this had now to happen within a far wider secular and political opening of windows: the colonial age was about to end. World War II; the decline in power of Britain, France, and Belgium; the ideology and activities of the United Nations Organization; the decolonization of Asia; all this and much else had produced pressures that brought the formal period of colonial rule to an end in most of black Africa in the early 1960s. There was a period of hasty economic, educational, and political preparation, both producing and deriving from new nationalisms, taking the form of a range of political parties, some progressive, others conservative or tribal in base. Effectively, by the later 1950s all the European powers ruling parts of Africa, except for Portugal, had decided that it was better to pull out in an atmosphere of good will than to fight both black nationalism and world opinion. The Suez Crisis of late 1956 was perhaps the point at which a policy of retaining African colonies was seen to be unrealistic. 1960 was the "Year of Africa" in which the Belgian Congo became independent in June and Nigeria in December, black Africa's two largest and most populous countries. Twelve other states of West Africa from Senegal to Congo (Brazzaville), formerly ruled by France, became independent the same year. They were followed by Tanganyika (now Tanzania) in 1961; Rwanda, Burundi, and Uganda in 1962; Kenya in 1963; Malawi and Zambia in 1964. This meant that the years of the Second Vatican Council and its preparation were years of extraordinarily rapid and complete political change: white governors disappeared almost overnight, black presidents took over their residences. Old flags were pulled down, new ones appeared. On the surface there was an extraordinary reversal of the previous order of things (a reversal, of course, wholly rejected in the south of the continent, from the Zambezi to the Cape). It was, however, in most places a remarkably peaceful and optimistic reversal. It was believed that this score or more of new states with their Western constitutions and very small educated elites were truly viable economically and politically. It was obvious, quite apart from the Council or any specific ecclesiastical policy of Africanization, that the churches had to respond to the new situation. White archbishops fitted well enough into the old colonial order. They stuck out like sore thumbs as heads of the church in the new world of Nkrumah, Mobutu, Kenyatta, and Nyerere.

Inevitably the political revolution was accompanied by a cultural one. In and for the young universities of Africa, history was being rewritten as something achieved by Africans themselves instead of something done by explorers and colonialists in Africa. African novels and plays were published—by Achebe, Ngugi, and Soyinka. African philosophies of society were produced by Nkrumah, Nyerere, and Kaunda. For the most part, friendly as the new order was to the main mission churches—most of its leaders had, after all, been educated in church schools, while some had been seminarians or even priests—it clearly called for a considerable change on their part: a change in personalities at the level of leadership, but a change also in ethos, in priorities, in the sense of relationship to African tradition, culture, and identity.

There was, then, an almost millennial sense of renewal in much of Africa in the early 1960s. That sense was, in its central thrust, or at least in the intention of its overt political leaders, secular enough. It could see religion with its multiple separa-tions between Christian, Moslem, and traditionalist, between Catholic and Protestant, mission church and independent church, as divisive enough, something for which there should not be too much place in the new nationalist political kingdom. The millenarian sense could also take a religious form hostile to the mission churches to produce in Zambia the *Lumpa* Church of Alice Lenshina, in Kenya the *Legio Maria* Church of Simeon Ondeto, and many others. It was, then, a moment of excitement, expectation, potential instability. But it was not, except marginally, antimissionary, and most of the new political leaders realized how much in the fields of education and health they needed the cooperation of the major churches. In providing such services the Catholic commitment was second to none.

All this meant that Pope John XXIII's announcement of an ecumenical council in January 1959 and the actual sessions of the Council between 1962 and 1965 responded in Africa to a situation very different from that almost anywhere else. The mood of the Council, its optimistic image of *aggiornamento* and the opening of win-dows, fitted extraordinarily well with the wider mood of Africa. The forward march, the vigor, an increasing sense of the need for new directions in the missionary church of the 1950s meant that, in an efficient but mostly quite untheoretical way, there was an ecclesial dynamism available to be harnessed to the new vision. In the early and mid 1960s other churches simply had neither the resources nor the sudden sense of a new wind, which the Catholic church experienced at this point, with which to respond to the new postcolonial situation.

Thus the 1960s may be seen as the high point of African Catholic history. Pre-viously, especially in British Africa, the Protestant missions had appeared to call the tune: they were both politically more akin to the British Colonial State, and intellec-tually more advanced in tackling the problems of Africanization. The African theo-logians of the 1960s—Harry Sawyerr, Bolaji Idowu, John Mbiti, and others—were mostly Anglicans, Methodists, or Presbyterians. The Catholic church in Africa had, hitherto, largely eschewed discussion of the problems of culture, marital practice, and traditional belief with which the more thoughtful leaders of other churches had long been wrestling. But now suddenly, galvanized by the Council, on the one hand, and political independence, on the other, and increasingly conscious of its own resources and strength, Catholicism entered into the debates and, for a while, with a vigor all its own. The years of the Council and immediately after the Council were for many Catholics in Africa a particularly exhilarating time, if often confusing and frustrating. Of course, that was not only true in Africa. It was the suddenness of it in Africa and the apparent providentiality with which the Council and its new guidelines responded to the secular needs of the postindependence situation that were special.

It is also true, however, that the ethos of the Council came through less easily to many remote dioceses of Africa than to those in more technically developed parts of the world. There were almost no *periti* from Africa and far fewer newspapers and journals to spread the news of day-to-day conciliar happenings. Most African Cath-olics knew no European language. For a long while the sermons of rural priests and, still more, rural catechists were almost unaffected. Yet as the majority of bishops were Europeans—especially French, Dutch, Germans, and Belgians—they were naturally in touch at the Council with the bishops and *periti* of their home countries, so that the missionary church tended naturally to learn from and side with the more progressive forces at the Council, whose message they saw anyway as pastorally appropriate for the dioceses of Africa. Theirs was not a major voice within the Council,[2] but they spoke responsibly and organized themselves effectively, thanks largely to moderate progressives like the Dutch bishop of Mwanza in Tanzania, Mgr. Blomjous, the South African archbishop of Durban, Denis Hurley, or Jean Zoa, a young African archbishop from Cameroon who just a few years before had been one of the slightly rebellious group of *Prêtres noirs* who published the symposium in 1956 that had so upset the old hands (several other contributors to the book were also now bishops). Already too, however, a certain division of sympathy started to appear. If some missionary bishops identified easily with the more progressive bishops of northern Europe, there were at least some African bishops whose training had been in Rome and who identified almost entirely with a Roman view of things. Their theology was wholly Roman and a certain caution made them feel that in practice diversification in the immensely subdivided world of tribal Africa could only lead to disaster. The unity of Latin and an unadapted canon law obscured the myriad problems of countries, including scores of different languages and cultural practices. Once one began to adapt to traditional culture where would it end?[3] Was polygamy, for instance, to be permitted? Ever since the Council, one of the complexities of the African Catholic quandary has been that the very scale of the case for Africanization provides an argument for its rejection, and this argument appeals particularly to some of the principal Roman-selected leaders of the African church, men like Cardinals Laurean Rugambwa of Dar es Salaam and Maurice Otunga of Nairobi.

The rapid implementation of important areas of the Council's constitution and decrees was, nevertheless, decisive for the future character of African Catholicism. Nowhere had the liturgical changes greater impact. It was fortunate that the decision to adopt the vernacular in the liturgy came after, and not before, political independence. If it had come in the 1950s, in the colonial period, it would have been hard not to agree to the celebration of mass in an almost unlimited number of tribal languages. Many were in fact accepted for liturgical use in the 1960s, but guidance could now to some extent be taken from the policy of the new states, anxious to unify rather than divide. This made it easier for the church to choose the overarching vernaculars, like Swahili, for use over a large area. Nevertheless, the number of African languages in which mass was being celebrated by the end of the decade was very great and the effect, in the transformation of worship, was enormous. With the vernacular went in many places several other, not unconnected things: a rehabilitation and extension of lay ministry for the thousands of priestless village communities, a reshaping of catechesis, and a musical revolution—the use of the drum and the development of African hymn styles in place of Western translations. It may seem odd, but it is probably true that in popular terms the most important single effect in Africa of the Council has been the change in singing, in hymns, in music, in the use of musical instruments.[4] The preconciliar African church had set its heart on the possession of a harmonium. The postconciliar African church glories in its use of drums.

The transformation of the liturgy in terms of popular participation was only part of a far wider pastoral revolution. With a Catholic population rising by 5 percent a year or more, an already bad and steadily worsening priest–people ratio, the increasing loss of control over church schools to the state, it was absolutely necessary to rejuvenate the already traditional pastoral shape of the African church. Its cornerstone from the end of the nineteenth century had been the village catechist. He, and he alone, had ensured regular prayer and a measure of simple instruction in the vast majority of village churches and primary schools. To begin with, he had been the school teacher himself, but then the two roles had split, the catechist remaining a churchman and a pastor, poorly paid if at all and poorly educated, while the teacher had improved in status, pay, and education but had become in due course a government-contracted professional. For a while, in the 1940s and 1950s, the church had almost completely given up training catechists in its preoccupation with schools and the meeting of government requirements. But then the schools themselves slipped away and the 1960s witnessed a massive rediscovery of the catechist, a reopening of catechist training schools, and a series of studies on the practice and even theology of this form of ministry.[5]

In addition to the catechist training centers, major new regional pastoral institutes, such as those at Lumku in South Africa, Kinshasa in Zaire, Abidjan in the Ivory Coast, and Gaba in Uganda, were opened. These have been the key institutions of the postconciliar African church in which every aspect of a new pastoral policy has been worked over. Crucial again was an alteration in attitude to the translation and use of the Bible. The preconciliar contrast between Catholic and Protestant biblical translations into African languages was striking indeed. In hardly any language had Catholics translated the complete Bible. In East Africa there were just three Catholic translations of the complete New Testament to stand against many complete Protestant Bibles and nearly fifty New Testaments.[6] The Pan-African Catechetical Study Week, meeting at Katigondo in Uganda in September 1964, passed as its first and most memorable resolution a plea to the hierarchies of all African territories to work together with the Protestant authorities for the early publication of both the Old and the New Testament in versions adequate both exegetically and linguistically.[7] Meanwhile it requested that Catholics be permitted to make use of Protestant editions. This was a truly revolutionary proposal. Hitherto Catholics had been almost everywhere forbidden to read a Protestant Bible. Within a couple of years after the Council, the Secretariat of Christian Unity came to a formal agreement with the Bible Societies, and Catholics joined translation teams set up by the Bible Societies in many parts of Africa.

This illustrates another aspect of what was happening: the rapid transformation in relations with Protestants. Previously these had varied. In some places they were courteous enough; in many others they had been characterized by bitter rivalry in which each side thought the very worst of the other. Catholics regarded Protestants as communists in disguise, Protestants denied that Catholics were Christians; each saw the other as an enemy comparable to Islam. The change in the course of the 1960s went far in places, particularly in the area of theological education, cooperation in the use of mass media, and scripture translation. Of course, at the grassroots level in most places relations had always been good, in that most ordinary families were divided according to what school they had attended. Vast numbers of marriages were mixed marriages between Catholic and Protestant, but as a dispensation was seldom given, this would normally mean their permanent subsequent exclusion from communion. Yet again, as so many other good Christians were excluded from communion for one reason or another (in many cases simply because they had not solemnized their marriage in church but only in customary form), the state of those in mixed marriages was in no way exceptional. It simply demonstrated how remote the formal canonical shape of the church was from the reality of popular Christian life.[8]

Finally, the Council brought about a considerable shift in the concern of the institutional church toward "development" work. This did not begin with the Council, but it was now much enlarged, particularly because far greater funds were henceforth available from Western countries for projects of this kind. Misereor and its likes became a dominant force in the life of the postconciliar African church. Hospitals had always been a high mission priority, but to these were now added agricultural and cooperative projects of one sort and another. Bishop Blomjous's Social Training Center at Nyegezi in Mwanza symbolized the new concern even if it predated the Council.

It has to be said in honesty that in almost all the things we have been speaking of, which so characterized the period up to the early 1970s, white priests took the lead. In the direction of the Pastoral Institutes and special study projects, editing journals, organizing renewal conferences, writing books about the renewal of African Catholicism characteristic of the time, it was almost always white missionaries who were still in front: Ton Simons, Eugene Hillman, Bernard Joinet, Aylward Shorter, to mention a few from East Africa. It was certainly a weakness in the whole movement. Up to 1968 in most countries there was still a majority of white bishops. This suddenly changed in the next two or three years, not so much as a result of the Council as of two other factors. One was the political realization that a white bishop was now an anomaly. The number of African priests had risen in most dioceses, and it seemed politically and pastorally opportune for the missionary to resign and for an African to take over. The second factor was different. By the end of the 1960s Rome was becoming alarmed by the radicalization of the reform program being proposed in Africa in the wake of the Council by both bishops and theologians, and it noticed that those who proposed the reforms were in most cases white foreigners. By appointing black instead of white bishops it hoped to relieve the pressure for radical change. In due course this indeed happened. As the 1970s advanced the radicals faded away.

The problems, however, did not. The high point of the confident postconciliar process of a moderate pastoral Africanization may be seen in the first and most memorable papal visit to Africa: that of Paul VI in 1969. "You may, and you must, have an African Christianity," he declared to the bishops assembled from the whole continent in Kampala for the opening meeting of SECAM, the new official organization of Catholic African bishops. Great things were still expected at that moment, even from SECAM, and episcopal conferences did in fact continue to make bold proposals for a while. However, the tide of postconciliar renewal had now turned. The Council's more straightforward decisions had been implemented to great effect but, despite the fact that they seemed insufficient to resolve the massive pastoral and institutional problems of the African church, for which they had anyway not been designed, it was becoming clear that additional major proposals for effecting an "African Christianity" were not acceptable.

Two clearly opposed models were now on offer, and the traditionalist one was chosen: "traditionalist" in a Western and Roman sense. The character of the priesthood was the most obvious issue at stake. The reformers had called for a far more diversified sacramental ministry including the ordination of married men.[9] There were numerous dioceses with hardly half a dozen African priests in them and little sign of many more coming. The number of missionaries was beginning to decline, due both to a falling off of vocations in the West and political pressures in Africa, while the number of the faithful was mounting as rapidly as ever. By the mid-1970s many dioceses had hardly one active priest for 8,000 faithful. Even in earlier years when the ratio was far better, the territorial size of dioceses, the badness of roads, and the multiplicity of small villages ensured that most Christians seldom saw a priest. All this was getting rapidly worse, especially when the rise in gasoline prices reduced the possibility of clerical travel. In these circumstances a number of African hierarchies, including Zambia, Central Africa, Cameroon, and South Africa, petitioned Rome to allow the ordination of married men in order "to answer the most elementary pastoral needs" (the words of the Central African and Cameroon request). These petitions were emphatically rejected. Indeed, the hierarchy of Zambia was abruptly ordered not even to discuss the matter further.

At this point (1969-1970) the main thrust of postconciliar reform in Africa in its logical development came to an end. The alternative model called for an increase in the number of seminarians and priests of the traditional type. Here it must be said that in numerical terms much has been done. The number of major seminarians in black Africa was 1,661 in 1960, 2,000 in 1967, 2,775 in 1971, 3,650 in 1974, and has risen much higher since then. By 1975 there were some 3,700 African priests in all. Twelve years later they were over 6,000. This still means less than twenty on average per diocese. In fact, they remain bunched in a minority of dioceses—in eastern Nigeria, parts of Zaire, Rwanda, Uganda, and Tanzania in particular—and are still exceedingly few in many other parts. Even where they are most numerous the priest-people ratio has deteriorated rather than improved under pressure of population growth and the decline in missionary numbers. Pastorally the situation is now, all in all, very much worse than in many parts of South America.

By the mid-1970s a logic of reform had given way to a logic of conservatism. Cautious as the *African Ecclesiastical Review* might appear in theological terms to a European or North American, African bishops could forbid their clergy to read it. Centers like Gaba were under continuous pressure to avoid innovation. An attempt to switch the argument away from the shortage of priests and the consequent "eucharistic starvation" to develop "local Christian communities" on a Latin American model essentially failed because it was an idea imposed rather woodenly from above and because such communities already existed: the church could not have survived at all if this were not the case. The multiplication of papal nuncios (one for each African country or for two together) and their presence at all meetings of episcopal conferences ensured that the line the bishops took would be that preferred by Rome. Where there were bishops of more originality or independence, such as Patrick Kalilombe of Lilongwe in Malawi or Emmanuel Milingo of Lusaka, they were forced to resign and move to Europe.[10] In comparison with the African church of the 1960s, that of the late 1970s and 1980s has become a Church of Silence.

This was not a merely ecclesiastical development. It relates to the whole state of Africa in this period. Compare Uganda in the early 1960s with its condition in the early 1980s. There was nothing odd or awkward about holding a large international conference at Katigondo in the Ugandan countryside in 1964. It was a peaceful, well-governed, and prosperous country. Twenty years later it had been through a series of awful despotisms and a civil war. The economy was ruined. Local government had almost broken down. The Gaba Institute had been moved to the more stable atmosphere of Kenya. But what had happened in Uganda had also happened in Chad, the Sudan, Ethiopia, Angola, and Mozambique, to name but a few of the more desperate examples. The 1960s were, on the whole, a decade of moderate progress and economic growth for most of Africa, but after that things went from bad to worse. Zaire had broken down immediately after independence. Elsewhere coups, military governments, tribal conflict, civil war (in places encouraged by South Africa, the Soviet Union, or a Western power), the rise in the price of oil, and recurrent droughts all contributed to produce a situation entirely different from that in which the Council had first been welcomed.

There was now no money for conferences, or even for buying books and theological journals, little gasoline even for the most elementary pastoral visiting. There was a recurrent state in many places of personal and communal danger. It was not an atmosphere in which the internal reform of the church was likely to flourish, but rather one in which the attention of the bishops was concentrated upon survival, upon the immediate strengthening of local support and traditional loyalties. If the anomalies were getting bigger and bigger in strictly theological terms, that was not evident to a laity with little theological education and only the most tenuous links with other parts of the church. It was not very evident even to the clergy, few of whom read any further theology after leaving the seminary or otherwise kept in touch with the church outside their own diocese. The local isolation of mission, parish, and diocese had long been a major characteristic of the African church scene. It diminished somewhat for about ten years in the 1960s. It then set in again. In such a situation the bishops felt strongly—just as East European bishops might feel—the value of the support of Rome. The last thing most wished to do would be to lessen the Roman link by arguing for a more decentralized church. A few theologians might do so but the bishops, desperate for financial assistance from abroad and a friend to appeal to in their need, would not. They could hardly be blamed for their caution.

The wider state of affairs also contributed to an overall sense of leaderlessness. The multiplicity of countries and the often antagonistic relations between neighboring countries (for instance, between Kenya and Tanzania or Kenya and Uganda, between Malawi and Zambia or Zaire and the Congo) made it difficult for any particular bishop to have a wider than national influence. When there were only a few African bishops in the early 1960s, they were widely known. Now no one was, and the interterritorial organizations intended to facilitate episcopal cooperation, such as SECAM and AMECEA (for Eastern Africa), were able to effect little. The problems of continental cooperation were simply too great both at a religious and at a secular level. Even within a single country the revival of tribal and regional conflict, at times resulting even in civil war, limited the scope for major ecclesiastical leadership, though undoubtedly—to take one example—Cardinal Nsubuga of Kampala exercised an important and truly national role across the many disasters that Uganda suffered. He did this by combining a cautious but courageous personal judgment with the powerful support of his own Ganda clergy and laity. His strength was essentially a local one. He had never studied abroad and had been appointed just after the Council ended. His theological and pastoral attitudes remained those of the church of his youth.

Among the considerable number of young priests and young sisters there was, undoubtedly, some sense of unrest. There were people who wanted to resume, and indeed, deepen, the interrupted 1960s agenda of Africanization. The weakness of the 1960s had been the continued effective dominance of outsiders, a young group of enthusiastic and efficient missionaries. If the agenda was to be retaken it would now be by Africans. Some attempt has been made to do so, but Africans lack an institutional base or easy recourse to the media. There is almost nothing of the more or less independent position which European and American theologians can find in the universities and elsewhere. There is also no sizable middle class urban laity to support their proposals. There are also few, if any, genuinely well-known names. African theology is lived rather than published.

What has happened most decisively and continuously in these years is a process that has gone on almost regardless of the Council: the rapid numerical enlargement of the Catholic community. Probably at least twice as many people call themselves Catholics today in Africa as did so in 1960. This is largely the consequence of the population explosion but also of the decline of traditional religion as a distinct allegiance. Catholicism has become the majority religion or the largest minority group in more and more areas. Where there were twenty African bishops when Pope John XXIII was elected, there are now more than 200; where there were over 600 African priests there are now over 6,000. Where there was no cardinal there are now twelve, including two curial cardinals, Bernardin Gantin and Francis Arinze.

Africa could still be almost disregarded in the run-up to the Council. It is now frequently cited as a major area of church growth and vitality. Many caveats may fairly be made in regard to that assessment. The proportion of Catholics ever contracting an ecclesiastically recognized marriage has fallen very low. A still largely priestless peasant religion prevails in most places almost as much in continuity with traditional religion as with missionary Christianity. Relations with other churches are less close than they were twenty years ago, and gone is the sense that Catholicism is providing a spiritual and intellectual leadership for other Christians. Wave after wave of evangelical born-again Protestantism, fueled from the United States, has flowed across Africa in the last few years, and it is influencing even the older and better-established churches. In comparison with this sort of activity, strident and well-financed, the African Catholic church often appears today inert and listless. It has almost no program for change or advance. Its bishops are cautiously anxious to displease neither local politicians nor the Roman Curia. Its theologians, insofar as they exist, are voiceless. Its strengths are those of the village, a capacity for endurance, a symbolic system of supernature that fits well—perhaps too well—with the legacy of tradition, a sense of identity, a community of both affliction and of hope.

South Africa is very different. Some of what has been said applies there too, since the shortage of African priests is particularly acute. In some ways the fact that black political hopes were here denied and white rule was maintained meant that the progressive development of the 1960s, which began rather later in South Africa than elsewhere, has continued with less of a break. The wise, moderately progressive leadership of Archbishop Hurley of Durban has extended over more than thirty years—one of the very few senior active members of the Council still in office in the late 1980s. But apartheid and the political state of the Republic has inevitably provided for the church within its frontiers a different agenda from that elsewhere, and an increasingly political agenda. To the north the church's agenda has become, for good or ill, rather obviously apolitical. In the south, on the contrary, the church has maintained and strengthened its participation in the ecumenical front established by liberal Christians against the racialism and oppression of government policy. For this a good deal is owed to the leadership of a few: Albert Nolan, a South African Dominican who refused election as master general of his order to continue his witness in South Africa; Patrick Mkhatshwa, general secretary of the Episcopal Conference, who has been in prison many times; Denis Hurley, who has learned with the times and yet kept ahead to provide again and again a presidency that encourages renewal. South Africa is a predominantly Protestant society. The sense of being socially at the center, which Catholicism undoubtedly experiences in Uganda, Tanzania, Rwanda, Zaire, or Zimbabwe is very different in South Africa where Catholics are essentially at the margin, at times a highly conformist margin, occasionally a quite creative one—even theologically creative. They are a more urban church than any other on the continent and that may be important for the future. They are also not leaderless.

The general characteristic of Catholicism elsewhere is quite different: it is that of being largely homogeneous with society, especially rural society, immensely numerous but with very little capacity to mobilize its membership for anything other than religious festivals. It was, without any possible doubt, immensely strengthened in its ability simply to be by the central reforms of Vatican II: the reform of the liturgy, the acceptance of the vernacular Bible, the wider validation of lay ministries. Without this much the prospect by the 1970s would have been bleak indeed. Maybe it was just enough to see the African Catholic church through a long dark tunnel without catastrophic loss. Only in the retrospect of the twenty-first century will it, perhaps, be possible to know. Meanwhile, buffeted by drought and war and waves of either corrupt or overideological government, the church stands loyal to the heroic mythology of its missionary past, glad to welcome the diversion of an occasional papal visit, but almost entirely unable to chart a course, analyze its problems, or perceive a future.

NOTES

1. See Adrian Hastings, *A History of African Christianity 1950–1975* (Cambridge: At the University Press, 1979).
2. George Conus, *L'Eglise d'Afrique au Concile Vatican II* (Immensee, Switzerland: Nouvelle Revue de Sciences Missionaires, 1975).
3. See, for instance, Vincent J. Donovan, *Christianity Rediscovered: An Epistle from the Masai* (Notre Dame, Ind.: Fides/Claretian, 1978); Eugene Hillman, *Polygamy Reconsidered* (Maryknoll, N.Y.: Orbis, 1975). Fr. Hillman's original paper with the same title was published as an appendix to *Pastoral Perspectives in Eastern Africa After Vatican II* (Nairobi: Amecea, 1967), pp. 127–38.

4. See, for instance, Boniface Luykx, *Culte chrétien en Afrique après Vatican II* (Immensee, Switzerland: Nouvelle Revue de Sciences Missionaires, 1974); A. M. Jones, *African Hymnody in Christian Worship* (Gwelo, Zimbabwe: Mambo Press, 1976).

5. See Aylward Shorter and Eugene Kataza, eds., *Missionaries to Yourselves: African Catechists Today* (London: Geoffrey Chapman, 1972).

6. J. Bessem, W. F., "Scripture Translations in East Africa," *African Ecclesiastical Review* 4 (July 1962): 201–211.

7. The full proceedings of the Pan-African Catechetical Study Week can be found in the *African Ecclesiastical Review* 6 (1964), n. 4.

8. Hastings, *Christian Marriage in Africa* (London: SPCK, 1973); Benezeri Kisembo, Laurenti Magesa, and Aylward Shorter, *African Christian Marriage* (London: Geoffrey Chapman, 1977).

9. Adrian Hastings, *Church and Mission in Modern Africa* (New York: Fordham University Press, 1967); Hastings, "Celibacy in Africa," *Concilium* 5 (Oct. 1972): 151–56; Hastings, "The Ministry of the Catholic Church in Africa 1960–1975," in *Christianity in Independent Africa*, ed. E. Fasholé-Luke et al. (London: Rex Collings, 1978), pp. 26–43; Raymond Hickey, *Africa: The Case for an Auxiliary Priesthood* (London: Geoffrey Chapman, 1980).

10. Emmanuel Milingo, *The World In Between* (London: C. Hurst & Co., 1984).

18

The Evolution of Catholicism in Western Africa: The Case of Cameroon

Meinrad P. Hebga, S.J.

Cameroon is bounded on the west by the Gulf of Guinea on the Atlantic, on the north by the Sahel, and in the south and east by Africa's equatorial zone. It covers an area of more than 180,000 square miles and has a population of 10 million. Rightly or wrongly, the country passes for black Africa in miniature. While this observation may be flattering, it is more often made in a derogatory sense, suggesting that a country composed of some 200 ethnic groups has yet to achieve either integration or unity. Like so many other nations on the black continent, Cameroon comprises human groups of various origins. In addition to the dominant Bantu element, people belonging to the so-called Sudanese branch settled there, as well as immigrants from neighboring Nigeria, Chad, Benin, Togo, Senegal, Conakry-Guinea, the Ivory Coast, and Burkina-Faso.

At the same time, Cameroon constitutes a religious crossroads. The animist religion of the natives (a term with little meaning, since animism is not a religion but a state of mind which can be found in the Bible, the Qur'ān, and any poetic literature) has withstood the iconoclastic assaults of Islam and Christianity.[1] Today, for good or ill, animism is trying to reorganize. Among the religions imported into Cameroon, Christianity has imposed itself most effectively. Islam has far less importance than it did under the dictatorship of the Muslim president Ahmadou Ahidjo (1958–1982), when the Western media complacently reiterated the official propaganda slogan: "The north is Muslim and the south is animist or Christian." Actually, among Cameroon's 10 million people one can count about 3 million Christians and barely half a million Muslims, with the rest belonging to various traditional cults. Within Christianity, it is Roman Catholicism that gives the impression of a solidly implanted, coherent, and massive institution in the midst of multiple and divergent Protestant denominations. Among these latter blows a brisk, healthy breeze of Christian freedom, and in fact the first Christian missionaries to Cameroon were Protestant—Dutch in the eighteenth century, British after 1845. How is it that Catholicism, a relative latecomer, seized a lion's share of the Christian population? The answer is easy: when Cameroon became a German colony in 1884, Bismarck simply decided that the coastal region would be Protestant and the inland country Catholic!

Emergence of the Cameroon Nation and Catholicism

Classical Colonial Period (1890–1957)

It is interesting to examine Catholic attitudes at a time when Europeans dominated urban populations as easily as they controlled land. The fashionable slogan was "civilizing mission": a Christian civilizing mission claimed by representatives of the Mission Societies and religious congregations, a lay civilizing mission brandished by the agents of German, British, or French colonialism. The true feelings of the heralds of the gospel then appeared clearly in their ideological and edifying discourse. They envisioned an ideal situation in which the white man possessed the aura of his race and military presence, of knowledge and absolute power over both the natural and supernatural world.

The Vatican state, which through its own special ministry assigned Catholic missionaries to territories to be evangelized, played a political and diplomatic game with the colonial powers—the only interlocutors it recognized. Subjugated populations had no right to speak. Both church and colonial powers reserved to themselves the right to define what the natives needed for eternal or temporal salvation without any concern for native opinion.

It is no secret that, at least with regard to Cameroon, the Congo, Oubangui-Chari (today's Central African Republic), Gabon, and other colonial territories of equatorial or West Africa, the European missionaries enthusiastically collaborated with the colonial powers within the framework of their mutual civilizing mission. Some of them were even considered heroes of the colonial epic and a grateful country solemnly granted them the Medal of Colonial Merit. Monsignor Augouard, first Apostolic Vicar of the Congo, is a typical example. As one French agent told his ecclesiastical colleague: "I serve a country which is also yours and you preach a religion which is also mine."[2]

Of course, close collaboration between Christian missionaries and the political authorities of their mother country was nothing new; it went back at least as far as the Conquistadores and the Patroados imposed on the peoples of Asia, America, and Africa by the Spanish, Portuguese, Dutch, British, and French, ratified by Popes Nicholas V (1453) and Alexander VI (1497), then legitimized by the theological and canonical reflections of men like Juan Ginez de Sepulveda, Bartholomé las Casas, Vitoria, and Suarez in the fifteenth and sixteenth centuries. Often, if not always, the missionaries, including bishops appointed by European kings and princes, behaved as loyal subjects of the crown. That mentality and practice, despite the undeniable progress in spiritual independence achieved by the heralds of the Gospel, have not disappeared. In the 1970s a scandal provoked considerable controversy in the United States: Republican Senator Mark Hatfield of Oregon, CIA director William Colby, and presidential adviser Philip Buchen admitted in writing that the use of missionaries as informants to the American administration was widespread. In December 1975 President Gerald Ford and Mr. Colby even declared that they had no intention of renouncing this practice or of ceasing to distribute secret CIA funds for this purpose.

As for Cameroon and the other colonial territories of Africa, rather cordial relations existed between the servants of God and the agents of Caesar, except for minor disputes over such matters as lay teachers in the schools or divorce. Both sides exercised equal zeal in promoting the cultural, political, and commercial interests of their country, especially through the schools. Young children, at a very vulnerable age, were impregnated with the language, customs, tastes, and ideology of the colonizers, and eschewed their native traditions and society. The champions of secularity and those who espoused so-called religious neutrality were filled with virtuous indignation over the rape of children's consciences by an inopportune catechesis, yet they felt no scruple about bombarding these same minds with chauvinistic and colonizing slogans. Cameroon's gratitude to the missionaries for their remarkable work cannot gainsay the essentially ambiguous character of the missionaries' general attitude toward African society: a mixture of disdain and compassion, racial segregation and devotedness—in a word, a condescending paternalism accompanied by ideological rhetoric about the civilizing mission of the church and of Europe. No doubt the same can be said of other colonies. It is certain, however, that the Cameroon people did not know what to think of priests who courageously undertook exhausting labor and severe deprivation to create converts, but who also rigorously separated them from their own flock and shared their meals, supplied by faithful natives, only with other Europeans. Moreover, these brave and zealous men of God refused to respond to the greetings of African polygamous people, even as they willingly dined at the houses of Europeans surrounded by their African concubines. This is perhaps what Saint Paul meant when he talked about sacrificing one's fortune and even one's life without burning with the love of one's neighbor.

Surely there were courageous exceptions who honored the authentic Christian mission. Some Western missionaries knew "how to become negroes with the negroes," as was said by Fr. Francis Libermann who founded the Holy Ghost Fathers. They became "all things to all men" in order to win everyone to Christ. But on the whole, the picture remained ambiguous.

Lucidity, sang-froid, and justice were especially rare in confronting traditional religious beliefs and practices; the almost general attitude was one of hostility and repression. Most of the heralds of the Gospel declared they had a duty to fight and destroy these horrible primitive and pagan superstitions. Both Catholics and Protestants, following Karl Barth and Hendrik Kraemer, showed the deepest contempt for what they called paganism in order to throw into bold relief, so they believed, the absolute transcendence of biblical revelation. One recognizes with what disdain Karl Barth rejected Thomas Aquinas's teachings on natural theology and his proposition that pagan religions contained positive elements that could lead people to Christian religion.[5] As too often happens, Europeans easily confused Western theological thought with Christianity and the Greco-Germanic expression of Christian faith with the whole Gospel. At the fourth Roman Synod of Bishops (1977) the chairman wrote without hesitation that the church must transmit to Africans "pure Christianity which they will clothe afterwards with their own culture." But this well-meaning statement fails to indicate in which coffer the pure metal of Christianity is sealed—a Christianity that would be neither Jewish nor Greek, Latin nor Germanic, Anglo-Saxon nor Slavic.

During the classical colonial period, which in fact extended beyond the years immediately following Vatican II, an ethnocentric and imperialist mentality dominated the Catholic fortress. The very notion of an African theology, which had begun to circulate at the University of Ibadan (Nigeria), Makerere College of Kampala (Uganda), and Lovanium University (in the former Belgian Congo), rang like heresy and blasphemy. It should not be surprising that audacious missionaries would dispute the validity of the Establishment's cultural imperialism and encourage creativity in theology and liturgy, going even so far as to recommend using local food for the Eucharist.

In sum, the rapport between Catholicism and the emerging nation of Cameroon during this period was one of an omniscient and all-powerful master with an ignorant, weak, and fundamentally bad apprentice. The responsibility of the master is to provide everything, to transform pagan savages into Christian civilized human beings; the apprentice's responsibility is to accept everything with docility and gratitude, yielding up his personality, pride, and all his culture.

The War of Independence (1955–1960)

Historians of Cameroon, with rare exception, sacrifice scientific objectivity to *griotisme*, that is, a flattering attitude toward existing power which pretends to ignore its origins coupled with a complacency regarding its former colonizer France, when they say that the UPC (Union of the Populations of Cameroon) made no significant contribution to the liberation of the country. The UPC was the true artisan of independence. Citing the January 1971 execution of UPC militants "for plotting against the security of the state," Cameroonian Célestin Monga reports his parents' explanation of this political murder. "It was a question of power for Yaoundé Ahmadou Ahidjo and the leaders of the UNC (the National Cameroon Union, Ahidjo's only political party); they had to liquidate the last true militants of the UPC so that they could quietly appropriate the origins of the fight for decolonization. The essential rule in politics is to falsify history."

The general secretary of the UPC, Ruben Um Nyobè, and the president of the same party, Félix Roland Moumié, were removed by the government—the first by gun shot, the second poisoned in Geneva. These two men were the most effective and prestigious nationalist leaders. Both were Protestant. While this factor does not seem to have motivated their deaths by a Muslim president in the service of unbelieving colonialists, it could have influenced the attitudes of the Catholic establishment at a time when the leaders of rival Christian churches cordially hated one another and encouraged their followers to do the same. When European and American pastors worried aloud about the growing popularity of a nationalist movement and labeled it communist, and when one of them went so far as to call Um Nyobè Satan from the pulpit, it was nonetheless the Catholic church that rose up as a stubborn adversary of the UPC, an adversary who did not worry about the means it used in service of a "good cause."

The Catholic church set in motion all its organizational machinery to crush this detested party. Priests thundered from the pulpit against "the hateful and communist propaganda of the UPC." In the confessional, turning over to the priest one's party card was a *sine qua non* for obtaining absolution. In legislative elections about which the government was extremely cautious and in which they openly had recourse to manipulation and intimidation, some priests in charge of voting booths did not hesitate to commit pious fraud on behalf of their brother Joseph Melonè to the detriment of Um Nyobè. Nyobè now wanted to leave the underground movement and enter the game of politics. A public lawsuit at Ekeka did not enhance the distinguished image of the Catholic church. The French governor, Roland Pré, first obtained the endorsement of the French bishop of Douala, Mgr. Pierre Bonneau, before acquitting the trickster. We must underline, however, that the most stubborn and most fanatical men who fought against the nationalist UPC were recruited not, as one might think, from among expatriate priests but from within the ranks of the Cameroon clergy.

However, it was the bishops, almost exclusively foreign-born, who struck the heaviest blow against the UPC in 1957 with a pastoral letter that irritated and provoked a large number of patriots from every religion. The letter condemned the UPC in the strongest terms, accused it of following a Marxist ideology, yet at the same time claimed not to oppose Cameroonian aspirations for independence. The day before the letter was published, the bishops spent an entire day with Governor Roland Pré at Nkongsamba, no doubt to decide with him the main lines of the letter if not its very wording. This obvious collusion with the colonial power only further tarnished the prestige of the bishops and the Catholic clergy in general. Grumbling was heard in churches and chapels and some young people even threatened the bishop of Douala, demanding that he step down from the pulpit as he was about to begin another typical anti-UPC homily.[6]

Finally in 1960 independence was proclaimed without any help from the Christian churches. The colonial power's eviction of the UPC and the government's creation of a body completely devoted to it deepened even more the rancor many people felt toward "the persecuting Catholic church." During the ten years when the underground nationalist movement undertook what they called the war of national liberation, the church paid a heavy price for its serious political errors—parishes destroyed, priests and nuns taken away and massacred.

The Impact of the Antagonism Between Liberal Revolution and Catholicism

Before Vatican II

We have already alluded to occasional minor conflicts between missionary churches and colonial authorities. Let us now examine what really happened.

It would be an exaggeration to characterize the time prior to Vatican II as a period of confrontation. But it is correct to say that fanatic heroes existed on both sides, that is, apostles of secularity vis-à-vis intransigent priests. Conflicts arose in three areas: the schools, matrimony, and social work.

With regard to schools the underlying issue cannot be sufficiently denounced: importing European political and religious antagonisms into an Africa already prey to countless ethnic divisions was a legacy it could have done without. Has anyone tried to measure the perplexity of young Africans whom foreign teachers educated to hate and despise the other camp and whom they taught to shout at one another: "Secular school, Godless school, children of the devil—go!" Or, "School of the priests, enemies of light and liberty—go!" I experienced this in my primary school. Once, I remember, the French priest, our headmaster, and our lay French teacher came to blows in front of their astonished pupils. That kind of education in a milieu of militant clericalism and anticlericalism puts a strong imprint on young people and prepares them for sectarian attitudes and behavior in later life.

In Cameroon this double sectarian prejudice has already brought much harm to national unity and cooperation. For decades French primary school teachers, filled with fanatic secularism, trained generations of native masters in an aggressive anticlericalism according to the Grand Orient of France, that wildly antireligious branch of French Freemasonry. On the other side, missionaries taught their pupils an aggressive horror of the secular school, considered as a workshop of immorality and Satanism. Now these children who were raised against one another are called to live and work together. A fine result of the civilizing mission of France so dear to Archbishop Lefebvre!

In April 1984, before a large gathering of Catholic and Protestant theologians who had come from more than thirty countries for the first international conference of its kind between Africans and Europeans, Cardinal Joseph Malula, archbishop of Kinshasa, sadly recalled a disturbing fact: black Africa is the only region in the world where Catholic couples are forced to contract a triple marriage. They must first celebrate the customary marriage in front of the two families—a procedure that can last years; then there is the matrimonial contract before a government official; and finally the ritual ceremony before a priest. In Cameroon, the three societies to which married couples belong—custom, the state, and the church—each believe only in its own rite. Marriage, therefore, becomes a privileged field of combat for these three authorities.

In the spirit of the liberalism that animated them, European colonial administrators brought with them a few clauses of their own matrimonial law, but they also codified certain African customs. Thus divorce, unusual in traditional Africa, became an accepted practice. Before the arrival of Europeans marriage ties were very difficult to break; in contrast to the individualistic mentality characteristic of the West, Africans were more concerned for the collectivity: both families were payees and felt committed to one another by the very union of their children. Today divorces are granted practically on demand. It is sufficient to invoke a pretext recognized by the law, such as incompatibility, unfaithfulness, or ill treatment, and to possess enough money for lawyers and court costs. Naturally, the Catholic church, which holds absolutely to the principle of the indissolubility of a Christian consummated marriage, condemned the laxity introduced into Africa by a liberal revolution. It refused to recognize the validity of divorces and second marriages. Remarried couples were excluded from the sacraments as long as their "concubinage" lasted. Such a firm attitude has considerably irritated public authorities. Judges sharply criticize the pettiness of the Vatican which, as they see it, grants divorce under the hypocritical guise of a declaration of nullity. But use of such privilege seems reserved for the rich and powerful in this world. These serious accusations undermine the church's credibility in the minds of many believers and encourage them to change their religious allegiance or even to abandon the Christian religion altogether.

But polygamous marriage, codified by the state and rejected by the church, forms the greatest stumbling block. Eugene Hillman, a former missionary in East Africa, has recently shown how offhandedly such a complex problem has been treated by Rome: a series of judicial laws not supported by any serious theological reflection.[7] Polygamy, or the close relationship of one man with several women, is practically a universal custom in Africa; still some people show condescending contempt toward those who throw away the mask of hypocrisy and openly acknowledge the truth of their lives. Pope Paul III's 1537 apostolic constitution *Altitudo* ordered converted African polygamists to divorce all their wives except the first. Recognizing that some clever men might suddenly lose their memories and think that the youngest, prettiest, or most fruitful of their wives was actually their first, Pius V (*Romani Pontificis,* 1571) obligingly allowed converts to choose the wife they preferred. All these interpretations of the "Pauline privilege" (cf. 1 Cor. 7:12–16), which favor the male over the repudiated spouses who are then doomed to prostitution or to another polygamous marriage, posed considerable difficulty for Catholic theologians and canonists whose job it was to find biblical justification for the church's teaching. Those intelligent men lost little time inventing the marvelous formula which has become known as the "Petrine privilege." But the colonial legislator who cared neither for the Bible nor for the juggling of biblical scholars declared according to common sense that all wives were equally legitimate in a society where polygamy has been institutionalized; there was a duty to scrupulously respect native custom. This was a declaration of war. The Catholic church protested energetically and fulminated unceasing condemnations. As always, it was the common people, the weak, those who have no voice, who paid for the conflict of the powerful.[8]

During colonization, the working relationship between European employers and salaried natives was very nearly that of master and slave, as is still the case for most South African enterprises: deplorable working conditions, lack of hygiene, no protection against accidents, miserly salaries, unpaid extra work, insults, blows, and sometimes unpunished homicides. This is no exaggeration. A certain M. Chamaulte, manager of a French plantation in Dzangue in Cameroon, used to shoot or drown his workmen for pleasure. He was never fined more than twenty-five centimes (less than a penny). On the administration side the situation was even worse. In the hell of a small Edea-Eseka railroad thousands of Africans died of malaria, dysentery, beatings, or . . . dynamite. One had to wait until the 1950s for the French militants of the left, especially the CGT (General Confederation of Workers) to introduce unions into Cameroon. Since then a tentative organization for the protection of workers has been slowly organized.

The Catholic church did not remain indifferent to the fate of the workers and sometimes showed courage in severely denouncing the injustice and cruelty of European private or government employers. Some priests were bold enough to free unfortunate men who were arbitrarily arrested in their homes, often at night, to be sent to places of extermination. When countries that call themselves free speak out against Soviet gulags and confer on people like Solzhenitsyn and Sakharov the honors of Western civilization, they too easily forget the gulags created by Westerners in a world where negro slaves labored for centuries either in the galleys of the sixteenth and seventeenth centuries or in the capitalist enterprises of the nineteenth and twentieth centuries that provoked the Marxist reaction, as well as the extermination camps of the very civilized Nazis or on the continent of Africa, which yielded without defense to the rapacity of colonialism. Catholic or Protestant missionaries often, but not always, defended the Africans in the name of human dignity or as children of God. But those whom they condemned replied that the Christian missions themselves exploited natives through nonpaid or underpaid jobs, especially the pupils of their schools and the "Sixa" women.[9]

Thus, with regard to schools, marriage, and social work, representatives of the liberal revolution and of Catholicism bickered, shouted, and condemned one another; but these professional quarrels made no dent in their collaboration in serving the culture, prestige, and glory of their mother country. For the missionaries in no way perceived this service as contradicting their sincere and obvious purpose: the glory of God and the salvation of souls.

After Vatican II

Surely Vatican II initiated a movement whose results the principal actors—John XXIII, Paul VI, or others of this international assembly—could not foresee. Gentle Pope John wished to open the windows of the church to some fresh air, releasing the stale air of an unhealthy fortress Catholicism. His wish was granted perhaps beyond his imagination. A certain openness now characterizes the Church of Rome, but how cautious it is! The new attitudes are embodied in the key conciliar decrees on religious liberty, the church in the modern world, and dialogue with other Christian churches and with non-Christian religions.

But during the Council, the efforts of the African bishops, even those of Vienna's Cardinal Franz Koenig, to see that African religions would be mentioned by name, fell on deaf ears, unable to overcome the European biases, latent racism, and ethnocentrism mentioned earlier. In the same proud spirit, at the 1983 Bishops' Synod on reconciliation, an eminent German prelate declared in response to the intervention of his African colleagues: "We do not need primitivism but technical science." However, during the 1970s on the eve of the Fourth Roman Synod, some members of the Roman Curia deigned to call traditional African cults religions, a belated gesture which hardly touched people in Cameroon and of which the schools of theology took no notice. In fact, the iron law requiring the almost exclusive teaching of Thomistic theology continued to be enforced in the major seminaries to the exclusion of any contemporary approaches, like those of Hans Küng or Edward Schillebeeckx. The seminary directors were even called to Rome to be told again that Thomism was exclusively to be taught; if this was not done, all financial subsidy would be withdrawn from their schools.

The dynamic of liberalization, however, proved stronger than the counteroffensive of conservative brakemen. The tonic of liberation theology finally arrived. Resisting the barely veiled threats hurled against it by champions of the confusion between European thought and Catholic or Protestant orthodoxy, the Ecumenical Association of African Theologians was consolidated. It created branches in various countries including Cameroon, and participated in international conferences of Third World theologians. The Congregation for the Doctrine of the Faith was harassing Catholic thinkers less frequently and seemed willing to respect human rights, notably the rights of self-defense and being heard before being condemned. As a result, African theologians felt they had room to breathe: if the Roman authorities received the giants of the new theology with tolerance and understanding, certainly the "small fry" of black Africa could proceed unobserved. What a mistake! Some articles which had seemed harmless in Africa were screened by inquisitive eyes, vehemently denounced as near-heresy, and finally labeled as primitive thought.

No matter. The general tendency now is toward vigilant tolerance. The Catholic church, fastidious about its own rights and authority and stern in exercising sacred power, is imperceptibly opening itself to the so-called Christian values that the liberal revolution claimed for itself: respecting freedom of conscience (even for priests and nuns) and putting a stop to the insult and annihilation of people in the name of "truth," church discipline, and the established order. These are improvements for which African Catholics are grateful. They are also grateful to their Protestant brothers and sisters who helped reconcile them both to forgotten evangelical values and to some very notable ideals of the liberal revolution which had been summarily denounced by the smug Catholicism of the nineteenth century.

As for ecumenism, its rapid growth is as certain in Cameroon as in the world at large, at least at the level of church leaders. Many groups remain walled up within their fierce doctrinal certainties and their contempt for others—"heretics" or "papists." The instinct for self-preservation, the fear of being nibbled at and finally devoured, often takes precedence over an attitude of sincere openness. Underneath, the current runs more smoothly. Especially because of the charismatic renewal movement Catholics have been able to discover one another, pray together, and interact. That spiritual awakening within the church owes its origin to the early-twentieth-century American Methodist pastor Charles Parham; curiously it has been shunned by the Protestant authorities in Cameroon at the same time that it flourishes in Catholic parishes, especially in the Ephphata groups launched in 1976 by a Cameroonian priest who had been exposed to the charismatic movement at John Carroll University in Cleveland, Ohio.

In schools the postconciliar period has been marked by greater tolerance of secularity. Moreover—and this is a novel phenomenon—a number of priests have pursued their primary and secondary studies not in Catholic schools, colleges, and seminaries but in public institutions. Catholic schools appear less and less as confessional ghettos: Protestant, even agnostic students and teachers are found there, and everyone's beliefs are generally respected.

The Marxist Revolution

Given the bloody demise of the UPC under the guise of its being a tiny Marxist cell, all talk about the impact of Marxist ideology in Cameroon is superfluous. A French proverb says: "the person who wants to drown his dog accuses it of rabies." In reality the UPC was not communist, although its nationalist rhetoric easily borrowed slogans from Saint-Simon, Proudhon, Marx, Mao-Zedong, and other theoreticians of the working class or national liberation. With the party suppressed and its leaders killed, neither the Catholic church nor the French-installed regime in Yaoundé were much concerned about it. If, however, Um Nyobè's gang had assumed power, its real or imagined former persecutors would have had to justify themselves. Such was the situation in those African colonies liberated from Portuguese domination. But let us first consider the Ndongmo affair, which made headlines in the early 1970s.

In its pitiless war against the underground forces of the UPC, the Ahidjo government and its French tutors leveled a spectacular lawsuit against the bishop of Nkongsamba Albert Ndongmo, who was tremendously popular especially among the youth. Accused of complicity with the underground he was arrested, but during the duration of the preliminary investigation the government organized a masquerade that undercut any credibility the lawsuit had. People met all over the country to demand the bishop's execution. The bishop's French attorneys were refused entry visas to the country, despite the convention between France and Cameroon which guaranteed that right. Abandoned by everyone, especially his fellow bishops who were paralyzed by fear, Ndongmo received no help for his defense from his local church; these men of God even refused to visit him in prison so as not to displease the Muslim dictator. Only one other bishop, Msgr. Bamileke—a West Cameroonian like Ndongmo—and the apostolic pro-nuncio, Msgr. Gallina, dared openly to show any sympathy or trust. African bishops from other countries took up his defense. The archbishops of Cotonon (then Dahomey, now Benin) and Ouagadougou (then Upper Volta, now Burkina-Faso) sent telegrams to president Ahidjo asking a pardon for the condemned Ndongma, whose guilt after all was far from established. Especially Pope Paul VI showed constant solicitude for bishop Ndongma until he was freed four years later. The surprising if not scandalous behavior of the Cameroon episcopate toward their colleague led some Catholics, particularly young people, to leave the church and turn to Marxist ideology. But their insignificant numbers and their bloody repression by a French-sponsored totalitarian regime crushed all opposition; they were never allowed to become a political force in the country or to cause problems for either the church or the state.

Other West African countries, however, have experienced a Marxist revolution, a reaction stimulated in large part by the unfortunate politics of the local Catholic church and the *realpolitik* of the Vatican in the early 1940s. Those who today condemn the Marxist takeovers of Angola and Mozambique, and of the former Portuguese colonies generally, do not carry their analysis far enough to denounce all those responsible for these deplorable situations. Perhaps they do not know about the 1940 concordat signed by Pius XII and Prime Minister Salazar which included a supplementary missionary agreement that gave civil rank and the salary of governor to all Portuguese bishops overseas. The corcordat also asserted that "the schools destined for local people and entrusted to the missionaries aim at the perfect nationalization [i.e., Portuguesization] of the population."[10] Thus, in the twentieth century the Vatican stood behind an international convention of Portuguese colonialism and imperialism that harked back to its earlier policy enunciated by the Borgia pope Alexander VI in his 1493 brief *Inter Coetera,* which traced the notorious meridian of Cape

Verde and quietly divided like a cake the whole world outside Europe into regions belonging to Portugal and to his own country, Spain. Needless to say, the missionary civil servants did their best to counter movements of national liberation. They discreetly collaborated with the sinister PIDE (International Police for State Defense) which hounded and assassinated patriots from Angola, Mozambique, and Cape Verde, even if they lived abroad.

Is it surprising that the freedom fighters considered the Catholic church among their most dangerous enemies? The only excuse (if there is one) is that forty years ago no one expected independence; it seemed good if not particularly evangelical policy to stand behind the stronger side. Later in the 1970s with victory in sight, the Vatican tried to correct its political position with regard to the Portuguese colonies. Deaf to the protests from Lisbon, which had provoked the 1940 concordat, Paul VI received the nationalist leaders at the Vatican. It was too little, too late. Rightly or wrongly, the Africans attributed victory to their friends in the socialist countries, notably the Soviet Union and Cuba. They believed, therefore, that they should organize their states according to a communist model despite the evident failure of this system everywhere in the world. Portugal and the church thus paid a high price for their stubborn blindness and ill-conceived political realism.

The Contemporary Scene

What is the current profile of Catholicism in Cameroon? On the strictly religious level, the Catholic church represents an autonomous cultural institution, brilliant in its tranquilizing conformity to the Roman model, subsisting under the vigilance of the apostolic pro-nuncio. It is a church without imagination and virtually without creative spirit, except for its music and vigorous hymn singing. The inculturation of the Christian message in Cameroon, that is, its Africanization in terms of liturgical, artistic, and especially theological expression is insignificant. The clergy does not bother about such matters, and proper African philosophical reflection penetrates the major seminaries only through the back door. In comparison to Zaire where inculturation is already well advanced, Cameroon is far behind. After Mobutu Sese Seko's nationalization of the prestigious Catholic Lovanium University, the faculty of Limete surged ahead; their publications are remarkable for solidity, boldness, and variety. There is nothing like this in Cameroon or in the other countries of West Africa, nothing that would compare with the grandiose Zaire mass or with the courageous attitudes regarding doctrine and discipline of Cardinal Joseph Malula, archbishop of Kinshasa. The bishops of Cameroon are managers of the foreign missionaries' heritage; they depend on a significant work force of expatriates and on financial support from overseas often acquired with great difficulty and considerable humiliation. They do not dare to seek church recognition of African marriage customs nor have they any interest in holding an African regional pastoral council. The church in Cameroon has grown numb in overconformity and a soporific "Romanità."

The Christian churches exert little social and political influence. True, the state pretends to respect them, but the politicians are rather secular oriented and more interested in esoteric groups like the Rosicrucians and Freemasons. A number of those in power received a Christian education; some were even candidates for the priesthood. But they appear to reject the church as an institution. Some boast an unoriginal anticlericalism that draws its worn-out slogans from the repertory of French colonialism. With awkward earnestness they work hard to have their authority felt by church officials, particularly in the areas of education and social welfare.

It should be noted that Protestants and Catholics do not always share the same attitude toward the secular state. Protestants are more at ease with it since they do not expect the protective apparel of an outside politico-religious tutelage. Roman Catholicism, in contrast, because of its authoritarian centralized structures and the civil status of the Vatican, plays a more direct role on the political and diplomatic scene through the nuncio-ambassador's interventions, of which the local church is often ignorant. At that level, pressure and compromise, if not surrender, is the rule — from state to state, from political power to politico-religious power.

The evolution of the African church since Vatican II has been minimal. This assessment derives in part from the insignificance of Africa's economy and geopolitics. The churches of the Third World are treated today as they were yesterday — as minor churches, "immature churches" in the charming phrase thrown in Cardinal Malula's face by Roman officials in 1986 when he discussed the project of an African regional pastoral council. To Rome, the fifty dioceses of Zaire, the more than 100 million African Catholics, are less important than the minuscule Dutch Catholic church which has the right to hold its own national pastoral council. The Netherlands is a Western country, an industrial power, financially respected; it has a long "Christian" history of war between Protestants and Catholics and of independent and rebellious communities. These are advantages of which the African church cannot boast, but which the policymakers in the Vatican take seriously.[11]

There is a long way to go before the universal church takes Africa seriously. If liberalism, Marxism, and Vatican II were all revolutions, one must recognize that their waves have hardly touched our shores.

NOTES

1. Meinrad P. Hebga, *Emancipation d'Eglises sous tutelle* (Paris: Edition Présence Africaine, 1976), pp. 123f.
2. Ibid., p. 35.
3. *The New York Times*, Jan. 29, 1976, p. 15.
4. *The Pilot*, Dec. 19, 1975, p. 20.
5. Karl Barth, *Church Dogmatics* (Edinburgh: T. & T. Clark, 1956), IV, i, pp. 556–57; II, i, p. 93.
6. See the review, *Jeune Afrique*, 1303–1304 (January 25, 1985–January 1, 1986), p. 86. See also Meinrad P. Hebga, "Les Etapes des Regroupements Africains," *Afrique Documents* (Dakar, 1958), pp. 194f.
7. Eugene Hillman, *Polygamy Reconsidered* (Maryknoll, N.Y.: Orbis Books, 1973).
8. Paul III relied on 1 Cor. 7:12f. interpreting very freely the text of the New Testament. The colonial administrators relied on the French Civil Code, on the one hand, and on customary law, on the other, faithfully interpreting these juridical references.

9. Girls and women whom the nuns prepared for marriage with housekeeping training on the territory of the Catholic mission. "Sixta" is a colloquial corruption of "Sister."

10. Accord, article 68. See *Portugal, Faits et Documents* 3 (May–June, 1959 and July–Aug., 1959), Lisbon, Secretariado Nacional da Informacao.

11. Meinrad P. Hebga, "Eglises dignes et églises indignes," *Concilium* 150 (1979), pp. 127f.

19

Christians of Lebanon and the Middle East Twenty Years After Vatican II

Jean Aucagne, S.J.

Before beginning any serious discussion of Catholicism in Lebanon and in the Middle East, we need first to demarcate the region under consideration. Boarded on the west by the Mediterranean, it is surrounded in the north by Turkey, in the east by Iran, in the south by Kuwait, Saudia Arabia, and the Sudan, and on the southwest by Libya. It is useful to recall some information about these adjoining states because of the influence they exercise and because of their similarity to the region we want to examine. In all these states except Sudan (where Latin Catholicism and Protestantism form a dynamic minority), Christianity is represented by Oriental churches reduced to the size of minute minorities in an overwhelmingly Muslim (or, in the case of Israel, Jewish) environment of ancient civilization.

Delimited in this way, the region includes six countries: Syria, Iraq, Lebanon, Israel, Jordan, and Egypt, comprising a total population of over 85 million inhabitants. About 9 million (10.5%) are Christian, of which less than 2 million (2%) are Catholic. Moreover, this minority Christianity is itself quite divided, even within the Catholic group. These divisions result from a historical heritage of which we will need to give a brief outline since, for better or worse, this history remains a live factor in interpreting the present situation. It is also necessary to say something briefly about the situation of each of the countries in the region, since even if they have similar characteristics, the size of the Christian community, its status in the cities, and its influence are each quite different. These considerations will help us to better under-

333

stand how these communities are presently evolving and what prospects the future
may hold.

Beliefs and Rites

Ecclesiastically, this region of the Middle East includes three of the great patriarchates established during the fifth century A.D. (Rome and Constantinople being
outside the region under consideration). The first is Antioch, whose domain roughly
corresponds to Syria, part of Iraq, and Lebanon. To this must be added two former
dependencies of the Antioch patriarchate which became independent during the fifth
century, forming national churches whose primate has the title *catholicos:* Baghdad
(with the official name Selucia-Ctesiphon for a neighboring city now in ruins), which
long ago spread as far east as China and India and from which remain the Syrian
Christians of Kerala, and Armenia, which today is divided between the primates of
Etchmiadzine (near Erivan in Soviet Armenia) and Sis in Cilicia (southeast of Turkey)
established at Antelias in Lebanon since 1930. The second patriarchate is Jerusalem,
whose territory corresponds to present-day Israel and Jordan. The third is Alexandria, which covers Egypt. Ethiopia, which earlier was a close dependent of Alexandria, is now an autonomous church.

These patriarchates, however, have been divided by various heresies and schisms
which also have cut across various ethnic groups and can be seen today in different
liturgical rites. Moreover, various unions with Rome have, as a rule, resulted in the
creation of uniate churches that have kept their own liturgical rites even while they
became Catholic. In chronological order these include the following:

In 431 A.D. the Council of Ephesus was convened without waiting for Syriacs of
the East (Catholics of the Selucia-Ctesiphon region) who were generally favorable to
Nestorius. These Syriacs, therefore, became Nestorians, holding that in Jesus there
were two persons, united by a single will. As early as the Middle Ages numerous
rival factions began to unite with Rome. By 1672 relationships were stabilized with
the creation of two churches—one Catholic, called "Chaldean," whose primate is
usually called patriarch; the other Nestorian, also called Assyrian. These Christians
are in great part Catholic and exist mostly in Iraq. Their liturgy follows the Eastern
Syriac rite and their language is oriental Syriac, of which one modern form (Sureth)
is still spoken in the mountains of Iraq.

In 451 A.D. the Council of Chalcedon was held in order to condemn a monophysite interpretation of the Council of Ephesus, but it was accepted neither by the
Armenians nor by most of the Western Syrians of Antioch nor by the Egyptians. The
Armenians all became monophysites. A small number united with Rome in 1740,
with the election of a pro-Catholic, Abraham Ardzivian, as *catholicos* of Sis in Cilicia;
his successors bear the title of Armenian Catholic Patriarch.

The non-Catholic Armenians are often called "Gregorian," after the name of the
apostle of the Armenian nation, Saint Gregory the Illuminator. They have at their
head two primates, one residing in Etchmiadzin, the other in Antelias (Lebanon). The
Gregorian archbishops of Istanbul and of Jerusalem bear the title of patriarch, but
they are simply autonomous under the primate of Etchmiadzin (under whose juris-

diction also fall the Egyptian Armenians). The non-Catholic Armenians in Lebanon, Syria, Iraq, and Iran are also subjects of the primate of Antelias.

The Armenian liturgy is close to the Byzantine liturgy of Saint Basil and is celebrated in Krapar (classical Armenian, as different from modern Armenian as middle English is from the English of today). The readings are often done in modern Armenian, as well as in Arabic for Catholic services.

The Syriacs of the West managed, in spite of the policing of the Byzantine empire, to reconstitute a monophysite hierarchy during the sixth century thanks to Jacobus Baradæus, with the complicity of the Empress Theodora (hence their name "Jacobites"). They have kept the proper liturgy of Antioch, using a western Syriac dialect. But in 1783 the Syriac patriarchate of Antioch was divided into two parts, one of which became Catholic. Especially among Catholics, Arabic has more and more replaced Syriac as the language of the liturgy. The faithful followers of the two patriarchs are especially numerous in Iraq and in Syria.

As early as the fifth century some of the Western Syriacs, grouped around the monastery of Saint Maron near Homs (Syria), accepted the Council of Chalcedon, as did the Hellenized groups of the region. But when the patriarch of Antioch took refuge in Constantinople because of the first Arab-Muslim invasion in 636, they elected their own patriarch. This is the origin of the Maronite patriarchate. The Maronites did not follow the Byzantine schism of 1054 and they are all Catholic. In order to avoid persecution they took refuge in the mountains of Lebanon, a country where they still comprise the most important Christian community (25% to 30% of the total population). The Maronite liturgy is very close to the liturgy of other Western Syrians, but it is almost completely celebrated in Arabic.

Finally, the generally Hellenized followers of the patriarchate of Antioch who, because of their fidelity to Constantinople, accepted the Council of Chalcedon also adopted its liturgy, especially after the beginning of the twelfth century. The Byzantine liturgy is profoundly different from the original liturgy of Antioch. It was, in the early days, translated into Syriac and is usually celebrated today in Arabic, with a few hymns in Greek. The orthodox faithful from Antioch followed — not without some reticence — the schism of Michael Cerulaire in 1054. In 1724, as a result of the dual election to the patriarchate of both a pro-Catholic candidate and a candidate loyal to the patriarch of Constantinople, two patriarchs of the Byzantine rite came into being. Consequently there are five patriarchs of Antioch: two Syriacs — one Jacobite (in Damascus), the other Catholic (in Beirut); one Maronite Catholic (in Lebanon); and two Byzantines — one orthodox (in Damascus), the other Catholic, also called "Melkite" (with residences in Damascus, Lebanon, and Cairo).

Egypt has experienced the same divisions described above, except that today only those groups of Hellenic origin remain faithful to orthodoxy. The whole of the Egyptian church (called Coptic) is, in principle, monophysite. In 1895 the small community of Copts who had become Catholic received authorization for their own patriarch. As with the Byzantine Catholic patriarch of Antioch, he was granted permission in 1838 to add to his title the names of Alexandria and Jerusalem for his followers of Syriac-Lebanese origin living in Egypt and in Palestine.

All those who followed the patriarchate of Jerusalem accepted the Council of Chalcedon. They later followed Cerulaine in his schism and adopted the Byzantine rite. But a Latin patriarchate was established by the Crusaders in 1099; although it later disappeared, it was reestablished in 1847 following the missionary efforts of the Franciscans and numerous conversions to Catholicism. It should also be noted that small Latin autonomous communities exist just about everywhere in the whole Middle East, with their own apostolic vicars in each country.

Finally, since believers who migrate from one country to another keep their own original liturgical rites and jurisdiction, cities like Beirut, Alep, and Cairo have five or six Catholic bishops (Byzantine, Armenian, Maronite, Syriac, Chaldean, Latin). Ecclesiastical considerations do not always coincide with these various jurisdictions, which complicates even more any communal pastoral activity. Except in Jerusalem and the Greek orthodox patriarchate of Alexandria, no patriarch resides in the city of which he holds the title, but instead lives in Lebanon, Damascus, or Cairo. In Antioch the Christians in fact number only about 5,000 Byzantine orthodox members.

Some Statistical Data

A word of caution is needed in interpreting statistical data from the Middle East. For one thing, the notions of state, individual, and residence are appreciably different from those commonly used in Western sociology. For another, "families" rather than "individuals" comprise the basic unit of measurement, and even here very young children and women are often not counted. Because an emigrant is always expected to return to his country, even when absent he continues to be listed according to his country of origin. Moreover, a non-Muslim immigrant cannot be granted nationality in the country in which he has established his residence if that country is Muslim. The situation is slightly different in Lebanon and in Israel where formalities are somewhat more difficult (one must take into account the confessional equilibrium in Lebanon and the status of non-Jews in Israel). As a result, available statistics provide only an approximate picture of the importance of Christians from the various patriarchates and in the different countries of the Middle East.

The Patriarchate of Alexandria
Byzantine rite: 25,000 (almost all Greek Orthodox); 6,000 Catholics (almost all of Syrian or Lebanese origin)
Coptic rite: 4–8 million monophysites; 140,000 Catholics

The Patriarchate of Antioch
Byzantine rite: 500,000 orthodox; 300,000 Catholics (almost all in Syria and Lebanon)
Western Syriac rite: 200,000 Jacobites; 900,000 Syriac-Catholics (Iraq, Syria, and Lebanon)
Maronite rite: 1,000,000 Catholics (Lebanon and Syria)
Armenian rite: 350,000 Gregorians; 70,000 Catholics (Syria and Lebanon)

The Patriarchate of Jerusalem
Byzantine rite: 100,000 orthodox; 70,000 Catholics
Latin rite: 60,000 Catholics
Other rites: a few hundred or thousand of each.

Some brief information about the surrounding countries may help to illuminate the situation of the Middle East region itself.

Turkey: 45 million inhabitants, of which 230,000 (5%) are Christian and 27,000 are Catholic. A few hundred of these Christians are genuinely Turkish (i.e., converted Muslims). For the others, one must distinguish their citizenship, which can be Turkish (Armenians especially), from their nationality, which counts as Armenian (80,000), Greek (60,000), Arabic, etcetera. Juridically there is religious freedom. But because Christianity itself is perceived as foreign in character, Christians are reticent to claim rights in which they hardly believe; and in the southern agricultural part of the country, where Syriacs and Assyrians live, the authorities turn a blind eye to bandits who victimize Christians. None of this is encouraging and Christians emigrate in large numbers.

Iran: 24 million inhabitants with 200,000 Christians, half of whom are Gregorian Armenians. The situation in Iran is similar to Turkey, but without any religious freedom.

Kuwait: 1.4 million inhabitants; 75,000 Christians; 44,000 Catholics (Indians, Filipinos, Palestinians, and Lebanese). All Christians are foreigners, but they enjoy freedom of worship (but worship only). Even this limited freedom, however, tends to be reduced under the influence of Muslim integralism. A similar, but slightly better, situation exists in Bahrein.

Saudi Arabia: 9 million inhabitants, almost 1,000,000 Christians (from India, the Philippines, and Lebanon), about half of whom are Catholic. Here, even the simple freedom of private worship (in homes or in the premises of foreign societies) can be revoked at any time; non-Muslim religious meetings of any kind are forbidden.

Sudan: 21 million inhabitants; 2,000,000 Christians, 1.5 million Catholics. The Catholics all belong to the Latin rite and to a church growing rapidly in the midst of persecution. The bishops have learned how to defend individual human rights and to speak out against abuses to human dignity, whereas the people have learned how to fight and to negotiate. The Sudan provides a unique example of dynamic and open Christianity in this Muslim area. It should be noted that serious observers estimate the number of Muslims in Sudan at 60 percent. This figure is not recognized by the authorities who regard all members of the northern part of the country as Muslim, where many in fact are animists coming from the south.

Libya: without interest or influence in the region, except for subsidizing Palestinian-Muslim extremist groups.

Syria: 9.7 million inhabitants, with 76 percent Sunnite Muslims, 12 percent Alawites, 3 percent Druze, and 2 percent Ismailian and other Muslim sects; Christians in Syria number 680,000 (7%) and Catholics 240,000 (2.5%). The most important Christian group is the Byzantine (200,000 orthodox and 100,000 Catholics), followed by the Armenian (100,000 Gregorians and 30,000 Catholics), and Syriac (80,000 Jacobites and 20,000 Catholics). Maronites, Latins, Chaldeans, Assyrians, and Protestants each number between 10,000 and 20,000. The country is ruled by the Baath, associated with other socialist parties which it closely controls. This Arab socialist theory, at least in principle, attracts a large number of Christians, particularly orthodox Byzantines. In fact, the atmosphere in the country is rather totalitarian, which results in a continuous emigration of Christians, mostly Armenians. In 1943, for example, Christians in Syria numbered 14 percent of the population.

Iraq: 14 million inhabitants, of which 45 percent are Sunni Muslims, 50 percent are Shiites, and 1.5 percent belong to other Muslim sects. Christians number about 490,000 (3.5%), Catholics about 390,000 (2.5%), of which 330,000 are Chaldeans and 50,000 are Syriac Catholics. As in Syria, the Baath party rules the country, but here is under Sunni influence and its laicism results in a positive view toward Christians, who are regarded as part and parcel of the national heritage. But there remains a strict dependence on the party which recruits informers even among the clergy. Christian emigration here is less notable than in Syria and is compensated for, at least in absolute numbers, by their high birth rate.

Lebanon: 3.3 million inhabitants; without doubt this figure exceeds 4 million when one includes the Palestinians (450,000), Syrians, and stateless people (e.g., Kurds of Turkey and Syria) living in the country. Shiite Muslims comprise about 25 percent of the population, Sunnis 22 percent, and Druze 6 percent; Christians make up almost 50 percent, with Catholics numbering 1,150,000 of which 900,000 are Maronite. The second largest Christian group is the Byzantine (with 200,000 orthodox and 170,000 Catholics). Lebanon is a parliamentary democracy in full decomposition. Historically, the country was founded with a higher proportion of Christians (51%), along with Druze, than other Middle Eastern nations. But the different demographic increases of each group, the arrival of many Palestinian refugees, and the growth of Muslim extremism (particularly pro-Khomeini Shiites) have broken the country's fragile equilibrium. The subsequent civil war has created regions that are more and more religiously homogeneous, where before the various religious communities overlapped and were to a greater extent integrated. Legally Lebanon upholds complete religious freedom, although in fact this is more or less limited to the seventeen religious communities officially recognized by the government.

Israel: 3.9 million inhabitants, of which 82.5 percent are Jews, 13 percent Muslims, and 1.2 percent Druze. Christians number about 100,000 (2.5%) and there are 55,000 Catholics, most of whom are Latin rite (24,000) and Greek Catholic (28,000). The non-Catholic Christians are, for the most part, Greek Orthodox. Israel is a parliamentary democracy which, as far as religious freedom is concerned, unites personal freedom of the Ottoman type with the modern principle of communal rights. For example, Christians who live in the kibbutzim receive paid trips to Cyprus in order to contract a civil marriage that is recognized in Israel. Similar arrangements exist in Lebanon. Nevertheless, the law in Israel is very strict against conversion. Christian Arabs can have the same rights as Jews if they do their military service (an option chosen by the Druze or bedouins). But they very rarely choose this option. The figures cited above include the annexed territories (East Jerusalem) but not the occupied territories (Judea, Samaria, and Gaza).

Jordan: 3.4 million inhabitants, 95 percent of whom are Sunni Muslims. Christians number 170,000 (5%), Catholics 70,000, of which most are Latin rite (40,000) and Greek Catholic (20,000). Eighty percent of the non-Catholic Christians in Jordan are Greek Orthodox. Jordan is a relatively liberal kingdom (recognizing freedom of worship only). The good will of the official authorities who are conscious of their responsibilities toward the Christians is often defeated by the influence of Muslim integralism within the administration.

Egypt: 45 million inhabitants, approximately 90 percent of whom are Sunni Muslims. Christians number from 4–7 million (8–14%); the first figure, although passionately dismissed by many, appears to be closer to reality. Catholics number about 160,000, of whom 140,000 are Coptic Catholics. Egypt represents an authoritarian democracy on the way to liberalization. But Islamic integralist groups provoke severe tension by regularly attacking students, destroying Christian places of worship, building mosques in the new Coptic districts, and making the erection of a church in the neighborhood illegal. The great economic misery of Egypt exacerbates these religious tensions, which easily turn into intolerance even toward the orthodox Copts who form 95 percent of the Christian population of the country.

Religious Practice

Christians feel strong attachment to their different communities. First, their personal status regarding marriage, divorce, inheritance, and child adoption depends on each group's religious authority. In all countries except Israel, to marry one must be baptized or become Muslim. Second, community identification is deep. There is an Arab word for this feeling, *ta'assub,* which is usually translated as fanaticism but has a more positive connotation; it means feeling bound together within the group. Through its history, beliefs, liturgy, and hierarchy the community forms a constitutive element of each person's identity. Third, natural religious piety is particularly strong among Syrians and Copts.

No statistics exist for religious practice, but among Catholics it is estimated that Sunday mass attendance varies between 30 and 80 percent, with fewer attending in urban areas (especially new suburbs) among the very rich or very poor. There is also fasting. Between 20 and 30 percent of the students fast more or less strictly during some part of Lent; many also refrain from smoking during the same period, especially the Lebanese Maronites and Egyptian Copts. The rate is higher in rural areas.

Families are large, with about four or five children in rural Lebanon and 2.8 children per family in middle or upper class Beirut. Iraqi and Egyptian Christians also have many children, urban Syrians fewer (especially in cities like Alep). Finally priestly and religious vocations are numerous, except among Greek Catholics, although fewer are entering Latin-rite women's congregations who recruit locally throughout the region.

General Overview

Two countries of the Middle East have rather homogeneous Christian groups — Egypt, which is massively Coptic, and Iraq, massively Syriac. The other four major countries of the region exhibit an important Byzantine Christian presence (comprising about 1 million people, 34-50 percent of whom are Catholic). Even in these countries, however, Syriacs (taking all their allegiances together) number approximately 1.5 million.

What, then, of the "national" Christian groups: the Byzantines, Syriacs, Copts, and in effect, the Armenians? Here the word "nation" must be understood in its Soviet meaning, which carefully distinguishes nationality from citizenship. Except for the Armenians — who are immigrants and for the most part descendants of refugees—these Christians have never been citizens of a state formed by the nation to which they claim allegiance and to which they are bound by extremely strong feeling. They are really subjects of successive empires: Persian, Greek, Norman, Byzantine, Islamic (Arab-Turkish). There have been continual efforts to resuscitate the Syriac and Coptic languages, and the Copts would even like to obtain for their pope a kind of "Vatican" which would at least enjoy the benefits of extraterritoriality. But all these efforts seem doomed to failure.

The Lebanese have tried to create a pluralistic state in which Christians should feel at home because they would have at least a slight numerical and political majority. In concept this effort seemed realistic, but it has not been able to withstand the rancor of the Palestinians and various pan-Islamic currents. The Copts, of course, closely watch the Lebanese Christians' struggle to maintain their own identity, which is one reason why they were held in such deep suspicion by Anwar Sadat.

The Byzantines alone, perhaps because they have inherited a certain "imperial" feeling and because they come from an empire where they were citizens, feel a common "Arab" identity. It is they who founded the Baath party, the party of "Arab Resurrection," and other pan-Syrian groups. It is they who are the militant members of the extreme wings of the P.L.O. (Bishop Capucci is a Greek Catholic; Georges Habrache, Nayef Hawatmet, and Scandar [Ahmed] Sibril are Greek Orthodox). Nevertheless, when the project of creating or integrating into an Arab national state fails, all these Christians, including the Byzantines, vote with their feet—by emigrating. Everywhere the proportions of Christians are in decline, partly because of a drop in the birth rate (which in the cities tends to follow the Western pattern except in Iraq and Egypt), but mostly because of emigration. Only the Copts have not experienced this phenomenon (until recently and in much smaller numbers) because of their strong attachment to the land of Egypt. But they are also the only group to have large numbers convert to Islam.

No doubt this strong pull toward emigration is partly due to economic factors. With a density of 400 inhabitants per square kilometer, Lebanon is clearly overpopulated. Egypt is even more so, when one takes into account its amount of usable land. (Ninety-five percent of its almost 1 million square kilometers is desert and the emigration from Egypt is less numerous.)

The essential fact is that Christians in the Middle East feel as if they were foreigners in their own country. No doubt the Muslims are fully Arab or have become Arab; but precisely for this reason they resent the present nation-states as a denial of their Arabic identity and, even more, of their Islamic identity. They want to form a single nation. This unitarian aspiration—pan-Arabic in origin at least for the political elites but more and more pan-Islamic today—can only serve to reinforce the Christians' feeling of being doubly foreign: they are not Muslims and because of their Christian allegiance they feel Armenian, Coptic, Syriac but not Arab (except for the Byzantines). Moreover, today's nation-states give little hope that their formal citizenship will become real, and there is no room for them in pan-Islamism.

At least the liberal capitalism of the 1930s did offer Christians some space for economic liberty in which they often excelled in commercial and technical competence. With the exception of Lebanon, Israel, and Jordan, these states have all become socialist. Technical competence is still appreciated, but even if Christians have achieved a high position (as the Egyptian Goutros Ghali) they are—and feel treated like—servants of an Islamic community of which they are foreigners, not citizens contributing to the common good. The Ottomon Empire, after all, enshrined in its vocabulary the essential foreignness of Christians by counting them not only as *dhimmis* (protected subjects) but as *millet* (an ethnic community).

The sociopolitical consequences of this fact are extremely serious. Counted as an ethnic and politically foreign community and having internalized this status, Christians are naturally inclined to defend their own interests and not the common good. The Maronites in Lebanon fight to keep sufficient political power to guarantee them real rights (and not just formal rights, as with the pretended laicism of neighboring countries). The Copts in Egypt protest against the threats of imposing the *shariʻah* (Qur'ānic law) by invoking the rights of their community, while the Sudanese bishops who do not have to carry this heavy historical heritage reject such imposition in the name of human rights. The Copts find themselves in a more difficult position since they seem to be defending privilege. The Sudanese present a more convincing case, even if they have not succeeded in eliciting strong international support or even an international Christian protest (as in the case of the international support for Soviet Jewry). Similarly, Christians in Israel (and Turkey) think almost entirely in terms of the limitations imposed on them by liberal or lay legislation, paying little attention to the opportunities it provides them to be full citizens (as the Druze and Bedouins have done). One may also ask if the massive bulk of Copts, Syriacs, and Armenians does not tend to a kind of "sociological monophysitism," which implies both a very narrow union, almost a fusion, between Christianity and nation, church and state, and, at the same time, a lack of interest in politics, since human nature is absorbed by divine nature. Apart from the work of Soloviev, who denounces such attitudes in Russia and the universal church, and a favorable brochure by the Armenian *catholicos,* Karekine II (Sarkissian), few studies of this phenomenon go beyond simple suggestions.

Undoubtedly another aspect of this "sociological monophysitism" is antisemitism, all too common, alas, among the Christians of the area. Cyril of Alexandria, it should be remembered, not only defended the unity of the person of Jesus against Nestorius but also invented the term "deicide" which provoked so many catastrophic tragedies in the following centuries. Islam itself is also deeply antisemitic. But here too one needs more studies in depth about Byzantines as well as other orthodox groups who are much more antisemitic than the monophysite Copts.

Developments After Vatican II

By its reminder that reforms are necessary in the life of the church and by its call for universal religious liberty, the Second Vatican Council opened the door to many positive initiatives. The attempted reforms, however, more often than not remained at the surface of the problems whose continuing seriousness threatens the very survival of Christianity—and Catholicism—in the Middle East.

Positive Points

I will speak now particularly about Lebanon since it is the country in the region I know best. In 1968 a meeting of the Young Christian Students (YCS) published a courageous analysis, "Our Church in Question." Unfortunately this initiative was doomed to failure from the start. Not only had the YCS, always few in numbers, shrunk to a few dozen militant members, but their analysis suffered from the fact that it was inspired by efforts, common in France, conceived in a society that was massively Christian (or even post-Christian). In Lebanon, however, as in the whole of the Middle East, one faces not a population more or less detached or alienated from the church but a surrounding Muslim society. The Marxist-socialist orientation of the document coupled with a radical liberalism in matters of doctrine undermined the credibility of the proposed reforms, despite the fact that much of what was called for appeared to be both just and timely—reforming the temporal administration of the church, more active church involvement in social problems, more interreligious collaboration.

The new Greek Catholic bishop of Beirut, Gregoire Haddad, participated in this YCS meeting, and his subsequent career was characterized by the same ambiguities present in the YCS analysis. As a pastor open to reform and anxious for the church to break out of its self-imposed ghetto, Haddad had undertaken many internal reforms in his own diocese: removing fixed stipends from ministries and leaving compensation to the generosity of the faithful, increasing social ministry to the poorest in the diocese without regard for their religious affiliation, and calling for a pastoral meeting of the whole city of Beirut which would bring together Catholics belonging to the six different ecclesiastical jurisdictions. Despite the fact that these reforms, as well as the charismatic personality of the bishop, generated considerable enthusiasm especially among educated laity, they also called into question much of the taken-for-granted religious reality in Beirut and challenged existing interests and canonical dispositions. As a result they elicited much opposition within the Greek Catholic hierarchy and among the Christian hierarchy in general. This opposition might have been lessened if Haddad had not had the unfortunate idea of linking his pastoral reforms (about which his views were generally correct) to doctrinal questions on which he seems not to have been well equipped. He therefore turned to two priests with a doubtful canonical status, trained in Germany in a theological radicalism that pushed to an extreme the theses of German liberal Protestantism and of the Catholic theologian Hans Küng. With these two priests, Haddad founded a magazine called "Afag" ("Horizons") which made the link between pastoral reforms and doctrinal extremism inextricable. The Greek-Catholic Synod got hold of the affair, and in order not to offend the influential laity favorable to Haddad, turned the matter over to Rome. Rome, however, recognized that any intervention was certain to inflame sentiments on both sides, and so returned the matter to the Synod which, in turn, referred it to theologians who sharply criticized the new theological perspectives. In the end, Haddad was forced to resign. Having been put in charge of social affairs in the diocese, he remained a bishop. In February 1976 he invited himself to attend the Islam-Christian seminar in Tripoli where he took the opportunity to proclaim Mohammad a "prophet of God, sent by God to all men." Rome preferred to ignore this action and Haddad remains a Roman Catholic bishop.

In the Maronite church, a group of priests and laity attempted a more discreet undertaking by founding the movement called "A Church for our World." It was so discreet that at first it limited itself only to Maronites and avoided anything that could have offended the bishops. In the beginning the movement attracted many important people. But paralyzed by its own discretion, unable to spell out a Christian position in the Lebanese conflict which exploded in 1975, the movement steadily declined. Today it is lost in the sands of immobility.

The charismatic movement in Lebanon has been more effective. There are numerous charismatic groups throughout the country, and since they are entirely religious, open to outsiders, and without any organizational ties to the hierarchy, they have generally escaped the suspicions of the police who frown upon any Christian meeting occurring outside the ordinary forms of worship. In the atmosphere of violence and misery that prevails in the area, these groups attract many followers sincerely desirous of a place for spontaneous communal prayer and for refuge. The strength of the movement rests on its ability to provide for precisely these needs, even if it shares the ambiguity of all Christian groups in Lebanon.

Several other groups could be classified along the same lines as the charismatic movement, although they are socially more active: *Foccolari* (centered in Lebanon but also touching Syria), which has a few Lebanese women as full-time members; *Faith and Light* (founded by Jean Vanier), which works with mentally handicapped people and their families and which fans out from Lebanon to all the areas of the region; and the groups that specialize in helping Mother Teresa's Missionaries of Charity. The *Community of the Lamb,* a mixed-monastic type group founded in France by a Protestant priest who later converted to Catholicism, has been active for several years at Amchit (40 kilometers from Beirut). Between thirty and 200 young people, mostly students, go to Amchit each weekend to participate in its religious services, which combine traditional devotions like the rosary and the exposition of the Blessed Sacrament with a kind of charismatic spontaneity. The community also distributes thousands of recorded cassettes on religious subjects which are passed from hand to hand throughout the whole Arab world. Here, then, we have a vibrant charismatic movement engaging in effective evangelization; two or three Lebanese young men have already joined this group of about ten French people as postulants. The action of "Frère Nour" is more original. About twenty years ago he began to live an eremitic life—going around barefoot and wearing a cloth sack for a garment. Today he has attracted several hundred followers who have founded a radio station (The Voice of Love) which broadcasts religious programs to which many people listen and contribute funds. Here again is charismatic reform with people trying to live a communal life.

Several common characteristics mark these movements: people who join belong to different religious groups; there is a stress on prayer, an absence of ritual and clerical divisions, and extreme poverty. When people belonging to these movements have lodgings, they are usually in premises made available without any contract. One thinks of the beginnings of the Franciscan movement. Unfortunately, there is only very sketchy information about such groups outside Lebanon. It is worth noting that the very precariousness of these groups renders them completely free from persecution by civil authorities; they are also largely free from any formal links to the hierarchy, which they criticize through their behavior, even if they generally refrain from doing so in their words. The hierarchy is understandably suspicious of these movements, although it has seldom gone beyond verbal warnings of the kind issued in the beginning of 1986 by the Maronite patriarch against the charismatics and the followers of Frère Nour.

Another phenomenon, even more common and exhibiting similar aspirations, is the increase of priestly vocations, especially in Lebanon and Egypt. Rather than representing a longing for renewal or reform, however, this growth seems more closely linked with the will to assert Christian identity in the difficult political, economic, and religious situation of the Middle East. Since 1955, the "monks" of Lebanon have become clerical religious orders, even though sociologically they retain much of their old Maronite and Lebanese roots. Exemption from direct hierarchical control has made them rather independent from the bishops and their support for the Christians at war has always been stronger than such support among the hierarchy, which has tried to hold a mediating position closer to the Vatican's. Closer to the people, these orders benefit most from increased vocations. With the recent foundation of the University of the Holy Spirit at Kaslik near Beirut, they have increased their cultural and social influence even more.

The renewal of the Coptic Orthodox church in Egypt is also linked to a monastic renewal. This began about thirty years ago when dozens of young university students arrived to join the monasteries, among whom was the current Coptic pope Shenouda, whose strong personality holds his church together. Yet priestly vocations are also numerous in the small Coptic Catholic community where there are no monks but only a Franciscan province. This renewal, however, is often accompanied by a kind of religious nationalism that is domineering, is often quick to take offense, and does not favor ecumenism, especially in Egypt. Women's congregations (mostly Latin rite or of Latin inspiration) are not experiencing the same increase in numbers. The traditional monastic congregations have never had much cultural or social influence.

Missed Opportunities

These promises of renewal, still fragile since they affect only a few thousand people, have sprung up quite independently of the official church. The hierarchy, however, was not short of opportunities to act immediately after Vatican II; but, divided between its various jurisdictions and preoccupied with its internal problems, the bishops have not been able to take hold of them. Nor has Rome given them much encouragement. Preoccupied with the Islamic–Christian dialogue, the Vatican has in fact discouraged the bishops from entering more actively into the fight against injustice and oppression.

The problem of the paralyzing multiplicity of competing Catholic jurisdictions came up during the Second Vatican Council with regard to the Oriental churches. But if two bishops from Lebanon (one Maronite and one Chaldean) proposed reforms, these were stopped by the common front of all the others who wanted to defend the status quo. The Oriental patriarchs strongly insisted that they should have full jurisdiction over the faithful of their own rite throughout the whole world. Not only does this approach universalize a system that has already proved incapable of adaptation but even more, it requires patriarchs to expend considerable time and personnel in Brazil or Australia, instead of dealing with the urgent problems of survival in the Middle East. It is also true that some patriarchs, when confronted with the mass of migrations from their areas, do not believe in the future of their churches, even if they express such doubts only confidentially. Could one say that opportunities for more ecumenical collaboration have been missed? Perhaps these opportunities never existed. Just after Vatican II, non-Catholics and even some Catholics themselves feared that they were about to be carried away by a very popular movement that looked as if it might get out of control. Later, the crisis within the Catholic church extinguished much of the earlier and more naive enthusiasm as well as the perceived danger. Part of the hesitance toward ecumenism, of course, arises from the fact that the churches own large assets. Who will dispose of them if Christian unity is accomplished? One proposal for Greek Catholics has involved the establishment of a double communion with Catholic Rome and Orthodox Antioch, but this solution is aimed principally at the communities of the two churches and still leaves many elements of confusion unresolved. Such a solution also assumes that the orthodox themselves are in doctrinal agreement, which they are not.

The Second Vatican Council's "Declaration on non-Christian Religions," under pressure from the Oriental bishops, aimed to exclude antisemitism from an authentic Catholicism. This declaration no doubt helped to create not only a more favorable climate for dialogue between Christians and Muslims but also a paralyzing pro-Muslim conformism. The inferior status of Christians in Muslim lands became aggravated, since the Muslims almost unanimously view an invitation to dialogue as a confession of weakness. The pressure from integralist Islam has continually increased, going as far as persecution of Christians in some cases.

This declaration also gave many Oriental bishops an opportunity to utter statements that are purely and simply antisemitic, more or less under the guise of anti-Zionism. One result has been an increase of the silent contempt Muslims usually have for the *dhimmis* and a reinforcement of Christian antisemitism. Copies of the "Protocols of the Wise Men of Zion" are for sale in all bookshops, and bishops never warn people about this perverse book. A shaykh can very well ask God in a Friday sermon "to send to the fires of hell the Jews who have been spared by the crematoria." This text appears in all the newspapers, but no Christian authority cares enough to warn the faithful against such blasphemy. And when, on the occasion of a synod in Lebanon in 1975, Joseph Raya, Greek Catholic bishop of Saint Joan of Arc (Akka, Israel) declared to the press that he willingly welcomes into his home Jews as well as Muslims, the outcry was even stronger among the Christians than among Muslims. He was forced to resign from his diocese and now lives in exile in Canada.

Gregoire Haddad surely continues to collaborate with Muslims in social welfare projects. The University of Saint Joseph in Lebanon sponsors an Islamic Christian Institute, giving classes in ethics and in theology taught alternately by a Christian and a Muslim. The University's Center for Studies of the Modern Arab World (CENAM) is a place for reflection and sociological, political, and even theological publications on Islam. All these efforts could bear considerable fruit in the future, but they do not have much effect on the present situation. Rather, the present is filled with a type of antisemitism (presented as anti-Zionism) as far as action for peace is concerned. There is no lack of kind Christian words in favor of peace, but either explicitly or implicitly they always exclude Israel from the peace in question. In the autumn of 1982, talks were begun between Israel and Lebanon, but neither in Rome nor in Lebanon did a single bishop take a position in favor of peace. In fact, only Pope John Paul I showed great joy at the prospects opened up by Camp David. And by continually refraining from establishing diplomatic relations with Israel, the Holy See lets it be known that Israel is an entity destined to disappear—an attitude that favors the worst kind of Arab warmongering.

Another opportunity was offered by Vatican II's "Declaration on Religious Freedom." But when, in Lebanon, a Muslim government minister chooses a Sunday (a legal holiday) for official examinations, nobody protests. The same type of silence is encountered when one learns that ten converts to Christianity have been imprisoned. Hundreds of Syrian attorneys, engineers, and doctors went on strike in 1980 to demand legislation that would show greater respect for human rights. Christians were not among them. Arrested and tortured, they did receive support from Amnesty International, but none from the local or international Christian churches. The truth is that the bishops do not believe in religious freedom. They fear it. If Muslims are converted, they fear complications: as in Algeria Christian baptism is refused to a Muslim even if the person requests it; the bishops are especially worried about losing their own Christians if the number of Muslim converts increases. This fear is not implausible. Christian lay people are so accustomed to depending on their bishops as the only competent persons even in civil matters to deal with their own personal concerns (e.g., marriage, divorce, inheritance) that many would no doubt leave the church, at least provisionally, if they were free to do so and would not at the same time have to become Muslims, since the status of "no religion" does not exist in a civil contract.

On all these issues (action for peace, human rights, religious liberty) not only are there divisions among Christians in multiple jurisdictions but various patriarchates also have jurisdiction over several different nation-states at the same time. As a result, coordinated action in any given country is practically impossible. Can a Christianity that has become incapable of being a "confessing church" really survive? In all these countries, in any case, the number of conversions is unfavorable to Christianity, except perhaps in Lebanon. There, the numbers are small (perhaps a few hundred). In Egypt thousands of Christians each year convert to Islam. The impact of these figures is in fact more disquieting than the numerous losses to the church through emigration.

There remains a Christian population in the Middle East with a solid faith capable of creating or welcoming new forms of charismatic Christian life. The real problem is to discover if these groups will be able to play the role of "acting minorities" working effectively to overcome the church's institutional inertia and a hostile environment.

20

The Philippines: Church at the Crossroads

John J. Carroll, S.J.

"Cory" Aquino and the events of February 1986, by putting the Philippines "on the map" of the world's consciousness, may finally have laid to rest the illusion that the country is Spanish-speaking and located somewhere near Cuba or Puerto Rico; or that it lies in mid-Pacific facing San Francisco. Manila in fact lies some 3,800 miles southwest of Hawaii, due south from Shanghai, and only 850 miles across the South China Sea from the coast of Vietnam. The archipelago extends northward to within 66 miles of Taiwan and southward to a point 30 miles from the coast of Borneo. Its 180,000 square miles of land area is slightly less than that of Japan but larger than the British Isles. The 56,600,000 inhabitants (1986) speak a variety of local languages of Malayo-Polynesian origin related to those of Indonesia; English is widely spoken as a second language, while Spanish is spoken hardly at all.[1]

But if geographically and linguistically the Philippines is unmistakably part of Southeast Asia, the illusions noted above do have certain cultural and historical bases in fact. In sharp contrast with the other nations of Asia, for example, 90 percent of Filipinos identify themselves as Christians, a consequence of four centuries of Spanish colonial and missionary effort. Thus the visitor, noting the Spanish-style churches and the colorful fiestas, as well as the *haciendas* or large agricultural plantations with their attendant social problems, is easily reminded of Latin America.

Moreover, in a very real sense, forty-five years of colonial experience under the United States taught the Filipino to look eastward to San Francisco and New York and Washington, rather than westward to Asia. One senses this in the widespread use of the English language, together with educational and political institutions modeled on those of the United States; continuing economic, political, and military ties to that country; and when times are hard, in the long lines of Filipinos outside the American embassy applying for visas.

These islands had been a crossroad of cultures and migrations from prehistoric times, and the underlying Malay culture had already been influenced in one region or another by Arabian, Chinese, and Hindu-Indonesian elements before the Spaniards arrived. Thus, Phillippine culture today is a blend of traits derived from many sources, with significant regional variations, and a remarkable resilience in absorbing new elements.

Church, State, and People Under Spain

When the Spaniards arrived, during the sixteenth century, they found a population of between 500,000 and 1,000,000 scattered along the coasts and river valleys with a few major seaport settlements such as Manila and Cebu. There was considerable regional variation in settlement type and economic activity: in the far south they found sea traders, slave raiders, fishermen, and pirates, living on houses built on piles over the sea, with extensive interregional contacts; around Manila and on the central plain of Luzon, village-dwelling rice cultivators with terraced fields; and in the central Philippines, coastal villagers making use of the sea but also engaged in shifting cultivation or gathering the products of forest, marsh, or swamp. Of the great world religions, only Islam had become established in the islands, and that only in the southern part of Mindanao and to some degree around seaports such as Manila. Elsewhere the religion of the people was directed toward ancestors and a variety of nature spirits; whether or not they had a clear belief in a supreme being is not certain. There were religious specialists, skilled in healing and in dealing with the supernatural, but no broader religious organization.[2]

Each community was headed by a *datu;* in the Muslim areas several *datu* might owe allegiance to a *rajah.* Class structure within the communities varied with the type of settlement and economic activity; it typically included a ruling class composed of the *datu* and his family; it could also include a class of hereditary warriors who served the *datu,* of freemen who worked the land, and of "slaves" of various types who owed labor service to the "owners." Irrigated land was the property of the community and allocated by the *datu* to families for their use; hillside land was available for whoever in the community wished to occupy and use it.[3]

With the exception of the Muslim south, these societies lacked the broader political organization necessary to resist occupation by the Spanish forces, beginning in 1665; and they were quickly "pacified." Quickly also, and again with the exception of the Muslim areas, the Christianity brought by the Spanish missionaries was accepted by the people, at least outwardly. Various explanations have been suggested for the rapidity of this conversion: the threat of Spanish arms, the perception by the people that the god of the Christians was more powerful than their gods since the Christians prevailed in battle, and the fact that none of the great world religions had yet established its hegemony in the area.

Other probable reasons for the success of the missionary effort have been documented: the evident self-sacrifice of the missionaries and the fact that they quickly came to be seen by the people as their protectors against abuse, whether by the

Spaniards or by their own leaders. Thus the very Augustinian friars who had accompanied Legazpi on his expedition publicly denounced the abuses of the Spanish soldiers, refusing to hear the confessions of those guilty of plundering the "Indios" (Filipinos) and unwilling to restore what they had stolen. In a message to the Spanish king himself they affirmed that "no part of these islands has come under the power of the Spaniards by a just title." The First Synod of Manila (1582–1586) took up a whole series of issues involving the rights of the local population and decreed that only a trained theologian be allowed to hear the confession of the governor, since his responsibility for the injustices committed by himself, his wife, and his associates was presumably both heavy and complex.[4]

The Spaniards had a variety of objectives in occupying the Philippines: the desire for gold and spices, the expansion of empire, and the missionary enterprise. Little gold or spices were found, and some Spaniards turned to collecting tribute from the "Indios" who were entrusted to their "care" under the *encomienda* system. Others turned to commerce, and Manila became a trading post where silk from China was exchanged for Mexican silver. Until the nineteenth century little effort was made to produce for export, and of the relatively few Spaniards who made the long trip to the Philippines, even fewer chose to live far from Manila. Spain was represented in the provinces principally by a provincial governor-judge, and by the missionaries. The former governed through the local *datu;* the latter learned the local languages rather than teaching the people Spanish. Hence there was probably less penetration and disruption of the older social and cultural systems than seems to have been the case in parts of Latin America. The clandestine practice of the traditional rites and rituals, and periodic revolts led by native religious figures and ruthlessly suppressed by the Spaniards, were testimony to the underground strength of the old beliefs.[5]

Nevertheless, the Spanish occupation did bring significant changes in social structure. The Spaniards themselves now constituted a new social class or caste possessing political, military, and ideological hegemony, superimposed on the system; and their administration of both civil and religious society was the first step in a long process of centralization of decision making in Manila. As part of the missionary enterprise, the clergy attempted with some success to gather the people together in towns or "reductions," "under the bell" of the parish church. Household slavery was abolished, but not debt-peonage or sharecropping. Private ownership of land was established, and in the process some communities seem to have lost their land through unscrupulous *datu* who sold it as if it were their own personal property. In the process the Spaniards acquired a strong economic base in the region around Manila.[6]

The position of the *datu,* who was now called *principal,* changed as well. It was strengthened by insertion into the Spanish bureaucratic system, and embellished with honorific titles and privileges; if he pleased the Spaniards he might be appointed magistrate, or given a grant of land, and his son educated in the house of the parish priest. He had lost some of his direct control over community land and labor, but instead was in charge of tax and tribute collections and organizing community labor services; since the tribute, forced deliveries of foodstuffs, and labor demands were very heavy, this new authority could be used as a means of enhancing his personal power.

The church and the religious clergy appear in a double role relative to the issues of tribute and obligatory labor. Religious institutions were the beneficiaries of unpaid labor services. At times, however, the clergy were active in opposing abuses, to the extent, it seems, of setting fire to forests where forced laborers were to have been employed in the back-breaking work of cutting logs for shipbuilding.[7]

Despite many conflicts with the state generated by the intricacies of church–state relations in the Spanish empire, and many internal conflicts as well, the church was active in developing educational and charitable activities, in continuing its missionary apostolate, and even in helping to fortify and protect Christian villages from the Muslim raids, which continued well into the nineteenth century. A major failure, however, was the slow and inadequate promotion and training of local clergy.[8]

Nationalism and Revolution

In the latter part of the eighteenth century, the Spaniards began to focus on the development of the local economy and foreign trade by promoting the production of export crops such as sugar, hemp, coffee, and tobacco. Educational reforms and prosperity permitted the sons of upper class Filipino families to study in Manila and abroad, while Spanish became more available as a medium of interregional communication among the elite. A consequence was the development of a national consciousness among these same elite, and a demand for social and political equality with the Spaniards, a demand echoed by the Filipino diocesan clergy, who by this time had come into conflict with Spanish religious over control of the parishes.

At the same time, the process of change had disastrous consequences for many of the poor, for example, weavers who were affected by foreign competition. With the monetization of the economy and the growing economic importance of mixed-blood Chinese families, land became a commercial commodity; many ordinary Filipinos lost their claims through debt or otherwise, and land ownership became more concentrated. Some land was taken out of rice production and devoted to cash crops. Tensions built up around the church-owned agricultural estates in the Manila area. The situation was exacerbated by the sheer ineptness of Spanish administration; and in 1872 the execution of three Filipino priests by the Spanish authorities united all nationalist groups against the Spaniards. These forces eventually coalesced in the first major nationalist war of liberation in Southeast Asia, the Philippine Revolution of 1896.

Many of the elite, Western-educated nationalist leaders had been influenced by Freemasonry and were bitterly anticlerical; they saw the friars, moreover, as the main bulwark of Spanish rule. A decline in numbers and quality of the Spanish clergy had given rise to complaints of avarice and immorality and provided the basis for a vast campaign of antifriar propaganda. Nevertheless, the revolution was not uniformly antireligious. Some revolutionary leaders protected the Spanish friars and ordered prayers to be offered for the souls of all, Filipinos and Spaniards, who had died in battle. Some Filipino priests took up arms, accepted posts of responsibility in the revolution, or preached it as a "holy war."[9] It has also been argued that the religious "Passion" (Pasyon) poetry, which depicted the sufferings of Christ and had become part of the popular culture in the area around Manila, provided the values, role models, and symbols that motivated the participation of the great mass of the people in the revolution.[10]

Nevertheless, the bishops, who were all Spanish, and the Spanish clergy were clearly opposed to the revolution. Some of the latter took up arms beside their countrymen; and some of them were tortured and killed by the revolutionary forces. The tensions thus generated eventually gave rise to the establishment of the schismatic "Aglipayan" or Philippine Independent Church.[11]

Elite Democracy

The Americans came to the Philippines in 1898 as allies of the Filipinos in their war against Spain. They remained as colonizers, after a costly and sometimes brutal process of "pacification" remembered by Filipinos as the Philippine–American War. Nevertheless, they were colonizers committed to self-government for Filipinos and eventual independence if the latter should wish it. The American authorities set vigorously about the process of transplanting to their new colony the institutions they believed to be essential for a viable democratic order: separation of church and state; a public school system with English as the language of instruction, staffed initially by American teachers; a system of local self-government. Protestant missionaries, some of them doubling as public school teachers, arrived in great numbers and began proselytizing. Later, American Freemasonry arrived to link up with Philippine Masonry, thus forming what became a dominant and anti-Catholic force in Philippine political life for two decades.[12]

The newcomers found the Catholic church in disarray and practically leaderless, besieged on all sides. The Spanish bishops were unable to function. By the beginning of 1904, three-fourths of the more than 1,000 Spanish clergy had left the country; there remained only about 600 Filipino priests, many of them poorly trained and some of less than exemplary personal lives. Hundreds of parishes were abandoned. The Aglipayan schism had drawn away perhaps one-fourth of the Catholic population and some of the priests, and had taken over the churches in many towns. The bishops and clergy had little knowledge of English or of American ways; the educated Filipino elite were typically anticlerical and of little help in dealing with the problems of civil marriage, religious instruction, control of church property, or anti-Catholic propaganda.[13]

In these circumstances, the fact that Catholicism survived as well as it did provided remarkable testimony to the faith of the Filipinos themselves. Eventually, and not without bitter internal struggles, the church was able to reorganize itself: new bishops were appointed, Americans at first and then Filipinos; missionaries arrived from Belgium and the Netherlands and later from elsewhere to replace the Spaniards who had left; seminaries were reopened and strengthened; Filipinos were accepted into the religious orders; the church's educational effort was renewed and lay Catholic organizations were established. By arrangement between the American government and the Holy See, the religious orders gave up their landed property. Gradually, most of those who had been lost to Aglipayanism were brought back.[14]

In 1907, elections were held for the First Philippine Assembly. The fact that, due to property qualifications, only 1.2 percent of the population voted, and that as late as 1938 only 11.2 percent voted, is indicative of the nature of the emerging democracy and also of a fundamental compromise which the American authorities had made. Americans needed the support of educated and influential Filipinos in "pacifying" the country and establishing their administration; yet the educated and influential had no stomach for sharing their power or wealth with the masses. Hence the Americans faced the dilemma: peace and order, or social change and reform; respect for local institutions, or social injustice? What eventually emerged was a "meeting of minds" among the "intelligent" leaders on both sides; social justice and social reform concerns were accordingly "put on the back burner" in favor of a slower, "educational" approach.[15]

The overall trend of economic policy was an intensification of agricultural production for export and of economic links to the United States. It was only in the 1930s, as the Philippines gained commonwealth status and internal self-government, that serious thought was directed to creating an independent and viable national economy; and this effort was largely aborted by World War II. Meanwhile, population pressure and the commercialization of agriculture created new social tensions in the rural areas north and south of Manila, tensions that were exacerbated by the activities of labor and peasant leaders with links to the world communist movement.[16]

Also by the 1930s, a new generation of Catholics less concerned with the issues of the past and more comfortable with the present had begun to make its voice heard on public issues. The bishops publicly challenged Manual Quezon, first president of the Commonwealth, on the issue of religious instruction in the public schools, much to his annoyance. And the students of Father Joseph Mulry, S.J., a professor at the Ateneo de Manila, began presenting articulate and witty radio plays and lectures that replied to attacks against the church but also took up issues such as communism and social justice.[17]

War and Independence: New Wine in Old Bottles

The Pacific War marked the end of the "American period" and the final burial of some of the issues inherited from the "Spanish period." Formal political independence had been programmed for July 4, 1946; it was achieved on schedule — but only after three years of Japanese occupation, heroic resistance on the part of the Philippine population, and a final desperate battle between Japanese and American forces which left the city of Manila in ruins. The constitution provided for a governmental structure modeled on that of the United States; it functioned for twenty-six years until 1972 when President Ferdinand Marcos declared martial law and imposed on the nation his own "constitutional authoritarianism."

By some standards the Philippine experiment with democracy might have been considered a success. The Filipinos in 1972 were the only nation in Southeast Asia ever to have *voted* an administration out of office, and they had done so regularly and enthusiastically. The economic growth rate of about 6 percent per year in real terms was impressive. Yet something obviously had gone wrong; and it appears that the root of failure lay in the continuation of the old pattern of elite democracy, despite the fact that the vote was now available to practically any adult Filipino who wished it.

In a sense, the postwar democracy had been "conceived in iniquity." In the immediate aftermath of the war, peasant groups of socialist or communist inspiration, which had fought the Japanese and then entered political life as the Democratic Alliance, had won six seats in the Philippine Congress. Congress, however, refused to seat them.[18] This precipitated an agrarian revolt which by 1952 threatened the city of Manila itself. The revolt was ultimately defeated, with considerable American support and "advice," but without any real attack on the fundamental issues of equality and participation.

Given the traditional dependence of the poor and weak on the wealthy and powerful, together with the failure of the Democratic Alliance, it is not surprising that elections simply became struggles between competing groups of leaders and followers, bound together by personal ties and only loosely identified with political parties. The parties themselves had no identifiable ideologies; their policies were determined by the personal interests of those in power and their concern to reward their followers with jobs and other forms of patronage in order to maintain their support.

In this context, democracy was hardly an instrument of social progress. Economic policy favored industrialization through import substitution and high-capital urban manufacturing, and almost totally neglected the rural areas. A study conducted by the International Labor Office in 1973 found that "the rural communities today are not radically different from the traditional rural economy of the prewar years." The intervening period had seen the development of a modern industrial sector; yet "satisfactory growth rates have been accompanied by more and more unacceptable outcomes in terms of employment and income distribution." In summary, "the particular growth path chosen in the past has tended to be adverse to the interests of the average worker, and even more so that of the below-average worker."[19]

The situation, and its disastrous human consequences, were a challenge to the Christian conscience. Fr. Mulry had died in a Japanese prison camp, but his social concern had been communicated to another American Jesuit, Fr. Walter Hogan, who in the late 1940s began working with labor unions and by the early 1950s was conducting labor classes at the Jesuit-run Institute of Social Order (ISO). Fr. Hogan was instrumental in establishing the Federation of Free Workers (FFW), which claimed the distinction of being inspired by the papal encyclicals and being free from government domination, communist domination, and control by racketeers. The early history of the FFW was stormy since it found itself pitted not only against government officials, communists, and racketeers, but also against various prominent Catholic laymen in the business world, as well as the Catholic University of Sto. Tomas, and eventually the archbishop of Manila, the apostilic nuncio, and the entire Philippine hierarchy. Fr. Hogan was forbidden to speak publicly on social matters by Archbishop (later Cardinal) Santos of Manila; yet the FFW and ISO survived, together with the Federation of Free Farmers (FFF), which was founded under similar inspiration by a Catholic layman, Jeremias Montemayor.[20]

After the silencing of Fr. Hogan, the ISO took a less controversial line, promoting the credit union and cooperative movements. Major new initiatives in the social field came in the wake of the Second Vatican Council, and of the month-long Priests'

Institute for Social Action organized by Fr. Hogan in Hong Kong in 1965 attended by a bishop and eighteen priests from the Philippines. Prominent among the new initiatives was the establishment in 1966 of the National Secretariat of Social Action (NASSA) of the Philippine hierarchy, with a full-time secretariat; it was instrumental in founding social action centers in the majority of dioceses, which undertook a wide range of social action projects. Another initiative was the National Catholic Rural Congress of 1967, which focused attention on the problems of the rural Philippines. Following the Congress, church support for the FFF became very evident, with chaplains being assigned and student groups joining in its organizational activities and demonstrations; the organization grew rapidly in numbers and influence. The Catholic Bishops' Conference issued a number of documents that reflected their deepening social awareness, and a new review, the *Philippine Priests' Forum* aimed at disseminating social concern among the clergy.

There were parallel developments in establishing new structures for communication, coordination, and formation within the church. The Catholic Bishops' Conference of the Philippines (CBCP) was strengthened, as were the Associations of Major Religious Superiors (AMRSP). In the south, the Mindanao-Sulu Pastoral Conference (MSPC) was established with representation of priests, religious, and laymen and a strong secretariat; its emphasis on Christian community building and the role of the laity pointed the way for the whole Philippine church. Established too were the Inter-Seminary Forum for seminarians in the Greater Manila area and the Sisters' Formation Institute. There were also the thousands of parishes, Catholic schools, radio stations and lay organizations, and older associations such as the Catholic Educational Association of the Philippines. This network of organizations gave to the church the potential as a social and cultural force in society, significant not so much in absolute terms (the ratio of priests to people was one of the lowest in the world) as in the absence of any competing network, especially in the rural areas.[21]

Slower and more painful was the change in relationships within the church itself. In the light of the principles of Vatican II, many priests and laymen became aware and resentful of what was seen as authoritarian and "triumphalistic" attitudes and a lack of social concern on the part of bishops, notably Rufino Cardinal Santos of Manila who was the dominant figure in the hierarchy. Their protests led to a fifty-seven day picket of the Manila Cathedral by a group of Catholic youth that explicitly took its inspiration from the Council, and eventually to a disturbance at the Cardinal's Midnight Mass on Christmas by a group of social activists. There were also bitter controversies within religious congregations between Filipino and foreign personnel, focusing on issues of nationalism and indigenization. The development of priests' senates was resisted by some of the hierarchy.

Meanwhile the underlying social problems were generating new tensions. A Maoist-oriented student movement came into being and soon dominated and disrupted academic life throughout the nation; it served also as a recruiting ground for the newly established Community party of the Philippines (CPP) and its military arm, the New People's Army (NPA). Catholic student groups also took more radical and aggressive lines. Community organizing, using the conflictual tactics of Saul Alinsky, was introduced under ecumenical church auspices in the Manila slums and elsewhere. There were efforts on the part of both church-related and radical groups to mobilize and organize the peasants; landlords and local politicians reacted by using "goons" and "private armies" against these "agitators." The government seemed incapable of controlling the rising tide of violence. Thus, in September 1972 President Marcos, who was approaching the end of his second and constitutionally last term of office, was able to declare that the security of the state and the constitutional order were in danger, and so to justify the imposition of martial law.

The Crucible

With the declaration of martial law the legislature was suspended; the media were at first suppressed and then taken over by trusted associates of the president; school campuses were put under strict surveillance; social action programs were closed; thousands of opposition figures, labor leaders, clergy, and media people were put under arrest; strikes and assemblies were prohibited; the write of habeas corpus was suspended. At the same time, Marcos promised to use the powers of the state to make equality and participation the basis for a "new society," the "cornerstone" of which was laid five days after the declaration of martial law when he proclaimed the whole nation a land reform area. By January 1973 a new constitution was "approved" *by show of hands* in nationwide "Citizens' Assemblies" and the Supreme Court found itself unable or unwilling to invalidate it. The constitution and subsequent amendments made it possible for Marcos to extend his rule indefinitely, and so enhanced the powers of the president that, when martial law was formally lifted in 1981, it made little difference.

In those first months there were many, including some churchmen, who were disillusioned with the failures of the "old society" and willing to give Marcos a chance, provided at least that basic human rights would be respected. Five days after the proclamation, the Administrative Council of the CBCP asked for calm and prayerful acceptance of the new situation, while urging the people to keep working for a more just society. The FFF leadership threw its support behind Marcos, banking on his promise of land reform. On the other hand, two days after the CBCP statement, seventeen bishops and seventeen members of the AMRSP signed a letter voicing a more critical reaction.

These differences of opinion occasioned bitter debate within the church and the CBCP. They reflected different theologies of the church, different readings of the situation, and different political options, which in turn reflected in part the different situations in which churchmen found themselves. The cardinals, archbishops, and others with heavy administrative responsibilities tended to avoid conflict with the state; some bishops of smaller rural dioceses and their social action directors, who had seen at first hand the arrest and sometimes torture and murder by the armed forces of dedicated social activists, took a far more critical stance. In its meeting in January 1973 the CBCP was unable to agree on a position and issued no statement. The divisions within the organization persisted until about 1977, and during this time the most outspoken episcopal statements came not from the CBCP as such but from individual bishops or groups of like-minded bishops.

The AMRSP as an organization was far more critical than the bishops. It supported an "above-ground" but illegal publication that documented military abuses and reappeared under a new name when closed down by the authorities. It also established a number of task forces, notably Task Force Detainees, to help meet the problems created by the new situation. The activism of the AMRSP at a time when the CBCP as a body was more cautious, gained for it some severe warnings from Rome.[22]

The years 1977–1983 saw a growth in unity among the bishops and a greater willingness to face delicate national issues and distance themselves from President Marcos. Behind this development were a number of factors: the ongoing discussions with the CBCP itself; the accumulating evidence that the promises of the regime were illusory and that government was favoring Marcos's rich and powerful friends at the expense of the poor, and thereby providing fuel for insurgency; and pressures from Christian activists who included a substantial number of priests and religious as well as many leaders of Basic Christian Communities and social action programs.

The communist-led insurgency itself was increasing in strength as repression drove social activists "underground"; there many Christian activists came into contact with cadres of the CPP, and discovered that they were alumni of the same pre-martial law training programs. The introduction in the mid-1970s of the technique of "structural analysis" provided them all with a common, though vastly oversimplified, vision of Philippine society and its ills.[23] Also by the late 1970s, the National Democratic Front (NDF), an "umbrella" organization founded by the CPP in which the latter has always been the dominant force, had incorporated many church-related groups attracted by its program of social reform and opposition to Marcos.

Christians linked to or sympathetic with the NDF had in fact been more active than many bishops in supporting human rights and in taking the risks associated with opposition to the regime. They included some very dedicated and articulate clergy and religious. But the commitment of these clergy and religious created problems of divided loyalties and suspicion with dioceses and religious congregations; some would say also of secrecy and deception. Moreover, a spirituality was developing in which the "people's struggle" and its demands, as understood from a certain point of view, became central and normative, and those elements of the Christian tradition that could not easily be integrated with this center were either reinterpreted or pushed to the margin. Finally, they helped to create an extensive network of communication and fund-raising, both locally and internationally, which projected the NDF as the only significant opposition to Marcos and systematically ignored or attacked opposition groups that were not aligned with themselves.[24]

In attempting to regain control of the situation, the bishops in the early 1980s had taken steps toward supervising NASSA more closely, and the Mindanao bishops eventually dissociated themselves from the secretariat of the MSPC. They thus found themselves forced to stake out a position of their own, one that would be basically moral and religious rather than "political" in the partisan sense; they did so in their "Dialogue for Peace" joint pastoral, issued in February 1983. In it they insisted that their role was to preach the Gospel, but also that the Gospel has something to say about public issues.

> Hence, we will have to reprobate any action or program that runs counter to the primary values of the Gospel: the torture and murder of citizens simply because they are of a different political persuasion from that of present or would-be power-holders;

the silencing of people, the suppression of media, merely because they speak the truth of our national situation; the increasing use of arms and violence, both by forces on the right and on the left, in the pursuit of their ends of power; and closer to home, the use of church funds, the manipulation of church programs, for the political purposes of ideological groups.[25]

The bishops went on to more specific criticisms of government policy in the areas of human rights and priorities for development, criticisms that were far from welcome to the regime. Church-state tensions mounted dramatically, and came to a head in August 1983 when the nation was shocked by the public assassination of Senator Benigno Aquino, a prominent opposition leader, presumably by members of the armed forces. As the custodian of many of the nation's symbols, but also as an institution possessing credibility and moral authority when those of the government were nil, as well as a degree of immunity from suppression by the state and a broad organizational network, the church could not be uninvolved during a moment of national crisis. The radio station operated by the archdiocese of Manila kept the nation informed at a time when the other media tended only to disinform; and the magnificent sermon of Cardinal Sin at Aquino's funeral helped to transfrom the event into a profoundly religious expression of hope and defiance rather than fear and hatred.

In the succeeding months the protest, now centered largely in the middle classes, which had been shocked out of their lethargy by the assassination, moved into more secular channels. It eventually focused on the presidential election of 1986. In a national situation that was deeply polarized, the bishops supported the "participation" option as against the "boycott" stance of the CPP and NDF, which condemned the election as an exercise in futility and an American stratagem to legitimate the Marcos regime. But the bishops also insisted vigorously on the duty of protecting the integrity of the ballot, and supported the National Movement for Free Elections (NAMFREL), of which the moving spirits were Catholic laypersons quite close to the hierarchy. NAMFREL fielded hundreds of thousands of volunteers to watch the polling places and protect the ballot boxes; priests, seminarians, and religious in their religious dress were assigned to some of the most critical and dangerous areas. When, despite everything, the election seemed about to be stolen by Marcos, the CBCP issued its now famous statement in which it stated that a fraudulent election could provide no moral legitimacy for the regime, and that if the people themselves agreed that the election had been stolen, then they should, by peaceful means, *oblige* the regime to respect their will.[26]

Beyond the Bloodless Revolution

The story of the "bloodless revolution" of February 1986, and the role played in it by Cardinal Sin and churchpeople generally, is well known and need not be repeated here. Nevertheless, some points must be underlined. First, the overthrow of Marcos was a victory of *moral* values over the sheer physical force on which he had relied. The stolen election was the climax of a series of moral outrages, and the military uprising together with Cardinal Sin's call to the streets galvanized the people into action. The people's determination that Filipinos were not to be allowed to shed the blood of their brother Filipinos effectively blocked the efforts of Marcos to use military force, and eventually won over the "enemy" soldiers themselves.

Second, the revolution was *not* the work of the NDF or of the groups associated with it, either Christian or Marxist. These groups had isolated themselves by their "boycott" stance and played almost no part in the February events. The roots of what happened lie elsewhere: in the mobilization of the middle classes by the Aquino assassination; in the movement for active nonviolence, which was promoted by church-related groups not identified with the NDF; in the "prayer vigils" organized among the military; and finally in the leadership provided by the CBCP with its postelection statement.[27]

At the same time, the February revolution was a *political* event, not a social revolution, and the story is far from over. The basic social issue that has plagued the nation for generations, namely, the concentration of wealth and power, still remains. It is clear that seventy years of free elections, a free press, separation of powers, and the other trappings of democracy did not bring the ordinary Filipino into the mainstream of national life. A more direct attack on the distribution of power and wealth in society is called for. And one wonders whether the middle and upper classes are more ready than were their predecessors of 1898 and 1946 for significant *social* change.

The NDF suffered a major setback by isolating itself from the election and its related events; but it has regrouped and, like its armed component, the NPA, remains strong. Its spokesmen, including priests and religious, dominate the lecture circuits where Philippine issues are discussed in Europe, North America, Australia. The NDF is keeping its options open and, should the Aquino government fail to deliver tangible benefits for the poor, an El Salvador-type situation could emerge from the consequent disillusionment of the people.

Clearly there is a continuing role here for the Catholic church. Some 84 percent of the population identify themselves as Roman Catholic; the remainder is divided among a wide variety of faiths: Aglipayans and Muslims with about 5 percent each; Protestants and the indigenous Iglesia ni Kristo together with another 4 or 5 percent; Buddhists and animists with 1 or 2 percent. Added to this numerical preponderance is the Catholic church's influence as a cultural force and custodian of many of the significant symbols of the people, and as a social force with an extensive network of communication in the form of parishes and schools, radio stations, social action programs, and thousands of trained and dedicated workers.

But the vast number of Catholics is also a liability. The church's resource base is weak, particularly in terms of professional personnel; geographically the population is widely scattered and in large part poorly educated. The ratio of one priest for 8,854 Catholics is one of the lowest in the world—only about one-tenth of that found in some of the countries of Europe and in North America; this ratio continues to decline as local vocations are insufficient to replace the foreign missionaries who die, retire, or leave the country. Many of the priests are not involved in parish work. Thus a sacramental Catholicism is virtually impossible, particularly in rural areas; it has been calculated that only 12–15 percent of Filipino Catholics attend mass each week and receive communion. For many of the people, therefore, religion is family-based and rooted in tradition, centered on local shrines and *fiestas,* rather than on an intellectual appropriation of the Christian message. Traditionally, too, religious practice has been seen as a matter for women and children, not for the men of the family.

The wide range of religious attitudes—from pre-Christian animists in the hills to post-Christian secular humanists in the universities—is further complicated by the rapid growth of sectarian movements. Some of these are fanatical groups, hardly Christian at all, led by individuals supposedly endowed with magical power and prone to violence; others have a spirituality of simplicity and gentleness. Fundamentalist Protestant sects are increasing in number and gaining members more rapidly than mainline and ecumenical churches; charismatic groups are particularly attractive to young people and students who apparently have not found much meaning in traditional Catholic belief and practice. Finally, the indigenous and bitterly anti-Catholic Iglesia ni Kristo has grown rapidly and in some areas has become a political force.

The most significant development within Catholicism in response to these challenges has been a growing Basic Christian Community movement, especially in rural areas, above all in Mindanao. Through it the church now reaches beyond the town to the barrio and small local settlement, and people are learning to reflect on the Gospel in common and to explore its meaning for their lives, while receiving communion from part-time lay ministers. Some suggest that the training in leadership and in articulating one's thoughts in these small gatherings and in the developing communication and action networks, which have already mobilized the communities in times of crisis, constitute a major social and religious development. In time this movement may link up with the growing social concern on the campuses of Catholic educational institutions and lay organizations, which until now have been urban-based and rather elitist. The Catholic church, therefore, remains a major social and cultural force with a unique network of institutions and a reservoir of credibility with the people. The question is, can and will it use its resources to delegitimate the *social* system as it used them to delegitimate the *political* system set up by Marcos? Can it promote the kind of solidarity on behalf of *social* justice which it promoted for *political* justice during the events of February? Can it overcome its internal polarization and establish dialogue among those of different points of view, a dialogue that will be based on the Gospel and transcend political and ideological differences? Can it lend its support to people's movements of all kinds, in which the "little man" can articulate his needs, link up with other "little men," and gain for himself a share in the decision making that affects his life?

An indication of the bishops' thinking may perhaps be found in a study which they commissioned of their pastoral priorities.[28] The bishops gave highest priority to the work of preaching the Gospel, administering the sacraments, promoting the prayer-life and faith-experience of the people. But they also insisted very strongly on the "integration of faith with daily concerns"; and a significant number of them saw the Basic Christian Community movement becoming the focus for a faith-life that expressed itself in communal prayer, service to the community, speaking out, and taking action on social issues—all carried out by lay men and women but with the support and encouragement of the clergy.

Thus as the nation and the church stand once again at a crossroads in their common history, the bishops look toward a church deeply rooted in the people, and will continue to address, from the viewpoint of the Gospel, the issues that affect the people. This will require leadership of a different type than that which once refused the sacraments to Spanish *conquistadores*, but no less demanding for all of that.

NOTES

1. In this paragraph and elsewhere I draw on material presented in my article, written under the pseudonym Benjamin A. McCloskey, "Les Philippines: une révolution dans l'impasse?" *Etudes,* 348/4 (April 1978):437–54.
2. John N. Schumacher, S.J., *Readings in Philippine Church History* (Quezon City: Loyola School of Theology, 1979), pp. 12–16.
3. William Henry Scott, "Filipino Class Structure in the Sixteenth Century," *Philippine Studies* 28 (1980):142–75. I have also made use of Scott's unpublished "Oripun and Alipin in the 16th Century Philippines," together with some notes taken during personal conversation with the author.
4. John F. Schumacher, S.J., "Has the Philippine Church Been on the Side of the Poor?," *Human Society* (series published by Human Development Research and Documentation, 2215 Pedro Gil, Manila), no. 26 (March 1984), p. 3.
5. Schumacher, *Readings in Philippine Church History,* pp. 72–73; also David R. Sturdevant, *Popular Uprisings in the Philippines, 1840–1940* (Ithaca, N.Y.: Cornell University Press, 1976).
6. John Leddy Phelan, *The Hispanization of the Philippines: Spanish Aims and Filipino Responses, 1565–1700* (Madison: University of Wisconsin Press, 1959), pp. 116–18; also Nicholas P. Cushner and John A. Larkin, "Royal Land Grants in the Colonial Philippines: Implications for the Formation of a Social Elite," *Philippine Studies* 26 (1978):102–111.
7. Nicholas P. Cushner, S.J., *Spain in the Philippines: From Conquest to Revolution* (Quezon City: Ateneo de Manila University Press, 1971), p. 120.
8. Schumacher, *Readings in Philippine Church History,* pp. 93–230.
9. John N. Schumacher, S.J., "The Religious Character of the Revolution in Cavite, 1896–97", *Philippine Studies* 24 (1976):399–417.
10. Reynaldo Clemena Ileto, *Pasyon and Revolution: Popular Movements in the Philippines, 1840–1910* (Quezon City: Ateneo de Manila University Press, 1979).
11. Schumacher, *Readings in Philippine Church History,* pp. 271–82, 317–33.
12. Ibid., p. 356.
13. Ibid., pp. 292–311.
14. Ibid., pp. 357–68.
15. Peter W. Stanley, "Introduction," in Peter W. Stanley (ed.), *Reappraising an Empire: New Perspectives on Philippine-American History* (Cambridge, Mass.: Harvard University Press, 1984).
16. John J. Carroll, S.J., "Philippine Labor Unions," *Philippine Studies* 9 (April 1961):220–54.
17. Schumacher, *Readings in Philippine Church History,* pp. 368–379.
18. This move in turn was intended to ensure the approval by Congress of the "parity" amendment to the constitution, granting to Americans equal rights with Filipinos in the exploitation of natural resources—a provision imposed by the U.S. Congress as a condition for completion of the war damage payments to the Philippines!
19. International Labour Office, *Sharing in Development: A Programme of Employment, Equity and Growth for the Phillipines* (Geneva, 1974), pp. 3, 13.

20. Wilfredo Fabros, "Socio-Economic Involvement of the Philippine Catholic Church: Proclamation and Action, 1930-1972," Ph.D. dissertaion, Loyala School of Theology, Ateneo de Manila University, 1983, pp. 132-54, 165-79, 215-45.

21. *Pro Mundi Vita*, 30 (1970), "The Philippines," pp. 19-28.

22. A chronological account of this period, focusing on the role of the hierarchy, is found in James Kroeger, M.M., *The Philippine Church and Evangelization, 1965-1984*, Ph.D. dissertation, Pontifical Gregorian University, 1985, pp. 169-274. See also my articles written under the pseudonym Benjamin A. McCloskey, "Operation Survival: The Church and Mr. Marcos," *America* 135 (Oct. 10, 1976), pp. 205-208; and "Church, State and Conflict in the Philippines," *The Month*, second new series, 10 (Aug. 1977), pp. 263-67.

23. Renato A. Ocampo, S.J., "Structural Analysis in the Philippines: Its Usefulness and Limitation in the Context of Social Transformation," *Pulso* (published by the Institute on Church and Social Issues, Loyola School of Theology, Ateneo de Manila University), 1 (1984):7-16.

24. John J. Carroll, S.J., "The Church: A Political Force?," *Human Society* 25 (Feb. 1984):18-22.

25. John J. Carroll, S.J., "The Philippine Bishops: Pastors or Politicos?," *Human Society* 37 (March 1985):9-11.

26. For documentation on the stand of the CBCP and of the discussions that preceded and followed it, see *Pulso* 1, no. 4 (1986).

27. John J. Carroll, S.J., "Looking Beyond EDSA," Parts I and II, *Human Society* 42 and 43 (May 1986).

28. John J. Carroll and Francisco F. Claver, "The Pastoral Priorities of the Philippine Bishops: A Report on a Survey Undertaken for the Catholic Bishops' Conference of the Philippines," May 31, 1984 (mimeo).

21

The Indian Catholic Community: A Minority in Search of Security

Walter Fernandes, S.J.

What is the Catholic community in India today? The question is not easy to answer. While Indian Catholicism faces the problems of socioeconomic development and cultural shock common to all Third World churches following a century of foreign occupation, one cannot really speak of the "Indian church" as a single community. India is larger than the whole of Europe (minus the Soviet Union). There may be a few underlying elements that link its various states in culture, political structure, and customs (more, probably, than among European countries) but the differences outnumber the similarities.

In delimiting India's Catholic community it is necessary to distinguish between six particular subgroups:

1. The Syrian Christians of Kerala, the oldest group (also known as Thomas Christians) who claim origin from the apostle Thomas. They comprise nearly one-fifth of the state's population and wield considerable power in its economic and political life.
2. The Konkan (or West) coast Catholics of Mangalore, Goa, and Bombay are products of Portuguese occupation of some territories in this region. Many of these Catholics were prominent in the British administration of India and today are found in private sector executive and clerical positions.
3. The Latin-rite Catholics of South India originate from three separate groups.

362

The Coromandel coast (known in Portuguese literature as the Fishery coast) fishermen of Tamilnadu and similar groups in Kerala were baptized by the Portuguese beginning in 1536. Another group in Tamilnadu, Andra Pradesh and Karnataka was converted by the missions founded by Roberto de Nobili in 1606.

4. Larger sections of the south belonging mainly to the "untouchable" caste were won over by the Paris Foreign Missionaries, Carmelites, and Jesuits, in the nineteenth century. Also during the nineteenth century, the Capuchins baptized many "untouchables" in north India.

5. Belgian Jesuits converted thousands of tribals in the Chotanagpur plateau of Bihar, Madhya Pradesh, West Bengal, and Orissa.

6. German Passionists and later the Salesians of Don Bosco converted several thousand tribals in northeastern India.

The Indian Catholic church constitutes the second largest Catholic community in Asia after the Philippines. In numbers, however, it comprises a mere fraction of India's vast population of almost 800 million people. Christians in India represent 2.6 percent of the total population; Catholics, about 1.6 percent. The church exhibits neither cultural homogeneity nor uniform jurisdiction. Nor are Catholics evenly distributed geographically. Kerala, with almost 4 percent of the nation's population and its highest literacy rate, has over 36 percent of India's Catholics; the four southern states with less than 25 percent of the population have nearly 70 percent. In the vast heartland of the subcontinent—the politically powerful northern states of Uttar Pradesh, Madya Pradesh, and Bihar—Catholics are practically nonexistent. This imbalance is also noticeable in the distribution of church personnel. Most of the clergy, religious, and active laity in the north and northeast come from the southern and western states. Despite its small numbers, however, the Catholic community owns and manages a vast complex of over 14,000 educational, medical, cultural, and charitable institutions. Such contrasts only complicate the task of understanding the heterogeneous quality of the Indian church.

Indian Catholicism's complexity is best approached through its history. Our first task, then, will be to identify the patterns of its development since independence in 1947. Political freedom did not represent a total break with the past; many actions of postindependence Catholicism flowed directly from attitudes built up during the colonial period and the freedom struggle. Hence, we also need to examine two main aspects of the nineteenth-century Indian church: the kinds of people who joined it and the origin of church-related institutions. These observations form a background for considering the situation of Indian Catholicism today. One topic that needs attention is the claim that Indian Christians have consistently preferred stability to change, that they supported the British until independence, and that over the last three decades they have been affiliated with the ruling Congress party. Some accuse them of thinking only of their own security and minority rights, keeping silent when others' human rights are violated. Others go further and attack the church for having a vested interest in the status quo.[1]

The present chapter proceeds on the alternative premise that any institution or social group is formed not so much by conscious strategy or deliberately expressed policy but by unconscious interaction with the changing situation of its surrounding environment. Hence, no effort will be made to pass judgment on the motives of church decision makers. Quite the contrary: we feel deep admiration for the people who have made the Indian church the important institution it is today.

Our analysis rests on the assumption that a social group develops in interaction with three particular poles or aspects of a society. First, the decision makers within a group declare certain interests that embody the vision (or goal) toward which the community as a whole is striving. This can be called the *legitimizing* pole. Indian Christian leaders have always articulated their aim as promoting the "good of the church," "saving souls," or "defending the rights of the minority"; it was this goal that justified their actions.

Second, both the members and leaders of a community perceive themselves and their society in a certain way. A group's interests, strategy, or "plan of action" are thus given practical orientation and may be modified in the process. This can be called the functional or *negotiating* pole. Missionaries in the nineteenth century, for example, perceived themselves as bearers of a saving message, their own group (the "baptized") as "redeemed," and Hindus as people who needed "to be saved from eternal damnation." As a result, missionaries felt the need of security in a foreign occupied India in order to better perform their tasks.

Third, the reality of a given society may not coincide with these perceptions. What decision makers do confronts society not as they perceive it but as it really exists. As a result, decisions may have consequences that were not originally foreseen or intended.[2] For example, the Catholic church opened schools for the upper class and dispensaries for the poor according to its perception of the Indian reality. But they might have proceeded differently.

These three poles provide the underlying framework for what will be discussed in the following pages.

The Postindependence Catholic Community

The post-1947 developments within Indian Catholicism are both quantitative and qualitative, and occurred in three areas: church organization, personnel, and institutions.

Organizational Changes

The Catholic church has experienced a dramatic increase in organizational size since independence—from 20 dioceses in 1886, when the Indian hierarchy was first established, to 48 in 1946, 106 in 1976, and 114 in 1986. The Thomas Christians have taken over dioceses in north India, which marks a missionary venture for the Kerala church.

In addition, there has been increased activity among Indian Catholics at the national level. The Catholic Bishops' Conference of India (CBCI) was founded in 1945; also in 1945 the Catholic Congress (of the laity), established originally in 1933, became the Catholic Union of India (CUI); India's First Plenary Council took place in 1950. The major superiors of religious communities formed a national conference in 1960. There now exist many national groups, for example, the Indian Catholic Hospital Association, the Xavier Board of Education (management), and the All-India Catholic University Federation (for students).

Ecumenical organizations have grown since independence. Many Protestant churches have joined together to form the Church of South India (CSI) and, later, the Church of North India (CNI). Catholic–Protestant encounters, however, began only in the 1960s when the two groups began to coordinate their activities, for example, the All India Association of Christian Higher Education (AIACHE) and other academic and development associations. Doubtless these two groups disagree on many points, but they continue to work together on issues of common interest.

Changes in Personnel

Parallel to this organizational development, the church has undergone a qualitative growth and Indianization of its personnel. It has also made a continuing serious effort at cultural adaptation. The first Latin-rite Indian bishop was appointed in 1923, the second in 1930. By independence there were only twelve Indians among the country's thirty-two bishops and archbishops; 40 percent of its priests and religious were foreigners. Today, only one Indian diocese is headed by a foreigner and fewer than a thousand of its 12,000 priests are foreign-born, most of them over sixty years of age.

A major feature of the Indian church is an abundance of priestly and religious vocations. Part of this growth results from the more than doubling of the Indian Catholic population over the last forty years, from a little less than 5 million to over 13 million in 1986. Over the same period, the number of priests trebled from 3,500 to over 12,000; religious sisters grew fourfold to about 50,000; religious brothers now number about 3,000, and seminarians more than 1,600.[3]

These patterns of growth reveal important regional differences. "Indianization" does not mean "regionalization"; the new personnel are not always local. Most, in fact, come from the south and west of India. During the first decade after independence, a greater proportion of higher church officials were held by the more Westernized Konkan coast groups (Mangalore-Goa-Bombay), but slowly the balance tilted in favor of the numerically strong and politically outgoing southern groups. Today, over 50 percent of all priests and 60 percent of all sisters come from Kerala. The same pattern is noticeable in the appointment of bishops and major religious superiors. Out of twelve Latin-rite bishops in 1946, five Tamils and three Keralites were bishops in their own states, and two each came from Mangalore and Andhra. Twenty years later, the thirty-eight Indian bishops comprised twelve Goans, four Mangaloreans, ten Tamilians, six Keralites (including one exarch in the north), four each from Andhra and Chotanagpur, and two from other groups. Today, apart from fifteen Syrian and eight Latin bishops in Kerala, there are twenty-four Keralite bishops in the north, and another ten bishops from the tribal groups. Thus, the Konkan coast group is slowing being confined to Karnataka and the western region, and most Tamil and Andhra bishops reside within their own states.[4]

This kind of regional imbalance can sometimes lead to competition and serious internal conflict. In 1972 demonstrations were staged in a Tamil diocese supporting the nomination of a bishop from a certain group. In 1974 a group of Orissa Catholics demanded the election of a "local" bishop in the place of those from other regions who had just been installed. The presidents of the CBCI and CUI visited the state to soothe local feelings and study the situation.[5] In other words, when regional imbalances lead to conflicts, national organizations intervene to try to solve such problems and maintain group solidarity. Often a solution cannot be found when both contending parties are strong. The problems in Orissa and Tamilnadu could be solved, at least temporarily, because the conflicting parties were not equal. It is more difficult to find solutions when the Thomas Christian bishops, for example, demand that a double jurisdiction be introduced in the north for the Kerala migrants.

Cultural adaptation is an important consequence of Indian Catholicism's growth in numbers. As a result, the Westernized character of certain urban groups and of seminary training becomes significant. Certainly the desire for more inculturation cannot be traced to a single cause. At the beginning, pressure for it was generated as a response to the assumptions of some of the freedom fighters in the 1940s who felt that Christians were agents of an alien colonial culture; and the Western appearance of the church was an obstacle to upper caste entry. More recently, pressure for inculturation has arisen from a deeper source: the concern to integrate elements of native Indian spirituality, philosophy, and culture with the Christian experience and its expression.

Institutional Changes

In addition to the remarkable growth in church personnel since independence, there has been a phenomenal increase in church-related institutions. In the last four decades university colleges have grown from 30 to over 150 and their student population has increased by over 1,000 percent. High schools have increased by 150 percent and the number of high school students by nearly 400 percent. Primary schools are up by 15 percent and their students by about 25 percent. Catholic hospitals have jumped from 53 to over 600 and dispensaries from 153 to about 750; other charitable institutions like orphanages, leprosaria, and homes for the aged and destitute have grown at a slower rate. In fact, the slowest growth has occurred in those institutions (e.g., primary schools and orphanages) most accessible to the poor.[6]

Besides an extraordinary vitality, these data also reveal interesting regional differences. Since independence institutional growth has been greater in the south, whereas before 1947 more institutions were established in the north. In Kerala, for example, only five (16.7%) of the thirty university colleges that existed in 1947 were Catholic; of the eighty Catholic university colleges founded in the first twenty-five years of independence, forty (50%) were located in Kerala.

Moreover, most of the new schools in the south are state-aided, do not charge fees, and use the regional language as the medium of instruction. Hence they are able to attract lower middle class students if they choose. With the exception of Chotanagpur, most schools in the north are English-medium, not aided by the state, and frequented by upper class non-Christians. Before independence these schools were mostly located in metropolitan areas, hill stations, military cantonments, and other British administrative centers and health resorts; since 1947 they have been located in the state capitals and newer industrial cities. Schools opened in small towns and semi-urban areas cater to middle class farmers who are becoming economically and politically powerful.

Besides regional differences, then, these patterns also reveal some of the pastoral priorities of postindependence Catholicism. There has been a steady shift from evangelizing the Hindu heartlands of the north to increasing Catholic resources in the culturally heterogeneous south and west where Christianity has long had its strength. The growth of church-related institutions has been more of an urban than a rural phenomenon; 60 percent of it has occurred in towns of more than 100,000, while 70 percent of India's population lives in rural areas. The beneficiaries of the church's services in the south belong mostly to the middle and lower classes. Those in the north come from the upper classes of the non-Christian majority. In other words, Catholicism has moved away from its "mission age" emphasis on conversion to what might be called "church buildings," that is, consolidating the community of the baptized—a shift clearly related to developments within Indian society at large and parallel to the "nation-building" efforts of the country. In order to understand this process we need to examine certain aspects of the nineteenth-century Indian church.

Nineteenth-Century Christians

Concentrating on the nineteenth century means that we must ignore the origin and presence of the powerful Catholic groups of Kerala, the Konkan coast, and other upper caste groups from Tamilnadu and Andhra. Their predominance is simply taken for granted in what follows; the institutional growth of Catholicism cannot be explained without them. Focusing on the nineteenth century is justified, however, because the process of conversion during this century formed many present-day attitudes within the Indian church. By and large, Catholic conversions in the nineteenth century were directed mostly at the "untouchables," who were open to receiving the Gospel and whose own interests intersected with those of the missionaries.

The Missionary's Interests

Until a few decades ago Christians were convinced that only the baptized could be saved. From this perspective it was imperative for missionaries to do everything in their power to save the souls of non-Christians and convert the largest number possible. Many missions started with the high castes, feeling that if these could be won others would follow. Slowly, however, it became evident that mass conversions would not occur among the Brahmins. Missionary efforts focused instead on the "untouchables," since they seemed more open to receiving the message of Christ.

The Convert's Interests

Conversion has sometimes been explained simply in terms of material allurements: nineteenth-century Christians are often called "rice Christians," that is, those converted "for a plate of rice." Certainly there have been such cases, but a large number of conversions took place long before famines and epidemics when material inducements were not decisive in changing religion. Other causes need to be examined, especially caste mobility.

The caste system is usually conceived as an unchangeable, rigid hierarchy. In reality, even though stratification has remained a permanent characteristic of the

Indian social structure, some kind of mobility has been integral to Hindu society for three millennia. Except for Brahmins who occupied the top rung of the social ladder and the "untouchables" who were kept outside the system, others rarely had a clear hierarchical identity. As a result, these groups continually struggled for higher social stratus. Acquiring land and political power, changing one's customs to suit the life-styles of the higher castes served as a means of mobility, which remained a struggle for promotion within the system, not away from it.

Caste stratification and the constant struggle for upward mobility has generated many reformist movements throughout Indian history. One of these was the four-teenth-century *Bhakti* (devotional) movement. Unlike the caste system, which assigned each caste a social status according to its occupation, the *Bhakti* movement declared that every kind of work possessed equal merit: no group could be called high or low because of its profession. Initially anticaste, the movement often turned out to be merely anti-Brahmin; but it did try to improve the lot of the "untouchables." Its influence continued into the nineteenth century but diminished with the consoli-dation of British power and the possibilities for mobility provided by Western edu-cation and the availability of administrative jobs.[7] The caste system thus lost its last chance for reform from within the Hindu fold.

Concurrently, the rural areas experienced little serious conflict. Traditional vil-lages followed the *Jajmani* system of economic independence and division of labor. Land was owned by one caste group, not by individuals or whole villages; farm labor and other services were divided among all castes and passed along by heredity; occu-pations, as well as the castes that practiced them, were hierarchically arranged. Although unjust from the viewpoint of individuals forced to retain their occupations and social status, the system did afford material security to every member of the village. By custom and law land-owning groups were obliged to provide for all the others. Every family received fixed amounts of grain in return for service, the quan-tity determined by the group's position in the hierarchy.[8]

The Historical Situation

In some areas, however, even this material security disappeared with the arrival of the British and the introduction of private property. Some low caste groups were the worst affected: they lost their material security without improving their social status. But the weakening of *Jajmani* also released them from a system that had perpetuated their low status; now they were free to seek liberation elsewhere.[9] In other words, the impact of British rule on the *Jajmani* system plus the aspirations raised by the *Bhakti* movement and other caste struggles combined to improve the chances of "outside elements" affecting the social situation. Christianity, therefore, could act as an alternative means of upward mobility.

A similar situation existed among the tribals of Chotanagpur in Bihar. Influenced by their contacts with other Hindu kings in the Mughal prisons of the seventeenth century, local chieftains who before had lived in simplicity began to imitate the more luxurious living of the *rajas*. To pay for this change in lifestyle they appointed *jagir-dars* and *thikedars* to collect taxes—a change that struck at the very roots of tribal society. Land owned by the whole village or by individual families formed the center of their culture, religion, and social relations. Previously the whole village contributed to maintaining their chieftain, but payment of a land tax was not only unknown but completely foreign to their traditions. Even after land taxation was introduced, the tribals retained ownership of their land. The British rulers, however, took for granted that landlordism—the common form of ownership in their own country—was a natural social system and transformed the *jagirdars* and *thikedars* into *zamindars*, that is, landlords of those areas for which they had only tax rights. For the tribals whose independence, self-respect, and human dignity were closely linked to their land, this change threatened to destroy their identity.[10]

The otherwise peaceful tribals revolted and the British, interested in maintaining peace for commercial purposes, sent in the army to quell the uprisings. Christianity—initially the Lutheran Gossner Mission and later Catholicism—mediated the conflict and helped the tribals adapt to changing circumstances. Fr. Constants Lievens's efforts to redress tribal grievances also met with evangelical success. The tribals believed that the mission was a source of land security; Lievens realized that the land lost to the *zamindars* affronted their human dignity. To help the tribals meant to stand with them against the powerful landlords and their British mentors, as well as their supposedly neutral judiciary.[11]

The results of this intersection of interests were ambivalent. The missionaries saw their work from the evangelical viewpoint of saving souls; their attitude toward caste was conditioned by this ideal. Protestant missionaries came mostly from countries where the egalitarian principles of the Enlightenment favored complete abolition of caste—the very antithesis of equality.[12] They stressed the individual not the group and so opposed mass conversions as a violation of an individual's freedom to follow his conscience, insisting instead on individual baptism.[13] The Catholics, in contrast, hailed mainly from the countries of southern Europe which had not passed through the political revolutions of the eighteenth century, or others, like France, that were experiencing a post-Napoleonic revival that gave little importance to the individual. They considered the monarchial estates system a natural social order, so that in India they viewed the caste system as simply another instance of legitimate stratification.[14] The converts, however, saw their conversion as linked to either social mobility or land security. To the "untouchables" and tribals, Christianity was not merely a religious phenomenon but a means of adapting to a new situation. They were ready to join any movement that promised equality. The late nineteenth and early twentieth centuries, therefore, witnessed mass conversions to Islam, Sikhism, Arya Samaj, and Christianity, all of which offered hope of liberation from oppression.[15]

Missionaries slowly realized that converts viewed conversion not as a suppression of caste but as social promotion—a new higher identity. Consequently, missionary attitudes to caste changed. In the 1850s, for example, when new converts began to use higher caste names rather than give up a caste identity, the Anglican bishop ordered all caste identification for Christians suppressed; he had to yield when converts threatened to join the more conservative Catholics or Leipzig Lutherans. Eventually, even many Protestants became more tolerant, feeling that caste solidarity helped rather than hampered conversion. God's work, they argued, could not be limited by spiritual criteria fixed by missionaries, and social liberation was after all a true sign of freedom in Christ.[16]

The real limits, however, to freedom from caste were posed not by missionaries but by older upper caste Christians who would not accept others as equals but continued to treat them as "untouchables." In seventeenth-century Tamilnadu, for example, a large number of lower castes had already entered the church. To ensure that the upper castes did not leave, de Nobili divided the mission in two, one section catering exclusively to upper caste Christians, the other to the low castes. When the "untouchables" converted in the nineteenth century, they and the low castes above them worshipped in the same church building but had to enter through different doors, kneel on opposite sides, and communicate at different railings. When in Pondicherry, Madurai, and Coimbatore new missionaries questioned this separation, the "pastoral wisdom" of the older missionaries prevailed. It was not ideal, they admitted, but was necessary to avert defections and save the souls of the Indians.[17] Not all the converts were prepared to accept this separation because it deprived them of social advancement. While Catholics in Tamilnadu continued the custom, Protestants (notably Anglicans) emphasized equality and tried to suppress it. The consequence was, as D. B. Forrester observes, that

> whereas Roman Catholic missionary strategy was directly largely toward group conversions, the Protestants who looked for individual decisions, attracted far more mass movements, for the tolerant Roman Catholic attitude to the caste system made conversion to Catholicism a less plausible escape from that system than conversion to Protestantism.[18]

Nineteenth-Century Christian Institutions

Besides churches, Christian groups also established educational, health, and other charitable institutions to serve evangelical purposes; but these too eventually adapted to the prevailing social reality. To understand this, one needs to place church-related institutions in the nineteenth century within the context of the colonial character of India, the missionary needs of the church, and the aspirations of various Christian and non-Christian groups.

Colonial society in nineteenth-century India was essentially three-tiered, with the rulers on top, upper caste Indians in the middle, the rest of the Indian population at the bottom. Educational and health institutions were organized according to the same scheme. Education is a medium of transmitting a society's cultural heritage and providing individuals with upward mobility; hence it preserves a social system by holding out the hope of eventual improvement, even if only a few benefit from it.[19] Schools in colonial India performed precisely these functions, although when the British replaced the Indian educational system with English language schools, they accepted the legal right of everyone to an education.[20] Within this apparent equality, however, lay the seeds of inequality. Colonial rule had to be consolidated through the colonizer's culture and language, but teaching English to the whole population was neither feasible nor necessary for this purpose. The British strategy demanded only that the colonizers educate a few influential elites assuming that they would pass British values to the others, legitimize colonial occupation, make Western dress and Western products respectable, and create a market for British industrial goods.[21] Education remained in private hands. Thus, only those who could pay for it, that is, only the upper classes, could send their children to school. Racial separation enforced from the beginning ensured that the educational system reproduced the three-tier colonial society.[22] While the British made education legally open to all castes they in fact attempted to introduce new classes in their place. As a result, the upper castes who already possessed socioeconomic power enhanced it by adding English education and administrative or professional status to their existing means of social control.[23]

The hospital system was introduced to take care of British residents and, later, upper class Indians. Moreover, medical colleges taught only Western medicine in a country where 90 percent of the population depended on local medicine. In this way church-related health organizations also reproduced the colonial system of stratification. Only the monied classes had access to it; the others depended on systems that were disparaged, neglected, and consequently stagnated.[24]

Missionaries, as we have said, introduced both these institutions for evangelical purposes. Convinced that education imparted through the medium of English was the "most fruitful means of converting Indians to Christianity by making them conscious of their superstition."[25] Alexander Duff, the best-known Protestant educator of the time, coined the term "downward filtration" to embody his conviction that once, because of English education, the upper classes recognized their superstition and were converted, Christian knowledge could filter down to the other classes.[26] Catholic interest in schools originated either because of local upper class Catholic aspiration to join the British administration or the fear that if Catholics did not form the upper classes, soon all educated Indians would be trained by the Protestants. A government run by British Protestants required some Catholic influence if their missions were to be made secure and the souls of Indian pagans were to be saved.[27]

Soon, however, social reality impinged on these perceptions. The Hindu (and later Muslim) upper class was interested only in receiving education that could improve their social status and help them join the British administration. "In every case," as Stephen Neil remarks, "the experience was very much the same—a brief period of enthusiastic popularity, the conversion of one or two promising students, tumults and disturbances, legal cases and accusations, the emptying of the schools, renewed popularity once the disturbance had passed."[28] But a change came between the two stages of popularity. After the initial disturbances schools reopened with little hope of making converts. They catered principally to upper class aspirations without realizing that in the process they had aligned themselves with the colonial and local forces of exploitation and were strengthening both of them.

Consequently a new justification for the schools had to be found, and the Protestants were first to find it. They argued that the schools aimed not merely at immediate conversion but also at long-term preparation for the filtration of Christian values which would eventually lead to mass conversions. Eventually, however, even this argument lost credibility, and the hope of exerting some Christian influence on the government became in fact merely a way to prepare the administrators and filtration agents of British cultural and commercial values.

As evangelization spread downward, other institutions were founded for the poorer classes. Primary schools often became part of the mission station, especially those established by the Paris Foreign Missions and the Jesuits. Even schools meant mainly for the rich educated poor Christians free of charge. Moreover, the missionaries made a significant contribution to women's education. "Indian" schools were often erected alongside European schools in order to serve the children of domestics and other servants of the British. The two groups were kept apart, and in that way the institutions themselves symbolized a "two-tier" church.

The charitable institutions organized by the church (hospitals, dispensaries, orphanages, and, later, technical schools) followed the same strategy. Unlike the schools, these institutions were built in mainly rural areas and catered mostly to the depressed classes. Whether relief centers or dispensaries, the missionaries viewed them as a means for spreading the Gospel. The converts found that here they were treated with respect and given facilities previously denied them. In this sense, the charitable institutions fulfilled the needs of the poor more than the needs of their oppressors. Since the "untouchables" experienced equality in these institutions, many conversions followed.

Missionaries themselves, of course, never thought in terms of separation between oppressors and oppressed or of the charitable institutions as symbols of equality. They were simply apostolic means for saving souls. But their interaction with the social reality of India had two distinct consequences: the schools strengthened the exploiter and charitable institutions fulfilled the aspirations of the oppressed.

The Situation in India Today

Against this background, what can be said about the Catholic community and its institutions today? In 1947 and the years following independence all discussions about the future of the church reiterated that evangelization coupled with service of the nation were Catholicism's twin objectives.[29] At the same time, Catholic leaders perceived India as a country controlled by a Hindu majority hostile to the Christian minority. The sense of insecurity that followed was expressed in various forms—by the secretary general of the CBCI in an interview with the Vatican News Agency Fides in December 1946, in the statement of the president of CUI, and in other articles published in Catholic weeklies at the time of India's independence.[30] Most of these statements stressed that Christians and Christian institutions should adapt themselves to Indian culture in order to better proclaim the Gospel, serve the country, and find security with the new government. One notices three aspects to these developments. First, until independence competition was mainly between the various Christian denominations (including "British Protestants") for more conversions and greater Christian influence in the British raj. After independence, Hindus became the ruling group. They were perceived as unfavorable to those who were friends of the colonizers. Insecurity led Christians to band together even with other minorities to defend their interests and safeguard their rights.

Second, Christian institutions constituted one of the major interests in need of defense. This mentality originated during the freedom struggle and the religiocultural revival at the turn of the century. When Hindu fanatics took control of the movement, they opposed proselytization both on religious grounds and because they viewed the conversion of the "untouchables" as a challenge to their society. Even moderate leaders like Gandhi and Nehru who took charge of the movement in the 1920s opposed conversions, but for different reasons. Proselytization, they felt, divided the country into competing religious groups vying with each other to gain new members. It was their concern to unite all Indians. Already the Muslims were numerically strong enough to demand a state of their own. What certainty was there that some other community would not become equally strong? Time and again Gandhi accused the charitable institutions of using material inducements to attract the poor. Other leaders suggested that privately owned English-medium schools had created a new class with vested interests in retaining a monopoly over education; these schools obstructed both the education of the masses and the equality of all citizens. For equality to be restored, all education must be in the hands of the state and should be given free of charge in Indian languages.[31]

These charges threatened the churches in just those areas in which they had felt secure under the British: conversion work and institutions, especially schools and colleges. When the constituent Assembly was formed in 1946, minorities demanded guarantees in both these domains. The right of minorities to own and manage their own institutions was granted without much debate. After considerable discussion the national leaders also granted the fundamental right to propagate one's own faith, since they felt the minorities would feel insecure in independent India without it.[32]

As already stated, church-related institutions have grown dramatically and the struggle for minority rights has mainly aimed at protecting them. There also have been official efforts to restrict the right to propagate one's faith. In some states an anticonversion Freedom of Religion Act has been passed; in 1954 the Niyogi Committee was appointed in Madya Pradesh to inquire into missionaries' use of material inducements and other unfair practices. Such actions have usually taken place in feudal states like Madya Pradesh, Orissa, and Bihar, where most Christians are tribals. They appear, therefore, as actions aimed at perpetuating the oppression of the tribals who, if they changed their religion, would have a chance for education and economic advancement. Christians, however, have viewed these actions not as anti-tribal but anti-Christian. As a result, they have increased Christian insecurity and intensified their desire to hold firmly to Christian institutions.[33]

This situation has partly changed over the last two decades. Some complain that too much attention has been given to running schools for the rich and they question their usefulness. Others wonder whether Christians are perceived simply as a group of good school administrators and disciplinarians, not as persons capable of taking new educational initiatives.[34] These queries have led to some soul-searching. For a long time Christians were sure they served the church and that their schools and hospitals contributed to evangelization. Today, some are not so certain they are serving the poor.

Third, at independence Catholics felt the need to enter the mainstream of national life. This desire took the form of cultural adaptation and service to the nation through institutions and economic development projects. The call for increasing cultural adaptation seems to reflect an effort to demonstrate that Christian groups are an integral part of the country's cultural life. Today both social activists and mission workers assert that the task of inculturation must include the struggle for justice. The continuing coexistence of great poverty amid great wealth gives such concerns pressing urgency, but the relation between social justice and evangelization is difficult to articulate.

All these developments indicate that, even though Christians may conceive of themselves as a minority different from others, they have in fact grown in interaction with the country as a whole. The present situation of Catholicism, therefore, can be explained largely in terms of an ongoing adaptation to larger changes, particularly in the economic and political life at postindependence India.

The pattern of planned development that India inaugurated in 1951 rested on the assumption that the Western political and economic experience could be duplicated in India. Leaders chose what they judged were the best elements in the two Western systems—democracy from the capitalist countries and planned economy from the socialist nations—and attempted to telescope the French and Russian revolutions in a single quick process of development. But India's situation was different. Political democracy had been shaped by the freedom movement initiated by people who had matriculated through British education with the hope of joining the colonial system and were disillusioned with it. Although the freedom struggle coopted all other tribal and working class movements, it remained strongly bourgeois.[35] Independence did not represent a total break with the past: educational and health institutions as well as the civil bureaucracy remained unchanged. Politically, individual liberty and equality were taken for granted. It was forgotten that colonialization had strengthened the already powerful groups in Indian society at the expense of the marginalized. These groups with a vested interest in maintaining the status quo took control of the new political structures and used them for their own protection.

Economic planning followed a similar path. Planners simply presumed that introducing advanced Western technology would solve India's problems, that the infrastructure of heavy industry built up in the first decade after independence should lead to mass consumer industries whose benefits would reach everyone. With the hope of rapid development, the government borrowed billions of dollars in foreign aid to finance high investment heavy industry. Social control of the means of production would ensure equitable distribution of goods. India's policymakers forgot, however, that Western nations had grown strong within the context of colonialism. Economic exploitation of the colonies, together with their role as suppliers of cheap raw materials and abundant capital and as buyers of its finished products had significantly contributed to Western economic development.

India, however, remained a colony. Though it had attained independence, its economy bore all the marks of foreign occupation. Despite the policymakers' socialist intentions, decisions remained in the hands of the dominant sectors and their vested interests. Hence, while some could afford to live by Western standards and the government could afford to export cereal and accumulate 30 million tons as buffer stock, a large part of the population remained undernourished and lacked purchasing power. What has resulted is a neocolonial economy short of goods, capital, services, and employment, with severe competition for limited resources. Weaker sections of society do not possess the strength required for such competition. In education, for example, poor students lack the cultural support, tradition of literacy, and parental motivation and guidance required to sustain them; failures are many. Only upper class children from educated families possess the ambition and resources needed for attaining high-status professions.[36]. In short, schools in India continue to operate on behalf of the existing social system in which everyone has theoretical equality but only a few achieve it.

What are the implications of this context for the Indian church? Three issues seem paramount.

First, the pattern of Catholic institutional growth reveals that church-related institutions of higher education have grown more than lower-level ones catering to the poor sections of society. This was not the result of deliberate policy as much as various interacting interests.

Second, the major factor motivating this growth seems to have been the community's search for security. A climate of insecurity inhibits analysis of the implications of decisions. Christian decision makers took the value of institutional development for granted and were unable to conceive of a different course that might have helped the country find another direction. Besides, there were considerable pressures from within the Catholic community to open new institutions. Like the postindependence government, which assumed that Western technology would benefit everyone, church leaders assumed that their institutions would enable them to serve the poor and eliminate illiteracy and illness. For the "good of the community" the church opened schools in state capitals and industrial centers; but the unintended consequences of these actions risked reinforcing a system of inequalities.

Third, the search for security seems unlikely to have been a contributing factor in the growth of Christian-sponsored hospitals. From the beginning these hospitals were built as charitable institutions for the poor. Even now, most provide free or subsidized medical facilities to many poor patients and retain a strong rural base. In 1974, for example, over half the Catholic hospitals were situated in rural areas.

The fact that more and better hospitals founded after independence are located in urban areas and that higher-level institutions have increased more rapidly than lower-level ones derives from the imperative of these institutions themselves. They exist in a competitive world; to survive they must keep pace with technological change. The more sophisticated the equipment, the more they require capital investment, expensive maintenance, and professional personnel. To meet these expenses while retaining their charitable character, hospitals have built paying wards for upper class patients; as costs escalate, more paying wards are needed with better amenities and more specialists at high salaries, thus further restricting clientele.

As for education, middle class Christians urge the church to build more schools to improve their children's competitive position. As mass education spreads, the church opens more high schools and colleges to meet their needs. In the process poorer groups, particularly those who once belonged to the "untouchable" castes (i.e., most of the nineteenth-century converts) benefit less from these services than other groups, especially those from the south who belong to the dominant class. Competition among dioceses, religious congregations, and Latin and Syrian churches (in Kerala) has led to the creation of many prestige projects and to greater investment in educational facilities. Foreign aid from Catholic churches abroad not only has made capital improvements easier but also has hampered the kind of self-examination possible at an earlier stage when these outside resources were not so available. Everyone took for granted that these works served the poor; few planners foresaw that the investments would benefit only a few and help consolidate inequalities.

Put briefly, Catholics today are growing as a community within a national, social, economic, and political system of shortages and competition. Led by their understanding of "the good of the community" and their self-perception as a minority threatened by a hostile Hindu majority, church leaders after independence became predominantly concerned with accumulating assets and institutions that would protect the community's existence, improve Catholics' bargaining position in the larger society, and neutralize upper class resistance to propagating the faith. As the possibility for making converts diminished, church-related institutions became the principal instruments of evangelization, interests to be safeguarded. In the circumstances of Indian socioeconomic and political life, church leaders unwittingly aligned themselves with those elements in society most interested in maintaining the status quo.

Today this strategy is under attack from people who accuse the church of being conservative and opportunistic. The preceding analysis reveals that such categorical judgments are unwarranted. Most Catholic groups have continually adapted to new situations attempting to elicit the cooperation of the dominant classes. This was not conservatism but a search for security. There is little evidence that the church has been blind to inequalities, much evidence that it feared taking a risk. Similarly, it is difficult to sustain the criticism that the church is simply a vested interest, that its actions are directed only at defending its rights and property. Initially, property represented security. Once accumulated, however, its preservation unconsciously became a vested interest with minority rights used to protect it. Moreover, association with elites through schools and other institutions confers status on both the institutions and the persons responsible for them. Admittedly, this can create a vested interest in its own right, especially when the cry "religion is in danger" is used to mobilize the masses in its support.

This is the context, then, within which the Catholic church has to consider its future. The first step will be to heighten its awareness of the broader national situation and examine the results of its actions on Indian society as a whole. Good intentions may no longer suffice, especially when what has been considered "good" may no longer serve its original purpose. Church leaders today call the church a church for the poor. To implement this sincere desire, however, means bringing the community as a whole to make a deliberate choice—a political option in favor of the poorest. A political option in this context does not mean a choice for one political party or ideology but a decision to initiate action in favor of the most disinherited and marginalized. To do this will require explicit reflection on the range of works sponsored by the church in terms of their impact on the poorest sections of society. A political option implies a search for genuine alternatives, even if this will demand reorienting existing works and reinterpreting the task of community building. What kind of community will it be: a closed community of the baptized seeking its own security and, in the process, becoming an unwitting instrument for those who want to maintain present injustices, or a community identified with the real majority who are powerless, exploited, and marginalized—a voice for those who, having no interests to promote, have no one to promote their own?

NOTES

1. See, among others, Gnana Robinson, "The Indian Church on the Fence Again?" *National Christian Council Review* 97 (Sept. 1977):422–25.
2. Henry Volken, Julian Gonalves, Sara Kathathara, *Moving Closer to the Rural Poor* (New Delhi: Indian Social Institute, 1979).
3. *Catholic Bishops Conference of India Directory*, 1986.
4. See the *Catholic Directory of India* 1964, 1969, 1972, 1977, and 1984.

5. See reports in the Catholic weeklies of India: *The New Leader* (Bangalore), Andhra Edition, Aug. 25, 1974; *The Examiner* (Bombay), July 20 and Sept. 7, 1974; *The Herald* (Calcutta), Aug. 8 and Sept. 5, 1974.

6. François Houtart et al., *The Catholic Hospital System in India* (Louvain: University of Louvain, 1975), p. 11.

7. Selig S. Harrison, *India: The Most Dangerous Decade* (Princeton, N.J.: Princeton University Press, 1960), pp. 64ff.

8. Santokh Singh Anant, *The Changing Concept of Caste in India* (Delhi: Vikas Publications, 1972), pp. 16-24.

9. D. B. Forrester, "The Depressed Classes and Conversion to Christianity." In *Religion in South Asia: Religious Conversion and Revival Movements in South Asia in Medieval and Modern Times*, ed. G. A. Oddie (Delhi: Manohar Book Service, 1977), pp. 41-42.

10. Fidelis de sa, *Crisis in Chotanagpur* (Bangalore: Redemptorist Publications, 1975), pp. 33-40, 46-47.

11. Ibid., pp. 107-138, 307-317.

12. G. A. Oddie, "Protestant Missions, Caste and Social Change in India," *Indian Economic and Social History Review* 6 (1969):274-77.

13. G. A. Oddie, *Social Movements in India: British Protestant Missionaries and Social Reforms 1850-1900* (Delhi: Manohar Book Service, 1978), pp. 30-46.

14. E. Germaine, *En Quel Dieu Croyons Nous?* (Paris: ISPC, 1975), pp. 1-27.

15. Surajit Sinha, "Tribal Solidarity Movements in India: A Review." In *Tribal Situation in India*, vol. 13, ed. K. Suresh Singh (Simla: Indian Institute of Advanced Studies, 1972).

16. Oddie, "Protestant Missions," pp. 264-68.

17. Julien Launay, *Histore des Missions des Indes*, Vol. 1 (Paris: MEP, 1860-1896), pp. 104ff.

18. D. B. Forrester, "The Depressed Classes," pp. 39-40.

19. Francis J. Brown, *Educational Sociology*, 2nd ed. (Bombay: Asia Publishing House, 1961), pp. 202-207.

20. J. P. Naik, *Equality, Quality and Quantity: The Elusive Triangle in Indian Education* (Delhi: Allied Publishers, 1975), p. 6.

21. S. M. Pathak, "Attitudes of the British and American Missionaries Towards the Growth of English Education in India in the First Three Quarters of the 19th Century," *Journal of Indian History* 48 (1970): 10; B. B. Misra, *The Indian Middle Classes: Their Growth in Modern Times* (London: Oxford University Press, 1961), pp. 149-152.

22. Howard S. Baker, "Schools and Systems of Stratification." In *Education, Economy and Society*, ed. A. H. Halsey, Jean Floud, and C. A. Anderson (New York: Free Press, 1961), pp. 94-96.

23. Naik, *Equality, Quality and Quantity*, pp. 7-9.

24. Gunnar Myrdal, *Asian Drama: A Study in the Poverty of Nations*, Vol. 3 (New York: Pantheon Books, 1968), pp. 1593-98.

25. Melvin J. Laird, *Missionaries and Education in Bengal 1793-1837* (Oxford: Oxford University Press, 1972), pp. 20-21.

26. Pathak, "Attitudes of the British and American Missionaries," pp. 102-104.

27. Launay, *Histoire des Missions des Indes*, Vol. 2, pp. 510-511.

28. Stephen Neil, *A History of Christian Missions* (Harmondsworth Penguin Books, 1964), p. 276.

29. Plenary Council of India Decrees, 1950, nos. 14, 20, 163-65, 168, 171, 185-89; Catholic Bishops Conference of India Report for 1951, pp. 56-62.

30. *The Examiner*, Jan. 3, 1947.

31. K. P. Karunakaran, *Religion and Political Awakening in India* (Meerut: Meenakshi Prakashan, 1969), pp. 17–18.

32. For various opinions of the Constituent Assembly members and the final concessions, see *Constituent Assembly Debates: Parliamentary Secretariate,* Vol. 7, pp. 399, 612, 819, 834, 863–71.

33. See the text of the CBCI Statement in *The Examiner,* Nov. 10, 1956.

34. See, for example, Joseph Currie, "Jesuit Educational Association Meeting Report," *The Clergy Monthly* 31 (Oct. 9, 1969):471–73.

35. Sumit Sarkar, *Modern India 1857–1947* (New Delhi: Macmillan, 1983).

36. R. Rath, "From Social Isolation to Stagnation: A Study of Scheduled Caste Groups," *Social Action* 24 (April–June 1974):106–108 and 115.

22

The Awakening of a Local Church: Japanese Catholicism in Tension Between Particularistic and Universal Values

Jan Swyngedouw

More than a hundred years have passed since in 1873, under strong foreign pressure, the Meiji government of Japan removed the public notices proscribing the "evil Christian religion." For the Catholic church it was a new beginning. Two and a half centuries of one of the cruelest persecutions in history had almost completely wiped out the achievement of the so-called Kirishitan period, which began in 1549 with the arrival of Jesuit missionary Francis Xavier and his companions and ended about ninety years later with a series of decrees closing the country to foreigners.[1] Compared to the results of that first period of Catholic missionary endeavor, the second one cannot yet be called a great success. By the end of the sixteenth century, Catholics in Japan numbered about 300,000 out of a total population of nearly 20 million; at the present time, Catholics comprise little more than 400,000 of a population of 120 million. Even when we add the roughly 600,000 Christians of various Protestant and other churches, Christianity still represents less than 1 percent of the Japanese population.

Admittedly, in the ten years immediately following World War II the church not only recovered but doubled its prewar strength of 120,000, which had been reduced

TABLE 22.1   Number of Japanese Catholics

YEAR	TOTAL NUMBER	NAGASAKI DIOCESE	TOKYO DIOCESE
1900	55,091	37,101	9,053
1920	76,404	56,339	10,502
1940	119,224	59,322	12,455
1946	108,324	54,502	8,455
1950	142,461	63,170	15,246
1955	212,318	71,164	26,586
1960	277,502	78,296	40,128
1965	323,880	74,300	48,929
1970	356,252	69,835	57,931
1975	377,687	72,104	61,554
1980	406,796	75,136	69,238
1985	432,851	75,553	76,509

by about 11,000 in 1945. This was a period of high growth for Catholicism, although not everyone joined the church for lofty spiritual reasons.[2] But by the end of the 1950s, the "rush" toward the church began to falter and a period of modest growth set in, with an annual increase of about 5,000 instead of the 15,000 of previous years (see Table 22.1). It seemed as if the church had run out of energy.

Any discussion of Catholicism in Japan, however, must take into account the basic fact that Christianity cannot be considered simply in terms of its numbers. Through its network of educational, welfare, and other institutions, Christianity exerts an influence on society much greater than its numerical strength would suggest. In the minds of most Japanese, Christianity is intrinsically linked to Western culture. While this perception creates a double burden of foreignness and heterogeneity which prevents any easy implantation into the soil of Japan, it also increases the church's visibility in the wider society.[3] Except for a few who may be attracted to Christianity precisely because of those features, most people keep at a safe distance claiming to defend their own Japaneseness. Still, they cannot afford to disregard this "agent of the Western world," since it is this world that remains for most Japanese the primary reference by which they evaluate their position in the rank order of nations. This is especially true for the Roman Catholic church, since many Japanese, particularly those involved in non-Christian religions, see behind it the international standing of the Vatican with its global religious and political influence. These factors continue to play a significant role in Japanese Catholicism's recent awakening.

The Internal Configuration of Japanese Catholicism

The most decisive internal factor to influence the development of Japan's Catholic church is the coexistence of two types of believers who, because of their different background, have often adopted very different attitudes toward the problems the church faces. One type is the so-called Nagasaki Christians, descendants of the approximately 15,000 believers who were "discovered" in 1865 and later and who were descendants of Christians baptized during the Kirishitan period. Because of their high birthrate, the number of Nagasaki Christians rose rapidly, and it was only natural that, when leading positions within the church were gradually given to the Japanese, this group received first consideration.

The second type is the "new" converts and their children who have mainly been recruited from large cities such as Tokyo and Osaka. Although the number of Nagasaki Christians has recently leveled off at about 75,000 (i.e., about 18 percent of the total Catholic population), the new converts have continued to grow in numerical strength and influence; today there are more Catholics in Tokyo than in Nagasaki (Table 22.1).[4]

Rivalry between these two groups has characterized Japanese Catholicism in the modern era, especially in the years since Vatican II, when the church has slowly but steadily become more open to the outside world and local (regional) churches have become more aware of their role within the universal church. Nagasaki Catholics have not been a positive force for renewal and openness; in fact, their decreasing strength might well have contributed to the growing self-confidence of the Japanese church as a whole. Nagasaki Catholicism has borne both the assets and liabilities of its legacy as a church born out of persecution. Its need to establish a strong self-identity with clearly fixed boundaries separating it from the surrounding society has driven it toward conservatism in social matters—closely knit, ghetto-type communities, mainly from lower social classes—and toward preserving clearly defined doctrine, expressed in a wide layer of rituals and pietistic devotions under the control of an authoritarian hierarchy.[5] The new converts, on the other hand, come mostly from the urban middle class and have generally been more open to change, although they too face their own peculiar obstacles in adapting to a changing church.

A second factor that strongly influences developments in Japanese Catholicism is the ratio between clergy and laity and the internal composition of each group. The church in Japan has always possessed a high number of clergy and religious compared to the number of Catholics. Indeed, clergy and religious presently constitute about 2.5 percent (10,500) of the total Catholic population. The number of female religious (about 7,000) is especially remarkable. This number may be partly explained by the propensity for prayer and meditation characteristic of Asian religion generally, as well as by the typically Japanese tendency for intensive commitment to a cause. Whatever the reasons, the high rate of vocations to the religious life has produced a church that is clergy-centered and, in a society already known for its stress on hierarchy and authority, one in which the role of the laity is downplayed.

A look at the composition of both priests and religious illuminates important elements in this picture (see Table 22.2). While female religious are 90 percent native-born, only since 1985 has the proportion of Japanese priests equaled that of foreign missionaries. In 1967 there were twice as many foreign missionaries as native-born priests; since then the number has gradually decreased while Japanese vocations have progressively accelerated. Since the beginning of World War II, because of government pressure, all bishops have been Japanese; but this should not obscure the fact that most of the other leading positions within the church and almost all the financial resources have long been in the hands of foreign clergy. Especially in recent years the Japanization of the church's central administration has progressed steadily. Nevertheless, the presence of foreigners still exerts a strong pressure on church policy. With a few exceptions, these foreigners belong to the religious clergy (of whom

TABLE 22.2 Clergy and Religious in the Japanese Church

| | PRIESTS | | | RELIGIOUS | | | |
| | FOREIGN (REL./MISS.) | JAPANESE | | BROTHERS | | SISTERS (INCLUDING SECULAR INSTITUTES) | |
Year		DIOCESAN	RELIGIOUS	FOREIGN	JAPANESE	FOREIGN	JAPANESE
1901	121	34			71		305
1920	92	37			151		505
1940	308	159			290		1,685
1946	253	151			332		1,578
1950	556	187		102 (in 1951)	169	664 (in 1951)	1,874
1955	952	220	59	157	255	1,019	2,518
1960	1,246	309	117	174	222	1,020	3,559
1965	1,246	397	210	182	241	1,059	4,780
1970	1,188	441	297	168	216	973	5,773
1975	1,103	479	341	165	225	810	6,197
1980	998	489	336	145	211	748	6,305
1985	922	503	407	124	205	627	6,336

45 percent are also Japanese). But even though many of them work in parishes under the leadership of Japanese bishops, their affiliation with a religious or foreign missionary order sometimes raises special problems, especially since whole regions have traditionally been assigned to the pastoral care of these orders.[6] It should be added that among the laity women are by far in the majority. If we remember that Japan as a whole is still a male-dominated society, this fact cannot but further strengthen the important role of the male clergy.

It is difficult to gauge the impact on church policies of both the clergy-laity ratio and the internal composition of both groups. It is evident that the diminishing number of foreign priests has not resulted in a surge toward inculturation on the level of ideas. Although it has become fashionable to stress the importance of the laity today—among whom are a high proportion of people with high social and academic standing—the transition from a church dominated by foreign clergy to one dominated by Japanese clergy has in many cases rendered the laity more subdued than one might have initially expected.

A third factor important to the internal configuration of Japanese Catholicism is religious practice. Given the relatively small number of Catholics in Japan, among whom are many first-generation Christians still establishing a Christian identity distinct from their countrymen, one might expect that Catholics would be eager to express their religion by strict observance of church practice. Statistics reveal the opposite. Overall Sunday mass attendance steadily hovers around 34 percent of the Catholic population; this percentage rises to 50-55 percent for church attendance at Easter; both figures have shown little change over the last several decades. And the dominant presence of women at religious services reveals a church particularly appealing to the female sector of society.

As might be expected, there are clear differences in church attendance between Catholics in the Nagasaki area and those elsewhere. Weekly observance for the whole diocese of Nagasaki—which today also contains a number of new converts—falls between 50 and 55 percent, while 70 percent make their Easter observance. Both these figures represent a slight decrease in recent years. For the diocese of Tokyo, however, only about 30 percent attend mass weekly, about 48-52 percent at Easter (the former slightly below the national average, the latter close to the national average). Dioceses outside the large urban centers even if they are not rural show a lower average weekly church attendance with some falling below 25 percent, although even here Easter observance approaches 50 percent.

There are several possible explanations for these rather low figures. Except for the Nagasaki Christians who, as long as they remain in their Catholic villages experience strong pressure to conform to traditional church practices, Japanese Catholics as a whole feel quite free with regard to church attendance. Since they live in a culture in which weekly religious observance is nonexistent, many Christians do not perceive Sunday mass as a strict obligation; many pastors now tacitly accept this situation. Also Easter church attendance does not carry the same cultural force as in Western countries. Although statistics are not available, it seems that many more Catholics attend mass at Christmas than at Easter and Christmas itself has been culturally adopted as a holiday in Japanese society at large. However, the main reason for these low figures may be that many converts silently stop attending church after a time. While this may especially apply to converts baptized during Catholicism's "golden years" immediately after the war, it seems no less applicable to more recent converts. These people generally remain enrolled on church membership lists. Most of them would not deny their church affiliation and still attend church irregularly, practicing their religion in more or less the same way as non-Christian Japanese. Among this group are a considerable number of people, particularly women, who are simply unable to attend church on a regular basis. Indeed, a look at Catholic marriage statistics indirectly confirms this interpretation. The vast majority of Christians celebrate a church wedding, but more than 75 percent of these are marriages between a Christian and a non-Christian. Outside large cities where Catholics are fewer, the proportion of mixed marriages is even higher. In Nagasaki, where church regulations in this regard used to be much stricter, marriages between Catholics outnumbered mixed marriages, but this trend has recently been reversed. While a mixed marriage does not signal an end to religious practice for the Catholic partner, in most cases it does not facilitate it. Moreover, "church weddings" have increasingly become a custom for non-Christian couples—a custom generally welcomed by the church as a means of evangelization. As a result, even for Catholics marrying in church is not necessarily a sign of continued religious practice.

External Factors

Although many tend to underestimate the impact of elements within Japanese society that have initiated change, it remains true that the major turning points in its history have come when Japan was forced to interact with alien cultures. Similarly, transitions in Japanese Catholicism have mainly been the result of external forces.

The Universal Church

Its youth, size, distance from the center, and the large number of foreign clergy in influential positions all give the Japanese church a special character. While remoteness from Rome might enhance independence, its small size has intensified the need of Japanese Catholicism to emphasize its membership in a universal church and its obedience to directives coming from the center. It is precisely the deep awareness of belonging to a broader entity with worldwide dimensions that has given the Japanese church its strongest foundation and safeguard for its identity. Lacking self-confidence as a local church, it has found its strength in the universal church. It has, as a result, been quite complacent in engaging actively in local causes in any independent way, waiting instead for general policies to come from Rome to which it would then loyally conform. This identity borrowed from the outside, with its often ghetto-like mentality, has strengthened the church's image among the Japanese as a *Fremdkörper* in their culture.

Only when after Vatican II the universal church began to move in new directions did the Japanese church move into action following directions from above, always careful not to proceed too quickly. Pressures for moving more quickly or independently came mostly from foreign missionaries who were generally better informed about what was occurring outside Japan and outside Rome. Changes were then begun, but the slow pace at which they proceeded in Japan was certainly related to the slow pace of change in Rome itself.

Pope John Paul II's visit in February 1981 might have been a turning point in the relationship between Japanese Catholicism and the center. Although it was widely covered in the secular media—exceptional in Japan for a religious leader and even for a foreign head of state—the visit did not result in any increased interest in the Gospel message among non-Christians.[7] But the visit did convey the message that, notwithstanding the Vatican's centralizing tendencies, the pope gave his blessing to Japanese efforts to build a strong local church, including efforts for inculturation, interreligious dialogue, and other related issues. Japanese Catholics received a strong sense of self-respect and self-confidence, which has led to a wider awakening and a firmer resolution to move forward in a more independent way.

Another element in this awakening is the deepening relationship between the Japanese church and its sister churches in Asia. Besides lack of confidence arising from their small size—particularly when compared to most other Asian countries, especially neighboring South Korea where conversions to Catholicism have been more numerous—the Japanese felt uneasy about interacting with fellow Asians because of the experience of World War II. Guilt feelings aside, at least an awareness that any effort to play an active role in Asia could be interpreted as reborn Japanese arrogance—a perception associated with Japan's economic penetration of Asia— has hindered the Japanese church from moving forward in this regard. It was, for example, only after much hesitation that the Japanese Bishops' Conference joined the Federation of Asian Bishops' Conference (FABC). Slowly, however, the Japanese church recognized it could no longer remain aloof from these internationalizing trends. Frequent appeals from the other Asian churches for greater involvement and support provided occasions for awakened Catholics in Japan to assume their responsibility as part of Asia—for example, the Japanese church's generous response to the refugee problem at the end of the Vietnam war, which set an example for the whole of Japanese society. The growing number of Japanese missionaries abroad, especially religious sisters, has also strengthened mutual ties, as has the increasingly active role of the Japanese Catholic Council for Justice and Peace, particularly with regard to the Philippines and South Korea. Finally, Japanese Catholicism cannot remain aloof from religious developments in mainland China and a special committee has been established to deal with this problem. All these factors have contributed to a new vitality in Japanese Catholicism.

The Ecumenical Movement

Since the Christian community in Japan is one of the smallest in the world, no single church can afford to disregard the existence of other churches in its mission to Japanese society.[8] This is the main reason why the need for ecumenical cooperation has been keenly felt and why, especially since the impetus provided by Vatican II, an ecumenical mood has led to a plethora of actions, such as a common Bible translation, ecumenical prayer meetings, and the adoption of a common stance on a number of social issues. This mood has not permeated the whole church down to the grassroots level. Since not a few Catholics are converts from Protestant denominations, there is some resentment to engaging in joint Catholic-Protestant activities. Still, the ecumenical movement has greatly influenced the general thinking of the Japanese Catholic church.

The impact of Protestant Christianity in Japan has been extremely diverse, reflecting the diversity of Japanese Protestantism itself. More so than the Catholic church with its worldwide dimension, the many small Protestant churches in Japan cling to their independence and to symbols that assert their individual identities. This defensiveness often manifests itself in a doctrinal rigidity which sets them apart not only from each other but also from Japanese society and culture as a whole. This has often been accompanied by intense involvement in social reform movements and by leftist political radicalism. Rigidity and radicalism have thus become the twin pillars on which many Protestant churches and believers have established their own identities, and this has produced new internal struggles and divisions within Protestantism itself.[9]

Growing contacts with Protestant Christianity since Vatican II, however, have raised Catholic consciousness precisely with regard to social and political affairs. Although Catholicism suffered less than most Protestant churches from the turmoils associated with the university struggles of the late 1960s and from other actions— opposition to the jointly sponsored Christian pavilion at the 1970 Osaka World Exposition and demands for a more explicit confession of war guilt—a more radical mood has spilled over into sectors of Japanese Catholicism and shaken its fundamental conservatism. This mood has especially influenced the Justice and Peace Council, and has found support in the demand of other Asian churches for more social activism and the worldwide popularity of liberation theology. Social activism today usually implies actions critical of government policies. Currently the most conspicious targets are the alleged revival of ultranationalism and militarism symbolized by efforts to mobilize government support for Shrine Shinto and the status of Korean and other minorities in a society that prides itself on its homogeneity. Many concerned Catholics find difficulty in harmonizing a reformist stance toward these issues with efforts to more fully inculturate the Christian Gospel into Japanese society and increase dialogue with non-Christian religions, since these latter actions seem to support the traditional Japanese model of a harmonious society.

Interreligious Encounters

Dialogue between Christianity and non-Christian religions has a long history in Japan, although until recently it was limited to individual contacts between people engaged in scholarly research. More Protestants than Catholics pioneered in this work and prepared the religious world for the "age of dialogue" initiated by the Second Vatican Council. Since the Council, leadership in this dialogue has clearly been taken over by the Catholic church, at least for the Christians of Japan. Catholicism has become the pivot around which the dialogue conducted by non-Christians religions takes place. Already in the 1950s some of the so-called new religions such as the Buddhist lay movement Risshō Kōseikai, which immediately after the war attracted many adherents, established organizations for conversation and mutual cooperation, partly because of the common threat they perceived from the Sōka Gokkai, a rival new Buddhist movement, both exclusivistic and missionary. The impetus of Vatican II provided the Catholic church with a golden opportunity to expand its interreligious activities and to play a role on the world scene by using the Vatican's global prestige.

The recent history of interreligious encounters in Japan is complicated and intriguing, and its details are still shrouded in mystery.[10] Without accusing any of Japan's religious leaders of deliberate manipulation, it is clear that political preoccupations and image enhancement have played a large role in dialogue fervor. Certainly more than religious aims are at stake. Symptomatic of this situation is the fact that Japanese religions engaged in dialogue prefer contacts directly with the Vatican over those with representatives of the local Japanese Catholic church, even though these latter contacts are not avoided. There are frequent visits to Rome and invitations to Roman officials—and others close to the center—to attend international religious conferences in Japan. In such efforts it is not difficult to discern both the rivalries among non-Christian religions themselves, engaged as they are in a power struggle for leadership in Japan's religious world, and attempts to enhance their prestige by courting the Vatican.

This complicated state of affairs puts the Japanese church in an extremely delicate and sometimes awkward position. As with the Catholic–Protestant ecumenical dialogue, Japan's interreligious encounter is not a grassroots movement. It remains the work of specialists. Nevertheless, its impact on the whole church cannot be underestimated. Interreligious dialogue has become one of the best known features of Japanese Catholicism abroad and is gradually opening the minds of many Japanese Christians to the religious world around them. But because of its many machinations, this dialogue has become a point of contention. While few would deny the need and significance of openness toward other religions in the spirit of Vatican II, most Japanese Catholics are not enthusiastic about concrete cooperation. First of all, for a church with many new Christians who are still establishing their own Christian identity, it is not easy to look back positively to the religion they left behind. They fear being manipulated. Second, at a time when more importance is being given to the local church, many Christians—especially church leaders—resent the preference for direct contact with the Vatican in gentle disregard of the opinion of the local church. Recent conflicts have led Rome to reappraise how it interacts with Japan's non-Christian religions and to formulate stricter rules about "friendly visits" to Rome, including more frequent consultation of the local church.[11] All these factors certainly do not arouse popular Catholic support for more interreligious dialogue. From another perspective, however, they are necessary adjustments toward a healthier and safer dialogue and in this sense represent progress.

Changes in Japanese Society and Culture

The fact that Christianity in Japan bears the mark, if not the stigma, of a foreign religion extraneous to Japanese society and culture does not prevent its being influenced by what happens in that society and culture at large. Japan shares the societal and cultural changes of the global community. It is also a country with its own problems and concerns, different in its own eyes from those occurring outside its boundaries. The interplay between these two elements—Japan as an international power and Japan as a nation-state—form the basis for whatever may be said about the country as a whole. This interplay also affects the changing situation of Christianity.

The quality of this global–domestic relationship is one of tension yet strongly inclined to subordinate the value of universalism (internationalism) to particularism (nationalism). Thus, whatever happens within the country easily takes precedence over other world issues; in turn, whatever occurs internationally tends to be judged in terms of its usefulness for enhancing the harmony and prestige of Japan.

Obviously, the application of this principle in an increasingly interdependent world meets some resistance, for example, foreign criticism of Japan's apparently ethnocentric economic and social behavior. Within Japan itself there are new calls for nurturing more "genuine" international feelings, although these voices often run afoul of social structures that impede universal openness or are silenced by the media's incessant emphasis on the uniqueness of Japanese culture, whether superior or inferior to other nations. A struggle is in progress and the outcome is far from certain.

The rapid economic growth of the 1960s has created a welfare society in which almost 90 percent of the population perceives itself as middle class. Social prosperity has been enhanced by political stability, except for the ripples created by the world-wide student unrest of the late 1960s. While memories of defeat in World War II still linger in the minds of older Japanese, the younger generation is primarily concerned with the present and the affluence it offers. Everyone, however, participates in the changes occurring in present-day society.

Observers of the religious scene often point to 1973 as a turning point in people's attitudes toward religion and culture. Some even speak of a "religious revival," especially among the young, following a period in which the importance of religious values had increasingly diminished.[12] That year was, of course, the year of the oil crisis, bringing with it a general change of consciousness that had repercussions on people's attitudes toward religion. This crisis ended the rapid economic growth of the 1960s. About the same time, however, Japan recognized that, in contrast to Western nations, it was much better equipped to overcome its own difficulties. Indeed, Western countries began to view Japan as "Number One." This adulation gave the Japanese new confidence in their own cultural values, including traditional religion, while it undermined their confidence in the extremely individualistic and rationalistic values imposed upon them after the war. This mixture of confidence lost and regained helped people to reflect on the deeper meaning of the material success they had acquired through scientific development.

Thus, in the early 1970s, the Japanese could afford to relax spiritually and begin considering what they thought important in life. They looked again at their own tradition and its spiritual roots. Japan recovered its soul and it should surprise no-one that this recovery implies a "quiet reversal" away from a kind of functional rationality that has no place for traditional Japanese religiosity toward a typically Japanese mixture of seemingly contradictory elements—including occasional leaps into the irrational—which balance one another and thus contribute to the harmony of the nation.[13]

An Awakening Local Church

It is against this background that the Japanese church has reacted to the impact of forces outside its small boundaries—the universal church, other Christian Japanese churches, and non-Christian religions. As a result of these many and often contradictory influences the Catholic church finds itself in tension between universal and particular values. On the one hand, it is asked and is increasingly willing to become more "Japanese," establishing an identity no longer borrowed from the outside but grounded in the soil of its own culture. On the other, it cannot cease proclaiming Christ's message of universal love with its prophetic witness to the danger of a narrow nationalism and, more concretely, the plight of those who fall outside the harmonious structure of Japanese society such as the Japanese *buraku* (outcasts) and foreigners, particularly Koreans and other Asians.

In June 1984 the Japanese Bishops' Conference published a statement on "Basic Policies and Priorities of the Catholic Church in Japan."[14] There has been no lack of bishops' statements in the postwar years, but most of them have reached only a few interested people, if they were not disregarded altogether. This latest document, however, found a wide audience. Not that all levels of the church suddenly awakened, but repeated references to it in Catholic publications and sermons gradually spread its message to the church at large. The statement represents a call to action directed at the whole church, reaffirming that "top priority should be given to proclaiming the Gospel and to evangelizing society and culture," especially since "in the 1980s we see that many people are becoming dissatisfied with mere material affluence and are looking for spiritual values." The first emphasis calls for direct evangelization, which leads to conversion and baptism. The second calls for an inculturation that recognizes that evangelical seeds are already embedded in Japanese culture, although mixed with elements of oppression and discrimination; cultivating the good seeds can change Japan into a society "that respects all and everyone."

Although the whole Japanese church is presently mobilizing for a new evangelization effort, not everyone agrees on its content or on the forms it should take.[15] Talk of direct evangelization triggers opposition from those who find it a disguised form of proselytism. Nor is the call for greater inculturation without critics. No one, apparently, objects to a greater role for the local church, but opinions differ about what this means. In particular the term inculturation does not arouse everyone's sympathy.

The image of Christianity still prevalent among Japanese is of a foreign religion incongruous with Japanese culture. Admittedly, this image is changing, and one could argue that the Japanese are increasingly adopting and adapting Christianity to their own culture in their own peculiar way. This is evident, for example, in the general popularity of church weddings for non-Christians and Christmas celebrations, which are seen to contribute to the harmony of personal and social life. Even here, however, Christianity remains a "foreign compartment" within the culture, which ultimately reinforces an allegedly pure Japanese identity. Both Japanese Christians and non-Christians, after all, have long cherished the idea that Christianity is "different." Abstracting and overemphasizing this difference gives both Christians and non-Christians a sense of self-identity. Calls for inculturation, especially when they come from outside the Japanese Catholic community, directly affect everyone's identity. Non-Christian Japanese, imbued with an image of Christianity intrinsically linked to Western culture, find it difficult to locate an "inculturated" Christianity. Especially in the present atmosphere of regained Japanese confidence, not a few regard the Christian attempt to become more Japanese as a subtle Western attempt to undermine Japanese cultural values from within. Many Christians, in turn, fear that inculturation will "Japanize" their religious life, that is, subordinate it to the supreme value of harmony, which is basically particularistic, since it puts one's nation above everything else. Still others interpret inculturation as a step backward, expressing a kind of romantic idea of a static Japanese culture at odds with a society undergoing rapid change, still questioning its own role in a world that is increasingly international and interdependent.

The church's problem thus mirrors the struggle of Japanese society as a whole: the tension between particularistic and universal values. But the starting point is different. The issue for Japanese society is how to break out of its enclosure and assume responsibilities as a full-fledged member of the world community without losing its own cultural identity. The church's problem is to recognize that it is part of Japanese culture and to express this in concrete form while preserving the credentials of universality it derives from the Gospel.

This tension in the Japanese church is manifested in the often expressed fear that fuller inculturation will prevent Christianity from exerting its prophetic role. The extent to which Christianity's image as a religion incongruous with Japanese culture persists if indeed it has not become stronger in recent years, is largely due to its public visibility in criticizing government policies. Protestants have been particularly active in this regard, but ecumenism has also heightened the social consciousness of parts of the Catholic community. It is no exaggeration to say that the slightest sign of appreciation for Japanese cultural and religious values, not to mention politics, is likely to arouse a storm of small but vocal protest that the purity of the Christian message is being jeopardized.[16] Single examples are generalized to indict the whole process of inculturation. At the same time, many do not yet understand how the church can simultaneously comfort and challenge; they prefer that the church move in the single direction of prophetically challenging particularistic values in the name of its own universality.

To what extent can inculturation make room for prophetic criticism of culture? Or more generally, how can the tension between particularism and universalism be understood not as contradictory but as complementary values? Japan's present-day obsession with theories about what it means "to be Japanese" is undoubtedly a defense against the incursion of alien values associated with internationalization. But this obsession might also be a sign that Japan is after all moving away from particularism toward universalism. The strong negative reaction to inculturation within the Christian churches is surely inspired by a genuine concern for the universal message of the Gospel. It might also signal that the church has resolutely determined to become genuinely incarnate in the soil of Japan. The history of the Catholic church in Japan over the last twenty years is a story of the slow awakening of a local church with a specific role. This transition involves many problems and tensions. The church's present task is to help people realize that these problems can be lived with, that they are in fact a sign of health and hope for the future.

NOTES

1. The classic work on this period is still C. R. Boxer, *The Christian Century in Japan 1549–1650* (Berkeley: University of California Press, 1951; rev. ed., 1967). Another less known but very valuable study is Joseph Jennes, *A History of the Catholic*

Church in Japan from Its Beginnings to the Early Meiji Era (Tokyo: Oriens Institute for Religious Research, 1973).

2. For a history of the modern period of the Catholic Church, see Joseph L. Van Hecken, *The Catholic Church in Japan Since 1859* (Tokyo: Enderle, 1963). Also informative is Joseph J. Spae, *Catholicism in Japan: A Sociological Study* (Tokyo: International Institute for the Study of Religions, 1964).

3. See James P. Colligan, ed., *The Image of Christianity in Japan: A Survey* (Tokyo: Institute of Christian Culture, Sophia University, 1980).

4. Although detailed statistics are not available, it should be noted that quite a few Catholics outside Nagasaki are in fact emigrants from that diocese. Also among the clergy, and especially the religious, Nagasaki Catholics still constitute a relatively high number. For example, in 1986 six of Japan's sixteen dioceses were led by Nagasaki-born bishops. Of course, not all Catholics in the Nagasaki diocese itself are descendants of the old Christians.

5. Symbolic in this respect is the fact that, at the time of the "discovery" of the Nagasaki Christians in 1865, the three main signs that led them to "recognize" the French missionaries as representatives of their own Christian religion were obedience to the Roman Pontiff, priestly celibacy, and veneration of the Virgin Mary.

6. Interesting is that, as of 1986, two-thirds of the members of the (male) Superiors' Conference of Japan were foreigners, while only one foreign sister was left in the (female) Major Superiors' Association.

7. In the same year (1981) Mother Teresa of Calcutta and the Polish Solidarity leader Lech Walesa also visited Japan. The general impact their visit made on the "image" of the Catholic church among the Japanese was apparently much deeper and not so quickly forgotten as the pope's festival-like appearance.

8. For more information on the ecumenical movement in Japan, and on the recent history of Christianity in general, see James M. Phillips, *From the Rising of the Sun: Christians and Society in Contemporary Japan* (Maryknoll, N.Y.: Orbis Books, 1981). Other valuable sources from a Protestant viewpoint are the journals *The Christian Quarterly* (Tokyo) and *Japanese Religions* (Kyoto).

9. See David Reid, "Secularization Theory and Japanese Christianity: The Case of the Nhon Kirisuto Kyōdan," *Japanese Journal of Religious Studies* 6 (March–June 1979):347–78.

10. This history has become a favorite topic for Japanese social critics specializing in religious affairs who like to indulge in fancies about a so-called Vatican strategy of world domination against the forces of communism and in collusion with Japan's new religions and, more recently, Shinto. Those Japanese religions are said to be "Vatican agents" for promoting this strategy within Japan since the Japanese Catholic church itself is too powerless to do so.

11. Recent examples are the commotion raised by the visit to the Vatican in 1985 of the founder of a controversial new religion, which was cleverly exploited in the mass media, and by the allegedly favored treatment by the Vatican of the Risshō Kōseikai, both events that occurred without the knowledge of the local church.

12. See NHK Hōsō Yoron-chōsa-sho, ed., Nihonjin no shūkyō-ishiki [The Religious Consciousness of the Japanese] (Tokyo: Nippon Hōsō Shuppankyōkai, 1984). For a comment on this survey, see my "Religion in Contemporary Japanese Society," *The Japan Foundation Newsletter* 13 (Jan. 1985):1–5.

13. In this connection mention should be made of the role played by Japanese companies in contributing to Japanese "harmony" by the mixture they provide of rational and nonrational elements, including religious rites. Japan's companies can be considered as the new "sacred communities." They have taken over the role of the old

agricultural communities as the *locus* of traditional Japanese religiosity centered on maintaining and enhancing harmonious life-power. See Swyngedouw, "Religion in Contemporary Japanese Society," 5–14.

14. See *The Japan Missionary Bulletin* (Tokyo) 38 (Sept. 1984):483–84.

15. The concrete modalities of this evangelization effort were to be taken up in a national convention of bishops, priests, religious, and laity scheduled for the autumn of 1987 and given the "Japanese" name of NAISU, from the English N.I.C.E. (National Incentive Congress for Evangelization).

16. An example is the refusal of many Protestant leaders, supported by sections in the Catholic church, to meet with Pope John Paul II when he visited Japan in 1981 because of his courtesy call on the emperor. Another example is the 1983 controversy that arose around the scheduled publication by the Episcopal Commission for non-Christian Religions of "Guidelines for Catholics with Regard to the Ancestors and the Dead." The positive attitude expressed in it toward traditional ancestor veneration practices and attending rituals of non-Christian religions was attacked as contributing to the revival of Shinto nationalism and emperor worship.

Index